Merriam-Webster's
Pocket
Rhyming
Dictionary

Merriam-Webster's
Pocket
Rhyming
Dictionary

MERRIAM-WEBSTER, INCORPORATED
Springfield, Massachusetts, U.S.A.

A GENUINE MERRIAM-WEBSTER

The name *Webster* alone is no guarantee of excellence. It is used by a number of publishers and may serve mainly to mislead an unwary buyer.

Merriam-Webster™ is the name you should look for when you consider the purchase of dictionaries or other fine reference books. It carries the reputation of a company that has been publishing since 1831 and is your assurance of quality and authority.

Copyright © 2001 by Merriam-Webster, Incorporated

Library of Congress Cataloging-in-Publication Data
Merriam-Webster's pocket rhyming dictionary.
  p.   cm.
"The words in this book come from Merriam-Webster's collegiate dictionary, tenth edition, and in some cases, from Webster's ninth new collegiate dictionary"—Explanatory notes
  ISBN 978-0-87779-516-2
  1. English language—Rhyme—Dictionaries. I. Title: Pocket rhyming dictionary. II. Merriam-Webster, Inc.
PE1519.M46   2001
423'.1—dc21   00-068238

MADE IN THE UNITED STATES OF AMERICA

10 11 12 13 TFP:RP 10 13

Explanatory Notes

Sources and content The words in this book come from *Merriam-Webster's Collegiate Dictionary, Tenth Edition,* and, in some cases, from *Webster's Ninth New Collegiate Dictionary.* Though many uncommon words can be found here, many highly technical or obscure words have been omitted, as have words whose only meanings are vulgar or offensive.

The rhyming sound The sounds we rhyme with come at the end of the word, beginning with the vowel sound in the word's last stressed syllable. That final stress may be primary, as in *Dundee* \ˌdən-'dē\, or secondary, as in *passkey* \'pas-ˌkē\. Both words fall into the category of words with one-syllable rhyming sounds, because they rhyme on the final syllable alone. Other words with one-syllable rhyming sounds are *wide* \'wīd\ (rhyming sound \īd\), *appeal* \ə-'pēl\ (rhyming sound \ēl\), *mongoose* \'män-ˌgüs\ (rhyming sound \üs\), and *undergrad* \'ən-dər-ˌgrad\ (rhyming sound \ad\).

This book also includes rhyming sounds of two and three syllables. Two-syllable rhyming sounds are found in words in which the final stressed syllable is the next-to-last syllable. *Cola* \'kō-lə\ and *remover* \rē-'mü-vər\ have two-syllable rhyming sounds; for *cola,* the rhyming sound is \ō-lə\; for *remover,* it is \ü-vər\.

Three-syllable rhyming sounds are found in words in which the third syllable from the end carries the stress. *Mutable* \'myüt-ə-bəl\ and *frivolity* \friv-'äl-ət-ē\ have three-syllable rhyming sounds, \üt-ə-bəl\ and \äl-ət-ē\, respectively.

Main entries The main entries in this dictionary consist of an entry form, a pronunciation, and a list of rhyming

words. The entry form is the most common spelling of
the rhyming sound shown in the pronunciation. To find
a rhyme for a given word, you need to know only the
spelling of the word and its rhyming sound. If, for instance, you wanted to find a word to rhyme with *deep,*
you would look up **eep,** because that is how the rhyming
sound is spelled. At **eep,** you would find the following
entry:

> **eep** \ēp\ beep, bleep,
> cheap, cheep, cleep,
> creep, deep, heap, jeep,
> Jeep, keep, . . .

If the word you wanted to find a rhyme for had
been *cheap,* you would have looked up **eap** and found
the following cross-reference entry:

> **eap** \ēp\ see EEP

When the same spelling is used for more than one
rhyming sound, superscript numbers are used to alert
users to all identically spelled entries. The user searching
for a rhyme for *give,* for example, would look up **ive** and
find the following entries:

> **¹ive** \īv\ chive, dive, drive,
> five, gyve, hive, I've, jive,
> live, . . .
> **²ive** \iv\ give, live, sheave,
> shiv, . . .
> **³ive** \ēv\ see ¹EAVE

The rhyming sound in *give* is pronounced \iv\, so the
second entry is the appropriate one.

Since many words have more than one standard
pronunciation, some words appear in more than one list,
and not every word on every list will rhyme for every
person.

An explanation of the pronunciation symbols is found on pages xiii–xiv.

Cross-reference entries Cross-reference entries reflect alternative spellings of the rhyming sound. The entry form **arten,** for instance, represents the rhyming sound \ärt-ᵊn\, and rhyming words listed there include *carton, martin, Spartan,* and *Sint Maarten,* among others. Because those words variously spell the rhyming sound **arton, artin, artan,** and **aartin,** there are cross-reference entries at each of those spellings directing the user to **arten.**

If a cross-reference entry directs users to an entry that is one of several spelled identically, the identification number ensures that users will find the correct entry:

> ¹ieve \iv\ see ²IVE
> ²ieve \ēv\ see ¹EAVE

The order of rhyming words The words that follow the entry form and the pronunciation are arranged by number of syllables. Words with the fewest syllables are listed alphabetically first, followed by groups of words with successively more syllables:

> **arten** \ärt-ᵊn\ Barton,
> carton, hearten, marten,
> martin, Martin, smarten,
> Spartan, tartan, baum
> marten, dishearten,
> Dumbarton, freemartin,
> Saint Martin, Sint
> Maarten, kindergarten

Unlisted rhyming words In order to save space, inflected forms of words have not been listed as entries or included in the lists of rhymes. Inflected forms are those forms that are created by adding grammatical endings to the base word. For instance, the base word *arm,* a noun, is made plural by adding *-s* to form *arms,* and the base word *walk,* a verb, forms its past tense by adding *-ed* to form *walked.* You will find *arm* listed under the entry **¹arm** \ärm\, which also includes such words as *farm* and *firearm.* There is no entry **arms** for the forms *arms, farms,* and *firearms,* however; users must go to entries for the base word in such cases.

Inflected and uninflected forms sometimes share a rhyming sound. For example, the uninflected forms *lox* and *paradox* share the \äks\ rhyming sound with the inflected forms *docks* and *socks.* In such cases, only the rhyming uninflected forms are listed, but a note at the end of the entry indicates where the base words of the rhyming inflected forms can be found:

> **ox** \äks\ box, cox, fox, . . .
> *—also -s, -'s, and -s' forms*
> *of nouns listed at* ¹OCK,
> *and -s forms of verbs*
> *listed there*

Such notes have been added whenever two or more rhyming words could be created by adding endings to the base word at the entry. (If only one such rhyme could be created, it has simply been added to the list.)

Other rhyming words that may not be listed fall into the category of derived words. A derived word, like an inflected word, is one to which an ending has been added. An inflected word represents the same part of speech as its uninflected form. For instance, when *-s* is added to *dog* to form *dogs,* the inflected word remains a noun; similarly, when *-ed* is added to *want* to form *wanted,* both forms are verbs. A derived word, however, generally represents a different part of speech from its base word. For instance, when *-ly* is added to the adjective *quick,* the derived word, *quickly,* is an adverb; likewise, when *-ness* is added to the adjective *glad*, the derived word, *gladness*, is a noun.

There is no entry for a rhyming sound if all the words that would be on the list are derived words created by adding an ending to words drawn from another list. For instance, there is no entry **arkly**, because the only rhyming words, *darkly* and *starkly*, are adverbs formed by adding *-ly* to the adjectives found at the entry **ark**. If, however, any of the rhyming words do not derive from other words in this fashion, a complete list is given. The entry **adly**, for instance, is included so as to list two words. The first, *Bradley*, is not a derived form. The second, the adjective *comradely*, is included because, for the purposes of this book, adjectives formed from nouns by adding *-ly* are not treated as derived words (since they are rare and adjectives are not normally created from nouns by adding *-ly*). Because the entry must contain those two words, the derived adverbs *badly*, *gladly*, *madly*, and *sadly* are also shown.

Editorial acknowledgments Like all Merriam-Webster publications, *Merriam-Webster's Pocket Rhyming Dictionary* is the product of a collective effort, especially that of the editors of *Webster's Compact Rhyming Dictionary* and *Merriam-Webster's Rhyming Dictionary*, from which it draws most of its content. The adaptation was carried out by Francesca M. Forrest, with pronunciation assistance from Joshua Guenter. Robert D. Copeland provided electronic support, and the text was typeset by the Clarinda Company.

Pronunciation Symbols

ə	banana, collide, abut	n	no, own
ᵊ	preceding \l\ and \n\, as in battle, mitten, and eaten; following \l\, \m\, \r\, as in French table, prisme, titre	ⁿ	preceding vowel or diphthong is pronounced with the nasal passages open, as in French un bon vin blanc \œⁿ-bōⁿ-vaⁿ-bläⁿ\
ər	further, merger, bird	ŋ	sing \'siŋ\, finger \'fiŋ-gər\, ink \iŋk\
a	mat, gag, sap		
ā	day, fade, aorta	ō	bone, know, beau
ä	bother, cot, father	ȯ	saw, all, caught
au̇	now, loud, Faust	ȯi	coin, destroy
b	baby, rib	p	pepper, lip
ch	chin, nature \'nā-chər\	r	red, car, rarity
		s	source, less
d	did, adder	sh	shy, mission, machine, special
e	bet, peck, help		
ē	fee, easy, media	t	tie, attack, late
f	fifty, phone, rough	th	thin, ether
g	go, big	t̲h̲	then, either
h	hat, ahead	ü	rule, fool, union \'yün-yən\, few \fyü\
i	tip, banish, active		
ī	site, buy, deny	u̇	pull, would, book
j	job, gem, judge	v	vivid, give
k	kin, cook, ache	w	we, away
ḵ	German ich, Buch	y	yard, cue \'kyü\, mute \'myüt\
l	lily, pool		
m	murmur, dim	z	zone, raise

zh vision, azure \\'a-zhər\

\\ slant line used in pairs to mark off pronunciations

ˈ precedes a syllable with primary (strongest) stress

ˌ precedes a syllable with secondary (medium) stress

- mark of syllable division

Merriam-Webster's
Pocket
Rhyming
Dictionary

A

¹**a** \ä\ aah, ah, baa, bah, blah, bra, dah, droit, fa, Fra, ha, Jah, Kwa, la, ma, na, nah, pa, pas, qua, Ra, rah, schwa, shah, ska, spa, à bas, aba, Accra, aha, Allah, Armagh, blah-blah, Borgia, bourgeois, brava, Casbah, chamois, Chang-sha, Chita, Degas, Dumas, éclat, fa la, faux pas, fellah, fetah, foie gras, gaga, galah, Galois, grandma, grandpa, ha-ha, halvah, Hama, hoo-ha, hoopla, Hsia, hurrah, huzzah, isba, Issa, Luda, Marat, markka, mudra, Oita, opah, orgeat, Oujda, quinoa, pai-hua, paisa, Para, pasha, patois, pooh-bah, prutah, pya, San'a, sangfroid, selah, Shema, sola, supra, tola, Tonghua, Ufa, Utah, Valois, Vaudois, viva, voilà, whoopla, abaca, Adana, agora, ahimsa, Akita, aloha, assignat, Aymara, baccarat, baklava, Bogotá, brouhaha, cervelat, Chippewa, coup d'état, Cumanà, Delacroix, entrechat, feria, habdalah, haftarah, haniwa, Kashiwa, koruna, Kostroma, la-di-da, Libera, ma-and-pa, Machida, Malinois, Mardi Gras, Modena, moussaka, Omaha, Oshawa, Ottawa, pakeha, panama, Panama, Paraná, parashah, pas de trois, persona, picara, pietà, podesta, polenta, polynya, port de bras, Quebecois, reseda, rufiyaa, Shangri-la, tempura, ulema, usquebaugh, Ahvenanmaa, Alma-Ata, ayatollah, Baha' Allah, caracara, con anima, coureur de bois, hispanidad, hors de combat, je ne sais quoi, Karaganda, ménage à trois, phenomena, res publica, sursum corda, tamandua, Alto Paraná, Haleakala, Katharevusa, Makhachkala, mousseline de soie, Nishinomiya, Isthmus of Panama, pâté de foie gras, Utsunomiya, Afars and the Isas, exempli gratia, Novaya Zemlya, Tokorozawa

²**a** \ä\ see ¹AY

³**a** \ȯ\ see ¹AW

¹**aa** \ä\ see ³AH

²**aa** \ä\ see ¹A

aachen \ä-kən\ Aachen, lochan

aag \äg\ see ¹OG

¹**aal** \äl\ see AIL

²**aal** \ȯl\ see ALL

³**aal** \äl\ see ¹AL

aam \äm\ see ¹OM

aan \an\ see ⁵AN

¹**aans** \äns\ see ²ANCE

²**aans** \änz\ see ONZE

aard \ärd\ see ¹ARD

aari \är-ē\ see ¹ARI

aaron \ar-ən\ see ²ARON

aarten \ärt-ᵊn\ see ARTEN

aas \äs\ see ¹OS

aatz \äts\ see OTS

¹**ab** \äb\ see ¹OB

²**ab** \äv\ see ²OLVE

³ab \ab\ blab, cab, crab, dab,
drab, flab, gab, grab, jab,
lab, Lab, Mab, nab, scab,
slab, stab, tab, Ahab, Moab,
baobab, Cantab, confab,
prefab, Rajab, rehab, smack-
dab, astrolabe, minilab,
pedicab, taxicab

aba \äb-ə\ Kaaba, Labe,
PABA, Saba, Sabah, casaba,
djellaba, indaba, Ali Baba,
Orizaba, Sorocaba,
jaboticaba, Pico de Orizaba

abah \äb-ə\ see ABA

abala \ab-ə-lə\ cabala,
cabbalah, parabola

abalist \ab-ə-ləst\ cabalist,
diabolist

abard \ab-ərd\ clapboard,
scabbard, tabard—also -ed
forms of verbs listed at
²ABBER

abatis \ab-ət-əs\ abatis,
habitus

abbalah \ab-ələ\ see ABALA

abbard \ab-ərd\ see ABARD

abbas \ab-əs\ see ABBESS

abbat \ab-ət\ see ABIT

¹abbed \ab-əd\ crabbed,
rabid

²abbed \abd\ blabbed,
stabbed—also -ed forms of
verbs listed at ³AB

¹abber \äb-ər\ see OBBER

²abber \ab-ər\ blabber,
clabber, crabber, dabber,
drabber, gabber, grabber,
jabber, slabber, stabber,
yabber, rehabber,
bonnyclabber

abbet \ab-ət\ see ABIT

abbey \ab-ē\ see ABBY

¹abbie \äb-ē\ see OBBY

²abbie \ab-ē\ see ABBY

abbin \ab-ən\ see ABIN

abbit \ab-ət\ see ABIT

abbitry \ab-ə-trē\ see
ABBITTRY

abbitt \ab-ət\ see ABIT

abbittry \ab-ə-trē\ Babbittry,
rabbitry

¹abble \äb-əl\ bauble, bobble,
cobble, gobble, hobble,
Kabul, nobble, obol,
squabble, wabble, wobble

²abble \ab-əl\ Babel, babble,
brabble, dabble, drabble,
gabble, grabble, habile,
rabble, scrabble, bedabble,
hardscrabble, psychobabble,
technobabble

abblement \ab-əl-mənt\
babblement, rabblement

abbler \ab-lər\ babbler,
dabbler, gabbler, grabbler,
rabbler, scrabbler

abbly \ab-lē\ see ABLY

abbot \ab-ət\ see ABIT

abby \ab-ē\ abbey, Abby,
blabby, cabbie, crabby,
flabby, gabby, grabby,
scabby, shabby, tabby,
kohlrabi, Panjabi, Punjabi

¹abe \āb\ babe, mabe, nabe,
astrolabe

²abe \ab\ see AB

³abe \ä-bə\ see ABA

abel \ā-bəl\ see ABLE

aben \äb-ən\ see OBIN

¹aber \ā-bər\ see ABOR

²aber \äb-ər\ see OBBER

abes \ā-bēz\ see ABIES

¹abi \äb-ē\ see OBBY

²abi \əb-ē\ see UBBY

³abi \ab-ē\ see ABBY

abia \ā-bē-ə\ Arabia, labia,
Swabia, Bessarabia, Saudi
Arabia

abian \ā-bē-ən\ Fabian,
gabion, Arabian, Bessarabian

abid \ab-əd\ see ABBED

abies \ā-bēz\ rabies, scabies,

tabes—*also* -s, -'s, *and* -s'
forms of nouns listed at ABY
abile \ab-əl\ see ²ABBLE
abilis \äb-ə-ləs\ obelus, annus
 mirabilis
abin \ab-ən\ cabin, rabbin
abion \ā-bē-ən\ see ABIAN
abit \ab-ət\ abbot, babbitt,
 Babbitt, Cabot, habit, rabbet,
 rabbit, sabbat, cohabit,
 inhabit, jackrabbit
abitant \ab-ət-ənt\ habitant,
 cohabitant, inhabitant
abitus \ab-ət-əs\ see ABATIS
able \ā-bəl\ Abel, able, Babel,
 cable, fable, Froebel, gable,
 label, Mabel, sable, stable,
 table, disable, enable,
 instable, pin-table, retable,
 round table, timetable,
 turntable, unable, unstable,
 worktable
abled \ā-bəld\ fabled,
 gabled—*also* -ed *forms of*
 verbs listed at ABLE
ablis \ab-lē\ see ABLY
ably \ab-lē\ chablis, drably,
 scrabbly
abola \ab-ə-lə\ see ABALA
abolist \ab-ə-ləst\ see
 ABALIST
abor \ā-bər\ caber, labor,
 neighbor, saber, tabor,
 belabor, von Weber,
 zeitgeber
aborer \ā-bər-ər\ laborer,
 taborer
abot \ab-ət\ see ABIT
abra \äb-rə\ sabra, Sabra,
 candelabra
abre \äb\ see ¹OB
abul \äb-əl\ see ¹ABBLE
abular \ab-yə-lər\ fabular,
 tabular, vocabular,
 acetabular
abulous \ab-yə-ləs\ fabulous,
 fantabulous

abulum \ab-yə-ləm\ pabulum,
 acetabulum, incunabulum
aby \ā-bē\ baby, gaby, maybe,
 crybaby, grandbaby
¹ac \ak\ see ²ACK
²ac \äk\ see ¹OCK
³ac \ò\ see ¹AW
¹aca \äk-ə\ see ¹AKA
²aca \ak-ə\ Dacca, Dhaka,
 paca, alpaca, malacca,
 Malacca, sifaka, portulaca,
 Strait of Malacca
acable \ak-ə-bəl\ see
 ACKABLE
acao \ō-kō\ see OCO
acas \ak-əs\ Bacchus, fracas,
 Gracchus, Caracas
¹acca \ak-ə\ see ACA
²acca \äk-ə\ see ¹AKA
accent \ak-sənt\ accent,
 relaxant
acchanal \ak-ən-ºl\ see
 ACONAL
acchic \ak-ik\ bacchic,
 halakic, stomachic,
 tribrachic, amphibrachic
acchus \ak-əs\ see ¹AKA
accid \as-əd\ see ACID
accio \ä-chē-ō\ bocaccio,
 Bocaccio, carpaccio
¹acco \ak-ə\ see ACA
²acco \ak-ō\ see ²AKO
acculus \ak-yə-ləs\ sacculus,
 miraculous
¹ace \ās\ ace, base, bass,
 brace, case, chase, dace,
 face, grace, Grace, lace,
 mace, Mace, pace, place,
 plaice, prase, race, res,
 space, Thrace, trace, vase,
 abase, airspace, Alsace,
 ambsace, apace, backspace,
 best-case, biface, birthplace,
 blackface, boldface,
 bookcase, bootlace,
 braincase, briefcase,
 crankcase, debase, deface,

ace

disgrace, displace, dogface, doughface, efface, embrace, emplace, encase, enchase, enlace, erase, firebase, fireplace, footpace, footrace, foreface, gyrase, half-space, hard case, headspace, Jerez, lightface, manes, millrace, milreis, misplace, notecase, null-space, outface, outpace, outrace, paleface, postface, Quilmes, replace, retrace, scapegrace, shoelace, showcase, showplace, slipcase, smearcase, someplace, staircase, subbase, subspace, suitcase, surbase, tailrace, tenace, typeface, ukase, unbrace, unlace, watchcase, wheelbase, whey-face, whiteface, workplace, worst-case, about-face, aerospace, anyplace, boniface, bouillabaisse, carapace, commonplace, contrabass, double-space, everyplace, interface, interlace, kilobase, lemures, lowercase, marketplace, pillowcase, Samothrace, single-space, steeplechase, thoroughbass, thoroughbrace, triple-space, uppercase, rarae aves, beta-lactamase, in medias res, Aguascalientes, Goya y Lucientes, superoxide dismutase, litterae humaniores

²**ace** \ä-sē\ see ACY
³**ace** \äs\ see ¹OS
⁴**ace** \as\ see ³ASS
⁵**ace** \äch-ē\ see OTCHY
⁶**ace** \äs-ə\ see ¹ASA
aceable \ā-sə-bəl\ placeable, traceable, displaceable, effaceable, embraceable, erasable, persuasible, replaceable, ineffaceable, irreplaceable
acean \ā-shən\ see ¹ATION
aced \āst\ based, baste, chaste, faced, geest, haste, laced, mayest, paste, taste, waist, waste, bald-faced, barefaced, bold-faced, distaste, dough-faced, foretaste, impaste, lambaste, lightfaced, moonfaced, pie-faced, po-faced, posthaste, rad waste, self-paced, shamefaced, shirtwaist, snail-paced, slipcased, stone-faced, straight-faced, straitlaced, toothpaste, two-faced, unchaste, unplaced, white-faced, aftertaste, brazen-faced, double-faced, Janus-faced, hatchet-faced, pantywaist, poker-faced, thorough-paced—*also* -ed *forms of verbs listed at* ¹ACE
aceless \ā-sləs\ baseless, faceless, graceless, laceless, placeless, spaceless, traceless
aceman \ā-smən\ baseman, placeman, spaceman
acement \ā-smənt\ basement, casement, placement, abasement, debasement, defacement, displacement, effacement, embracement, emplacement, encasement, enlacement, misplacement, replacement, self-effacement
acence \ās-ᵊns\ see ¹ASCENCE
acency \ās-ᵊn-sē\ adjacency, complacency, subjacency
acent \ās-ᵊnt\ nascent, adjacent, complacent, complaisant, subjacent, circumjacent, superjacent
aceor \ā-sər\ see ¹ACER

aceous \ā-shəs\ see ACIOUS

¹acer \ā-sər\ baser, bracer, chaser, facer, pacer, placer, racer, spacer, tracer, defacer, disgracer, effacer, embraceor, embracer, eraser, replacer, subchaser, steeplechaser

²acer \as-ər\ see ASSER

acery \ās-rē\ tracery, embracery

¹acet \ā-sət\ hic jacet, non placet

²acet \as-ət\ asset, facet, tacet, tacit

acewalking \ās-wȯ-kiŋ\ racewalking, spacewalking

acey \ā-sē\ see ACY

¹ach \äk\ Bach, saugh, Pesach, pibroch, Offenbach, Mönchengladbach

²ach \äk\ see ¹OCK

³ach \ak\ see ²ACK

⁴ach \ach\ see ⁴ATCH

acha \äch-ə\ cha-cha, dacha, kwacha, viscacha

achary \ak-ə-r-ē\ see ²ACKERY

¹ache \äk\ see ¹AKE

²ache \ash\ see ³ASH

³ache \äch-ē\ see OTCHY

⁴ache \ach-ē\ see ATCHY

acheal \ā-kē-əl\ brachial, tracheal

ached \acht\ attached, detached, unattached, semidetached—*also* -ed *forms of verbs listed at* ⁴ATCH

acher \ā-kər\ see ¹AKER

achet \ach-ət\ see ATCHET

achi \äch-ē\ see OTCHY

achial \ā-kē-əl\ see ACHEAL

achian \ā-shən\ see ¹ATION

achic \ak-ik\ see ACCHIC

aching \ā-kiŋ\ see ¹AKING

¹achio \ash-ō\ mustachio, pistachio

²achio \ash-ē-ō\ mustachio, pistachio

achm \am\ see ²AM

achment \ach-mənt\ see ATCHMENT

achne \ak-nē\ see ACNE

acho \äch-ō\ muchacho, quebracho

achou \ash-ü\ see ASHEW

achsen \äk-sən\ see OXEN

acht \ät\ see ¹OT

achtsman \ät-smən\ see OTSMAN

achy \ā-kē\ see AKY

acia \ā-shə\ Dacia, fascia, geisha, acacia, Croatia, Dalmatia, ex gratia, Galatia, prima facie, exempli gratia

acial \ā-shəl\ facial, glacial, racial, spatial, abbatial, bifacial, biracial, englacial, palatial, primatial, subglacial, interfacial, interglacial, interracial, multiracial

acian \ā-shən\ see ¹ATION

acias \ā-shəs\ see ACIOUS

acid \as-əd\ acid, Chasid, flaccid, Hasid, jassid, placid, Abbasid, antacid

acie \ā-shə\ see ACIA

acient \ā-shənt\ see ATIENT

¹acier \ā-shər\ see ¹ASURE

²acier \ā-zhər\ see AZIER

acile \as-əl\ see ²ASSEL

acing \ā-siŋ\ bracing, casing, facing, lacing, racing, spacing, tracing, catfacing, effacing, all-embracing, interfacing, letterspacing, self-effacing—*also* -ing *forms of verbs listed at* ¹ACE

acious \ā-shəs\ gracious, spacious, audacious, bodacious, capacious, ceraceous, cretaceous, crustaceous, curvaceous,

edacious, fallacious,
flirtatious, fugacious,
herbaceous, Horatius,
Ignatius, loquacious,
mendacious, mordacious,
pomaceous, predaceous,
pugnacious, rapacious,
sagacious, salacious,
sebaceous, sequacious,
setaceous, tenacious,
testaceous, ungracious,
veracious, vexacious,
vinaceous, vivacious,
voracious, alliaceous,
arenaceous, argillaceous,
carbonaceous,
contumacious, coriaceous,
disputatious, efficacious,
farinaceous, foliaceous,
ostentatious, pectinaceous,
perspicacious, pertinacious,
saponaceous, scire facias,
stercoraceous, violaceous,
inefficacious, fieri facias

acis \as-ē\ see ASSY
acist \ā-səst\ see ASSIST
acit \as-ət\ see ²ACET
¹acity \as-tē\ see ²ASTY
²acity \as-ət-ē\ audacity,
capacity, fugacity, loquacity,
mendacity, opacity, rapacity,
sagacity, tenacity, veracity,
vivacity, voracity, efficacity,
incapacity, overcapacity
acive \ā-siv\ see ASIVE
¹ack \äk\ see ¹OCK
²ack \ak\ back, black, clack,
claque, crack, flack, flak,
hack, jack, Jack, knack, lac,
lack, mac, Mac, Mack,
pack, plaque, quack, rack,
sac, Sac, sack, sacque,
shack, slack, smack, snack,
stack, tach, tack, thwack,
track, Wac, whack, wrack,
yak, aback, ack-ack, alack,
amtrac, Anzac, Arak, attack,

backpack, backtrack,
Balzac, bareback, blackjack,
blue-black, bootblack,
bootjack, brushback,
bushwhack, buyback,
callback, calpac, champac,
cheapjack, Coalsack,
coatrack, cognac, come
back, comeback, cookshack,
cossack, crackback,
crookback, cut back,
cutback, Dayak, dieback,
draw back, drawback, fall
back, fallback, fastback, fast-
track, fatback, feedback,
finback, fireback, flapjack,
flareback, flashback, fullback,
gimcrack, graywacke,
greenback, gripsack, guaiac,
halfback, half-track,
hardback, hardhack,
hardtack, hatchback,
hayrack, haystack, hijack,
hogback, hold back,
holdback, hopsack,
horseback, humpback,
hunchback, Iraq, jam-pack,
jet-black, kayak, Kazak,
Kazakh, kickback,
knapsack, knickknack,
Kodak, kulak, kyack, laid-
back, lampblack, leaseback,
linac, macaque, man jack,
manpack, Micmac,
mossback, muntjac, Muzak,
notchback, offtrack, outback,
packsack, payback, pitch-
black, play back, playback,
plow back, plowback,
pullback, quillback,
racetrack, ransack, rickrack,
roll back, rollback,
roorback, rucksack,
runback, scatback, serac, set
back, setback, shellac,
shellback, shoeblack,
shoepac, sidetrack, six-pack,

skewback, skipjack, skyjack, slapjack, slotback, Slovak, smokejack, smokestack, snap back, snapback, snowpack, softback, sumac, swayback, sweepback, swept-back, switchback, tailback, tarmac, thornback, throw back, throwback, thumbtack, ticktack, tieback, tie tack, tombac, touchback, tow sack, trictrac, tripack, unpack, Welsbach, wetback, whaleback, wingback, wisecrack, woolpack, woolsack, yashmak, Yurak, zwieback, almanac, amberjack, anorak, antiblack, applejack, Arawak, Armagnac, birdyback, bivouac, bric-a-brac, camelback, canvasback, cardiac, carryback, celiac, coeliac, cornerback, Cousin Jack, crackerjack, cul-de-sac, diamondback, fiddleback, fishyback, Frontenac, gunnysack, hackmatack, haversack, high-low-jack, huckaback, hydrocrack, iliac, ipecac, Kodiak, ladder-back, leatherback, lumberjack, maniac, medevac, minitrack, moneyback, nunatak, otomac, paperback, Pasternak, pickaback, piggyback, Pontiac, portapak, quarterback, razorback, retropack, running back, sandarac, Sarawak, Sazerac, silverback, single-track, Skaggerak, snapper-back, solonchak, steeplejack,

stickleback, supplejack, Syriac, tamarack, tenure-track, theriac, tokamak, turtleback, umiak, zodiac, Adirondack, ammoniac, amnesiac, Aniakchak, biofeedback, celeriac, counterattack, demoniac, elegiac, insomniac, Monterey Jack, paranoiac, simoniac, tacamahac, aphrodisiac, coprophiliac, Dionysiac, dipsomaniac, egomaniac, hemophiliac, hypochondriac, intracardiac, kleptomaniac, melancholiac, monomaniac, mythomaniac, necrophiliac, neophiliac, nymphomaniac, pedophiliac, pyromaniac, Rhodesian Ridgeback, sacroiliac, sal ammoniac, megalomaniac, Cyrano de Bergerac

ackable \ak-ə-bəl\ packable, placable, stackable, implacable

ackage \ak-ij\ package, trackage, prepackage, repackage

ackal \ak-əl\ see ACKLE

acked \akt\ see ACT

acken \ak-ən\ blacken, bracken, flacon, slacken, Arawakan

ackened \ak-ənd\ blackened—also -ed forms of verbs listed at ACKEN

acker \ak-ər\ backer, clacker, cracker, hacker, jacker, knacker, lacquer, packer, sacker, slacker, smacker, stacker, tacker, tracker, whacker, attacker, backpacker, bushwhacker, firecracker, hijacker, kayaker, linebacker, nutcracker, racetracker,

ransacker, safecracker,
shellcracker, skyjacker,
unpacker, wisecracker,
simulacre, counterattacker
ackeray \ak-ə-rē\ see ACKERY
ackerel \ak-rəl\ see ACRAL
ackery \ak-ə-rē\ flackery,
quackery, Thackeray,
Zachary, gimcrackery
acket \ak-ət\ bracket, jacket,
packet, placket, racket,
bluejacket, straitjacket,
yellowjacket
ackey \ak-ē\ see ACKY
ackguard \ag-ərd\ see
AGGARD
ackie \ak-ē\ see ACKY
acking \ak-iŋ\ backing,
blacking, cracking, packing,
sacking, smacking, tracking,
whacking, bushwhacking,
kayaking, linebacking,
meatpacking, nerve-racking,
nerve-wracking,
safecracking, skyjacking—
also -ing *forms of verbs listed
at* ²ACK
ackish \ak-ish\ blackish,
brackish, quackish
ackle \ak-əl\ cackle, crackle,
grackle, hackle, jackal,
macle, rackle, shackle,
spackle, tackle, debacle,
gang-tackle, ramshackle,
unshackle, tabernacle
ackly \ak-lē\ blackly, crackly,
hackly, abstractly, compactly,
exactly, inexactly
ackman \ak-mən\ hackman,
packman, trackman
ackney \ak-nē\ see ACNE
ackneyed \ak-nēd\ see ACNED
acko \ak-ō\ see ²AKO
acksman \ak-smən\ see
AXMAN
ackson \ak-sən\ see AXON
acky \ak-ē\ hackie, Jackie,

Jacky, khaki, lackey, tacky,
wacky, ticky-tacky
¹**acle** \ik-əl\ see ICKLE
²**acle** \äk\ see ¹OCK
³**acle** \äk-əl\ see OCKLE
⁴**acle** \ak-əl\ see ACKLE
acne \ak-nē\ acne, hackney,
Hackney, Arachne
acned \ak-nēd\ acned,
hackneyed
aco \äk-ō\ see OCCO
¹**acon** \ā-kən\ see ¹AKEN
²**acon** \ak-ən\ see ACKEN
aconal \ak-ən-ᵊl\ bacchanal,
diaconal, archidiaconal
¹**acque** \ak\ see ²ACK
²**acque** \äk\ see ¹OCK
acquer \ak-ər\ see ACKER
acques \äk\ see ¹OCK
acral \ak-rəl\ mackerel,
sacral
¹**acre** \ā-kər\ see ¹AKER
²**acre** \ak-ər\ see ACKER
acrum \ak-rəm\ sacrum,
simulacrum
act \akt\ act, backed, bract,
cracked, fact, packed, pact,
stacked, tact, tracked, tract,
abstract, attract, coact,
compact, contact, contract,
crookbacked, detract,
didact, diffract, distract,
enact, entr'acte, epact,
exact, extract, half-tracked,
humpbacked, hunchbacked,
impact, infract, intact,
mossbacked, playact,
protract, react, redact,
refract, subtract,
swaybacked, transact,
unbacked, abreact, artifact,
cataract, chain-react,
counteract, cross-react,
inexact, interact, overact,
paperbacked, precontact,
razor-backed, reenact,
subcompact, subcontract,

underact, vacuum-packed, ventifact, autodidact, matter-of-fact, overreact, semiabstract, underreact—*also -ed forms of verbs listed at* ²ACK

actable \ak-tə-bəl\ actable, tractable, abstractable, attractable, compactible, contractible, distractable, extractable, intractable

actance \ak-təns\ attractance, reactance

actant \ak-tənt\ attractant, reactant, surfactant, interactant

¹acte \äkt\ see OCKED

²acte \akt\ see ACT

acted \ak-təd\ fracted, abstracted, impacted—*also -ed forms of verbs listed at* ACT

acter \ak-tər\ see ACTOR

actery \ak-trē\ see ACTORY

actible \ak-tə-bəl\ see ACTABLE

actic \ak-tik\ lactic, tactic, atactic, climactic, didactic, galactic, syntactic, ataractic, chiropractic, parallactic, paratactic, prophylactic, anaphylactic, anticlimactic, autodidactic, extragalactic, intergalactic, intragalactic, stereotactic

actical \ak-ti-kəl\ practical, tactical, didactical, impractical, syntactical

actice \ak-təs\ cactus, practice, malpractice, cataractous

actics \ak-tiks\ tactics, didactics, syntactics, phonotactics—*also -s, -'s, and -s' forms of nouns listed at* ACTIC

actile \ak-t³l\ dactyl, tactile,

contractile, protractile, refractile, retractile, polydactyl, pterodactyl

acting \ak-tiŋ\ acting, exacting, self-acting—*also -ing forms of verbs listed at* ACT

action \ak-shən\ action, faction, fraction, taction, traction, abstraction, attraction, bolt-action, coaction, compaction, contraction, detraction, diffraction, distraction, exaction, extraction, impaction, inaction, infraction, olfaction, protraction, reaction, redaction, refraction, retraction, subtraction, transaction, benefaction, counteraction, interaction, liquefaction, malefaction, overaction, petrifaction, putrefaction, rarefaction, retroaction, satisfaction, single-action, stupefaction, tumefaction, dissatisfaction, photoreaction, self-satisfaction

actional \ak-shnəl\ factional, fractional, tractional, abstractional, contractional, redactional, transactional, interactional, rarefactional

actious \ak-shəs\ factious, fractious

active \ak-tiv\ active, tractive, abstractive, attractive, coactive, contractive, detractive, distractive, extractive, impactive, inactive, proactive, reactive, refractive, subtractive, bioactive, counteractive, hyperactive, interactive, overactive, psychoactive,

putrefactive, retroactive,
unattractive, radioactive
actly \ak-lē\ see ACKLY
actor \ak-tər\ actor, factor,
tractor, abstractor, attractor,
cofactor, compactor,
contractor, detractor,
enactor, exactor, extractor,
g-factor, impactor, infractor,
protractor, reactor, redactor,
refractor, retractor,
subtracter, transactor,
benefactor, chiropractor,
malefactor, subcontractor,
bioreactor, campylobacter
actory \ak-trē\ factory,
olfactory, phylactery,
refractory, calefactory,
manufactory, satisfactory,
dissatisfactory,
unsatisfactory
actous \ak-təs\ see ACTICE
actress \ak-trəs\ actress,
benefactress
actual \ak-chəl\ actual,
factual, tactual, artifactual,
counterfactual
acture \ak-chər\ facture,
fracture, contracture,
manufacture, remanufacture
actus \ak-təs\ see ACTICE
actyl \ak-t³l\ see ACTILE
acular \ak-yə-lər\ macular,
oracular, spectacular,
spiracular, tentacular,
vernacular, tabernacular
aculate \ak-yə-lət\ maculate,
ejaculate, immaculate
aculous \ak-yə-ləs\ see
ACCULUS
acy \ā-sē\ Basie, lacy, pace,
précis, racy, spacey, Stacey,
Stacy, Tracey, Tracy,
O'Casey, prima facie,
Sulawesi, Veronese
acyl \as-əl\ see ²ASSEL
¹**ad** \ä\ see ¹A

²**ad** \äd\ see ¹OD
³**ad** \ad\ ad, add, bad, bade,
brad, cad, chad, Chad, clad,
dad, fad, gad, Gad, glad,
grad, had, lad, mad, pad,
plaid, rad, sad, scad, shad,
tad, Thad, trad, Akkad,
aoudad, Baghdad, Belgrade,
Carlsbad, caudad, comrade,
Conrad, crawdad, doodad,
dorsad, dryad, dyad, egad,
farad, footpad, forbade,
gonad, granddad, heptad,
hexad, horn-mad, ironclad,
keypad, launchpad, maenad,
Mashad, monad, naiad,
nicad, nomad, notepad,
pentad, pleiad, Sinbad,
Sindbad, tetrad, thinclad,
triad, triclad, Troad, armor-
clad, Ashkhabad, cephalad,
chiliad, ennead, Galahad,
hebdomad, helipad,
Hyderabad, laterad, mediad,
oread, overplaid, Pythiad,
undergrad, Volgograd,
superadd, Trinidad,
Allahabad, bromeliad,
gesneriad, hamadryad,
hispanidad, Kaliningrad,
Kirovograd, olympiad,
seminomad, Upanishad,
Voroshilovgrad
¹**ada** \ä-dä\ Dada, Dhu'l-Qa
dah, aficionada
²**ada** \äd-ə\ nada, sadhe,
tsade, Agada, Agade,
Aggada, armada, cicada,
gelada, Granada, Haggadah,
Jumada, Nevada, panada,
posada, tostada, autostrada,
empanada, enchilada,
Ensenada, Theravada,
aficionada, Ponta Delgada,
Vijayawada, cascara sagrada,
Sierra Nevada
³**ada** \ād-ə\ Ada, Veda,

armada, cicada, Grenada, alameda, Avellaneda

adable \ád-ə-bəl\ gradable, tradable, wadable, abradable, degradable, evadable, persuadable, biodegradable

a'dah \äd-ä\ see ¹ADA

adah \äd-ə\ see ²ADA

adal \ad-°l\ see ADDLE

adam \ad-əm\ Adam, madam, macadam, tarmacadam

adams \ad-əmz\ Adams—also -s, -s', -'s, and -s' forms of nouns listed at ADAM

¹**adan** \ad-n\ see ADDEN

²**adan** \äd-n\ see ODDEN

adant \ad-°nt\ cadent, abradant, decadent

add \ad\ see ³AD

adden \ad-°n\ gladden, madden, sadden, Aladdin, Ibadan

adder \ad-ər\ adder, bladder, ladder, madder, stepladder—also -er forms of adjectives listed at ³AD

addie \ad-ē\ see ADDY

addik \äd-ik\ see ODIC

addin \ad-°n\ see ADDEN

adding \ad-iŋ\ cladding, madding, padding—also -ing forms of verbs listed at ³AD

¹**addish** \äd-ish\ see ODDISH

²**addish** \ad-ish\ see ADISH

addison \ad-ə-sən\ Addison, Madison

addle \ad-°l\ addle, paddle, raddle, saddle, staddle, straddle, astraddle, foresaddle, gonadal, packsaddle, sidesaddle, skedaddle, unsaddle, fiddle-faddle

¹**addler** \äd-lər\ see ODDLER

²**addler** \ad-lər\ saddler, paddler, straddler, skedaddler

addo \ad-ō\ see ADOW

¹**addock** \ad-ik\ see ²ADIC

²**addock** \ad-ək\ haddock, paddock, shaddock

¹**addy** \ad-ē\ baddie, caddie, caddy, daddy, faddy, laddie, paddy, forecaddie, granddaddy, finnan haddie

²**addy** \äd-ē\ see ¹ODY

¹**ade** \ād\ aid, aide, bade, blade, braid, cade, clade, fade, glade, grade, jade, lade, laid, made, maid, paid, raid, rayed, shade, spade, stade, staid, suede, they'd, trade, wade, Wade, abrade, afraid, aggrade, arcade, Band-Aid, barmaid, Belgrade, blockade, bondmaid, bridesmaid, brigade, brocade, cascade, Cascade, charade, clichéd, cockade, corrade, cross-trade, crusade, decade, degrade, dissuade, downgrade, evade, eyeshade, fair-trade, forebade, gainsaid, glissade, grenade, handmade, handmaid, homemade, housemaid, inlaid, invade, limeade, low-grade, man-made, mermaid, milkmaid, navaid, nightshade, nursemaid, outlaid, parade, persuade, pervade, plain-laid, pomade, postpaid, repaid, sacheted, scalade, sea-maid, self-made, shroud-laid, souffléed, stockade, sunshade, switchblade, tirade, torsade, twayblade, twice-laid, unbraid, unlade, unmade, unpaid, upbraid, upgrade, waylaid, accolade, Adelaide, ambuscade, aquacade,

autocade, balustrade, barricade, bastinade, cable-laid, cannonade, carronade, cavalcade, centigrade, chambermaid, chiffonade, colonnade, countertrade, custom-made, dairymaid, defilade, enfilade, escalade, escapade, esplanade, everglade, fusillade, gallopade, gasconade, grant-in-aid, hawser-laid, intergrade, lemonade, marinade, marmalade, masquerade, medicaid, motorcade, orangeade, orthograde, overtrade, palisade, pasquinade, plantigrade, promenade, ready-made, renegade, retrograde, serenade, stock-in-trade, tailor-made, underlaid, fanfaronade, harlequinade, overpersuade, rodomontade

²ade \ăd\ see ¹OD

³ade \ad\ see ³AD

⁴ade \ä-ə\ see ²ADA

aded \ād-əd\ bladed, arcaded, brocaded, cockaded, colonnaded—*also* -ed *forms of verbs listed at* ¹ADE

adeless \ād-ləs\ fadeless, gradeless, shadeless

adely \ad-lē\ see ADLY

¹aden \ād-°n\ Aden, laden, maiden, handmaiden, menhaden

²aden \ad-ən\ Aden, Wiesbaden

adent \ād-°nt\ see ADANT

ader \ād-ər\ aider, braider, cheder, fader, grader, heder, nadir, raider, seder, shader, spader, trader, wader, blockader, crusader, degrader, dissuader, evader,

invader, persuader, masquerader, serenader

¹ades \ād-ēz\ ladies, Hades, quaker-ladies

²ades \ādz\ AIDS, Glades, Cascades, antitrades, Everglades, jack-of-all-trades—*also* -s, -'s, *and* -s' *forms of nouns listed at* ¹ADE, *and* -s *forms of verbs listed there*

adge \aj\ badge, cadge, hajj, Madge

adger \aj-ər\ badger, cadger

adh \äd\ see ¹OD

¹adhe \ād-ə\ see ²ADA

²adhe \ād-ē\ see ¹ODY

adia \ād-ē-ə\ stadia, Acadia, arcadia, Arcadia, palladia

adial \ād-ē-əl\ radial, biradial, interstadial

adian \ād-ē-ən\ Acadian, Akkadian, arcadian, Arcadian, Barbadian, Canadian, circadian, Orcadian, Palladian

adiant \ād-ē-ənt\ gradient, radiant

¹adic \äd-ik\ Vedic, tornadic

²adic \ad-ik\ Braddock, haddock, paddock, balladic, dyadic, faradic, haggadic, hexadic, maenadic, monadic, nomadic, sporadic, tetradic, tornadic, triadic, Iliadic, seminomadic

adie \ād-ē\ see ADY

adient \ād-ē-ənt\ see ADIANT

adies \ād-ēz\ see ¹ADES

ading \ād-iŋ\ braiding, lading, shading, arcading, degrading, downgrading, unfading—*also* -ing *forms of verbs listed at* ¹ADE

adir \ād-ər\ see ADER

adish \ad-ish\ caddish, faddish, radish, horseradish

adison \ad-ə-sən\ see ADDISON

¹**adist** \òd-əst\ broadest, sawdust, haggadist

²**adist** \ad-əst\ see ODEST

adium \ād-ē-əm\ radium, stadium, caladium, palladium, vanadium

adle \ād-ᵊl\ cradle, dreidel, ladle, wedel

adley \ad-lē\ see ADLY

adly \ad-lē\ badly, Bradley, gladly, madly, sadly, comradely

adness \ad-nəs\ badness, gladness, madness, sadness

¹**ado** \ad-ō\ bravado, camisado, carbonado, cruzado, Manado, mikado, passado, stoccado, strappado, avocado, bastinado, Colorado, Coronado, desperado, El Dorado, hacendado, amontillado, zapateado, aficionado, incommunicado, Llano Estacado

²**ado** \ad-ō\ dado, credo, crusado, gambado, strappado, teredo, tornado, barricado, bastinado, camisado, carbonado, desperado, El Dorado, fettuccine Alfredo

ados \ā-dəs\ see ADUS

adow \ad-ō\ Caddo, shadow, foreshadow, overshadow

adrate \ād-rət\ see ODERATE

adre \ad-rē\ see ADERY

adrian \ā-drē-ən\ Adrian, Adrienne, Hadrian

adrienne \ā-drē-ən\ see ADRIAN

adt \ät\ see ¹OT

adual \aj-əl\ see AGILE

adus \ā-dəs\ Padus,

Barbados—*also* -s, -'s, and -s' *forms of nouns listed at* ³ADA

ady \ād-ē\ cedi, glady, lady, Sadie, shady, forelady, landlady, milady, saleslady

¹**ae** \ā\ see ¹AY

²**ae** \ē\ see ¹EE

³**ae** \ī\ see ¹Y

aea \ē-ə\ see ¹IA

aean \ē-ən\ see ¹EAN

aedal \ēd-ᵊl\ see EEDLE

aedile \ēd-ᵊl\ see EEDLE

aedra \ē-drə\ see EDRA

¹**aegis** \ā-jəs\ see AGEOUS

²**aegis** \ē-jəs\ see EGIS

ael \āl\ see AIL

aeli \ā-lē\ see AILY

¹**aelic** \äl-ik\ see ¹OLIC

²**aelic** \al-ik\ see ALLIC

aemon \ē-mən\ see ¹EMON

aen \äⁿ\ see ¹ANT

¹**aena** \ā-nä\ scena, faena

²**aena** \ē-nə\ see ²INA

¹**aenia** \ē-nē-ə\ see ¹ENIA

²**aenia** \ē-nyə\ see ²ENIA

aens \äⁿs\ see ¹ANCE

aeon \ē-ən\ see ¹EAN

aera \ir-ə\ see ²ERA

¹**aere** \er-ē\ see ¹ARY

²**aere** \ir-ē\ see EARY

¹**aerial** \er-ē-əl\ see ARIAL

²**aerial** \ir-ē-əl\ see ERIAL

¹**aerie** \ā-rē\ aerie, aery, faerie, fairy

²**aerie** \er-ē\ see ¹ARY

³**aerie** \ir-ē\ see EARY

¹**aero** \er-ō\ see ²ERO

²**aero** \ar-ō\ see ²ARROW

¹**aeroe** \ar-ō\ see ²ARROW

²**aeroe** \er-ō\ see ²ERO

¹**aery** \ā-rē\ see ¹AERIE

²**aery** \er-ē\ see ¹ARY

aesar \ē-zər\ see ¹EASER

aese \ā-zə\ see ²ESA

aestor \ē-stər\ see EASTER

aestus \es-təs\ see ESTIS

aet \āt\ see ¹ATE

aetor \ēt-ər\ see ¹EATER

aeum \ē-əm\ see ¹EUM

aeus \ē-əs\ see ¹EUS

af \af\ see APH

¹afe \āf\ chafe, safe, strafe, waif, fail-safe, vouchsafe, bathyscaphe

²afe \af\ see APH

afel \äf-əl\ offal, waffle, falafel, pantofle, rijsttafel

afer \ā-fər\ chafer, safer, strafer, wafer, cockchafer

aff \af\ see APH

affable \af-ə-bəl\ affable, laughable

affe \af\ see APH

affed \aft\ see ²AFT

¹affer \äf-ər\ see ¹OFFER

²affer \af-ər\ chaffer, gaffer, Kaffir, kafir, Kafir, laugher, staffer, zaffer, paragrapher, polygrapher

affia \af-ē-ə\ raffia, agraphia

affic \af-ik\ see APHIC

affick \af-ik\ see APHIC

affir \af-ər\ see ²AFFER

affish \af-ish\ raffish, giraffish

¹affle \äf-əl\ see AFEL

²affle \af-əl\ baffle, raffle, snaffle

affron \af-rən\ saffron, Biafran

affy \af-ē\ chaffy, daffy, taffy

afic \af-ik\ see APHIC

afir \af-ər\ see ²AFFER

afran \af-rən\ see AFFRON

¹aft \äft\ toft, waft, gemeinschaft, gesellschaft— also -ed forms of verbs listed at ¹OFF

²aft \aft\ aft, craft, daft, draft, graft, haft, kraft, raft, shaft, Taft, waft, abaft, aircraft, campcraft, camshaft, crankshaft, engraft, handcraft, indraft, kingcraft, rockshaft, scoutcraft, seacraft, spacecraft, stagecraft, statecraft, updraft, witchcraft, woodcraft, countershaft, fore-and-aft, handicraft, Hovercraft, overdraft, rotorcraft, turboshaft, understaffed, watercraft, antiaircraft

aftage \af-tij\ graftage, waftage

after \af-tər\ after, dafter, drafter, grafter, laughter, rafter, hereafter, thereafter, fore-and-after, handicrafter, hereinafter, thereinafter

aftness \af-nəs\ daftness, Daphnis, halfness

aftsman \af-smən\ craftsman, draftsman, raftsman, handcraftsman, handicraftsman

afty \af-tē\ crafty, drafty

ag \ag\ bag, brag, crag, dag, drag, fag, flag, gag, hag, jag, lag, mag, nag, quag, rag, sag, scag, scrag, shag, slag, snag, sprag, stag, swag, tag, wag, YAG, zag, beanbag, blackflag, chin-wag, dirtbag, dishrag, fleabag, gasbag, greylag, handbag, hangtag, mailbag, postbag, ragbag, ragtag, ratbag, sandbag, schoolbag, scumbag, seabag, sleazebag, washrag, wigwag, windbag, workbag, zigzag, ballyrag, bullyrag, carpetbag, litterbag, lollygag, saddlebag, scalawag, tucker-bag

¹aga \äg-ə\ quagga, raga, saga, anlage, vorlage 's Gravenhage

²aga \ā-gə\ Vega, bodega, omega, rutabaga

³aga \eg-ə\ see ¹EGA

⁴aga \ó-gə\ see AUGA

agan \ā-gən\ see AGIN

¹**agar** \ā-gər\ Hagar, jaeger

²**agar** \äg-ər\ see ¹OGGER

³**agar** \əg-ər\ see ¹UGGER

agary \ag-ə-rē\ see AGGERY

agate \ag-ət\ see AGGOT

¹**age** \äj\ dodge, lodge, raj,
stodge, wodge, barrage,
collage, corsage, dislodge,
garage, hodgepodge, Karaj,
massage, swaraj,
camouflage, espionage,
counterespionage

²**age** \äzh\ plage, assuage,
barrage, collage, corsage,
dressage, frottage, gavage,
lavage, massage, ménage,
mirage, montage, moulage,
portage, potage, treillage,
triage, arbitrage, assemblage,
badinage, bon voyage,
bricolage, cabotage,
camouflage, colportage,
curettage, decoupage,
empennage, enfleurage,
entourage, fuselage,
Hermitage, maquillage,
persiflage, repechage,
sabotage, vernissage,
décolletage, espionage,
photomontage, rite de
passage, counterespionage

³**age** \āj\ age, cage, mage, page,
Gage, gauge, mage, page,
rage, sage, stage, swage,
wage, assuage, backstage,
birdcage, broad-gauge,
downstage, encage, engage,
enrage, forestage, front-page,
greengage, offstage, onstage,
Osage, outrage, presage,
rampage, restage, soundstage,
space-age, substage, teenage,
uncage, upstage, disengage,
multistage, ossifrage, overage,
saxifrage, underage

⁴**age** \äg\ see ¹EG

⁵**age** \äzh\ see ¹EIGE

⁶**age** \äg-ə\ see ¹AGA

ageable \ā-jə-bəl\ gaugeable,
stageable, unassuageable

aged \ājd\ aged, gauged,
broad-gauged, engaged,
unpaged, middle-aged—
also -ed *forms of verbs listed
at* ³AGE

agel \ā-gəl\ bagel, Hegel,
plagal, finagle, inveigle,
wallydraigle

ageless \āj-ləs\ ageless,
wageless

¹**agen** \ā-gən\ see AGIN

²**agen** \ā-gən\ see OGGIN

agenous \aj-ə-nəs\ see
AGINOUS

ageous \ā-jəs\ aegis,
ambagious, courageous,
contagious, outrageous,
rampageous, umbrageous,
advantageous,
disadvantageous

¹**ager** \ā-jər\ gauger, major,
Major, pager, stager, wager,
teenager, Canis Major,
golden-ager, middle-ager,
Ursa Major

²**ager** \äg-ər\ see ¹OGGER

agey \ā-jē\ see AGY

agga \äg-ə\ see ¹AGA

aggar \äg-ər\ see ¹OGGER

aggard \ag-ərd\ blackguard,
haggard, laggard

agged \ag-əd\ cragged,
jagged, ragged

agger \ag-ər\ bagger, bragger,
dagger, dragger, gagger,
jagger, lagger, nagger, sagger,
stagger, swagger, wagger,
foot dragger, four-bagger,
one-bagger, sandbagger,
three-bagger, two-bagger,
carpetbagger

aggery \ag-ə-rē\ jaggery,
staggery, vagary, waggery,
carpetbaggery

aggie \ag-ē\ see ²AGGY

agging \ag-iŋ\ bagging, flagging, lagging, nagging, brown bagging, foot-dragging, unflagging, carpetbagging—*also -ing forms of verbs listed at* AG

aggish \ag-ish\ haggish, waggish

aggle \ag-əl\ draggle, gaggle, haggle, raggle, straggle, waggle, bedraggle, raggle-taggle

aggly \ag-lē\ scraggly, straggly, waggly

aggot \ag-ət\ agate, faggot, fagot, maggot

¹**aggy** \äg-ē\ see ¹OGGY

²**aggy** \ag-ē\ aggie, baggy, braggy, craggy, draggy, jaggy, quaggy, ragi, scraggy, shaggy, snaggy, staggy, swaggy

agh \ä\ see ¹A

¹**agi** \äg-ē\ see ¹OGGY

²**agi** \ag-ē\ see ²AGGY

agian \ā-jən\ see AJUN

agic \aj-ik\ magic, tragic, choragic, pelagic

agile \aj-əl\ agile, fragile, gradual, vagile

agin \ā-gən\ fagin, pagan, Reagan, Copenhagen

aginal \aj-ən-ᵊl\ paginal, vaginal, imaginal

aging \ā-jiŋ\ aging, raging, staging, unaging—*also -ing forms of verbs listed at* ³AGE

aginous \aj-ə-nəs\ collagenous, farraginous, plumbaginous, viraginous, cartilaginous, mucilaginous, oleaginous

agion \ā-jən\ see AJUN

agious \ā-jəs\ see AGEOUS

¹**aglia** \äl-yə\ see ¹AHLIA

²**aglia** \al-yə\ see ALUE

aglio \al-yō\ intaglio, seraglio

agm \am\ see ²AM

agma \ag-mə\ magma, syntagma

agman \ag-mən\ bagman, flagman, swagman

agna \än-yə\ see ¹ANIA

agne \ān\ see ¹ANE

agnes \ag-nəs\ Agnes, Albertus Magnus

agnum \ag-nəm\ magnum, sphagnum

agnus \ag-nəs\ see AGNES

¹**ago** \äg-ō\ lago, Chicago, farrago, galago, virago, Asiago, Calinago, Santiago, solidago

²**ago** \ā-gō\ sago, farrago, galago, imago, lumbago, plumbago, sapsago, Tobago, virago, solidago, San Diego, Tierra del Fuego

³**ago** \äŋ-gō\ see ONGO

agon \ag-ən\ dragon, flagon, lagan, wagon, bandwagon, jolt-wagon, Pendragon, snapdragon, battlewagon

agonal \ag-ən-ᵊl\ agonal, diagonal, heptagonal, hexagonal, octagonal, pentagonal, tetragonal

agora \ag-ə-rə\ agora, mandragora

agoras \ag-ə-rəs\ Protagoras, Pythagoras

agot \ag-ət\ see AGGOT

agrance \ā-grəns\ flagrance, fragrance

agrancy \ā-grən-sē\ flagrancy, fragrancy, vagrancy

agrant \ā-grənt\ flagrant, fragrant, vagrant, conflagrant

agster \ag-stər\ dragster, gagster

agua \äg-wə\ majagua,

Managua, piragua, Aconcagua, Nicaragua

¹ague \ag\ see ¹EG

²ague \āg\ see ¹OG

aguey \eg-ē\ see EGGY

agus \ā-gəs\ magus, Tagus, choragus, Las Vegas, Simon Magus

agy \ā-jē\ cagey, Meiji, stagy

¹ah \ä\ see ¹A

²ah \o\ see ¹AW

³ah \a\ baa, nah, nah, pas de chat

aha \ä-hä\ Baja, Naha, Praha

aham \ā-əm\ see AHUM

ahd \äd\ see ¹OD

ahdi \äd-ē\ see ¹ODY

ahdom \äd-əm\ see ODOM

ahib \äb\ see ¹OB

ahl \äl\ see ¹AL

ahler \äl-ər\ see OLLAR

¹ahlia \äl-yə\ dahlia, passacaglia

²ahlia \al-yə\ see ALUE

³ahlia \ä-lē-ə\ see ¹ALIA

¹ahma \ä-mə\ see ³AMA

²ahma \äm-ə\ see ²AMA

³ahma \am-ə\ see ⁴AMA

¹ahman \äm-ən\ see OMMON

²ahman \am-ən\ see AMMON

ahn \än\ see ¹ON

ahms \ämz\ see ALMS

ahnda \än-də\ see ONDA

ahr \är\ see ³AR

ahru \ä-rü\ see ARU

aht \ät\ see ¹OT

ahua \ä-wə\ see ¹AWA

ahum \ā-əm\ Graham, mayhem, Nahum, Te Deum

ahveh \ä-vä\ see ¹AVE

¹ai \ā\ see ¹AY

²ai \ē\ see ¹EE

³ai \ī\ see ¹Y

⁴ai \oi\ see OY

⁵ai \ä-ē\ see AII

a'i \ī\ see ¹Y

¹aia \ä-ə\ Freya, Aglaia, cattleya, Hosea, Isaiah,

Nouméa, Himalaya, Kilauea, Mauna Kea, Meghalaya

²aia \ī-ə\ see ¹AH

¹aiad \ā-əd\ naiad, pleiad

²aiad \ī-əd\ see YAD

aiah \ä-ə\ see AIA

aias \ä-əs\ see ¹AIS

aic \ā-ik\ laic, alcaic, Altaic, archaic, Chaldaic, deltaic, Hebraic, Incaic, Judaic, Mishnaic, Mithraic, mosaic, Mosaic, prosaic, Romaic, spondaic, stanzaic, trochaic, voltaic, algebraic, Aramaic, Cyrenaic, faradaic, formulaic, pharisaic, Ptolemaic, apotropaic, paradisaic, photomosaic, Ural-Altaic

aica \ā-ə-k-ə\ Judaica, Cyrenaica

aical \ā-ə-kəl\ laical, pharisaical, paradisaical

aice \äs\ see ¹ACE

aich \āk\ see AIGH

aiche \esh\ see ¹ESH

aicos \ā-kəs\ see ECAS

¹aid \äd\ see ¹ADE

²aid \ed\ see ¹EAD

³aid \ad\ see ³AD

aida \ī-də\ see ²IDA

¹aide \äd\ see ¹ADE

²aide \īd-ē\ see IDAY

aiden \äd-ᵊn\ see ADEN

aider \äd-ər\ see ADER

aiding \äd-iŋ\ see ADING

aido \ī-dō\ see ¹IDO

aids \ädz\ see ²ADES

aiety \ā-ət-ē\ see AITY

aif \āf\ see ¹AFE

aig \āg\ see ¹EG

aiga \ī-gə\ taiga, Auriga

aigh \āk\ laigh, quaich

aight \āt\ see ¹ATE

aighten \āt-ᵊn\ see ¹ATEN

aightly \āt-lē\ see ¹ATELY

aign \ān\ see ¹ANE

aigne \ān\ see ¹ANE

aignment \ān-mənt\ see AINMENT

aii \ä-ē\ Hawaii, Tubuai

aiian \ä-yən\ zayin, Hawaiian

aijin \ī-jēn\ gaijin, hygiene

aik \īk\ see ²IKE

aika \ī-kə\ see ¹ICA

ail \āl\ ail, ale, baal, bail, bale, brail, braille, Braille, dale, Dale, drail, fail, flail, frail, Gael, gale, Gale, Gayle, grail, hail, hale, Hale, jail, kale, mail, male, nail, pail, pale, quail, Quayle, rail, sail, sale, scale, shale, snail, stale, swale, tael, tail, taille, tale, they'll, trail, vail, vale, veil, wail, wale, whale, Yale, abseil, airmail, assail, avail, bangtail, bewail, blackmail, blacktail, bobtail, broadscale, broadtail, bucktail, canaille, cattail, Clydesdale, coattail, cocktail, contrail, curtail, derail, detail, doornail, dovetail, downscale, ducktail, E-mail, entail, exhale, fantail, female, fishtail, folktale, foresail, foxtail, full-scale, Glendale, greenmail, guardrail, Hallel, handrail, hangnail, headsail, hightail, hobnail, horntail, horsetail, impale, inhale, Longueuil, lugsail, mainsail, oxtail, pass-fail, percale, pigtail, pintail, pinwale, portrayal, prevail, rattail, regale, resale, rescale, retail, ringtail, Sangreal, sei whale, shavetail, shirttail, skysail, small-scale, springtail, spritsail, staysail, surveil, swordtail, taffrail, telltale, thumbnail, timescale, toenail, topsail, travail, treenail, trysail, unnail, unveil, upscale, ventail, wagtail, wassail, whitetail, wholesale, abigail, Abigail, aventail, betrayal, bristletail, Chippendale, Corriedale, cottontail, countervail, defrayal, disentail, draggle-tail, farthingale, fingernail, flickertail, forestaysail, gaff-topsail, galingale, martingale, monorail, montadale, nightingale, Nightingale, overscale, ponytail, romeldale, scissortail, swallowtail, tattletale, tripletail, trundle-tail, yellowtail, self-betrayal, Fort Lauderdale, Oregon Trail, Santa Fe Trail

ailable \ā-lə-bəl\ bailable, mailable, sailable, salable, scalable, assailable, available, resalable, unassailable

ailand \ī-lənd\ see IGHLAND

ailant \ā-lənt\ see ALANT

aile \ī-lē\ see YLY

ailed \āld\ mailed, nailed, sailed, scaled, tailed, veiled, detailed, engrailed, hobnailed, pigtailed, ring-tailed, unveiled, ponytailed, swallow-tailed—also -ed forms of verbs listed at AIL

ailer \ā-lər\ alar, bailer, bailor, baler, bailer, jailer, mailer, malar, nailer, sailer, sailor, scalar, scaler, tailer, tailor, Taylor, trailer, wailer, waler, whaler, blackmailer, curtailer, derailleur, detailer, entailer, inhaler, loud-haler, retailer, wassailer, wholesaler, semitrailer—also -er forms of adjectives listed at AIL

ailey \ā-lē\ see AILY

ailful \āl-fəl\ see ALEFUL

ailie \ā-lē\ see AILY

ailiff \ā-ləf\ bailiff, caliph

ailing \ā-liŋ\ failing, grayling, mailing, paling, railing, sailing, tailing, veiling, whaling, boardsailing, prevailing, retailing, self-mailing, unfailing, parasailing, unavailing—*also* -ing *forms of verbs listed at* AIL

¹aille \āl\ see AIL

²aille \ī\ see ¹Y

³aille \īl\ see ¹ILE

⁴aille \ä-yə\ see ¹AYA

ailles \ī\ see ¹Y

ailleur \ā-lər\ see AILER

ailment \āl-mənt\ ailment, bailment, curtailment, derailment, entailment, impalement

ailor \ā-lər\ see AILER

ails \ālz\ see ALES

ailsman \ālz-mən\ see ALESMAN

aily \ā-lē\ bailey, Bailey, bailie, daily, gaily, grayly, paly, scaly, shaley, wally, Bareilly, Bareli, Disraeli, Israeli, shillelagh, triticale, ukulele

aim \ām\ see ¹AME

aima \ī-mə\ see YMA

aimable \ā-mə-bəl\ see AMABLE

aiman \ā-mən\ see ¹AMEN

aimant \ā-mənt\ see AYMENT

aiment \ā-mənt\ see AYMENT

aimer \ā-mər\ blamer, claimer, flamer, framer, gamer, tamer, declaimer, defamer, disclaimer, exclaimer—*also* -er *forms of adjectives listed at* ¹AME

aimless \ām-ləs\ see AMELESS

¹ain \ā-ən\ see ¹AYAN

²ain \ān\ see ¹ANE

³ain \en\ see ¹EN

⁴ain \in\ see ¹IN

⁵ain \in\ see ¹INE

⁶ain \aⁿ\ see ⁴IN

aina \ī-nə\ see ¹INA

ainable \ā-nə-bəl\ stainable, trainable, attainable, containable, explainable, maintainable, restrainable, retrainable, sustainable, inexplainable

ainder \ān-dər\ attainder, remainder

¹aine \ān\ see ¹ANE

²aine \en\ see ¹EN

ained \ānd\ brained, caned, craned, drained, grained, maned, pained, paned, stained, vaned, strained, veined, birdbrained, bloodstained, close-grained, coarse-grained, crackbrained, cross-grained, edge-grained, harebrained, ingrained, lamebrained, mad-brained, membraned, restrained, tearstained, unfeigned, featherbrained, rattlebrained, scatterbrained, self-contained, unrestrained—*also* -ed *forms of verbs listed at* ¹ANE

ainer \ā-nər\ caner, drainer, feigner, gainer, planar, planer, seiner, stainer, strainer, trainer, veiner, campaigner, complainer, container, coplanar, cordwainer, detainer, lupanar, maintainer, ordainer, profaner, restrainer, retainer, sustainer, Trakehner, entertainer—*also* -er *forms of adjectives listed at* ¹ANE

ainful \ān-fəl\ baneful,
gainful, painful, disdainful

aininess \ā-nē-nəs\ braininess,
graininess

aining \ā-niŋ\ veining,
complaining, sustaining, self-
sustaining, uncomplaining—
*also -ing forms of verbs listed
at* ¹ANE

ainish \ā-nish\ brainish,
Danish, swainish

ainless \ān-ləs\ brainless,
painless, stainless

ainly \ān-lē\ mainly, plainly,
thegnly, vainly, humanely,
insanely, profanely,
ungainly, inhumanely

ainment \ān-mənt\
arraignment, attainment,
containment, detainment,
detrainment, enchainment,
entrainment, ordainment,
refrainment, entertainment,
preordainment, self-
containment

aino \ī-nō\ see ¹INO

ains \ānz\ Keynes, reins,
cremains, Great Plains,
Mains Plains, remains—*also
-s, -'s, and -s' forms of nouns
listed at* ¹ANE, *and -s forms of
verbs listed there*

ainsman \ānz-mən\
plainsman, reinsman

aint \ānt\ ain't, faint, feint,
mayn't, paint, plaint, quaint,
saint, taint, 'tain't, acquaint,
attaint, bepaint, complaint,
constraint, distraint,
greasepaint, impaint,
restraint, unconstraint,
unrestraint

ain't \ānt\ see AINT

ainting \ān-tiŋ\
underpainting—*also -ing
forms of verbs listed at*
AINT

aintly \ānt-lē\ faintly,
quaintly, saintly

ainy \ā-nē\ brainy, grainy,
meiny, rainy, veiny, zany,
Allegheny

ainz \īnz\ see ³INES

aipse \āps\ see APES

¹air \er\ see ⁴ARE

²air \ir\ see ¹IRE

aira \ī-rə\ see YRA

aird \erd\ see AIRED

¹aire \er\ see ⁴ARE

²aire \ir\ see ²EER

³aire \īr\ see ¹IRE

aired \ard\ caird, haired,
laird, fair-haired, impaired,
long-haired, misleared,
prepared, shorthaired,
unpaired, wirehaired,
multilayered, underprepared,
unimpaired—*also -ed forms
of verbs listed at* ⁴ARE

airer \er-ər\ see ¹EARER

¹aires \er\ see ⁴ARE

²aires \ar-ēs\ see ²ARES

¹airess \er-əs\ see ERROUS

²airess \ar-əs\ see ²ARIS

airie \er-ē\ see ¹ARY

airing \er-iŋ\ see ¹ARING

airish \er-ish\ see ¹ARISH

airist \er-əst\ see ARIST

airly \er-lē\ fairly, ferlie,
rarely, squarely

airn \ern\ see ¹ERN

airo \ī-rō\ see ¹YRO

airs \erz\ theirs, backstairs,
downstairs, nowheres,
somewheres, upstairs,
unawares—*also -s, -'s, and -s'
forms of nouns listed at* ⁴ARE,
*and -s forms of verbs listed
there*

¹airy \er-ē\ see ¹ARY

²airy \ā-rē\ see ¹AERIE

¹ais \ā-əs\ dais, Laius, Isaias,
Menelaus

²ais \ā\ see ¹AY

¹aisal \ā-zəl\ see ²ASAL
²aisal \ī-səl\ see ¹ISAL
aisance \ās-ᵊns\ see ¹ASCENCE
aisant \ās-ᵊnt\ see ACENT
¹aise \āz\ see ¹AZE
²aise \ez\ see ¹AYS
aisement \āz-mənt\ see AZEMENT
¹aiser \ā-zər\ see AZER
²aiser \ī-zər\ see IZER
aisian \ā-zhən\ see ASION
aisin \āz-ᵊn\ see AZON
aising \ā-ziŋ\ braising, glazing, hazing, phrasing, appraising, fund-raising, hair-raising, hell-raising, house-raising, stargazing, trailblazing—also -ing forms of verbs listed at ¹AZE
aisle \īl\ see ¹ILE
aisley \āz-lē\ paisley, nasally
aisne \ān\ see ¹ANE
aisse \ās\ see ACE
aisson \ās-ᵊn\ see ¹ASON
¹aist \ā-əst\ see AYEST
²aist \āst\ see ACED
³aist \āst\ see ¹OST
aisy \ā-zē\ see AZY
¹ait \ā\ see ¹AY
²ait \āt\ see ¹ATE
³ait \īt\ see ¹ITE
⁴ait \at\ see ⁵AT
aite \īt\ see ¹ITE
aited \āt-əd\ see ATED
aiten \āt-ᵊn\ see ¹ATEN
aiter \āt-ər\ see ATOR
aith \āth\ eighth, faith, Faith, saithe, scathe, wraith, unfaith, interfaith
aithe \āth\ see AITH
aithless \āth-ləs\ faithless, natheless
aitt \āt-ē\ see ATY
aitian \ā-shən\ see ¹ATION
aiting \āt-iŋ\ see ATING
aitly \āt-lē\ see ¹ATELY
aitor \āt-ər\ see ATOR

aitorous \āt-ə-rəs\ see ATERESS
aitour \āt-ər\ see ATOR
aitress \ā-trəs\ traitress, waitress, aviatress
aity \ā-ət-ē\ deity, gaiety, laity, corporeity, spontaneity, synchroneity, diaphaneity, contemporaneity, extemporaneity
¹aius \ā-əs\ see ¹AIS
²aius \ī-əs\ see ¹IAS
aiva \ī-və\ see ¹IVA
aive \āv\ see ²AVE
aix \ā\ see ¹AY
aize \āz\ see ¹AZE
aj \āj\ see ¹AGE
¹aja \ä-hä\ see AHA
²aja \ī-ə\ see ¹IAH
ajan \ā-jən\ see AJUN
ajj \aj\ see ADGE
ajor \ā-jər\ see ¹AGER
ajos \ā-əs\ see ¹AIS
ajun \ā-jən\ Cajun, Trajan, contagion, Pelagian, reagin
¹ak \āk\ see ¹OCK
²ak \ak\ see ²ACK
¹aka \äk-ə\ Dacca, Dhaka, kaka, paca, taka, Lusaka, maraca, medaka, Oaxaca, Osaka, pataca, Mbandaka, saltimbocca, Toyonaka, Lake Titicaca, Higashiosaka
²aka \ak-ə\ see ²ACA
akable \ā-kə-bəl\ breakable, makable, shakable, mistakable, unslakable, unmistakable
¹akan \äk-ən\ see ²AKEN
²akan \ak-ən\ see ACKEN
akar \ak-ər\ see OCKER
¹ake \āk\ ache, bake, Blake, brake, break, cake, crake, drake, Drake, fake, flake, hake, jake, Jake, lake, make, quake, rake, sake, shake,

sheikh, slake, snake, spake,
stake, steak, strake, take,
wake, Wake, awake,
backache, beefcake,
beefsteak, betake,
blacksnake, canebrake,
caretake, cheesecake,
clambake, corncrake,
cupcake, daybreak, earache,
earthquake, firebreak,
firedrake, forsake, friedcake,
fruitcake, grubstake,
handshake, headache,
heartache, heartbreak,
hoecake, hotcake,
housebreak, intake,
jailbreak, keepsake,
lapstrake, mandrake,
Marsquake, mistake,
moonquake, muckrake,
namesake, newsbreak,
oatcake, opaque, outbreak,
outtake, Pan-Cake, pancake,
partake, remake, retake,
rewake, seaquake, seedcake,
sheldrake, shortcake,
snowflake, sweepstake,
toothache, unmake, uptake,
windbreak, youthquake,
bellyache, give-and-take,
halterbreak, johnnycake,
kittiwake, make-or-break,
microquake, overtake, pat-a-
cake, patty-cake, put-and-
take, rattlesnake,
stomachache, undertake,
wapentake, wideawake,
semiopaque

²ake \ak\ see ²ACK

³ake \äk-ē\ see OCKY

aked \ākt\ awaked, half-
baked, ringstraked,
sunbaked—*also* -ed *forms of
verbs listed at* ¹AKE

akeless \ā-kləs\ brakeless,
wakeless

¹aken \ā-kən\ bacon, Bacon,

Macon, waken, shaken,
taken, awaken, partaken,
retaken, betaken, forsaken,
mistaken, rewaken, well-
taken, godforsaken,
overtaken, undertaken

²aken \äk-ən\ kraken,
Arawakan

¹aker \ā-kər\ acre, baker,
breaker, faker, laker, maker,
nacre, quaker, Quaker,
raker, saker, shaker, taker,
waker, backbreaker,
bookmaker, caretaker,
carmaker, comaker,
dressmaker, drugmaker,
earthshaker, filmmaker,
glassmaker, groundbreaker,
grubstaker, hatmaker,
haymaker, heartbreaker,
homemaker, housebreaker,
icebreaker, jawbreaker,
kingmaker, lawbreaker,
lawmaker, mapmaker,
matchmaker, mistaker,
muckraker, mythmaker,
noisemaker, oddsmaker,
pacemaker, peacemaker,
phrasemaker, platemaker,
playmaker, printmaker,
rainmaker, saltshaker,
shirtmaker, shoemaker,
snowmaker, stavesacre,
steelmaker, strikebreaker,
tastemaker, tiebreaker,
toolmaker, trailbreaker,
watchmaker, windbreaker,
wiseacre, automaker,
bellyacher, boilermaker,
merrymaker, moneymaker,
moviemaker, papermaker,
simulacre, troublemaker,
undertaker, cabinetmaker,
holidaymaker, policymaker

²aker \ak-ər\ see ACKER

akery \ā-krē\ bakery, fakery

akes \āks\ jakes, cornflakes,

at Lakes, sweepstakes—
-s, -'s *and* -s' *forms of*
nouns listed at ¹AKE, *and*
forms of verbs listed
there

ake-up \ā-kəp\ break-up,
breakup, make-up, makeup,
shake-up, shakeup, take-up,
wake-up

akey \ā-kē\ see AKY

¹akh \äk\ see ¹OCK

²akh \ak\ see ²ACK

¹aki \äk-ē\ see OCKY

²aki \ak-ē\ see ACKY

akian \äk-ē-ən\ see OCKIAN

akic \ak-ik\ see ACCHIC

¹aking \ā-kiŋ\ aching,
making, waking,
bookmaking, breathtaking,
caretaking, dressmaking,
earthshaking, filmmaking,
glassmaking,
groundbreaking,
heartbreaking,
housebreaking, lawbreaking,
lawmaking, leave-taking,
lovemaking, mapmaking,
matchmaking, mythmaking,
noisemaking, pacemaking,
painstaking, pathbreaking,
peacemaking, phrasemaking,
printmaking, rainmaking,
snowmaking, stocktaking,
strikebreaking, toolmaking,
watchmaking, world-
shaking, merrymaking,
moneymaking,
moviemaking, papermaking,
undertaking, cabinetmaking,
policymaking—*also -ing
forms of verbs listed at* ¹AKE

²aking \ak-iŋ\ see ACKING

¹ako \äk-ō\ see OCCO

²ako \ak-ō\ shako, wacko,
tobacco

aku \äk-ü\ Bunraku, gagaku,
nunchaku

akum \ā-kəm\ vade mecum,
shalom aleichem

aky \ā-kē\ achy, braky,
cakey, flaky, laky, shaky,
snaky, headachy

¹al \äl\ Bâle, col, dahl, dal,
doll, loll, moll, nal, pol, sol,
Sol, Taal, toile, Algol, atoll,
austral, Baikal, Bhopal,
cabal, Chagall, chorale,
grand mal, gun moll, hamal,
jacal, mistral, narwhal,
Natal, nopal, Pascal, petrol,
quetzal, real, rial, riyal,
Shawwal, tical, timbale,
Transvaal, à cheval, aerosol,
Emmenthal, falderal, femme
fatale, folderol, Heyerdahl,
parasol, pastoral, pastorale,
protocol, Provençal,
Simmental, urial, Wuppertal,
entente cordiale,
Neanderthal, procès-verbal,
sublittoral, succès de
scandale

²al \el\ see ¹EL

³al \òl\ see ALL

⁴al \al\ Al, gal, Hal, pal, rale,
sal, Val, banal, cabal, canal,
Chagall, chorale, copal,
corral, decal, fal-lal, grand
mal, joual, La Salle, Laval,
locale, mescal, moral,
morale, nopal, pall-mall,
pascal, percale, quetzal,
salal, serval, vinal,
bacchanal, caracal,
chaparral, femme fatale,
musicale, pastoral, pastorale,
pedocal, rationale, retinal,
Seconal, Guadalcanal,
kilopascal, sublittoral

¹ala \äl-ä\ à la, Allah, gala

²ala \äl-ə\ Allah, olla, tala,
wallah, cabala, cantala,
Chapala, chuckwalla, cicala,
corolla, Douala, halala,

Kampala, koala, Lingala, marsala, nyala, tambala, Tlaxcala, Valhalla, Walhalla, ayotollah, Guatemala, Gujranwala

³ala \ä-lə\ ala, gala, Venezuela, zarzuela

⁴ala \al-ə\ see ALLOW

alaam \ä-ləm\ Balaam, golem, Salem, Winston-Salem

alable \ä-lə-bəl\ see AILABLE

alace \al-əs\ see ²ALIS

alad \al-əd\ see ²ALID

alam \äl-əm\ see OLUMN

alamine \al-ə-mən\ allemande, calamine

alan \al-ən\ see ALLON

alance \al-əns\ balance, valance, imbalance, outbalance, unbalance, counterbalance, overbalance

alant \ä-lənt\ assailant, bivalent, covalent, exhalent, inhalant, multivalent, pentavalent, quadrivalent, surveillant, tetravalent, trivalent, univalent

alap \al-əp\ see ²ALLOP

alar \ä-lər\ see AILER

¹alary \al-rē\ see ALLERY

²alary \al-ə-rē\ calorie, gallery, Mallory, Malory, salary, Valerie, Valery, kilocalorie

alas \al-əs\ see ²ALIS

alate \al-ət\ see ²ALLET

¹alcon \ò-kən\ see ¹ALKIN

²alcon \al-kən\ falcon, gyrfalcon, grimalkin

¹ald \òld\ bald, scald, skald, walled, close-hauled, keelhauled, kobold, piebald, ribald, skewbald, so-called, sunscald, Archibald, coveralled, overalled—*also* -ed *forms of verbs listed at* ALL

²ald \àlt\ see ALT

alder \òl-dər\ alder, balder, Balder

aldi \òl-dē\ Bartholdi, Vivaldi, Garibaldi

aldron \òl-drən\ aldron, caldron, cauldron, chaldron

¹ale \ä-lē\ see AILY

²ale \äl\ see AIL

³ale \äl\ see ¹AL

⁴ale \al\ see ⁴AL

⁵ale \äl-ē\ see ¹OLLY

⁶ale \al-ē\ see ⁴ALLY

alea \ä-lē-ə\ see ¹ALIA

¹aleck \el-ik\ see ²ELIC

²aleck \al-ik\ see ALLIC

aled \äld\ see AILED

aleful \āl-fəl\ baleful, wailful

¹aleigh \äl-ē\ see ¹OLLY

²aleigh \òl-ē\ see AWLY

alem \ä-ləm\ see ALAAM

alement \āl-mənt\ see AILMENT

alen \ä-lən\ see ⁵OLLEN

alence \ä-ləns\ valence, surveillance

alends \al-ənz\ see ALLANS

¹alent \al-ənt\ see ALLANT

²alent \ä-lənt\ see ALANT

alep \al-əp\ see ²ALLOP

¹aler \ä-lər\ see AILER

²aler \äl-ər\ see OLLAR

alerie \al-ə-re\ see ²ALARY

alery \al-ə-rē\ see ²ALARY

¹ales \älz\ sales, Wales, entrails, Marseilles, New South Wales, Prince of Wales, cat-o'-nine-tails—*also* -s, -'s, *and* -s' *forms of nouns listed at* AIL, *and* -s *forms of verbs listed there*

²ales \äl-əs\ see OLIS

alesman \älz-mən\ bailsman, dalesman, salesman, talesman

alet \al-ət\ see ²ALLET

alette \al-ət\ see ²ALLET

aley \ä-lē\ see AILY

alf \af\ see APH
alfa \al-fə\ see ALPHA
alfness \af-nəs\ see AFTNESS
algia \al-jə\ neuralgia, nostalgia
¹ali \äl-ē\ see ¹OLLY
²ali \al-ē\ see ⁴ALLY
³ali \ȯ-lē\ see AWLY
⁴ali \ā-lē\ see AILY
¹alia \ā-lē-ə\ dahlia, Australia, azalea, battalia, realia, regalia, vedalia, Westphalia, bacchanalia, genitalia, glossolalia, inter alia, Lupercalia, marginalia, Orientalia, paraphernalia, penetralia, saturnalia
²alia \al-yə\ dahlia, battalia, et alia, passacaglia
¹alian \ā-lē-ən\ alien, Australian, Daedalian, Deucalion, Hegelian, mammalian, Pygmalion, Uralian, bacchanalian, Lupercalian, saturnalian, Episcopalian, sesquipedalian, tatterdemalion
²alian \al-yən\ see ALLION
alic \al-ik\ see ALLIC
alice \al-əs\ see ²ALIS
³alid \äl-əd\ see OLID
²alid \al-əd\ ballad, pallid, salad, valid, invalid
alie \al-yə\ see ¹AHLIA
alien \ā-lē-ən\ see ¹ALIAN
aling \ā-liŋ\ see AILING
alinist \al-ə-nəst\ see OLONIST
alinn \al-ən\ see ALLON
¹alion \ā-lē-ən\ see ¹ALIAN
²alion \al-yən\ see ALLION
aliph \ā-ləf\ see AILIFF
¹alis \ā-ləs\ see AYLESS
²alis \al-əs\ Alice, balas, callous, callus, chalice, Dallas, gallus, malice, palace, Pallas, phallus, talus, thallous, thallus, oxalis,

digitalis, hemerocallis, aurora borealis, Corona Borealis
alist \al-əst\ ballast, callused, gallused, cabalist, sodalist
¹ality \äl-ət-ē\ jollity, polity, quality, equality, frivolity, coequality, inequality
²ality \al-ət-ē\ anality, banality, brutality, carnality, causality, centrality, duality, extrality, fatality, feudality, finality, formality, frontality, frugality, legality, locality, mentality, modality, morality, mortality, nasality, natality, neutrality, nodality, orality, plurality, primality, rascality, reality, regality, rurality, sodality, tonality, totality, venality, vitality, vocality, abnormality, actuality, amorality, animality, atonality, axiality, bestiality, bimodality, bipedality, cardinality, classicality, coevality, comicality, commonality, communality, conjugality, cordiality, corporality, criminality, criticality, ethicality, externality, factuality, farcicality, fictionality, functionality, generality, geniality, hospitality, ideality, illegality, immorality, immortality, informality, integrality, internality, irreality, lexicality, liberality, lineality, literality, logicality, musicality, mutuality, nationality, notionality, nuptiality, optimality, partiality, personality, physicality, principality, punctuality, rationality,

seasonality, sexuality,
sociality, spaciality,
speciality, subnormality,
technicality, temporality,
topicality, triviality,
unmorality, unreality,
verticality, virtuality,
whimsicality, asexuality,
atypicality, bisexuality,
collaterality, collegiality,
colloquiality, commerciality,
conceptuality, conditionality,
congeniality, connaturality,
conventionality, conviviality,
corporeality, dimensionality,
directionality, effectuality,
emotionality, ephemerality,
equivocality, essentiality,
ethereality, eventuality,
exceptionality, extensionality,
fantasticality, grammaticality,
illiberality, illogicality,
impersonality, impracticality,
inhospitality, instrumentality,
irrationality, materiality,
microtonality,
monumentality, municipality,
originality, orthogonality,
pansexuality, paranormality,
polytonality, potentiality,
provinciality, self-partiality,
sentimentality, spirituality,
substantiality, theatricality,
transexuality, triaxiality,
universality, veridicality,
ambisexuality, artificiality,
circumstantiality,
confidentiality,
consequentiality,
constitutionality,
homosexuality,
hypersexuality,
immateriality, individuality,
ineffectuality,
insubstantiality,
intellectuality,
internationality,

intersexuality,
paradoxicality,
psychosexuality,
referentiality, superficiality,
supranationality,
territoriality,
tridimensionality, two-
dimensionality,
uncongeniality,
unconventionality,
ungrammaticality,
unisexuality,
unsubstantiality,
exterritoriality,
heterosexuality,
inconsequentiality,
unconstitutionality,
unidimensionality,
extraterritoriality

alium \al-ē-əm\ see ALLIUM
alius \ä-lē-əs\ alius, Sibelius
alk \ȯk\ auk, balk, calk,
caulk, chalk, gawk, hawk,
Koch, Salk, Sauk, squawk,
stalk, talk, walk, Bartok,
Black Hawk, bemock,
boardwalk, cakewalk,
catwalk, chalktalk,
cornstalk, crosswalk,
duckwalk, eyestalk, fast-
talk, goshawk, jaywalk,
langue d'oc, leafstalk,
Mohawk, nighthawk,
Norfolk, outtalk, ropewalk,
shoptalk, sidewalk, skywalk,
sleepwalk, Suffolk, sweet-
talk, belle epoque,
catafalque, double-talk,
Swainson's hawk,
tomahawk
alkan \ȯl-kən\ see ¹ALKIN
alker \ȯ-kər\ balker, caulker,
gawker, hawker, squawker,
stalker, walker, cakewalker,
deerstalker, floorwalker,
jayhawker, jaywalker,
nightwalker, ropewalker,

sleepwalker, spacewalker, streetwalker, trackwalker, double-talker

alkie \ȯ-kē\ balky, chalky, gawky, gnocchi, pawky, stalky, talkie, talky, Milwaukee, Handie-Talkie, walkie-talkie, Winnipesaukee

¹**alkin** \ȯ-kən\ Balkan, falcon, malkin, grimalkin, gyrfalcon

²**alkin** \al-kən\ see ²ALCON

alking \ȯ-kiŋ\ caulking, walking, racewalking, spacewalking, streetwalking—*also* -ing *forms of verbs listed at* ALK

alkland \ȯk-lənd\ see AUCKLAND

alky \ȯ-kē\ see ALKIE

¹**all** \ȯl\ all, awl, ball, bawl, brawl, call, caul, crawl, doll, drawl, fall, Gall, Gaul, hall, Hall, haul, kraal, mall, maul, moll, pall, Paul, pawl, Saul, scall, scrawl, shawl, small, Sol, spall, sprawl, squall, stall, tall, thrall, trawl, wall, y'all, yauld, yawl, Algol, ALGOL, appall, argol, air ball, ashfall, at all, atoll, AWOL, baseball, Baikal, beanball, befall, Bengal, best-ball, birdcall, blackball, Bokmål, bookstall, boxhaul, bradawl, broomball, catcall, catchall, COBOL, cornball, Cornwall, cure-all, curveball, deadfall, de Gaulle, dewfall, dodgeball, downfall, downhaul, drywall, enthrall, eyeball, fastball, fireball, floodwall, football, footfall, footstall, footwall, forestall, forkball, four-ball, free-fall, gadwall, goofball, googol, grease ball, guildhall, hair ball, handball, hardball,

headstall, heelball, highball, holdall, icefall, install, keelhaul, know-all, landfall, Landsmål, line-haul, lowball, meatball, menthol, Metol, miscall, mothball, naphthol, Nepal, nightfall, nutgall, oddball, outfall, outhaul, pitfall, plimsoll, pratfall, pub-crawl, puffball, punchball, pushball, rainfall, rainsquall, recall, rial, rial, Riksmål, riyal, rockfall, rorqual, Saint Paul, save-all, screwball, seawall, short-haul, shortfall, sidewall, sleazeball, slimeball, snowball, snowfall, softball, speedball, spitball, Stendhal, stickball, stonewall, stoopball, T-ball, tell-all, three-ball, trackball, Tyrol, Walsall, waterfall, what all, Whitehall, whitewall, windfall, windgall, withal, withdrawal, you-all, aerosol, alcohol, barbital, basketball, bucky ball, butterball, buttonball, cannonball, carryall, caterwaul, cover-all, coverall, Demerol, disenthrall, Donegal, entresol, evenfall, free-for-all, gasohol, girasole, Grand Guignol, haute école, know-it-all, knuckleball, Komsomol, methanol, minié ball, Montreal, Nembutal, overall, overcall, overhaul, paddleball, parasol, Parsifal, Pentothal, protocol, racquetball, Seconal, Senegal, superball, tattersall, tetherball, therewithal, timolol, volleyball, wherewithal, cholesterol, Costa del Sol, Mariupol,

Massif Central, Neanderthal, Sevastopol, Transalpine Gaul, Vincent de Paul, be-all and end-all

²all \äl\ see ¹AL

³all \ȯl\ see ⁴AL

¹alla \äl-ə\ see ²ALA

²alla \al-ə\ see ⁴ALLOW

allable \ȯ-lə-bəl\ callable, spallable

allace \äl-əs\ see OLIS

allacy \al-ə-sē\ fallacy, jalousie

allad \al-əd\ see ²ALID

allage \al-ə-jē\ see ²ALOGY

¹allah \äl-ä\ see ¹ALA

²allah \äl-ə\ see ²ALA

³allah \al-ə\ see ⁴ALLOW

allan \al-ən\ see ALLON

allans \al-ənz\ calends, Lallans—*also* -s, -'s, *and* -s' *forms of nouns listed at* ALLON

allant \al-ənt\ callant, gallant, talent, topgallant, fore-topgallant

allas \al-əs\ see ²ALIS

allasey \äl-ə-sē\ see OLICY

allast \al-əst\ see ALIST

¹alle \al\ see ⁴AL

²alle \al-ē\ see ⁴ALLY

³alle \äl-ē\ see OLLY

alled \ȯld\ see ALD

allee \al-ē\ see ⁴ALLY

allemande \al-ə-mən\ see ALAMINE

¹allen \ȯ-lən\ fallen, stollen, befallen, chapfallen, chopfallen, crestfallen, downfallen, tarpaulin, unfallen

²allen \al-ən\ see ALLON

¹aller \ȯ-lər\ bawler, brawler, caller, drawler, faller, hauler, mauler, scrawler, squaller, trawler, fireballer, footballer, forestaller, installer, stonewaller, knuckleballer

²aller \al-ər\ caller, pallor, valor

alles \ī-əs\ see ¹IAS

¹allet \äl-ət\ see OLLET

²allet \al-ət\ ballot, callet, mallet, palate, palette, pallet, sallet, shallot, valet

alley \al-ē\ see ⁴ALLY

alli \al-ē\ see ⁴ALLY

alliard \al-yərd\ galliard, halyard

allic \al-ik\ Gaelic, Gallic, malic, phallic, salic, Salic, thallic, cephalic, italic, mandalic, medallic, metallic, smart aleck, Uralic, Vandalic, vocalic, genitalic, intervallic, ithyphallic, nonmetallic, postvocalic, prevocalic, intervocalic

allid \al-əd\ see ²ALID

allie \al-ē\ see ⁴ALLY

alling \ȯ-liŋ\ balling, calling, drawling, falling, galling, hauling, mauling, Pauling, stalling, infalling, name-calling—*also* -ing *forms of verbs listed at* ¹ALL

alinn \al-ən\ see ALLON

allion \al-yən\ scallion, stallion, battalion, Italian, medallion, rapscallion, tatterdemalion

¹allis \al-əs\ see ²ALIS

²allis \al-ē\ see ⁴ALLY

³allis \äl-əs\ see OLIS

allish \ȯ-lish\ Gaulish, smallish, tallish

allit \ä-lət\ see OLLET

¹allith \äl-əs\ see OLIS

²allith \äl-ət\ see OLLET

allium \al-ē-əm\ allium, gallium, pallium, thallium, Valium

allment \ȯl-mənt\

enthrallment, forestallment,
installment

allo \äl-ō\ see ¹OLLOW

allon \al-ən\ Alan, Allan,
Allen, Allyn, gallon, lallan,
Talinn, talon

¹**allop** \äl-əp\ see OLLOP

²**allop** \al-əp\ gallop, galop,
jalap, salep, Salop, scallop,
shallop, escallop

allor \al-ər\ see ²ALLER

¹**allory** \al-re\ see ALLERY

²**allory** \al-ə-rē\ see ²ALARY

allot \al-ət\ see ²ALLET

allous \al-əs\ see ²ALIS

¹**allow** \el-ō\ see ELLO

²**allow** \äl-ə\ see ²ALA

³**allow** \äl-ō\ see ¹OLLOW

⁴**allow** \al-ə\ Allah, callow,
fallow, gala, Galla, hallow,
sallow, shallow, tallow,
cavalla, impala, unhallow,
Valhalla

⁵**allow** \al-ō\ aloe, callow,
fallow, hallow, mallow,
sallow, shallow, tallow,
unhallow

allowed \al-ōd\ hallowed,
unhallowed

allows \al-ōz\ gallows,
Allhallows—*also* -s, -'s, *and*
-s' *forms of nouns listed at*
⁵ALLOW

alls \ȯlz\ Angel Falls,
Niagara Falls—*also* -s, -'s,
and -s' *forms of nouns listed*
at ALL, *and* -s *forms of verbs*
listed there

allsy \ȯl-zē\ see ALSY

allus \al-əs\ see ²ALIS

allused \al-əst\ see ALIST

¹**ally** \ā-lē\ see AILY

²**ally** \ä-lē\ see ¹OLLY

³**ally** \ȯ-lē\ see AWLY

⁴**ally** \al-ē\ alley, bally, challis,
dally, galley, gally, mallee,
pally, rally, sallie, sally, Sally,

tally, valley, Aunt Sally, bialy,
crevalle, Death Valley, finale,
Nepali, tomalley, dillydally,
Mexicali, shilly-shally,
teocalli, Great Rift Valley

allyn \al-ən\ see ALLON

alm \äm\ see ¹OM

alma \al-mə\ Alma, halma

almar \äm-ər\ see ¹OMBER

almer \äm-ər\ see ¹OMBER

almily \äm-ə-lē\ see OMALY

almish \äm-ish\ see ¹AMISH

almist \äm-əst\ palmist,
psalmist, Islamist

almody \äm-əd-ē\ see
OMEDY

almon \am-ən\ see AMMON

almoner \äm-ə-nər\ see
OMMONER

alms \ämz\ alms, Brahms,
Psalms—*also* -s, -'s, *and* -s'
forms of nouns listed at ¹OM,
and -s *forms of verbs listed*
there

almy \äm-ē\ see ¹AMI

alo \äl-ō\ see ¹OLLOW

aloe \al-ō\ see ⁵ALLOW

¹**alogist** \äl-ə-jəst\ see
OLOGIST

²**alogist** \al-ə-jəst\ analogist,
dialogist, mammalogist,
genealogist

¹**alogy** \äl-ə-jē\ see OLOGY

²**alogy** \al-ə-jē\ analogy,
hypallage, mammalogy,
tetralogy, mineralogy

alom \äl-əm\ see OLUMN

alon \al-ən\ see ALLON

alop \al-əp\ see ²ALLOP

¹**alor** \äl-ər\ see OLLAR

²**alor** \al-ər\ see ²ALLER

¹**alorie** \al-rē\ see ¹ALLERY

²**alorie** \al-ə-rē\ see ²ALARY

¹**alory** \al-rē\ see ALLERY

²**alory** \al-ə-rē\ see ²ALARY

alousie \al-ə-sē\ see ALLACY

alp \alp\ alp, salp, scalp

alpa \al-pə\ salpa, catalpa, Tegucigalpa

alpal \al-pəl\ palpal, scalpel

alpel \al-pəl\ see ALPAL

alpha \al-fə\ alpha, alfalfa

¹**alque** \ók\ see ALK

²**alque** \alk\ calque, talc, catafalque

als \älz\ see OLS

alsa \ól-sə\ balsa, salsa

alse \óls\ false, waltz

alsey \ól-zē\ see ALSY

alsy \ól-zē\ ballsy, Halsey, palsy

alt \ólt\ fault, gault, halt, malt, salt, smalt, vault, volt, Walt, asphalt, assault, basalt, cobalt, default, desalt, exalt, footfault, gestalt, Great Salt, Schwarzwald, stringhalt, double-fault, somersault, pepper-and-salt

alta \äl-tə\ Malta, Saita, Volta, Yalta

altar \ól-tər\ see ALTER

alter \ól-tər\ altar, alter, falter, halter, palter, Psalter, salter, vaulter, Walter, defaulter, desalter, exalter, Gibraltar, pole-vaulter

altery \ól-trē\ see ALTRY

¹**alti** \al-tē\ Balti, difficulty

²**alti** \ól-tē\ see ALTY

altic \ól-tik\ Baltic, asphaltic, cobaltic, systalic, peristaltic

alting \ól-tiŋ\ halting, salting, vaulting—*also* -ing forms of verbs listed at ALT

altless \ólt-ləs\ faultless, saltless

alto \al-tō\ alto, contralto, rialto

alton \ólt-ᵊn\ Alton, dalton, Dalton, Walton

altry \ól-trē\ paltry, psaltery, psaltry

alty \ól-tē\ Balti, faulty, malty, salty, vaulty

altz \óls\ see ALSE

alu \äl-ü\ Yalu, Tuvalu

alue \al-yü\ value, devalue, disvalue, misvalue, revalue, transvalue, overvalue, undervalue

¹**alus** \ā-ləs\ see AYLESS

²**alus** \al-əs\ see ²ALIS

¹**alve** \äv\ see ²OLVE

²**alve** \alv\ salve, valve, bivalve, univalve, inequivalve

³**alve** \av\ calve, halve, have, salve

alver \al-vər\ salver, salvor, quacksalver

alvin \al-vən\ Alvin, Calvin

alvor \al-vər\ see ALVER

aly \al-ē\ see ⁴ALLY

alyard \al-yərd\ see ALLIARD

alysis \al-ə-səs\ analysis, dialysis, paralysis, cryptanalysis, metanalysis, self-analysis

¹**am** \äm\ see ¹OM

²**am** \am\ am, cam, cham, clam, cram, dam, damn, damned, drachm, dram, DRAM, flam, gam, Graham, gram, ham, Ham, jam, jamb, lam, lamb, Lamb, ma'am, Pam, pram, ram, RAM, Sam, SAM, scam, scram, sham, slam, swam, tam, tram, wham, yam, Annam, ashram, Assam, dirham, Edam, ngram, exam, flimflam, goddamn, grandam, iamb, logjam, madame, mailgram, milldam, nizam, Priam, program, quondam, tam-tam, thiram, trigram, whim-wham, ziram, Abraham, aerogram, Amsterdam, anagram, Birmingham,

Boulder Dam, cablegram, centigram, Christogram, chronogram, cofferdam, cryptogram, decagram, deprogram, diagram, diaphragm, dithyramb, epigram, fluid dram, hexagram, histogram, Hohokam, hologram, Hoover Dam, kilogram, logogram, mammogram, milligram, Minicam, monogram, nomogram, oriflamme, pentagram, phonogram, pictogram, reprogram, Rotterdam, scattergram, skiagram, Smithfield ham, sonogram, subprogram, Surinam, telegram, tetradrachm, thank-you-ma'am, Uncle Sam, ad nauseam, cardiogram, heliogram, ideogram, in personam, microprogram, New Amsterdam, Omar Khayyam, parallelogram

¹ama \äm-ə\ Brahma, comma, drama, Kama, lama, llama, mama, momma, squama, Rama, Bahama, pajama, Toyama, Atacama, cyclorama, Dalai Lama, diorama, docudrama, Fujiyama, Fukuyama, Matsuyama, melodrama, monodrama, Mount Mazama, Okayama, panorama, photodrama, psychodrama, Suriname, Wakayama, Yokohama, Fuji-no-Yama, Puna de Atacama

²ama \am-ə\ Brahma, drama, gamma, grama, mamma, da Gama, Manama, Miami, pajama, Alabama, anadama,

cyclorama, diorama, docudrama, melodrama, monodrama, panorama, photodrama, psychodrama

amble \ā-mə-bəl\ blamable, claimable, framable, nameable, tamable, irreclaimable

amah \äm-ä\ see ¹AMA

¹aman \ä-mən\ see ¹AMEN

²aman \äm-ən\ see OMMON

¹amant \ā-mənt\ see AYMENT

²amant \am-ənt\ see ²AMENT

amas \am-əs\ see AMICE

amash \äm-ish\ see ¹AMISH

amateur \am-ət-ər\ see AMETER

amatist \am-ət-əst\ dramatist, epigrammatist, melodramatist

amba \äm-bə\ gamba, mamba, samba, Zomba, Cochabamba, viola da gamba

¹ambar \äm-bər\ see ²OMBER

²ambar \am-bər\ amber, Amber, camber, sambar, timbre, liquidambar

ambe \am-bē\ see AMBY

ambeau \am-bō\ see AMBO

¹amber \am-bər\ see ²AMBAR

²amber \am-ər\ see AMMER

ambia \am-bē-ə\ Gambia, Zambia

ambit \am-bət\ ambit, gambit

¹amble \äm-bəl\ see ¹EMBLE

²amble \am-bəl\ amble, bramble, gamble, gambol, ramble, scramble, shamble, preamble, unscramble, skimble-skamble

ambler \am-blər\ ambler, gambler, rambler, scrambler, unscrambler

ambo \am-bō\ crambo, jambeau, sambo, Ovambo

ambol \am-bəl\ see ²AMBLE

ambray \am-brē\ see AMBRY

ambry \am-brē\ ambry, chambray

ambulant \am-byə-lənt\ ambulant, somnambulant

amby \am-bē\ crambe, Dushanbe, namby-pamby

¹**ame** \ām\ aim, blame, came, claim, dame, fame, flame, frame, game, hame, kame, lame, maim, name, same, shame, tame, wame, A-frame, acclaim, aflame, airframe, became, byname, cross-claim, declaim, defame, disclaim, endgame, enframe, exclaim, forename, freeze-frame, grandame, inflame, mainframe, misname, nickname, place-name, prename, proclaim, quitclaim, reclaim, selfsame, surname, counterclaim, overcame, Niflheim

²**ame** \äm\ see ¹OM

³**ame** \am\ see ²AM

⁴**ame** \äm-ə\ see ¹AMA

ameable \ā-mə-bəl\ see AMABLE

amed \āmd\ famed, named, ashamed, forenamed, unashamed—also -ed forms of verbs listed at ¹AME

ameful \ām-fəl\ blameful, shameful

amel \am-əl\ see AMMEL

ameless \ām-ləs\ aimless, blameless, nameless, shameless, tameless

amely \ām-lē\ gamely, lamely, namely, tamely

¹**amen** \ā-mən\ bayman, Bremen, caiman, Cayman, Damon, drayman, flamen, Haman, layman, shaman, stamen, Yemen, examen, gravamen, highwayman

²**amen** \äm-ən\ see OMMON

ameness \ām-nəs\ gameness, lameness, sameness, tameness

¹**ament** \ā-mənt\ see AYMENT

²**ament** \am-ənt\ ament, clamant

amer \ā-mər\ see AIMER

ames \āmz\ James—also -s, -'s, and -s' forms of nouns listed at ¹AME, and -s forms of verbs listed there

ameter \am-ət-ər\ amateur, decameter, diameter, heptameter, hexameter, octameter, parameter, pentameter, tetrameter

¹**amfer** \am-pər\ see ²AMPER

²**amfer** \am-fər\ camphor, chamfer

¹**ami** \äm-ē\ balmy, commie, mommy, palmy, qualmy, swami, Tommy, gourami, pastrami, Sagami, salami, tatami, tsunami, origami

²**ami** \am-ə\ see ⁴AMA

³**ami** \am-ē\ see AMMY

amia \ā-mē-ə\ lamia, zamia, Mesopotamia

¹**amic** \ō-mik\ see ²OMIC

²**amic** \am-ik\ gamic, Adamic, agamic, balsamic, ceramic, dynamic, adynamic, cleistogamic, cryptogrammic, cycloramic, dioramic, exogamic, panoramic, phonogrammic, polygamic, aerodynamic, biodynamic, hydrodynamic, hypothalamic, ideogramic, thermodynamic, magnetodynamic

amice \am-əs\ amice, camas, chlamys, Lammas

amics \äm-iks\ see OMICS

¹**amie** \ā-mē\ Amy, Jamie,

Mamie, ramie, cockamamie, cockamamy

²**amie** \am-ē\ see AMMY

¹**amil** \äm-əl\ see ¹OMMEL

²**amil** \am-əl\ see AMMEL

amily \am-lē\ family, profamily, stepfamily

amin \am-ən\ see AMMON

amina \am-ə-nə\ lamina, stamina

aminal \am-ən-ᵊl\ laminal, foraminal

aminant \am-ə-nənt\ contaminant, examinant

aminar \am-ə-nər\ see ²AMINER

amine \am-ən\ see AMMON

¹**aminer** \äm-ə-nər\ see OMMONER

²**aminer** \am-ə-nər\ laminar, gewurztraminer

aming \ā-min\ flaming, framing, gaming—also -ing forms of verbs listed at ¹AME

¹**amish** \äm-ish\ Amish, qualmish, quamash, schoolmarmish

²**amish** \am-ish\ Amish, famish

amist \äm-əst\ see ALMIST

amity \am-ət-ē\ amity, calamity

amlet \am-lət\ camlet, hamlet, Hamlet, samlet

amlets \am-ləts\ Tower Hamlets—also -s, -'s, and -s' forms of nouns listed at AMLET

amma \am-ə\ see ⁴AMA

ammable \am-ə-bəl\ flammable, programmable, diagrammable

ammal \am-əl\ see AMMEL

ammany \am-ə-nē\ see AMMONY

ammar \am-ər\ see AMMER

ammas \am-əs\ see AMICE

ammatist \am-ət-əst\ see AMATIST

amme \am\ see ²AM

ammel \am-əl\ camel, mammal, stammel, Tamil, trammel, enamel

emmer \am-ər\ clamber, clammer, clamor, clamour, crammer, dammar, gammer, glamour, grammar, hammer, jammer, lamber, rammer, shammer, slammer, stammer, yammer, clawhammer, enamor, flimflammer, jackhammer, programmer, sledgehammer, trip-hammer, windjammer, katzenjammer, monogrammer, ninnyhammer, yellowhammer

ammes \äm-əs\ see OMISE

ammie \am-ē\ see AMMY

ammies \am-ēz\ jammies—also -s, -'s, and -s' forms of nouns listed at AMMY

amming \am-in\ damning, programming—also -ing forms of verbs listed at ²AM

ammock \am-ək\ drammock, hammock, mammock

ammon \am-ən\ Brahman, famine, gamin, gammon, mammon, salmon, backgammon, examine, cross-examine

ammony \am-ə-nē\ scammony, Tammany

ammy \am-ē\ chamois, clammy, gammy, Grammy, hammy, mammy, ramie, Sammie, Sammy, shammy, whammy, Miami

amn \am\ see ²AM

amned \am\ see ²AM

amning \am-in\ see AMMING

amois \am-ē\ see AMMY

¹**amon** \ā-mən\ see ¹AMEN

²**amon** \äm-ən\ see OMMON

amor \am-ər\ see AMMER

amorous \am-rəs\ amorous, clamorous, glamorous

amos \ā-məs\ see AMOUS

amour \am-ər\ see AMMER

amous \ā-məs\ Amos, famous, shamus, squamous, biramous, mandamus, ignoramus, Nostradamus

¹**amp** \ämp\ see ¹OMP

²**amp** \äⁿ\ see ¹ANT

³**amp** \amp\ amp, camp, champ, clamp, cramp, damp, gamp, gramp, guimpe, lamp, ramp, samp, scamp, stamp, tamp, tramp, vamp, blackdamp, C-clamp, chokedamp, decamp, encamp, firedamp, headlamp, off-ramp, on-ramp, preamp, revamp, sunlamp, unclamp, afterdamp, aide-de-camp, minicamp

¹**ampean** \äm-pē-ən\ pampean, tampion

²**ampean** \am-pē-ən\ see ²AMPION

¹**amper** \äm-pər\ see OMPER

²**amper** \am-pər\ camper, chamfer, damper, hamper, pamper, scamper, stamper, tamper

amphor \am-fər\ see ²AMFER

¹**ampi** \äm-pē\ see OMPY

²**ampi** \am-pē\ see AMPY

ampian \am-pē-ən\ see ²AMPION

¹**ampion** \äm-pē-ən\ see ¹AMPEAN

²**ampion** \am-pē-ən\ campion, champion, Grampian, pampean, rampion, tampion

ample \am-pəl\ ample, sample, trample, ensample, example, subsample, counterexample

ampler \am-plər\ sampler, trampler

ampo \äm-pō\ see OMPO

ampos \am-pəs\ see AMPUS

ampsia \am(p)-sē-ə\ eclampsia, preeclampsia

ampton \am-tən\ Hampton, Easthampton, Northampton, Southampton, Wolverhampton

ampus \am-pəs\ Campos, campus, grampus, hippocampus

ampy \am-pē\ campy, scampi

ams \amz\ Jams—*also* -s, -'s, *and* -s' *forms of nouns listed at* ²AM, *and* -s *forms of verbs listed there*

amson \am-sən\ damson, Samson

amster \am-stər\ hamster, lamster

amsun \äm-sən\ Hamsun, Thompson

amulus \am-yə-ləs\ famulus, hamulus

¹**amus** \ā-məs\ see AMOUS

²**amus** \äm-əs\ see OMISE

amy \ā-mē\ see ¹AMIE

amys \am-əs\ see AMICE

¹**an** \äⁿ\ see ¹ANT

²**an** \än\ see ¹ON

³**an** \ən\ see UN

⁴**an** \aŋ\ see ²ANG

⁵**an** \an\ an, Ann, Anne, ban, bran, can, clan, crayon, Dan, fan, Fan, flan, Jan, Klan, man, Mann, nan, Nan, pan, Pan, panne, plan, ran, scan, San, Shan, span, Stan, tan, van, Van, adman, Afghan, aidman, ape-man, ashcan, Bataan, bedpan, began, Bhutan, birdman, boardman,

brainpan, brogan, caftan, caiman, cancan, capstan, captan, caveman, Cayman, Cèzanne, chessman, Cheyenne, chlordan, Chopin, claypan, clubman, Cohan, cooncan, corban, cowman, Cruzan, cyan, deadpan, deskman, Dian, Diane, Diann, Dianne, dishpan, divan, doorman, dustpan, fancy-dan, fan-tan, fibranne, flyman, foreran, FORTRAN, freedman, freeman, frogman, G-man, gagman, Georgeann, glucan, Gosplan, hardpan, he-man, iceman, inspan, Iran, japan, Japan, jazzman, Joann, Joanne, Kazan, kneepan, Koran, Kurgan, leadman, Leanne, legman, liftman, loran, Luanne, madman, Mandan, Marfan, mailman, merman, Milan, milkman, newsman, oilcan, oilman, outran, pavane, pecan, plowman, postman, preman, pressman, propman, Queen Anne, Qur'an, ragman, rattan, reedman, reman, rodman, Roseanne, routeman, Roxanne, Ruthann, Saipan, sampan, sandman, Saran, saucepan, scalepan, schoolman, sedan, sideman, snowman, soundman, soutane, spaceman, Spokane, stewpan, stickman, stockman, strongman, stuntman, Sudan, suntan, Susanne, Suzanne, T-man, TACAN, taipan, Tarzan, tisane, toucan, trainman, trashman, trepan, Tristan, unman, vegan, Walkman, wingspan, yardman, yes-

man, Alcoran, allemande, also-ran, Ameslan, anchorman, Andaman, astrakhan, Astrakhan, ataman, Athelstan, attackman, automan, balmacaan, Baluchistan, Bantustan, bartizan, Belmopan, black-and-tan, bogeyman, boogeyman, businessman, Caliban, cameraman, caravan, catalan, cattleman, Civitan, colorman, cornerman, counterman, counterplan, countryman, courtesan, dairyman, defenseman, everyman, exciseman, expressman, fellowman, funnyman, gamelan, garageman, garbageman, Hamadan, handyman, harmattan, Hindustan, hotelman, Isle of Man, jerrican, Juliann, Julianne, Kazakhstan, Ku Klux Klan, Kurdistan, Kyrgyzstan, man-for-man, man-to-man, Marianne, Maryann, Maryanne, middleman, minuteman, Monaghan, moneyman, Occitan, ombudsman, Omdurman, overman, overran, Pakistan, Parmesan, partisan, pattypan, Peter Pan, pivotman, plainclothesman, Port Sudan, Powhatan, Ramadan, repairman, rewrite man, Ryazan, safetyman, selectman, serviceman, shandrydan, Shantyman, shovelman, signalman, spick-and-span, superman, tallyman, tamarin, Teheran, teleman, teleran, triggerman,

trimaran, turbofan,
weatherman, workingman,
yataghan, Yucatan,
Afghanistan, arrière-ban,
bipartisan, catamaran, catch-
as-catch-can, cavalryman,
committeeman, deliveryman,
Kalimantan, newspaperman,
orangutan, radioman, salary
man, Tajikistan,
Turkmenistan, Uzbekistan

⁶an \än-yə\ see ¹ANIA

⁷an \äng\ see ¹ONG

⁸an \änt\ see ²ANT

¹ana \än-ə\ ana, anna, Anna,
bwana, Dona, donna, Donna,
fauna, Ghana, Kana, Lana,
Lonna, mana, Botswana,
chicana, gymkhana, iguana,
jacana, lantana, liana,
Madonna, mañana, nagana,
nirvana, piranha, Purana,
ruana, Tijuana, Tirane,
Toscana, zenana, Africana,
belladonna, epifauna, French
Guiana, Guadiana, Haryana,
Hinayana, hiragana, ikebana,
Ludhiana, Mahayana,
marijuana, parmigiana,
pozzolana, prima donna,
Rajputana, Rosh Hashanah,
Tatiana, Americana, fata
morgana, Lincolniana,
Ljubljana, nicotiana,
Shakespeareana, Victoriana,
Ciudad Guyana

²ana \ā-nə\ ana, Dana, Lana,
Africana, cantilena,
Cartagena, nicotiana,
Shakespeareana

³ana \an-ə\ ana, Anna, canna,
manna, Ghana, Hannah,
Lana, nana, banana,
bandanna, cabana, Deanna,
Diana, Dianna, Fermanagh,
goanna, Guiana, Guyana,
gymkhana, Havana,

hosanna, Joanna, Johanna,
Montana, savanna,
Savannah, sultana, Susanna,
Susannah, Africana, Indiana,
Juliana, Mariana, Marianna,
poinciana, Pollyanna, Santa
Ana, Americana, fata
morgana, Louisiana,
nicotiana, Shakespeareana,
Victoriana

aña \än-yə\ see ¹ANIA

anacle \an-i-kəl\ see ANICAL

anage \an-ij\ manage,
tannage, stage-manage,
micromanage

anagh \an-ə\ see ³ANA

¹anah \ō-nə\ see ¹ONA

²anah \an-ə\ see ¹ANA

anal \än-ᵊl\ anal, banal

analyst \an-ᵊl-əst\ analyst,
annalist, panelist,
cryptanalyst, psychoanalyst

anan \an-ən\ see ANNON

anape \an-ə-pē\ see ANOPY

¹anary \än-rē\ see ANERY

²anary \an-rē\ see ²ANNERY

anate \an-ət\ see ANNET

anative \an-ət-iv\ sanative,
explanative

anbe \am-bē\ see AMBY

¹anc \aⁿ\ see ¹ANT

²anc \aŋ\ see ²ANG

³anc \aŋk\ see ANK

anca \aŋ-kə\ Kanka,
barranca, Casablanca, lingua
franca, Salamanca

¹ance \äⁿs\ Reims, nuance,
outrance, Provence, Saint-
Saëns, séance, à outrance,
diligence, Fort-de-France,
ordonnance, renaissance,
mésalliance, par excellence,
concours d'elegance, pièce
de résistance

²ance \äns\ Hans, nonce,
sconce, brisance, ensconce,
faience, nuance, response,

seance, Afrikaans, complaisance, fer-de-lance, nonchalance, provenance, renaissance, pièce de résistance

³**ance** \ans\ chance, dance, France, glance, lance, Lance, manse, Nantes, prance, stance, trance, trans, Vance, advance, askance, bechance, enhance, entrance, expanse, finance, mischance, perchance, romance, Romance, side-glance, sweatpants, circumstance, complaisance, contredanse, country-dance, fer-de-lance, happenchance, happenstance, Liederkranz, Port-au-Prince, refinance, smarty-pants, underpants— *also* -s, -'s, *and* -s' *forms of nouns listed at* ⁵ANT, *and* -s *forms of verbs listed there*

anceable \an-sə-bəl\ see ANSIBLE

anced \anst\ canst, circumstanced, underfinanced—*also* -ed *forms of verbs listed at* ³ANCE

ancel \an-səl\ cancel, chancel, handsel, expansile, precancel

anceler \an-slər\ canceler, chancellor, vice-chancellor

ancellor \an-slər\ see ANCELER

ancement \an-smənt\ advancement, enhancement

ancer \an-sər\ answer, cancer, dancer, glancer, lancer, prancer, advancer, enhancer, free-lancer, merganser, romancer, ropedancer, anticancer, geomancer, necromancer, rhabdomancer

ances \an(t)-səs\ see ANCIS

ancet \an-sət\ lancet, Narragansett

¹**anch** \änch\ see ¹AUNCH

²**anch** \ónch\ see ²AUNCH

³**anch** \anch\ blanch, Blanche, branch, ranch, rebranch, avalanche

¹**anche** \ä ⁿsh\ tranche, carte blanche, revanche

²**anche** \anch\ see ³ANCH

³**anche** \an-chē\ see ANCHY

¹**ancher** \ón-chər\ see AUNCHER

²**ancher** \an-chər\ ceinture, rancher

anchi \an-chē\ see ANCHY

anchion \an-chən\ see ANSION

anchor \aŋ-kər\ see ANKER

anchoress \aŋ-krəs\ see ANKEROUS

anchy \an-chē\ branchy, Ranchi, Comanche

ancial \an-chəl\ see ANTIAL

ancis \an(t)-səs\ Frances, Francis, Aransas—*also* -s, -'s, *and* -s' *forms of nouns listed at* ³ANCE, *and* -s *forms of verbs listed there*

anck \äŋk\ see ¹ONK

anco \äŋ-kō\ see ONCO

ancolin \aŋ-klən\ see ANKLIN

ancor \aŋ-kər\ see ANKER

ancorous \aŋ-krəs\ see ANKEROUS

ancre \aŋ-kər\ see ANKER

ancrous \aŋ-krəs\ see ANKEROUS

anct \aŋt\ see ANKED

ancy \an-sē\ chancy, fancy, Nancy, unchancy, chiromancy, geomancy, hydromancy, necromancy, pyromancy, rhabdomancy, sycophancy, oneiromancy

¹**and** \ä ⁿ\ see ¹ANT

²**and** \änd\ see ¹OND

³**and** \and\ and, band, bland,

brand, canned, gland, grand,
hand, land, manned, NAND,
rand, Rand, sand, Sand,
stand, strand, armband,
backhand, backland,
badland, bandstand,
benchland, blackland,
broadband, brushland,
bushland, cabstand,
cloudland, coastland,
command, cowhand, crash-
land, cropland, deckhand,
demand, disband, dockhand,
dockland, downland,
dreamland, dryland,
duneland, expand,
farmhand, farmland,
fenland, filmland, firebrand,
firsthand, flatland, forehand,
four-hand, free hand,
freehand, gangland, glad-
hand, Gotland, grandstand,
grassland, handstand,
hardstand, hatband,
headband, headstand,
heartland, heathland,
homeland, Iceland, inkstand,
inland, Inland, kickstand,
Kokand, Lapland, left-hand,
longhand, mainland,
marshland, misbrand,
newsstand, nightstand,
northland, noseband,
offhand, outland, outstand,
parkland, pineland, playland,
proband, Queensland,
quicksand, rangeland,
remand, repand, Rheinland,
Rhineland, ribband, right-
hand, rimland, roband,
Saarland, scabland,
screenland, scrubland,
seastrand, shorthand,
sideband, softland,
southland, spaceband,
stagehand, summand,
swampland, sweatband,

Thailand, thirdhand,
tideland, trainband, unhand,
unmanned, waistband,
washstand, wasteland,
watchband, wetland,
wildland, withstand,
wristband, ampersand,
beforehand, behindhand,
bellyband, belly-land,
borderland, bottomland,
confirmand, contraband,
countermand, Damavand,
Dixieland, fairyland,
fatherland, Ferdinand,
forestland, four-in-hand,
graduand, hand-to-hand,
hand to hand, hinterland,
Krugerrand, lotusland,
meadowland, motherland,
Nagaland, narrowband, no-
man's-land, operand,
ordinand, overhand,
overland, pastureland,
reprimand, Rio Grande,
Samarkand, saraband,
secondhand, Swaziland,
tableland, Talleyrand,
timberland, Togoland,
underhand, undermanned,
understand, wonderland,
Zululand, analysand,
Bechuanaland, cloud-
cuckoo-land, fantasyland,
misunderstand, multiplicand,
Prince Rupert's Land,
Somaliland, Sudetenland,
vacationland, videoland,
Witwatersrand,
Matabeleland, Alice-in-
Wonderland—also *-ed forms
of verbs listed at* ⁵AN
⁴**and** \än\ see ¹ON
⁵**and** \änt\ see ²ANT
¹**anda** \an-də\ Ganda, panda,
Amanda, Luanda, Luganda,
Miranda, Uganda, veranda,
jacaranda, memoranda,

nomina conservanda,
propaganda
²**anda** \än-də\ see ONDA
andable \an-də-bəl\ mandible,
commandable, demandable,
expandable, understandable
andaed \an-dəd\ see ANDED
andal \an-dᵊl\ see ANDLE
andaled \an-dᵊld\ handled,
sandaled, well-handled—*also*
-ed *forms of verbs listed at*
ANDLE
andall \an-dᵊl\ see ANDLE
andalous \an-dləs\ see
²ANDLESS
andam \an-dəm\ see
ANDUM
andant \an-dənt\ see ANDENT
andar \ənd-ər\ see UNDER
andarin \an-drən\ mandarin,
alexandrine, salamandrine
¹**ande** \ən\ see UN
²**ande** \an\ see ⁵AN
³**ande** \an-dē\ see ANDY
⁴**ande** \and\ see ³AND
⁵**ande** \än-də\ see ONDA
anded \an-dəd\ banded,
branded, candid, handed,
landed, stranded,
backhanded, bare-handed,
cleanhanded, forehanded,
four-handed, freehanded,
ham-handed, hardhanded,
high-handed, ironhanded,
left-handed, light-handed,
offhanded, one-handed, red-
handed, right-handed,
shorthanded, sure-handed,
three-handed, two-handed,
unbranded, verandaed,
empty-handed, evenhanded,
heavy-handed, openhanded,
overhanded, singlehanded,
underhanded—*also* -ed *forms
of verbs listed at* ³AND
andel \an-dᵊl\ see ANDLE
andem \an-dəm\ see ANDUM

andent \an-dənt\ candent,
scandent, demandant
¹**ander** \en-dər\ see ENDER
²**ander** \än-dər\ see ¹ONDER
³**ander** \an-dər\ bander,
brander, candor, dander,
gander, grandeur, lander,
pander, sander, slander,
strander, zander, auslander,
backhander, blackhander,
bystander, commander,
demander, expander,
flatlander, germander, glad-
hander, goosander,
grandstander, inlander,
Leander, left-hander,
mainlander, meander,
outlander, philander,
pomander, right-hander,
scrimshander, soft-lander,
Uitlander, Africander,
alexander, Alexander,
calamander, coriander,
gerrymander, oleander,
salamander, single-
hander—*also* -er *forms of
adjectives listed at* ³AND
anderous \an-drəs\ see
ANDROUS
anders \an-dərz\ Flanders,
Bouvier des Flandres, golden
alexanders—*also* -s, -'s, *and*
-s' *forms of nouns listed at*
³ANDER, *and* -s *forms of verbs
listed there*
andery \an-drē\ see ANDRY
andes \an-dēz\ Andes—*also*
-s, -'s, *and* -s' *forms of nouns
listed at* ANDY, *and* -s *forms
of verbs listed there*
¹**andeur** \an-dər\ see ³ANDER
²**andeur** \an-jər\ see ⁴ANGER
andhi \an-dē\ see ANDY
andi \an-dē\ see ANDY
andible \an-də-bəl\ see
ANDABLE
andid \an-dəd\ see ANDED

anding \an-diŋ\ standing,
commanding, crossbanding,
freestanding, hardstanding,
long-standing, outstanding,
upstanding, mind-expanding,
notwithstanding,
understanding—*also* -ing
forms of verbs listed at ³AND

andish \an-dish\ blandish,
brandish, standish, Standish,
outlandish

andist \an-dəst\
contrabandist,
propagandist—*also* -est
forms of adjectives listed at
³AND

andit \an-dət\ bandit, pandit

andle \an-dᵊl\ candle, dandle,
Handel, handle, Randall,
sandal, scandal, vandal,
footcandle, manhandle,
mishandle, panhandle,
stickhandle, coromandel,
Coromandel

andled \an-dᵊl\ see ANDALED

andler \an-lər\ candler,
chandler, handler,
panhandler, stickhandler

andless \an-ləs\ see ANLESS

andly \an-lē\ see ²ANLY

andment \an-mənt\
commandment,
disbandment

ando \an-dō\ Fernando,
Orlando

andom \an-dəm\ see ANDUM

andor \an-dər\ see ³ANDER

andra \an-drə\ Sandra,
Cassandra, Alexandra,
pachysandra

andrea \an-drē-ə\ see ANDRIA

andrel \an-drəl\ mandrel,
mandrill, spandrel

andres \an-dərz\ see ANDERS

andria \an-drē-ə\ Andrea,
Alexandria

andrill \an-drəl\ see ANDREL

andrine \an-drən\ see
ANDARIN

andros \an-drəs\ see ANDROUS

androus \an-drəs\ Andros,
slanderous, gynandrous,
meandrous, polyandrous

andry \an-drē\ commandery,
monandry, polyandry

ands \anz\ Badlands,
Lowlands, Canyonlands

andsel \an-səl\ see ANCEL

andsman \anz-mən\
bandsman, clansman,
Klansman, landsman

andsome \an-səm\ see ANSOM

andum \an-dəm\ fandom,
grandam, random, tandem,
memorandum, nomen
conservandum, subpoena ad
testificandum

andy \an-dē\ Andy, bandy,
brandy, Brandy, candy,
dandy, handy, Handy,
pandy, randy, Randy,
sandhi, sandy, Sandy,
shandy, jim-dandy, unhandy,
Rio Grande, modus
operandi

¹ane \ān\ ain, Aisne, ane,
bane, blain, Blaine, brain,
Cain, cane, chain, crane,
Crane, Dane, deign, drain,
Duane, Dwain, Dwayne,
fain, fane, feign, gain, grain,
Jane, Jayne, lane, Lane,
main, Maine, mane, pain,
Paine, pane, plain, plane,
quean, rain, reign, rein, sain,
sane, seine, Seine, skein,
slain, Spain, sprain, stain,
stane, strain, swain, thane,
thegn, train, twain, Twain,
vain, vane, vein, wain, wane,
Wayne, Zane, abstain, again,
airplane, amain, arcane,
arraign, attain, Bahrain,
Bassein, Beltane, biplane,

birdbrain, Biscayne, bloodstain, bugbane, campaign, champagne, champaign, Champlain, checkrein, chicane, chilblain, chow mein, cinquain, cocaine, Cockaigne, coxswain, complain, constrain, contain, cordwain, cowbane, crackbrain, demesne, deplane, destain, detain, detrain, devein, disdain, distain, distrain, dogbane, domain, drivetrain, Duane, dumbcane, edgegrain, Elaine, emplane, enchain, engrain, enplane, entrain, explain, eyestrain, fleabane, floatplane, floodplain, Fort Wayne, Gawain, germane, grosgrain, Helaine, Helene, henbane, house-train, humane, Hussein, Igraine, immane, inane, ingrain, insane, lamebrain, lightplane, lo mein, Loraine, Lorraine, maintain, marchpane, membrane, migraine, Montaigne, montane, moraine, mortmain, Moulmein, mundane, neckrein, obtain, octane, ordain, pertain, plain-Jane, profane, ptomaine, purslane, quatrain, refrain, remain, restrain, retain, retrain, romaine, sailplane, sea-lane, seaplane, seatrain, sustain, tearstain, terrain, terrane, triplane, Touraine, Ukraine, unchain, urbane, vervain, vicereine, villein, volplane, warplane, wolfsbane, aeroplane, appertain, aquaplane, Aquitaine, ascertain, avellane,

Bloemfontein, cellophane, Charlemagne, Charles's Wain, chatelain, chatelaine, counterpane, de Montaigne, entertain, featherbrain, foreordain, frangipane, gyroplane, hurricane, hydroplane, hyperplane, inhumane, Kwajalein, La Fontaine, marocain, Mary Jane, mise-en-scène, monoplane, Novocain, neutercane, novocaine, overlain, paravane, paper-train, peneplain, Port of Spain, port-wine stain, preordain, rattlebrain, scatterbrain, shaggymane, Spanish Main, sugarcane, suzerain, Tamburlaine, Tamerlane, terreplein, tramontane, transmontane, windowpane, Alsace-Lorraine, auf Wiedersehen, balletomane, convertiplane, demimondaine, elecampane, extramundane, intermontane, Lake Pontchartraine, legerdemain, ultramontane, trichalomethane

²ane \an\ see ⁵AN

³ane \än-ə\ see ¹ANA

⁴ane \än\ see ¹ON

anen \ä-nē-ə\ see ²ANIA

anean \ā-nē-ən\ see ²ANIAN

aned \änd\ see AINED

anee \an-ē\ see ANNY

aneful \ān-fəl\ see AINFUL

anel \an-ᵊl\ see ANNEL

anelist \an-ᵊl-əst\ see ANALYST

aneous \ā-nē-əs\ cutaneous, extraneous, spontaneous, coetaneous, consentaneous, instantaneous, miscellaneous, porcelaneous, simultaneous, succedaneous, contemporaneous, extemporaneous

¹aner \ā-nər\ see AINER

²aner \än-ər\ see ¹ONOR

anery \än-rē\ granary, chicanery

anet \an-ət\ see ANNET

aneum \ā-nē-əm\ see ANIUM

aney \ō-nē\ see ¹AWNY

anford \an-fərd\ Sanford, Stanford

¹ang \äŋ\ see ¹ONG

²ang \aŋ\ bang, bhang, clang, dang, fang, Fang, gang, gangue, hang, pang, prang, rang, sang, slang, spang, sprang, stang, tang, twang, whang, yang, cliff-hang, defang, ginseng, harangue, linsang, meringue, mustang, orang, parang, Pinang, press-gang, probang, shebang, slam-bang, straphang, trepang, whizbang, boomerang, charabanc, overhang, parasang, siamang, interrobang, orangutan

³ang \óŋ\ see ²ONG

anga \äŋ-gə\ see ONGA

angar \aŋ-ər\ see ²ANGER

¹ange \ä"zh\ blancmange, mélange

²ange \ānj\ change, grange, mange, range, strange, arrange, derange, downrange, estrange, exchange, free-range, gearchange, long-range, outrange, short-range, shortchange, counterchange, disarrange, interchange, omnirange, Great Dividing Range

³ange \anj\ flange, phalange

angel \aŋ-gəl\ see ANGLE

angell \aŋ-gəl\ see ANGLE

angement \ānj-mənt\ arrangement, derangement, estrangement, disarrangement

angency \an-jən-sē\ plangency, tangency

angent \an-jənt\ plangent, tangent

¹anger \ān-jər\ changer, danger, granger, manger, ranger, stranger, bushranger, endanger, estranger, exchanger, shortchanger, interchanger

²anger \aŋ-ər\ banger, clanger, clangor, clangour, ganger, hangar, hanger, languor, Sanger, twanger, cliff-hanger, straphanger, haranguer, paperhanger

³anger \aŋ-gər\ anger, clangor

⁴anger \an-jər\ flanger, grandeur, phalanger

angi \aŋ-ē\ see ²ANGY

angible \an-jə-bəl\ frangible, tangible, infrangible, intangible, refrangible

angie \aŋ-ē\ see ²ANGY

¹anging \ān-jiŋ\ bushranging, unchanging, wide-ranging—*also* -ing *forms of verbs listed at* ²ANGE

²anging \aŋ-iŋ\ hanging, cliff-hanging, paperhanging—*also* -ing *forms of verbs listed at* ²ANG

angle \aŋ-gəl\ angle, bangle, dangle, jangle, mangel, mangle, spangle, strangle, tangle, wangle, wrangle, embrangle, entangle, Mount Wrangell, pentangle, quadrangle, rectangle, triangle, untangle, wide-angle, disentangle

angled \aŋ-gəld\ angled,

tangled, newfangled, oldfangled, right-angled, star-spangled—*also* -ed *forms of verbs listed at* ANGLE

anglement \aŋ-gəl-mənt\ tanglement, embranglement, entanglement, disentanglement

angler \aŋ-glər\ angler, dangler, jangler, mangler, strangler, wangler, wrangler, entangler

angles \aŋ-gəlz\ Angles, strangles—*also* -s, -'s, *and* -s' *forms of nouns listed at* ANGLE, *and* -s *forms of verbs listed there*

anglian \aŋ-glē-ən\ Anglian, ganglion

angling \aŋ-gliŋ\ angling, gangling—*also* -ing *forms of verbs listed at* ANGLE

anglion \aŋ-glē-ən\ *see* ANGLIAN

angly \aŋ-glē\ gangly, jangly, tangly

ango \aŋ-gō\ mango, tango, Durango, fandango

¹angor \aŋ-ər\ *see* ²ANGER

²angor \aŋ-gər\ *see* ³ANGER

angorous \aŋ-ə-rəs\ clangorous, languorous

angour \aŋ-ər\ *see* ²ANGER

angster \aŋ-stər\ gangster, prankster

anguage \aŋ-gwij\ language, slanguage, metalanguage, paralanguage, protolanguage

angue \aŋ\ *see* ²ANG

anguer \aŋ-ər\ *see* ²ANGER

anguish \aŋ-gwish\ anguish, languish

anguor \aŋ-ər\ *see* ²ANGER

anguorous \aŋ-ə-rəs\ *see* ANGOROUS

angus \aŋ-gəs\ Angus, Brangus

¹angy \ān-jē\ mangy, rangy

²angy \aŋ-ē\ tangy, twangy, Ubangi, collieshangie

anha \än-ə\ *see* ¹ANA

anhope \an-əp\ *see* ANNUP

¹ani \än-ē\ Bonnie, bonny, Connie, Donnie, fawny, johnny, Ronnie, tawny, afghani, Fulani, chalcedony, Kisangani, maharani, Nuristani, quadriphony, Rajasthani, mulligatawny

²ani \an-ē\ *see* ANNY

¹ania \än-yə\ Agana, España, lasagna, Titania, Emilia-Romagna

²ania \ā-nē-ə\ mania, titania, Titania, Urania, Acarnania, Anglomania, Aquitania, collectanea, dipsomania, egomania, hypomania, kleptomania, Lithuania, Mauretania, Mauritania, miscellanea, monomania, mythomania, nymphomania, Oceania, Pennsylvania, Pomerania, pyromania, Transylvania, balletomania, bibliomania, decalcomania, megalomania—*also* ³ANIA

³ania \än-yə\ Campania, Catania, Hispania, Titania, Aquitania, malaguena, Tripolitania—*also* ²ANIA

¹anian \än-ē-ən\ Kiwanian, Araucanian, Turanian

²anian \ā-nē-ən\ Albanian, Dardanian, Iranian, Romanian, Rumanian, Sassanian, Turanian, Ukrainian, Uranian, vulcanian, Lithuanian, Pennsylvanian, Pomeranian, Ruritanian, subterranean, Indo-Iranian, Mediterranean

aniard \an-yərd\ lanyard, Spaniard

anic \an-ik\ manic, panic,
tannic, Brahmanic,
Britannic, cyanic, firemanic,
galvanic, Germanic,
Hispanic, Koranic,
mechanic, melanic, organic,
Romanic, satanic, shamanic,
Sudanic, titanic, tympanic,
volcanic, aldermanic,
Alemannic, councilmanic,
epiphanic, inorganic,
messianic, oceanic, Ossianic,
pre-Hispanic, talismanic,
theophanic, Indo-Germanic,
megalomanic, Rhaeto-
Romanic, suboceanic,
transoceanic

anical \an-i-kəl\ manacle,
panicle, sanicle, botanical,
mechanical, tyrannical,
puritanical

anice \an-əs\ see ANISE

anicle \an-i-kəl\ see ANICAL

anics \an-iks\ annex,
mechanics—*also* -s, -'s, *and*
-s' *forms of nouns listed at*
ANIC, *and* -s *forms of verbs
listed there*

¹**anid** \ā-nəd\ ranid, tabanid

²**anid** \an-əd\ canid, ranid,
Sassanid

¹**aniel** \an-ᵊl\ see ANNEL

²**aniel** \an-yəl\ see ANUAL

anigan \an-i-gən\ see
ANNIGAN

anikin \an-i-kən\ see ANNIKIN

animous \an-ə-məs\ animus,
magnanimous, unanimous,
pusillanimous

animus \an-ə-məs\ see
ANIMOUS

¹**anion** \ān-yən\ see ¹ONYON

²**anion** \an-yən\ banyan,
canon, canyon, fanion,
companion, Grand Canyon,
Hells Canyon

anis \an-əs\ see ANISE

anise \an-əs\ anise, Janice,
Janis, stannous, johannes,
Johannes, pandanus,
titanous, Scipio Africanus

¹**anish** \ā-nish\ see AINISH

²**anish** \an-ish\ banish,
clannish, mannish, planish,
Spanish, tannish, vanish,
Pollyannish, Judeo-Spanish

anist \än-əst\ see ONEST

anister \an-ə-stər\ banister,
canister, ganister

anite \an-ət\ see ANNET

anity \an-ət-ē\ sanity, vanity,
humanity, inanity, insanity,
profanity, urbanity,
Christianity, churchianity,
inhumanity, superhumanity

anium \ā-nē-əm\ cranium,
geranium, uranium,
succedaneum

ank \aŋk\ bank, blank,
brank, clank, crank, dank,
drank, flank, franc, frank,
Frank, hank, lank, plank,
prank, rank, sank, shank,
shrank, spank, stank, swank,
tank, thank, yank, Yank,
Burbank, claybank, embank,
foreshank, gangplank,
greenshank, nonbank,
outflank, outrank,
pickthank, point-blank,
redshank, sandbank,
sheepshank, snowbank,
mountebank, riverbank,
clinkety-clank

¹**anka** \äŋ-kə\ concha, tanka,
Sri Lanka

²**anka** \aŋ-kə\ see ANCA

ankable \aŋ-kə-bəl\ bankable,
frankable

anked \aŋt\ shanked, tanked,
spindle-shanked,
sacrosanct—*also* -ed *forms of
verbs listed at* ANK

ankee \an-kē\ see ANKY

anken \aŋ-kən\ flanken, Rankine

anker \aŋ-kər\ anchor, banker, canker, chancre, flanker, franker, hanker, rancor, ranker, spanker, tanker, thanker, co-anchor, unanchor—*also* -er *forms of adjectives listed at* ANK

ankerous \aŋ-krəs\ anchoress, cankerous, chancrous, rancorous, cantankerous

ankh \äŋk\ *see* ¹ONK

ankie \an-kē\ *see* ANKY

ankine \aŋ-kən\ *see* ANKEN

ankish \aŋ-kish\ Frankish, prankish

ankle \aŋ-kəl\ ankle, crankle, rankle

ankly \aŋ-klē\ blankly, dankly, frankly

anks \aŋs\ *see* ANX

ankster \aŋ-stər\ *see* ANGSTER

anky \aŋ-kē\ cranky, hankie, lanky, swanky, Yankee, hanky-panky

anless \an-ləs\ handless, manless, planless

anley \an-lē\ *see* ²ANLY

anli \an-lē\ *see* ²ANLY

¹anly \än-lē\ fondly, thrawnly, wanly

²anly \an-lē\ blandly, grandly, manly, Stanley, Osmanli, unmanly

¹ann \an\ *see* ⁵AN

²ann \än\ *see* ¹ON

¹anna \än-ə\ *see* ¹ANA

²anna \an-ə\ *see* ³ANA

annage \an-ij\ *see* ANAGE

annah \an-ə\ *see* ³ANA

annalist \an-ᵊl-əst\ *see* ANALYST

annan \an-ən\ *see* ANNON

anne \an\ *see* ⁵AN

anned \and\ *see* ³AND

annel \an-ᵊl\ channel, Channel, Daniel, flannel, panel, scrannel, spaniel, impanel, English Channel

annequin \an-i-kən\ *see* ANNIKIN

anner \an-ər\ banner, canner, fanner, lanner, manner, manor, planner, scanner, spanner, tanner, vanner, deadpanner, japanner, caravanner

¹annery \än-rē\ ornery, swannery

²annery \an-rē\ cannery, granary, tannery

annes \an-əs\ *see* ANISE

anness \än-nəs\ fondness, wanness

annet \an-ət\ gannet, granite, Janet, planet, pomegranate

annexe \an-iks\ *see* ANICS

annibal \an-ə-bəl\ cannibal, Hannibal

annic \an-ik\ *see* ANIC

annie \an-ē\ *see* ANNY

annigan \an-i-gən\ brannigan, shenanigan

annikin \an-i-kən\ cannikin, manikin, mannequin, pannikin

annin \an-ən\ *see* ANNON

annish \an-ish\ *see* ²ANISH

annon \an-ən\ cannon, canon, Shannon, tannin, Buchanan, Clackmannan, colcannon

annous \an-əs\ *see* ANISE

anns \anz\ *see* ⁴ANS

annual \an-yəl\ *see* ANUAL

annular \an-yə-lər\ annular, cannular, granular

annulate \an-yə-lət\ annulate, annulet, campanulate

annulet \an-yə-lət\ *see* ANNULATE

annum \an-əm\ *see* ²ANUM

annup \an-əp\ sannup, stanhope

anny \an-ē\ Annie, canny, cranny, Danny, fanny, granny, Lanny, nanny, afghani, ca'canny, kokanee, uncanny, frangipani, Hindustani, hootenanny

¹**ano** \än-ō\ guano, Kano, llano, mano, mono, Chicano, Marrano, Nagano, piano, Romano, Serrano, soprano, altiplano, boliviano, fortepiano, mezzo piano, mezzo-soprano, Città del Vaticano

²**ano** \ä-nō\ ripieno, volcano

³**ano** \an-ō\ Hispano, piano, soprano, fortepiano, mezzo-soprano

¹**anon** \an-ən\ see ANNON

²**anon** \an-yən\ see ²ANION

anopy \an-ə-pē\ canape, canopy

anor \an-ər\ see ANNER

anous \an-əs\ see ANISE

anqui \än-kē\ see ONKY

¹**ans** \äns\ see ²ANCE

²**ans** \änz\ see ONZE

³**ans** \ans\ see ³ANCE

⁴**ans** \anz\ banns, Hans, sans, trans, Sextans—also -s, -'s, and -s' forms of nouns listed at ⁵AN, and -s forms of verbs listed there

⁵**ans** \aⁿ\ see ¹ANT

ansard \an-sərd\ see ANSWERED

¹**ansas** \an(t)-səs\ see ANCIS

²**ansas** \an-zəs\ Kansas, Arkansas

anse \ans\ see ³ANCE

ansea \än-zē\ see ANZY

anser \an-sər\ see ANCER

anset \an-sət\ see ANCET

ansett \an-sət\ see ANCET

ansible \an-sə-bəl\ danceable, expansible

ansile \an-səl\ see ANCEL

ansing \an-siŋ\ Lansing—also -ing forms of verbs listed at ³ANCE

ansion \an-chən\ mansion, scansion, stanchion, expansion

ansk \änsk\ Bryansk, Gdansk, Murmansk, Saransk

ansman \anz-mən\ see ANDSMAN

ansom \an-səm\ handsome, hansom, ransom, transom, unhandsome

anst \anst\ see ANCED

answer \an-sər\ see ANCER

answered \an-sərd\ answered, mansard, unanswered

ansy \an-zē\ pansy, tansy, chimpanzee

¹**ant** \äⁿ\ Caen, Gant, arpent, beurre blanc, croissant, en banc, Mont Blanc, riant, roman, Rouen, Tátouan, savant, versant, accouchement, aide-de-camp, au courant, battement, ci-devant, contretemps, debridement, denouement, en passant, Maupassant, Mitterand, Orléans, Perpignan, rapprochement, revenant, se tenant, soi-disant, vol-au-vent, arrondissement, chateaubriand, Chateaubriand, Clermont-Ferrand, de Maupassant, idiot savant, ressentiment, sauvignon blanc

²**ant** \änt\ aunt, can't, daunt, flaunt, font, fount, gaunt, taunt, vaunt, want, wont, avant, avaunt, bacchant, bacchante, Balante, Beaumont, bouffant, brisant, courante, détente, entente,

Fremont, gallant, grandaunt,
piedmont, Piedmont,
piquant, romaunt, Rostand,
savant, sirvente, Vermont,
bon vivant, commandant,
complaisant, confidant,
debridement, debutant,
debutante, dilettante, John
of Gaunt, intrigant,
nonchalant, poste restante,
restaurant, symbiont,
dicynodont, subdebutante,
Montcalm de Saint Veran,
sinfonia concertante

³ant \ȯnt\ see ¹ONT

⁴ant \ȯnt\ see ¹AUNT

⁵ant \ant\ ant, aunt, brant,
cant, can't, chant, grant,
Grant, hant, Kant, pant,
plant, rant, scant, shan't,
slant, aslant, bacchant,
bacchante, bezant, courante,
decant, descant, discant,
displant, eggplant, enceinte,
enchant, explant, extant,
formant, gallant, grandaunt,
houseplant, implant, incant,
leadplant, levant, Levant,
pieplant, pissant, plainchant,
pourpoint, preplant, replant,
rampant, recant, replant,
savant, supplant, transplant,
adamant, commandant,
complaisant, confidant,
cormorant, corposant,
Corybant, covenant,
demipointe, dilettante,
disenchant, gallivant,
hierophant, interplant,
sycophant

anta \ant-ə\ anta, manta,
Atlanta, infanta, vedanta,
Atalanta

antage \ant-ij\ vantage,
advantage, coign of
vantage, disadvantage

antain \ant-³n\ see ²ANTON

¹antal \änt-³l\ see ¹ONTAL

²antal \ant-³l\ see ²ANTLE

antam \ant-əm\ bantam,
phantom

antar \ant-ər\ see ²ANTER

antasist \ant-ə-səst\ see
ANTICIST

¹ante \än-tā\ Brontë, Dante,
andante, Asante, volante,
Belo Horizonte

²ante \änt\ see ²ANT

³ante \änt\ see ⁵ANT

⁴ante \änt-ē\ see ⁴ANTI

⁵ante \ant-ē\ ante, canty,
chantey, pantie, scanty,
shanty, slanty, andanti,
Asante, Ashanti, Chianti,
infante, non obstante,
penny-ante, vigilante,
pococurante, status quo
ante

antean \ant-ē-ən\ Dantean,
Atlantean, post-Kantian

anteau \an-tō\ see ²ANTO

anted \an-təd\
disenchanted—*also* -ed
forms of verbs listed at ⁵ANT

antel \ant-³l\ see ANTLE

antelet \ant-lət\ mantelet,
plantlet

¹anter \änt-ər\ see ¹AUNTER

²anter \ant-ər\ antre, banter,
canter, cantor, chanter,
granter, grantor, plantar,
planter, ranter, scanter,
decanter, implanter,
instanter, levanter,
transplanter, trochanter,
covenanter, covenantor,
disenchanter

¹antes \an-tēz\ Cervantes—
also -s, -'s, *and* -s' *forms of
nouns listed at* ⁵ANTE, *and* -s
forms of verbs listed there

²antes \ans\ see ³ANCE

antey \ant-ē\ see ⁵ANTE

anth \anth\ amaranth,

coelacanth, perianth,
tragacanth

antha \an-thə\ Samantha,
polyantha, pyracantha

anthemum \an-thə-məm\
chrysanthemum,
mesembryanthemum

anther \an-thər\ anther,
panther

anthropy \an-thrə-pē\
lycanthropy, misanthropy,
philanthropy

anthus \an-thəs\ acanthus,
ailanthus, dianthus,
agapanthus, amianthus,
polyanthus, Rhadamanthus

¹anti \änt-ē\ Brontë, jaunty,
monte, Monte, Monty,
vaunty, andante, Asante,
Ashanti, Chianti

²anti \ant-ē\ see ⁵ANTE

antial \an-chəl\ financial,
substantial, circumstantial,
consubstantial, insubstantial,
transsubstantial,
unsubstantial,
supersubstantial

¹antian \änt-ē-ən\ see ONTIAN

²antian \ant-ē-ən\ see ANTEAN

¹antic \änt-ik\ see ONTIC

²antic \ant-ik\ antic, frantic,
mantic, Atlantic, bacchantic,
gigantic, pedantic, romantic,
semantic, Vedantic,
corybantic, geomantic,
hierophantic, necromantic,
sycophantic, transatlantic

anticist \ant-ə-səst\ fantasist,
Atlanticist, romanticist,
semanticist

antid \ant-əd\ mantid,
Quadrantid—also -ed *forms
of verbs listed at* ⁵ANT

antie \ant-ē\ see ⁵ANTE

antine \ant-ⁿn\ see ²ANTON

¹anting \ant-iŋ\ anting,
canting, disenchanting—*also*

-ing *forms of verbs listed at*
⁵ANT

²anting \ont-iŋ\ see UNTING

antis \ant-əs\ cantus, mantis,
Santos, Atlantis

antish \ant-ish\ dilettantish,
sycophantish

antle \ant-ⁿl\ cantle, mantel,
mantle, quintal, dismantle,
quadrantal, consonantal,
covenantal, overmantel,
determinantal

antlet \ant-lət\ see ANTELET

antling \ant-liŋ\ bantling,
scantling, dismantling

¹anto \än-tō\ Squanto, bel
canto, Toronto, Esperanto

²anto \an-tō\ canto, panto,
coranto, Otranto,
portmanteau, Esperanto,
Strait of Otranto

antom \ant-əm\ see
ANTAM

¹anton \änt-ⁿn\ see ONTON

²anton \ant-ⁿn\ Anton,
canton, Canton, plantain,
Scranton, Stanton,
adamantine

antor \ant-ər\ see ²ANTER

¹antos \an-təs\ see ANTIS

²antos \än-təs\ Santos,
Propontis

antra \an-trə\ tantra,
yantra

antre \ant-ər\ see ²ANTER

antry \an-trē\ chantry,
gantry, pantry

ants \ans\ see ³ANCE

antua \anch-wə\ mantua,
Gargantua

antus \ant-əs\ see ANTIS

anty \ant-ē\ see ⁵ANTE

¹anual \an-yəl\ Daniel,
spaniel, Nathaniel

²anual \an-yə-wəl\ annual,
manual, Manuel, biannual,
bimanual, Emanuel,

Emmanuel, Immanuel, semi-
annual, Victor Emmanuel

anuel \an-yəl\ see ²ANUAL

anular \an-yə-lər\ see
ANNULAR

anulate \an-yə-lət\ see
ANNULATE

¹anum \ā-nəm\ paynim,
arcanum

²anum \an-əm\ per annum,
solanum

¹anus \ā-nəs\ see AYNESS

²anus \an-əs\ see ANISE

anx \aŋs\ Manx, thanks,
Grand Banks, phalanx—
*also -s, -'s, and -s' forms of
nouns listed at* ANK, *and -s
forms of verbs listed there*

¹any \ā-nē\ see AINY

²any \en-ē\ see ENNY

anyan \an-yən\ see ²ANION

anyard \an-yərd\ see ANIARD

anyon \an-yən\ see ²ANION

anz \ans\ see ³ANCE

¹anza \än-zə\ kwanza,
Kwanza, Kwanzaa, Sancho
Panza

²anza \an-zə\ stanza, zanza,
bonanza, organza, Sancho
Panza, extravaganza

anzaa \än-zə\ see ¹ANZA

anzee \an-zē\ see ANSY

anzer \än-sər\ see ONSOR

anzo \än-zō\ gonzo, garbanzo

anzy \än-zē\ bronzy, Ponzi,
Swansea

¹ao \ā-ō\ see ¹EO

²ao \ō\ see ¹OW

³ao \au̇\ see ²OW

⁴ao \ä-ō\ Caliao, Mindanao

aoedic \ēd-ik\ see ¹EDIC

aoighis \äsh\ see ²ECHE

aole \au̇-lē\ see ²OWLY

aône \ōn\ see ¹ONE

aori \au̇r-ē\ see OWERY

¹aos \au̇s\ see ²OUSE

²aos \ā-äs\ chaos, Laos

aotian \ō-shən\ see OTION

aow \au̇\ see ²OW

¹ap \āp\ see ¹OP

²ap \əp\ see UP

³ap \ap\ cap, chap, clap, crap,
flap, frap, gap, gape, hap,
knap, lap, Lapp, map, nap,
nape, nappe, pap, rap, sap,
scrap, slap, snap, strap, tap,
trap, wrap, yap, Yap, zap,
backslap, backwrap,
blackcap, bootstrap, burlap,
catnap, claptrap, dewlap,
dognap, earflap, entrap,
enwrap, firetrap, flatcap,
foolscap, giddap, heeltap,
hubcap, jockstrap, kidnap,
kneecap, lagniappe, livetrap,
madcap, mantrap, mayhap,
mishap, mobcap, mousetrap,
nightcap, pinesap, rattrap,
recap, redcap, remap, riprap,
satrap, shiplap, shrink-wrap,
skullcap, skycap, snowcap,
steel-trap, stopgap, unsnap,
unstrap, unwrap, verb sap,
whitecap, wiretap, afterclap,
gingersnap, handicap,
overlap, rattletrap,
thunderclap, verbum sap,
wentletrap, Venus's-flytrap

¹apa \äp-ə\ grappa, Joppa,
papa, poppa, tapa, Jalapa,
jipijapa

²apa \ap-ə\ kappa, tapa, Phi
Beta Kappa

apable \ā-pə-bəl\ capable,
drapable, shapable,
escapable, incapable,
inescapable

apal \ā-pəl\ see APLE

apas \äp-əs\ Chiapas—*also
-s, -'s, and -s' forms of
nouns listed at* ¹APA

apboard \ab-ərd\ see ABARD

¹ape \āp\ ape, cape, chape,
crape, crepe, drape, gape,

grape, jape, nape, rape, scape, scrape, shape, tape, agape, broomrape, cloudscape, duct tape, escape, landscape, moonscape, North Cape, reshape, seascape, shipshape, snowscape, streetscape, townscape, transshape, undrape, waveshape, cityscape, masking tape, waterscape, Xeriscape, audiotape, stereotape, videotape

²ape \ap\ see ³AP

³ape \äp-ē\ see OPPY

⁴ape \ap-ē\ see APPY

aped \āpt\ bell-shaped—*also* -ed *forms of verbs listed at* ¹APE

apel \ap-əl\ see APPLE

apelin \ap-lən\ see APLAIN

apen \ā-pən\ capon, shapen, unshapen

aper \ā-pər\ caper, draper, gaper, paper, scraper, shaper, taper, tapir, vapor, vapour, curlpaper, endpaper, flypaper, glasspaper, landscaper, newspaper, notepaper, sandpaper, skyscraper, wallpaper, wastepaper, run-of-paper

aperer \ā-pər-ər\ paperer, taperer, vaporer

apery \ā-prē\ drapery, japery, napery, papery, vapory, sandpapery

apes \āps\ traipse, jackanapes— *also* -s, -'s, *and* -s' *forms of nouns listed at* ¹APE, *and* -s *forms of verbs listed there*

apey \ā-pē\ crepey, drapy, grapey, grapy, kepi, scrapie

aph \af\ caff, calf, chaff, daff, gaff, gaffe, graph, half,

laugh, quaff, raff, sclaff, staff, staph, Waf, waff, agrafe, behalf, carafe, chiffchaff, cowlstaff, digraph, distaff, Falstaff, flagstaff, giraffe, half-staff, horselaugh, kenaf, mooncalf, paraph, pikestaff, riffraff, tipstaff, autograph, barograph, bathyscaphe, cenotaph, chronograph, cryptograph, epigraph, epitaph, half-and-half, hectograph, holograph, homograph, hygrograph, kymograph, lithograph, logograph, micrograph, monograph, pantograph, paragraph, phonograph, photograph, pictograph, polygraph, quarterstaff, seismograph, serigraph, shadowgraph, shandygaff, spectrograph, sphygmograph, telegraph, thermograph, typograph, understaff, cardiograph, choreograph, heliograph, ideograph, mimeograph, oscillograph, pseudepigraph, radiograph, chromolithograph, cinematograph, encephalograph, photomicrograph, radiotelegraph, electrocardiograph, electroencephalograph

aphael \af-ē-əl\ see APHIAL

¹aphe \āf\ see ¹AFE

²aphe \af\ see APH

apher \af-ər\ see ²AFFER

aphia \af-ē-ə\ see AFFIA

aphial \af-ē-əl\ Raphael, epitaphial

aphic \af-ik\ graphic, maffick, sapphic, traffic, digraphic,

edaphic, serafic, triaphic,
allographic, autographic,
barographic, biographic,
calligraphic, cartographic,
cosmographic,
cryptographic, demographic,
epigraphic, epitaphic,
ethnographic, geographic,
hectographic, homographic,
hydrographic, lithographic,
logographic, mammographic,
monographic, orthographic,
pantographic, paragraphic,
petrographic, phonographic,
photographic, pictographic,
polygraphic, pornographic,
reprographic, stenographic,
stratigraphic, telegraphic,
tomographic, topographic,
typographic, xerographic,
bibliographic,
choreographic,
crystallographic,
hagiographic,
homolographic,
iconographic, ideographic,
lexicographic,
oceanographic,
stereographic,
autobiographic,
cinematographic,
echocardiographic,
historiographic,
electroencephalographic

aphical \af-i-kǝl\ graphical,
biographical, cartographical,
cosmographical,
cryptographical,
epigraphical, ethnographical,
geographical, orthographical,
petrographical,
topographical,
typographical,
bibliographical,
choreographical,
hagiographical,
iconographical,

lexicographical,
oceanographical,
autobiographical,
historiographical

aphics \af-iks\ graphics,
demographics,
micrographics, supergraphics

aphnis \af-nǝs\ see AFTNESS

aphora \a-fǝ-rǝ\ anaphora,
cataphora

api \äp-ē\ see OPPY

apid \ap-ǝd\ rapid, sapid,
vapid

aple \ā-pē\ see APEY

apin \ap-ǝn\ see APPEN

apine \ap-ǝn\ see APPEN

apir \ā-pǝr\ see APER

apis \ā-pǝs\ Apis, Priapus,
Serapis

apist \ā-pǝst\ rapist, escapist,
landscapist

aplain \ap-lǝn\ capelin,
chaplain, chaplin, sapling

aple \ā-pǝl\ maple, papal,
staple

aples \ā-pǝlz\ Naples—*also* -s,
-'s, *and* -s' *forms of nouns
listed at* APLE, *and* -s *forms of
verbs listed there*

apless \ap-lǝs\ hapless,
napless, sapless, strapless

aplin \ap-lǝ-n\ see APLAIN

aply \ap-lē\ see APTLY

apnel \ap-nᵊl\ grapnel,
shrapnel

apo \äp-ō\ capo, da capo,
gestapo, Mount Apo

apolis \ap-ǝ-lǝs\ Annapolis,
Minneapolis, Indianapolis

apon \ā-pǝn\ see APEN

apor \ā-pǝr\ see APER

aporer \ā-pǝr-ǝr\ see APERER

apory \ā-prē\ see APERY

apour \ā-pǝr\ see APER

app \ap\ see ³AP

¹appa \äp-ǝ\ see ¹APA

²appa \ap-ǝ\ see ²APA

appable \ap-ə-bəl\ flappable,
mappable, recappable,
unflappable

appalli \äp-ə-lē\ see OPOLY

appe \ap\ see ³AP

apped \apt\ see APT

appen \ap-ən\ happen, lapin,
rapine

¹**apper** \äp-ər\ see OPPER

²**apper** \ap-ər\ capper, clapper,
dapper, flapper, knapper,
rapper, sapper, scrapper,
snapper, strapper, tapper,
wrapper, zapper, backslapper,
catnapper, didapper,
kidnapper, knee-slapper,
petnapper, wiretapper,
handicapper, snippersnapper,
understrapper,
whippersnapper

appet \ap-ət\ lappet, tappet

apphic \af-ik\ see APHIC

appie \äp-ē\ see OPPY

appily \ap-ə-lē\ happily,
scrappily, snappily,
unhappily

appiness \ap-ē-nəs\
happiness, sappiness,
scrappiness, snappiness,
unhappiness

apping \ap-iŋ\ capping,
mapping, strapping,
trapping, wrapping,
kneecapping, petnapping—
also -ing forms of verbs listed
at ³AP

apple \ap-əl\ apple, chapel,
dapple, grapple, scrapple,
mayapple, pineapple,
antechapel

apps \aps\ see APSE

appy \ap-ē\ crappy, flappy,
gappy, happy, nappy, pappy,
sappy, scrappy, snappy,
zappy, satrapy, serape,
slaphappy, unhappy,
triggerhappy

aps \aps\ see APSE

apse \aps\ apse, chaps, craps,
lapse, schnapps, taps, traps,
collapse, elapse, perhaps,
prolapse, relapse, synapse,
time-lapse—also -s, -'s, and
-s' forms of nouns listed at
³AP, and -s forms of verbs
listed there

apt \apt\ apt, napped, rapt,
adapt, black-capped, coapt,
dewlapped, enrapt, inapt,
snowcapped, unapt,
untapped, periapt—also -ed
forms of verbs listed at ³AP

apter \ap-tər\ captor,
chapter, raptor, adapter

aption \ap-shən\ caption,
adaption, contraption

aptive \ap-tiv\ captive,
adaptive, maladaptive,
preadaptive

aptly \ap-lē\ aptly, haply,
raptly, inaptly, unaptly

aptor \ap-tər\ see APTER

apture \ap-chər\ rapture,
enrapture, recapture

apular \ap-yə-lər\ papular,
scapular

apus \ā-pəs\ see APIS

¹**apy** \ā-pē\ see APEY

²**apy** \ap-ē\ see APPY

¹**aq** \äk\ see ¹OCK

²**aq** \ak\ see ²ACK

aqi \äk-ē\ see OCKY

¹**aque** \āk\ see ¹AKE

²**aque** \ak\ see ²ACK

aqui \äk-ē\ see OCKY

¹**ar** \er\ see ⁴ARE

²**ar** \ȯr\ see ¹OR

³**ar** \är\ ar, are, bar, barre,
car, carr, char, charr, czar,
far, gar, gnar, guar, jar, Lar,
mar, moire, noir, our, par,
parr, R, quare, Saar, scar,
spar, SPAR, star, tar, tahr,
Thar, tsar, tzar, yare, Adar,

afar, ajar, all-star, armoire,
attar, bazaar, beaux arts,
Bihar, bizarre, boudoir,
boxcar, boyar, briard,
bulbar, Bulgar, bursar,
canard, catarrh, Cathar,
chukar, cigar, clochard,
cougar, couloir, crossbar,
crowbar, Dakar, daystar,
debar, decare, devoir, dinar,
disbar, drawbar, Dunbar,
durbar, earthstar, Elgar,
eschar, eyebar, feldspar, five-
star, flatcar, four-star,
fulmar, gazar, guitar,
Gunnar, Hagar, handcar,
Hoggar, horsecar, hussar,
Invar, Ishtar, Kolar, Loire,
Iyar, jack-tar, jowar,
Khowar, lahar, Lamar,
lekvar, lodestar, Magyar,
memoir, Mizar, Mylar,
Navarre, nightjar, paillard,
peignoir, petard, Pindar,
pissoir, planar, plantar,
polestar, pourboire, pulsar,
qintar, quasar, radar, railcar,
rebar, Renoir, Safar, Samar,
sandbar, scalar, shikar,
shofar, sidebar, sidecar,
sirdar, sitar, sofar, solar,
sonar, streetcar, Svalbard,
tramcar, trocar, unbar, volar,
voussoir, Weimar, abattoir,
acinar, Ahaggar, Aligarh,
aide-memoire, au revoir,
avatar, bete noire, beurre
noir, bolivar, Bolívar, café
noir, caviar, cinnabar,
commissar, communard,
coplanar, Côte d'Ivoire,
cultivar, deciare, deodar,
Dreyfusard, escolar,
escritoire, exemplar,
fluorspar, handlebar, insofar,
isobar, Issachar, jacamar,
jaguar, Kandahar, Kashgar,

kilobar, Krasnodar, Malabar,
megabar, megastar, millibar,
minicar, montagnard,
motorcar, Mudejar, muscle
car, Myanmar, Nicobar,
objet d'art, pinot noir,
Qiqihar, registrar, rent-a-car,
repertoire, reservoir,
ricercar, samovar, scimitar,
seminar, simular, steak
tartare, subahdar, superstar,
tutelar, turbocar, VCR,
Veadar, zamindar, Zanzibar,
budgerigar, conservatoire,
Gulf of Mannar, Hubli-
Dharwar, kala-azar,
Kathiawar, proseminar

¹ara \är-ə\ Kara, Laura,
Mara, Nara, para, vara,
Asmara, Bambara,
begorra, Bukhara,
Camorra, Ferrara,
Gomorrah, saguaro,
Samara, samsara, tantara,
tiara, capybara, carbonara,
Connemara, deodara,
Gemarara, Guanabara,
solfatara, tuatara,
Guadalajara, Ogasawara,
Sagamihara, Tarahumara,
Timisoara

²ara \er-ə\ see ¹ERA

³ara \ar-ə\ see ¹ARROW

⁴ara \ȯr-ə\ see ORA

arab \ar-əb\ Arab, Carib,
carob, scarab, Shatt al Arab

arable \ar-ə-bəl\ arable,
bearable, parable, shareable,
spareable, wearable,
declarable, unbearable,
inenarrable

aracen \ar-ə-sən\ see ARISON

aracin \ar-ə-sən\ see ARISON

arad \ar-əd\ see ARID

araday \ar-əd-ē\ faraday,
parody

arage \ar-ij\ see ARRIAGE

aragon \ar-ə-gən\ paragon, tarragon

¹**arah** \er-ə\ see ¹ERA

²**arah** \ar-ə\ see ¹ARROW

¹**aral** \ar-əl\ see ²ARREL

²**aral** \ar-əl\ see ERRAL

¹**aralee** \ar-ə-lē\ Marilee, Saralee

²**aralee** \er-ə-lē\ see ARILY

¹**aran** \er-ən\ see ¹ARON

²**aran** \ar-ən\ see ²ARON

¹**arant** \er-ənt\ see ¹ARENT

²**arant** \ar-ənt\ see ²ARENT

¹**araoh** \er-ō\ see ²ERO

²**araoh** \ar-ō\ see ²ARROW

araph \ar-əf\ see ARIFF

aras \är-əs\ see ¹ORRIS

arass \ar-əs\ see ²ARIS

arat \ar-ət\ Barrett, carat, caret, carrot, claret, garret, Garrett, karat, parrot, disparate

arate \ar-ət\ see ARAT

¹**arative** \er-ət-iv\ declarative, imperative

²**arative** \ar-ət-iv\ narrative, comparative, declarative, preparative, reparative

arator \ar-ət-ər\ barrator, apparitor, comparator, preparator

arb \ärb\ barb, barbe, carb, darb, garb, bicarb, rhubarb

arbel \är-bəl\ see ¹ARBLE

arber \är-bər\ see ARBOR

arbered \är-bərd\ see ARBOARD

arbin \är-bən\ see ARBON

¹**arble** \är-bəl\ barbel, garble, marble

²**arble** \ȯr-bəl\ see ORBEL

arboard \är-bərd\ barbered, larboard, starboard, astarboard, unbarbered

arbon \är-bən\ carbon, Harbin

arbor \är-bər\ arbor, barber, harbor, Pearl Harbor

¹**arc** \äk\ see ¹OCK

²**arc** \ärk\ see ¹ARK

arca \är-kə\ see ¹ARKA

¹**arce** \ers\ scarce, Nez Percé

²**arce** \ärs\ see ¹ARSE

arcel \är-səl\ see ARSAL

arcener \ärs-nər\ larcener, parcener, coparcener

arch \ärch\ arch, larch, march, March, parch, starch, cornstarch, frog-march, countermarch

archal \är-kəl\ darkle, sparkle, exarchal, monarchal, hierarchal, matriarchal, patriarchal

archate \är-kət\ see ARKET

arche \ärsh\ see ARSH

arched \ärcht\ arched, parched—*also* -ed *forms of verbs listed at* ARCH

archer \är-chər\ archer, marcher, departure

arches \är-chəz\ Arches, Marches

archic \är-kik\ anarchic, autarchic, autarkic, monarchic, tetrarchic, hierarchic, oligarchic

archical \är-ki-kəl\ autarchical, autarkical, monarchical, oligarchical

archon \är-kən\ see ARKEN

archy \är-kē\ barky, charqui, larky, snarky, anarchy, autarchy, autarky, dyarchy, eparchy, exarchy, heptarchy, malarkey, menarche, monarchy, pentarchy, squirearchy, tetrarchy, triarchy, trierarchy, hierarchy, matriarchy, patriarchy, oligarchy

arck \ärk\ see ¹ARK

arco \är-kō\ arco, narco

arct \ärkt\ see ARKED

¹arctic \ärk-tik\ arctic, Arctic, antarctic, Antarctic, Holarctic, Nearctic, subarctic, Palearctic, subantarctic

²arctic \ärt-ik\ see ¹ARTIC

arcy \är-sē\ farcy, Parsi

¹ard \ärd\ bard, barred, card, chard, Dard, fard, guard, hard, lard, nard, pard, sard, shard, yard, Asgard, backyard, bankcard, barnyard, Bernard, blackguard, blowhard, boatyard, bombard, boneyard, brassard, brickyard, canard, churchyard, courtyard, deeryard, die-hard, diehard, discard, dockyard, dooryard, farmyard, filmcard, fireguard, foreyard, foulard, Gerard, graveyard, ill-starred, jacquard, junkyard, lifeguard, Lombard, mansard, Midgard, milliard, mudguard, noseguard, petard, placard, postcard, poularde, rear guard, rearguard, regard, retard, ritard, safeguard, scorecard, shipyard, spikenard, steelyard, stockyard, switchyard, tabard, tanyard, tiltyard, unbarred, unguard, vanguard, vizard, avant-garde, Beauregard, bodyguard, boulevard, disregard, goliard, Hildegard, interlard, Kierkegaard, Langobard, leotard, Longobard, no-holds-barred, lumberyard, Saint Bernard, Savoyard, Scotland Yard, self-regard, undercard, unitard,

camelopard—*also* -ed *forms of verbs listed at* ³AR

²ard \är\ see ³AR

³ard \ȯrd\ see OARD

ardant \ärd-ᵊnt\ ardent, guardant, regardant, retardant

arde \ärd\ see ¹ARD

¹arded \ärd-əd\ guarded, mansarded, retarded, unguarded—*also* -ed *forms of verbs listed at* ¹ARD

²arded \ȯrd-əd\ corded, sordid, swarded, warded—*also* -ed *forms of verbs listed at* OARD

ardee \ȯrd-ē\ see ¹ORDY

¹arden \ärd-ᵊn\ Arden, Dardan, garden, harden, pardon, bombardon, case-harden, Kincardine

²arden \ȯrd-ᵊn\ cordon, Gordon, Jordan, warden, churchwarden

ardener \ärd-nər\ gardener, hardener, pardner, pardoner, partner

ardent \ärd-ᵊnt\ see ARDANT

¹arder \ärd-ər\ ardor, carder, guarder, harder, larder, discarder, green-carder

²arder \ȯrd-ər\ see ORDER

ardi \ärd-ē\ see ARDY

¹ardian \ärd-ē-ən\ guardian, Edwardian, Lombardian

²ardian \ȯrd-ē-ən\ see ORDION

ardic \ärd-ik\ bardic, Dardic, Lombardic, Sephardic, goliardic, Longobardic

ardine \ärd-ⁿ\ see ¹ARDEN

arding \ȯrd-iŋ\ see ¹ORDING

ardingly \ȯrd-iŋ-lē\ see ORDINGLY

ardom \ärd-əm\ czardom, stardom, superstardom

ardon \ärd-ᵊn\ see ¹ARDEN

ardoner \ärd-nər\ see
ARDENER

ardor \ärd-ər\ see ¹ARDER

ardy \ärd-ē\ hardy, Hardy,
lardy, tardy, foolhardy,
Lombardy, Sephardi

¹**are** \er-ē\ see ¹ARY

²**are** \är\ see ³AR

³**are** \är-ē\ see ¹ARI

⁴**are** \er\ air, Ayr, bare, bear,
Blair, blare, chair, chare,
Claire, Clare, dare, Dare,
e'er, ere, err, eyre, fair, fare,
flair, flare, glair, glare, hair,
hare, Herr, heir, lair, mare,
ne'er, pair, pare, pear,
prayer, quare, rare, rear,
scare, share, snare, spare,
square, stair, stare, swear,
tare, tear, their, there,
they're, vair, ware, wear,
weir, where, yare, affair,
aglare, airfare, Ajmer, Altair,
armchair, au pair, aware,
barware, Basseterre,
Baudelaire, beachwear,
beware, bricklayer, bugbear,
caneware, carfare, clayware,
cochair, coheir, compare,
compere, confrere,
cookware, corsair,
courseware, creamware,
cudbear, day-care, daymare,
decare, declare, delftware,
despair, dishware, éclair,
elsewhere, enclair, ensnare,
eyewear, fanfare, fieldfare,
firmware, flatware, Flaubert,
footwear, forbear, forebear,
forswear, foursquare,
funfair, galère, giftware,
glassware, Great Bear,
Gruyère, hardware, hectare,
horsehair, impair, infare,
Khmer, Kildare, knitwear,
Lake Eyre, life-care,
longhair, loungewear,

menswear, meunière, midair,
mohair, Molière, neckwear,
nightmare, outstare,
outwear, Pierre, playwear,
plein air, plowshare, Poor
Clare, portiere, premiere,
prepare, pushchair,
rainwear, redware, repair,
Saint Pierre, Sancerre,
shorthair, skiwear,
sleepwear, slipware,
software, somewhere,
spongeware, sportswear,
stemware, stoneware,
swimwear, threadbare,
tinware, torchère, tracklayer,
trouvère, tuyere, unfair,
unhair, unswear, Voltaire,
warfare, welfare, wheelchair,
wirehair, workfare,
aftercare, air-to-air, antiair,
anywhere, bayadere, bêche-
de-mer, billionaire,
boutonniere, Camembert,
chinaware, crackleware,
cultivar, debonair, deciare,
de la Mare, Delaware,
derriere, dinnerware,
disrepair, doctrinaire,
earthenware, étagère,
everywhere, Cape Finisterre,
fourragère, Frigidaire,
graniteware, hollowware,
ironware, jasperware,
kitchenware, laissez-faire,
Lake Saint Clair, laquerware,
legionnaire, luminaire,
lusterware, maidenhair, mal
de mer, medicare,
metalware, millionaire,
minaudière, minelayer, Mon-
Khmer, Mousquetaire, nom
de guerre, otherwhere,
outerwear, overbear,
overwear, potty-chair, porte
cochere, questionnaire,
rivière, Robespierre,

Santander, savoir faire, self-aware, self-despair, silverware, solitaire, tableware, thoroughfare, unaware, underwear, vaporware, Venushair, vivandière, willowware, woodenware, yellowware, zillionaire, chargé d'affaires, chemin de fer, commissionaire, concessionaire, couturiere, Croix de guerre, devil-may-care, enamelware, memoriter, pied-à-terre, ready-to-wear, son et lumière, vin ordinaire, cordon sanitaire

area \er-ē-ə\ see ARIA

¹areable \er-ə-bəl\ see ¹EARABLE

²areable \ar-ə-bəl\ see ARABLE

areal \er-ē-əl\ see ARIAL

¹arean \er-ē-ən\ see ¹ARIAN

²arean \ar-ē-ən\ see ²ARIAN

ared \erd\ see AIRED

aredness \ar-əd-nəs\ see ARIDNESS

arel \ar-əl\ see ²ARREL

¹arely \er-lē\ see AIRLY

²arely \ar-lē\ see ARLIE

arem \er-əm\ see ²ARUM

¹arence \er-əns\ clarence, Clarence, Terence, Terrance, Terrence, forbearance, transparence

²arence \ar-ən(ts)\ see ARENTS

¹arent \er-ənt\ daren't, errant, parent, aberrant, afferent, apparent, declarant, deferent, efferent, godparent, grandparent, inapparent, inerrant, knight-errant, sederunt, stepparent, transparent, semitransparent

²arent \ar-ənt\ arrant, daren't, parent, apparent, declarant, godparent, grandparent, stepparent, transparent, inapparent, semitransparent

¹aren't \er-ənt\ see ¹ARENT

²aren't \ar-ənt\ see ²ARENT

arents \ar-ən(t)s\ Barents, Clarence—*also* -s, -'s, *and* -s' *forms of nouns listed at* ²ARENT

arer \er-ər\ see ¹EARER

¹ares \erz\ see AIRS

²ares \ar-ēz\ Ares, caries, nares, Antares, Buenos Aires, primus inter pares—*also* -s, -'s, *and* -s' *forms of nouns listed at* ³ARRY, *and* -s *forms of verbs listed there*

³ares \är-əs\ see ¹ORRIS

aret \ar-ət\ see ARAT

areve \är-və\ see ARVA

¹arey \ar-ē\ see ³ARRY

²arey \er-ē\ see ARY

arez \är-əs\ see ¹ORRIS

¹arf \ärf\ barf, scarf

²arf \ȯrf\ see ORPH

arfarin \ȯr-fə-rən\ warfarin, hematoporphyrin

argain \är-gən\ bargain, jargon, plea-bargain

arge \ärj\ barge, charge, large, marge, Marge, parge, sarge, sparge, targe, discharge, enlarge, litharge, recharge, surcharge, take-charge, uncharge, by and large, hypercharge, overcharge, supercharge, undercharge

argent \är-jənt\ argent, margent, sargent, sergeant

arger \är-jər\ charger, discharger, enlarger, recharger, supercharger,

turbocharger,
turbosupercharger

arget \är-gət\ argot, garget,
target, nontarget

argle \är-gəl\ gargle, argle-
bargle

argo \är-gō\ Argo, argot,
cargo, Fargo, largo, Margo,
Margot, embargo,
supercargo

argon \är-gən\ see ARGAIN

¹**argot** \är-gət\ see ARGET

²**argot** \är-gō\ see ARGO

arh \är\ see ³AR

¹**ari** \är-ē\ Bari, gharry, laari,
sari, scarry, sorry, starry,
Bihari, curare, Imari, safari,
scalare, shikari, tamari,
calamari, cheboksary,
Kalahari, Stradivari,
zamindari, certiorari

²**ari** \er-ē\ see ¹ARY

³**ari** \är-ē\ see ³ARRY

aria \er-ē-ə\ area, Beria, feria,
kerria, varia, Bavaria,
Bulgaria, hysteria, malaria,
planaria, Samaria, adularia,
Carpentaria, cineraria,
fritillaria, laminaria,
luminaria, militaria,
sanguinaria, calceolaria,
opera seria, acetabularia

arial \er-ē-əl\ aerial, areal,
Ariel, burial, gharial,
glossarial, notarial, subaerial,
vicarial, actuarial,
adversarial, estuarial,
secretarial, prothonotarial

¹**arian** \er-ē-ən\ Arian, Aryan,
Carian, Marian, Marion,
parian, Parian, agrarian,
Aquarian, barbarian,
Bavarian, Bulgarian,
Cancerian, cesarean,
Caesarian, cnidarian,
frutarian, grammarian,
Hungarian, Khymerian,

librarian, Maid Marian,
ovarian, Pierian, riparian,
rosarian, Rotarian, sectarian,
Sumerian, Tartarean,
Tartarian, Tocharian,
Tractarian, Vulgarian,
Wagnerian, antiquarian,
apiarian, centenarian,
culinarian, Indo-Aryan,
jubilarian, lapidarian,
libertarian, millenarian,
nonsectarian, postlapsarian,
prelapsarian, Presbyterian,
proletarian, Rastafarian,
Ripuarian, Sabbatarian,
Sagittarian, sanitarian,
seminarian, trinitarian,
Trinitarian, unitarian,
Unitarian, vegetarian,
zoantharian, abecedarian,
Austro-Hungarian,
authoritarian,
communitarian,
disciplinarian,
documentarian, egalitarian,
equalitarian, futilitarian,
hereditarian, humanitarian,
majoritarian, necessitarian,
nonagenarian, octogenarian,
parliamentarian,
postmillinarian,
premillinarian,
predestinarian, radiolarian,
Sacramentarian,
sexagenarian, totalitarian,
utilitarian, veterinarian,
establishmentarian,
inegalitarian, latitudinarian,
platitudinarian,
septuagenarian,
solitudinarian,
uniformitarian,
valetudinarian,
disestablishmentarian

²**arian** \ar-ē-ən\ Arian, Aryan,
carrion, clarion, Marian,
Marion, parian, Parian,

agrarian, Aquarian,
barbarian, Bavarian,
Bulgarian, caesarean,
Caesarian, cesarean,
contrarian, Hungarian,
Megarian, ovarian, rosarian,
Tartarean, Tartarian,
Tocharian, vulgarian, Indo-
Aryan, Rastafarian, Austro-
Hungarian

ariance \ar-ē-əns\ tarriance,
variance, covariance,
vicariance

ariant \ar-ē-ənt\ variant,
vicariant

¹**ariat** \er-ē-ət\ heriot, lariat,
variate, bivariate, salariat,
vicariate, commissariat,
multivariate, proletariat,
secretariat, undersecretariat

²**ariat** \är-ē-ət\ see ¹AUREATE

³**ariat** \ar-ē-ət\ chariot, lariat,
bivariate, salariat,
commissariat, proletariat,
Judas Iscariot

ariate \er-ē-ət\ see ¹ARIAT

arib \ar-əb\ see ARAB

aric \ar-ik\ barrack, carrack,
Amharic, barbaric, Dinaric,
Megaric, Pindaric, isobaric,
Balearic

arice \ar-əs\ see ²ARIS

aricide \ar-ə-sīd\ see
ARRICIDE

arid \ar-əd\ arid, farad,
semiarid

aridin \ar-ə-dᵊn\ see ARRIDAN

aridness \ar-əd-nəs\ aridness,
preparedness

¹**aried** \er-ēd\ see ERRIED

²**aried** \ar-ēd\ see ARRIED

ariel \er-ē-əl\ see ARIAL

¹**arier** \er-ē-ər\ see ERRIER

²**arier** \ar-ē-ər\ see ²ARRIER

aries \ar-ēz\ see ²ARES

ariff \ar-əf\ paraph, tariff

aril \ar-əl\ see ²ARREL

¹**arilee** \ar-ə-lē\ see ARALEE

²**arilee** \ar-ə-lē\ see ARILY

arily \er-ə-lē\ Marilee,
merrily, Merrily, Saralee,
scarily, sterily, verily,
contrarily, primarily,
arbitrarily, customarily,
dietarily, exemplarily,
fragmentarily, honorarily,
literarily, mercenarily,
militarily, momentarily,
necessarily, salutarily,
sanguinarily, sanitarily,
secondarily, temporarily,
unitarily, voluntarily,
contemporarily,
elementarily, extemporarily,
extraordinarily, hereditarily,
imaginarily, involuntarily,
preliminarily, rudimentarily,
subsidiarily, unnecessarily,
documentarily,
evolutionarily,
revolutionarily

arin \är-ən\ florin, foreign,
Lauren, Orrin, sarin,
sporran, warren, Warren,
Gagarin

arinate \ar-ə-nət\ see ARONET

arinet \ar-ə-nət\ see ARONET

¹**aring** \er-iŋ\ airing, Bering,
fairing, flaring, glaring,
herring, paring, raring,
sparing, tearing, wearing,
cheeseparing, childbearing,
seafaring, time-sharing,
unerring, unsparing,
wayfaring—*also* -ing *forms of
verbs listed at* ⁴ARE

²**aring** \er-ən\ see ¹ARON

ario \er-ē-ō\ stereo, Ontario

¹**arion** \ar-ē-ən\ see ²ARIAN

²**arion** \er-ē-ən\ see ¹ARIAN

ariot \ar-ē-ət\ see ³ARIAT

arious \ar-ē-əs\ Arius,
carious, Darious, scarious,
various, Aquarius,

burglarious, calcareous,
contrarious, denarius,
gregarious, guarnerius,
hilarious, nefarious,
precarious, senarius,
vagarious, vicarious,
multifarious, omnifarious,
septenarius, Stradivarius,
Sagittarius, temerarious

¹aris \är-əs\ see ¹ORRIS

²aris \ar-əs\ arras, arris,
Clarice, harass, Harris,
heiress, Paris, parous, varus,
coheiress, embarrass, Polaris,
disembarrass, millionairess,
Lewis with Harris, plaster of
paris

¹arish \er-ish\ bearish,
cherish, fairish, garish,
perish, squarish, nightmarish

²arish \ar-ish\ garish, marish,
parish

arison \ar-ə-sən\ characin,
garrison, Garrison, Harrison,
Saracen, warison, caparison,
comparison

arist \er-əst\ Marist, querist,
aquarist, pleinairist,
scenarist, apiarist—*also* -est
forms of adjectives listed at
⁴ARE

aritan \er-ət-ⁿn\ see ERATIN

aritor \ar-ət-ər\ see ARATOR

¹arity \er-ət-ē\ see ERITY

²arity \ar-ət-ē\ carroty,
charity, clarity, parity, rarity,
barbarity, disparity, hilarity,
imparity, polarity, unclarity,
vulgarity, angularity,
familiarity, insularity,
peculiarity, popularity,
regularity, similarity,
singularity, solidarity,
complementarity,
dissimilarity, irregularity,
particularity, unfamiliarity,
unpopularity

arium \er-ē-əm\ barium,
aquarium, herbarium,
sacrarium, samarium,
solarium, terrarium,
velarium, vivarium,
cinerarium, columbarium,
honorarium, leprosarium,
oceanarium, planetarium,
sanitarium, syllabarium,
termitarium,
armamentarium

arius \er-ē-əs\ see ARIOUS

¹ark \ärk\ arc, ark, bark,
Clark, Clarke, dark, hark,
lark, marc, Marc, mark,
Mark, marque, narc, nark,
park, Park, quark, sark,
shark, spark, stark,
aardvark, airpark, anarch,
ballpark, birchbark,
birthmark, Bismarck,
bookmark, debark, demark,
Denmark, earmark, embark,
endarch, exarch, footmark,
futhark, Graustark,
hallmark, ironbark,
landmark, Lake Clark,
Lamarck, monarch, ostmark,
Ozark, Petrarch, pitch-dark,
Plutarch, pockmark,
postmark, pressmark,
pugmark, reichsmark,
remark, remarque,
Remarque, ringbark,
seamark, shagbark,
sitzmark, skylark,
soapbark, tanbark, tetrarch,
tidemark, titlark,
touchmark, trademark,
acritarch, cutty sark,
deutsche mark, disembark,
double-park, hierarch, Joan
of Arc, matriarch,
meadowlark, metalmark,
minipark, oligarch,
patriarch, stringybark,
telemark, trierarch,

watermark, heresiarch, symposiarch

²**ark** \òrk\ see ²ORK

³**ark** \ərk\ see ¹ORK

¹**arka** \är-kə\ charka, parka, anasarca, Hamilcar Barca

²**arka** \ər-kə\ see ¹URKA

arke \ärk\ see ¹ARK

arked \ärkt\ marked, chop-marked, infarct, ripple-marked, unremarked—*also* -ed *forms of verbs listed at* ¹ARK

arken \är-kən\ darken, hearken

arker \är-kər\ barker, larker, marker, parker, Parker, sparker, bookmarker, skylarker, nosey parker—*also* -er *forms of adjectives listed at* ¹ARK

arket \är-kət\ market, down-market, mass-market, newmarket, test-market, upmarket, aftermarket, hypermarket, matriarchate, patriarchate, supermarket

arkey \är-kē\ see ARCHY

arkian \är-kē-ən\ Graustarkian, Lamarckian, Monarchian

arkic \är-kik\ see ARCHIC

arking \är-kiŋ\ barking, Barking, carking, parking, loan-sharking—*also* -ing *forms of verbs listed at* ¹ARK

arkle \är-kəl\ see ARCHAL

arks \ärks\ Marks, parks—*also* -s, -'s, *and* -s' *forms of nouns listed at* ¹ARK, *and* -s *forms of verbs listed there*

arky \är-kē\ see ARCHY

arl \ärl\ carl, Carl, farl, gnarl, jarl, Karl, marl, parle, quarrel, snarl, ensnarl, housecarl, unsnarl, Albemarle

arla \är-lə\ Carla, Darla, Karla, Marla

arlan \ä-lən\ see ARLINE

arland \är-lənd\ garland, Garland, Harland

arlatan \är-lət-ᵊn\ charlatan, tarlatan

arlay \är-lē\ see ARLIE

arle \ärl\ see ARL

arlen \är-lən\ see ARLINE

arler \är-lər\ see ARLOR

arless \är-ləs\ Carlos, parlous, scarless, starless

arlet \är-lət\ charlotte, Charlotte, harlot, scarlet, starlet, varlet

arley \är-lē\ see ARLIE

arlic \är-lik\ garlic, pilgarlic

arlie \är-lē\ barley, charlie, Charlie, gnarly, Harley, marly, parlay, parley, snarly, yarely, bizarrely, Mr. Charlie

arlin \är-lən\ see ARLINE

arline \är-lən\ Arlen, carline, Harlan, marlin, Marlin, marline, Marlyn

arling \är-liŋ\ carling, darling, Darling, starling—*also* -ing *forms of verbs listed at* ARL

arlor \är-lər\ parlor, quarreler, snarler

arlos \är-ləs\ see ARLESS

arlot \är-lət\ see ARLET

arlotte \är-lət\ see ARLET

arlous \är-ləs\ see ARLESS

arlow \är-lō\ Barlow, Harlow

arly \är-lē\ see ARLIE

arlyn \är-lən\ see ARLINE

¹**arm** \ärm\ arm, barm, charm, farm, harm, smarm, alarm, disarm, firearm, forearm, gendarme, gisarme, poor farm, rearm, sidearm, stiff-arm, straight-arm, strong-arm, tonearm, unarm, yardarm, overarm, underarm

²**arm** \äm\ see ¹OM

³**arm** \órm\ see ²ORM

¹**arma** \är-mə\ dharma, karma, Parma

²**arma** \ər-mə\ see ERMA

arman \är-mən\ barman, Carmen, carmine, Harmon

armed \ärmd\ armed, charmed, unarmed—*also* -ed *forms of verbs listed at* ¹ARM

armen \är-mən\ see ARMAN

arment \är-mənt\ garment, varmint, debarment, disbarment, undergarment, overgarment

¹**armer** \är-mər\ armor, charmer, farmer, harmer, disarmer

²**armer** \òr-mər\ see ¹ORMER

armic \ər-mik\ see ERMIC

armine \är-mən\ see ARMAN

¹**arming** \är-miŋ\ charming, farming, alarming, disarming—*also* -ing *forms of verbs listed at* ¹ARM

²**arming** \òr-miŋ\ see ORMING

armint \är-mənt\ see ARMENT

armless \ärm-ləs\ armless, charmless, harmless

armoir \är-mər\ see ¹ARMER

armon \är-mən\ see ARMAN

army \är-mē\ army, barmy, smarmy

¹**arn** \ärn\ Arne, barn, darn, Marne, tarn, yarn, carbarn, lucarne

²**arn** \órn\ see ¹ORN

arna \ər-nə\ see ERNA

arnal \ärn-ᵊl\ see ARNEL

arnate \är-nət\ Barnet, garnet, discarnate, incarnate

¹**arne** \ärn\ see ¹ARN

²**arne** \är-nē\ see ARNY

arnel \ärn-ᵊl\ carnal, charnel, darnel

¹**arner** \är-nər\ darner, garner, yarner

²**arner** \òr-nər\ see ORNER

arness \är-nəs\ harness, bizarreness

arnet \är-nət\ see ARNATE

arney \är-nē\ see ARNY

arnhem \är-nəm\ see ARNUM

arning \òr-niŋ\ see ORNING

arnish \är-nish\ garnish, tarnish, varnish

arnum \är-nəm\ Arnhem, Barnum

arny \är-nē\ Barney, barny, blarney, carny, Killarney, chili con carne

¹**aro** \er-ō\ see ²ERO

²**aro** \ar-ō\ see ²ARROW

³**aro** \är-ə\ see ARA

⁴**aro** \är-ō\ see ¹ORROW

arob \är-əb\ see ARAB

arody \ar-əd-ē\ see ARADAY

¹**aroe** \ar-ō\ see ²ARROW

²**aroe** \er-ō\ see ²ERO

arol \ar-əl\ see ²ARREL

¹**arold** \ar-əld\ Darold, Harold

²**arold** \är-əld\ see ERALD

arole \ar-əl\ see ²ARREL

arom \er-əm\ see ²ARUM

¹**aron** \er-ən\ Aaron, Charon, Erin, garron, heron, perron, raring, Sharon, Sharron, sierran, rose of Sharon, sub-Saharan

²**aron** \ar-ən\ Aaron, baron, barren, Charon, garron, Sharon, Sharron, rose of Sharon, sub-Saharan

aronet \ar-ə-nət\ baronet, carinate, clarinet

¹**arous** \er-əs\ see ERROUS

²**arous** \ar-əs\ see ²ARIS

¹**arp** \ärp\ carp, harp, scarp, sharp, tarp, cardsharp, Jews harp, Autoharp, vibraharp

²**arp** \órp\ see ORP

arpen \är-pən\ sharpen, tarpon

arper \är-pər\ carper, harper, scarper, sharper, cardsharper

arple \är-pē\ see ARPY

arpon \är-pən\ see ARPEN

arpy \är-pē\ harpy, sharpie

arque \ärk\ see ¹ARK

arquetry \är-kə-trē\ marquetry, parquetry

arqui \är-kē\ see ARCHY

arrable \ar-ə-bəl\ see ARABLE

¹arrack \ar-ik\ see ARIC

²arrack \ar-ək\ arrack, barrack, carrack

arrage \är-ij\ see ¹orage

arragon \ar-ə-gən\ see ARAGON

arral \ar-əl\ see ²ARREL

arram \ar-əm\ see ²ARUM

¹arrant \ar-ənt\ see ²ARENT

²arrant \òr-ənt\ see ORRENT

arras \ar-əs\ see ²ARIS

arrass \ar-əs\ see ²ARIS

arrative \ar-ət-iv\ see ²ARATIVE

arrator \ar-ət-ər\ see ARATOR

arre \är\ see ³AR

arred \ärd\ see ¹ARD

¹arrel \òrl\ see ²ORL

²arrel \ar-əl\ Aral, aril, barrel, carol, Carol, Carole, Caryl, carrel, Carroll, Darrel, Darrell, Darryl, Daryl, Karol, parol, parral, parrel, apparel, cracker-barrel, double-barrel

³arrel \òr-əl\ see ¹ORAL

arreler \är-lər\ see ARLOR

arrell \ar-əl\ see ²ARREL

arrely \är-lē\ see ARLIE

¹arren \ar-ən\ see ARON

²arren \òr-ən\ see ¹ORIN

³arren \ar-ən\ see ARIN

arrener \òr-ə-nər\ see ORONER

arreness \är-nəs\ see ARNESS

arret \ar-ət\ see ARAT

arrett \ar-ət\ see ARAT

arrh \är\ see ³AR

arriage \ar-ij\ carriage,

marriage, disparage, miscarriage, intermarriage, undercarriage

arriance \ar-ē-əns\ see ARIANCE

arricide \ar-ə-sīd\ parricide, acaricide

arridan \ar-ə-dᵊn\ harridan, cantharidin

arrie \ar-ē\ see ³ARRY

arried \ar-ēd\ harried, married, varied, unmarried

¹arrier \òr-ē-ər\ see ARRIOR

²arrier \ar-ē-ər\ barrier, carrier, farrier, harrier, varier, ballcarrier, spear-carrier

arrion \ar-ē-ən\ see ²ARIAN

arrior \òr-ē-ər\ quarrier, sorrier, warrior

arris \ar-əs\ see ²ARIS

arrison \ar-ə-sən\ see ARISON

arro \är-ō\ see ¹ORROW

arroll \ar-əl\ see ²ARREL

arron \ar-ən\ see ²ARON

arrot \ar-ət\ see ARAT

arroty \ar-ət-ē\ see ²ARITY

¹arrow \ar-ə\ Clara, jarrah, Kara, Sara, Sarah, Tara, Bukhara, cascara, mascara, Sahara, samara, Tamara, tantara, tiara, capybara, caracara, marinara, Santa Clara

²arrow \ar-ō\ aero, arrow, barrow, Darrow, Faeroe, faro, Faroe, farrow, harrow, Harrow, marrow, narrow, pharaoh, sparrow, taro, tarot, yarrow, handbarrow, Point Barrow, wheelbarrow

arrowy \ar-ə-wē\ arrowy, marrowy

¹arry \är-ē\ see ¹ARI

²arry \òr-ē\ see ORY

³arry \ar-ē\ Barrie, Barry, Carey, Carrie, carry, Cary,

chary, Gary, Garry, gharry,
harry, Harry, Larry, marry,
nary, parry, Shari, tarry,
glengarry, miscarry, safari,
shikari, cash-and-carry, hari-
kari, intermarry, Stradivari;
Tom, Dick, and Harry

arryl \ar-əl\ see [2]ARREL

ars \ärz\ Lars, Mars, ours—
also -s, -'s, *and* -s' *forms of
nouns listed at* [3]AR, *and* -s
forms of verbs listed there

arsal \är-səl\ parcel, versal,
tarsal, metatarsal

[1]**arse** \ärs\ arse, farce, marse,
parse, sparse

[2]**arse** \ärz\ see ARS

arsh \ärsh\ harsh, marsh,
demarche

arshal \är-shəl\ see ARTIAL

arshall \är-shəl\ see ARTIAL

arshen \är-shən\ harshen,
martian

arsi \är-sē\ see ARCY

arsis \är-səs\ see ARSUS

arsle \äs-əl\ see OSSAL

arson \ärs-ᵊn\ arson, Carson,
parson

arsus \är-səs\ arsis, tarsus,
Tarsus, catharsis,
metatarsus

[1]**art** \ärt\ art, Art, Bart, cart,
chart, Chartres, dart, fart,
hart, Harte, heart, kart, mart,
part, Sartre, scart, smart, start,
tart, apart, blackheart,
compart, depart, Descartes,
dispart, dogcart, Earhart,
flowchart, forepart, go-cart,
greenheart, handcart, Hobart,
impart, jump-start, Mozart,
mouthpart, outsmart, oxcart,
oxheart, pushcart, rampart,
redstart, restart, street-smart,
Stuttgart, sweetheart, tipcart,
upstart, à la carte, anti-art,
applecart, Bonaparte,

counterpart, heart-to-heart,
purpleheart, underpart,
upperpart

[2]**art** \ȯrt\ see [1]ORT

arta \är-tə\ Marta, Sparta,
Jakarta, Magna Carta, Santa
Marta, Surakarta,
yogyakarta

artable \ärt-ə-bəl\ see ARTIBLE

[1]**artan** \ärt-ᵊn\ see ARTEN

[2]**artan** \ȯrt-ᵊn\ see ORTEN

artar \ärt-ər\ see [1]ARTER

[1]**arte** \ärt-ē\ see [1]ARTY

[2]**arte** \ärt\ see [1]ART

[1]**arted** \ärt-əd\ see EARTED

[2]**arted** \ȯrt-əd\ see ORTED

arten \ärt-ᵊn\ Barton, carton,
hearten, marten, martin,
Martin, smarten, Spartan,
tartan, baum marten,
dishearten, Dumbarton,
freemartin, Saint Martin,
Sint Maarten, kindergarten

[1]**arter** \ärt-ər\ barter, carter,
Carter, charter, darter,
garter, martyr, starter,
tartar, nonstarter, self-
starter, protomartyr—*also* -
er *forms of adjectives listed at*
[1]ART

[2]**arter** \ȯt-ər\ see [1]ATER

[3]**arter** \ȯrt-ər\ see ORTER

artern \ȯrt-ərn\ see AUTERNE

artery \ärt-ə-rē\ artery,
martyry

artes \ärt\ see [1]ART

artford \ärt-fərd\ Hartford,
Hertford

arth \ärth\ garth, Garth,
hearth, Hogarth

arti \ärt-ē\ see [1]ARTY

artial \är-shəl\ marshal,
Marshal, Marshall, martial,
Martial, partial, court-
martial, impartial

artian \är-shən\ see ARSHEN

artible \ärt-ə-bəl\ partible,

startable, impartible,
restartable

¹artic \ärt-ik\ arctic, Arctic,
antarctic, Antarctic,
cathartic, Nearctic, Palearctic

²artic \órt-ik\ quartic, aortic

article \ärt-i-kəl\ article,
particle, microparticle

artile \órt-ºl\ see ORTAL

artily \ärt-ºl-ē\ artily,
heartily

artin \ärt-ºn\ see ARTEN

arting \ärt-iŋ\ carting,
charting, karting, parting,
starting, flowcharting, self-
starting—also -ing forms of
verbs listed at ¹ART

artisan \ärt-ə-zən\ artisan,
bartizan, partisan,
bipartisan, nonpartisan

artist \ärt-əst\ artist, chartist,
Chartist, Bonapartist

artizan \ärt-ə-zən\ see
ARTISAN

artless \ärt-ləs\ artless,
heartless

artlet \ärt-lət\ martlet,
partlet, tartlet

¹artly \ärt-lē\ partly,
smartly, tartly

²artly \órt-lē\ see ORTLY

artment \ärt-mənt\
apartment, compartment,
department

artner \ärt-nər\ partner,
kindergartner

¹arton \órt-ºn\ see ORTON

²arton \ärt-ºn\ see ARTEN

artre \ärt\ see ¹ART

artres \ärt\ see ¹ART

artridge \är-trij\ cartridge,
partridge

¹arts \är\ see ³AR

²arts \ärts\ Hartz —also -s,
's, and -s' forms of nouns
listed at ¹ART, and -s forms
of verbs listed there

arture \är-chər\ see ARCHER

¹arty \ärt-ē\ arty, hearty, party,
smarty, tarty, Astarte, ex
parte, Havarti, Buonaparte,
commedia dell'arte

²arty \órt-ē\ see ORTY

artyr \ärt-ər\ see ¹ARTER

artyry \ärt-ə-rē\ see ARTERY

artz \órts\ see ORTS

²artz \ärts\ see ²ARTS

aru \ä-rü\ Bukaru,
Pakanbaru, Johor Baharu

¹arum \är-əm\ larum,
alarum

²arum \er-əm\ arum, carom,
harem, Sarum, Muharram,
harum-scarum, arbiter
elegantiarum

arus \ar-əs\ see ²ARIS

arva \är-və\ larva, Marva,
parve, pareve

arval \är-vəl\ see ARVEL

¹arve \ärv\ carve, starve,
varve

²arve \är-və\ see ARVA

arvel \är-vəl\ carvel, larval,
marvel

arven \är-vən\ carven,
Marvin, Caernarvon

arvin \är-vən\ see ARVEN

arvon \är-vən\ see ARVEN

¹ary \er-ē\ aerie, aery, airy,
berry, bury, Carey, Cary,
Cherie, cherry, Cherry,
chary, clary, dairy, Derry,
faerie, fairy, ferry, Gary,
Garry, Gerry, glairy, glary,
hairy, Jere, Jeri, Jerrie, Jerry,
kerry, Kerry, Mary, marry,
merry, Merry, nary, perry,
Perry, prairie, quaere, query,
scary, serry, Shari, Sheri,
Sherrie, sherry, Sherry,
skerry, terry, Terry, vary,
very, wary, wherry,
baneberry, barberry,
bayberry, bearberry,

bilberry, blackberry,
blaeberry, blueberry,
Bradbury, bunchberry,
Burberry, canary, Canary,
chokeberry, chokecherry,
cloudberry, contrary,
coralberry, costmary,
cowberry, cranberry,
crowberry, deerberry,
dewberry, equerry,
gooseberry, ground-cherry,
hackberry, hegari, inkberry,
Juneberry, knobkerrie,
library, mulberry, nondairy,
pokeberry, primary,
raspberry, rosemary,
Rosemary, scalare,
shadberry, sheepberry,
snowberry, soapberry,
strawberry, summary,
teaberry, tilbury, twinberry,
unwary, vagary, wolfberry,
youngberry, actuary,
adversary, airy-fairy,
ancillary, antiquary, apiary,
arbitrary, aviary, axillary,
beriberi, bestiary, biliary,
boysenberry, breviary,
budgetary, calamari,
calamary, candleberry,
Canterbury, capillary,
cartulary, cassowary,
catenary, cautionary,
cavitary, cemetery,
centenary, certiorari,
chartulary, checkerberry,
chinaberry, ciliary, cinerary,
cometary, commentary,
commissary, condottiere,
corollary, coronary,
culinary, customary,
dictionary, dietary, dignitary,
dingleberry, dromedary,
dysentery, elderberry,
emissary, estuary,
farkleberry, February,
formicary, formulary,

fragmentary, fritillary,
functionary, funerary,
honorary, huckleberry,
intermarry, janissary,
January, lamasery, lapidary,
lectionary, legendary,
legionary, limitary,
lingonberry, literary,
loganberry, luminary,
mammillary, mandatary,
maxillary, medullary,
mercenary, miliary, military,
millenary, milliary, millinery,
miserere, missionary,
momentary, monastery,
monetary, mortuary,
necessary, ordinary, ossuary,
papillary, parcenary,
partridgeberry, pensionary,
phalanstery, pigmentary,
plagiary, planetary,
Pondicherry, prebendary,
presbytery, pulmonary,
pupillary, quaternary,
questionary, reliquary,
rowanberry, salivary,
salmonberry, salutary,
sanctuary, sanguinary,
sanitary, secondary,
secretary, sedentary,
seminary, serviceberry,
silverberry, solitary,
stationary, stationery,
statuary, Stradivari,
subcontrary, sublunary,
sugarberry, sumptuary,
syllabary, temporary,
termitary, tertiary, textuary,
thimbleberry, Tipperary,
Tom and Jerry, topiary,
tributary, tutelary, unitary,
urinary, vestiary, visionary,
voluntary, vulnerary,
Waterbury, whortleberry,
winterberry, ablutionary,
accretionary, antiphonary,
apothecary, bicentenary,

bilmillenary, concessionary,
conclusionary,
concretionary,
confectionary,
confectionery, consigliere,
constabulary, contemporary,
convulsionary, coparcenary,
depositary, delusionary,
digressionary, disciplinary,
discretionary, distributary,
diversionary, electuary,
epistolary, exclusionary,
expansionary, expeditionary,
extempory, extortionary,
extraordinary, fiduciary,
hereditary, illusionary,
imaginary, incendiary,
inflationary, insanitary,
intercalary, involuntary,
itinerary, judiciary,
libationary, obituary,
officiary, pecuniary,
petitionary, precautionary,
preliminary, presidiary,
previsionary, probationary,
proprietary, provisionary,
reactionary, recessionary,
reflationary, residuary,
reversionary, revisionary,
stagflationary, stipendiary,
subliterary, subsidiary,
subversionary, tercentenary,
traditionary, tumultuary,
unnecessary, veterinary,
vocabulary, voluptuary,
abolitionary, beneficiary,
consuetudinary,
deflationary, devolutionary,
disinflationary, domiciliary,
eleemosynary, elocutionary,
evidentiary, evolutionary,
extraliterary, intermediary,
paramilitary, penitentiary,
quatercentenary,
revolutionary,
semicentenary,
semilegendary,

sesquicentenary,
superciliary, **supernumerary**,
tintinnabulary,
transdisciplinary,
usufructuary, **valetudinary**,
interdisciplinary,
plenipotentiary,
counterrevolutionary

²**ary** \ar-ē\ see ³ARRY
³**ary** \är-ē\ see ¹ARI
¹**aryan** \er-ē-ən\ see ¹ARIAN
²**aryan** \ar-ē-ən\ see ²ARIAN
aryl \ar-əl\ see ²ARREL
¹**as** \ash\ see ³ASH
²**as** \as\ see ³ASS
³**as** \az\ see AZZ
⁴**as** \ä\ see ¹A
⁵**as** \äsh\ see ¹ASH
⁶**as** \äz\ see ¹OISE
⁷**as** \əz\ see ¹EUSE
⁸**as** \äs\ see ¹OS
⁹**as** \ȯ\ see ¹AW
¹**asa** \äs-ə\ casa, fossa, glossa,
   Lhasa, Ossa, kielbasa,
   Kinshasa, Landrace,
   Mombasa, tabula rasa
²**asa** \äz-ə\ see ¹AZA
³**asa** \as-ə\ see ASSA
¹**asable** \ā-zə-bəl\ grazeable,
   persuasible, paraphrasable
²**asable** \ā-sə-bəl\ see
   ACEABLE
¹**asal** \ā-səl\ basal, Basil, stay
   sail, forestay sail
²**asal** \ā-zəl\ basal, Basil,
   hazel, Hazel, nasal, phrasal,
   appraisal, Azazel
asally \āz-lē\ see AISLEY
asca \as-kə\ see ASKA
ascal \as-kəl\ paschal, rascal
ascan \as-kən\ see ASKIN
ascar \as-kər\ see ASKER
¹**ascence** \ās-ⁿns\ nascence,
   complacence, complaisance,
   renascence
²**ascence** \as-ⁿns\ nascence,
   renascence

¹**ascent** \as-ᵊnt\ nascent, passant, renascent

²**ascent** \ās-ᵊnt\ see ACENT

¹**asch** \ask\ see ASK

²**asch** \äsh\ see ¹ASH

³**asch** \ȯsh\ see ²ASH

aschal \as-kəl\ see ASCAL

¹**ascia** \ā-shə\ see ACIA

²**ascia** \ash-ə\ see ²ASHA

ascible \as-ə-bəl\ see ASSABLE

ascicle \as-i-kəl\ see ASSICAL

¹**asco** \äs-kō\ see OSCOE

²**asco** \as-kō\ fiasco, Tabasco

ascon \as-kən\ see ASKIN

ascot \as-kət\ see ASKET

ascus \as-kəs\ Damascus, Velazquez

¹**ase** \ās\ see ¹ACE

²**ase** \āz\ see ¹AZE

³**ase** \äz\ see ¹OISE

asel \äz-əl\ see OZZLE

ased \āst\ see ACED

aseless \ā-sləs\ see ACELESS

aseman \ā-smən\ see ACEMAN

asement \ās-mənt\ basement, casement, debasement, bargain-basement

¹**aser** \ā-sər\ see ¹ACER

²**aser** \ā-zər\ see AZER

asey \ā-sē\ see ACY

¹**ash** \äsh\ bosh, cosh, Fosh, frosh, gosh, gouache, josh, Mâche, nosh, posh, quash, slosh, squash, swash, tosh, wash, awash, backwash, blackwash, cohosh, czardas, Dias, Diaz, downwash, eyewash, galosh, ganache, goulash, kibosh, midrash, mishmash, mouthwash, musquash, panache, rainwash, Siwash, whitewash, wish-wash, hamantasch, mackintosh, McIntosh

²**ash** \ȯsh\ Bosch, Foch, gosh, grosz, quash, slosh, squash, swash, wash, awash, backwash, Balkhash, blackwash, brainwash, brioche, Bydgoszcz, downwash, eyewash, hogwash, lasi, mouthwash, outwash, rainwash, Siwash, whitewash, wish-wash, hamantasch

³**ash** \ash\ ash, bash, brash, cache, cash, clash, crash, dash, fash, flash, gash, gnash, hash, lash, mash, nash, pash, plash, splash, stash, thrash, thresh, trash, abash, backlash, backsplash, Balkhash, calash, Chumash, czardas, encash, eyelash, goulash, mishmash, moustache, mustache, panache, potash, rehash, slapdash, soutache, stramash, tongue-lash, unlash, whiplash, baiderdash, calabash, succotash

¹**asha** \äsh-ə\ kasha, pasha, quassia, Falasha

²**asha** \ash-ə\ cassia, fascia, pasha

ashan \ash-ən\ see ASSION

¹**ashed** \ȯsht\ sloshed, stonewashed, unwashed—*also -ed forms of verbs listed at* ²ASH

²**ashed** \asht\ dashed, Rasht, smashed, unabashed—*also -ed forms of verbs listed at* ³ASH

ashen \ash-ən\ see ASSION

¹**asher** \äsh-ər\ josher, nosher, squasher, swasher, washer, dishwasher

²**asher** \ȯsh-ər\ swasher, washer, brainwasher, dishwasher, whitewasher

³**asher** \ash-ər\ Asher, basher,

brasher, clasher, crasher,
dasher, flasher, masher,
rasher, slasher, smasher,
splasher, thrasher, gate-
crasher, haberdasher
ashew \ash-ü\ cachou, cashew
¹**ashi** \äsh-ē\ see ¹ASHY
²**ashi** \ash-ē\ see ²ASHY
ashing \ash-iŋ\ crashing,
dashing, flashing, mashing,
slashing, smashing—*also* -ing
forms of verbs listed at ³ASH
ashion \ash-ən\ see ASSION
asht \asht\ see ²ASHED
¹**ashy** \äsh-ē\ dashi, Iasi,
Kashi, squashy, washy,
Funabashi, Lubumbashi,
Toyohashi, wishy-washy
²**ashy** \ash-ē\ ashy, flashy,
Kashi, splashy, trashy
¹**asi** \äs-ē\ see ¹OSSY
²**asi** \äz-ē\ see ¹AZI
³**asi** \òsh\ see ²ASH
⁴**asi** \äsh-ē\ see ¹ASHY
asia \ā-zhə\ Asia, aphasia,
Eurasia, fantasia, Malaysia,
Anastasia, Australasia,
euthanasia, antonomasia
¹**asian** \ā-shən\ see ¹ATION
²**asian** \ā-zhən\ see ASION
asible \ā-zə-bəl\ see ¹ASABLE
asic \ā-zik\ basic, phasic,
biphasic, diphasic,
multiphasic, polyphasic
asid \as-əd\ see ACID
asie \ā-sē\ see ACY
¹**asil** \as-əl\ see ²ASSEL
²**asil** \az-əl\ see AZZLE
³**asil** \äs-əl\ see ¹ASAL
⁴**asil** \äz-əl\ see ²ASAL
⁵**asil** \äz-əl\ see OZZLE
asin \äs-ⁿn\ see ¹ASON
¹**asing** \ā-siŋ\ see ACING
²**asing** \ā-ziŋ\ see AISING
asion \ā-zhən\ Asian, suasion,
abrasion, Caucasian,
corrasion, dissuasion,

equation, Eurasian, evasion,
invasion, occasion,
persuasion, pervasion,
Amerasian, Athanasian,
dermabrasion, Rabelaisian,
overpersuasion
asional \āzh-nəl\ equational,
occasional
¹**asis** \ā-səs\ basis, stasis, oasis
²**asis** \as-əs\ see ²ASSIS
asium \ā-zē-əm\ dichasium,
gymnasium
asive \ā-siv\ suasive, abrasive,
assuasive, corrasive,
dissuasive, embracive,
evasive, invasive, persuasive,
pervasive, noninvasive
ask \ask\ ask, bask, Basque,
cask, casque, flask, mask,
masque, Pasch, task,
unmask, photomask
aska \as-kə\ Alaska, Itasca,
Nebraska, Athabaska
askan \as-kən\ see ASKIN
asked \ast\ see ²AST
asker \as-kər\ lascar, masker,
masquer, Madagascar
asket \as-kət\ ascot, basket,
casket, gasket, breadbasket,
handbasket, wastebasket,
workbasket
askin \as-kən\ gascon, gaskin,
Alaskan, Tarascan,
Athapaskan
asking \as-kiŋ\ multitasking
—*also* -ing *forms of verbs
listed at* ASK
asm \az-əm\ chasm, plasm,
spasm, chiasm, orgasm,
phantasm, sarcasm, chiliasm,
ectoplasm, pleonasm,
enthusiasm, blepharospasm,
iconoclasm
asma \az-mə\ asthma, plasma,
chiasma, miasma,
phantasma
asman \az-mən\ see ASMINE

asmine \az-mən\ jasmine, Tasman

asn't \əz-ᵊnt\ doesn't, wasn't

¹aso \as-ō\ see ¹ASSO

²aso \äs-ō\ see ²ASSO

¹ason \ās-ᵊn\ basin, caisson, chasten, hasten, Jason, mason, Mason, Foxe Basin, Freemason, Great Basin, stonemason, washbasin, diapason, Donets Basin

²ason \az-ᵊn\ see AZON

asp \asp\ asp, clasp, gasp, grasp, hasp, rasp, enclasp, handclasp, last-gasp, unclasp

asper \as-pər\ clasper, jasper, Jasper

asperate \as-prət\ aspirate, exasperate

aspirate \as-prət\ see ASPERATE

asque \ask\ see ASK

asquer \as-kər\ see ASKER

¹ass \ās\ see ¹ACE

²ass \äs\ see ¹OS

³ass \as\ as, ass, bass, Bass, brass, class, crass, frass, gas, glass, grass, has, lass, mass, pass, sass, sauce, strass, tace, tasse, trass, vas, wrasse, admass, alas, Alsace, amass, avgas, badass, bagasse, band-pass, bluegrass, bromegrass, bunchgrass, bypass, cordgrass, crabgrass, crevasse, cuirass, cut-grass, declass, degas, Donbas, Drygas, eelgrass, en masse, eyeglass, first-class, groundmass, harass, hard-ass, high-class, hourglass, impasse, jackass, knotgrass, Kuzbass, landmass, Madras, morass, outclass, outgas, palliasse, Petras, plateglass, repass, ribgrass, rubasse, ryegrass, sandglass,

shortgrass, spyglass, subclass, sunglass, surpass, switchgrass, tallgrass, teargas, trespass, Troas, wineglass, wiseass, witchgrass, biogas, biomass, demiglace, demitasse, fiberglass, gallowglass, gravitas, Hallowmas, hardinggrass, hippocras, isinglass, Kiribati, lemongrass, lower-class, middle-class, overpass, pampas grass, peppergrass, Plexiglas, sassafras, superclass, underclass, underpass, upper-class, weatherglass

assa \as-ə\ massa, Lake Nyasa, Manasseh

assable \as-ə-bəl\ chasuble, passable, passible, impassable, impassible, irascible

assail \äs-əl\ see OSSAL

assailer \äs-ə-lər\ see OSSULAR

assal \as-əl\ see ²ASSEL

assant \as-ᵊnt\ see ¹ASCENT

assar \as-ər\ see ASSER

¹asse \as\ see ³ASS

²asse \äs\ see ¹OS

assed \ast\ see ²AST

assee \as-ē\ see ASSY

asseh \as-ə\ see ASSA

¹assel \äs-əl\ see OSSAL

²assel \as-əl\ acyl, basil, castle, facile, gracile, hassle, Kassel, passel, tassel, vassal, wrestle, forecastle, Newcastle

asser \as-ər\ crasser, gasser, Nasser, placer, harasser, antimacassar

asset \as-ət\ see ²ACET

¹assia \ash-ə\ see ²ASHA

²assia \äsh-ə\ see ¹ASHA

assian \ash-ən\ see ASSION

assible \as-ə-bəl\ see ASSABLE

assic \as-ik\ classic, Jurassic, Liassic, thalassic, Triassic, neoclassic, pseudoclassic, semiclassic

assical \as-i-kəl\ classical, fascicle, postclassical, unclassical, semiclassical

assid \as-əd\ see ACID

¹**assie** \as-ē\ see ASSY

²**assie** \äs-ē\ see ¹OSSY

¹**assim** \äs-əm\ see OSSUM

²**assim** \as-əm\ passim, sargassum

assin \as-ᵊn\ see ²ASTEN

assion \ash-ən\ ashen, fashion, passion, ration, Circassian, compassion, dispassion, impassion, refashion, Wakashan

assional \ash-nəl\ see ³ATIONAL

¹**assis** \as-ē\ see ASSY

²**assis** \as-əs\ classis, stasis, Parnassus, Halicarnassus

assist \as-əst\ bassist, racist, contrabassist

assive \as-iv\ massive, passive, impassive

assle \as-əl\ see ²ASSEL

assless \as-ləs\ classless, glassless, massless

assment \as-mənt\ blastment, amassment, harassment

assness \as-nəs\ see ASTNESS

¹**asso** \as-ō\ basso, lasso, El Paso, Picasso, sargasso, Sargasso, Bobo-Dioulasso

²**asso** \äs-ō\ Campo Basso, Burkina Faso

assock \as-ək\ cassock, hassock

assum \as-əm\ see ²ASSIM

assus \as-əs\ see ASSIS

assy \as-ē\ brassy, chassis, classy, gassy, glacis, glassie,

glassy, grassy, lassie, massy, sassy, saucy, Malagasy, Tallahassee, Haile Salassie

¹**ast** \əst\ see ¹UST

²**ast** \ast\ bast, blast, cast, caste, clast, fast, gast, ghast, hast, last, mast, past, vast, aghast, avast, bedfast, Belfast, bombast, broadcast, bypast, contrast, dicast, dismast, downcast, dynast, fantast, flypast, forecast, foremast, forepassed, gymnast, half-caste, half-mast, handfast, holdfast, lightfast, mainmast, makefast, march-past, miscast, newscast, oblast, offcast, outcast, outcaste, precast, recast, repast, roughcast, sandblast, sandcast, shamefast, soothfast, sportscast, steadfast, sunfast, topmast, trade-last, typecast, unasked, upcast, windblast, acid-fast, chiliast, cineast, colorcast, colorfast, flabbergast, fore-topmast, hard-and-fast, main-topmast, mizzenmast, narrowcast, opencast, overcast, pederast, rebroadcast, scholiast, simulcast, telecast, weathercast, ecdysiast, encomiast, enthusiast, iconoclast, radiocast, symposiast, radiobroadcast—*also* -ed *forms of verbs listed at* ³ASS

¹**asta** \äs-tə\ see OSTA

²**asta** \as-tə\ Rasta, canasta, Jocasta, Mount Shasta

astable \at-ə-bəl\ see ATIBLE

astard \as-tərd\ bastard, dastard, mastered, plastered

¹**aste** \āst\ see ACED

²**aste** \ast\ see ²AST

asted \as-təd\ blasted, masted, plastid—*also* -ed *forms of verbs listed at* ²AST

¹**asten** \ās-ᵊn\ see ¹ASON

²**asten** \as-ᵊn\ fasten, assassin, unfasten

¹**aster** \ā-stər\ taster, waster

²**aster** \as-tər\ aster, Astor, caster, castor, Castor, faster, gaster, master, pastor, plaster, raster, bandmaster, broadcaster, bushmaster, cadastre, choirmaster, disaster, drillmaster, headmaster, linecaster, loadmaster, paymaster, piaster, pilaster, postmaster, quizmaster, remaster, ringmaster, schoolmaster, scoutmaster, shinplaster, shipmaster, sportscaster, spymaster, taskmaster, three-master, toastmaster, truckmaster, wharfmaster, whoremaster, yardmaster, alabaster, burgomaster, concertmaster, criticaster, ironmaster, oleaster, overmaster, poetaster, quartermaster, rallymaster, stationmaster, weathercaster, Zoroaster, cotoneaster

astered \as-tərd\ see ASTARD

astering \as-tə-riŋ\ overmastering —*also* -ing *forms of verbs listed at* ASTER

astes \as-tēz\ cerastes, Ecclesiastes—*also* -s, -'s, *and* -s' *forms of nouns listed at* ²ASTY

asthma \az-mə\ see ASMA

astian \as-chən\ see ASTION

astic \as-tik\ drastic, mastic, plastic, spastic, bombastic, dynastic, elastic, fantastic, gymnastic, monastic, sarcastic, scholastic, stochastic, anelastic, Hudibrastic, inelastic, onomastic, orgiastic, paraphrastic, pederastic, periphrastic, superplastic, ecclesiastic, enthusiastic, iconoclastic, interscholastic, semimonastic

astics \as-tiks\ gymnastics, slimnastics

astid \as-təd\ see ASTED

astie \as-tē\ see ²ASTY

astiness \ā-stē-nəs\ hastiness, pastiness

¹**asting** \ā-stiŋ\ basting, wasting—*also* -ing *forms of verbs listed at* ACED

²**asting** \as-tiŋ\ typecasting, everlasting, narrowcasting, overcasting—*also* -ing *forms of verbs listed at* ²AST

astion \as-chən\ bastion, Erastian

astle \as-əl\ see ²ASSEL

astly \ast-lē\ ghastly, lastly

astment \as-mənt\ see ASSMENT

astness \as-nəs\ crassness, fastness, gastness, pastness

asto \as-tō\ impasto, antipasto

astor \as-tər\ see ²ASTER

astoral \as-trəl\ see ASTRAL

astral \as-trəl\ astral, gastral, pastoral, plastral, cadastral

astre \as-tər\ see ²ASTER

astric \as-trik\ gastric, nasogastric

astrophe \as-trə-fē\ anastrophe, catastrophe

¹**asty** \ā-stē\ hasty, pasty, tasty

²**asty** \as-tē\ blastie, nasty, pasty, vasty, capacity, contrasty, pederasty, angioplasty, bepharoplasty, osteoplasty, overcapacity

asuble \as-ə-bəl\ see ASSABLE

¹asure \ā-shər\ glacier, Glacier, rasure, erasure

²asure \ā-zhər\ see AZIER

asy \as-ē\ see ASSY

¹at \ä\ see ¹A

²at \ät\ see ¹OT

³at \ət\ see ¹UT

⁴at \ȯt\ see ¹OUGHT

⁵at \at\ bat, batt, blat, brat, cat, Cat, chat, chert, drat, fat, flat, frat, gat, gnat, hat, mat, matt, Matt, matte, pat, Pat, plait, plat, rat, Rat, sat, scat, scatt, skat, slat, spat, splat, sprat, stat, tat, that, vat, all that, at bat, backchat, begat, bobcat, brickbat, bullbat, Cassatt, chitchat, combat, comsat, cowpat, cravat, Croat, defat, dingbat, doormat, expat, fiat, firebrat, format, Hallstatt, hellcat, hepcat, high-hat, jurat, meerkat, muscat, Muscat, muskrat, nonfat, polecat, Sadat, savate, Sno-Cat, stand pat, standpat, stonechat, strawhat, Surat, thereat, tipcat, tomcat, whereat, whinchat, wildcat, wombat, acrobat, apparat, Ararat, assignat, autocrat, Automat, bureaucrat, butterfat, caveat, cervelat, concordat, copycat, democrat, diplomat, Dixiecrat, Eurocrat, habitat, Kattegat, Laundromat, marrowfat, mobocrat, monocrat, Montserrat, ochlocrat, pas de quatre, photostat, pit-a-pat, plutocrat, pussycat, rat-a-tat, scaredy-cat, semimatte, technocrat, theocrat, thermostat, tit for tat, Uniate, ziggurat, aristocrat,

gerontocrat, heliostat, Jehoshaphat, magnificat, meritocrat, Physiocrat, requiescat, thalassocrat, proletariat, professoriat, secretariat

⁶at \ə\ see ³AH

¹ata \ät-ə\ cotta, data, kata, balata, cantata, Carlotta, errata, fermata, frittata, La Plata, Maratha, Niigata, non grata, pinata, pro rata, reata, riata, regatta, sonata, Sorata, toccata, caponata, Hirakata, Mar del Plata, serenata, terracotta, Uspallata, Basilicata, desiderata, inamorata, medulla oblongata, missa cantata, persona grata, res judicata, persona non grata, res adjudicata, Rio de la Plata

²ata \ät-ə\ beta, data, eta, strata, theta, zeta, muleta, peseta, potato, pro rata, substrata, tomato, viewdata, corona radiata

³ata \at-ə\ data, errata, mulatto, non grata, pro rata, reata, regatta, riata, viewdata, paramatta, Paramatta, persona grata, persona non grata

¹atable \āt-ə-bəl\ datable, ratable, statable, debatable, dilatable, inflatable, locatable, rotatable, translatable, allocatable, circulatable, confiscatable, correlatable, detonatable, undebatable

²atable \at-ə-bəl\ see ATIBLE

atal \āt-ᵊl\ fatal, natal, ratel, shtetl, hiatal, postnatal, prenatal, antenatal, neonatal, perinatal

atalie \at-ᵊl-ē\ see ATTILY

atally \āt-ªl-ē\ fatally, natally,
postnatally, prenatally,
antenatally, neonatally,
perinatally

atalyst \at-ªl-əst\ catalyst,
philatelist

¹atan \āt-ən\ see ¹ATEN

²atan \at-ªn\ see ²ATIN

atancy \āt-ªn-sē\ blatancy,
latency, dilatancy

¹atant \āt-ªnt\ blatant, latent,
natant, patent, statant

²atant \at-ªnt\ patent,
combatant, noncombatant

atany \at-ªn-ē\ atony,
rhatany

atar \āt-ər\ see OTTER

atary \āt-ə-rē\ see OTTERY

¹atch \ech\ see ETCH

²atch \äch\ see OTCH

³atch \óch\ see ¹AUCH

⁴atch \ach\ bach, batch,
catch, cratch, hatch, klatch,
latch, match, natch, patch,
ratch, scratch, snatch,
thatch, attach, book-match,
crosshatch, crosspatch,
despatch, detach, dispatch,
nuthatch, outmatch,
potlatch, rematch,
Sasquatch, throatlatch,
unlatch, Wasatch, coffee
klatch, kaffeeklatsch,
overmatch

¹atcher \äch-ər\ botcher,
watcher, bird-watcher,
clock-watcher, debaucher,
topnotcher

²atcher \ach-ər\ batcher,
catcher, hatcher, matcher,
scratcher, stature, thatcher,
cowcatcher, dispatcher,
dogcatcher, eye-catcher,
flycatcher, gnatcatcher,
oyster catcher

atchet \ach-ət\ hatchet,
latchet, rachet, ratchet

atchily \ach-ə-lē\ patchily,
patchouli

atching \ach-iŋ\ back-
scratching, cross-hatching,
eye-catching,
nonmatching—*also* -ing
forms of verbs listed at ⁴ATCH

atchman \äch-mən\ see
OTCHMAN

atchment \ach-mənt\
catchment, hatchment,
attachment, detachment

atchouli \ach-ə-lē\ see
ATCHILY

atchy \ach-ē\ catchy, patchy,
scratchy, Apache

¹ate \āt\ ait, ate, bait, bate,
blate, cate, Cate, crate, date,
eight, fate, fete, freight, gait,
gate, grate, great, haet, hate,
Kate, late, mate, pate, plait,
plate, prate, quoit, rate, sate,
skate, slate, spate, state,
straight, strait, trait, wait,
wait, weight, abate, ablate,
adnate, aerate, age-mate,
agnate, airdate, airfreight,
alate, arête, await, backdate,
baldpate, bedmate, bedplate,
berate, birthrate, bistate,
bookplate, breastplate,
casemate, castrate, caudate,
cerate, cheapskate,
checkmate, chordate,
classmate, clavate, cognate,
collate, comate, conflate,
connate, cordate, create,
cremate, crenate, curate,
cut-rate, deadweight, debate,
deflate, delate, dentate,
derate, dictate, dilate,
disrate, donate, doorplate,
downstate, drawplate, elate,
equate, estate, faceplate,
falcate, fellate, filtrate, first-
rate, fishplate, fixate,
flatmate, floodgate,

flyweight, formate, frustrate,
gelate, gestate, gyrate,
hamate, hastate, headgate,
helpmate, housemate,
hydrate, ice-skate, inflate,
ingrate, inmate, innate,
instate, irate, jailbait, jugate,
khanate, Kuwait, lactate,
legate, liftgate, ligate,
lightweight, liquate, lobate,
locate, lunate, lustrate, lych-
gate, lyrate, magnate,
makebate, makeweight,
mandate, messmate, migrate,
misstate, mutate, nameplate,
narrate, negate, Newgate,
nitrate, notate, nutate,
oblate, orate, ornate, ovate,
palmate, palpate, peltate,
phonate, pinnate, placate,
playmate, plicate, portrait,
postdate, predate, primate,
probate, prolate, prorate,
prostate, prostrate, pulsate,
punctate, pupate, quadrate,
ramate, rebate, red-bait,
relate, restate, roommate,
rostrate, rotate, saccate,
schoolmate, seatmate,
sedate, sensate, septate,
serrate, shipmate, short
weight, soleplate, spectate,
spicate, squamate, stagnate,
stalemate, stellate, striate,
sublate, substrate, sulcate,
summate, tailgate, teammate,
Tebet, tenth-rate, ternate,
terneplate, testate, third-rate,
tinplate, toeplate, tollgate,
tractate, translate, tristate,
truncate, unweight, update,
uprate, upstate, V-8, vacate,
vallate, valvate, vibrate,
virgate, vulgate, whitebait,
workmate, zonate, abdicate,
abnegate, abrogate,
absorbate, acclimate,

acerbate, acetate, activate,
actuate, acylate, adsorbate,
advocate, adulate,
adumbrate, aggravate,
aggregate, agitate, allocate,
altercate, alternate,
ambulate, amputate,
animate, annotate, annulate,
antedate, antiquate,
apartheid, apostate,
approbate, approximate,
arbitrate, arcuate, arrogate,
aspirate, automate, aviate,
bantamweight, bifurcate,
billingsgate, bipinnate,
boilerplate, bombinate,
brachiate, cachinnate,
calculate, calibrate,
caliphate, candidate,
cantillate, capitate, captivate,
carbonate, carbon-date,
carinate, castigate, catenate,
cavitate, celebrate,
cerebrate, circinate,
circulate, city-state, cogitate,
collimate, collocate,
commentate, commutate,
compensate, complicate,
concentrate, condensate,
confiscate, conglobate,
conjugate, consecrate,
constellate, consternate,
constipate, consummate,
contemplate, copperplate,
copulate, coronate,
correlate, corrugate,
coruscate, counterweight,
crenulate, crepitate,
criminate, cruciate,
cucullate, culminate,
cultivate, cumulate, cuneate,
cupulate, cuspidate,
cyclamate, decimate,
decollate, decorate,
decussate, dedicate,
defalcate, defecate, delegate,
demarcate, demonstrate,

denigrate, deviate, deprecate,
depredate, derivate,
derogate, desecrate,
desiccate, designate,
desolate, detonate, devastate,
deviate, digitate, diplomate,
discarnate, dislocate,
dissertate, dissipate,
distillate, divagate, dominate,
duplicate, edentate, educate,
elevate, elongate, eluate,
emanate, emigrate, emirate,
emulate, enervate, ephorate,
escalate, estimate, estivate,
excavate, exculpate,
execrate, expiate, explicate,
expurgate, exsiccate,
extirpate, extricate, exudate,
fabricate, fascinate,
featherweight, fecundate,
federate, fenestrate,
festinate, fibrillate, flabellate,
flagellate, flocculate,
fluctuate, fluoridate, foliate,
formulate, fornicate,
fractionate, fragmentate,
fulminate, fumigate,
fustigate, geminate, generate,
germinate, glaciate, Golden
Gate, graduate, granulate,
gratulate, gravitate,
heavyweight, hebetate,
herniate, hesitate, hibernate,
hundredweight, hyphenate,
ideate, illustrate, imamate,
imbricate, imitate,
immigrate, immolate,
impetrate, implicate,
imprecate, impregnate,
incarnate, increase, incubate,
inculcate, inculpate,
incurvate, indagate, indicate,
indurate, infiltrate,
innervate, innovate,
insensate, insolate,
inspissate, instigate, insulate,
interstate, intestate, intimate,

intonate, intraplate,
inundate, invocate, iodate,
irrigate, irritate, isolate,
iterate, jubilate, juniorate,
lacerate, laminate, Latinate,
laureate, legislate, levigate,
levitate, liberate, liquidate,
litigate, littermate, lubricate,
macerate, machinate,
magistrate, marginate,
margravate, marinate,
masticate, masturbate,
maturate, mediate, medicate,
meditate, meliorate,
menstruate, microstate,
micturate, middleweight,
militate, ministrate,
miscreate, mithridate,
mitigate, moderate,
modulate, motivate,
multistate, mutilate, nation-
state, nauseate, navigate,
neonate, nictitate, niobate,
nominate, numerate,
obfuscate, objurgate,
obligate, obovate, obviate,
operate, opiate, orchestrate,
ordinate, oscillate, osculate,
out-of-date, overstate,
overweight, ovulate,
paginate, palliate, palpitate,
paperweight, patinate,
peculate, penetrate,
pennyweight, percolate,
perennate, perforate,
permeate, perorate,
perpetrate, personate,
pollinate, populate,
postulate, potentate,
predicate, procreate,
profligate, promulgate,
propagate, prorogate,
pullulate, pulmonate,
punctuate, quantitate,
rabbinate, radiate, re-create,
reclinate, recreate, regulate,
reinstate, relegate, relocate,

reluctate, remonstrate,
renovate, replicate,
reprobate, resonate,
retardate, retranslate,
roseate, rubricate, ruminate,
runagate, rusticate, sagittate,
salivate, sanitate, satiate,
saturate, scintillate, second-
rate, segregate, separate,
sequestrate, seriate, sibilate,
simulate, sinuate, situate,
speculate, spoliate,
stablemate, stimulate,
stipulate, strangulate,
stridulate, stylobate,
subjugate, sublimate,
subrogate, subulate,
suffocate, sultanate,
supplicate, surrogate,
syncopate, syndicate,
tablemate, tabulate,
terminate, tessellate, tête-à-
tête, thirty-eight, titillate,
titivate, tolerate,
transmigrate, transudate,
tribulate, tribunate,
trifurcate, trilobate,
tripinnate, triplicate,
tunicate, turbinate, ulcerate,
ululate, umbellate, uncinate,
underrate, understate,
underweight, undulate,
ungulate, urinate, vaccinate,
vacillate, validate, valuate,
variate, vaticinate, vegetate,
venerate, ventilate,
vertebrate, vicarate,
vindicate, violate, vitiate,
Watergate, welterweight,
abbreviate, abominate,
accelerate, accentuate,
accommodate, acculturate,
accumulate, acidulate,
adjudicate, administrate,
adulterate, affiliate,
agglomerate, agglutinate,
alienate, alleviate, alliterate,

amalgamate, ameliorate,
annihilate, annunciate,
anticipate, apostolate,
appreciate, appropriate,
articulate, asphyxiate,
assassinate, asseverate,
assimilate, associate,
attenuate, authenticate,
barbiturate, bicarbonate,
calumniate, campanulate,
capacitate, capitulate,
catholicate, certificate,
circumvallate, coagulate,
coelenterate, collaborate,
commemorate, commiserate,
communicate,
compassionate, concatenate,
concelebrate, conciliate,
confabulate, confederate,
conglomerate, congratulate,
consociate, consolidate,
contaminate, cooperate,
coordinate, corroborate, de-
escalate, deaerate, debilitate,
decapitate, decerebrate,
deconcentrate, deconsecrate,
decrepitate, defibrinate,
defribrillate, degenerate,
deliberate, delineate,
demodulate, denominate,
depopulate, depreciate,
deregulate, desegregate,
desiderate, devaluate,
diaconate, dilapidate,
discriminate, disintegrate,
disseminate, dissimilate,
dissimulate, dissociate,
divaricate, domesticate,
edulcorate, effectuate,
ejaculate, elaborate,
electroplate, eliminate,
elucidate, elucubrate,
elutriate, emaciate,
emancipate, emarginate,
emasculate, encapsulate,
enumerate, enunciate,
episcopate, equilibrate,

equivocate, eradicate,
etiolate, evacuate, evaluate,
evaporate, eventuate,
eviscerate, exacerbate,
exaggerate, exasperate,
excogitate, excoriate,
excruciate, exfoliate,
exhilarate, exonerate,
expatiate, expatriate,
expectorate, expostulate,
expropriate, extenuate,
exterminate, extrapolate,
extravagate, exuberate,
facilitate, fantasticate,
felicitate, gesticulate,
habilitate, habituate,
hallucinate, homologate,
humiliate, hypothecate,
illuminate, impersonate,
inactivate, inaugurate,
incarcerate, incinerate,
incorporate, incriminate,
indoctrinate, inebriate,
infatuate, infuriate,
ingratiate, ingurgitate,
initiate, inoculate,
inosculate, inseminate,
insinuate, instantiate,
intenerate, intercalate,
interpellate, interpolate,
interrelate, interrogate,
intimidate, intoxicate,
invaginate, invalidate,
investigate, invigilate,
invigorate, irradiate,
italianate, itinerate,
lanceolate, legitimate,
luxuriate, machicolate,
mandarinate, manipulate,
matriarchate, matriculate,
Merthiolate, necessitate,
negotiate, noncandidate,
obliterate, obnubilate,
officiate, orientate, originate,
oxygenate, participate,
particulate, patriarchate,
patriciate, penicillate,

perambulate, peregrinate,
perpetuate, pontificate,
potentiate, precipitate,
predestinate, predominate,
prefabricate, premeditate,
prenominate, preponderate,
prevaricate, procrastinate,
prognosticate, proliferate,
propitiate, proportionate,
quadruplicate, quintuplicate,
reciprocate, recriminate,
recuperate, redecorate,
redintegrate, reduplicate,
reeducate, refrigerate,
regenerate, regurgitate,
reincarnate, reintegrate,
reiterate, rejuvenate,
remunerate, renominate,
repatriate, repristinate,
repudiate, resupinate,
resuscitate, retaliate,
reticulate, revaluate,
revegetate, reverberate,
scholasticate, self-portrait,
seventy-eight, sextuplicate,
somnambulate, sophisticate,
stereobate, subordinate,
substantiate, syllabicate,
tergiversate, transliterate,
transvaluate, triangulate,
variegate, vituperate,
vociferate, beneficiate,
circumambulate,
circumnavigate,
circumstantiate,
contraindicate,
decontaminate, deteriorate,
differentiate, disaffiliate,
disambiguate, disarticulate,
disassociate,
discombobulate,
disintoxicate, disorientate,
disproportionate,
domiciliate, excommunicate,
free-associate,
hyperventilate, incapacitate,
individuate, intermediate,

interpenetrate, lithium
niobate, superheavyweight,
microencapsulate,
misappropriate, multivariate,
ratiocinate, recapitulate,
rehabilitate, renegotiate,
superannuate, superelevate,
superordinate, supersaturate,
transilluminate,
transubstantiate,
underestimate,
intercommunicate,
diammonium phosphate,
phosphoenolpyruvate,
peroxyacetyl nitrate

²ate \at\ see ⁵AT

³ate \ät\ see ¹OT

⁴ate \ät-ē\ see ATI

⁵ate \ət\ see ¹UT

ated \āt-əd\ gaited, lated,
pated, stated, belated, ill-
fated, outdated, pustulated,
related, striated, three-
gaited, truncated, unbated,
X-rated, aberrated,
addlepated, animated,
asteriated, calculated,
capsulated, carbonated,
carburated, castellated,
complicated, crenellated,
disrelated, elevated,
fenestrated, fimbriated,
floriated, foliated,
inspissated, intoxicated,
laminated, marginated,
mentholated, perforated,
pileated, pixilated, saturated,
tessellated, trabeated,
unabated, uncreated,
understated, variegated,
affiliated, configurated,
coordinated, decaffeinated,
domesticated, incorporated,
inebriated, interrelated,
intoxicated, opinionated,
sophisticated, uncalculated,
uncelebrated,

uncomplicated,
underinflated, unmediated,
unmitigated, unsaturated,
unsegregated, unadulterated,
unanticipated, unarticulated,
unconsolidated,
undereducated,
underpopulated,
undissociated,
unsophisticated,
polyunsaturated,
underappreciated—*also* -ed
forms of verbs listed at ¹ATE

ateful \āt-fəl\ fateful, grateful,
hateful, ungrateful

¹atel \ət-ᵊl\ see OTTLE

²atel \āt-ᵊl\ see ATAL

ateless \āt-ləs\ dateless,
stateless, weightless

atelist \at-ᵊl-əst\ see ATALYST

¹ately \āt-lē\ greatly, lately,
stately, straightly, straitly,
innately, irately, ornately,
up-to-dately, Johnny-come-
lately

²ately \at-ᵊl-ē\ see ATTILY

atem \āt-əm\ see ¹ATUM

atement \āt-mənt\ statement,
abatement, debatement,
misstatement, restatement,
overstatement,
reinstatement,
understatement

¹aten \āt-ᵊn\ greaten, laten,
Satan, straighten, straiten,
Keewatin

²aten \at-ᵊn\ see ²ATIN

³aten \ät-ᵊn\ see OTTEN

¹atent \āt-ᵊnt\ see ¹ATANT

²atent \at-ᵊnt\ see ²ATANT

¹ater \ȯt-ər\ daughter,
slaughter, tauter, water,
backwater, bathwater,
blackwater, breakwater,
cutwater, dewater,
deepwater, dishwater,
firewater, floodwater,

forequarter, freshwater,
goddaughter, granddaughter,
groundwater, headwater,
hindquarter, jerkwater,
limewater, manslaughter,
meltwater, rainwater,
rosewater, saltwater,
seawater, self-slaughter,
shearwater, springwater,
stepdaughter, tailwater,
tidewater, wastewater, milk-
and-water, polywater,
underwater

²ater \āt-ər\ see ATOR

ateral \at-ə-rəl\ lateral,
bilateral, collateral,
trilateral, contralateral,
dorsolateral, equilateral,
ipsilateral, multilateral,
quadrilateral, unilateral,
ventrolateral, posterolateral

aterer \ȯt-ər-ər\ slaughterer,
waterer, dewaterer

ateress \āt-ə-rəs\ cateress,
traitorous

atering \ȯt-ə-riŋ\ mouth-
watering —also -ing forms of
verbs listed at ¹ATER

¹atery \āt-ə-rē\ see OTTERY

²atery \ȯt-ə-rē\ cautery,
watery

¹ates \āts\ Yeats, Gulf States,
Papal States, Persian Gulf
States, United States,
Federated Malay States,
United Arab Emirates —
also -s, -'s, and -s' forms of
nouns listed at ¹ATE, and -s
forms of verbs listed there

²ates \āt-ēz\ nates, Achates,
Euphrates, Penates—also -s,
-'s, and -s' forms of nouns
listed at ATY

atest \āt-əst\ latest, statist—
also -est forms of adjectives
listed at ¹ATE

atey \āt-ē\ see ATY

¹ath \äth\ see ¹OTH

²ath \ȯth\ see ²OTH

³ath \ath\ bath, hath, lath,
math, path, rathe, snath,
strath, wrath, birdbath,
bloodbath, bypath, footbath,
footpath, sunbath, towpath,
warpath, aftermath,
polymath, psychopath,
telepath, naturopath,
osteopath, sociopath

atha \ät-ə\ see ¹ATA

¹athe \äth\ swathe, enswathe,
unswathe

²athe \āth\ bathe, lathe,
rathe, saithe, scathe, spathe,
swathe, sunbathe, unswathe

³athe \ath\ see ³ATH

atheless \āth-ləs\ see AITHLESS

¹ather \äth-ər\ bother, father,
pother, rather, forefather,
godfather, grandfather,
housefather, stepfather

²ather \ōth-ər\ see ¹OTHER

³ather \ath-ər\ blather,
Cather, gather, lather,
Mather, rather, slather,
forgather, ingather, wool-
gather

athering \ath-riŋ\
ingathering,
woolgathering—also -ing
forms of verbs listed at
³ATHER

athi \ät-ē\ see ATI

athic \ath-ik\ empathic,
amphipathic, psychopathic,
telepathic, homeopathic,
idiopathic, sociopathic

athlon \ath-lən\ biathlon,
decathlon, pentathlon,
triathlon

athy \ath-ē\ Cathie, Cathy,
Kathie, Kathy, wrathy,
allelopathy

¹ati \ät-ē\ Ate, Dottie, dotty,
Dotty, grotty, knotty,

naughty, plotty, potty,
Scottie, Scotty, snotty,
spotty, squatty, Amati,
basmati, chapati, coati,
flokati, karate, Marathi,
metate, Scarlatti, Tol'yatti,
glitterati, Gujarati,
Hakodate, literati,
manicotti, illuminati

²ati \atē\ see ATTY

³ati \äts\ see OTS

⁴ati \as\ see ³ASS

atia \ā-shə\ see ACIA

atial \ā-shəl\ see ACIAL

atian \ā-shən\ see ¹ATION

atians \ā-shənz\ see ATIONS

atible \at-ə-bəl\ compatible,
getatable, incompatible, self-
compatible, biocompatible,
self-incompatible

¹atic \ät-ik\ see ¹OTIC

²atic \at-ik\ attic, Attic, batik,
phatic, static, vatic, agnatic,
aquatic, astatic, asthmatic,
chromatic, climatic, comatic,
dalmatic, dogmatic, dramatic, ecstatic, emphatic,
erratic, fanatic, hepatic,
judgmatic, komatik,
lymphatic, magmatic,
neumatic, phlegmatic,
plasmatic, pneumatic,
pragmatic, prismatic,
protatic, quadratic,
rheumatic, schematic,
schismatic, sciatic, sematic,
Socratic, somatic, spermatic,
stigmatic, sylvatic, thematic,
traumatic, villatic,
achromatic, acrobatic,
Adriatic, aerobatic, anabatic,
antistatic, aromatic,
astigmatic, autocratic,
automatic, bureaucratic,
charismatic, cinematic,
democratic, dilemmatic,
diplomatic, Dixiecratic,

Eleatic, emblematic,
enigmatic, enzymatic,
fungistatic, Hanseatic,
hieratic, Hippocratic,
kerygmatic, leviratic,
melismatic, miasmatic,
mobocratic, monocratic,
morganatic, numismatic,
ochlocratic, operatic,
phonematic, plutocratic, pre-
Socratic, problematic,
programmatic, symptomatic,
syntagmatic, systematic,
technocratic, theocratic,
timocratic, undogmatic,
undramatic, anagrammatic,
apothegmatic, aristocratic,
asymptomatic, axiomatic,
conglomeratic,
diagrammatic,
diaphragmatic,
epigrammatic, gerontocratic,
gynecocratic, homeostatic,
idiomatic, logogrammatic,
melodramatic, meritocratic,
monochromatic,
monodramatic,
monogrammatic,
pantisocratic, paradigmatic,
physiocratic,
psychodramatic,
psychosomatic, semiaquatic,
theorematic, undemocratic,
undiplomatic,
antidemocratic,
Austroasiatic, biosystematic,
ideogrammatic,
semiautomatic

atica \at-i-kə\ Attica,
hepatica, sciatica, viatica

atical \at-i-kəl\ statical,
dogmatical, erratical,
fanatical, grammatical,
piratical, pragmatical,
sabbatical, schismatical,
autocratical, emblematical,
enigmatical, magistratical,

mathematical, ochlocratical,
problematical, systematical,
theocratical, timocratical,
ungrammatical,
anagrammatical,
diagrammatical,
epigrammatical,
pantisocratical

atics \at-iks\ statics,
chromatics, dogmatics,
dramatics, pneumatics,
pragmatics, acrobatics,
informatics, mathematics,
numismatics, systematics,
melodramatics,
psychosomatics—*also* -s, -s,
and -s' *forms of nouns listed
at* ²ATIC

atie \āt-ē\ *see* ATY

atiens \ā-shənz\ *see* ATIONS

atient \ā-shənt\ patient,
impatient, inpatient,
outpatient, rubefacient,
somnifacient, abortifacient

atik \at-ik\ *see* ²ATIC

atile \at-ᵊl-ē\ *see* ATTILY

atim \ät-əm\ *see* ²ATUM

¹**atin** \āt-ᵊn\ *see* OTTEN

²**atin** \at-ᵊn\ batten, fatten,
flatten, gratin, Latin, latten,
matin, paten, patten, Patton,
platan, platen, ratton, satin,
cisplatin, manhattan,
Manhattan, Powhatan,
lovastatin, Neo-Latin

³**atin** \āt-ᵊn\ *see* ¹ATEN

atinate \at-ᵊn-ət\ concatenate,
Palatinate, Rhineland-
Palatinate

ating \āt-iŋ\ bating, grating,
plating, rating, skating,
slating, abating, bearbaiting,
bullbaiting, frustrating, self-
rating, calculating,
lancinating, maid-in-waiting,
nauseating, operating,
titillating, humiliating, lady-

in-waiting, nonterminating,
self-liquidating, self-
regulating, self-replicating,
subordinating, uncalculating,
undeviating, unhesitating,
indiscriminating, self-
incriminating—*also* -ing
forms of verbs listed at ¹ATE

atinous \at-nəs\ *see* ATNESS

¹**ation** \ā-shən\ Asian, Haitian,
nation, Nation, ration,
station, Thracian, ablation,
agnation, Alsatian,
carnation, castration,
causation, cessation,
cetacean, chrismation,
citation, cognation,
collation, conation,
conflation, creation,
cremation, crenation,
Croatian, crustacean,
cunctation, dalmatian,
damnation, deflation,
dictation, dilation, donation,
duration, elation, enation,
equation, Eurasian,
filtration, fixation, flotation,
formation, foundation,
frustration, furcation,
gestation, gradation,
gustation, gyration,
hydration, illation, inflation,
lactation, laudation, lavation,
legation, libation, libration,
ligation, location, lustration,
mentation, migration,
mutation, narration,
natation, negation, nitration,
notation, novation, nutation,
oblation, oration, outstation,
ovation, phonation,
planation, plantation,
plication, potation,
predation, privation,
probation, pronation,
proration, prostration,
pulsation, purgation,

quotation, reflation, relation, rogation, rotation, saltation, salvation, sedation, sensation, serration, slumpflation, squamation, stagflation, stagnation, starvation, striation, stylization, sublation, substation, summation, tarnation, taxation, temptation, translation, truncation, vacation, venation, vexation, vibration, vocation, workstation, zonation, abdication, aberration, abjuration, abnegation, acceptation, acclamation, acclimation, accusation, activation, actuation, adaptation, adjuration, admiration, adoration, adulation, adumbration, advocation, affectation, affirmation, aggravation, aggregation, allegation, allocation, amputation, alteration, altercation, alternation, Amerasian, angulation, animation, annexation, annotation, annulation, antiquation, Appalachian, appellation, application, approbation, arbitration, aspiration, assentation, assignation, attestation, augmentation, Aurignacian, automation, aviation, avocation, blaxploitation, botheration, brachiation, cachinnation, calculation, calibration, cancellation, capitation, captivation, carbonation, carburation, castigation, celebration, cementation, cerebration, circulation,

claudication, cogitation, collocation, coloration, combination, commendation, commination, commutation, compellation, compensation, compilation, complication, compurgation, computation, concentration, condemnation, condensation, condonation, confirmation, confiscation, conflagration, conformation, confrontation, confutation, congelation, congregation, conjugation, conjuration, connotation, consecration, conservation, consolation, conspiration, constellation, consternation, constipation, consultation, consummation, contemplation, contestation, conurbation, conversation, convocation, copulation, coronation, corporation, correlation, corrugation, coruscation, crenellation, culmination, cupellation, cuspidation, cybernation, decimation, declamation, declaration, declination, decoration, dedication, defalcation, defamation, defecation, defloration, deformation, degradation, degustation, dehydration, delectation, delegation, demarcation, demonstration, denegation, denigration, denotation, depilation, deportation, depravation, depredation, deprivation, deputation, derivation, derogation, desecration, desiccation, designation, desolation, desperation, destination, detestation, detonation, devastation, deviation, dilatation, disclamation, disinflation, dislocation, dispensation, disputation, disrelation, dissertation, dissipation, distillation, divination, domination, dubitation, duplication, education, elevation, elongation, emanation, embarkation, embrocation, emendation, emigration, emulation, encrustation, enervation, epilation, equitation, eructation, escalation, estimation, estivation, evocation, exaltation, excavation, excitation, exclamation, exculpation, execration, exhalation, exhortation, expectation, expiation, expiration, explanation, explication, exploitation, exploration, exportation, expurgation, extirpation, extrication, exudation, exultation, fabrication, fascination, federation, fenestration, fermentation, fibrillation, figuration, filiation, flagellation, fluoridation, fluctuation, foliation, fomentation, formulation, fornication, fragmentation, fulguration, fulmination, fumigation, gemination, generation, germination, glaciation, graduation, granulation, gravitation, habitation, hesitation, hibernation, hyphenation, ideation, illustration, imbrication, imitation, immigration, immolation, implantation, implication,

importation, imprecation, imputation, incantation, incarnation, incitation, inclination, incrustation, incubation, inculcation, indentation, indexation, indication, indignation, induration, infestation, infiltration, inflammation, information, inhalation, innovation, insolation, inspiration, installation, instauration, insufflation, insulation, intonation, inundation, invitation, invocation, irrigation, irritation, isolation, iteration, jactitation, jubilation, laceration, lacrimation, lamentation, lamination, legislation, levitation, liberation, limitation, lineation, liquidation, literation, litigation, lubrication, lucubration, maceration, machination, maculation, malformation, malversation, margination, mastication, masturbation, maturation, mediation, medication, meditation, melioration, menstruation, mensuration, metrication, ministration, moderation, modulation, molestation, motivation, navigation, nomination, numeration, obfuscation, objurgation, obligation, observation, obturation, occultation, occupation, operation, orchestration, ordination, oscillation, osculation, ostentation, ovulation, oxidation, ozonation, pagination, palliation, palpitation, patination, penetration, perforation, permeation, permutation, peroration, perpetration, perspiration, perturbation, pigmentation, pixilation, pollination, population, postulation, predication, preformation, prelibation, preparation, presentation, proclamation, procreation, procuration, profanation, prolongation, propagation, prorogation, protestation, provocation, publication, punctuation, radiation, recitation, reclamation, recordation, re-creation, recreation, reformation, refutation, registration, regulation, relaxation, relocation, reparation, replantation, replication, reprobation, reputation, reservation, resignation, respiration, restoration, retardation, revelation, revocation, ruination, salivation, salutation, sanitation, satiation, saturation, scatteration, scintillation, segmentation, segregation, separation, sequestration, sexploitation, simulation, situation, solmization, speciation, speculation, spoliation, sternutation, stimulation, stipulation, strangulation, structuration, subjugation, sublimation, subrogation, suffocation, suspiration, susurration, sustentation, syncopation, syndication, tabulation, termination, tessellation, titillation, titivation, toleration, transformation,

translocation, transmigration, transmutation, transpiration, transplantation, transportation, trepidation, tribulation, trituration, ulceration, ululation, undulation, urination, usurpation, vaccination, vacillation, validation, valuation, variation, vegetation, veneration, ventilation, vindication, violation, visitation, abbreviation, abomination, acceleration, accentuation, accommodation, accreditation, acculturation, accumulation, actualization, adjudication, administration, adulteration, affiliation, afforestation, agglomeration, agglutination, alienation, alleviation, alliteration, amalgamation, amelioration, amortization, amplification, analyzation, anglicization, annihilation, annunciation, anticipation, appreciation, appropriation, approximation, argumentation, articulation, asphyxiation, assassination, asseveration, assimilation, association, attenuation, authorization, autoxidation, barbarization, bastardization, beautification, bowdlerization, brutalization, canalization, canonization, capacitation, capitulation, carbonylation, centralization, certification, cicatrization, civilization, clarification, classification, coagulation, coeducation,

cohabitation, colonization,
collaboration, columniation,
commemoration,
commiseration,
communication,
communization,
compartmentation,
complementation,
concatenation, conciliation,
confabulation,
confederation, configuration,
conglomeration,
congratulation,
consideration, consociation,
consolidation,
contamination, continuation,
cooperation, coordination,
corroboration, crustification,
crystallization, deactivation,
debilitation, decapitation,
decompensation,
defenestration, deforestation,
degeneration, deglaciation,
deification, deliberation,
delineation, denomination,
denunciation, depopulation,
depreciation, deregulation,
desegregation, despoliation,
determination, devaluation,
dilapidation,
diphthongization,
disapprobation,
discoloration,
discrimination,
disembarkation,
disinclination,
disinformation,
disintegration, dissemination,
dissimilation, dissimulation,
dissociation, divarication,
documentation,
domestication,
dramatization, echolocation,
edification, ejaculation,
elaboration, elicitation,
elimination, elucidation,
emaciation, emancipation,

emasculation, enumeration,
enunciation, epoxidation,
equalization, equivocation,
eradication, evacuation,
evagination, evaluation,
evaporation, evisceration,
exacerbation, exaggeration,
examination, exasperation,
excoriation, excruciation,
exercitation, exhilaration,
exoneration, expostulation,
expropriation, extenuation,
extermination, extrapolation,
facilitation, factorization,
falsification, fantastication,
feminization, fertilization,
Finlandization,
formalization, formulization,
fortification, fossilization,
fructification, gasification,
gentrification, gesticulation,
glamorization, globalization,
glorification, glycosylation,
gratification, habituation,
hallucination,
harmonization,
haruspication, hellenization,
humanization,
hyperinflation, idolization,
illumination, imagination,
immunization,
impersonation,
implementation,
improvisation, inauguration,
incarceration, incardination,
incineration, incorporation,
incrimination,
indoctrination, inebriation,
infatuation, ingratiation,
inhabitation, initiation,
inoculation, insemination,
insinuation, instrumentation,
internalization,
interpretation, interrelation,
intimidation, intoxication,
invagination, investigation,
invigoration, irradiation,

itemization, jollification, justification, labanotation, laicization, latinization, legalization, lionization, localization, machicolation, magnetization, magnification, maladaptation, manifestation, masculinization, matriculation, maximization, mechanization, miscegenation, mobilization, modernization, modification, mollification, mongrelization, monopolization, moralization, mortification, multiplication, mystification, nationalization, naturalization, necessitation, negotiation, neutralization, normalization, notarization, notification, novelization, nullification, optimization, organization, orientation, ornamentation, ossification, pacification, paralyzation, participation, pasteurization, patronization, penalization, perambulation, perpetuation, perseveration, personalization, plasticization, pluralization, petrification, polarization, pontification, preadaptation, precipitation, predestination, prefiguration, premeditation, preoccupation, preregistration, prettification, procrastination, prognostication, proliferation, pronunciation, propitiation, pulverization, purification, qualification, quantification, ramification, randomization, ratification, ratiocination, realization, reciprocation, recombination, recommendation, recrimination, recuperation, redecoration, reduplication, reforestation, refrigeration, regeneration, regimentation, regurgitation, reification, reincarnation, reintegration, remediation, remuneration, renunciation, representation, republication, repudiation, reticulation, retrogradation, reverberation, robotization, romanization, sanctification, sanitization, scarification, secularization, sedimentation, sensitization, Serbo-Croatian, signification, simplification, socialization, solemnization, solicitation, solidification, sophistication, specialization, specification, stabilization, standardization, sterilization, stratification, stultification, subalternation, subinfeudation, subordination, subpopulation, subsidization, summarization, supplementation, syllabication, symbolization, synchronization, systemization, teleportation, tergiversation, terrorization, theorization, transfiguration, transliteration, transvaluation, traumatization, triangulation, trivialization, uglification, unification, unionization, urbanization, vandalization, vaporization, variegation, vaticination,

velarization, verbalization,
verification, versification,
victimization, vilification,
vinification, vitalization,
vituperation, vocalization,
vociferation, vulgarization,
westernization, x-radiation,
acclimatization,
allegorization,
alphabetization,
autocorrelation,
automatization,
beneficiation, capitalization,
characterization,
circumnavigation,
codetermination,
commercialization,
conceptualization,
consubstantiation,
containerization,
counterreformation,
criminalization, cross-
examination,
cryopreservation,
decarboxylation,
decimilization, de-
Stalinization,
decasualization,
decentralization,
declassification,
decontamination,
dehumanization,
dehydrogenation,
delegitimation,
demystification,
derealization, derivitization,
desulfurization,
deterioration, differentiation,
disassociation,
discombobulation,
disorientation,
disorganization,
disproportionation,
disqualification,
diversification,
dolomitization,
electrification,

excommunication,
exemplification,
experimentation,
extemporization,
externalization,
familiarization,
federalization,
generalization,
homogenization,
hospitalization,
hyperventilation,
idealization, identification,
immobilization,
immortalization,
incapacitation,
inconsideration,
incoordination,
indemnification,
indetermination,
indiscrimination,
individuation,
institutionalization,
insubordination,
intensification,
intermediation,
intermodulation,
intrapopulation, italicization,
legitimization, lexicalization,
maladministration,
mathematization,
megacorporation,
militarization,
miniaturization,
misappropriation,
miscommunication,
misinterpretation,
mispronunciation,
misrepresentation,
noncooperation,
nonproliferation,
overcompensation,
overpopulation,
palatalization, periodization,
personification,
photoduplication,
photoexcitation,
popularization,

predetermination,
prestidigitation,
proselytization,
radicalization,
ratiocination,
rationalization,
reafforestation,
recapitulation,
reconciliation,
reconsideration,
rehabilitation,
reinterpretation,
renegotiation,
reorganization,
revitalization, ritualization,
Schrödinger equation,
subvocalization,
supererogation,
syllabification,
tintinnabulation,
transubstantiation,
unappreciation,
underestimation,
undervaluation,
unsophistication,
visualization,
Americanization,
automanipulation,
decriminalization,
depersonalization,
electrodesiccation,
intercommunication,
industrialization,
materialization,
oversimplification,
particularization,
pictorialization,
photointerpretation,
pseudosophistication,
recapitalization,
spiritualization,
telecommunication,
universalization,
biodeterioration,
deindustrialization,
intellectualization,
reindustrialization,

internationalization,
deinstitutionalization

²**ation** \ā-zhən\ see ASION

³**ation** \ash-ən\ see ASSION

¹**ational** \ā-shnəl\ stational,
citational, formational,
gestational, gradational,
migrational, narrational,
notational, relational,
sensational, vocational,
aberrational, adaptational,
avocational, compensational,
computational,
conformational,
confrontational,
congregational,
conjugational, connotational,
conservational,
conversational,
convocational, derivational,
educational, fluctuational,
generational, gravitational,
ideational, informational,
innovational, inspirational,
invitational, irrotational,
limitational, navigational,
observational, operational,
orchestrational,
postranslational,
prevocational,
progestational, recreational,
reformational, situational,
transformational,
communicational,
coeducational,
denominational,
improvisational,
interpretational,
investigational,
organizational,
representational,
nonrepresentational,
reorganizational,
interdenominational

²**ational** \āzh-nəl\ see
ASIONAL

³**ational** \ash-nəl\ national,

passional, rational,
binational, cross-national,
irrational, transnational,
international, multinational,
supranational, suprarational

ationist \ā-shnəst\
salvationist, vacationist,
annexationist,
confrontationist,
conservationist, educationist,
integrationist, isolationist,
liberationist, operationist,
preservationist, recreationist,
segregationist, separationist,
preservationist,
accomodationist,
administrationist,
assimilationist, associationist,
collaborationist,
emancipationist

ations \ā-shənz\ Galatians,
impatiens, relations,
Lamentations, Revelations,
United Nations, Rhode
Island and Providence
Plantations

atious \ā-shəs\ see ACIOUS

¹**atis** \at-əs\ see ³ATUS

²**atis** \ät-əs\ see OTTIS

atist \āt-əst\ see ATEST

atitude \at-ə-tüd\ see
ATTITUDE

atium \ā-shē-əm\ Latium,
pancratium, solatium

atius \ā-shəs\ see ACIOUS

ative \āt-iv\ dative, native,
stative, ablative, constative,
creative, dilative, mutative,
rotative, summative, aggregative,
translative, aggregative,
agitative, alterative,
applicative, carminative,
cogitative, combinative,
commutative, connotative,
consecrative, consultative,
contemplative, copulative,
corporative, cumulative,

decorative, denotative,
dissipative, educative,
explicative, facultative,
federative, generative,
germinative, imitative,
implicative, innovative,
integrative, irritative,
iterative, legislative,
limitative, meditative,
meliorative, motivative,
nominative, nuncupative,
operative, palliative,
pejorative, penetrative,
procreative, propagative,
qualitative, quantitative,
recreative, regulative,
replicative, separative,
speculative, terminative,
vegetative, accelerative,
accumulative,
administrative,
agglutinative, alliterative,
appreciative, assimilative,
associative, authoritative,
collaborative,
commemorative,
commiserative,
communicative,
contaminative, continuative,
cooperative, corroborative,
degenerative, deliberative,
delineative, determinative,
discriminative, evaporative,
exhilarative, exonerative,
illuminative, interpretative,
investigative, justificative,
multiplicative, obliterative,
opinionative, originative,
postoperative, premeditative,
preoperative, proliferative,
reciprocative, recuperative,
regenerative, remunerative,
reverberative, significative,
vituperative,
excommunicative,
incommunicative,
noncooperative, quasi-

legislative, semiquantitative,
uncommunicative

atl \ät-ᵊl\ see OTTLE

atlas \at-ləs\ atlas, Atlas,
hatless

atless \at-ləs\ see ATLAS

atli \ät-lē\ see OTLY

atling \at-liŋ\ fatling, flatling,
rattling—*also* -ing *forms of
verbs listed at* ATTLE

atly \at-lē\ flatly, rattly

atnam \ət-nəm\
Machilipatnam,
Vishakhapatnam

atness \at-nəs\ fatness,
flatness, platinous,
gelatinous

¹ato \ät-ō\ auto, blotto,
grotto, lotto, motto, otto,
Otto, potto, annatto,
castrato, legato, marcato,
mulatto, rabato, rebato,
ridotto, rubato, sfumato,
spiccato, staccato, agitato,
animato, ben trovato,
Guanajuato, moderato,
obbligato, ostinato, pizzicato

²ato \ät-ō\ Cato, Plato,
Orvieto, potato, tomato,
Barquisimeto

atomist \at-ə-məst\ atomist,
anatomist

atomy \at-ə-mē\ atomy,
anatomy

aton \at-ᵊn\ see ²ATIN

atony \at-ᵊn-ē\ see ATANY

ator \āt-ər\ baiter, cater,
crater, Crater, dater, faitour,
freighter, gaiter, gator,
grater, hater, krater, later,
mater, plater, rater, satyr,
skater, slater, stater, stator,
tater, traitor, waiter, aerator,
collator, Bay Stater, creator,
curator, debater, Decatur,
dictator, donator,
dumbwaiter, equator, first-
rater, glossator, headwaiter,
levator, locator, mandator,
Mercator, narrator,
pronator, pulsator, rotator,
spectator, tailgater, testator,
theater, third-rater,
translator, upstater, vibrator,
actuator, abdicator,
activator, adulator,
advocate, agitator, alligator,
allocator, alternator,
animator, annotator,
applicator, arbitrator,
aspirator, aviator,
buccinator, calculator,
captivator, carburetor,
celebrator, circulator,
commentator, commutator,
compensator, compurgator,
concentrator, confiscator,
congregator, consecrator,
consummator, contemplator,
corporator, correlator,
depredator, desecrater,
desecrator, designator,
detonator, deviator,
dissipater, dominator,
duplicator, dura mater,
educator, elevator, emulator,
escalator, estimator,
excavator, explicator,
expurgator, extirpator,
fascinator, formulator,
fornicator, generator,
gladiator, hibernator,
illustrator, incubator,
indicator, infiltrator,
innovator, inhalator,
inspirator, insulator,
integrator, lacrimator,
liquidator, literator,
mediator, moderator,
motivator, navigator,
nomenclator, nominator,
numerator, obturator,

operator, orchestrator, oscillator, percolator, perpetrator, pia mater, pollinator, postulator, procreator, procurator, propagator, radiator, regulator, resonator, respirator, revelator, second-rater, selling-plater, separator, simulator, subjugator, syndicator, tabulator, terminator, valuator, ventilator, violator, accelerator, accommodator, accumulator, administrator, adulterator, alienator, alleviator, annihilator, annunciator, anticipator, appreciator, appropriator, assassinator, attenuator, continuator, calumniator, collaborator, commemorator, communicator, conciliator, congratulator, consolidator, contaminator, cooperator, coordinator, corroborator, defibrillator, delineator, denominator, depreciator, determinator, discriminator, disseminator, dissimulator, ejaculator, eliminator, emancipator, enumerator, equivocator, eradicator, evaluator, evaporator, exterminator, extrapolator, impersonator, improvisator, incinerator, inseminator, interrogator, intimidator, investigator, negotiator, oxygenator, pacificator, perambulator, predestinator, procrastinator, purificator, redecorator, refrigerator, regenerator, resuscitator, totalizator, subordinator, excommunicator,

rehabilitator, turbogenerator, immunomodulator—*also* -er *forms of adjectives listed at* [1]ATE

[1]**atre** \ätrͦ\ coup de theatre, pas de quatre

[2]**atre** \at\ *see* [5]AT

atric \a-trik\ Patrick, sympatric, theatric, allopatric, geriatric, pediatric, podiatric, psychiatric

atrick \a-trik\ *see* ATRIC

atrics \a-triks\ theatrics, pediatrics

atrist \a-trͦst\ geriatrist, physiatrist

atrix \ā-triks\ matrix, cicatrix, testatrix, aviatrix, dominatrix, mediatrix, administratrix

atron \ā-trͦn\ matron, natron, patron

[1]**ats** \äts\ *see* OTS

[2]**ats** \ats\ bats, rats, ersatz—*also* -s, -'s, *and* -s' *forms of nouns listed at* [5]AT, *and* -s *forms of verbs listed there*

atsa \ät-sͦ\ *see* [1]ATZO

atsch \ach\ *see* [4]ATCH

atsk \ätsk\ Bratsk, Okhotsk, Petrozavodsk

atsu \ät-sü\ Hamamatsu, shiatsu, shiatzu, Takamatsu

atsy \at-sē\ *see* [3]AZI

[1]**att** \at\ *see* [5]AT

[2]**att** \ät\ *see* [1]OT

atta \ät-ͦ\ *see* [1]ATA

attage \ät-ij\ *see* OTTAGE

attan \at-ͦn\ *see* [2]ATIN

atte \at\ *see* [5]AT

atted \a-tͦd\ superfatted —*also* -ed *forms of verbs listed at* [5]AT

attel \at-ͦl\ *see* ATTLE

atten \at-ᵊn\ see ²ATIN

atter \at-ər\ attar, batter, blatter, chatter, clatter, fatter, flatter, hatter, latter, matter, natter, patter, plaiter, platter, ratter, satyr, scatter, shatter, smatter, spatter, splatter, tatter, backscatter, bespatter, flat-hatter, standpatter, wildcatter, antimatter, pitter-patter

attering \at-ə-riŋ\ nattering, smattering, backscattering, earth-shattering, self-flattering, unflattering, Rayleigh scattering—*also* -ing *forms of verbs listed at* ATTER

attern \at-ərn\ pattern, Saturn, slattern

attery \at-ə-rē\ battery, cattery, clattery, flattery, mattery, Cape Flattery, self-flattery

¹**atti** \ät-ē\ see ¹ATI

²**atti** \at-ē\ see ATTY

attic \at-ik\ see ²ATIC

attica \at-i-kə\ see ATICA

¹**attice** \at-əs\ see ³ATUS

²**attice** \at-ish\ see ATTISH

attie \at-ē\ see ATTY

attily \at-ᵊl-ē\ cattily, chattily, Natalie, Nathalie, nattily, rattly, philately, sal volatile

atting \at-iŋ\ batting, matting, tatting—*also* -ing *forms of verbs listed at* ⁵AT

attish \at-ish\ brattish, fattish, flattish

attitude \at-ə-tüd\ attitude, latitude

attle \at-ᵊl\ battle, brattle, cattle, chattel, prattle, rattle, tattle, embattle, Seattle, tittle-tattle

attler \at-lər\ battler, prattler, rattler, tattler

attling \at-liŋ\ see ATLING

¹**attly** \at-ᵊl-ē\ see ATTILY

²**attly** \at-lē\ see ATLY

¹**atto** \at-ə\ see ³ATA

²**atto** \ät-ō\ see ¹ATO

atton \at-ᵊn\ see ²ATIN

atty \at-ē\ batty, catty, bratty, chatty, fatty, Hattie, natty, Patti, Pattie, patty, Patty, platy, ratty, scatty, tattie, tatty, Cincinnati

¹**atum** \ät-əm\ bottom, datum, satem, erratum, pomatum, desideratum

²**atum** \ät-əm\ datum, pomatum, substratum, verbatim, ageratum, literatim, seriatim, ultimatum, corpus allatum, corpus striatum, desideratum

³**atum** \at-əm\ atom, datum, erratum, substratum, seriatim

atuous \ach-wəs\ fatuous, ignis fatuus

atur \āt-ər\ see ATOR

atural \ach-rəl\ natural, connatural, transnatural, unnatural, preternatural, seminatural, supernatural

¹**ature** \ā-chər\ nature, denature, 4-H'er, magistrature, nomenclature, supernature

²**ature** \ach-ər\ see ²ATCHER

aturn \at-ərn\ see ATTERN

¹**atus** \āt-əs\ flatus, gratis, status, stratus, afflatus, hiatus, meatus, apparatus, coitus reservatus

²**atus** \ät-əs\ see OTTIS

³**atus** \at-əs\ brattice, gratis, lattice, status, stratus, clematis, altostratus,

apparatus, cirrostratus, nimbostratus

atute \ach-ət\ see ATCHET

atuus \ach-wəs\ see ATUOUS

aty \āt-ē\ eighty, Haiti, Katie, Katy, Leyte, matey, platy, slaty, weighty, yeti, 1080, Papeete

atyr \āt-ər\ see ATOR

¹atz \ats\ see ²ATS

²atz \äts\ see OTS

¹atzo \ät-sə\ matzo, tazza, Hidatsa, piazza

²atzo \ät-sō\ see ¹AZZO

atzu \ät-sü\ see ATSU

¹au \ō\ see ¹OW

²au \ü\ see ¹EW

³au \aú\ see ²OW

⁴au \ó\ see ¹AW

aub \äb\ see ¹OB

auba \ó-bə\ carnauba, Catawba

aube \ōb\ see ¹OBE

auber \ōb-ər\ dauber, Micawber

auble \äb-əl\ see ¹ABBLE

¹auce \as\ see ³ASS

²auce \ós\ see ¹OSS

aucer \ó-sər\ see OSSER

aucet \äs-ət\ see OSSET

¹auch \óch\ nautch, watch, debauch

²auch \ách\ see OTCH

auche \ōsh\ see ²OCHE

auchely \ōsh-lē\ see OCIALLY

auckland \ók-lənd\ Auckland, Falkland

aucous \ó-kəs\ caucus, glaucous, raucous

aucus \ó-kəs\ see AUCOUS

aucy \as-ē\ see ASSY

¹aud \ód\ awed, baud, bawd, broad, Claud, Claude, clawed, fraud, gaud, god, jawed, laud, Maud, Maude, yod, abroad, applaud, belaud, defraud, dewclawed,

maraud, whipsawed, eisteddfod, lantern-jawed, quartersawed— *also* -ed *forms of verbs listed at* ¹AW

²aud \äd\ see ¹OD

audable \ód-ə-bəl\ audible, laudable, applaudable, illaudable, inaudible

audal \ód-ᵊl\ caudal, caudle, dawdle

audative \ód-ət-iv\ see AUDITIVE

¹aude \aúd-ē\ see OWDY

²aude \ód-ē\ see AWDY

³aude \aúd-ə\ howdah, cum laude, magna cum laude, summa cum laude

⁴aude \ód\ see ¹AUD

audible \ód-ə-bəl\ see AUDABLE

auding \ód-iŋ\ auding, applauding, self-applauding— *also* -ing *forms of verbs listed at* ¹AUD

audit \ód-ət\ audit, plaudit

auditive \ód-ət-iv\ auditive, laudative

audle \ód-ᵊl\ see AUDAL

¹audy \äd-ē\ see ¹ODY

²audy \ód-ē\ see AWDY

auer \aúr\ see ²OWER

auf \aúf\ see OWFF

auffeur \ō-fər\ see OFER

auga \ó-gə\ massasauga, Mississauga, Onondaga

auge \āj\ see ³AGE

augeable \ā-jə-bəl\ see AGEABLE

auged \ājd\ see AGED

¹auger \ó-gər\ see ²OGGER

²auger \ā-jər\ see ¹AGER

¹augh \af\ see APH

²augh \ä\ see ¹A

³augh \äk\ see ¹ACH

⁴augh \ó\ see ¹AW

aughable \af-ə-bəl\ see AFFABLE

augham \óm\ see ¹AUM
¹aughn \än\ see ¹ON
²aughn \ón\ see ³ON
¹aught \ät\ see ¹OT
²aught \ót\ see ¹OUGHT
¹aughter \af-tər\ see AFTER
²aughter \ót-ər\ see ¹ATER
aughterer \ót-ər-ər\ see
  ATERER
¹aughty \ót-ē\ haughty,
  naughty, zloty, Michelangelo
  Buonarroti
²aughty \ät-ē\ see ATI
augre \óg-ər\ see ²OGGER
augur \óg-ər\ see ²OGGER
augury \ó-gə-rē\ see ²OGGERY
aui \aú-ē\ see OWIE
auk \ók\ see ALK
aukee \ó-kē\ see ALKIE
aul \ól\ see ALL
aulay \ó-lē\ see AWLY
¹auld \ól\ see ALL
²auld \ō\ see ¹OW
auldron \ól-drən\ see
  ALDRON
auled \óld\ see ALD
auler \ó-lər\ see ¹ALLER
aulin \ó-lən\ see ALLEN
auling \ó-liŋ\ see ALLING
aulish \ó-lish\ see ALLISH
aulk \ók\ see ALK
aulker \ó-kər\ see ALKER
aulking \ó-kiŋ\ see ALKING
aulle \ól\ see ¹ALL
aulm \óm\ see ¹AUM
¹ault \ólt\ see ALT
²ault \ō\ see ¹OW
aulter \ól-tər\ see ALTER
aulting \ól-tiŋ\ see ALTING
aultless \ólt-ləs\ see ALTLESS
aulty \ól-tē\ see ALTY
¹aum \óm\ gaum, haulm,
  Maugham, poem, qualm,
  shawm, meerschaum,
  Radom
²aum \äm\ see ¹OM
¹aun \än\ see ¹ON

²aun \ən\ see UN
³aun \ón\ see ³ON
⁴aun \aún\ see ²OWN
¹auna \än-ə\ see ¹ANA
²auna \ón-ə\ see ¹ONNA
aunce \óns\ jaunce, launce
¹aunch \änch\ conch, cranch,
  craunch, paunch, raunch,
  stanch, Romansh
²aunch \ónch\ craunch,
  haunch, launch, paunch,
  raunch, stanch, staunch
auncher \ón-chər\ launcher,
  stancher, stauncher
aunchy \ón-chē\ paunchy,
  raunchy
aund \ónd\ awned, maund—
  also -ed *forms of verbs listed
  at* ³ON
¹aunder \ón-dər\ launder,
  maunder
²aunder \än-dər\ see ¹ONDER
aunish \än-ish\ see ONISH
¹aunt \ónt\ daunt, flaunt,
  gaunt, haunt, jaunt, taunt,
  vaunt, want, wont, avant,
  avaunt, keeshond, romaunt,
  John of Gaunt
²aunt \ant\ see ⁵ANT
³aunt \änt\ see ²ANT
aunted \ónt-əd\ see ONTED
¹aunter \änt-ər\ saunter,
  taunter, mishanter,
  rencontre
²aunter \ónt-ər\ gaunter,
  haunter, saunter, taunter
aunty \ónt-ē\ flaunty, jaunty,
  vaunty
²aunty \änt-ē\ see ¹ANTI
aunus \än-əs\ see ¹ONUS
aup \óp\ gawp, scaup, whaup,
  yawp
aupe \óp\ see OPE
auphin \ó-fən\ see OFFIN
¹aur \aúr\ see ²OWER
²aur \ór\ see ¹OR
¹aura \ór-ə\ see ORA

²**aura** \är-ə\ see ¹ARA

aural \ór-əl\ see ¹ORAL

aure \ór\ see ¹OR

aurea \ór-ē-ə\ see ORIA

aurean \ór-ē-ən\ see ORIAN

¹**aureate** \är-ē-ət\
baccalaureate, commisariat

²**aureate** \ór-ē-ət\ aureate,
laureate, baccalaureate,
professoriat

aurel \ór-əl\ see ¹ORAL

¹**auren** \är-ən\ see ARIN

²**auren** \ór-ən\ see ¹ORIN

aurence \ór-ən(t)s\ see
AWRENCE

aureus \ór-ē-əs\ see ORIOUS

auri \aúr-ē\ see OWERY

aurian \ór-ē-ən\ see ORIAN

auric \ór-ik\ see ORIC

¹**aurice** \är-əs\ see ¹ORRIS

²**aurice** \ór-əs\ see AURUS

auricle \ór-i-kəl\ see ORICAL

¹**aurie** \ór-ē\ see ORY

²**aurie** \är-ē\ see ARI

aurous \ór-əs\ see AURUS

aurus \ór-əs\ aurous, Boris,
chorus, Doris, Flores,
Horace, Horus, loris,
Maurice, morris, Morris,
Norris, orris, porous, sorus,
Taurus, Torres, torus,
canorous, Centaurus,
clitoris, decorous, Delores,
Dolores, pelorus,
phosphorous, sonorous,
thesaurus, allosaurus,
brontosaurus, deoch an
doris, doch-an-dorris,
stegosaurus, apatosaurus,
tyrannosaurus

aury \ór-ē\ see ORY

¹**aus** \ā-əs\ see ¹AIS

²**aus** \aús\ see ²OUSE

³**aus** \óz\ see ¹AUSE

ausal \ó-zəl\ causal, clausal,
menopausal, postmenopausal

¹**ause** \óz\ Broz, cause, clause,

gauze, hawse, pause, tawse,
yaws, applause, because,
kolkhoz, sovkhoz,
aeropause, diapause,
menopause, Santa Claus—
*also -s, -'s, and -s' forms of
nouns listed at* ¹AW, *and* -s
forms of verbs listed there

²**ause** \əz\ see ¹EUSE

auseous \ó-shəs\ see AUTIOUS

auser \ó-zər\ causer, hawser

ausey \ó-zē\ causey, gauzy

auss \aús\ see ¹OUSE

¹**aussie** \äs-ē\ see ¹OSSY

²**aussie** \ó-sē\ see ²OSSY

¹**aust** \aúst\ see OUST

²**aust** \óst\ see ³OST

austen \ós-tən\ see OSTON

austin \ós-tən\ see OSTON

austless \óst-ləs\ costless,
exhaustless

¹**austral** \äs-trəl\ see OSTREL

²**austral** \ós-trəl\ see
¹OSTRAL

¹**aut** \ó\ see ¹OW

²**aut** \aút\ see ³OUT

³**aut** \ät\ see ¹OT

⁴**aut** \ót\ see ¹OUGHT

autch \óch\ see ¹AUCH

aute \ót\ see OAT

auten \ót-ᵊn\ boughten,
tauten

auterne \ót-ərn\ quartern,
sauterne, sauternes

auternes \ót-ərn\ see
AUTERNE

autery \ót-ə-rē\ see ATERY

autic \ót-ik\ orthotic,
aeronautic, astronautic

autical \ót-i-kəl\ nautical,
aeronautical, astronautical

autics \ät-iks\ see OTICS

aution \ó-shən\ caution,
groschen, incaution,
precaution

autious \ó-shəs\ cautious,
nauseous, incautious

¹**auto** \ȯt-ō\ auto, Giotto, risotto

²**auto** \ät-ō\ see ¹ATO

auve \ōv\ see ²OVE

auze \ȯz\ see ¹AUSE

auzer \au̇-zər\ see OUSER

auzy \ȯ-zē\ see AUSEY

¹**av** \äv\ see ²OLVE

²**av** \av\ see ²ALVE

¹**ava** \äv-ə\ brava, fava, guava, java, Java, kava, lava, baklava, cassava, ottava, balaclava, Bratislava, Costa Brava, lavalava, piassava, Warszawa

²**ava** \av-ə\ java, Ungava, balaclava

avage \av-ij\ ravage, savage

avan \ā-vən\ see ¹AVEN

avant \av-ənt\ haven't, savant

avarice \av-rəs\ see AVEROUS

¹**ave** \äv-ā\ ave, clave, grave, Jahveh, soave

²**ave** \āv\ brave, clave, cave, crave, Dave, fave, gave, glaive, grave, knave, lave, nave, pave, rave, save, shave, slave, stave, they've, trave, waive, wave, Wave, airwave, behave, concave, conclave, deprave, dissave, drawshave, enclave, engrave, enslave, exclave, forgave, Great Slave, margrave, octave, outbrave, p-wave, palsgrave, shortwave, spokeshave, after-shave, architrave, biconcave, microwave, contraoctave, photoengrave

³**ave** \av\ see ³ALVE

⁴**ave** \äv\ see ²OLVE

aved \āvd\ waved, depraved, unsaved—*also* -ed *forms of verbs listed at* ²AVE

avel \av-əl\ cavil, gavel, gravel, ravel, travel, unravel

aveless \āv-ləs\ graveless, waveless

aveling \av-liŋ\ raveling, traveling—*also* -ing *forms of verbs listed at* AVEL

avement \āv-mənt\ pavement, depravement, enslavement

¹**aven** \ā-vən\ Avon, Cavan, craven, graven, haven, maven, raven, shaven, New Haven, riboflavin, Stratford-upon-Avon

²**aven** \av-ən\ see AVIN

aven't \av-ənt\ see AVANT

¹**aver** \äv-ər\ slaver, palaver, windhover

²**aver** \ā-vər\ caver, claver, favor, flavor, graver, haver, laver, quaver, raver, saver, savor, shaver, slaver, waiver, waver, disfavor, enslaver, face-saver, flag-waver, lifesaver, semiquaver, demisemiquaver, hemidemisemiquaver—*also* -er *forms of adjectives listed at* ²AVE

³**aver** \av-ər\ slaver, cadaver, palaver

avern \av-ərn\ cavern, klavern, tavern

averous \av-rəs\ avarice, cadaverous

avery \āv-rē\ bravery, knavery, quavery, savory, slavery, wavery, unsavory

avey \ā-vē\ see AVY

avia \ā-vē-ə\ Moldavia, Moravia, Scandinavia

avial \ā-vē-əl\ gavial, margravial

avian \ā-vē-ən\ avian, Shavian, Moravian, Scandinavian

avid \av-əd\ avid, gravid, pavid

avie \ā-vē\ see AVY

avil \av-əl\ see AVEL

avin \av-ən\ Avon, raven, ravin, savin, spavin

aving \ā-viŋ\ caving, craving, paving, raving, saving, shaving, flagwaving, lifesaving, timesaving, laborsaving—*also* -ing *forms of verbs listed at* ²AVE

avis \ā-vəs\ Davis, favus, mavis, Mavis, rara avis

¹**avish** \ā-vish\ knavish, slavish

²**avish** \av-ish\ lavish, ravish

avist \äv-əst\ Slavist, suavest, Pan-Slavist

avity \av-ət-ē\ cavity, gravity, concavity, depravity, antigravity, microgravity, supergravity

avl \äv-əl\ see ¹OVEL

¹**avo** \äv-ō\ bravo, Bravo, centavo, octavo

²**avo** \ä-vō\ octavo, relievo, mezzo relievo

¹**avon** \ā-vən\ see ¹AVEN

²**avon** \a-vən\ see AVIN

avor \ā-vər\ see ²AVER

avored \ā-vərd\ favored, flavored, ill-favored, well-favored—*also* -ed *forms of verbs listed at* ²AVER

avory \āv-rē\ see AVERY

avus \ā-vəs\ see AVIS

avvy \av-ē\ navvy, savvy

avy \ā-vē\ cavy, Davey, Davy, gravy, navy, shavie, slavey, wavy

¹**aw** \o\ aw, awe, blaw, braw, ca, caw, chaw, claw, craw, daw, draw, faugh, flaw, gnaw, haugh, haw, jaw, la, law, maw, pa, paw, pshaw, Ra, rah, raw, saw, shah, shaw, Shaw, slaw, spa, squaw, straw, tau, taw, thaw, yaw, backsaw, bashaw, bedstraw, bucksaw, bylaw, catclaw, cat's-paw, coleslaw, cumshaw, cushaw, Danelaw, declaw, dewclaw, Esau, forepaw, fretsaw, grandma, grandpa, guffaw, hacksaw, handsaw, hawkshaw, hee-haw, hurrah, in-law, jackdaw, jackstraw, jigsaw, kickshaw, lockjaw, macaw, Nassau, old-squaw, outdraw, outlaw, pasha, pooh-bah, ricksha, rickshaw, ringtaw, ripsaw, scofflaw, scrimshaw, seesaw, southpaw, trishaw, tussah, undraw, Utah, vizsla, Warsaw, whipsaw, windflaw, wiredraw, withdraw, Arkansas, Chickasaw, Chippewa, clapperclaw, decree-law, foofaraw, jinrikisha, Kiowa, Mackinac, mackinaw, Omaha, Ottawa, overawe, overdraw, oversaw, overslaugh, padishah, panama, son-in-law, usquebaugh, Wichita, williwaw, windlestraw, Yakima, brother-in-law, daughter-in-law, father-in-law, mother-in-law, pipsissewa, serjeant-at-law, sister-in-law, Straits of Mackinac

²**aw** \äv\ see ²OLVE

³**aw** \of\ see ²OFF

⁴**aw** \äf\ see ¹OFF

¹**awa** \ä-wə\ Chihuahua, Tarawa, Urawa, Fujisawa, Ichikawa, Kanazawa, Okinawa, Ahashikawa

²**awa** \ä-və\ see ¹AVA

awain \aú-ən\ see ²OWAN

swan \aú-ən\ see ²OWAN

awar \aúr\ see ²OWER

awba \ó-bə\ see AUBA

¹**awber** \äb-ər\ see OBBER

²**awber** \ób-ər\ see AUBER

awd \ód\ see ¹AUD

awddle \äd-ºl\ see ODDLE

awdle \ód-ºl\ see AUDAL

awdry \ó-drē\ Audrey, tawdry

awdust \ód-əst\ see ¹ADIST

awdy \ód-ē\ bawdy, gaudy, summa cum laude

awe \ó\ see ¹AW

awed \ód\ see ¹AUD

aweless \ó-ləs\ see AWLESS

awer \ór\ see ¹OR

awers \órz\ see OORS

awful \ó-fəl\ awful, coffle, lawful, offal, god-awful, unlawful

awfully \óf-ə-lē\ awfully, lawfully, offaly, unlawfully

awing \óin\ cloying, drawing, wappenschawing—*also* -ing *forms of verbs listed at* ¹AW

awk \ók\ see ALK

awker \ó-kər\ see ALKER

awkes \óks\ Fawkes —*also* -s, -'s, *and* -s' *forms of nouns listed at* ALK, *and* -s *forms of verbs listed there*

awkish \ó-kish\ gawkish, hawkish, mawkish

awky \ó-kē\ see ALKIE

awl \ól\ see ALL

awler \ó-lər\ see ¹ALLER

awless \ó-ləs\ aweless, flawless, lawless

awling \ó-lin\ see ALLING

awly \ó-lē\ brawly, crawly, dolly, drawly, Raleigh, scrawly, squally, Bengali, Macaulay

awm \óm\ see ¹AUM

¹**awn** \än\ see ¹ON

²**awn** \ón\ see ³ON

awned \ónd\ see AUND

¹**awner** \ón-ər\ fawner, goner, pawner, prawner, spawner

²**awner** \än-ər\ see ¹ONOR

awney \ó-nē\ see ¹AWNY

awning \än-in\ see ¹ONING

awnly \än-lē\ see ¹ANLY

¹**awny** \ó-nē\ brawny, fawny, lawny, sawney, scrawny, Taney, tawny, mulligatawny

²**awny** \än-ē\'see ¹ANI

awp \óp\ see AUP

awrence \ór-ən(t)s\ Florence, Laurence, Lawrence, Torrence, abhorrence, Saint Lawrence —*also* -s, -'s, *and* -s' *forms of nouns listed at* ORRENT, *and* -s *forms of verbs listed there*

awry \ór-ē\ see ORY

aws \óz\ see ¹AUSE

awse \óz\ see ¹AUSE

awser \ó-zər\ see AUSER

awsi \aú-sē\ see ²OUSY

awy \ói\ see OY

awyer \ó-yər\ lawyer, sawyer

¹**ax** \äks\ see OX

²**ax** \aks\ ax, fax, flax, lax, max, Max, pax, rax, sax, tax, wax, addax, Ajax, anthrax, banjax, beeswax, borax, broadax, climax, coax, earwax, galax, gravlax, hyrax, meat-ax, panchax, pickax, poleax, pretax, relax, smilax, storax, styrax, surtax, syntax, thorax, toadflax, aftertax, battle-ax, Halifax, minimax, overtax, parallax, supertax, anticlimax, Astyanax—*also* -s, -'s, *and* -s' *forms of nouns listed at* ²ACK, *and* -s *forms of verbs listed there*

axant \ak-sənt\ see ACCENT

axen \ak-sən\ see AXON

axi \ak-sē\ see AXY

axic \ak-sik\ ataraxic, stereotaxic

axis \ak-səs\ axis, Naxos, praxis

axman \ak-smən\ axman, cracksman

axon \ak-sən\ flaxen, Jackson, Klaxon, Saxon, waxen, Port Jackson, Anglo-Saxon

axos \ak-səs\ see AXIS

axy \ak-sē\ flaxy, maxi, taxi, waxy

¹ay \ā\ a , ae, aye, bay, bey, blae, brae, bray, chez, clay, Clay, day, dey, dray, eh, fay, Fay, Faye, fey, flay, fley, frae, fray, Frey, gay, Gay, gey, gley, gray, Gray, greige, Grey, hae, hay, he, hey, Hue, j, jay, Jay, Jaye, k, kay, Kay, Kaye, lay, lei, may, May, nay, né, née, neigh, pay, pe, play, pray, prey, qua, quai, quay, Rae, ray, Ray, re, say, sei, shay, slay, sleigh, spae, spay, splay, spray, stay, stray, sway, they, tray, trey, way, weigh, whey, yea, abbé, affray, agley, airplay, airway, all-day, allay, allée, Angers, Anhui, Anhwei, archway, array, ashtray, assay, astray, Augier, away, aweigh, backstay, ballet, beignet, belay, beltway, benday, Benet, beret, betray, bewray, bidet, bikeway, birthday, Biscay, Bizet, blasé, bobstay, Bombay, bombe, bouchée, bouclé, boule, bouquet, bourrée, breezeway, Broadway, buffet, byplay, byway, cachet, café, cahier, Cambay, Cape May, Cartier, Cathay, causeway, chaîné, chalet, chambray, chassé, ciré, cliché, cloqué, congé, convey, corvée, coudé, coupé, crawlway, crochet, croquet, crossway, cube, curé, cy pres, DA, daresay,

decay, deejay, defray, delay, dengue, dismay, display, distrait, DJ, donnée, doomsday, doorway, dossier, downplay, dragée, driveway, duvet, embay, entrée, épée, essay, estray, Ewe, fairway, filé, filet, fillet, fireclay, fishway, flambé, floodway, flyway, folkway, footway, foray, forebay, foreplay, forestay, formée, forte, fouetté, four-way, fourchée, foyer, franglais, frappé, freeway, frieze, frisé, fumet, gainsay, Galway, gamay, gangway, Gaspé, gateway, gelée, glacé, godet, gourmet, Green Bay, greenway, guideway, gunplay, halfway, hallway, hatchway, headway, hearsay, Hebei, Hefei, heyday, highway, homestay, hooray, horseplay, Hubei, in re, inlay, inveigh, issei, jackstay, jeté, keyway, Kobe, koine, kouprey, lamé, laneway, leeway, lifeway, Lomé, Lough Neagh, lwei, lycée, M-day, maguey, mainstay, Malay, maigré, man-day, Mande, Manet, manqué, margay, Marseilles, massé, maté, May Day, Mayday, melee, metier, meze, midday, Midway, Millay, Millet, mislay, misplay, moiré, Monet, moray, nevé, Niamey, nisei, noonday, Norway, nosegay, obey, OK, olé, ombré, osprey, outlay, outré, outstay, outweigh, oyez, **PA**, parfait, parkway, parlay, parquet, partway, passé, pâté, pathway, pavé, payday, per se, pince-nez, piqué,

piquet, PK, plié, plissé,
pommée, Pompeii, portray,
prepay, projet, pulque,
puree, purvey, quale,
raceway, railway, rappee,
relay, Rene, Renee, repay,
replay, risqué, roadway, role-
play, ropeway, rosé, rosebay,
Roubaix, roué, routeway,
runway, sachet, Salé, sansei,
sashay, sauté, screenplay,
seaway, semé, shar-pei,
shipway, short-day, sideway,
Skopje, skyway, slideway,
slipway, sluiceway, soigné,
soiree, someday, someway,
soothsay, soufflé, speedway,
spillway, stairway, sternway,
stingray, straightway,
strathspey, subway, survey,
swordplay, Taipei, tempeh,
thoughtway, three-way,
thruway, tideway, Tigré,
today, Tokay, tollway,
Torbay, touché, toupee,
trackway, tramway, unlay,
unsay, valet, V-day, veejay,
vide, visé, Vouvray,
walkway, waylay, weekday,
windway, wireway,
wordplay, workday, X ray, x-
ray, Yaoundé, Adige, A-OK,
alleyway, anyway, appliqué,
arrivé, atelier, attaché,
ballonet, Beaujolais, beurre
manié, BHA, botonée,
braciole, breakaway, bustier,
cabaret, cableway,
Camagüey, canapé, cap-a-
pie, caraway, carriageway,
Cartier, cassoulet, castaway,
champlevé, chansonnier,
chardonnay, Charolais,
chevalier, Chippewa,
cloisonné, consommé,
coryphée, croupier, crudités,
cutaway, day-to-day,

debauchee, déclassé, dégagé,
degree-day, démodé,
devotee, disarray, disobey,
distingué, divorcé, divorcée,
DNA, émigré, engagé,
entranceway, entremets,
entryway, espalier, etoufée,
everyday, exposé,
expressway, fadeaway,
fallaway, faraday, Faraday,
faraway, fiancé, fiancée,
flageolet, flyaway, foldaway,
Galloway, Georgian Bay,
getaway, giveaway, gratiné,
gratinée, guillemet, Harare,
haulageway, Hemingway,
hereaway, hideaway, HLA,
Hogmanay, holiday, Hugh
Capet, IgA, inter se,
interplay, intraday, IPA,
IRA, Joliet, Kootenay,
Kutenai, kyrie, lackaday,
latter-day, layaway, lingerie,
macramé, Mandalay,
Massenet, matinee, MIA,
Molise, Monterrey,
motorway, muscadet,
negligee, overlay, overplay,
overstay, overweigh,
Paraguay, passageway,
patissier, Petare, photoplay,
pikake, piolet, pis aller, play-
by-play, poly (A), Ponape,
popinjay, pourparler,
pousse-café, present-day,
protégé, protégée, Rabelais,
rambouillet, ratiné,
recamier, rechauffé,
recherché, reconvey,
repartee, repoussé, résumé,
retroussé, ricochet, right-of-
way, rockaway, rondelet,
roundelay, RNA, runaway,
Saguenay, San Jose, San
José, Santa Fe, São Tomé,
semplice, sobriquet,
sommelier, steerageway,

standaway, stowaway,
straightaway, Table Bay,
taboret, take-away, tarsier,
taxiway, tearaway,
teleplay, Tempere,
Tenebrae, thataway,
throwaway, Thunder
Bay, Udine, underlay,
underpay, underplay,
underway, Uruguay,
velouté, Venite, vérité,
vertebra, virelay, walkaway,
waterway, wellaway,
Whitsunday, workaday,
Yenisey, Zuider Zee, Agnus
Dei, areaway, auto-da-fé,
bichon frisé, boulevardier,
cabriolet, café au lait,
cantabile, cDNA,
communiqué, costumier,
couturier, décolleté,
diamanté, Dies Irae,
eglomisé, felo-de-se, Fiesole,
garde-manger, habitué,
Jubilate, laissez-passer,
Lavoisier, marrons glacé,
mezzo forte, Morgan le Fay,
objet trouvé, out-of-the-way,
papier collé, papier-mâché,
pas de bourrée, photo-essay,
Port Philip Bay, pouilly-
fuissé, Pouilly-Fumé, prêt-à-
porter, roche moutonnée,
roman à clef, roturier, sine
die, sub judice,
superhighway, ukiyo-e,
Ulan-Ude, yerba maté, Alto
Adige, arrière pensée,
Guanabara Bay, lettre de
cachet, catalogue raisonné,
cinema verité, Dumfries and
Galloway, vers de société,
video verité, sinfonia
concertante, Trentino-Alto
Adige

²**ay** \ē\ see ¹EE

³**ay** \ī\ see ¹Y

¹**aya** \ä-yə\ ayah, maya, taille,
Malaya, Koshigaya

²**aya** \ī-ə\ see ¹IAH

³**aya** \ä-ə\ see ¹AIA

ayable \ā-ə-bəl\ payable,
playable, sayable, defrayable,
displayable, unsayable

ayah \ī-ə\ see ¹IAH

ayal \āl\ see AIL

¹**ayan** \ā-ən\ crayon,
Chilean, Malayan, ouabain,
papain, Pompeian,
Pompeiian, Galilean,
Himalayan

²**ayan** \ī-ən\ see ¹ION

¹**aybe** \ā-bē\ see ABY

²**aybe** \eb-ē\ see EBBY

ayday \ā-dā\ Ede, Mayday,
May Day

ayden \īd-ᵊn\ see IDEN

¹**aye** \ā\ see ¹AY

²**aye** \ī\ see ¹Y

ayed \ād\ see ¹ADE

¹**ayer** \ā-ər\ brayer, layer,
mayor, payer, player, prayer,
preyer, sayer, player, prayer,
strayer, ballplayer, betrayer,
bilayer, bricklayer,
cardplayer, conveyer,
crocheter, decayer, delayer,
doomsayer, doomsdayer,
gainsayer, horseplayer,
inlayer, essayer, forayer,
inveigher, obeyer,
manslayer, minelayer,
portrayer, purveyor,
ratepayer, soothsayer,
swordplayer, surveyor,
taxpayer, tracklayer, yea-
sayer, disobeyer, holidayer—
also -er *forms of adjectives
listed at* ¹AY

²**ayer** \er\ see ⁴ARE

ayered \erd\ see AIRED

ayest \ā-əst\ mayest, sayest,
épéeist, essayist, fideist,
Hebraist, Mithraist—*also*

-est *forms of adjectives listed at* ¹AY

¹**ayin** \ī-ən\ see ¹ION

²**ayin** \in\ see ¹INE

³**ayin** \ä-yən\ see AIIAN

aying \ā-iŋ\ gleying, maying, playing, saying, bricklaying, long-playing, soothsaying, surveying, taxpaying, tracklaying—*also* -ing *forms of verbs listed at* ¹AY

ayish \ā-ish\ clayish, grayish

ayist \ā-əst\ see AYEST

ayle \āl\ see AIL

ayless \ā-ləs\ rayless, talus, wayless, Morelos, aurora australis, Corona Australis

ayling \ā-liŋ\ see AILING

aylor \ā-lər\ see AILER

ayly \ā-lē\ see AILY

ayman \ā-mən\ see ¹AMEN

ayment \ā-mənt\ ament, claimant, clamant, payment, raiment, co-payment, embayment, prepayment, underlayment, underpayment

ayne \ān\ see ¹ANE

ayness \ā-nəs\ anus, feyness, gayness, grayness, heinous, Janus, manus, awayness, uranous, Uranus, everydayness

aynim \ā-nəm\ see ¹ANUM

ayn't \ā-ənt\ see EYANT

¹**ayo** \ā-ō\ see ¹EO

²**ayo** \ī-ō\ see ¹IO

¹**ayon** \an\ see ⁵AN

²**ayon** \ā-ən\ see ¹AYAN

ayor \ā-ər\ see ¹AYER

¹**ayou** \ī-ə\ see ¹IAH

²**ayou** \ī-ō\ see ¹IO

ayr \er\ see ⁴ARE

¹**ays** \ez\ fez, Fez, Geez, prez, says, Cortez, gainsays, Inez, Suez, unsays, crème anglaise, Louis Seize, Louis Treize,

Isthmus of Suez, Vincente López

²**ays** \āz\ see ¹AZE

aysia \ā-zhə\ see ASIA

ay-so \ā-sō\ see ¹ESO

ayton \āt-ᵊn\ Clayton, Dayton, Layton

¹**ayyid** \ī-əd\ see YAD

²**ayyid** \ēd-ē\ see EEDY

¹**az** \az\ see AZZ

²**az** \äz\ see ¹OISE

³**az** \äts\ see OTS

¹**aza** \äz-ə\ Gaza, plaza, piazza, tabula rasa

²**aza** \az-ə\ plaza, piazza

¹**azar** \az-ər\ see OZZER

²**azar** \az-ər\ lazar, alcazar, Belshazzar

azard \az-ərd\ hazard, mazard, mazzard, haphazard

¹**aze** \āz\ baize, blaze, braise, braze, chaise, craze, days, daze, Draize, faze, feaze, fraise, gaze, glaze, graze, Hays, haze, lase, laze, maize, maze, phase, phrase, praise, raise, rase, raze, smaze, vase, ways, ablaze, agaze, amaze, appraise, breadthways, catchphrase, crossways, deglaze, dispraise, edgeways, emblaze, endways, flatways, foodways, gainsays, hereways, leastways, lengthways, liaise, malaise, mores, pj's, sideways, slantways, stargaze, ukase, upraise, weekdays, anyways, chrysoprase, cornerways, crème anglaise, holidays, Louis Seize, Louis Treize, lyonnaise, mayonnaise, metaphrase, multiphase, nowadays, overglaze, overgraze, paraphrase, polonaise, polyphase, single-phase, underglaze—*also* -s,

-'s, *and* -s' *forms of nouns
listed at* ¹AY, *and* -s *forms of
verbs listed there*

²**aze** \äz\ *see* ¹OISE

³**aze** \äz-ē\ *see* ¹AZI

azeabie \ä-zə-bəl\ *see*
¹ASABLE

azed \āzd\ unfazed—*also* -ed
forms of verbs listed at ¹AZE

azel \ā-zəl\ *see* ²ASAL

azement \āz-mənt\
amazement, appraisement

azen \āz-ᵊn\ *see* AZON

azer \ā-zər\ blazer, brazer,
Fraser, gazer, glazer, grazer,
hazer, laser, maser, mazer,
praiser, razer, razor,
appraiser, fund-raiser, hair-
raiser, hell-raiser, stargazer,
trailblazer, paraphraser, free-
electron laser

¹**azi** \äz-ē\ quasi, Swazi,
Benghazi, Anasazi, kamikaze

²**azi** \az-ē\ *see* AZZY

³**azi** \āt-sē\ Nazi, patsy, Patsy,
neo-Nazi

⁴**azi** \ät-sē\ Nazi, neo-Nazi

azier \ā-zhər\ brazier, Frasier,
glacier, glazier, grazier,
leisure, measure, pleasure,

rasure, treasure, admeasure,
embrasure, erasure

azing \ā-ziŋ\ *see* AISING

azo \az-ō\ diazo, terrazzo

azon \āz-ᵊn\ blazon, brazen,
raisin, emblazon,
Marquesan, diapason,
hexenbesen

azor \ā-zər\ *see* AZER

azquez \as-kəs\ *see* ASCUS

azy \ā-zē\ crazy, daisy, Daisy,
hazy, lazy, mazy, stir-crazy,
witch of Agnesi

azz \az\ as, has, jazz, razz,
spaz, Hejaz, La Paz, pizzazz,
topaz, whenas, whereas,
razzmatazz

¹**azza** \az-ə\ *see* ²AZA

²**azza** \äz-ə\ *see* ¹AZA

³**azza** \ät-sə\ *see* ¹ATZO

azzar \az-ər\ *see* ²AZAR

azzard \az-ərd\ *see* AZARD

azzle \az-əl\ basil, Basil,
dazzle, frazzle, bedazzle,
razzle-dazzle

¹**azzo** \ät-sō\ matzo, palazzo,
terrazzo, paparazzo

²**azzo** \az-ō\ *see* AZO

azzy \az-ē\ jazzy, snazzy,
Ashkenazi

E

¹e \ā\ see ¹AY
²e \ē\ see ¹EE
³e \ə\ see ³U
é \ā\ see ¹AY
¹ea \ā\ see ¹AY
²ea \ä-ə\ see ¹AIA
³ea \ē\ see ¹EE
⁴ea \ē-ə\ see ¹IA
eabee \ē-bē\ see ¹EBE
eace \ēs\ see IECE
eaceable \ē-sə-bəl\ see ¹EASABLE

each \ēch\ beach, beech, bleach, breach, breech, each, fleech, leach, leech, peach, pleach, preach, reach, screech, speech, teach, beseech, forereach, impeach, Long Beach, outreach, unteach, overreach, practice-teach, Huntington Beach

eachable \ē-chə-bəl\ bleachable, leachable, reachable, teachable, impeachable, unimpeachable

eacher \ē-chər\ bleacher, creature, feature, leacher, preacher, reacher, screecher, teacher, defeature, schoolteacher

eacherous \ech-rəs\ see ECHEROUS

eachery \ech-rē\ see ECHERY

eaching \ē-chiŋ\ see EECHING

eachment \ēch-mənt\ preachment, impeachment

eachy \ē-chē\ beachy, chichi, Nietzsche, peachy, preachy, screechy, caliche, Campeche

eacle \ē-kəl\ see ¹ECAL

eacly \ē-klē\ see EEKLY

eacon \ē-kən\ beacon, deacon, sleeken, weaken, archdeacon, Mohican, subdeacon, Neorican

¹ead \ed\ bed, bled, bread, bred, dead, dread, ed, Ed, fed, fled, Fred, head, Jed, lead, led, med, Ned, ped, pled, read, red, Red, redd, said, shed, shred, sled, sped, thread, tread, wed, zed, abed, afraid, ahead, airhead, baldhead, beachhead, bedspread, bedstead, beebread, behead, bestead, bighead, biped, blackhead, blockhead, bloodred, bloodshed, bobsled, bonehead, bridgehead, brown bread, bulkhead, bullhead, cathead, childbed, coed, cokehead, corn-fed, cowshed, crispbread, crossbred, crosshead, daybed, deadhead, death's-head, deathbed, dispread, dogsled, dopehead, drophead, drumhead, dumbhead, egghead, embed, far-red, farmstead, fathead, flatbed, forehead, foresaid, gainsaid, Gateshead, godhead, green-head, half-bred, hardhead, highbred, hogshead, homebred, homestead, hophead, hotbed, hothead, ill-bred, inbred, instead, jarhead, juicehead, lamed, light bread, longhead, lowbred, lunkhead,

masthead, meathead, misled, misread, moped, naled, nonsked, outspeed, outspread, packthread, phys ed, pinhead, pithead, pothead, premed, printhead, purebred, railhead, re-tread, redhead, retread, riverbed, roadbed, roadstead, Roundhead, saphead, scarehead, seabed, seedbed, sheep ked, sheepshead, sheetfed, shewbread, shortbread, sickbed, skinhead, snowshed, softhead, sorehead, spearhead, springhead, steelhead, straightbred, streambed, subhead, sweetbread, swellhead, thickhead, thunderhead, toolhead, toolshed, towhead, trailhead, unbred, undead, unread, unsaid, unthread, untread, warhead, webfed, well-bred, well-read, wellhead, white-bread, whitehead, widespread, wingspread, woodshed, woolshed, acidhead, aforesaid, arrowhead, barrelhead, Birkenhead, bubblehead, bufflehead, chowderhead, chucklehead, colorbred, copperhead, dragonhead, dunderhead, featherbed, featherhead, fiddlehead, figurehead, fire-engine red, fountainhead, gingerbread, go-ahead, hammerhead, infrared, interbred, knucklehead, letterhead, loggerhead, lowlihead, maidenhead, newlywed, overhead, overspread, pinniped, pointy-head, poppyhead,

quadruped, saddlebred, Saint John's bread, Samoyed, showerhead, sleepyhead, slugabed, standardbred, straight-ahead, timberhead, thoroughbred, underbred, underfed, watershed, woodenhead, far-infrared, near-infrared, West Quoddy Head, parallelepiped

²**ead** \ēd\ see EED

³**ead** \əd\ see ¹UD

¹**eadable** \ēd-ə-bəl\ kneadable, pleadable, readable

²**eadable** \ed-ə-bəl\ see EDIBLE

¹**eaded** \ed-əd\ bedded, headed, bareheaded, bigheaded, bullheaded, clearheaded, coolheaded, eggheaded, embedded, fatheaded, hardheaded, hotheaded, light-headed, longheaded, lunkheaded, pigheaded, pinheaded, roundheaded, sapheaded, softheaded, soreheaded, swelled-headed, swellheaded, thickheaded, towheaded, bubbleheaded, chowderheaded, chuckleheaded, dunderheaded, featherheaded, unleaded, white-headed, empty-headed, hydra-headed, knuckleheaded, levelheaded, muddleheaded, pointy-headed, puzzleheaded, woodenheaded, woolly-headed

²**eaded** \ē-dəd\ see EEDED

eaden \ed-ᵊn\ deaden, leaden, redden, steading, Armageddon

¹**eader** \ēd-ər\ bleeder, breeder, cedar, ceder, feeder,

kneader, leader, pleader, reader, seeder, speeder, weeder, bandleader, cheerleader, conceder, impeder, lip-reader, newsreader, nonreader, proofreader, repleader, ringleader, seceder, stampeder, stockbreeder, succeeder, copyreader, interpleader

²**eader** \ed-ər\ bedder, cheddar, chedar, header, shedder, shredder, sledder, spreader, tedder, threader, treader, wedder, homesteader, doubleheader, triple-header

eadily \ed-ʰl-ē\ headily, readily, unsteadily

¹**eading** \ed-iŋ\ bedding, heading, Reading, steading, wedding, bobsledding, farmsteading, subheading, wide-spreading—*also -ing forms of verbs listed at* ¹EAD

²**eading** \ed-ʰn\ see EADEN

³**eading** \ēd-ʰn\ see EDON

⁴**eading** \ēd-iŋ\ see ¹EEDING

¹**eadle** \ed-ʰl\ see ¹EDAL

²**eadle** \ēd-ʰl\ see EEDLE

eadly \ed-lē\ see EDLEY

ead of \ed-ə\ see EDDA

eadow \ed-ə\ see EDDA

¹**eadsman** \edz-mən\ headsman, leadsman

²**eadsman** \ēdz-mən\ see EEDSMAN

¹**eady** \ed-ē\ Eddie, eddy, Eddy, Freddie, heady, leady, ready, steady, Teddie, teddy, Teddy, thready, already, makeready, unsteady, gingerbready, rough-and-ready

²**eady** \ēd-ē\ see EEDY

¹**eaf** \ef\ see ¹EF

²**eaf** \ēf\ see ¹IEF

eafless \ē-fləs\ see IEFLESS

eafy \ē-fē\ see EEFY

eag \ēg\ see IGUE

eagan \ā-gən\ see AGIN

eager \ē-gər\ eager, leaguer, meager, beleaguer, intriguer, Xinjiang Uygur

eagh \ā\ see ¹AY

eagle \ē-gəl\ see EGAL

eague \ēg\ see IGUE

eaguer \ē-gər\ see EAGER

eah \ē-ə\ see ¹IA

¹**eak** \ēk\ beak, bleak, cheek, chic, cleek, clique, creak, creek, Creek, eke, flic, freak, geek, gleek, Greek, keek, leak, leek, meek, peak, peek, peke, pic, pique, reek, screak, seek, sheik, sheikh, shriek, sic, Sikh, sleek, sneak, speak, squeak, steek, streak, streek, teak, tweak, weak, week, wreak, antique, apeak, batik, Belgique, Belleek, bespeak, bezique, boutique, cacique, caique, critique, debeak, forepeak, forespeak, grosbeak, hairstreak, halfbeak, houseleek, misspeak, muzhik, mystique, newspeak, nonpeak, oblique, off-peak, outspeak, perique, physique, Pikes Peak, pip-squeak, pratique, relique, technic, technique, Tajik, unique, unspeak, workweek, biunique, Bolshevik, Chesapeake, dominique, doublespeak, ecofreak, fenugreek, hide-and-seek, Lassen Peak, Martinique, Menshevik, Mozambique, semi-antique, verd antique, Veronique, electroweak, opéra comique, realpolitik

²**eak** \āk\ see ¹AKE

³**eak** \ek\ see ECK

eakable \ā-kə-bəl\ see AKABLE

eake \ēk\ see ¹EAK

¹**eaked** \ē-kəd\ peaked, streaked

²**eaked** \ēkt\ beaked, freaked, peaked, streaked, apple-cheeked—*also* -ed *forms of verbs listed at* ¹EAK

³**eaked** \ik-əd\ see ¹ICKED

eaken \ē-kən\ see EACON

¹**eaker** \ē-kər\ beaker, leaker, reeker, seeker, sneaker, speaker, squeaker, loudspeaker, self-seeker, sunseeker, doublespeaker—*also* -er *forms of adjectives listed at* ¹EAK

²**eaker** \ā-kər\ see ¹AKER

¹**eaking** \ē-kiŋ\ freaking, sneaking, speaking, streaking, heat-seeking, self-seeking—*also* -ing *forms of verbs listed at* ¹EAK

²**eaking** \ā-kiŋ\ see ¹AKING

eakish \ē-kish\ bleakish, cliquish, freakish, weakish

eakly \ē-klē\ see EEKLY

eaky \ē-kē\ cheeky, cliquey, creaky, freaky, leaky, piki, reeky, sneaky, screaky, squeaky, streaky, tiki, daishiki, dashiki, Tajiki, cock-a-leekie, Kurashiki, Manihiki

¹**eal** \ē-əl\ empyreal, hymeneal, laryngeal, apophyseal, pharmacopeial

²**eal** \ēl\ ceil, chiel, creel, deal, deil, eel, feel, heal, heel, he'll, keel, Kiel, kneel, leal, meal, Neal, Neil, peal, peel, real, reel, seal, seel, she'll, shiel, speel, spiel, squeal, steal, steel, Steele, Streel,

teal, tuille, veal, weal, we'll, wheal, wheel, zeal, aiguille, allheal, anneal, appeal, Arbil, bastille, Bastille, bonemeal, bonspiel, Camille, Castile, cartwheel, Cecile, chainwheel, chenille, cogwheel, conceal, congeal, cornmeal, enwheel, Erbil, flywheel, forefeel, four-wheel, freewheel, genteel, handwheel, ideal, inchmeal, Irbil, irreal, Kuril, Lucille, misdeal, mobile, Mobile, newsreel, nosewheel, oatmeal, O'Neill, ordeal, pastille, piecemeal, pinwheel, repeal, reveal, schlemiel, self-heal, side-wheel, singspiel, somedeal, stabile, surreal, tahsil, Tarheel, thumbwheel, unreal, unreel, unseal, acetyl, airmobile, Ardabil, bidonville, beau ideal, blastocoel, bloodmobile, Bogomil, bookmobile, campanile, chamomile, cochineal, cockatiel, commonweal, difficile, dishabille, down-at-heel, glockenspiel, goldenseal, Guayaquil, manchineel, megadeal, mercantile, pimpmobile, skimobile, snowmobile, thunderpeal, waterwheel, automobile, Solomon's seal, varicocele

³**eal** \āl\ see AIL

⁴**eal** \il\ see ILL

ealable \ē-lə-bəl\ peelable, reelable, stealable, appealable, concealable, revealable, repealable, irrepealable, unappealable

ealand \ē-lənd\ see ELAND

eald \ēld\ see IELD

ealed \ēld\ see IELD

ealer \ē-lər\ dealer, feeler, healer, heeler, kneeler, peeler, reeler, sealer, spieler, squealer, stealer, stelar, vealer, velar, wheeler, appealer, concealer, four-wheeler, freewheeler, newsdealer, repealer, revealer, scene-stealer, side-wheeler, stern-wheeler, three-wheeler, two-wheeler, double-dealer, eighteen-wheeler, 18-wheeler, snowmobiler, wheeler-dealer

ealie \ē-lē\ see EELY

ealing \ē-liŋ\ see EELING

¹eally \ē-ə-lē\ leally, ideally, hymeneally, industrially

²eally \il-ē\ see ILLY

³eally \ē-lē\ see EELY

ealm \elm\ see ELM

ealment \ēl-mənt\ concealment, congealment, revealment

ealot \el-ət\ see ELLATE

ealotry \el-ə-trē\ see ELOTRY

ealous \el-əs\ Ellis, Hellas, jealous, trellis, zealous, cancellous, ocellus

ealousy \el-ə-sē\ see ELACY

ealth \elth\ health, stealth, wealth, commonwealth

ealthy \el-thē\ healthy, stealthy, wealthy, unhealthy

ealty \ēl-tē\ fealty, realty

¹eam \ēm\ beam, bream, cream, deem, deme, dream, gleam, mime, neem, Nîmes, ream, scheme, scream, seam, seem, seme, steam, stream, team, teem, theme, abeam, agleam, airstream, berseem, beseem, bireme, blaspheme, bloodstream, centime, daydream, downstream, esteem, extreme, grapheme,

Gulf Stream, hakim, headstream, hornbeam, ice cream, inseam, kilim, lexeme, mainstream, midstream, millime, millstream, moonbeam, morpheme, onstream, phoneme, redeem, regime, sememe, sidestream, slipstream, sunbeam, supreme, Tarim, taxeme, toneme, trireme, unseam, upstream, academe, disesteem, double-team, enthymeme, misesteem, monotreme, self-esteem, succès d'estime, treponeme

²eam \im\ see ¹IM

eaman \ē-mən\ see ¹EMON

¹eamed \emt\ see EMPT

²eamed \emd\ beamed, steamed, teamed—also -ed forms of verbs listed at ¹EAM

eamer \ē-mər\ creamer, dreamer, femur, lemur, reamer, schemer, screamer, seamer, steamer, streamer, blasphemer, daydreamer, redeemer—also -er forms of adjectives listed at ¹EAM

eaming \ē-miŋ\ see EEMING

eamish \ē-mish\ beamish, squeamish

eamless \ēm-ləs\ dreamless, seamless

eamon \ē-mən\ see ¹EMON

eamster \ēm-stər\ seamster, teamster

eamy \ē-mē\ beamy, creamy, dreamy, gleamy, preemie, seamy, steamy, polysemy

¹ean \ē-ən\ aeon, eon, Ian, Leon, paean, peon, paeon, zein, Achaean, Actaeon, Aegean, Antaean, Archean, Augean, Chaldean, Chilean,

Fijian, Korean, Kuchean,
Linnaean, Mandaean,
Matthean, pampean,
plebeian, protean,
pygmaean, Tupi-Guaranian,
Tupian, apogean, Aramaean,
Atlantean, Caribbean,
Cerberean, circadian,
cyclopean, Clytherean,
Damoclean, empyrean,
epigean, European, Galilean,
Hasmonaean, Herculean,
Jacobean, kallikrein,
Maccabean, Manichaean,
Mycenaean, Odyssean,
panacean, perigean,
Sadducean, Sisyphean,
Typhoean, Tyrolean,
antipodean, epicurean,
Laodicean, Ponce de Leon,
proboscidean, Pythagorean,
terpsichorean, un-European,
epithalamion, Indo-
European

²ean \ēn\ see ³INE
³ean \ȯn\ see ³ON
⁴ean \ä-ən\ see ¹AYAN
eane \ēn\ see ³INE
eaner \ē-nər\ cleaner, gleaner,
keener, meaner, preener,
teener, weaner, weiner,
wiener, congener, convener,
demeanor, fourteener,
carabiner, contravener,
intervenor, misdemeanor,
submariner, trampoliner
eanery \ēn-rē\ beanery,
deanery, greenery, scenery,
machinery, turbomachinery
eanid \ē-ə-nəd\ Leonid,
Oceanid
eanie \ē-nē\ see ¹INI
eaning \ē-niŋ\ greening,
leaning, meaning, screening,
housecleaning, spring-
cleaning, sunscreening,
unmeaning, well-meaning,

overweening—*also* -ing
forms of verbs listed at ³INE
¹eanist \ē-nəst\ see ²INIST
²eanist \ē-ə-nist\ see IANIST
eanliness \en-lē-nəs\ see
ENDLINESS
eanling \ēn-liŋ\ greenling,
weanling, yeanling
¹eanly \ēn-lē\ cleanly,
greenly, leanly, meanly,
queenly, pristinely,
routinely, serpentinely,
uncleanly
²eanly \en-lē\ see ENDLY
eanne \ēn\ see ³INE
eanness \ēn-nəs\ cleanness,
greenness, meanness,
betweenness, uncleanness
eannie \ē-nē\ see ¹INI
eano \ē-nō\ see ²INO
eanor \ē-nər\ see EANER
eanse \enz\ see ¹ENS
eant \ent\ see ¹ENT
eany \ē-nē\ see ¹INI
eap \ēp\ see EEP
eapen \ē-pən\ see EEPEN
eaper \ē-pər\ see EEPER
eapie \ē-pē\ see EEPY
eapish \ē-pish\ see EEPISH
eapo \ē-pō\ see EPOT
¹ear \er\ see ⁴ARE
²ear \ir\ see ²EER
¹earable \er-ə-bəl\ bearable,
shareable, terrible, wearable,
unbearable, unwearable
²earable \ar-ə-bəl\ see
ARABLE
earage \ir-ij\ see EERAGE
¹earance \ir-əns\ see ¹ERENCE
²earance \er-əns\ see ARENCE
earch \ərch\ see URCH
earchist \ər-chəst\ see
URCHLESS
eard \ird\ beard, eared,
tiered, weird, afeard, bat-
eared, bluebeard, crop-
eared, dog-eared, graybeard,

lop-eared, misleared, whitebeard, chandeliered, engineered, pre-engineered—*also* -ed *forms of verbs listed at* ²EER

²**eard** \ərd\ *see* IRD

eare \ir\ *see* ²EER

earean \ir-ē-ən\ *see* ¹ERIAN

¹**eared** \erd\ *see* AIRED

²**eared** \ird\ *see* ¹EARD

¹**earer** \er-ər\ airer, bearer, carer, error, sharer, terror, casebearer, crossbearer, cupbearer, declarer, furbearer, live-bearer, pallbearer, seafarer, talebearer, torchbearer, trainbearer, wayfarer, color-bearer, standard-bearer, stretcher-bearer—*also* -er *forms of adjectives listed at* ⁴ARE

²**earer** \ir-ər\ cheerer, clearer, fearer, hearer, mirror, shearer, smearer, coherer, sheepshearer, veneerer, electioneerer—*also* -er *forms of adjectives listed at* ²EER

earful \ir-fəl\ cheerful, earful, fearful, tearful

earies \ir-ēz\ *see* ERIES

¹**earing** \ir-iŋ\ clearing, earing, earring, gearing, God-fearing, sheepshearing, fictioneering, hard-of-hearing, orienteering—*also* -ing *forms of verbs listed at* ²EER

²**earing** \er-iŋ\ *see* ¹ARING

earish \er-ish\ *see* ¹ARISH

earl \ərl\ *see* ¹IRL

earle \irl\ *see* ¹IRL

earler \ər-lər\ *see* IRLER

earless \ir-ləs\ cheerless, fearless, gearless, peerless, tearless

¹**earling** \ir-liŋ\ shearling, yearling

²**earling** \ər-lən\ *see* ERLIN

¹**early** \ir-lē\ clearly, dearly, merely, nearly, queerly, yearly, austerely, biyearly, severely, sincerely, cavalierly, semiyearly, insincerely

²**early** \ər-lē\ *see* URLY

earn \ərn\ *see* URN

earned \ərnd\ *see* URNED

earner \ər-nər\ *see* URNER

earnist \ər-nəst\ *see* ERNIST

earnt \ərnt\ burnt, learnt, weren't

earring \ir-iŋ\ *see* ¹EARING

earsal \ər-səl\ *see* ¹ERSAL

earse \ərs\ *see* ERSE

earser \ər-sər\ *see* URSOR

earst \ərst\ *see* URST

eart \ärt\ *see* ¹ART

earted \ärt-əd\ hearted, parted, bighearted, coldhearted, downhearted, fainthearted, freehearted, good-hearted, greathearted, halfhearted, hard-hearted, kindhearted, largehearted, lighthearted, proudhearted, softhearted, stouthearted, truehearted, uncharted, warmhearted, weakhearted, wholehearted, brokenhearted, chickenhearted, heavyhearted, ironhearted, lionhearted, openhearted, single-hearted, stonyhearted, tenderhearted—*also* -ed *forms of verbs listed at* ¹ART

¹**earth** \ärth\ *see* ARTH

²**earth** \ərth\ *see* IRTH

eartha \ər-thə\ *see* ERTHA

earthen \ər-thən\ *see* URTHEN

earthy \ər-thē\ *see* ORTHY

eartily \ärt-ᵊl-ē\ *see* ARTILY

eartless \ärt-ləs\ see ARTLESS

earty \ärt-ē\ see ¹ARTY

eary \ir-ē\ aerie, beery, bleary, cheery, dreary, eerie, Erie, leery, Peary, peri, quaere, query, smeary, sphery, teary, veery, weary, aweary, Kashmiri, Lake Erie, Valkyrie, world-weary, hara-kiri, miserere, overweary, whigmaleerie, Mount Dhaulagiri

eas \ē-əs\ see ¹EUS

¹easable \ē-sə-bəl\ peaceable, increasable

²easable \ē-zə-bəl\ see EASIBLE

¹easand \iz-ᵊn\ see ²ISON

²easand \ez-ᵊnd\ see EASONED

¹ease \ēs\ see IECE

²ease \ēz\ see EZE

¹eased \.ēzd\ pleased, diseased—*also* -ed *forms of verbs listed at* EZE

²eased \ēst\ see ¹EAST

easel \ē-zəl\ bezel, deasil, diesel, easel, measle, teasel, weasel

easeless \ē-sləs\ ceaseless, creaseless, greaseless

easelly \ē-zlē\ see EASLY

easement \ēz-mənt\ easement, appeasement

¹easer \ē-sər\ creaser, greaser, piecer, degreaser, increaser, one-piecer, releaser, two-piecer

²easer \ē-zər\ Caesar, freezer, geezer, greaser, pleaser, seizer, sneezer, squeezer, teaser, tweezer, appeaser, brainteaser, crowd-pleaser, degreaser, misfeasor, stripteaser, timepleaser

eash \ēsh\ see ²ICHE

easible \ē-zə-bəl\ feasible, squeezable, appeasable,

defeasible, infeasible, inappeasable, indefeasible, unappeasable

easil \ē-zəl\ see EASEL

easily \ēz-lē\ see EASLY

¹easing \ē-siŋ\ leasing, unceasing—*also* -ing *forms of verbs listed at* IECE

²easing \ē-ziŋ\ pleasing, subfreezing—*also* -ing *forms of verbs listed at* EZE

easingly \ē-siŋ-lē\ decreasingly, increasingly, unceasingly

easle \ē-zəl\ see EASEL

easly \ēz-ə-lē\ easily, measly, weaselly

eason \ēz-ᵊn\ reason, season, seisin, treason, disseisin, off-season, unreason, diocesan

easonable \ēz-nə-bəl\ reasonable, seasonable, treasonable, unreasonable, unseasonable

easoned \ēz-ᵊnd\ weasand, unreasoned—*also* -ed *forms of verbs listed at* EASON

easoning \ēz-niŋ\ reasoning, seasoning, unreasoning

easonless \ēz-ᵊn-ləs\ reasonless, seasonless

easor \ē-zər\ see ²EASER

¹east \ēst\ beast, east, East, feast, fleeced, geest, least, piste, priest, reest, triste, yeast, archpriest, artiste, batiste, deceased, Far East, hartebeest, modiste, Near East, northeast, southeast, tachiste, arriviste, dirigiste, hartebeest, Middle East, north-northeast, pointillist, wildebeest—*also* -ed *forms of verbs listed at* IECE

²east \ēst\ see EST

easted \es-təd\ see ESTED

easter \ē-stər\ Dniester,

Easter, keister, leister, quaestor, down-easter, northeaster, southeaster
eastie \ē-stē\ see EASTY
eastly \ēst-lē\ beastly, Priestley, priestly
easy \ē-stē\ beastie, yeasty
easurable \ezh-rə-bəl\ pleasurable, treasurable, immeasurable
¹**easure** \ezh-ər\ leisure, measure, pleasure, treasure, admeasure, displeasure, countermeasure
²**easure** \ā-zhər\ see AZIER
easurer \ezh-ər-ər\ measurer, treasurer
¹**easy** \ē-zē\ breezy, cheesy, easy, greasy, queasy, sleazy, sneezy, wheezy, pachisi, Parcheesi, speakeasy, uneasy, Zambezi
²**easy** \ē-sē\ see EECY
¹**eat** \ēt\ beat, beet, bleat, cheat, cleat, Crete, deet, eat, feat, fleet, Geat, gleet, greet, heat, keet, lied, meat, meet, mete, neat, peat, Pete, pleat, seat, sheet, skeet, sleet, street, suite, sweet, teat, treat, tweet, weet, wheat, accrete, aesthete, afreet, athlete, backbeat, backseat, backstreet, bedsheet, bolete, Bradstreet, broadsheet, browbeat, buckwheat, bystreet, clipsheet, compete, compleat, complete, conceit, concrete, crabmeat, deadbeat, deceit, defeat, delete, deplete, discreet, discrete, disseat, downbeat, drumbeat, effete, elite, en suite, entreat, escheat, esthete, excrete, facete, forcemeat, foresheet, groundsheet, heartbeat, heat-

treat, helpmeet, hoofbeat, ill-treat, mainsheet, maltreat, mesquite, mincemeat, mistreat, offbeat, petite, preheat, receipt, recheat, regreet, repeat, replete, retreat, secrete, slip-sheet, sweetmeat, terete, unmeet, unseat, upbeat, vegete, volkslied, zizith, aquavit, biathlete, bittersweet, cellulite, corps d'elite, countryseat, decathlete, exegete, incomplete, indiscreet, indiscrete, lorikeet, marguerite, Marguerite, Masorete, meadowsweet, Nayarit, obsolete, overeat, overheat, Paraclete, parakeet, pentathlete, plebiscite, polychaete, progamete, self-conceit, semisweet, superheat, triathlete, winding-sheet
²**eat** \āt\ see ¹ATE
³**eat** \et\ see ¹ET
⁴**eat** \it\ see ¹IT
eatable \ēt-ə-bəl\ eatable, heatable, treatable, depletable, escheatable, repeatable, unbeatable
¹**eated** \ēt-əd\ heated, pleated, conceited, deep-seated, repeated, overheated, superheated—*also* -ed *forms of verbs listed at* ¹EAT
²**eated** \et-əd\ see ETID
³**eated** \it-əd\ see ITTED
¹**eaten** \ēt-ᵊn\ eaten, beaten, Cretan, cretin, Eaton, Eton, neaten, sweeten, wheaten, browbeaten, moth-eaten, secretin, unbeaten, worm-eaten, overeaten, weather-beaten
²**eaten** \āt-ᵊn\ see ¹ATEN

¹eater \ēt-ər\ beater, bleater, cheater, eater, fetor, greeter, heater, liter, meter, peter, Peter, pleater, praetor, rhetor, seater, sheeter, skeeter, teeter, treater, tweeter, anteater, beefeater, blue peter, Demeter, drumbeater, eggbeater, excreter, fire-eater, flowmeter, man-eater, Main Streeter, maltreater, preheater, propraetor, repeater, saltpeter, secretor, seedeater, toadeater, Wall Streeter, windcheater, world-beater, altimeter, centiliter, centimeter, deciliter, decimeter, drunkometer, lotus-eater, milliliter, millimeter, overeater, taximeter—*also -er forms of adjectives listed at* ¹EAT

²eater \et-ər\ see ETTER

eatery \ēt-ə-rē\ see ETORY

¹eath \ēth\ eath, heath, Keith, Meath, neath, sheath, wreath, beneath, bequeath, hadith, monteith, underneath

²eath \ēth\ see EATHE

eathe \ēth\ breathe, Meath, seethe, sheathe, teethe, wreathe, bequeath, ensheathe, enwreathe, inbreathe, unsheathe, unwreathe, Westmeath

eathean \ē-thē-ən\ lethean, Promethean

¹eather \eth-ər\ see ¹ETHER

²eather \ē-thər\ see EITHER

eathern \eth-ərn\ see ETHERN

eathery \eth-rē\ feathery, heathery, leathery

eathing \ē-thiŋ\ breathing, sheathing, teething, firebreathing—*also -ing forms of verbs listed at* EATHE

eathless \eth-ləs\ breathless, deathless

eathy \ē-thē\ heathy, lethe, wreathy

eating \ēt-iŋ\ beating, eating, fleeting, meeting, seating, sheeting, sweeting, breast-beating, drumbeating, fire-eating, man-eating, unweeting, Sunday-go-to-meeting—*also -ing forms of verbs listed at* ¹EAT

eatise \ēt-əs\ see ETUS

¹eatly \āt-lē\ see ¹ATELY

²eatly \ēt-lē\ see EETLY

eaton \ēt-ᵊn\ see ¹EATEN

¹eats \ēts\ Keats—*also -s, -'s, and -s' forms of nouns listed at* ¹EAT, *and -s forms of verbs listed there*

²eats \āts\ see ¹ATES

eature \ē-chər\ see EACHER

eaty \ēt-ē\ meaty, peaty, sleety, sweetie, treaty, ziti, entreaty, Tahiti, Dolomiti, spermaceti

eau \ō\ see ¹OW

eaucracy \äk-rə-sē\ see OCRACY

eauteous \üt-ē-əs\ see UTEOUS

eautiful \üt-i-fəl\ see UTIFUL

eauty \üt-ē\ see ¹OOTY

eaux \ō\ see ¹OW

eavable \ē-və-bəl\ see EIVABLE

eaval \ē-vəl\ see IEVAL

¹eave \ēv\ breve, cleave, eve, Eve, greave, grieve, heave, leave, lief, peeve, reave, reeve, reive, scrieve, sheave, shrieve, sleave, sleeve, steeve, Steve, thieve, weave, weve, Abib, achieve, aggrieve, believe, bereave, conceive, deceive, inweave, khedive, Maldive, motive, naive, perceive, qui vive, receive, relieve, reprieve, retrieve,

shirtsleeve, unreeve,
unweave, upheave,
apperceive, by-your-leave,
disbelieve, Genevieve,
interleave, interweave,
Laccadive, make-believe,
misbelieve, misconceive,
preconceive, semibreve, Tel
Aviv, undeceive, recitative, ticket-of-
leave, underachieve, Saint
Agnes' Eve
²**eave** \iv\ see ²IVE
eaved \ēvd\ leaved, sleeved,
aggrieved, bereaved,
relieved—*also* -ed *forms of
verbs listed at* ¹EAVE
eavement \ēv-mənt\ see
EVEMENT
eaven \ev-ən\ devon, Devon,
Evan, heaven, Kevin,
leaven, levin, Nevin, seven,
Sevin, sweven, eleven,
replevin, South Devon
eaver \ē-vər\ see IEVER
eavers \ē-vərz\ cleavers,
vivers
eaves \ēvz\ eaves, Treves,
shirtsleeves
eavey \ē-vē\ peavey,
divi-divi
eaward \ē-wərd\ see EEWARD
¹**eaze** \ēz\ see EZE
²**eaze** \āz\ see ¹AZE
eazo \ē-zō\ see ¹IZO
eazy \ē-zē\ see ¹EASY
eb \eb\ bleb, deb, ebb, neb,
pleb, reb, Reb, web, ardeb,
celeb, cobweb, cubeb,
Deneb, Horeb, subdeb,
Zagreb, zineb, cause
célèbre, Johnny Reb,
spiderweb
eba \ē-bə\ Chiba, Reba,
Sheba, amoeba, zareba,
copaiba, Curitiba
ebate \ab-ət\ see ABIT

ebb \eb\ see EB
ebble \eb-ē\ see EBBY
ebble \eb-əl\ pebble, rebel,
treble
ebbuck \eb-ək\ kebbuck,
rebec
ebby \eb-ē\ blebby, Debbie,
Debby, maybe, webby,
cobwebby
¹**ebe** \ē-bē\ BB, freebie,
Hebe, phoebe, Phoebe,
Seabee, caribe, Galibi
²**ebe** \ēb\ glebe, grebe, plebe,
ephebe, sahib
ebec \eb-ək\ see EBBUCK
ebel \eb-əl\ see EBBLE
eber \ā-bər\ see ABOR
ebes \ēbz\ Thebes—*also* -s,
-'s, *and* -s' *forms of nouns
listed at* ²EBE
eble \eb-əl\ see EBBLE
ebo \ē-bō\ see IBO
ebral \ē-brəl\ cerebral,
palpebral, vertebral
ebrity \eb-rət-ē\ celebrity,
muliebrity
¹**ebs** \eps\ see EPS
²**ebs** \ebz\ Debs—*also* -s,
-'s, *and* -s' *forms of nouns
listed at* EB, *and* -s *forms of
verbs listed there*
ebt \et\ see ¹ET
ebted \et-əd\ see ETID
ebtor \et-ər\ see ETTER
ebus \ē-bəs\ Phoebus, rebus,
ephebus
¹**ec** \ek\ see ECK
²**ec** \ets\ see ETS
eca \ē-kə\ see ¹IKA
ecal \ē-kəl\ cecal, fecal,
meikle, treacle, intrathecal,
bibliothecal
ecan \ek-ən\ see ECKON
ecant \ē-kənt\ piquant,
secant
ecas \ā-kəs\ Turks and
Caicos, Zacatecas

ecca \ek-ə\ Decca, mecca, Mecca, weka, Rebecca, Rebekah, Rijeka

eccable \ek-ə-bəl\ see ECKABLE

eccan \ek-ən\ see ECKON

ecce \ek-ē\ see ECKY

ecco \ek-ō\ see ECHO

ecency \ēs-ᵊn-sē\ decency, recency, indecency

ecent \ēs-ᵊnt\ decent, recent, indecent, obeisant

eces \ē-sēz\ see ECIES

¹ech \ek\ see ECK

²ech \ək\ see UCK

³ech \esh\ see ¹ESH

¹eche \āsh\ crèche, flèche, Laoighis, Leix, resh, seiche, bobeche, Bangladesh, tête-bêche, Andhra Pradesh, Madhya Pradesh, Uttar Pradesh, Himadral Pradesh, Arunachal Pradesh

²eche \esh\ see ¹ESH

³eche \ē-chē\ see EACHY

êche \esh\ see ¹ESH

èche \esh\ see ¹ESH

eched \echt\ see ᴇTCHED

echerous \ech-rəs\ lecherous, treacherous

echery \ech-rē\ lechery, treachery

echie \ek-ē\ see ECKY

echin \ek-ən\ see ECKON

echo \ek-ō\ deco, echo, gecko, secco, El Greco, reecho

echnical \ek-ni-kəl\ technical, biotechnical, geotechnical

echt \ekt\ see ECT

ecia \ē-shə\ see ¹ESIA

ecially \esh-lē\ see ESHLY

ecian \ē-shən\ see ¹ETION

ecibel \es-ə-bəl\ see ESSIBLE

¹ecie \ē-sē\ see EECY

²ecie \ē-shē\ see ISHI

ecies \ē-sēz\ feces, species, theses, prostheses, subspecies, exegeses

¹ecil \ē-səl\ Cecil, diesel

²ecil \es-əl\ see ¹ESTLE

ecile \es-əl\ see ¹ESTLE

ecily \es-ə-lē\ see ESSALY

ecimal \es-ə-məl\ see ESIMAL

eciman \es-mən\ see ESSMAN

ecious \ē-shəs\ specious, capricious, facetious, Lucretius

ecium \ē-shē-əm\ aecium, lutecium, technetium, zoecium, androecium, apothecium, gynoecium, paramecium, perithecium

eck \ek\ beck, check, cheque, Czech, deck, dreck, fleck, heck, lek, neck, pec, peck, reck, sec, sneck, spec, speck, trek, wreak, wreck, Aztec, Baalbek, backcheck, bedeck, breakneck, Capek, cromlech, crookneck, cross-check, cusec, ewe-neck, exec, flyspeck, fore-check, foredeck, gooseneck, haček, hatcheck, henpeck, high tech, kopeck, limbeck, low-tech, Lubeck, Mixtec, paycheck, pinchbeck, Quebec, rebec, ringneck, roll-neck, roughneck, samekh, shipwreck, spot-check, Steinbeck, tenrec, Toltec, Uzbek, wryneck, xebec, afterdeck, à la grecque, Aquidneck, biotech, bodycheck, bottleneck, Chiang Kai-shek, countercheck, demi-sec, discotheque, double-check, double-deck, hunt-and-peck, leatherneck, littleneck, Pont l'évêque, quarterdeck, rubberneck, triple sec, turtleneck, Yucatec, Zapotec, cinematheque,

Melchizedek, Toulouse-Lautrec

eckable \ek-ə-bəl\ checkable, impeccable

ecked \ekt\ see ECT

ecker \ek-ər\ checker, chequer, decker, pecker, trekker, wrecker, exchequer, three-decker, woodpecker, dominicker, double-decker, rubbernecker, triple-decker

ecking \ek-iŋ\ decking, necking—also -ing forms of verbs listed at ECK

ecklace \ek-ləs\ see ECKLESS

eckle \ek-əl\ deckle, freckle, heckle, shekel, speckle, kenspeckle

eckless \ek-ləs\ feckless, checkless, necklace, reckless, affectless

ecko \ek-ō\ see ECHO

eckon \ek-ən\ beckon, Brecon, Deccan, reckon, zechin, Aztecan, misreckon, Toltecan, Yucatecan

ecks \ecks\ eks\ see EX

ecky \ek-ē\ Becky, recce, techie, Shimonoseki

econ \ek-ən\ see ECKON

¹**econd** \ek-ənd\ see ECUND

²**econd** \ek-ənt\ see ECCANT

ecque \ek\ see ECK

ecs \eks\ see EX

ect \ekt\ necked, sect, specked, abject, affect, aspect, bisect, cathect, collect, confect, connect, convect, correct, defect, deflect, deject, detect, direct, dissect, effect, eject, elect, erect, ewe-necked, expect, goosenecked, infect, inflect, inject, insect, inspect, neglect, object, pandect, perfect, porrect,

prefect, prelect, project, prospect, protect, rednecked, refect, reflect, reject, resect, respect, ringnecked, select, stiff-necked, subject, suspect, traject, transect, trisect, Utrecht, V-necked, acrolect, architect, circumspect, deselect, dialect, disaffect, disconnect, disinfect, disrespect, double-decked, genuflect, grapholect, incorrect, indirect, intellect, interject, intersect, introject, introspect, misdirect, preselect, re-collect, recollect, redirect, reelect, resurrect, retrospect, self-respect, turtlenecked, vivisect, aftereffect, hypercorrect, idiolect, interconnect, megaproject, semierect, semi-indirect—also -ed forms of verbs listed at ECK

ecta \ek-tə\ dejecta, ejecta, perfecta, trifecta

ectable \ek-tə-bəl\ affectable, collectible, correctable, deflectable, delectable, detectable, ejectable, erectable, expectable, inflectable, injectable, electable, indefectible, perfectible, projectable, respectable, disrespectable, indefectible

ectacle \ek-ti-kəl\ see ECTICAL

ectal \ek-t²l\ see ECTILE

ectance \ek-təns\ expectance, reflectance

ectant \ek-tənt\ expectant, humectant, injectant, protectant, disinfectant

ectar \ek-tər\ see ECTOR

ectarous \ek-trəs\ see
ECTRESS

ectary \ek-tə-rē\ sectary,
insectary

ected \ek-təd\ affected,
collected, complected,
dejected, recollected, self-
affected, self-collected, self-
elected, self-selected,
unaffected, undirected,
unexpected, unselected,
inner-directed, other-
directed—*also -ed forms of
verbs listed at* ECT

ecten \ek-tən\ nekton, pecten,
pectin, fibronectin,
ivermectin

ecter \ek-tər\ see ECTOR

ectible \ek-tə-bəl\ see
ECTABLE

ectic \ek-tik\ hectic, pectic,
cathectic, eclectic, synectic,
anorectic, apoplectic,
catalectic, dialectic

ectical \ek-ti-kəl\ spectacle,
dialectical

ectile \ek-tᵊl\ sectile, erectile,
insectile, projectile,
colorectal, dialectal

ectin \ek-tən\ see ECTEN

ecting \ek-tiŋ\ affecting, self-
respecting, self-correcting—
*also -ing forms of verbs listed
at* ECT

ection \ek-shən\ flexion,
lection, section, abjection,
advection, affection,
bisection, collection,
complexion, confection,
connection, connexion,
convection, correction, C-
section, defection,
deflection, dejection,
detection, direction,
dissection, ejection, election,
erection, evection, infection,
inflection, injection,

inspection, midsection,
objection, perfection,
prelection, projection,
protection, refection,
reflection, rejection,
resection, selection,
subjection, subsection,
trajection, transection,
trisection, by-election,
circumspection, disaffection,
disconnection, disinfection,
genuflection, imperfection,
indirection, introjection,
introspection, insurrection,
intellection, interjection,
intersection, misdirection,
predilection, preselection,
recollection, redirection,
reelection, reinfection,
resurrection, retroflexion,
retrospection, vivisection,
antirejection,
hypercorrection,
interconnection, Cesarean
section

ectional \ek-shnəl\ sectional,
affectional, bisectional,
complexional, connectional,
convectional, correctional,
cross-sectional, directional,
inflectional, projectional,
reflectional, bidirectional,
introspectional,
interjectional, resurrectional,
vivisectional,
omnidirectional,
unidirectional

ectionist \ek-shə-nəst\
perfectionist, projectionist,
protectionist, selectionist,
introspectionist,
resurrectionist, vivisectionist

ective \ek-tiv\ advective,
affective, adjective, bijective,
collective, connective,
convective, corrective,
defective, deflective,

detective, directive, effective, elective, ejective, infective, inflective, injective, invective, objective, perfective, perspective, projective, prospective, reflective, respective, selective, subjective, cost-effective, imperfective, ineffective, intellective, introspective, nondirective, nonobjective, retrospective, cryoprotective, intersubjective

ectless \ek-ləs\ see ECKLESS

ectly \ekt-lē\ abjectly, correctly, directly, erectly, incorrectly, indirectly

ectness \ekt-nəs\ abjectness, correctness, directness, erectness, selectness, incorrectness, indirectness, hypercorrectness

ecto \ek-tō\ recto, perfecto

ectomy \ek-tə-mē\ mastectomy, vasectomy, appendectomy, hysterectomy, tonsillectomy, clitoridectomy

ector \ek-tər\ hector, Hector, lector, nectar, rector, sector, specter, vector, bisector, collector, convector, corrector, defector, deflector, detector, director, dissector, effector, ejector, elector, erector, infector, injector, inspector, neglecter, objector, perfecter, projector, prospector, protector, reflector, selector, trisector, vivisector

ectoral \ek-trəl\ spectral, pectoral, electoral, protectoral, multispectral

ectorate \ek-tə-rət\ rectorate, directorate, electorate, inspectorate, protectorate

ectory \ek-tə-rē\ rectory, directory, protectory, refectory, trajectory, ex-directory

ectral \ek-trəl\ see ECTORAL

ectress \ek-trəs\ nectarous, directress, electress, protectress

ectrix \ek-triks\ rectrix, directrix

ectrum \ek-trəm\ plectrum, spectrum, electrum

¹ectual \ek-chə-wəl\ effectual, ineffectual, intellectual, anti-intellectual

²ectual \eksh-wəl\ see EXUAL

ectually \ek-chə-lē\ effectually, ineffectually, intellectually

¹ectural \ek-chə-rəl\ conjectural, prefectural, architectural

²ectural \ek-shrəl\ flexural, conjectural, architectural

ecture \ek-chər\ lecture, conjecture, prefecture, architecture

ectus \ek-təs\ conspectus, prospectus

ecular \ek-yə-lər\ secular, specular, molecular

ecum \ē-kəm\ vade mecum, subpoena duces tecum

ecund \ek-ənd\ fecund, second, femtosecond, microsecond, millisecond, nanosecond—*also* -ed *forms of verbs listed at* ECKON

ecutive \ek-ət-iv\ consecutive, executive, inconsecutive

ed \ed\ see ¹EAD

e'd \ēd\ see EED

¹eda \ēd-ə\ Freda, Frieda, Leda, Vida, Machida, alameda, olla podrida

²**eda** \ed-ə\ see ³ADA

¹**edal** \ed-²l\ heddle, medal, meddle, pedal, peddle, treadle, backpedal, bipedal, soft-pedal, intermeddle

²**edal** \ēd-²l\ see EEDLE

edance \ēd-²ns\ see EDENCE

¹**edar** \ed-ər\ see ²EADER

²**edar** \ēd-ər\ see ¹EADER

edator \ed-ət-ər\ see EDITOR

edd \ed\ see ¹EAD

edda \ed-ə\ Jedda, Vedda

eddar \ed-ər\ see ²EADER

edded \ed-əd\ see EADED

edden \ed-²n\ see EADEN

edder \ed-ər\ see ²EADER

eddie \ed-ē\ see ¹EADY

edding \ed-iŋ\ see ¹EADING

eddle \ed-²l\ see ¹EDAL

eddler \ed-lər\ meddler, medlar, peddler, intermeddler

eddon \ed-²n\ see EADEN

eddy \ed-ē\ see ¹EADY

¹**ede** \ād\ see ¹ADE

²**ede** \ēd\ see EED

³**ede** \ā-dā\ see AYDAY

edeas \ēd-ē-əs\ see ¹EDIOUS

eded \ē-dəd\ see EEDED

edel \ād-²l\ see ADLE

eden \ēd-²n\ Eden, Sweden, Dunedin

edence \ed-²ns\ credence, impedance, precedence, antecedence

edent \ēd-²nt\ credent, needn't, decedent, precedent, succedent, antecedent

¹**eder** \ād-ər\ see ADER

²**eder** \ēd-ər\ see ¹EADER

edes \ē-dēz\ Archimedes, Diomedes

edge \ej\ dredge, edge, fledge, hedge, kedge, ledge, pledge, sedge, sledge, veg, wedge, allege, frankpledge, gilt-edge, two-edged, hard-edge, knife-

edge, nutsedge, straightedge, featheredge, sortilege

edged \ejd\ edged, wedged, alleged, full-fledged, gilt-edged, two-edged, unfledged, deckle-edged, double-edged—*also* -ed *forms of verbs listed at* EDGE

edger \ej-ər\ dredger, edger, hedger, ledger, leger, pledger

edgie \ej-ē\ see EDGY

edgy \ej-ē\ edgy, ledgy, Reggie, sedgy, veggie, wedgie, wedgy, Himeji

edi \ād-ē\ see ADY

edia \ēd-ē-ə\ media, Media, acedia, cyclopedia, via media, encyclopedia

edial \ēd-ē-əl\ medial, predial, remedial

edian \ēd-ē-ən\ median, comedian, tragedian

ediant \ēd-ē-ənt\ see EDIENT

edible \ed-ə-bəl\ credible, edible, spreadable, incredible, inedible

¹**edic** \ēd-ik\ comedic, cyclopedic, logaoedic, orthopedic, encyclopedic

²**edic** \ed-ik\ Eddic, medic, comedic, paramedic, samoyedic

³**edic** \ād-ik\ see ¹ADIC

edicable \ed-i-kə-bəl\ medicable, predicable, immedicable

edical \ed-i-kəl\ medical, pedicle, premedical, biomedical, paramedical

edicate \ed-i-kət\ dedicate, predicate

edicle \ed-i-kəl\ see EDICAL

edience \ēd-ē-əns\ expedience, obedience, disobedience, inexpedience

edient \ēd-ē-ənt\ mediant, expedient, ingredient,

obedient, submediant, disobedient, inexpedient

ediment \ed-ə-mənt\ pediment, sediment, impediment

edin \ēd-ᵊn\ see EDEN

eding \ēd-in\ see ¹EEDING

¹**edious** \ēd-ē-əs\ tedious, supersedeas

²**edious** \ē-jas\ see EGIS

edist \ēd-əst\ orthopedist, encyclopedist

edit \ed-ət\ credit, edit, accredit, coedit, discredit, noncredit, reedit, subedit, copyedit

editor \ed-ət-ər\ creditor, editor, predator, coeditor, subeditor

edium \ēd-ē-əm\ medium, tedium, cypripedium

edlar \ed-lər\ see EDDLER

edley \ed-lē\ deadly, medley, redly, chance-medley

edly \ed-lē\ see EDLEY

¹**edo** \ēd-ō\ credo, lido, Lido, speedo, aikido, libido, Toledo, torpedo, tuxedo

²**edo** \ād-ō\ see ²ADO

³**edo** \ēd-ə\ see ¹EDA

⁴**edo** \e-dō\ Edo, meadow, Yedo

edom \ēd-əm\ see EDUM

edon \ēd-ᵊn\ bleeding, Eden, steading, Sarpedon, boustrophedon

edouin \ed-wən\ see EDWIN

edra \ē-drə\ Phaedra, cathedra

edral \ē-drəl\ cathedral, dihedral, trihedral, hemihedral, holohedral, octahedral, pentahedral, polyhedral, procathedral, tetrahedral, dodecahedral, icosahedral, tetartohedral

edro \ā-drō\ Pedro,

Murviedro

edulous \ej-ə-ləs\ credulous, sedulous, incredulous

edum \ēd-əm\ Edam, Edom, freedom, sedum

edure \ē-jər\ besieger, procedure, supersedure

edwin \ed-wən\ Edwin, bedouin

¹**ee** \ē\ b, be, bee, Brie, c, cay, cee, Cree, d, dee, Dee, dree, e, fee, flea, flee, free, g, gee, ghee, gie, glee, gree, he, key, Key, Klee, knee, lea, lee, Lee, Leigh, li, me, mi, p, pea, plea, pree, quay, re, scree, sea, see, she, shri, si, ski, spree, sri, t, tea, tee, the, thee, three, ti, tree, Tshi, twee, Twi, v, vee, we, wee, whee, ye, z, zee, agley, aiguille, agree, alee, ani, Bacchae, bailee, Bangui, banshee, bargee, bawbee, Belgae, Black Sea, bohea, bootee, bougie, buckshee, bungee, burgee, Bt, Capri, carefree, Castries, CB, CD, Chablis, Chaldee, chick-pea, Chi-li, chili, confit, cowpea, croquis, curie, Curie, Dead Sea, debris, decree, deep-sea, degree, Denis, donee, DP, draftee, drawee, Dundee, emcee, ennui, esprit, etui, farci, feoffee, foresee, fusee, GB, germfree, glacis, goatee, grand prix, grandee, grantee, GT, heart-free, he/she, HIV, Horae, IC, IV, Jaycee, jaygee, jayvee, knock-knee, KP, latchkey, lessee, look-see, low-key, LP, mame, maquis, Marie, marquee, MC, métis, Midi, mille-feuille, muggee, must-see, Nancy, ngwee, OD,

off-key, ogee, Osee, Parcae, pardie, passkey, Pawnee, payee, PC, perdie, per se, PG, pledgee, pongee, post-free, précis, puree, puttee, qt, raki, rani, razee, rooftree, rupee, rushee, RV, sati, scotfree, settee, Shaanxi, Shanxi, Shawnee, s/he, sightsee, signee, sirree, spadille, spahi, spondee, squeegee, squilgee, standee, strophe, suttee, sycee, T₃, T-3, TB, testee, 3-D, titi, to-be, topee, towhee, townee, trainee, trustee, trusty, Tupi, turfski, turnkey, tutee, Tutsi, tutti, TV, unbe, vendee, vestee, Volsci, vouchee, whangee, whoopee, would-be, Yang-Tze, yen-shee, abatis, ABC, ABD, absentee, addressee, adoptee, advisee, alienee, allottee, ambergris, AMP, amputee, appellee, appointee, après-ski, arrestee, assignee, attendee, B.V.D., Bahai, barley-bree, batterie, billi-bi, bonhomie, booboisie, bourgeoisie, brasserie, brusquerie, bumblebee, camporee, cap-a-pie, causerie, CCD, chickaree, chimpanzee, coati, Coligny, committee, conferee, consignee, counselee, context-free, counterplea, Danae, DDD, Debussy, departee, DDT, debauchee, DDE, deportee, dernier cri, deshabille, designee, detainee, devisee, devotee, diploe, disagree, dischargee, dishabille, divorcé, divorcée, DME, DMT, dungaree, duty-free, eau-de-vie, employee, endorsee, enlistee, enrollee,

epopee, escadrille, escapee, ESP, evictee, expellee, FAD, fancy-free, fantasie, fantasy, fedayee, filigree, fleur-de-lis, formulae, franchisee, fricassee, galilee, Galilee, garnishee, gaucherie, Gemini, GTP, guarani, guarantee, Hawaii, honeybee, honoree, humble-bee, hydro-ski, IgE, IgG, inductee, internee, invitee, IUD, jacquerie, jamboree, Jiangxi, jus soli, Kayseri, kidnappee, LCD, LED, legatee, libelee, licensee, LSD, maître d', manatee, Medici, millidegree, murderee, NAD, nominee, obligee, oversea, oversee, parolee, parti pris, patentee, pedigree, peppertree, picotee, piroshki, point d'appui, potpourri, praecipe, presentee, promisee, rapparee, referee, refugee, rejectee, renminbi, repartee, retiree, retrainee, returnee, Rosemarie, RPV, saddletree, Sadducee, San Luis, sangaree, Savaii, selectee, Semele, shivaree, snickersnee, SST, STD, Tenebrae, Tennessee, thirty-three, TNT, toile de Jouy, torii, transferee, undersea, Urümqi, vaccinee, value-free, verdigris, VIP, vis-à-vis, warrantee, Adar Sheni, Agri Dagi, alienee, biographee, bouquet garni, casus belli, charcuterie, charivari, chincherinchee, chinoiserie, covenantee, DBCP, dedicatee, de Medici, delegatee, distributee, ESOP, evacuee, examinee, exuviae, facetiae, fait accompli, felo-

de-se, fortunately, Galilei,
HTLV, interrogee,
interviewee, jaborandi,
Jiamusi, minutiae, Omega-3,
Pasiphae, patisserie, prima
facie, reliquiae, relocatee,
Sargasso Sea, Simon Legree,
Sault Sainte Marie,
Southend on Sea,
communicatee, HTLV-III,
taedium vitae, Tupi-
Guarani, ignoratio elenchi,
petitio principii

²ee \ā\ see ¹AY

ée \ā\ see ¹AY

eeable \ē-ə-bəl\ seeable,
skiable, agreeable,
foreseeable, disagreeable

eeble \ē-bē\ see ¹EBE

eece \ēs\ see IECE

eeced \ēst\ see ¹EAST

eech \ēch\ see EACH

eecher \ē-chər\ see EACHER

eeches \ich-əz\ see ITCHES

eeching \ē-chiŋ\ breeching,
far-reaching—*also* -ing
forms of verbs listed at EACH

eechy \ē-chē\ see EACHY

eecy \ē-sē\ fleecy, greasy,
specie, Tbilisi, AC/DC

eed \ēd\ bead, Bede, bleed,
brede, breed, cede, creed,
deed, feed, Gide, glede,
gleed, greed, he'd, heed,
keyed, knead, kneed, lead,
mead, Mead, Mede, meed,
need, plead, read, rede,
reed, Reed, Reid, screed,
seed, she'd, speed, steed,
swede, Swede, treed, tweed,
Tweed, we'd, weed, accede,
airspeed, allseed, bindweed,
birdseed, blueweed, bourride,
breast-feed, bugseed,
burweed, cheerlead,
chickweed, concede,
crossbreed, cudweed,

debride, degreed, duckweed,
exceed, fairlead, fireweed,
flaxseed, Godspeed,
gulfweed, half-breed, hand-
feed, hawkweed, hayseed,
high-speed, horseweed,
impede, implead, inbreed,
indeed, ironweed, Jamshid,
jetbead, knapweed,
knotweed, Lake Mead,
linseed, lip-read, milkweed,
misdeed, mislead, misread,
moonseed, nosebleed, off-
speed, oilseed, pigweed,
pinweed, pokeweed,
pondweed, Port Said,
precede, proceed, proofread,
ragweed, rapeseed, recede,
reseed, rockweed, seaweed,
secede, self-feed, Siegfried,
sight-read, silkweed,
smartweed, snakeweed,
sneezeweed, speed-read,
spoon-feed, stall-feed,
stampede, stickseed,
stickweed, stinkweed,
succeed, ten-speed, tickseed,
weak-kneed, witchweed,
wormseed, aniseed,
antecede, beggarweed,
bitterweed, bottle-feed,
bugleweed, butterweed,
carpetweed, centipede,
copyread, cottonseed,
cottonweed, crazyweed,
Ganymede, interbreed,
intercede, interplead,
jewelweed, jimsonweed,
locoweed, millipede,
overfeed, pedigreed,
pickerelweed, pumpkinseed,
retrocede, riverweed,
rosinweed, Runnymede,
silverweed, supersede,
thimbleweed, tumbleweed,
underfeed, waterweed,
velocipede

eedal \ēd-ᵊl\ see EEDLE

eeded \ē-dəd\ beaded, deeded, kneaded, receded—*also* -ed *forms of verbs listed at* EED

eeder \ēd-ər\ see ¹EADER

eedful \ēd-fəl\ heedful, needful

¹eeding \ēd-iŋ\ bleeding, breeding, leading, reading, reeding, inbreeding, linebreeding, lipreading, outbreeding, preceding, speed-reading—*also* -ing *forms of verbs listed at* EED

²eeding \ēd-ᵊn\ see EDON

eedle \ēd-ᵊl\ aedile, beadle, credal, creedal, daedal, needle, wheedle

eedless \ēd-ləs\ deedless, heedless, needless, seedless

eedn't \ēd-ᵊnt\ see EDENT

eedo \ēd-ō\ see ¹EDO

eedom \ēd-əm\ see EDUM

eeds \ēdz\ Leeds, needs, Beskids, proceeds—*also* -s, -'s, *and* -s' *forms of nouns listed at* EED, *and* -s *forms of verbs listed there*

eedsman \ēdz-mən\ beadsman, seedsman

eedy \ēd-ē\ beady, deedy, greedy, needy, reedy, seedy, speedy, tweedy, weedy

eef \ēf\ see ¹IEF

eefe \ēf\ see ¹IEF

eefy \ē-fē\ beefy, leafy, reefy

eegee \ē-jē\ see IJI

eeing \ē-iŋ\ seeing, skiing, farseeing, ill-being, sight-seeing, turfskiing, well-being, heli-skiing, waterskiing—*also* -ing *forms of verbs listed at* ¹EE

¹eek \ik\ see ICK

²eek \ēk\ see ¹EAK

eeked \ēkt\ see ²EAKED

eeken \ē-kən\ see EACON

eeker \ē-kər\ see ¹EAKER

eekie \ē-kē\ see EAKY

eeking \ē-kiŋ\ see ¹EAKING

eekly \ē-klē\ bleakly, chicly, sleekly, weakly, weekly, treacly, biweekly, midweekly, newsweekly, triweekly, semiweekly

eeks \ēks\ see ¹IXE

eeky \ē-kē\ see EAKY

eel \ēl\ see ²EAL

eelable \ē-lə-bəl\ see EALABLE

eele \ēl\ see ²EAL

eeled \ēld\ see IELD

eeler \ē-lər\ see EALER

eeley \ē-lē\ see EELY

eelie \ē-lē\ see EELY

eelin \ē-lən\ see ELIN

eeling \ē-liŋ\ ceiling, dealing, Ealing, feeling, peeling, shieling, wheeling, appealing, Darjeeling, freewheeling, self-dealing, self-feeling, self-sealing, unfeeling, double-dealing, self-revealing, snowmobiling, unappealing—*also* -ing *forms of verbs listed at* ²EAL

eelson \el-sən\ see ELSON

eely \ē-lē\ Chi-li, dele, eely, Ely, freely, Greeley, mealie, mealy, really, seely, steelie, steely, stele, surreally, syli, vealy, wheelie, scungilli, Swahili, campanile, contumely, Isle of Ely, monostele, touchy-feely

eem \ēm\ see ¹EAM

eeman \ē-mən\ see ¹EMON

eemer \ē-mər\ see EAMER

eemie \ē-mē\ see EAMY

eeming \ē-miŋ\ seeming, streaming, redeeming, unbeseeming—*also* -ing *forms of verbs listed at* ¹EAM

eemly \ēm-lē\ seemly, supremely, unseemly

¹**een** \in\ see ¹IN

²**een** \ēn\ see ³INE

e'en \ēn\ see ³INE

eena \ē-nə\ see ²INA

eene \ēn\ see ³INE

eener \ē-nər\ see EANER

eenery \ēn-rē\ see ²EANERY

eening \ē-niŋ\ see EANING

eenling \ēn-liŋ\ see EANLING

eenly \ēn-lē\ see ¹EANLY

eenness \ēn-nəs\ see EANNESS

eens \ēnz\ Queens, teens, Grenadines, Philippines, smithereens

eenwich \in-ich\ see INACH

eeny \ē-nē\ see ¹INI

eep \ēp\ beep, bleep, cheap, cheep, clepe, creep, deep, heap, jeep, Jeep, keep, leap, neap, neep, peep, reap, seep, sheep, sleep, sneap, steep, sweep, threap, veep, weep, asleep, barkeep, bopeep, dustheap, househeap, knee-deep, skin-deep, upkeep, upsweep, overleap, oversleep, Lakshadweep, Louis Philippe

eepage \ē-pij\ creepage, seepage

eepen \ē-pən\ cheapen, deepen, steepen

eepence \əp-əns\ see UPPANCE

eepenny \əp-nē\ see OPENNY

eeper \ē-pər\ beeper, creeper, keeper, leaper, Dnieper, peeper, reaper, sleeper, sweeper, weeper, barkeeper, beekeeper, bookkeeper, crowkeeper, doorkeeper, gamekeeper, gatekeeper, goalkeeper, greenkeeper, groundskeeper, housekeeper, innkeeper, lockkeeper, minesweeper, peacekeeper, scorekeeper, shopkeeper, stockkeeper, storekeeper, timekeeper, zookeeper, honeycreeper— *also* -er *forms of adjectives listed at* EEP

eeple \ē-pē\ see EEPY

eeping \ē-piŋ\ creeping, keeping, weeping, beekeeping, bookkeeping, gatekeeping, housekeeping, minesweeping, peacekeeping, safekeeping, timekeeping— *also* -ing *forms of verbs listed at* EEP

eepish \ē-pish\ cheapish, sheepish

eeple \ē-pəl\ see EOPLE

eepy \ē-pē\ cheapie, creepy, seepy, sleepy, sweepy, tepee, tipi, weepie, weepy

¹**eer** \ē-ər\ freer, seer, skier, we're, CBer, decreer, foreseer, sightseer, overseer, water-skier

²**eer** \ir\ beer, bier, blear, cere, cheer, clear, dear, deer, drear, ear, fear, fere, fleer, gear, hear, here, jeer, Lear, leer, mere, mir, near, peer, pier, Pierre, queer, rear, schmear, sear, seer, sere, shear, sheer, skirr, smear, sneer, spear, speer, sphere, spier, steer, tear, tier, Trier, Tyr, veer, we're, year, adhere, Aesir, Ajmer, ambeer, appear, arrear, Asir, austere, Ayrshire, Berkshire, besmear, brassiere, Cape Fear, career, cashier, cashmere, Cheshire, chimere, clavier, cohere, compeer, destrier, dog-ear, Ellesmere, emir, Empire, endear, ensphere, eyrir, Fafnir, Fifeshire, Flintshire, footgear, frontier, gambier, Goodyear, haltere, Hampshire, headgear,

inhere, Izmir, Kashmir, kefir, killdeer, laveer, light-year, man-year, menhir, mishear, monsieur, mouse-ear, nadir, Nairnshire, out-year, Pamir, Perthshire, pickeer, portiere, premier, premiere, redear, rehear, reindeer, revere, Revere, Robespierre, revers, Saint Pierre, santir, severe, Shakespeare, Shropshire, sincere, slick-ear, tapir, uprear, Vanir, veneer, vizier, voir dire, wheatear, Wiltshire, Ymir, Yorkshire, zaire, Zaire, atmosphere, auctioneer, balladeer, bandolier, bayadere, Bedfordshire, Bedivere, belvedere, biosphere, black-tailed deer, bombardier, boutonniere, brigadier, buccaneer, budgeteer, Cambridgeshire, cameleer, cannoneer, cassimere, cavalier, chandelier, chanticleer, chevalier, chiffonier, chocolatier, commandeer, corsetiere, cuirassier, Denbighshire, Derbyshire, diapir, disappear, domineer, Dumfriesshire, ecosphere, Elzevir, engineer, fictioneer, financier, fourdrinier, fusilier, gadgeteer, gasolier, gazetteer, Gloucestershire, gondolier, grenadier, Guinevere, halberdier, hemisphere, Herefordshire, Hertfordshire, IJsselmere, insincere, interfere, jardiniere, junketeer, kerseymere, Lanarkshire, Lancashire, lavaliere, leafleteer, marketeer,

Meyerbeer, missileer, Monmouthshire, Morayshire, mountaineer, Mount Ranier, muleteer, musketeer, mutineer, Oxfordshire, overhear, overseer, oversteer, pamphleteer, Pembrokeshire, persevere, pioneer, pistoleer, pontonier, privateer, profiteer, puppeteer, racketeer, Radnorshire, rocketeer, Rutlandshire, scrutineer, Selkirkshire, sloganeer, sonneteer, souvenir, Staffordshire, stratosphere, summiteer, Tyne and Wear, understeer, volunteer, Warwickshire, white-tailed deer, Windermere, Worcestershire, yesteryear, acyclovir, animalier, black marketeer, Buckinghamshire, Clackmannanshire, carabineer, Caernarvonshire, Cardiganshire, Carmarthenshire, charioteer, conventioneer, Dunbartonshire, electioneer, Eskisehir, Glamorganshire, free-marketeer, harquebusier, Huntingdonshire, Invernessshire, Kincardineshire, Montgomeryshire, Northamptonshire, Nottinghamshire, Merionethshire

e'er \er\ see ⁴ARE

eerage \ir-ij\ peerage, steerage, arrearage

eered \ird\ see ¹EARD

eerer \ir-ər\ see ²EARER

eeress \ir-əs\ see EROUS

eerful \ir-fəl\ see EARFUL

¹eerie \ir-ē\ see EARY

²eerie \ē-rē\ see EIRIE

eering \ir-iŋ\ see ¹EARING

eerist \ir-əst\ see ¹ERIST

eerless \ir-ləs\ see EARLESS

eerly \ir-lē\ see ¹EARLY

eersman \irz-mən\ steersman, frontiersman

eerut \ir-ət\ see IRIT

eery \ir-ē\ see BARY

ees \ēz\ see EZE

eese \ēz\ see EZE

eesh \ēsh\ see ²ICHE

eesi \ē-zē\ see ¹EASY

eesia \ē-zhə\ see ²ESIA

eesome \ē-səm\ gleesome, threesome

¹eest \āst\ see ACED

²eest \ēst\ see ¹EAST

eesy \ē-zē\ see ¹EASY

eet \ēt\ see ¹EAT

eetah \ēt-ə\ see ²ITA

eete \āt-ē\ see ATY

eeten \ēt-ᵊn\ see ¹EATEN

eeter \ēt-ər\ see ¹EATER

eethe \ē<u>th</u>\ see EATHE

eether \ē-<u>th</u>ər\ see EITHER

eething \ē-<u>th</u>iŋ\ see EATHING

eetie \ēt-ē\ see EATY

eeting \ēt-iŋ\ see EATING

eetle \ēt-ᵊl\ see ETAL

eetly \ēt-lē\ featly, fleetly, neatly, sweetly, completely, concretely, discreetly, discretely, effetely, bittersweetly, incompletely, indiscreetly

eety \ēt-ē\ see EATY

ee-um \ē-əm\ see ¹EUM

eeve \ēv\ see ¹EAVE

eeved \ēvd\ see EAVED

eeves \ēvz\ see EAVES

eevil \ē-vəl\ see IEVAL

eevish \ē-vish\ peevish, thievish

eeward \ē-wərd\ leeward, Leeward, seaward

eewee \ē-wē\ kiwi, peewee, pewee

eewit \ü-ət\ see UET

eez \ēz\ see EZE

eezable \ē-zə-bəl\ see EASIBLE

eeze \ēz\ see EZE

eezer \ē-zər\ see ²EASER

eezing \ē-ziŋ\ see ²EASING

eezy \ē-zē\ see ¹EASY

¹ef \ef\ chef, clef, deaf, ef, f , lev, ref, teff, aleph, Brezhnev, enfeoff, H-F, Kiev, Lwiw, stone-deaf, tone-deaf, emf, Kishinev

²ef \ā\ see ¹AY

³ef \ēf\ see ¹IEF

efanie \ef-ə-nē\ see EPHONY

efany \ef-ə-nē\ see EPHONY

efe \ef-ē\ see EFFIE

eferable \ef-rə-bəl\ preferable, referable

eference \ef-rəns\ deference, preference, reference, cross-reference

eferent \ef-rənt\ deferent, referent

eff \ef\ see ¹EF

effer \ef-ər\ see EPHOR

efic \ef-ik\ Efik, benefic, malefic

eficence \ef-ə-səns\ beneficence, maleficence

efik \e-fik\ see EFIC

efsk \efsk\ Izhefsk, Profopyevsk

eft \eft\ cleft, deft, eft, heft, klepht, left, theft, weft, bereft

efty \ef-tē\ hefty, lefty

¹eg \āg\ Craig, plague, vague, stravage, The Hague

²eg \eg\ beg, Craig, dreg, egg, gleg, Greg, Gregg, keg, leg, peg, reg, skeg, yegg, blackleg, bootleg, bowleg,

dogleg, foreleg, jackleg, jake
leg, muskeg, nutmeg, redleg,
renege, roughleg, Tuareg,
unpeg, Winnipeg, mumblety-
peg

³**eg** \ej\ see EDGE

¹**ega** \eg-ə\ omega, rutabaga

²**ega** \ä-gə\ see ²AGA

³**ega** \ē-gə\ see ¹IGA

egal \ē-gəl\ beagle, eagle,
egal, legal, regal, illegal,
porbeagle, spread-eagle,
viceregal, extralegal,
paralegal, medicolegal

egan \ē-gən\ Megan, vegan,
Mohegan

egas \ā-gəs\ see AGUS

¹**ege** \ezh\ barege, cortege,
Liège, manege, solfege

²**ege** \eg\ see ²EG

³**ege** \ej\ see EDGE

⁴**ege** \ēg\ see IGUE

⁵**ege** \ig\ see IG

eged \ejd\ see EDGED

egel \āgəl\ see AGEL

egent \ē-jənt\ regent, rejant,
allegiant, vice-regent

eger \ej-ər\ see EDGER

egg \eg\ see ²EG

eggar \eg-ər\ see EGGER

eggary \eg-ə-rē\ beggary,
Gregory

egger \eg-ər\ beggar,
bootlegger, Heidegger,
thousand-legger

eggie \ej-ē\ see EDGY

eggio \ej-ē-ō\ Reggio,
arpeggio, solfeggio

eggs \egz\ see EGS

eggy \eg-ē\ dreggy, eggy,
leggy, Peggy, plaguey,
Carnegie

egia \ē-jə\ Ouija, aqua regia,
aquilegia, paraplegia,
quadriplegia

egian \ē-jən\ see EGION

egiant \ē-jənt\ see EGENT

egiate \ē-jət\ collegiate, elegit,
intercollegiate

egic \ē-jik\ strategic,
paraplegic, quadriplegic

egie \eg-ē\ see EGGY

egion \ē-jən\ legion, region,
Norwegian, subregion,
collegian

egious \ē-jəs\ see EGIS

egis \ē-jəs\ aegis, egis, Regis,
tedious, egregious

egit \ē-jət\ see EGIATE

egm \em\ see ¹EM

egn \ān\ see ¹ANE

egnant \eg-nənt\ pregnant,
regnant, impregnant,
unpregnant

egnly \ān-lē\ see AINLY

egno \ān-yō\ see ¹ENO

¹**ego** \ē-gō\ chigoe, ego, Vigo,
amigo, alter ego, impetigo,
superego

²**ego** \ā-gō\ see ²AGO

egory \eg-ə-rē\ see EGGARY

egs \egz\ sheerlegs,
yellowlegs, butter-and-eggs,
daddy longlegs—*also* -s, -'s,
and -s' *forms of nouns listed
at* ²EG, *and* -s *forms of verbs
listed there*

egular \eg-lər\ see EGLER

¹**eh** \ā\ see ¹AY

²**eh** \ä\ see ³AH

ehen \ān\ see ¹ANE

ehner \ā-nər\ see AINER

¹**ei** \ēk\ dreich, skeigh

²**ei** \ā\ see ¹AY

³**ei** \ī\ see ¹Y

¹**eia** \ē-ə\ see ¹IA

²**eia** \ī-ə\ see ¹IAH

eial \ē-əl\ see ¹EAL

¹**eian** \ē-ən\ see ¹EAN

²**eian** \ā-ən\ see ¹AYAN

eic \ē-ik\ oleic, epigeic,
logorrheic, mythopoeic,
onomatopoeic

eich \ēk\ see ¹EI

eiche \āsh\ see ¹ECHE

eickel \ī-kəl\ see YCLE

¹eid \āt\ see ¹ATE

²eid \īt\ see ¹ITE

³eid \ēd\ see EED

¹eidel \ād-əl\ see ADLE

²eidel \īd-ᵊl\ see IDAL

eidi \īd-ē\ see IDAY

eidon \īd-ᵊn\ see IDEN

eier \īr\ see ¹IRE

eifer \ef-ər\ see EPHOR

¹eige \āzh\ beige, assuage

²eige \ā\ see ¹AY

eiger \ī-gər\ see IGER

¹eigh \ā\ see ¹AY

²eigh \ē\ see ¹EE

eighbor \ā-bər\ see ABOR

¹eight \āt\ see ¹ATE

²eight \īt\ see ¹ITE

eighter \āt-ər\ see ATOR

eightless \āt-ləs\ see ATELESS

eights \īts\ see IGHTS

eighty \āt-ē\ see ATY

eign \ān\ see ¹ANE

eigner \ā-nər\ see AINER

eii \ā\ see ¹AY

eiian \ā-ən\ see ¹AYAN

eiji \ā-jē\ see AGY

eik \ēk\ see ¹EAK

eikh \ēk\ see ¹EAK

eikle \ē-kəl\ see ECAL

¹eil \āl\ see AIL

²eil \el\ see ¹EL

³eil \ēl\ see ¹EAL

⁴eil \īl\ see ¹ILE

eila \ē-lə\ see ¹ELA

eiled \āld\ see AILED

eiler \ī-lər\ see ILAR

¹eiling \ā-liŋ\ see AILING

²eiling \ē-liŋ\ see EELING

eill \el\ see ²EAL

eillance \ā-ləns\ see ALENCE

eillant \ā-lənt\ see ALANT

¹eilles \ā\ see ¹AY

²eilles \ālz\ see ALES

eilly \ā-lē\ see AILY

¹eim \ām\ see ¹AME

²eim \īm\ see ¹IME

eimer \ī-mər\ see ¹IMER

¹eims \äⁿs\ see ¹ANCE

²eims \ēmz\ Reims,
Rheims—*also* -s, -'s, *and* -s'
forms of nouns listed at ¹EAM,
and -s *forms of verbs listed*
there

¹ein \ān\ see ¹ANE

²ein \ē-ən\ see ¹EAN

³ein \īn\ see ³INE

⁴ein \in\ see ¹INE

¹eine \ān\ see ¹ANE

²eine \ēn\ see ³INE

³eine \ī-nə\ see ¹INA

⁴eine \en\ see ¹EN

eined \ānd\ see AINED

¹einer \ā-nər\ see AINER

²einer \ē-nər\ see EANER

eing \ē-iŋ\ see EEING

einie \ī-nē\ see ¹INY

eining \ā-niŋ\ see AINING

einous \ā-nəs\ see AYNESS

eins \ānz\ see AINS

einsman \ānz-mən\ see
AINSMAN

eint \ānt\ see AINT

einte \ant\ see ⁵ANT

einture \an-chər\ see
²ANCHER

einy \ā-nē\ see AINY

eipt \ēt\ see ¹EAT

eir \er\ see ⁴ARE

eira \ir-ə\ see ¹ERA

eird \ird\ see ¹EARD

eiress \ar-əs\ see ²ARIS

eiric \ī-rik\ see YRIC

eiro \er-ō\ see ²ERO

eirs \erz\ see AIRS

¹eis \īs\ see ¹ICE

²eis \ē-əs\ see ¹EUS

³eis \īs\ see ¹ICE

eisant \ēs-ᵊnt\ see ECENT

eise \ēz\ see EZE

eisel \ī-zəl\ see ²ISAL

eisen \īz-ᵊn\ see ¹IZEN

¹eiser \ī-sər\ see ICER

¹**eiser** \ī-zər\ see IZER

¹**eisha** \ā-shə\ see ACIA

²**eisha** \ē-shə\ see ¹ESIA

eisin \ēz-ᵊn\ see EASON

eiss \īs\ see ¹ICE

eissen \īs-ᵊn\ see ¹ISON

¹**eist** \ā-əst\ see AYEST

²**eist** \īst\ see ¹IST

¹**eister** \ī-stər\ shyster, tryster, concertmeister, kapellmeister

²**eister** \ē-stər\ see EASTER

eisure \ē-zhər\ see EIZURE

¹**eit** \ē-ət\ fiat, albeit, howbeit

²**eit** \it\ see ¹IT

³**eit** \ēt\ see ¹EAT

⁴**eit** \īt\ see ¹ITE

eited \ēt-əd\ see ¹EATED

¹**eiter** \it-ər\ see ITTER

²**eiter** \ī-tər\ see ¹ITER

eith \ēth\ see ¹EATH

either \ē-t͟hər\ breather, either, neither, teether

eitus \īt-əs\ see ITIS

eity \ē-ət-ē\ deity, velleity, corporeity, spontaneity, synchroneity, diaphaneity, homogeneity, incorporeity, instantaneity, contemporaneity, extemporaneity, heterogeneity, inhomogeneity

eivable \ē-və-bəl\ cleavable, achievable, believable, conceivable, deceivable, perceivable, receivable, relievable, retrievable, imperceivable, inconceivable, irretrievable, unbelievable, unconceivable

eive \ēv\ see ¹EAVE

eiver \ē-vər\ see IEVER

eix \āsh\ see ¹ECHE

¹**eize** \āz\ see ¹AZE

²**eize** \ēz\ see EZE

eizure \ē-zhər\ leisure, seizure

ejant \ē-jənt\ see EGENT

eji \ej-ē\ see EDGY

ejo \ā-ō\ see ¹EO

ek \ek\ see ECK

¹**eka** \ek-ə\ see ECCA

²**eka** \ē-kə\ see ¹IKA

ekah \ek-ə\ see ECCA

eke \ēk\ see ¹EAK

ekel \ek-əl\ see ECKLE

ekh \ek\ see ECK

eki \ek-ē\ see ECKY

ekker \ek-ər\ see ECKER

ekoe \ē-kō\ see ICOT

ekton \ek-tən\ see ECTEN

¹**el** \el\ bell, bell, Bell, belle, cel, cell, dell, dwell, el, ell, fell, gel, Hel, hell, jell, knell, l, mell, quell, sel, sell, shell, smell, snell, spell, swell, tell, they'll, well, yell, Adele, Ardell, artel, barbell, befell, Blackwell, bluebell, boatel, bombshell, Boswell, botel, bridewell, cadelle, cartel, carvel, chandelle, clamshell, compel, cormel, cornel, corral, cowbell, Cromwell, cupel, Danielle, diel, dispel, doorbell, dumbbell, duxelles, echelle, eggshell, Estelle, excel, expel, farewell, fjeld, foretell, gabelle, gazelle, Giselle, gromwell, handbell, hard-shell, harebell, hotel, impel, indwell, inkwell, jurel, lampshell, lapel, marcel, maxwell, Maxwell, micelle, Michele, Michelle, misspell, morel, Moselle, motel, nacelle, Nobel, noel, nouvelle, nutshell, oat-cell, Orel, Orwell, outsell, pall-mall, Parnell, pastel, pell-mell, pixel, pointelle, presell, propel, quenelle, rakehell, rappel, Ravel, rebel, refel,

repel, respell, retell, riel,
Rochelle, rondel, saurel,
scalpel, seashell, sequel,
Seychelles, soft-shell, solgel,
speedwell, spinel, stairwell,
unsell, unwell, upwell,
Weddell, wind-bell,
Annabelle, APL, aquarelle,
asphodel, Azazel, bagatelle,
BAL, barbicel, bechamel,
brocatelle, Camberwell,
caramel, caravel, carousel,
cascabel, chanterelle,
chaparral, Charles Martel,
citadel, clientele, cockleshell,
Cozumel, damozel, decibel,
demoiselle, fare-thee-well,
fontanel, immortelle, Isabel,
Isabelle, Jezebel, kiss-and-
tell, lenticel, mangonel,
muscatel, ne'er-do-well,
Neufchatel, nonpareil,
organelle, oversell, parallel,
pedicel, pennoncel,
personnel, petronel,
Philomel, pimpernel, show-
and-tell, tortoiseshell,
undersell, T4 cell, villanelle,
William Tell, zinfandel, Aix-
la-Chapelle, au naturel,
crème caramel,
mademoiselle, maître
d'hôtel, matériel, Mont-
Saint-Michel, spirituel,
T-helper cell, Thompson's
gazelle, VLDL, antiparallel,
antipersonnel, AWOL

²el \äl\ see AIL

¹ela \ē-lə\ Gila, Leila, Lela,
selah, sheila, Sheila, stela,
Vila, Braila, candela, tequila,
weigela, sheila, Coahuila,
Philomela, sinsemilla,
Tutuila

²ela \ā-lə\ see ³ALA

³ela \el-ə\ see ELLA

elable \el-ə-bəl\ see ELLABLE

elacy \el-ə-sē\ jealousy,
prelacy

elagh \ā-lē\ see AILY

elah \ē-lə\ see ¹ELA

eland \ē-lənd\ eland, Leland,
Zealand, New Zealand

elanie \el-ə-nē\ see ELONY

elar \ē-lər\ see EALER

elate \el-ət\ see ELLATE

elatin \el-ət-ᵊn\ see ELETON

elative \el-ət-iv\ relative,
appellative, correlative,
irrelative

elba \el-bə\ Elba, Elbe, Melba

elbe \el-bə\ see ELBA

elbert \el-bərt\ Delbert,
Elbert, Mount Elbert

elch \elch\ belch, squelch,
welch, Welch, Welsh

¹eld \eld\ eld, geld, held,
meld, shelled, weld, beheld,
danegeld, handheld, hard-
shelled, upheld, withhold,
jet-propelled, self-propelled,
unparalleled—*also -ed forms
of verbs listed at* ¹EL

²eld \el\ see ¹EL

³eld \elt\ see ELT

elda \el-də\ Zelda, Dar el
Belda

eldam \el-dəm\ see ELDOM

elder \el-dər\ elder, welder

eldom \el-dəm\ beldam,
seldom, hoteldom

eldon \el-dən\ Sheldon,
Weldon

eldt \elt\ see ELT

ele \ā-lē\ see AILY

²ele \el\ see ¹EL

³ele \el-ē\ see ELLY

⁴ele \ē-lē\ see EELY

¹eled \eld\ see ¹ELD

²eled \ēld\ see IELD

elen \el-ən\ see ELON

elena \el-ə-nə\ Elena, Helena

elens \el-ənz\ Saint Helens,
Mount Saint Helens—*also -s,*

-'s, *and* -s' *forms of nouns
listed at* ELON

eleon \ēl-yən\ *see* ²ELIAN

eletal \el-ət-ᵊl\ pelletal,
skeletal

eleton \el-ət-ᵊn\ gelatin,
skeleton

eleus \ē-lē-əs\ *see* ELIOUS

elf \elf\ elf, Guelf, pelf, self,
shelf, bookshelf, herself,
hisself, himself, itself, meself,
myself, nonself, oneself,
ourself, top-shelf, thyself,
yourself, mantelshelf, do-it-
yourself

elfish \el-fish\ elfish, selfish,
unselfish

elhi \el-ē\ *see* ELLY

eli \el-ē\ *see* ELLY

¹elia \ēl-yə\ Delia, Lelia,
Shelia, Amelia, camellia,
Camellia, Cecilia, Cornelia,
Karelia, lobelia, obelia,
Ophelia, Rumelia, sedilia,
stapelia, psychedelia,
seguidilla

²elia \il-ē-ə\ *see* ¹ILIA

elial \ē-lē-əl\ Belial, epithelial

¹elian \ē-lē-ən\ Melian, Pelion,
abelian, Karelian, Mendelian

²elian \ēl-yən\ anthelion,
aphelion, carnelian,
chameleon, cornelian,
Mendelian, parhelion,
perihelion, Aristotelian,
Mephistophelian

³elian \ē-lē-ən\ *see* ELLIAN

elible \el-ə-bəl\ *see* ELLABLE

¹elic \ē-lik\ parhelic, autotelic

²elic \el-ik\ melic, relic, telic,
angelic, Goidelic, smart
aleck, archangelic, autotelic,
philatelic, psychedelic

elical \el-i-kəl\ helical,
pellicle, angelical, double-
helical, evangelical

elier \el-yer\ *see* ELURE

elin \ē-lən\ shieling, theelin

¹elion \el-ē-ən\ *see* ELLIAN

²elion \ēl-yən\ *see* ²ELIAN

³elion \ē-lē-ən\ *see* ¹ELIAN

elios \ē-lē-əs\ *see* ELIOUS

elious \ē-lē-əs\ Helios, Peleus,
Cornelius, contumelious

elish \el-ish\ *see* ELLISH

elist \el-əst\ cellist, trellised,
Nobelist, pastelist

¹elius \ā-lē-əs\ *see* ALIUS

²elius \ē-lē-əs\ *see* ELIOUS

elix \ē-liks\ Felix, helix,
double helix

¹elk \elk\ elk, whelk

²elk \ilk\ *see* ILK

ell \el\ *see* ¹EL

e'll \ēl\ *see* ²EAL

ella \el-ə\ Celle, Della, Ella,
fella, fellah, stella, Stella,
Benguela, candela, Capella,
Estella, favela, Gisela,
glabella, lamella, Luella,
Marcella, Mandela, novella,
paella, patella, prunella,
quiniela, rubella, sequela,
umbrella, vanilla, a cappella,
Cinderella, citronella,
columella, fraxinella,
Isabella, mortadella,
mozzarella, panatela,
salmonella, sarsaparilla,
subumbrella, tarantella,
villanella, valpolicella

ellable \el-ə-bəl\ fellable,
gelable, compellable,
expellable, indelible

ellah \el-ə\ *see* ELLA

ellan \el-ən\ *see* ELON

ellant \el-ənt\ gellant,
appellant, flagellant,
propellant, repellent, water-
repellent

ellar \el-ər\ *see* ELLER

ellas \el-əs\ *see* EALOUS

ellate \el-ət\ helot, pellet,
prelate, zealot, appellate,

flagellate, haustellate,
lamellate, scutellate
ellative \el-ət-iv\ see ELATIVE
¹elle \el\ see ¹EL
²elle \el-ə\ see ELLA
ellean \el-ē-ən\ see ELLIAN
elled \eld\ see ¹ELD
ellen \el-ən\ see ELON
ellent \el-ənt\ see ELLANT
eller \el-ər\ cellar, dweller,
feller, heller, Keller, seller,
sheller, smeller, speller,
stellar, teller, yeller, best-
seller, bookseller,
compeller, expeller,
foreteller, glabellar,
impeller, indweller,
lamellar, ocellar, patellar,
propeller, rathskeller,
repeller, rostellar, saltcellar,
tale-teller, cerebellar,
circumstellar, columellar,
fortune-teller, interstellar,
Rockefeller, storyteller
¹elles \el\ see ¹EL
²elles \elz\ see ELLS
ellet \el-ət\ see ELLATE
elletal \el-ət-ᵊl\ see ELETAL
elley \el-ē\ see ELLY
elli \el-ē\ see ELLY
ellia \ēl-yə\ see ELIA
ellian \el-ē-ən\ Chellean,
Boswellian, pre-Chellean,
Sabellian, triskelion,
Pantagruelian,
Machiavellian
ellicle \el-i-kəl\ see ELICAL
ellie \el-ē\ see ELLY
elline \el-ən\ see ELON
elling \el-iŋ\ belling, selling,
spelling, swelling, telling,
bookselling, compelling,
indwelling, misspelling, tale-
telling, upwelling, fortune-
telling, self-propelling—*also*
-*ing forms of verbs listed at*
¹EL

ellington \el-iŋ-tən\
Ellington, Wellington, beef
Wellington
ellion \el-yən\ hellion,
rebellion
ellis \el-əs\ see EALOUS
ellised \el-əst\ see ELIST
ellish \el-ish\ hellish, relish,
disrelish, embellish
ellist \el-əst\ see ELIST
ello \el-ō\ bellow, Bellow,
cello, fellow, Jell-O, mellow,
yellow, Yellow, bargello,
bedfellow, bordello, duello,
hail-fellow, Longfellow,
marshmallow, morello,
niello, Othello, playfellow,
schoolfellow, yokefellow,
Pirandello, punchinello,
ritornello, saltarello, Robin
Goodfellow, violoncello
ell-o \el-ō\ see ELLO
ellous \el-əs\ see EALOUS
¹ellow \el-ə\ see ELLA
²ellow \el-ō\ see ELLO
ells \elz\ Welles,
Dardanelles—*also* -s, -'s,
and -s' *forms of nouns listed
at* ¹EL, *and* -s *forms of verbs
listed there*
ellum \el-əm\ blellum,
skellum, vellum,
postbellum, rostellum,
antebellum, cerebellum
ellus \el-əs\ see EALOUS
elly \el-ē\ belly, Delhi, deli,
felly, jelly, Kellie, Kelly,
Nellie, shelly, Shelley,
Shelly, smelly, tele, telly,
wellie, New Delhi, nice-
nelly, potbelly, rakehelly,
sowbelly, Boticelli, nervous
Nellie, underbelly,
vermicelli, Machiavelli,
Dadra and Nagar Haveli
ellyn \el-ən\ see ELON
elm \elm\ elm, helm, realm,

whelm, overwhelm,
underwhelm
elma \el-mə\ Selma, Velma
elmar \el-mər\ see ELMER
elmer \el-mər\ Delmar,
Delmer, Elmer
elmet \el-mət\ helmet,
Helmut, pelmet
elmut \el-mət\ see ELMET
elo \ē-lō\ see ²ILO
elon \el-ən\ Ellen, Ellyn,
felon, Helen, melon, avellan,
Magellan, McClellan,
muskmelon, Snellen,
vitelline, Mary Ellen,
watermelon, Strait of
Magellan
elony \el-ə-nē\ felony, Melanie
elop \el-əp\ develop, envelop,
redevelop, overdevelop
elopment \el-əp-mənt\
development, envelopment,
redevelopment,
overdevelopment
elos \ā-ləs\ see AYLESS
elot \el-ət\ see ELLATE
elotry \el-ə-trē\ helotry,
zealotry
elp \elp\ help, kelp, skelp,
whelp, yelp
elsea \el-sē\ see ELSIE
elsh \elch\ see ELCH
elsie \el-sē\ Chelsea, Elsie,
Kensington and Chelsea
elson \el-sən\ keelson, nelson,
Nelson
elt \elt\ belt, celt, Celt, dealt,
delt, dwelt, felt, gelt, melt,
pelt, Scheldt, smelt, spelt,
svelte, veld, welt, black belt,
flybelt, forefelt, greenbelt,
heartfelt, hot-melt,
jacksmelt, Krefeld, self-belt,
snowbelt, snowmelt, Sunbelt,
Bielefeld, Roosevelt,
shelterbelt
elte \elt\ see ELT

elted \el-təd\ bias-
belted—*also* -ed *forms of
verbs listed at* ELT
elter \el-tər\ belter, melter,
pelter, shelter, skelter,
smelter, spelter, swelter,
welter, helter-skelter
eltered \el-tərd\ earth-
sheltered—*also* -ed *forms of
verbs listed at* ELTER
elting \el-tiŋ\ belting, felting,
melting, pelting—*also* -ing
forms of verbs listed at ELT
elure \el-yər\ velure, hotelier
elve \elv\ delve, helve, shelve,
twelve
elves \elvz\ elves, ourselves,
theirselves, themselves,
yourselves—*also* -s, -'s, *and*
-s' *forms of nouns listed at*
ELVE, *and* -s *forms of verbs
listed there*
elvin \el-vən\ Elvin, Kelvin,
Melvin, Melvyn
elvyn \el-vən\ see ELVIN
ely \ē-lē\ see EELY
¹em \em\ Clem, crème, em,
femme, gem, hem, m, mem,
phlegm, REM, Shem, stem,
them, ad rem, ahem, AM,
Arnhem, Belem, bluestem,
condemn, contemn, FM,
idem, in rem, item, mayhem,
millieme, modem, poem,
problem, pro tem, proem,
Shechem, ABM, anadem,
apothegm, apothem,
Bethlehem, diadem,
exanthem, ibidem, IgM,
meristem, OEM, SAM,
stratagem, ad hominem,
carpe diem, crème de la
crème, ICBM, post
meridiem, star-of-Bethlehem,
terminus ad quem
²em \əm\ see ¹UM
ema \ē-mə\ bema, Lima,

Pima, schema, Colima,
eczema, edema, diastema,
emphysema, Hiroshima, Iwo
Jima, Kagoshima,
Matsushima, terza rima,
Tokushima, ottava rima

emacist \em-ə-səst\ see
EMICIST

¹**eman** \em-ən\ see ²EMON

²**eman** \ē-mən\ see ¹EMON

emane \em-ə-nē\ see EMONY

emanence \em-ə-nəns\ see
EMINENCE

emanent \em-ə-nənt\ see
EMINENT

ematis \em-ət-əs\ see EMITUS

ematist \em-ət-əst\ see
EMITIST

ematous \em-ət-əs\ see
EMITUS

ember \em-bər\ ember,
member, December,
dismember, November,
remember, September,
disremember

¹**emble** \äm-bəl\ wamble,
ensemble

²**emble** \em-bəl\ tremble,
assemble, atremble,
dissemble, resemble,
disassemble

embler \em-blər\ temblor,
trembler, assembler,
dissembler

emblor \em-blər\ see
EMBLER

embly \em-blē\ trembly,
assembly, disassembly, self-
assembly, subassembly

¹**eme** \em\ see ¹EM

²**eme** \ēm\ see ¹EAM

emel \ā-məl\ see EMILE

emely \ēm-lē\ see EEMLY

¹**emen** \ē-mən\ see ¹EMON

²**emen** \em-ən\ see ²EMON

³**emen** \ā-mən\ see ¹AMEN

emer \ē-mər\ see EAMER

emeral \em-rəl\ femoral,
ephemeral

emery \em-rē\ emery, Emery,
Emory, memory

emesis \em-ə-səs\ emesis,
nemesis

emi \em-ē\ see EMMY

emia \ē-mē-ə\ anemia,
bohemia, Bohemia,
leukemia, toxemia,
academia, septicemia,
thalassemia, hypoglycemia,
hypokalemia, beta-
thalassemia

emian \ē-mē-ən\ anthemion,
Bohemian

¹**emic** \ē-mik\ emic, anemic,
graphemic, morphemic,
lexemic, phonemic, taxemic,
tonemic, epistemic

²**emic** \em-ik\ chemic,
alchemic, endemic,
pandemic, polemic,
sachemic, systemic, totemic,
academic, epidemic,
epistemic

emical \em-i-kəl\ chemical,
alchemical, polemical,
academical, biochemical,
epidemical, petrochemical,
biogeochemical

emicist \em-ə-səst\ polemicist,
supremacist

emics \ē-miks\ graphemics,
morphemics, phonemics,
proxemics

emile \ā-məl\ Emile, Memel

eminal \em-ən-ᵊl\ geminal,
seminal

eminate \em-ə-nət\ geminate,
effeminate

eminence \em-ə-nəns\
eminence, remanence,
preeminence

eminent \em-ə-nənt\ eminent,
remanent, preeminent

eming \em-iŋ\ Fleming,

Heminge, lemming—*also*
-ing *forms of verbs listed at*
¹EM

eminge \em-iŋ\ see EMING
emini \em-ə-nē\ see EMONY
eminy \em-ə-nē\ see EMONY
emion \ē-mē-ən\ see EMIAN
emis \ē-məs\ see EMUS
emish \em-ish\ blemish,
Flemish
emist \em-əst\ chemist,
polemist, biochemist
emitist \em-ət-əst\ Semitist,
systematist
emitus \em-ət-əs\ clematis,
fremitus, edematous
emlin \em-lən\ gremlin,
kremlin
emma \em-ə\ Emma, gemma,
lemma, stemma, dilemma
emme \em\ see ¹EM
emmer \em-ər\ emmer,
hemmer, stemmer, tremor,
condemner, contemner
emming \em-iŋ\ see EMING
emmy \em-ē\ Emmy, gemmy,
jemmy, phlegmy, semi,
stemmy
emn \em\ see ¹EM
emner \em-ər\ see EMMER
emnity \em-nət-ē\ indemnity,
solemnity
emo \em-ō\ demo, memo
¹emon \ē-mən\ demon,
freeman, Freeman, gleeman,
Piman, seaman, semen, Lake
Leman, pentstemon,
Philemon, cacodemon,
Lacedaemon
²emon \em-ən\ Bremen,
leman, lemon, Yemen
emone \em-ə-nē\ see EMONY
emony \em-ə-nē\ Gemini,
lemony, anemone, bigeminy,
Gethsemane, hegemony
emor \em-ər\ see EMMER
emoral \em-rəl\ see EMERAL

emory \em-rē\ see EMERY
emous \ē-məs\ see EMUS
emp \emp\ hemp, kemp,
temp
emperer \em-pər-ər\ emperor,
temperer
emperor \em-pər-ər\ see
EMPERER
emplar \em-plər\ Templar,
exemplar
emple \em-pəl\ semple,
temple
emps \äⁿ\ see ¹ANT
empt \emt\ dreamt, kempt,
tempt, attempt, contempt,
exempt, preempt,
undreamed, unkempt, tax-
exempt
emptable \em-tə-bəl\
attemptable, contemptible
emptible \em-tə-bəl\ see
EMPTABLE
emption \em-shən\
exemption, preemption,
redemption
emptive \em-tiv\ preemptive,
redemptive
emptor \em-tər\ tempter,
preemptor, caveat emptor
emptory \em-trē\ peremptory,
redemptory
emulous \em-yə-ləs\ emulous,
tremulous
emur \ē-mər\ see EAMER
emus \ē-məs\ Remus, in
extremis, Polyphemus,
polysemous
emy \ē-mē\ see EAMY
¹en \en\ ben, Ben, den, en,
fen, gen, glen, Glen, Glenn,
Gwen, hen, ken, Ken, Len,
men, n, pen, Penn, Rennes,
Seine, sen, Sten, ten, then,
wen, when, wren, Wren, yen,
Zen, again, amen, Ardennes,
Big Ben, Cayenne, Cevennes,
Cheyenne, Chosen, Dairen,

doyen, doyenne, Duchenne,
Fulcien, hapten, hymen,
Karen, La Tène, moorhen,
peahen, pigpen, Phnom
Penh, playpen, RN,
Touraine, Tynmen,
somewhen, Adrienne,
Debrecen, DPN, five-and-ten, FMN, julienne,
Kerguelen, La Fontaine,
LPN, madrilene, mise-en-scène, samisen, Sun Yat-sen,
TPN, carcinogen,
comedienne, equestrienne,
tamoxifen, tragedienne,
Valenciennes
²en \ēn\ see ³INE
³en \aⁿ\ see ⁴IN
⁴en \ən\ see UN
⁵en \äⁿ\ see ¹ANT
¹ena \ā-nä\ see ¹AENA
²ena \ā-nə\ see ²ANA
³ena \än-yə\ see ³ANIA
⁴ena \ē-nə\ see ²INA
enable \en-ə-bəl\ tenable,
amenable, untenable
enace \en-əs\ see ¹ENIS
enacle \en-i-kəl\ see ENICAL
enae \e-nē\ see ¹INI
enal \ēn-ᵊl\ penal, renal,
venal, adrenal, vaccinal,
duodenal
enancy \en-ən-sē\ tenancy,
lieutenancy, subtenancy
enant \en-ənt\ pennant,
tenant, lieutenant, se tenant,
subtenant, sublieutenant,
undertenant
enary \en-ə-rē\ hennery,
plenary, senary, venery,
centenary, millenary,
bicentenary, bimillenary,
quincentenary, tercentenary,
quatercentenary,
semicentenary,
sesquicentenary
enas \ē-nəs\ see ¹ENUS

enate \en-ət\ see ENNET
enator \en-ət-ər\ see ENITOR
ençal \en-səl\ see ENCIL
¹ence \ens\ see ENSE
²ence \äⁿs\ see ¹ANCE
³ence \äns\ see ²ANCE
encel \en-səl\ see ENCIL
enceless \en-sləs\ see
ENSELESS
encer \en-sər\ see ENSOR
ench \ench\ bench, blench,
clench, drench, french,
French, mensch, quench,
stench, tench, trench, wench,
wrench, entrench,
luftmensch, retrench,
unclench, workbench,
Anglo-French, Mariana
Trench
enchant \en-chənt\ see
ENTIENT
enched \encht\ trenched,
unblenched—also -ed forms
of verbs listed at ENCH
encher \en-chər\ see ENTURE
enchman \ench-mən\
Frenchman, henchman
encia \en-chə\ see ENTIA
encil \en-səl\ mensal, pencel,
pencil, stencil, tensile, blue-pencil, commensal, extensile,
Provençal, prehensile, red-pencil, utensil, intercensal
ençon \en-sən\ see ENSIGN
ency \en-sē\ Montmorency,
residency, nonresidency
end \end\ bend, blend,
blende, end, fend, friend,
lend, mend, rend, scend,
send, shend, spend, tend,
trend, vend, wend, Wend,
addend, amend, append,
ascend, attend, augend,
befriend, Big Bend, bookend,
boyfriend, closed-end,
commend, compend,
contend, dead end, dead-end,

defend, depend, descend,
distend, downtrend, emend,
expend, extend, forfend,
girlfriend, godsend,
hornblende, impend, intend,
Land's End, low-end,
missend, misspend, offend,
outspend, perpend,
pitchblende, portend,
pretend, propend, protend,
rear-end, resend, South
Bend, stipend, subtend,
suspend, transcend, unbend,
unkenned, upend, uptrend,
weekend, year-end,
adherend, apprehend, bitter
end, comprehend,
condescend, Damavend,
discommend, dividend,
minuend, overspend,
recommend, repetend,
reprehend, subtrahend,
vilipend, hyperextend,
misapprehend, overextend,
superintend—*also* -ed
forms of verbs listed at
¹EN

enda \en-də\ Brenda, Glenda,
Venda, addenda, agenda,
pudenda, corrigenda,
hacienda, referenda,
definienda

endable \en-də-bəl\ lendable,
mendable, spendable,
vendible, amendable,
ascendable, commendable,
defendable, dependable,
descendible, expendable,
extendable, unbendable,
comprehendable,
recommendable

endal \en-dᵊl\ Grendel,
Kendall, Mendel, Wendell,
prebendal, pudendal

endall \en-dᵊl\ see ENDAL

endance \en-dəns\ see
ENDENCE

endancy \en-dən-sē\ see
ENDENCY

endant \en-dənt\ see ENDENT

¹**ende** \end\ see END

²**ende** \en-dē\ see ENDI

ended \en-dəd\ ended,
splendid, befriended,
unfriended, double-ended,
open-ended,
undescended—*also* -ed *forms
of verbs listed at* END

endel \en-dᵊl\ see ENDAL

endell \en-dᵊl\ see ENDAL

endence \en-dəns\ tendance,
ascendance, attendance,
intendance, resplendence,
transcendence,
condescendence,
independence,
Independence,
superintendence

endency \en-dən-sē\
pendency, tendency,
ascendancy, dependency,
resplendency, transcendency,
superintendency,
independency

endent \en-dənt\ pendant,
pendent, splendent,
appendant, ascendant,
attendant, defendant,
dependent, descendant,
impendent, intendant,
respendent, transcendent,
independent, superintendent,
semi-independent

ender \en-dər\ bender,
blender, fender, gender,
lender, mender, render,
sender, slender, spender,
splendor, tender, vendor,
amender, ascender, attender,
auslander, bartender,
commender, contender,
defender, descender,
emender, engender,
expender, extender, fork-

tender, goaltender,
hellbender, intender,
offender, pretender,
surrender, suspender,
tailender, weekender,
double-ender, moneylender,
over-spender, self-surrender

endi \en-dē\ bendy, Mende,
trendy, Wendy, effendi,
modus vivendi

endible \en-də-bəl\ see
ENDABLE

endid \en-dəd\ see ENDED

ending \en-diŋ\ bending,
ending, pending, sending,
ascending, attending, fence-
mending, goaltending,
heartrending, mind-bending,
unbending, unending,
uncomprehending,
unpretending,
uncomprehending—*also* -ing
forms of verbs listed at END

endium \en-dē-əm\
compendium, antependium

endless \end-ləs\ endless,
friendless

endliness \en-lē-nəs\
cleanliness, friendliness,
uncleanliness, unfriendliness

endly \en-lē\ cleanly, friendly,
loop of Henle, uncleanly,
unfriendly

endment \en-mənt\
amendment, intendment

endo \en-dō\ kendo,
crescendo, stringendo,
decrescendo, innuendo,
diminuendo

endor \en-dər\ see ENDER

endous \en-dəs\ horrendous,
stupendous, tremendous

endron \en-drən\
philodendron, rhododendron

ends \enz\ see ¹ENS

endum \en-dəm\ addendum,
agendum, pudendum,

corrigendum, referendum,
definiendum

endy \en-dē\ see ENDI

¹**ene** \ā-nā\ nene, sene

²**ene** \en\ see ¹EN

³**ene** \en-ē\ see ENNY

⁴**ene** \ē-nē\ see ¹INI

⁵**ene** \ēn\ see ³INE

⁶**ene** \ān\ see ¹ANE

enel \en-ᵊl\ see ENNEL

eneous \ē-nē-əs\ genius,
homogeneous,
heterogeneous

ener \ē-nər\ see EANER

enerable \en-rə-bəl\
generable, venerable,
regenerable

eneracy \en-rə-sē\
degeneracy, regeneracy

enerate \en-rət\ degenerate,
regenerate, unregenerate

enerative \en-rət-iv\
generative, degenerative,
regenerative,
neurodegenerative

eneris \en-ə-rəs\ mons
veneris, sui generis

¹**enery** \en-ə-rē\ see ²ENARY

²**enery** \ēn-rē\ see EANERY

¹**enet** \en-ət\ see ENNET

²**enet** \ē-nət\ see EANUT

¹**eng** \aŋ\ see ²ANG

²**eng** \əŋ\ see ¹UNG

enge \enj\ venge, avenge,
revenge, Stonehenge

engi \eŋ-gē\ dengue, sengi

english \iŋ-glish\ English,
Yinglish

engo \eŋ-gō\ marengo,
camerlengo

¹**ength** \eŋth\ length, strength,
full-length, half-length,
wavelength, understrength,
industrial-strength

²**ength** \enth\ see ENTH

engthen \eŋ-thən\ lengthen,
strengthen

engue \eŋ-gē\ see ENGI

enh \en\ see ¹EN

¹enia \ē-nē-ə\ taenia, Slovenia, sarracenia, schizophrenia

²enia \ē-nyə\ Armenia, Encaenia, Eugenia, gardenia, Ruthenia, Tigrinya

enial \ē-nē-əl\ genial, menial, venial, congenial

enian \ē-nē-ən\ Fenian, Armenian, Essenian, Icenian, sirenian, Slovenian, Tyrrhenian, Achaemenian, Magdalenian

¹enic \ēn-ik\ genic, scenic

²enic \en-ik\ fennec, pfennig, phrenic, splenic, sthenic, arsenic, asthenic, Edenic, Essenic, eugenic, Hellenic, hygienic, irenic, transgenic, allergenic, androgenic, autogenic, calisthenic, chromogenic, cryogenic, cryptogenic, hygienic, mutagenic, Panhellenic, pathogenic, photogenic, Saracenic, schizophrenic, telegenic, carcinogenic, cariogenic, hallucinogenic, hypoallergenic

enical \en-i-kəl\ cenacle, arsenical, galenical, ecumenical

enice \en-əs\ see ¹ENIS

enicist \en-ə-səst\ eugenicist, ecumenicist

enics \en-iks\ eugenics, euphenics, euthenics, hygienics, calisthenics, cryogenics—also -s, -'s, and -s' forms of nouns listed at ²ENIC

¹enie \en-ē\ see ENNY

²enie \ē-nē\ see ¹INI

enlence \ē-nyəns\ lenience, convenience, provenience, inconvenience

enlent \ēn-yənt\ convenient, prevenient

enim \en-əm\ see ENOM

enin \en-ən\ see ENNON

enior \ē-nyər\ senior, monsignor

¹enis \en-əs\ Denis, Dennis, Denys, genus, menace, tenace, tennis, Venice, frontenis, summum genus

²enis \ē-nəs\ see ¹ENUS

¹enison \en-ə-sən\ benison, Tennyson, venison

²enison \en-ə-zən\ benison, denizen, venison

enist \en-əst\ tennist, euthenist

enitive \en-ət-iv\ genitive, lenitive, philoprogenitive, polyphiloprogenitive

enitor \en-ət-ər\ senator, progenitor, primogenitor

enity \en-ət-ē\ see ENTITY

enium \ē-nē-əm\ hymenium, proscenium

enius \ē-nē-əs\ see ENEOUS

enizen \en-ə-zən\ see ²ENISON

enn \en\ see ¹EN

enna \en-ə\ Glenna, henna, senna, antenna, duenna, Gehenna, sienna, Vienna

ennae \en-ē\ see ENNY

ennant \en-ənt\ see ENANT

¹enne \en\ see ¹EN

²enne \en-ē\ see ENNY

³enne \an\ see ⁵AN

ennec \en-ik\ see ²ENIC

enned \end\ see END

ennel \en-ᵊl\ crenel, fennel, kennel, unkennel

enner \en-ər\ see ¹ENOR

ennery \en-ə-rē\ see ²ENARY

ennes \en\ see ¹EN

ennet \en-ət\ Bennett, genet,

jennet, rennet, senate,
sennet, sennit, tenet

ennett \en-ət\ see ENNET

enney \en-ē\ see ENNY

enni \en-ē\ see ENNY

ennial \en-ē-əl\ biennial,
centennial, decennial,
millennial, perennial,
quadrennial, quinquennial,
septennial, triennial,
vicennial, bicentennial,
bimillennial, postmillennial,
premillennial,
quincentennial,
tercentennial,
semicentennial,
sesquicentennial,
quadricentennial

ennies \en-ēz\ tennies—also
-s, -'s, and -s' forms of nouns
listed at ENNY

ennig \en-ik\ see ²ENIC

ennin \en-ən\ see ENNON

ennis \en-əs\ see ¹ENIS

ennist \en-əst\ see ENIST

ennit \en-ət\ see ENNET

ennium \en-ē-əm\ biennium,
decennium, millennium,
quadrennium,
quinquennium, triennium

ennon \en-ən\ Lenin, pennon,
rennin, tenon, antivenin

enny \en-ē\ any, benne,
benny, Benny, blenney,
Dene, Denny, fenny, genie,
Jennie, jenny, Jenny, many,
penni, penny, Penny,
antennae, catchpenny,
halfpenny, Kilkenny, Na-
dene, pinchpenny, sixpenny,
tenpenny, threepenny,
truepenny, twopenny,
lilangeni, spinning jenny

ennyson \en-ə-sən\ see
¹ENISON

¹eno \ān-yō\ segno, dal segno,
jalapeño

²eno \en-ō\ steno, ripieno

³eno \ā-nō\ see ²ANO

enoch \ē-nik\ see ¹INIC

enom \en-əm\ denim, plenum,
venom, envenom

enon \en-ən\ see ENNON

¹enor \en-ər\ Brenner, Jenner,
tenner, tenor, tenour,
countertenor, heldentenor

²enor \ē-nər\ see EANER

enour \en-ər\ see ¹ENOR

enous \ē-nəs\ see ¹ENUS

¹ens \enz\ cleanse, gens, lens,
amends, beam-ends,
weekends, sapiens, definiens,
locum tenens—also -s, -'s,
and -s' forms of nouns listed
at ¹EN, and -s forms of verbs
listed there

²ens \ens\ see ENSE

ensable \en-sə-bəl\ see
ENSIBLE

ensal \en-səl\ see ENCIL

ensary \ens-rē\ see ENSORY

ensch \ench\ see ENCH

ense \ens\ cense, dense,
fence, flense, gens, hence,
mense, pence, sense, spence,
tense, thence, whence,
commence, condense,
defense, dispense, expense,
immense, incense, intense,
missense, nonsense, offense,
prepense, pretense,
propense, sequence,
sixpence, subsequence,
suspense, twopence,
accidence, antisense,
commonsense, confidence,
consequence, diffidence,
evidence, frankincense,
multisense, nondefense,
providence, Providence,
recompense, residence, self-
defense, subsequence,
coincidence, ego-defense,
inconsequence, New

Providence, nonresidence,
self-confidence, self-evidence

enseful \ens-fəl\ menseful,
senseful, suspenseful

enseless \en-sləs\ fenceless,
senseless, defenseless,
offenseless

ensem \en-səm\ see ENSUM

enser \en-sər\ see ENSOR

ensian \en-chən\ see ENSION

ensible \en-sə-bəl\ sensible,
compensable, condensable,
defensible, dispensable,
distensible, extensible,
insensible, ostensible,
apprehensible,
commonsensible,
comprehensible,
incondensable, indefensible,
indispensable, reprehensible,
supersensible,
incomprehensible

ensign \en-sən\ ensign,
alençon

ensil \en-səl\ see ENCIL

ensile \en-səl\ see ENCIL

ension \en-chən\ gentian,
mention, pension, tension,
abstention, ascension,
attention, contention,
convention, declension,
descension, detention,
dimension, dissension,
distension, extension,
indention, intension,
intention, invention,
Laurentian, low-tension,
posttension, prehension,
pretension, prevention,
recension, retention,
subvention, suspension,
sustention, Vincentian,
Waldensian, Albigensian,
apprehension,
circumvention,
comprehension,
condescension,

contravention, hypertension,
hypotension, inattention,
reinvention, reprehension,
salientian, incomprehension,
misapprehension,
nonintervention,
overextension,
Premonstratensian

ensional \ench-nəl\ tensional,
ascensional, attentional,
conventional, declensional,
dimensional, extensional,
intensional, intentional,
unconventional,
tridimensional,
unidimensional

ensioner \ench-nər\ see
ENTIONER

ensis \en-səs\ see ENSUS

ensitive \en-sət-iv\ sensitive,
insensitive, hypersensitive,
oversensitive, photosensitive,
supersensitive

ensity \en-sət-ē\ density,
tensity, extensity, immensity,
intensity, propensity

ensive \en-siv\ pensive,
tensive, ascensive, defensive,
expensive, extensive,
intensive, offensive,
ostensive, protensive,
suspensive, apprehensive,
coextensive, comprehensive,
hypertensive, hypotensive,
inexpensive, inoffensive,
reprehensive, self-defensive,
counteroffensive, labor-
intensive

ensor \en-sər\ censer, censor,
fencer, sensor, spencer,
Spencer, Spenser, tensor,
commencer, condenser,
dispenser, extensor,
precensor, sequencer,
suspensor, biosensor—*also*
-er *forms of adjectives listed at*
ENSE

ensory \ens-rē\ sensory, dispensary, suspensory, extrasensory, multisensory, supersensory

¹**ensual** \en-chəl\ see ENTIAL

²**ensual** \ench-wəl\ see ¹ENTUAL

ensum \en-səm\ sensum, per mensem

ensurable \ens-rə-bəl\ censurable, mensurable, commensurable, immensurable, incommensurable

ensure \en-chər\ see ENTURE

ensus \en-səs\ census, consensus, dissensus, amanuensis

¹**ent** \ent\ bent, Brent, cent, dent, gent, Ghent, Gwent, hent, Kent, leant, lent, Lent, meant, pent, rent, scent, sent, sklent, spent, sprent, tent, Trent, vent, went, absent, accent, Advent, anent, ascent, assent, augment, besprent, cement, chimkent, comment, concent, consent, content, convent, descent, detent, dissent, docent, event, extent, ferment, foment, forewent, forspent, fragment, frequent, hellbent, indent, intent, invent, lament, loment, low-rent, mordent, outspent, outwent, percent, pigment, portent, present, prevent, quitrent, relent, repent, resent, segment, Tashkent, torment, unbent, wellmeant, wisent, accident, aliment, argument, circumvent, compartment, complement, compliment, confident, devilment,

diffident, discontent, document, evident, heaven-sent, implement, instrument, Jack-a-Lent, malcontent, nonevent, Occident, ornament, orient, president, provident, regiment, reinvent, represent, re-present, resident, sediment, self-content, Stoke on Trent, subsequent, supplement, underwent, coincident, disorient, experiment, ferrocement, inconsequent, misrepresent, nonresident, privatdocent, self-evident

²**ent** \änt\ see ²ANT

³**ent** \äⁿ\ see ¹ANT

enta \ent-ə\ menta, yenta, magenta, momenta, placenta, polenta, tegmenta, tomenta, irredenta, impedimenta

entable \ent-ə-bəl\ fermentable, presentable, preventable, documentable, representable, sedimentable

entacle \ent-i-kəl\ see ENTICAL

entage \ent-ij\ tentage, ventage, percentage

ental \ent-ᵊl\ cental, dental, dentil, gentle, lentil, mental, rental, cliental, fragmental, judgmental, parental, placental, segmental, accidental, adjustmental, apartmental, biparental, compartmental, complemental, condimental, continental, departmental, detrimental, developmental, documental, excremental, elemental, environmental, firmamental, fundamental, governmental,

grandparental, incidental,
incremental, instrumental,
managemental, monumental,
nonjudgmental, occidental,
oriental, ornamental,
regimental, rudimental,
sacramental, sentimental,
supplemental,
temperamental,
transcendental, vestamental,
coincidental, developmental,
experimental,
presentimental,
subcontinental,
transcontinental,
uniparental,
intercontinental,
interdepartmental,
intergovernmental,
semigovernmental

entalist \ent-ᵊl-əst\ gentlest,
mentalist, documentalist,
fundamentalist,
governmentalist,
incrementalist,
instrumentalist, orientalist,
sacramentalist,
sentimentalist,
transcendentalist,
environmentalist,
experimentalist

entalness \ent-ᵊl-nəs\ see
ENTLENESS

entance \ent-ᵊns\ see
ENTENCE

entary \en-trē\ gentry,
sentry, passementerie,
reentry, subentry,
alimentary, complementary,
complimentary,
documentary, elementary,
filamentary, integumentary,
parliamentary, rudimentary,
sedimentary,
supplementary, tenementary,
testamentary,
uncomplimentary,

unparliamentary,
semidocumentary

entative \ent-ət-iv\ tentative,
augmentative, fermentative,
frequentative, presentative,
preventative, argumentative,
representative,
misrepresentative

¹**ente** \en-tā\ al dente,
lentamente

²**ente** \ent-ē\ see ENTY

³**ente** \änt\ see ²ANT

ented \ent-əd\ tented,
augmented, contented,
demented, lamented,
segmented, untented,
battlemented, malcontented,
oriented, self-contented,
unfrequented,
unprecedented,
overrepresented,
underrepresented—*also* -ed
forms of verbs listed at ¹ENT

enten \ent-ᵊn\ Benton, dentin,
Denton, Kenton, Lenten,
Quentin, Trenton

entence \ent-ᵊns\ sentence,
repentance

enter \ent-ər\ center, enter,
mentor, renter, stentor,
tenter, venter, assenter,
augmentor, cementer,
concenter, consenter,
dissenter, incenter, indenter,
fermenter, frequenter,
inventor, precentor,
preventer, rack-renter,
reenter, repenter, subcenter,
tormentor, documenter,
epicenter, representer,
supplementer, hypocenter,
metacenter, experimenter,
hundred-percenter—*also*
-er *or* -or *nouns formed from
verbs listed at* ¹ENT

entered \en-tərd\ centered,
face-centered, self-centered,

body-centered—*also* -ed
forms of verbs listed at ENTER

enterie \en-trē\ see ENTARY

entful \ent-fəl\ eventful,
resentful, uneventful

enth \enth\ nth, strength,
tenth, crème de menthe

enthe \enth\ see ENTH

enthesis \en-thə-səs\
epenthesis, parenthesis

enti \ent-ē\ see ENTY

entia \en-chə\ dementia,
Florentia, sententia,
Valencia, differentia, in
absentia

ential \en-chəl\ cadential,
consensual, credential,
demential, essential,
eventual, potential,
prudential, sciential,
sentential, sequential,
tangential, torrential,
componential, conferential,
confidential, consequential,
deferential, differential,
evidential, existential,
expediential, exponential,
inessential, inferential,
influential, nonessential,
penitential, pestilential,
preferential, presidential,
providential, referential,
residential, reverential,
transferential, unessential,
circumferential,
equipotential, experiential,
inconsequential,
intelligential, interferential,
jurisprudential,
multipotential,
reminiscential

entialist \en-chə-ləst\
essentialist, existentialist

entian \en-chən\ see ENSION

entiary \ench-rē\ century,
penitentiary, plenipotentiary

entic \ent-ik\ lentic, argentic,

authentic, crescentic,
identic, inauthentic

entical \ent-i-kəl\ denticle,
penticle, tentacle,
conventicle, identical,
nonidentical, self-identical

entice \ent-əs\ see ENTOUS

enticle \ent-i-kəl\ see ENTICAL

entient \en-chənt\ penchant,
sentient, trenchant,
dissentient, insentient,
presentient

entil \ent-²l\ see ENTAL

entin \ent-²n\ see ENTEN

enting \ent-iŋ\ dissenting,
unrelenting—*also* -ing *forms
of verbs listed at* ¹ENT

ention \en-chən\ see ENSION

entionable \ench-nə-bəl\
mentionable, pensionable,
unmentionable

entional \ench- nəl\ see
ENSIONAL

entioned \en-chənd\
aforementioned, well-
intentioned—*also* -ed *forms
of verbs listed at* ENSION

entioner \ench-nər\
mentioner, pensioner,
tensioner

entious \en-chəs\
abstentious, contentious,
dissentious, licentious,
pretentious, sententious,
tendentious, conscientious,
unpretentious

entis \ent-əs\ see ENTOUS

entist \ent-əst\ dentist,
cinquecentist, irredentist

entity \en-ət-ē\ entity,
amenity, identity, nonentity,
obscenity, serenity,
coidentity, self-identity

entium \ent-ē-əm\ jus
gentium, unnilpentium

entive \ent-iv\ adventive,
attentive, incentive,

inventive, pendentive,
preventive, retentive,
argumentive, disincentive,
inattentive

entle \ent-ᵊl\ see ENTAL

entleness \ent-ᵊl-nəs\
gentleness, accidentalness

entment \ent-mənt\
contentment, presentment,
resentment, discontentment,
self-contentment

ento \en-tō\ cento, lento,
Trento, memento, pimento,
pimiento, seicento, trecento,
cinquecento, papiamento,
portamento, quatrocento,
Sacramento, aggiornamento,
divertimento,
pronunciamento,
risorgimento

enton \ent-ᵊn\ see ENTEN

entor \ent-ər\ see ENTER

entous \ent-əs\ prentice,
apprentice, argentous,
momentous, portentous,
compos mentis, filamentous,
ligamentous, non compos
mentis, in loco parentis

entral \en-trəl\ central,
ventral, subcentral,
dorsiventral

entress \en-trəs\ gentrice,
inventress

entric \en-trik\ centric,
acentric, concentric,
dicentric, eccentric,
acrocentric, androcentric,
Christocentric, egocentric,
ethnocentric, Eurocentric,
geocentric, phallocentric,
polycentric, theocentric,
topocentric,
anthropocentric, areocentric,
Europocentric, heliocentric,
selenocentric

entrice \en-trəs\ see ENTRESS

entry \en-trē\ see ENTARY

ents \ents\ gents, events,
dollars-and-cents—*also* -s,
-'s, *and* -s' *forms of nouns
listed at* ¹ENT, *and* -s *forms of
verbs listed there*

¹**entual** \en-chə-wəl\ sensual,
accentual, consensual,
conventual, eventual

²**entual** \en-chəl\ see ENTIAL

entum \ent-əm\ centum,
mentum, cementum,
momentum, per centum,
tegmentum, tomentum,
argumentum

enture \en-chər\ bencher,
censure, denture, drencher,
trencher, venture, wencher,
adventure, backbencher,
debenture, front-bencher,
indenture, misventure,
misadventure, peradventure

enturer \ench-rər\ censurer,
venturer, adventurer

enturess \ench-rəs\ see
ENTUROUS

enturous \ench-rəs\
venturous, adventuress,
adventurous

entury \ench-rē\ see ENTIARY

enty \ent-ē\ plenty, sente,
senti, tenty, twenty, aplenty,
licente, cognoscente, twenty-
twenty, Deo volente, dolce
far niente

enuis \en-yə-wəs\ see ENUOUS

enum \en-əm\ see ENOM

enuous \en-yə-wəs\ strenuous,
tenuis, tenuous, ingenuous,
disingenuous

¹**enus** \ē-nəs\ genus, lenis,
penis, venous, Venus,
Campinas, Delphinus,
Maecenas, Quirinus, silenus,
intravenous

²**enus** \en-əs\ see ¹ENIS

eny \ā-nē\ see AINY

enys \en-əs\ see ¹ENIS

¹enza \en-zə\ Penza, cadenza, credenza, influenza

²enza \en-sə\ Polenza, Vicenza, Piacenza

¹eo \ā-ō\ mayo, Mayo, cacao, paseo, rodeo, aparejo, Bulawayo, cicisbeo, zapateo, Montevideo

²eo \ē-ō\ see ²IO

¹eoff \ef\ see ¹EF

²eoff \ēf\ see ¹IEF

eoffor \ef-ər\ see EPHOR

eolate \ē-ə-lət\ triolet, alveolate, areolate, urceolate

eoman \ō-mən\ see OMAN

¹eon \ē-ən\ see ¹EAN

²eon \ē-än\ eon, freon, neon, prion

eonid \ē-ə-nəd\ see EANID

eopard \ep-ərd\ jeopard, leopard, peppered, shepard, shepherd

eopardess \ep-ərd-əs\ shepherdess, leopardess

eople \ē-pəl\ people, pipal, steeple, craftspeople, dispeople, laypeople, newspeople, salespeople, spokespeople, townspeople, tradespeople, tribespeople, unpeople, workpeople, anchorpeople, businesspeople, congresspeople

eopled \ē-pəld\ unpeopled—*also* -ed *forms of verbs listed at* EOPLE

eordie \ord-ē\ see ¹ORDY

eorem \ir-əm\ see ERUM

eorge \orj\ see ORGE

eorgian \or-jən\ see ORGIAN

eorist \ir-əst\ see ¹ERIST

eoul \ōl\ see ¹OLE

eous \ē-əs\ see ¹EUS

ep \ep\ hep, pep, prep, rep, schlepp, skep, step, steppe, strep, yep, Alep, crowstep, doorstep, footstep, goose-step, instep, lockstep, misstep, one-step, quickstep, salep, sidestep, two-step, unstep, corbiestep, demirep, overstep, step-by-step, Gaziantep

eparable \ep-rə-bəl\ reparable, separable, inseparable, irreparable

epard \ep-ərd\ see EOPARD

epe \āp\ see ¹APE

epee \ē-pē\ see EEPY

eper \ep-ər\ see EPPER

eperous \ep-rəs\ leprous, obstreperous

epey \ā-pē\ see APEY

eph \ef\ see ¹EF

epha \ē-fə\ ephah, Recife, synalepha, synaloepha

ephalin \ef-ə-lən\ cephalin, encephalon, enkephalin, acanthocephalan

ephaly \ef-ə-lē\ anencephaly, brachycephaly, microcephaly

ephen \ē-vən\ see EVEN

epherd \ep-ərd\ see EOPARD

epherdess \ep-ərd-əs\ see EOPARDESS

ephone \ef-ə-nē\ see EPHONY

ephony \ef-ə-nē\ Stefanie, Stefany, Persephone, telephony

ephor \ef-ər\ deafer, ephor, feoffor, heifer, zephyr, hasenpfeffer

ephrine \ef-rən\ epinephrine, norepinephrine

epht \eft\ see EFT

ephyr \ef-ər\ see EPHOR

epi \ā-pē\ see APEY

epid \ep-əd\ tepid, trepid, intrepid

epo \ēp-ō\ see EPOT

epot \ēp-ō\ depot, Ipo, pepo, el cheapo

epp \ep\ see EP

eppe \ep\ see EP

epped \ept\ see EPT

epper \ep-ər\ hepper, leper, pepper, stepper, Colepeper, Culpeper, sidestepper

eppy \ep-ē\ peppy, preppy, orthoepy

eprous \ep-rəs\ see EPEROUS

eps \eps\ biceps, forceps, triceps, quadriceps, editio princeps—*also* -s, -'s, *and* -s' *forms of nouns listed at* EP, *and* -s *forms of verbs listed there*

epsis \ep-səs\ skepsis, prolepsis, syllepsis, omphaloskepsis

epsy \ep-sē\ catalepsy, epilepsy, narcolepsy, nympholepsy

ept \ept\ crept, kept, sept, slept, stepped, swept, wept, accept, adept, backswept, concept, except, incept, inept, percept, precept, transept, upswept, windswept, yclept, high-concept, intercept, nympholept, overslept, self-concept—*also* -ed *forms of verbs listed at* EP

eptable \ep-tə-bəl\ see EPTIBLE

eptacle \ep-ti-kəl\ skeptical, conceptacle, receptacle

epter \ep-tər\ see EPTOR

eptible \ep-tə-bəl\ acceptable, perceptible, susceptible, imperceptible, insusceptible, unacceptable

eptic \ep-tik\ peptic, septic, skeptic, aseptic, dyspeptic, eupeptic, proleptic, sylleptic, antiseptic, cataleptic, epileptic, narcoleptic, nympholeptic

eptical \ep-ti-kəl\ see EPTACLE

eptile \ep-t^əl\ see EPTAL

eption \ep-shən\ conception, deception, exception, inception, perception, reception, subreption, apperception, contraception, interception, misconception, preconception, self-conception, self-perception

eptional \ep-shnəl\ conceptional, deceptional, exceptional, unexceptional

eptive \ep-tiv\ acceptive, conceptive, deceptive, exceptive, inceptive, perceptive, preceptive, receptive, susceptive, apperceptive, contraceptive, imperceptive

eptor \ep-tər\ scepter, accepter, acceptor, inceptor, preceptor, receptor, intercepter, interceptor

eptual \ep-chəl\ conceptual, perceptual

eptus \ep-təs\ conceptus, textus receptus

epy \ep-ē\ see EPPY

epys \ēps\ Pepys—*also* -s, -'s, *and* -s' *forms of nouns listed at* EEP, *and* -s *forms of verbs listed there*

equal \ē-kwəl\ equal, prequel, sequel, coequal, unequal

eque \ek\ see ECK

equel \ē-kwəl\ see EQUAL

equence \ē-kwəns\ frequence, sequence, infrequence, subsequence

equency \ē-kwən-sē\ frequency, sequency, infrequency

equent \ē-kwənt\ frequent, sequent, infrequent

equer \ek-ər\ see ECKER

¹**er** \ā\ see ¹AY

²**er** \er\ see ⁴ARE

³**er** \ər\ see ¹EUR

⁴**er** \ir\ see ²EER

¹**era** \er-ə\ era, Sara, Sarah, sclera, terra, caldera, Rivera, sierra, tiara, aloe vera, ciguatera, cordillera, guayabera, habanera, Halmahera, riviera, Riviera, Santa Clara

²**era** \ir-ə\ era, gerah, Hera, lira, Pyrrha, sera, sirrah, Vera, wirra, chimaera, chimera, hetaera, lempira, Madeira, mbira, Altamira

erable \ər-ə-bəl\ thurible, conferrable, deferrable, deterrable, inferable, preferable, transferable

erah \ir-ə\ see ²ERA

¹**eral** \ir-əl\ Cyril, feral, seral, spheral, virile

²**eral** \er-əl\ see ERIL

³**eral** \ər-əl\ see ERRAL

erald \er-əld\ Gerald, Harold, herald, Jerald, Jerold, Jerrold, Fitzgerald, FitzGerald

eraph \er-əf\ see ERIF

erapy \er-əld\ therapy, chemotherapy, chronotherapy, aromatherapy

eratin \er-ət-ᵊn\ keratin, Sheraton, Samaritan

erative \er-ət-iv\ see ¹ARATIVE

eraton \er-ət-ᵊn\ see ERATIN

erb \ərb\ blurb, curb, herb, kerb, Serb, verb, acerb, adverb, disturb, exurb, perturb, potherb, pro-verb, proverb, reverb, suburb, superb

erbal \ər-bəl\ burble, gerbil, herbal, verbal, deverbal, nonverbal, preverbal

erbalist \ər-bə-ləst\ herbalist, verbalist, hyperbolist

erbally \ər-bə-lē\ verbally, hyperbole, nonverbally

erber \ər-bər\ see URBER

erberis \ər-bər-əs\ berberis, Cerberus

erberus \ər-bər-əs\ see ERBERIS

erbet \ər-bət\ see URBIT

erbia \ər-bē-ə\ see URBIA

erbial \ər-bē-əl\ adverbial, proverbial

erbid \ər-bəd\ see URBID

erbil \ər-bəl\ see ERBAL

erbium \ər-bē-əm\ erbium, terbium, ytterbium

erbole \ər-bə-lē\ see ERBALLY

erbolist \ər-bə-ləst\ see ERBALIST

erby \ər-bē\ derby, Derby, herby, Kirby

ercal \ər-kəl\ see IRCLE

erce \ərs\ see ERSE

ercé \ers\ see ¹ARCE

ercel \ər-səl\ see ¹ERSAL

ercement \ər-smənt\ amercement, disbursement, reimbursement

ercer \ər-sər\ see URSOR

ercery \ərs-rē\ see URSARY

erch \ərch\ see URCH

ercia \ər-shə\ see ERTIA

ercial \ər-shəl\ Herschel, Hershel, commercial, inertial, controversial, uncommercial, semicommercial

ercian \ər-shən\ see ERTIAN

ercible \ər-sə-bəl\ see ERSIBLE

ercion \ər-zhən\ see ¹ERSION

ercis \ər-səs\ see ERSUS

ercive \ər-siv\ see ERSIVE

ercular \ər-kyə-lər\ see IRCULAR

ercy \ər-sē\ Circe, mercy,

Percy, pursy, gramercy,
controversy

erd \ərd\ see IRD

¹erde \erd\ see AIRED

²erde \ərd\ see IRD

³erde \ərd-ē\ see URDY

erder \ərd-ər\ birder, girder,
herder, murder, self-murder,
sheepherder

erderer \ərd-ər-ər\ see
URDERER

¹erdi \ər-dē\ see URDY

²erdi \er-dē\ Verdi,
Monteverdi

erdin \ərd-²n\ see URDEN

erding \ərd-iŋ\ wording,
sheepherding—*also* -ing
forms of verbs listed at IRD

erdu \ər-dü\ perdu, perdue,
Urdu

erdue \ər-dü\ see ERDU

erdure \ər-jər\ see ERGER

¹ere \er\ see ⁴ARE

²ere \er-ē\ see ¹ARY

³ere \ir\ see ²EER

⁴ere \ir-ē\ see EARY

⁵ere \ər\ see ¹EUR

e're \ē-ər\ see ¹EER

ère \er\ see ⁴ARE

ereal \ir-ē-əl\ see ERIAL

ereid \ir-ē-əd\ see ERIOD

erek \erik\ see ¹ERIC

erely \ir-lē\ see ¹EARLY

erement \er-ə-mənt\ see
ERIMENT

¹erence \ir-əns\ clearance,
adherence, appearance,
coherence, inherence,
incoherence, interference,
perseverance

²erence \ər-əns\ see URRENCE

³erence \er-əns\ see ARENCE

erency \ir-ən-sē\ coherency,
vicegerency

²erency \er-ən-sē\ see
ERRANCY

¹erent \ir-ənt\ gerent,

adherent, coherent, inherent,
sederunt, vicegerent,
incoherent

²erent \er-ənt\ see ¹ARENT

¹eren't \ərnt\ see EARNT

²eren't \ər-ənt\ see URRENT

ereo \er-ē-ō\ see ARIO

ereous \ir-ē-əs\ see ERIOUS

erer \ir-ər\ see ²EARER

¹eres \erz\ see AIRS

²eres \ir-ēz\ see ERIES

³eres \ərs\ see ERS

eresy \er-ə-sē\ clerisy, heresy

ereth \er-ət\ see ERIT

ereus \ir-ē-əs\ see ERIOUS

erf \ərf\ see URF

erg \ərg\ berg, burg, erg,
Augsburg, Boksburg,
exergue, hamburg, Hamburg,
Hapsburg, homburg, iceberg,
Lemberg, Limburg,
Lindbergh, Newburg,
Pittsburgh, Salzburg,
Sandburg, Strasbourg,
svedberg, Tilburg,
Drakensberg, Gutenberg,
Harrisburg, Inselberg,
Königsberg, Luxembourg,
Magdeburg, Nuremberg,
Toggenburg, Venusberg,
Wallenberg, Württemberg,
Rube Goldberg,
Johannesburg, St.
Petersburg, von Hindenburg,
Baden-Württemberg,
Pietermaritzburg,
Yekaterinburg, Roodepoort-
Maraisburg

ergative \ər-gə-tir\ ergative,
purgative

erge \ərj\ see URGE

ergeant \är-jənt\ see ARGENT

ergen \ər-gən\ Bergen,
Spitzbergen

ergence \ər-jəns\ convergence,
divergence, emergence,
immergence, insurgence,

resurgence, submergence

ergency \ər-jən-sē\ urgency, convergency, detergency, divergency, emergency, insurgency, counterinsurgency

ergent \ər-jənt\ see URGENT

ergeon \ər-jin\ see URGEON

erger \ər-jər\ merger, perjure, purger, scourger, urger, verdure, verger, deterger

ergh \ərg\ see ERG

ergic \ər-jik\ allergic, synergic, theurgic, demiurgic, dramaturgic, thaumaturgic, alpha-adrenergic, beta-adrenergic

ergid \ər-jid\ see URGID

¹ergne \ərn\ see URN

²ergne \ern\ see ²ERN

ergo \ər-gō\ ergo, Virgo

ergue \ərg\ see ERG

ergy \ər-jē\ see URGY

¹eri \er-ē\ see ¹ARY

²eri \ir-ē\ see EARY

¹eria \ir-ē-ə\ feria, Styria, Syria, Algeria, Assyria, asteria, bacteria, collyria, criteria, diphtheria, Egeria, franseria, Illyria, Liberia, Nigeria, plumeria, porphyria, Siberia, wisteria, cafeteria, cryptomeria, latimeria, sansevieria, washateria, opera seria

²eria \er-ē-ə\ see ARIA

erial \ir-ē-əl\ aerial, cereal, ferial, serial, arterial, bacterial, empyreal, ethereal, funereal, imperial, material, sidereal, venereal, vizierial, immaterial, magisterial, managerial, ministerial, presbyterial

¹erian \ir-ē-ən\ Adlerian, Assyrian, Aterian,

Cimmerian, criterion, Hesperian, Hutterian, Hyperion, Iberian, Illyrian, Mousterian, Mullerian, Pierian, Shakespearean, Spencerian, Spenglerian, Sumerian, valerian, Valerian, Wagnerian, Hanoverian, Presbyterian, Thraco-Illyrian

²erian \er-ē-ən\ see ¹ARIAN

¹eric \er-ik\ Berwick, cleric, Derek, derrick, Eric, Erich, Erik, ferric, Herrick, xeric, aspheric, chimeric, choleric, cholesteric, entheric, generic, Homeric, mesmeric, numeric, alphanumeric, atmospheric, climacteric, congeneric, dysenteric, esoteric

²eric \ir-ik\ lyric, pyric, pyrrhic, spheric, xeric, aspheric, chimeric, empiric, satiric, satyric, atmospheric, hemispheric, stratospheric, panegyric

erica \er-i-kə\ erica, Erica, Erika, America, esoterica, North America, South America, Latin America

¹erical \er-i-kəl\ clerical, chimerical, numerical, anticlerical

²erical \ir-i-kəl\ lyrical, miracle, spherical, spiracle, empirical, hemispherical

erich \erik\ see ¹ERIC

erics \er-iks\ sferics, hysterics—*also -s, -'s, and -s' forms of nouns listed at* ¹ERIC

eried \ir-ē-əd\ see ERIOD

eries \ir-ēz\ Ceres, series, dundrearies, miniseries—*also -s, -'s, and -s' forms of nouns listed at* EARY, *and -s forms of verbs listed there*

erif **152**

erif \er-əf\ seraph, serif, sheriff, teraph, sans serif

eriff \er-əf\ see ERIF

erik \erik\ see ¹ERIC

erika \er-i-kə\ see ERICA

eril \er-əl\ beryl, Beryl, Cheryl, Errol, feral, ferrule, ferule, Merrill, peril, Sherrill, Sheryl, sterile, Terrell, Terrill, imperil, chrysoberyl

erilant \er-ə-lənt\ see ERULENT

erile \er-əl\ see ERIL

erilous \er-ə-ləs\ perilous, querulous, glomerulus

eriment \er-ə-mənt\ cerement, experiment, gedankenexperiment

erin \er-ən\ see ¹ARON

ering \ar-iŋ\ see ¹ARING

eriod \ir-ē-əd\ myriad, nereid, Nereid, period, photoperiod

erion \ir-ē-ən\ see ¹ERIAN

erior \ir-ē-ər\ querier, anterior, exterior, inferior, interior, posterior, superior, ulterior, Lake Superior—also -er forms of adjectives listed at EARY

eriot \er-ē-ət\ see ¹ARIAT

erious \ir-ē-əs\ cereus, Nereus, serious, Sirius, cinereous, delirious, Guarnerius, imperious, mysterious, Tiberius, deleterious

¹eris \ir-əs\ see EROUS

²eris \er-əs\ see ERROUS

¹erist \ir-əst\ querist, theorist, verist, careerist, panegyrist—also -est forms of adjectives listed at ²EER

²erist \er-əst\ see ARIST

erisy \er-ə-sē\ see ERESY

erit \er-ət\ ferret, merit, terret, demerit, inherit, disinherit, Shemini Atzereth

eritable \er-ət-ə-bəl\ heritable,

veritable, inheritable

eritor \er-ət-ər\ ferreter, heritor, inheritor

erity \er-ət-ē\ ferity, ferrety, rarity, verity, asperity, celerity, dexterity, legerity, posterity, prosperity, severity, sincerity, temerity, insincerity, ambidexterity, subsidiarity

erium \ir-ē-əm\ Miriam, criterium, bacterium, collyrium, delirium, imperium, psalterium, atmospherium, magisterium, archaeobacterium

¹erius \er-ē-əs\ see ARIOUS

²erius \ir-ē-əs\ see ERIOUS

erjure \ər-jər\ see ERGER

erjury \ərj-rē\ perjury, surgery, microsurgery, neurosurgery

erk \ərk\ see ¹ORK

erker \ər-kər\ see ¹ORKER

erkin \ər-kən\ see IRKIN

erking \ər-kiŋ\ see ORKING

erkly \ər-klē\ clerkly, berserkly

erky \ər-kē\ birkie, jerky, murky, perky, smirky, turkey, Turkey, Turki, Albuquerque, herky-jerky

erle \ərl\ see ¹IRL

erlie \er-lē\ see AIRLY

erlin \ər-lən\ merlin, Merlin, merlon, Merlyn, purlin, yearling

erling \ər-liŋ\ see URLING

erlon \ər-lən\ see ERLIN

erlyn \ər-lən\ see ERLIN

erm \ərm\ see ¹ORM

erma \ər-mə\ dharma, Erma, herma, Irma, scleroderma, terra firma

ermal \ər-məl\ dermal, thermal, nonthermal, subdermal, transdermal, ectodermal, endothermal, epidermal, exothermal, hydrothermal, hypodermal, hypothermal

erman \ər-mən\ ermine, german, German, germen, Herman, Hermann, merman, sermon, Sherman, Thurman, vermin, determine, extermine, Mount Hermon, predetermine, cousin-german, Tibeto-Burman

ermanent \ərm-nənt\ permanent, determinant, impermanent, semipermanent

ermann \ər-mən\ see ERMAN

ermary \ərm-rē\ see IRMARY

erment \ər-mənt\ averment, conferment, deferment, determent, interment, preferment, disinterment

ermer \ər-mər\ see URMUR

ermes \ər-mēz\ Hermes, kermes

ermi \ər-mē\ see ERMY

ermic \ər-mik\ dharmic, thermic, geothermic, hypodermic, taxidermic, electrothermic

ermin \ər-mən\ see ERMAN

erminable \ərm-nə-bəl\ terminable, determinable, interminable, indeterminable

erminal \ərm-nəl\ germinal, terminal, preterminal, subterminal

erminant \ərm-nənt\ see ERMANENT

ermine \ər-mən\ see ERMAN

ermined \ər-mənd\ ermined, determined, self-determined, overdetermined

erminous \ər-mə-nəs\ terminus, verminous,

conterminous, coterminous

erminus \ər-mə-nəs\ see ERMINOUS

ermis \ər-məs\ dermis, kermis, kirmess, thermos, endodermis, epidermis, exodermis

ermit \ər-mət\ hermit, Kermit, Thermit

ermon \ər-mən\ see ERMAN

ermos \ər-məs\ see ERMIS

ermy \ər-mē\ fermi, germy, squirmy, wormy, diathermy, endothermy, taxidermy

¹**ern** \ern\ bairn, Bern, cairn, hern, Nairn, Auvergne, moderne, Pitcairn, Sauternes, Ygerne, art moderne

²**ern** \orn\ see URN

erna \ər-nə\ dharna, Myrna, sterna, Verna, cisterna

ernal \ərn-²l\ colonel, journal, kernel, sternal, vernal, diurnal, eternal, external, fraternal, hibernal, infernal, internal, maternal, nocturnal, paternal, supernal, coeternal, sempiternal, semidiurnal

ernary \ər-nə-rē\ fernery, ternary, turnery, quaternary

¹**erne** \ern\ see ¹ERN

²**erne** \orn\ see URN

erned \ornd\ see URNED

ernel \ərn-²l\ see ERNAL

erner \ər-nər\ see URNER

¹**ernes** \ern\ see ¹ERN

²**ernes** \orn\ see URN

ernest \ər-nəst\ see ERNIST

ernia \ər-nē-ə\ hernia, Hibernia

ernian \ər-nē-ən\ Hibernian, quaternion, Saturnian

ernible \ər-nə-bəl\ see URNABLE

ernie \ər-nē\ see ¹OURNEY

ernier \ər-nē-ər\ see OURNEYER

ernion \ər-nē-ən\ see ERNIAN

ernist \ər-nəst\ earnest, Earnest, Ernest, internist

ernity \ər-nət-ē\ eternity, fraternity, maternity, modernity, paternity, quaternity, coeternity, confraternity, sempiternity

ernment \ərn-mənt\ adjournment, attornment, concernment, discernment, internment

ernum \ər-nəm\ see URNUM

erny \ər-nē\ see ¹OURNEY

¹ero \ē-rō\ giro, gyro, hero, Hero, Nero, zero, subzero, antihero, superhero

²ero \er-ō\ aero, cero, Duero, Faeroe, faro, Faroe, pharaoh, taro, tarot, bolero, bracero, cruzeiro, Guerrero, Herero, Madero, montero, pampero, primero, ranchero, sombrero, torero, vaquero, burladero, caballero, Mescalero, novillero, banderillero, carabinero, embarcadero, Rio de Janeiro

³ero \ir-ō\ giro, guiro, gyro, hero, zero, primero

erod \er-əd\ Herod, out-Herod, viverrid

erold \er-əld\ see ERALD

eron \er-ən\ see ¹ARON

erous \ir-əs\ cerous, cirrous, cirrus, Eris, peeress, Pyrrhus, scirrhous, scirrhus, seeress, serous

erp \ərp\ see URP

erpe \ər-pē\ see IRPY

erque \ər-kē\ see ERKY

¹err \er\ see ⁴ARE

²err \ər\ see ¹EUR

erra \er-ə\ see ¹ERA

errable \ər-ə-bəl\ see ERABLE

errace \er-əs\ see ERROUS

erral \ər-əl\ bharal, scurrile, squirrel, conferral, deferral, demurral, referral, transferal

errance \er-əns\ see ARENCE

errancy \er-ən-sē\ errancy, aberrancy, coherency, inerrancy

errand \er-ənd\ errand, gerund

errant \er-ənt\ see ¹ARENT

erre \er\ see ⁴ARE

errell \er-əl\ see ERIL

¹errence \ər-əns\ see URRENCE

²errence \er-əns\ see ARENCE

errent \ər-ənt\ see URRENT

errer \ər-ər\ blurrer, stirrer, conferrer, deferrer, demurer, demurrer, deterrer, inferrer, preferrer, referrer, transferrer

erret \er-ət\ see ERIT

erreter \er-ət-ər\ see ERITOR

erria \er-ē-ə\ see ARIA

errible \er-ə-bəl\ see ¹EARABLE

erric \er-ik\ see ¹ERIC

errick \er-ik\ see ¹ERIC

errid \er-əd\ see EROD

errie \er-ē\ see ¹ARY

erried \er-ēd\ berried, serried, varied—also -ed forms of verbs listed at ¹ARY

errier \er-ē-ər\ burier, terrier, varier, bullterrier—also -er forms of adjectives listed at ¹ARY

errill \er-əl\ see ERIL

errily \er-ə-lē\ see ARILY

¹erring \ar-iŋ\ see ¹ARING

²erring \ər-iŋ\ see URRING

erris \er-əs\ see ERROUS

errol \er-əl\ see ERIL

errold \er-əld\ see ERALD

erron \er-ən\ see ¹ARON

error \er-ər\ see ¹EARER

errous \er-əs\ derris, Eris, ferrous, parous, terrace, nonferrous, millionairess

errule \er-əl\ see ERIL

erry \er-ē\ see ¹ARY

¹ers \ərz\ furze, hers, somewheres, Voyageurs—*also* -s, -'s, *and* -s' *forms of nouns listed at* ¹EUR, *and* -s *forms of verbs listed there*

²ers \ā\ see ¹AY

ersa \ər-sə\ bursa, Bursa, vice versa

ersable \ər-sə-bəl\ see ERSIBLE

¹ersal \ər-səl\ bursal, tercel, versal, dispersal, rehearsal, reversal, transversal, traversal, universal

²ersal \är-səl\ see ARSAL

ersant \ərs-ᵊnt\ versant, conversant

ersary \ərs-rē\ see URSARY

erse \ərs\ birse, burse, curse, Erse, hearse, nurse, perse, purse, terce, terse, thyrse, verse, worse, adverse, amerce, asperse, averse, coerce, commerce, converse, cutpurse, disburse, disperse, diverse, immerse, inverse, Nez Perce, obverse, perverse, rehearse, reverse, sesterce, stress-verse, submerse, transverse, traverse, intersperse, reimburse, universe

ersed \ərst\ see URST

erser \ər-sər\ see URSOR

ersey \ər-zē\ furzy, jersey, Jersey, kersey, Mersey, New Jersey

erschel \ər-shəl\ see ERCIAL

ershel \ər-shəl\ see ERCIAL

ersial \ər-shəl\ see ERCIAL

ersian \ər-zhən\ see ¹ERSION

ersible \ər-sə-bəl\ coercible, conversable, dispersible, eversible, immersible, reversible, submersible, traversable, incoercible, irreversible, semisubmersible

¹ersion \ər-zhən\ Persian, version, aspersion, aversion, coercion, conversion, dispersion, diversion, emersion, eversion, excursion, immersion, incursion, inversion, perversion, recursion, reversion, submersion, subversion, ambiversion, extroversion, interspersion, introversion, reconversion, retroversion, animadversion, seroconversion

²ersion \ər-shən\ see ERTIAN

ersional \ərzh-nəl\ versional, conversional, reversional

ersionist \ərzh-nəst\ diversionist, excursionist

¹ersity \ər-sət-ē\ adversity, diversity, multiversity, university, biodiversity

²ersity \ər-stē\ see IRSTY

ersive \ər-siv\ cursive, ambersive, aversive, coercive, detersive, discursive, dispersive, excursive, inversive, perversive, recursive, subversive, extroversive, introversive

erson \ərs-ᵊn\ person, worsen, chairperson, craftsperson, draftsperson, houseperson, MacPherson, newsperson, nonperson, salesperson, spokesperson, unperson, anchorperson, businessperson, gentleperson, weatherperson

erst \ərst\ see URST

ersted \ər-stəd\ oersted, worsted, kilooersted

ersus \ər-səs\ cercis, thyrsus, versus, excursus

ersy \ər-sē\ see ERCY

¹**ert** \ərt\ Bert, blurt, Burt, chert, curt, dirt, flirt, girt, hurt, Kurt, pert, quirt, shirt, skirt, spurt, squirt, sturt, vert, wert, wort, advert, alert, assert, avert, bellwort, birthwort, Blackshirt, brownshirt, Cape Vert, colewort, concert, convert, covert, desert, dessert, dissert, divert, evert, exert, expert, exsert, figwort, fleawort, frankfurt, glasswort, hoopskirt, hornwort, inert, insert, invert, lousewort, lungwort, madwort, milkwort, nightshirt, outskirt, overt, pervert, pilewort, ragwort, redshirt, revert, ribwort, saltwort, sandwort, Schubert, seagirt, soapwort, spearwort, spleenwort, stitchwort, stonewort, subvert, sweatshirt, toothwort, T-shirt, ungirt, undershirt, bladderwort, ambivert, butterwort, controvert, disconcert, extrovert, feverwort, inexpert, introvert, liverwort, malapert, miniskirt, mitrewort, moneywort, overshirt, overskirt, pennywort, pettiskirt, preconcert, reconvert, Saint-John's-wort, spiderwort, swallowwort, thoroughwort, undershirt, underskirt, animadvert, interconvert

²**ert** \er\ see ⁴ARE

³**ert** \at\ see ⁵AT

erta \ərt-ə\ Gerta, Alberta, Roberta

ertain \ərt-ᵊn\ burton, Burton, certain, curtain, Merton, uncertain

ertant \ərt-ᵊnt\ see ERTENT

erted \ərt-əd\ skirted, concerted, perverted, T-shirted, extroverted, miniskirted, undershirted— also -ed forms of verbs listed at ¹ERT

ertedly \ərt-əd-lē\ assertedly, concertedly, pervertedly

ertence \ərt-ᵊns\ advertence, inadvertence

ertent \ərt-ᵊnt\ advertent, revertant, inadvertent

erter \ərt-ər\ blurter, skirter, squirter, stertor, converter, inverter, subverter, controverter—also -er forms of adjectives listed at ¹ERT

¹**ertes** \ərt-ēz\ certes, Laertes

²**ertes** \ərts\ see ERTS

ertford \ärt-fərd\ see ARTFORD

erth \ərth\ see IRTH

ertha \ər-thə\ Bertha, Eartha

ertia \ər-shə\ Mercia, Murcia, inertia

ertial \ər-shəl\ see ERCIAL

ertian \ər-shən\ Mercian, tertian, assertion, Cistercian, desertion, exertion, insertion, self-assertion

ertible \ərt-ə-bəl\ convertible, invertible, controvertible, inconvertible, incontrovertible, interconvertible

ertile \ərt-ᵊl\ curtal, fertile, hurtle, kirtle, myrtle, Myrtle, spurtle, turtle, cross-fertile, exsertile, infertile, interfertile

ertinence \ərt-ᵊn-əns\

pertinence, purtenance,
appurtenance, impertinence

¹ertinent \ərt-ᵊn-ənt\
pertinent, appurtentant,
impertinent

²ertinent \ərt-nənt\ see
IRTINENT

erting \ərt-iŋ\ shirting,
skirting, disconcerting, self-
asserting—*also* -ing *forms of
verbs listed at* ¹ERT

ertion \ər-shən\ see ERTIAN

ertisement \ərt-əs-mənt\
advertisement,
divertissement

ertium \ər-shəm\ see URTIUM

ertive \ərt-iv\ furtive,
assertive, self-assertive,
unassertive

erton \ərt-n\ see ERTAIN

ertor \ərt-ər\ see ERTER

erts \ərts\ certes, hertz,
nerts, weltschmerz,
gigahertz, kilohertz,
megahertz—*also* -s, -'s, *and*
-s' *forms of nouns listed at*
¹ERT, *and* -s *forms of verbs
listed there*

erty \ər-tē\ see IRTY

ertz \ərts\ see ERTS

erule \er-əl\ see ERIL

erulent \er-ə-lənt\ sterilant,
puberulent, pulverulent

erulous \er-ə-ləs\ see
ERILOUS

erum \ir-əm\ theorem, serum

erund \er-ənd\ see ERRAND

erunt \er-ənt\ see ¹ARENT

erval \ər-vəl\ see ERVIL

ervancy \ər-vən-sē\ see
ERVENCY

ervant \ər-vənt\ fervent,
servant, maidservant,
manservant, observant

ervative \ər-vət-iv\
conservative, preservative,
archconservative,

neoconservative,
semiconservative

ervator \ər-vət-ər\ see
ERVITOR

erve \ərv\ curve, MIRV,
nerve, serve, swerve, verve,
conserve, deserve, disserve,
hors d'oeuvre, incurve,
observe, preserve, reserve,
self-serve, subserve,
unnerve, unreserve

erved \ərvd\ nerved,
decurved, deserved, recurved,
reserved, underserved,
unreserved— *also* -ed *forms
of verbs listed at* ERVE

ervency \ər-vən-sē\ fervency,
conservancy

ervent \ər-vənt\ see ERVANT

erver \ər-vər\ fervor, server,
deserver, observer,
preserver, timeserver

ervice \ər-vəs\ nervous,
service, disservice, full-
service, in-service, self-
service, interservice

ervil \ər-vəl\ chervil, serval,
servile

ervile \ər-vəl\ see ERVIL

erviness \ər-vē-nəs\
nerviness, topsy-turviness

erving \ər-viŋ\ Irving,
serving, deserving, self-
serving, timeserving,
unswerving—*also* -ing *forms
of verbs listed at* ERVE

ervitor \ər-vət-ər\ servitor,
conservator

ervor \ər-vər\ see ERVER

ervous \ər-vəs\ see ERVICE

ervy \ər-vē\ see URVY

erwick \er-ik\ see ¹ERIC

erwin \ər-wən\ Irwin,
Sherwin

¹ery \er-ē\ see ¹ARY

²ery \ir-ē\ see EARY

eryl \er-əl\ see ERIL

erz \erts\ see ¹ERTZ

¹es \ā\ see ¹AY

²es \äs\ see ¹ACE

³es \āz\ see ¹AZE

⁴es \es\ see ESS

⁵es \ēz\ see EZE

e's \ēz\ see EZE

¹esa \ā-sə\ mesa, Mesa, presa, omasa, Teresa, Theresa

²esa \ā-zə\ presa, impresa, marchesa, Bel Paese, Maria Theresa

esage \es-ij\ see ESSAGE

¹esan \āz-ᵊn\ see AZON

²esan \ēz-ᵊn\ see EASON

esant \ez-ᵊnt\ bezant, peasant, pheasant, pleasant, present, unpleasant, omnipresent

esas \ā-zəs\ Marquesas—*also* -s, -'s, *and* -s' *forms of nouns listed at* ²ESA

esce \es\ see ESS

escence \es-ᵊns\ essence, candescence, concrescence, excrescence, florescence, fluorescence, pearlescence, pubescence, putrescence, quiescence, quintessence, senescence, tumescence, turgescence, virescence, acquiescence, adolescence, arborescence, coalescence, convalescence, decalescence, defervescence, deliquescence, detumescence, effervescence, efflorescence, evanescence, incandescence, inflorescence, iridescence, juvenescence, luminescence, obsolescence, opalescence, prepubescence, preadolescence

escency \es-ᵊn-sē\ excrescency, incessancy

escent \es-ᵊnt\ crescent, Crescent, candescent,
canescent, concrescent, decrescent, depressant, excrescent, fluorescent, frutescent, incessant, increscent, liquescent, pearlescent, pubescent, putrescent, quiescent, rufescent, senescent, suppressant, tumescent, turgescent, virescent, acaulescent, acquiescent, adolescent, coalescent, convalescent, detumescent, effervescent, efflorescent, arborescent, evanescent, incandescent, inflorescent, intumescent, irridescent, juvenescent, luminescent, opalescent, phosphorescent, prepubescent, recrudescent, viridescent, antidepressant, preadolescent

escible \es-ə-bəl\ see ESSIBLE

escience \ēsh-əns\ nescience, prescience

escive \es-iv\ see ESSIVE

esco \es-kō\ alfresco, barbaresco

escue \es-kyü\ fescue, rescue

¹ese \ēs\ see IECE

²ese \ēz\ see EZE

³ese \ā-sē\ see ACY

esence \ez-ᵊns\ pleasance, presence, omnipresence

eseus \ē-sē-əs\ Theseus, Tiresias

¹esh \esh\ crèche, flèche, flesh, fresh, mesh, thresh, afresh, bobeche, calèche, crème fraîche, enmesh, gooseflesh, horseflesh, immesh, parfleche, refresh, tête-bêche, Bangladesh, Gilgamesh, intermesh, Marrakech, Andhra Pradesh, Madhya Pradesh, Uttar

Pradesh, Himachral Pradesh, Arunachal Pradesh

²esh \ash\ see ¹ECHE

³esh \ash\ see ³ASH

eshed \esht\ fleshed, meshed—*also* -ed *forms of verbs listed at* ¹ESH

eshen \esh-ən\ see ESSION

eshener \esh-nər\ see ESSIONER

esher \esh-ər\ see ESSURE

eshly \esh-lē\ fleshly, freshly, specially, especially

eshment \esh-mənt\ fleshment, enmeshment, refreshment

¹esi \ā-zē\ see AZY

²esi \ā-sē\ see ACY

¹esia \ē-shə\ geisha, Moesia, Letitia, Lucretia, Magnesia, Phoenicia, alpoecia

²esia \ē-zhə\ freesia, amnesia, esthesia, frambesia, magnesia, rafflesia, Silesia, Tunisia, analgesia, anesthesia, Austronesia, Indonesia, Melanesia, Micronesia, Polynesia, synesthesia

esial \ē-zē-əl\ mesial, ecclesial

¹esian \ē-zhən\ Friesian, Frisian, lesion, adhesion, Cartesian, cohesion, etesian, Salesian, Austronesian, holstein-friesian, Indonesian, Melanesian, Micronesian, Polynesian

²esian \ē-shən\ see ¹ETION

esias \ē-sē-əs\ see ESEUS

esicant \es-i-kənt\ see ESICCANT

esiccant \es-i-kənt\ desiccant, vesicant

esidency \ez-əd-ən-sē\ presidency, residency, nonresidency, vice-presidency

esident \ez-əd-ənt\ president, resident, nonresident, vice-president

esima \es-ə-mə\ Quinquagesima, Sexagesima, Septuagesima

esimal \es-ə-məl\ centesimal, millesimal, vigesimal, duodecimal, planetesimal, sexagesimal, infinitesimal

esin \ez-ⁿn\ resin, muezzin, oleoresin

esion \ē-zhən\ see ¹ESIAN

esis \ē-səs\ Croesus, thesis, tmesis, ascesis, askesis, esthesis, mimesis, prosthesis, anamnesis, catachresis, catechesis, Dionysus, exegesis, hyperkinesis, Peloponnesus, psychokinesis, telekinesis, amniocentesis

esium \ē-zē-əm\ see EZIUM

esive \ē-siv\ adhesive, cohesive, self-adhesive

esk \esk\ see ESQUE

esley \es-lē\ see ESSLY

eslie \es-lē\ see ESSLY

esne \ēn\ see ³INE

¹eso \ā-sō\ peso, say-so

²eso \ā-ō\ see ESSO

espass \es-pəs\ Thespis, trespass

espis \es-pəs\ see ESPASS

espite \es-pət\ see ESPOT

espot \es-pət\ despot, respite

esque \esk\ desk, grotesque, moresque, arabesque, Bunyanesque, copydesk, gigantesque, humoresque, Junoesque, Kafkaesque, picaresque, picturesque, plateresque, Rubenesque, Romanesque, sculpturesque, statuesque, churrigueresque

ess \es\ bless, cess, chess, cress, dress, ess, fess, guess,

Hesse, jess, less, loess, mess,
ness, press, s, stress, tress,
yes, abscess, access, address,
aggress, assess, caress,
clothespress, coatdress,
compress, confess, CS,
depress, digress, distress,
duress, egress, excess,
express, finesse, handpress,
headdress, housedress,
impress, ingress, largess,
Meknes, nightdress, noblesse,
obsess, oppress, outguess,
pantdress, possess, precess,
prestress, princess, process,
profess, progress, re-press,
recess, redress, regress,
repress, shirtdress, sidedress,
SS, success, sundress,
suppress, top-dress,
transgress, undress, unless,
winepress, ABS, acquiesce,
baroness, coalesce,
convalesce, DES,
decompress, deliquesce,
derepress, dispossess,
effervesce, effloresce,
evanesce, gentilesse, GR-S,
IHS, in-process, incandesce,
intumesce, inverness,
Inverness, letterpress,
luminesce, Lyonnesse,
minidress, nonetheless,
obsolesce, otherguess,
overdress, pennycress,
phosphoresce, politesse,
prepossess, preprocess,
recrudesce, repossess,
reprocess, retrogress, second-
guess, SOS, sweaterdress,
unsuccess, watercress,
window-dress, another-guess,
nevertheless

essa \es-ə\ see ³ESSE
essable \es-ə-bəl\ see ESSIBLE
essage \es-ij\ message,
presage, expressage

essaly \es-ə-lē\ Cecily,
Thessaly
essamine \es-mən\ see
ESSMAN
essan \es-ᵊn\ see ESSEN
essancy \es-ᵊn-sē\ see ESCENCY
essant \es-ᵊnt\ see ESCENT
¹esse \es\ see ESS
²esse \es-ē\ see ESSY
³esse \es-ə\ Hesse, Odessa,
Vanessa
essed \est\ see EST
essedly \es-əd-lē\ blessedly,
confessedly, professedly,
possessedly, self-possessedly
essel \es-əl\ see ¹ESTLE
essen \es-ᵊn\ Essen, lessen,
lesson, messan, delicatessen
essence \es-ᵊns\ see ESCENCE
esser \es-ər\ see ESSOR
essex \es-iks\ Essex, Wessex
essful \es-fəl\ stressful,
distressful, successful,
unsuccessful
essian \esh-ən\ see ESSION
essible \es-ə-bəl\ decibel,
accessible, addressable,
compressible, confessable,
depressible, expressible,
impressible, processable,
putrescible, suppressible,
inaccessible, incompressible,
inexpressible, insuppressible,
irrepressible
essie \es-ē\ see ESSY
essile \es-əl\ see ¹ESTLE
ession \esh-ən\ cession,
freshen, hessian, session,
accession, aggression,
compression, concession,
confession, depression,
digression, discretion,
egression, expression,
impression, ingression,
obsession, oppression,
possession, precession,
procession, profession,

progression, recession,
refreshen, regression,
repression, secession,
succession, suppression,
transgression,
decompression,
dispossession, indiscretion,
intercession, intersession,
introgression,
misimpression,
prepossession, reimpression,
repossession, retrogression,
self-confession, self-
expression, self-possession,
supersession

essional \esh-nəl\ sessional,
accessional, concessional,
congressional, diagressional,
expressional, obsessional,
possessional, precessional,
processional, professional,
progressional, recessional,
successional,
preprofessional,
subprofessional,
paraprofessional,
semiprofessional

essioner \esh-nər\ freshener,
concessioner

essionist \esh-nəst\
expressionist,
impressionist, repressionist,
secessionist

essity \es-tē\ see ESTY

essive \es-iv\ crescive,
aggressive, caressive,
compressive, concessive,
degressive, depressive,
digressive, excessive,
expressive, impressive,
ingressive, obsessive,
oppressive, possessive,
progressive, recessive,
regressive, successive,
suppressive, transgressive,
inexpressive, retrogressive,
unexpressive, manic-
depressive

essly \es-lē\ Leslie, Lesley,
Wesley, expressly

essman \es-mən\ chessman,
pressman, expressman,
jessamine, specimen

essment \es-mənt\ see
ESTMENT

esso \es-ō\ gesso, espresso

esson \es-ᵊn\ see ESSEN

essor \es-ər\ dresser,
guesser, lesser, pressor,
stressor, addresser,
aggressor, assessor,
caresser, compressor,
confesser, depressor,
expressor, hairdresser,
oppressor, processor,
professor, regressor,
repressor, successor,
suppresssor, transgressor,
vinedresser, antecessor,
dispossessor, intercessor,
predecessor, repossessor,
second-guesser,
microprocessor,
multiprocessor

essory \es-ə-rē\ pessary,
accessory, possessory,
intercessory

essure \esh-ər\ pressure,
impressure, low-pressure,
refresher, acupressure,
overpressure

essy \es-ē\ Bessie, dressy,
Jesse, Jessie, messy

est \est\ best, breast, Brest,
chest, crest, gest, geste,
guest, hest, jessed, jest, lest,
nest, pest, prest, quest, rest,
test, tressed, vest, west,
West, wrest, zest, abreast,
appressed, armrest, arrest,
attest, backrest, beau geste,
behest, bequest, bird's-nest,
celeste, Celeste, compressed,
congest, conquest, contest,

detest, devest, digest, divest,
egest, field-test, flight-test,
footrest, gabfest, hard-
pressed, headrest, hillcrest,
houseguest, imprest, incest,
infest, ingest, inquest,
interest, invest, low-test, Mae
West, Midwest, molest,
northwest, posttest, pretest,
professed, protest, redbreast,
repressed, request, retest,
revest, slugfest, southwest,
suggest, trapnest, Trieste,
t-test, unblessed, undressed,
unrest, unstressed, almagest,
anapest, Bucharest,
Budapest, decongest,
disinfest, disinvest, empty-
nest, galley-west, manifest,
north-northwest, palimpsest,
predigest, reinvest,
rinderpest, second-best, self-
addressed, self-confessed,
self-interest, self-possessed,
supraprotest, sweatervest,
uninterest, unprofessed,
autosuggest, disinterest,
robin redbreast, underinvest,
thirty-second rest—*also* -ed
forms of verbs listed at ESS

esta \es-tə\ cesta, cuesta,
testa, vesta, Vesta, Avesta,
celesta, egesta, fiesta,
ingesta, siesta, Zend-Avesta

estable \es-tə-bəl\ see ESTIBLE

estae \es-tē\ see ESTY

estal \es-tᵊl\ crestal, pestle,
vestal

estan \es-tən\ see ESTINE

estant \es-tənt\ arrestant,
contestant, infestant,
protestant, Protestant,
decongestant, disinfestant,
manifestant

este \est\ see EST

ested \es-təd\ bested, crested,
nested, tested, vested, time-

tested, barrel-chested,
double-breasted, hairy-
chested, indigested,
single-breasted—*also* -ed
forms of verbs listed at
EST

ester \es-tər\ Chester, ester,
Esther, fester, Hester, jester,
Leicester, Lester, nester,
Nestor, pester, quaestor,
quester, questor, nester,
tester, wester, yester, zester,
ancestor, arrester, contester,
detester, digester, infester,
investor, Manchester,
molester, northwester,
Rochester, semester,
sequester, southwester,
sou'wester, suggester,
Sylvester, trimester,
Winchester, arbalester,
empty-nester, monoester,
polyester

esti \es-tē\ see ESTY

estial \es-tē-əl\ celestial,
forestial

estible \es-tə-bəl\ testable,
comestible, detestable,
digestible, ingestible,
investable, suggestible,
incontestable, indigestible

estic \es-tik\ gestic, domestic,
majestic, anapestic,
catachrestic

estical \es-ti-kəl\ see ESTICLE

esticle \es-ti-kəl\ testicle,
catachrestical

estimate \es-tə-mət\ estimate,
guesstimate

estinate \es-tə-nət\ festinate,
predestinate

estine \es-tən\ destine,
Preston, Avestan,
clandestine, intestine,
predestine

esting \es-tiŋ\ cresting,
vesting, westing,

arresting—*also* -ing *forms of
verbs listed at* EST

estion \es-chən\ question,
congestion, cross-question,
digestion, egestion, ingestion,
self-question, suggestion,
decongestion, indigestion,
self-suggestion,
autosuggestion

estis \es-təs\ cestus, testis,
Alcestis, asbestos,
Hephaestus

estival \es-tə-vəl\ estival,
festival

estive \es-tiv\ festive, restive,
congestive, digestive,
egestive, ingestive,
suggestive, decongestive

¹**estle** \es-əl\ Bessel, Cecil,
decile, nestle, pestle, sessile,
trestle, vessel, wrestle,
Indian-wrestle

²**estle** \as-əl\ see ²ASSEL

³**estle** \əs-əl\ see USTLE

estless \est-ləs\ crestless,
restless

estment \es-mənt\ vestment,
arrestment, assessment,
divestment, impressment,
investment, disinvestment,
reinvestment

esto \es-tō\ pesto, presto,
manifesto

eston \es-tən\ see ESTINE

estor \es-tər\ see ESTER

estos \es-təs\ see ESTIS

estra \es-trə\ fenestra,
orchestra, palaestra,
Clytemnestra

estral \es-trəl\ estral, kestrel,
ancestral, campestral,
fenestral, semestral,
orchestral

estrel \es-trəl\ see ESTRAL

estress \es-trəs\ see ESTRUS

estrial \es-trē-əl\ semestrial,
terrestrial, extraterrestrial

estrian \es-trē-ən\ equestrian,
pedestrian

estrous \es-trəs\ see ESTRUS

estrum \es-trəm\ estrum,
sequestrum

estrus \es-trəs\ estrous,
estrus, ancestress

estry \es-trē\ vestry, ancestry

estuous \es-chə-wəs\
incestuous, tempestuous

esture \es-chər\ gesture,
vesture

estus \es-təs\ see ESTIS

esty \es-tē\ chesty, testae,
testy, pesty, zesty, res gestae,
necessity, Tibesti

esus \ē-səs\ see ESIS

¹**et** \et\ bet, Bret, Brett, debt,
et, fret, get, jet, let, Lett,
met, net, pet, ret, set, stet,
sweat, Tet, threat, vet, wet,
whet, yet, abet, aigrette,
Annette, asset, Babette,
backset, baguette, banquette,
barbette, Barnet, Barnett,
barquette, barrette, beget,
beset, blanquette, boneset,
brevet, briquette, brochette,
brunet, burette, burnet,
cadet, cassette, cermet,
Claudette, Colette, coquet,
corvette, coset, courgette,
croquette, curette, curvet,
cuvette, daleth, dinette,
diskette, dragnet, duet, egret,
fan-jet, fishnet, flechette,
forget, frisette, gazette,
georgette, Georgette, gillnet,
godet, grisette, handset,
hard-set, headset, ink-jet,
inlet, inset, Janette, Jeanette,
Jeannette, Juliet, kismet,
layette, lorgnette, lunette,
Lynette, maquette,
Marquette, mind-set,
moonset, moquette, motet,

musette, Nanette, Nannette,
noisette, nonet, nymphet,
octet, offset, onset, Osset,
outlet, outset, paillette, palet,
pallette, palmette, Paulette,
pipette, piquet, planchette,
poussette, preset, quartet,
quickset, quintet, raclette,
ramet, regret, reset, revet,
rocket, roomette, rosette,
roulette, saw-whet, septet,
sestet, sextet, sharp-set,
soubrette, spinet, stylet,
sublet, subset, sunset,
Syrette, tacet, thickset,
Tibet, toilette, tonette, trijet,
twinset, typeset, unset, upset,
vedette, vignette, well-set,
Yvette, aiguillette, alphabet,
anchoret, andouilette,
anisette, Antoinette, avocet,
banneret, basinet, bassinet,
bayonet, Bernadette,
bobbinet, briolette,
burgonet, calumet, canzonet,
castanet, cellarette,
chemisette, cigarette,
clarinet, consolette, coronet,
corselet, crepe suzette,
dragonet, electret, en
brochette, epaulet, epithet,
etiquette, falconet,
farmerette, featurette,
flageolet, flannelette,
guillemet, heavyset, jaconet,
Juliett, kitchenette,
Lafayette, landaulet,
lanneret, launderette,
Leatherette, luncheonette,
maisonette, majorette,
marmoset, marquisette,
martinet, mignonette,
minaret, minuet, miquelet,
novelette, Olivet, oubliette,
parapet, paupiette, photoset,
pirouette, quodlibet,
rondelet, Samoset, satinet,

scilicet, sermonette,
serviette, silhouette,
sobriquet, solleret, somerset,
Somerset, soviet, spinneret,
statuette, stockinette,
suffragette, superjet,
swimmeret, taboret,
thermoset, towelette,
trebuchet, tricolette,
underlet, usherette,
vinaigrette, wagonette,
analphabet, bachelorette,
drum majorette, electrojet,
Hospitalet, marionette,
microcassette, micropipette,
musique concrète, photo-
offset, videlicet,
audiocassette, caulifloweret,
hail-fellow-well-met, Marie
Antoinette, videocassette

²et \ā\ see ¹AY

³et \ät\ see ¹ATE

⁴et \es\ see ESS

²eta \ät-ə\ see ²ATA

³eta \et-ə\ see ETTA

³eta \ēt-ə\ see ²ITA

¹etable \et-ə-bəl\ see
ETTABLE

²etable \ēt-ə-bəl\ see EATABLE

¹etal \ēt-ᵊl\ beetle, betel, fetal,
decretal, excretal

²etal \et-ᵊl\ see ETTLE

¹etan \et-ᵊn\ Breton, threaten,
Cape Breton, Tibetan

²etan \ēt-ᵊn\ see ¹EATEN

etch \ech\ catch, etch, fetch,
fletch, ketch, kvetch, lech,
letch, retch, sketch, stretch,
vetch, wretch, backstretch,
homestretch, outstretch

etched \echt\ teched,
farfetched—*also* -ed *forms of
verbs listed at* ETCH

etcher \ech-ər\ etcher,
catcher, fetcher, fletcher,
Fletcher, lecher, sketcher,
stretcher, cowcatcher,

dogcatcher, eye-catcher,
flycatcher, gnatcatcher

etching \ech-iŋ\ etching,
fletching—*also* -ing *forms of
verbs listed at* ETCH

etchy \ech-ē\ sketchy,
stretchy, tetchy

¹ete \āt\ *see* ¹ATE

²ete \et\ *see* ¹ET

³ete \ēt\ *see* ¹EAT

⁴ete \āt-ē\ *see* ATY

ête \āt\ *see* ¹ATE

eted \ād\ *see* ¹ADE

etel \ēt-ᵊl\ *see* ETAL

etely \ēt-lē\ *see* EETLY

eteor \ēt-ē-ər\ meteor,
confiteor—*also* -er *forms of
adjectives listed at* EATY

eter \ēt-ər\ *see* ¹EATER

etera \e-trə\ *see* ETRA

eterate \et-ə-rət\ *see* ETERIT

eterit \et-ə-rət\ preterit,
inveterate

etes \ēt-əs\ *see* ETUS

¹eth \eth\ Beth, breath,
breadth, death, saith, Seth,
snath, daleth, handbreadth,
hairbreadth, Macbeth,
Ashtoreth, isopleth,
megadeath, shibboleth,
Elisabeth, Elizabeth

²eth \ās\ *see* ¹ACE

³eth \āt\ *see* ¹ATE

⁴eth \et\ *see* ¹ET

etha \ē-thə\ Aretha, Ibiza

ethane \e-thān\ ethane,
methane, nitromethane,
dichloroethane

ethe \ē-thē\ *see* EATHY

¹ether \eth-ər\ blether,
feather, heather, Heather,
leather, nether, tether,
weather, wether, whether,
aweather, pinfeather, together,
untether, altogether, get-
together

²ether \ōth-ər\ *see* ¹OTHER

ethic \eth-ik\ ethic, erethic

ethral \ē-thrəl\ urethral,
bulbourethral

ethyl \eth-əl\ bethel, Ethel,
ethyl, methyl, triethyl

¹eti \ēt-ē\ *see* EATY

²eti \āt-ē\ *see* ATY

etia \ē-shə\ *see* ¹ESIA

etian \ē-shən\ *see* ¹ETION

¹etic \ēt-ik\ thetic, acetic,
docetic

etic \et-ik\ etic, thetic,
aesthetic, ascetic, athletic,
balletic, bathetic, cosmetic,
docetic, eidetic, emetic,
frenetic, gametic, genetic,
hermetic, kinetic, limnetic,
magnetic, mimetic, noetic,
Ossetic, paretic, pathetic,
phenetic, phonetic,
phrenetic, phyletic, poetic,
prophetic, prosthetic,
pyretic, splenetic, syncretic,
syndetic, synthetic, tonetic,
Venetic, alphabetic,
analgetic, anesthetic,
antithetic, apathetic,
asyndetic, copacetic,
cybernetic, diabetic, dietetic,
digenetic, diphyletic,
diuretic, empathetic,
energetic, epithetic, geodetic,
homiletic, Masoretic,
nomothetic, parenthetic,
sympathetic, synergetic,
synesthetic, aeromagnetic,
antimagnetic, antipathetic,
antipoetic, antipyretic,
apologetic, epexigetic,
epigenetic, ferrimagnetic,
ferromagnetic, geomagnetic,
gyromagnetic, homogametic,
hydrokinetic,
hydromagnetic,
hyperkinetic, isomagnetic,
monophyletic,

morphogenetic, ontogenetic, optokinetic, palingenetic, paramagnetic, pathogenetic, peripatetic, phylogenetic, polyphyletic, psychokinetic, telekinetic, thermomagnetic, aposiopetic, cyanogenetic, electrokinetic, electromagnetic, heterogametic, parasympathetic, parthenogenetic, psychotomimetic, unapologetic, onomatopoetic

etical \et-i-kəl\ metical, reticle, aesthetical, genetical, heretical, phonetical, antithetical, arithmetical, catechetical, cybernetical, epithetical, exegetical, geodetical, hypothetical, parenthetical, theoretical, atheoretical, epexegetical

eticist \et-ə-səst\ geneticist, kineticist, cyberneticist

etics \et-iks\ aesthetics, athletics, genetics, kinetics, phonetics, poetics, tonetics, cybernetics, dietetics, homiletics, apologetics, cytogenetics, immunogenetics—*also* -s, -'s, *and* -s' *forms of nouns listed at* ETIC

etid \et-əd\ fetid, fretted, sweated, indebted, parapeted—*also* -ed *forms of verbs listed at* ¹ET

etin \et-ᵊn\ *see* ¹EATEN

¹etion \ē-shən\ Grecian, accretion, Capetian, completion, concretion, deletion, depletion, excretion, Ossetian, Phoenician, repletion, secretion, suppletion, Tahitian, Austronesian, Diocletian, Melanesian, Polynesian, Taracahitian

²etion \esh-ən\ *see* ESSION

etious \ē-shəs\ *see* ECIOUS

¹etis \ēt-əs\ *see* ETUS

²etis \et-əs\ *see* ETTUCE

etist \et-əst\ cornetist, librettist, vignettist, clarinetist, exegetist, operettist—*also* -est *forms of adjectives listed at* ¹ET

etitive \et-ət-iv\ competitive, repetitive, uncompetitive, anticompetitive

etium \ē-shē-əm\ *see* ECIUM

etius \ē-shəs\ *see* ECIOUS

etive \ēt-iv\ accretive, completive, decretive, depletive, secretive, suppletive

¹etl \āt-ᵊl\ *see* ATAL

²etl \et-ᵊl\ *see* ETTLE

etland \et-lənd\ Shetland, wetland

etment \et-mənt\ abetment, besetment, curettement, revetment

¹eto \āt-ō\ *see* ²ATO

²eto \ēt-ō\ *see* ¹ITO

eton \ēt-ᵊn\ *see* ¹EATEN

¹etor \et-ər\ *see* ETTER

²etor \ēt-ər\ *see* ¹EATER

etory \ēt-ə-rē\ eatery, decretory, secretory, suppletory

etous \ēt-əs\ *see* ETUS

¹etra \e-trə\ Petra, tetra, etcetera

²etra \ē-trə\ Petra, Kenitra

¹etral \e-trəl\ petrel, retral

²etral \e-trəl\ *see* ¹ETREL

être \etrᵊ\ fête champêtre, raison d'être

¹etrel \e-trəl\ petrel, petrol, retral

²etrel \ē-trəl\ *see* ¹ETRAL

etric \e-trik\ metric, obstetric,

symmetric, asymmetric,
barometric, decametric,
dekametric, diametric,
dissymmetric, geometric,
hypsometric, isometric,
optometric, psychometric,
telemetric, volumetric,
acidometric, amperometric,
sociometric

etrical \e-tri-kəl\ metrical,
obstetrical, symmetrical,
asymmetrical, barometrical,
diametrical, geometrical,
unsymmetrical

etrics \e-triks\ obstetrics,
geometrics, isometrics,
sabermetrics

etrist \e-trəst\ metrist,
belletrist

etrol \e-trəl\ see ¹ETREL

ets \ets\ let's, Donets, rillettes,
Steinmetz, pantalets,
solonetz, Sosnowiec—*also* -s,
-'s, *and* -s' *forms of nouns
listed at* ¹ET, *and* -s *forms of
verbs listed there*

etsk \etsk\ Donetsk,
Kuznetsk, Lipetsk,
Novokuznetsk

ett \et\ *see* ¹ET

etta \et-ə\ betta, Etta, feta,
geta, Greta, Quetta, biretta,
cabretta, galleta, Loretta,
mozzetta, pancetta,
poinsettia, Rosetta, Valletta,
vendetta, anchoveta, arietta,
cabaletta, Henrietta,
Marietta, operetta,
sinfonietta

ettable \et-ə-bəl\ retable,
wettable, forgettable,
regrettable, unforgettable

ette \et\ *see* ¹ET

etter \et-ər\ better, bettor,
debtor, fetter, getter, letter,
netter, rhetor, setter,
sweater, tetter, wetter,

whetter, abettor, begetter,
bonesetter, enfetter, gill-
netter, go-getter, jet-setter,
newsletter, pacesetter,
pinsetter, red-letter, regretter,
trendsetter, typesetter,
unfetter, vignetter,
carburettor—*also* -er *forms of
adjectives listed at* ¹ET

ettered \et-ərd\ fettered,
lettered, unfettered,
unlettered

ettes \ets\ *see* ETS

ettia \et-ə\ *see* ETTA

ettie \et-ē\ *see* ¹ETTY

ettier \it-ē-ər\ *see* ITTIER

ettiness \it-ē-nəs\ *see* ITTINESS

etting \et-iŋ\ netting, setting,
bed-wetting, bloodletting,
go-getting, onsetting,
typesetting, thermosetting,
phototypesetting—*also* -ing
forms of verbs listed at ¹ET

ettish \et-ish\ fetish, Lettish,
pettish, wettish, coquettish,
novelettish

ettle \et-°l\ fettle, kettle,
metal, mettle, nettle, petal,
settle, shtetl, bimetal,
gunmetal, nonmetal,
teakettle, unsettle,
Citlaltepetl, Popocatepetl

ettlesome \et-°l-səm\
mettlesome, nettlesome

ettling \et-liŋ\ fettling,
settling, unsettling—*also*
-ing *forms of verbs listed at*
ETTLE

etto \et-ō\ ghetto, stretto,
cavetto, falsetto, in petto,
larghetto, libretto, palmetto,
stiletto, zucchetto,
allegretto, amaretto,
amoretto, fianchetto, **Kazan
Retto**, lazaretto, Tintoretto,
vaporetto

ettor \et-ər\ *see* ETTER

ettuce \et-əs\ lettuce, Thetis, Hymettus

ettus \et-əs\ see ETTUCE

¹**etty** \et-ē\ Betty, jetty, Nettie, netty, petit, petty, sweaty, yeti, brown Betty, cavetti, confetti, libretti, machete, Rossetti, spaghetti, amoretti, cappelletti, cavalletti, Donizetti, Serengeti, spermacetti, vaporetti

²**etty** \it-ē\ see ITTY

etum \ēt-əm\ pinetum, arboretum, equisetum

etus \ēt-əs\ Cetus, fetus, Thetis, treatise, acetous, Admetus, boletus, coitus, quietus, diabetes

etzsche \ē-chē\ see EACHY

euben \ü-bən\ Cuban, Reuben, Ruben, von Steuben

euce \üs\ see ¹USE

euced \ü-səd\ see UCID

eucey \ü-sē\ see UICY

euch \ük\ see UKE

euchre \ü-kər\ see UCRE

eucid \ü-səd\ see UCID

¹**eud** \üd\ see UDE

²**eud** \óid\ see ¹OID

eudal \üd-ᵊl\ see OODLE

eudist \üd-əst\ see ¹UDIST

eudo \üd-ō\ see UDO

eue \ü\ see ¹EW

euer \ü-ər\ see ¹EWER

euil \āl\ see AIL

euille \ē\ see ¹EE

euk \ük\ see UKE

eukin \ü-kən\ see UCAN

¹**eul** \əl\ see ¹ULL

²**eul** \ərl\ see ¹IRL

eulah \ü-lə\ see ULA

eulean \ü-lē-ən\ see ULEAN

¹**eum** \ē-əm\ geum, lyceum, museum, no-see-um, odeum, per diem, Te Deum, athenaeum, coliseum,

colosseum, hypogeum, mausoleum

²**eum** \ä-əm\ see AHUM

³**eum** \üm\ see ¹OOM

euma \ü-mə\ see UMA

eume \üm\ see ¹OOM

eumon \ü-mən\ see UMAN

eumy \ü-mē\ see OOMY

eunice \ü-nəs\ see EWNESS

eunt \ünt\ see ¹UNT

eunuch \ü-nik\ see UNIC

¹**eur** \ər\ birr, blur, buhr, burr, Burr, chirr, churr, cur, curr, err, fir, for, fur, her, knur, murre, myrrh, per, purr, shirr, sir, skirr, slur, spur, stir, thir, 'twere, were, whir, your, you're, à deux, as per, astir, auteur, aver, bestir, chasseur, chauffeur, claqueur, coiffeur, concur, confer, danseur, defer, demur, deter, douceur, du jour, farceur, flaneur, friseur, frondeur, hauteur, him/her, his/her, incur, infer, inter, jongleur, larkspur, liqueur, longspur, masseur, Malmö, millefleur, occur, Pasteur, poseur, prefer, recur, refer, sandbur, sandspur, seigneur, transfer, voyeur, accoucheur, amateur, cocklebur, colporteur, connoisseur, cri de coeur, cross-refer, cubature, curvature, de rigueur, disinter, force majeure, franc-tireur, monseigneur, nonconcur, pasticheur, prosateur, raconteur, rapporteur, regisseur, saboteur, secateur, underfur, voyageur, arbitrageur, carillonneur, conglomerateur, entrepreneur, litterateur,

provocateur, restaurateur, agent provocateur

²eur \ur\ see ¹URE

eure \ər\ see ¹EUR

eurial \ur-ē-əl\ see ¹URIAL

eurish \ər-ish\ see OURISH

eurs \ərz\ see ¹ERS

eury \ur-ē\ see URY

¹eus \ē-əs\ Aeneas, Aggeus, Alpheus, Arius, Chryseis, Linnaeus, Micheas, Piraeus, uraeus, coryphaeus, epigeous, scarabaeus, prelate nullius, Duque de Caxias, Judas Maccabaeus

²eus \üs\ see ¹USE

¹euse \əz\ buzz, 'cause, coz, does, fuzz, 'twas, was, abuzz, because, outdoes, undoes, overdoes

²euse \üs\ see ¹USE

³euse \üz\ see ²USE

¹eusel \ü-səl\ see ¹USAL

²eusel \ü-zəl\ see ²USAL

eut \üt\ see UTE

euter \üt-ər\ see UTER

euth \üth\ see ²OOTH

eutian \ü-shən\ see UTION

eutic \üt-ik\ see UTIC

eutical \üt-i-kəl\ see UTICAL

eutics \üt-iks\ toreutics, hermeneutics, therapeutics

eutist \üt-əst\ see UTIST

euton \üt-ᵊn\ see UTAN

eutonist \üt-ᵊn-əst\ see UTENIST

euve \əv\ see ¹OVE

euver \ü-vər\ see ³OVER

¹eux \ü\ see ¹EW

²eux \ər\ see ¹EUR

¹ev \ef\ see ¹EF

²ev \öf\ see ²OFF

eva \ē-və\ see ²IVA

eval \ē-vəl\ see IEVAL

evalent \ev-ə-lənt\ see EVOLENT

¹evan \ē-vən\ see EVEN

²evan \ev-ən\ see EAVEN

¹eve \ev\ breve, rev, Sevres, Negev, alla breve

²eve \ēv\ see ¹EAVE

evel \ev-əl\ bevel, devil, level, Neville, revel, baselevel, bedevil, bi-level, daredevil, dishevel, go-devil, split-level, entry-level

eveler \ev-lər\ leveler, reveler

evelly \ev-ə-lē\ heavily, levelly, reveille

evement \ēv-mənt\ achievement, aggrievement, bereavement, underachievement

even \ē-vən\ even, Stephen, Steven, breakeven, break-even, Genevan, Kesteven, uneven

eventh \ev-ənth\ seventh, eleventh

¹ever \ev-ər\ clever, ever, lever, never, sever, Trevor, dissever, endeavor, forever, however, soever, whatever, whenever, wherever, whichever, whoever, whomever, cantilever, howsoever, live-forever, whatsoever, whencesoever, whensoever, wheresoever, whichsoever, whomsoever, whosesoever, whosoever, whithersoever

²ever \ē-vər\ see IEVER

everage \ev-rij\ beverage, leverage

everence \ev-rəns\ reverence, severance, disseverance, irreverence

every \ev-rē\ every, reverie

eves \ēvz\ see EAVES

eviate \ē-vē-ət\ deviate, qiviut

evice \ev-əs\ clevis, crevice, Ben Nevis

evil \ē-vəl\ see IEVAL

eville \ev-əl\ see EVEL

evilry \ev-əl-rē\ devilry, revelry

evin \ev-ən\ see EAVEN

evious \ē-vē-əs\ devious, previous

¹**evis** \ev-əs\ see EVICE

²**evis** \ē-vəs\ see EVUS

evity \ev-ət-ē\ brevity, levity, longevity

evo \ē-vō\ in vivo, relievo, ring-a-lievo, alto-relievo, basso-relievo, mezzo-relievo, recitativo, Antananavivo

evocable \ev-ə-kə-bəl\ evocable, revocable, irrevocable

evolence \ev-ə-ləns\ prevalence, benevolence, malevolence

evolent \ev-ə-lənt\ prevalent, benevolent, malevolent

evor \ev-ər\ see ¹EVER

evous \ē-vəs\ grievous, Nevis, nevus, longevous, redivivus, Saint Kitts and Nevis

evsk \efsk\ see EFSK

evus \ē-vəs\ see EVOUS

evy \ev-ē\ bevy, heavy, levee, levy, replevy, top-heavy

¹**ew** \ü\ blue, boo, brew, chew, clew, clue, coo, coup, crew, cue, dew, do, doux, drew, due, ewe, few, flew, flu, flue, fou, glue, gnu, goo, hew, hue, Hugh, Jew, knew, lieu, loo, Lou, mew, moo, moue, mu, new, nu, ooh, pew, phew, piu, pooh, prau, q, queue, roux, rue, screw, shoe, shoo, shrew, Sioux, skew, slew, slough, slue, smew, sou, sous, spew, sprue, stew, strew, sue, Sue, thew, threw, thro, through, to, too, true, two, u, view, whew, who, woo, Wu, xu,

yew, you, zoo, accrue, adieu, ado, aircrew, airscrew, anew, Anjou, askew, au jus, Baku, bamboo, battu, battue, bedew, beshrew, bestrew, bijou, boubou, brand-new, breakthrough, burgoo, cachou, can-do, canoe, caoutchouc, Cebu, Cheng-du, Chongju, Chonju, construe, Corfu, corkscrew, coypu, CQ, debut, ecu, endue, ensue, eschew, floor-through, fondue, fordo, foreknew, Gansu, Gentoo, Gifu, gansun, gumshoe, guru, hairdo, hereto, Honshu, horseshoe, how-to, HQ, Hutu, imbrue, imbue, IQ, jackscrew, K2, Kansu, karoo, Karoo, kazoo, Khufu, kung fu, Kwangju, leadscrew, lean-to, make-do, Matthew, me-too, mildew, milieu, miscue, misdo, misknew, muumuu, Nehru, non-U, old-shoe, one-two, outdo, outgrew, perdu, Peru, poilu, preview, pursue, purview, ragout, redo, renew, Ren Crew, review, revue, rough-hew, run-through, sandshoe, see-through, set-to, setscrew, shampoo, Shih Tzu, skiddoo, snafu, snowshoe, soft-shoe, span-new, subdue, surtout, taboo, Taegu, tattoo, thank-you, thereto, thumbscrew, to-do, too-too, undo, undue, unglue, unscrew, untrue, vatu, vendue, venue, vertu, virtu, wahoo, walk-through, wherethrough, whereto, who's who, withdrew, worldview, aperçu, avenue, babassu, ballyhoo, barbecue, barley-broo, billet-doux, black-and-blue, buckaroo, bugaboo, callaloo, caribou, catechu, clerihew, cockapoo, cockatoo, Cotonou, counterview, déjà vu, derring-do, detinue, feverfew, follow-through, gardyloo, hitherto, honeydew, Ignaçu, ingenue, interview, IOU, jabiru, Jiangsu, kangaroo, Kathmandu, kinkajou, loup-garou, Makalu, manitou, marabou, Masaru, Montague, Montesquieu, ormolu, overdo, overdue, overflew, overgrew, overshoe, overstrew, overthrough, overview, parvenu, parvenue, pas de deux, passe-partout, PDQ, peekaboo, Port Salut, rendezvous, residue, retinue, revenue, Richelieu, Ryukyu, seppuku, Shikoku, succès fou, switcheroo, talking-to, teleview, Telugu, thereunto, thirty-two, thitherto, Timbuktu, tinamou, trou-de-loup, twenty-two, view halloo, vindaloo, w, wallaroo, waterloo, well-to-do, whoop-de-do, Xanadu, Aracaju, Brian Boru, didgeridoo, hullabaloo, Kota Bharu, Nova Iguaçu, Ouagadougou, pirarucu, Port du Salut, tu-whit tu-whoo, Vanuatu, Daman and Diu, Guangxi Zhuangzu, Ningxia Huizu, Havant and Waterloo

ew \ō\ see ¹OW

¹**ewable** \ō-ə-bəl\ see ¹OWABLE

²**ewable** \ü-ə-bəl\ see UABLE

ewage \ü-ij\ brewage, sewage

ewal \ü-əl\ see ¹UEL

ewar \ü-ər\ see ¹EWER

¹**eward** \ûrd\ see ¹URED

²**eward** \ü-ərd\ Seward, steward

ewd \üd\ see UDE

ewdness \üd-nəs\ see UDINOUS

¹**ewe** \ō\ see ¹OW

²**ewe** \ü\ see ¹EW

ewed \üd\ see UDE

ewee \ē-wē\ see EEWEE

ewel \ü-əl\ see ¹UEL

eweled \üld\ see OOLED

ewell \ü-əl\ see ¹UEL

¹**ewer** \ü-ər\ brewer, chewer, dewar, doer, ewer, fewer, hewer, queuer, screwer, sewer, skewer, spewer, suer, viewer, wooer, you're, horseshoer, me-tooer, misdoer, previewer, renewer, reviewer, shampooer, snowshoer, tattooer, undoer, wrongdoer, barbecuer, evildoer, interviewer, revenuer, televiewer—also -er forms of adjectives listed at ¹EW

²**ewer** \ûr\ see ¹URE

³**ewer** \ō-ər\ see ⁴OER

ewerage \ûr-ij\ see ¹OORAGE

ewery \ûr-ē\ see ¹URY

ewey \ü-ē\ see EWY

ewie \ü-ē\ see EWY

¹**ewing** \ō-iŋ\ see ¹OING

²**ewing** \ü-iŋ\ see ²OING

ewis \ü-əs\ see ²OUIS

ewish \ü-ish\ bluish, Hewish Jewish, newish, shrewish, aguish

ewl \ül\ see ¹OOL

ewless \ü-ləs\ clueless, crewless, dewless, shoeless, viewless

ewly \ü-lē\ see ULY

ewman \ü-mən\ see UMAN

ewment \ü-mənt\ strewment, accruement

ewn \ün\ see ¹OON

ewness \ü-nəs\ blueness, dueness, Eunice, newness, skewness, Tunis, askewness

ewpie \ü-pē\ see OOPY

ewry \ùr-ē\ see ¹URY

ews \üz\ see ²USE

ewsman \üz-mən\ bluesman, newsman

ewsy \ü-zē\ see OOZY

ewt \üt\ see UTE

ewter \üt-ər\ see UTER

ewterer \üt-ər-ər\ see UITERER

ewton \üt-²n\ see UTAN

ewy \ü-ē\ bluey, buoy, chewy, Dewey, dewy, flooey, gluey, gooey, hooey, Louie, Louis, newie, phooey, rouille, screwy, sloughy, viewy, chop suey, mildewy, Port Louis, ratatouille, waterzooi

ex \eks\ dex, ex, flex, hex, lex, rex, Rex, sex, specs, vex, x, annex, apex, carex, codex, complex, convex, cortex, culex, desex, duplex, DX, fourplex, ibex, ilex, index, Kleenex, Lastex, latex, mirex, murex, MX, narthex, perplex, Perspex, pollex, Pyrex, reflex, remex, Rx, scolex, silex, silvex, simplex, spandex, telex, Tex-Mex, triplex, unsex, vertex, videotex, vortex, analects, belowdecks, biconvex, circumflex, cross-index, googolplex, haruspex, intersex, Malcolm X, Middlesex, multiplex, PBX, pontifex, retroflex, spinifex, subindex, unisex—*also* -s, -'s, *and* -s' *forms of nouns listed*

at ECK, *and* -s *forms of verbs listed there*

exas \ek-səs\ see EXUS

exed \ekst\ see EXT

exedly \ek-səd-lē\ vexedly, perplexedly

exer \ek-sər\ flexor, hexer, duplexer, indexer, multiplexer, demultiplexer

exia \ek-sē-ə\ dyslexia, anorexia

exic \ek-sik\ dyslexic, anorexic

exical \ek-si-kəl\ lexical, indexical, nonlexical

exion \ek-shən\ see ECTION

exis \ek-səs\ see EXUS

exity \ek-sət-ē\ complexity, convexity, perplexity

exor \ek-sər\ see EXER

ext \ekst\ next, sexed, sext, text, vexed, context, deflexed, inflexed, perplexed, plaintext, pretext, reflexed, subtext, urtext, ciphertext, oversexed, teletext, undersexed—*also* -ed *forms of verbs listed at EX*

extant \ek-stənt\ extant, sextant

exterous \ek-strəs\ dexterous, ambidextrous

extrous \ek-strəs\ see EXTEROUS

extual \eks-chəl\ textual, contextual, subtextual

exual \eksh-wəl\ sexual, asexual, bisexual, effectual, pansexual, transsexual, ambisexual, homosexual, hypersexual, intersexual, parasexual, psychosexual, unisexual, heterosexual, sociosexual, anti-intellectual

exural \ek-shrəl\ see ²ECTURAL

exus \ek-səs\ lexis, nexus, plexus, texas, Alexis

exy \ek-sē\ prexy, sexy, apoplexy

¹ey \ā\ see ¹AY

²ey \ē\ see ¹EE

³ey \ī\ see ¹Y

¹eya \ā-ə\ see ¹AIA

²eya \ē-ə\ see ¹IA

eyance \ā-əns\ abeyance, conveyance, purveyance, surveillance, reconveyance

eyant \ā-ənt\ mayn't, abeyant, surveillant

eyas \ī-əs\ see IAS

ey'd \ād\ see ¹ADE

eye \ī\ see ¹Y

¹eyed \ēd\ see EED

²eyed \īd\ see ¹IDE

eyedness \id-nəs\ eyedness, snideness, cockeyedness

eyeless \ī-ləs\ see ILUS

eyelet \ī-lət\ see ILOT

eyen \īn\ see ¹INE

¹eyer \ā-ər\ see ¹AYER

²eyer \īr\ see ¹IRE

eyes \īz\ see IZE

eying \ā-iŋ\ see AYING

¹ey'll \āl\ see AIL

²ey'll \el\ see ¹EL

eyn \in\ see ¹IN

eynes \ānz\ see AINS

eyness \ā-nəs\ see AYNESS

eyor \ā-ər\ see ¹AYER

ey're \er\ see ⁴ARE

eyre \er\ see ⁴ARE

eyrie \īr-ē\ see ¹IRY

eys \ēz\ see EZE

eyser \ī-zər\ see IZER

eyte \ā-tē\ see ATY

ey've \āv\ see ²AVE

¹ez \ez\ see ¹AYS

²ez \ā\ see ¹AY

³ez \ās\ see ¹ACE

eza \ē-zə\ Giza, Lisa, Pisa, visa, mestiza, lespedeza

eze \ēz\ bise, breeze, cheese, ease, feaze, feeze, freeze, frieze, he's, jeez, lees, please, res, seize, she's, sleaze, sneeze, squeeze, tease, tweeze, wheeze, Andes, appease, Aries, Belize, betise, Burmese, camise, Castries, cerise, chemise, Chinese, deep-freeze, Deep-freeze, degrease, Denise, disease, displease, disseise, d.t.'s, Elise, fasces, fauces, Ganges, headcheese, heartsease, Hermes, Kirghiz, Louise, Maltese, marquise, menses, nates, Pisces, quick-freeze, Ramses, reprise, sharp-freeze, soubise, striptease, Tabriz, Thales, trapeze, unease, unfreeze, Xerxes, Amboinese, Androcles, Annamese, antifreeze, Assamese, Balinese, Brooklynese, Cantonese, Cervantes, Chersonese, Congolese, Cyclades. Damocles, diocese, Eloise, Erinyes, expertise, Faeroese, federalese, genovese, gourmandise, Hebrides, Heracles, Hercules, Hunanese, Hyades, Japanese, Javanese, Johnsonese, journalese, Kanarese, Lake Louise, legalese, litotes, manganese, Nipponese, overseas, Pekinese, Pekingese, Pericles, Pleiades, Portuguese, Pyrenees, Siamese, Silures, Sinhalese, Socrates, Sophocles, Sporades, Albigenses, antipodes, Aragonese, archdiocese, Averroës, bona fides, bureaucratese, cheval-de-frise, computerese, Diogenes, Dodecanese,

Eumenides, Euripides,
Florida Keys, Gaucher's
disease, governmentese,
Great Pyrenees, Hesperides,
Hippocrates, Hippomenes,
Hodgkin's disease, Indo-
Chinese, nephritides,
officialese, pentagonese,
Philoctetes, Sammarinese,
superficies, telegraphese,
Themistocles, Thucydides,
Vietnamese, Alcibiades,
Aristophanes, educationese,
ferromanganese, Lou

Gehrig's disease,
Mephistopheles, sociologese,
sword of Damocles, muscae
volitantes, Pillars of
Hercules—*also* -s, -'s, *and* -s'
forms of nouns listed at ¹EE,
and -s *forms of verbs listed
there*

ezel \ē-zəl\ *see* EASEL
ezi \ē-zē\ *see* ¹EASY
ezium \ē-zē-əm\ cesium,
magnesium, trapezium
ezzle \ez-əl\ bezel, embezzle

I

¹i \ē\ see ¹EE

²i \ī\ see ¹Y

³i \ā\ see ¹AY

¹ia \ē-ə\ Gaea, kea, Leah, Mia, rhea, Rhea, rya, via, Achaea, Crimea, althaea, Apia, Bahia, buddleia, cabrilla, cattleya, Chaldea, Euboea, Hygeia, idea, Judea, Kaffiyeh, Korea, mantilla, Maria, Medea, mens rea, Morea, Nicaea, ohia, Omiya, Oriya, ouguiya, rupiah, sangria, Sofia, Sophia, spirea, tortilla, Baile Atha Cliath, Banranquilla, barathea, bougainvillea, camarilla, Caesarea, cascarilla, Cytherea, dulcinea, Eritrea, fantasia, Galatea, gonorrhea, granadilla, hamartia, Hialeah, Idumea, Ikaria, Jicarilla, Kampuchea, latakia, Latakia, logorrhea, Manzanilla, mausolea, mythopoeia, Nabatea, Nicosia, panacea, Parousia, pizzeria, ratafia, sabadilla, Santeria, sapodilla, seguidilla, sinfonia, Tanzania, trattoria, alfilaria, Andalucia, Andalusia, Ave Maria, Cassiopeia, Diego Garcia, echeveria, Ismailia, peripeteia, pharmacopoeia, prosopopoeia, onomatopoeia, Joseph of Arimathea

²ia \ī-ə\ see ¹IAH

³ia \ä\ see ¹A

¹iable \ī-ə-bəl\ dryable, dyeable, flyable, friable, liable, pliable, triable, viable, deniable, inviable, reliable, certifiable, classifiable, justifiable, liquefiable, notifiable, pacifiable, qualifiable, quantifiable, rectifiable, satisfiable, specifiable, undeniable, unifiable, verifiable, emulsifiable, identifiable, unfalsifiable

²iable \ē-ə-bəl\ see EEABLE

iacal \ī-ə-kəl\ dandiacal, heliacal, maniacal, theriacal, zodiacal, ammoniacal, elegiacal, simoniacal, dipsomaniacal, egomaniacal, hypochondriacal, monomaniacal, nympomaniacal, pyromaniacal, paradisiacal, bibliomaniacal, megalomaniacal

iad \ī-əd\ see YAD

¹iah \ī-ə\ ayah, maya, Maya, playa, Praia, stria, via, Aglaia, Mariah, messiah, papaya, pariah, Thalia, Hezekiah, jambalaya, Jeremiah, Nehemiah, Obadiah, Surabaja, Zechariah, Zephaniah, Atchafalaya, Iphigenia, peripeteia

²iah \ē-ə\ see ¹IA

¹ial \ī-əl\ dial, diel, pial, redial

²ial \īl\ see ¹ILE

ialer \ī-lər\ see ILAR

ially \ē-ə-lē\ see ¹EALLY

iam \ī-əm\ Priam, per diem

¹ian \ē-ən\ see ¹EAN

²ian \ī-ən\ see ¹ION

iance \ī-əns\ science, affiance, alliance, appliance, compliance, defiance, nonscience, reliance, mesalliance, misalliance

iancy \ī-ən-sē\ pliancy, compliancy

ianist \ē-t-nist\ pianist, Indo-Europeanist

iant \ī-ənt\ Bryant, client, giant, pliant, riant, affiant, compliant, defiant, reliant, incompliant, self-reliant, supergiant

iao \aŭ\ see ²OW

iaour \aŭr\ see ²OWER

iaper \ī-pər\ see IPER

iar \īr\ see ¹IRE

¹iary \ī-ə-rē\ diary, fiery, miry, priory

²iary \īr-ē\ see ¹IRY

¹ias \ī-əs\ Aias, bias, dais, eyas, Laius, Lias, pious, Pius, Abdias, Elias, Messias, Nehemias, Tobias, Ananias, Jeremias, Malachias, Roncesvalles, Sophonias, Zacharias, Mount Saint Elias

²ias \ē-əs\ see ¹EUS

³ias \äsh\ see ¹ASH

iasis \ī-ə-səs\ diesis, diocese, archdiocese, psoriasis, acariasis, amebiasis, ascariasis, bilharziasis, helminthiasis, leishmaniasis, satyriasis, elephantiasis, hypochondriasis, schistosomiasis

¹iat \ē-ət\ see ¹EIT

²iat \ī-ət\ see IET

iate \ī-ət\ see IET

¹iath \ī-əth\ Wyeth, Goliath

²iath \ē-ə\ see ¹IA

iatry \ī-ə-trē\ podiatry, psychiatry

iaus \aŭs\ see ²OUSE

iaz \äsh\ see ¹ASH

¹ib \ib\ bib, bibb, crib, drib, fib, gib, glib, jib, lib, nib, rib, sib, squib, ad-lib, corncrib, midrib, sahib, memsahib

²ib \ēb\ see ²EBE

³ib \ēv\ see ¹EAVE

iba \ē-bə\ see EBA

ibable \ī-bə-bəl\ bribable, ascribable, describable, indescribable

ibal \ī-bəl\ bible, Bible, libel, scribal, tribal

ibb \ib\ see ¹IB

ibband \ib-ən\ see IBBON

ibbed \ibd\ bibbed, rock-ribbed—*also* -ed *forms of verbs listed at* ¹IB

ibber \ib-ər\ bibber, cribber, dibber, fibber, gibber, glibber, jibber, ribber

ibbet \ib-ət\ gibbet, exhibit, inhibit, prohibit, flibbertigibbet

ibbing \ib-iŋ\ cribbing, ribbing—*also* -ing *forms of verbs listed at* ¹IB

ibble \ib-əl\ dibble, dribble, fribble, gribble, kibble, nibble, quibble, scribble, sibyl, Sibyl

ibbler \ib-lər\ dribbler, nibbler, quibbler, scribbler

ibbly \ib-lē\ dribbly, ghibli, glibly

ibbon \ib-ən\ gibbon, Gibbon, ribbon, inhibin

ibby \ib-ē\ Libby, ribby

¹ibe \īb\ bribe, gibe, gybe, jibe, kibe, scribe, tribe, vibe, ascribe, conscribe, describe, imbibe, inscribe, prescribe, proscribe, subscribe, transcribe, circumscribe, diatribe, redescribe, superscribe, oversubscribe

²ibe \ē-bē\ see ¹EBE

ibel \ī-bəl\ see IBAL

iber \ī-bər\ briber, fiber, giber, Khyber, scriber, Tiber, describer, inscriber, prescriber, proscriber, subscriber, transcriber

ibi \ē-bē\ see ¹EBE

ibia \i-bē-ə\ Lybia, tibia, Namibia

ibin \ib-ən\ see IBBON

ibit \ib-ət\ see IBBET

ibitive \ib-ət-iv\ exhibitive, prohibitive

ibitor \ib-ət-ər\ exhibitor, inhibitor, ACE inhibitor

ible \ī-bəl\ see IBAL

iblet \ib-lət\ driblet, giblet, riblet

ibli \ib-lē\ see IBBLY

ibly \ib-lē\ see IBBLY

ibo \ē-bō\ Ibo, Kibo, gazebo

iboly \i-ə-lē\ see YBELE

ibrous \ī-brəs\ fibrous, hybris

ibs \ibz\ dibs, nibs, spareribs—*also* -s, -'s, *and* -s' *forms of nouns listed at* ¹IB, *and* -s *forms of verbs listed there*

ibular \ib-yə-lər\ fibular, mandibular, vestibular, infundibular

¹ibute \ib-yət\ tribute, attribute, contribute, distribute, redistribute

²ibute \ib-ət\ see IBBET

ibutive \ib-yət-iv\ attributive, contributive, distributive, retributive, redistributive

ibutor \ib-ət-ər\ see IBITOR

ibyl \ib-əl\ see IBBLE

¹ic \ik\ see ICK

²ic \ēk\ see ¹EAK

¹ica \ī-kə\ mica, Micah, pica, pika, plica, spica, Spica, Formica, lorica, balalaika

²ica \ē-kə\ see ¹IKA

icable \ik-ə-bəl\ despicable, explicable, extricable, inexplicable, inextricable

icah \ī-kə\ see ¹ICA

ical \ik-əl\ see ICKLE

icament \ik-ə-mənt\ medicament, predicament

ican \ē-kən\ see EACON

icar \ik-ər\ see ¹ICKER

icative \ik-ət-iv\ fricative, siccative, affricative, explicative, indicative, vindicative, multiplicative

iccative \ik-ət-iv\ see ICATIVE

iccio \ē-chō\ capriccio, pasticcio

ice \īs\ Bryce, dice, fice, fyce, gneiss, ice, lice, lyse, mice, nice, pice, price, rice, rise, slice, spice, splice, syce, thrice, trice, twice, vice, vise, advice, allspice, Brandeis, bride-price, concise, cut-price, deice, device, entice, excise, precise, suffice, beggars-lice, cockatrice, edelweiss, imprecise, merchandise, overprice, paradise, point-device, sacrifice, underprice, imparadise, self-sacrifice

²ice \ē-chə\ see ¹ICHE

³ice \ēs\ see IECE

⁴ice \ī-sē\ see ICY

⁵ice \īz\ see IZE

⁶ice \ēt-zə\ see ¹ITZA

iceless \ī-sləs\ iceless, priceless

icely \is-lē\ see ISTLY

iceous \ish-əs\ see ¹ICIOUS

icer \ī-sər\ dicer, Dreiser, nicer, pricer, ricer, slicer, splicer, deicer, sufficer, sacrificer, self-sacrificer

ices \ī-sēz\ Pisces, Anchises, Polynices, Coma Berenices

icety \ī-stē\ see EISTY

icey \ī-sē\ see ICY

¹ich \ich\ see ITCH

ich \ik\ see ICK

ichael \ī-kəl\ see ¹YCLE

¹iche \ē-chā\ ceviche, seviche, Beatrice, cantatrice

²iche \ēsh\ fiche, leash, quiche, sneesh, baksheesh, corniche, hashish, maxixe, pastiche, schottische, unleash, microfiche, nouveau riche

³iche \ish\ see ¹ISH

⁴iche \ich\ see ITCH

⁵iche \ē-chē\ see EACHY

ichen \ī-kən\ lichen, liken, proteoglycan

²ichen \ich-ən\ see ITCHEN

ichener \ich-nər\ see ITCHENER

icher \ich-ər\ see ITCHER

iches \ich-əz\ see ITCHES

¹ichi \ē-chē\ see EACHY

²ichi \ē-shē\ see ISHI

ichment \ich-mənt\ see ITCHMENT

ichore \ik-rē\ see ICKERY

ichu \ish-ü\ see ¹ISSUE

¹icia \ish-ə\ see ITIA

²icia \ēsh-ə\ see ¹ESIA

icial \ish-əl\ altricial, comitial, initial, judicial, official, simplicial, solstitial, surficial, artificial, beneficial, cicatricial, interstitial, prejudicial, sacrificial, superficial

ician \ē-shən\ see ¹ETION

icience \ish-əns\ omniscience, insufficience

iciency \ish-ən-sē\ deficiency, efficiency, proficiency, sufficiency, inefficiency, immunodeficiency

icient \ish-ənt\ deficient, efficient, omniscient, proficient, sufficient,

coefficient, cost-efficient, inefficient, insufficient, self-sufficient

icinable \is-nə-bəl\ see ISTENABLE

icinal \is-ᵊn-əl\ vicinal, medicinal, officinal, vaticinal

¹icing \ī-siŋ\ icing, splicing, self-sufficing—also -ing forms of verbs listed at ¹ICE

²icing \ī-ziŋ\ see IZING

¹icious \ish-əs\ vicious, ambitious, auspicious, capricious, delicious, factitious, fictitious, flagitious, judicious, lubricious, malicious, Mauritius, nutritious, officious, pernicious, propitious, pumiceous, seditious, sericeous, suspicious, adscititious, adventitious, avaricious, expeditious, inauspicious, injudicious, meretricious, prejudicious, subreptitious, superstitious, suppositious, surreptitious, excrementitious, supposititious

²icious \ē-shəs\ see ECIOUS

icipal \is-ə-bəl\ see ISSIBLE

icipant \is-ə-pənt\ anticipant, participant

icit \is-ət\ licit, complicit, elicit, explicit, illicit, implicit, solicit, inexplicit

¹icitor \is-ət-ər\ elicitor, solicitor

²icitor \is-tər\ see ISTER

icitous \is-ət-əs\ complicitous, duplicitous, felicitous, solicitous, infelicitous

¹icity \is-ət-ē\ basicity, causticity, centricity, chronicity, complicity, conicity, cyclicity, duplicity,

ethnicity, felicity, lubricity,
mendicity, plasticity,
publicity, rhythmicity,
seismicity, simplicity,
spasticity, sphericity,
tonicity, toxicity, triplicity,
atomicity, authenticity,
canonicity, catholicity,
concentricity, domesticity,
eccentricity, elasticity,
electricity, ellipticity,
endemicity, ergodicity,
historicity, iconicity,
impudicity, infelicity,
multiplicity, organicity,
pneumaticity, quadruplicity,
specificity, synchronicity,
volcanicity, aperiodicity,
aromaticity, automaticity,
ecumenicity, egocentricity,
epidemicity, ethnocentricity,
hydrophilicity,
hydrophobicity,
inauthenticity, inelasticity,
pathogenicity, periodicity,
theocentricity, aeroelasticity,
anthropocentricity,
carcinogenicity,
homoscedasticity,
quasiperiodicity

²icity \is-tē\ christie, Christie,
misty, twisty, wristy, Corpus
Christi, sacahuiste

ick \ik\ brick, chick, click,
crick, creek, Dick, flick,
hick, kick, KWIC, lick,
mick, nick, Nick, pic, pick,
prick, quick, rick, shtick, sic,
sick, slick, snick, stick,
strick, thick, tic, tick, trick,
wick, airsick, alsike,
bluetick, bootlick, boychick,
brainsick, broomstick,
carsick, chopstick, cowlick,
crabstick, dabchick, dead-
stick, detick, dik-dik,
dipstick, drop-kick,

drumstick, firebrick,
flagstick, goldbrick,
greensick, handpick,
hayrick, heartsick,
homesick, joystick, lipstick,
lovesick, matchstick, moujik,
muzhik, nightstick, nitpick,
nonstick, nutpick, outslick,
peacenik, pigstick, pinprick,
placekick, redbrick, rubric,
seasick, self-stick, shashlik,
sidekick, slapstick, slipstick,
Tajik, toothpick, topkick,
unpick, unstick, uptick,
yardstick, bailiwick, biopic,
Bolshevik, candlestick,
candlewick, Dominic,
dominick, Dominick,
double-quick, EBCDIC,
fiddlestick, hemistich,
heretic, lunatic, Menshevik,
meterstick, overtrick, politic,
politick, polyptych,
Reykjavik, singlestick,
taperstick, undertrick,
Watson-Crick, arithmetic,
carrot-and-stick,
computernik, impolitic,
kinnikinnick

icka \ē-kə\ see ¹IKA
¹icked \ik-əd\ picked, wicked
²icked \ikt\ see ¹ICT
ickel \ik-əl\ see ICKLE
icken \ik-ən\ chicken,
quicken, sicken, stricken,
thicken, awestricken, panic-
stricken, planet-stricken,
poverty-stricken
ickens \ik-ənz\ dickens,
Dickens, pickings—*also* -s,
-'s, *and* -s' *forms of nouns
listed at* ICKEN, *and* -s *forms
of verbs listed there*
¹icker \ik-ər\ bicker, dicker,
flicker, icker, kicker, liquor,
nicker, picker, pricker,
sicker, slicker, snicker,

sticker, ticker, tricker, vicar,
whicker, wicker, billsticker,
bootlicker, dropkicker, flea-
flicker, nitpicker, pigsticker,
placekicker, pot likker,
ragpicker, dominicker,
politicker—*also -er forms of
adjectives listed at* ICK

²**icker** \ek-ər\ *see* ECKER

ickery \ik-rē\ chicory,
flickery, hickory, snickery,
trickery, Terpsichore

icket \ik-ət\ cricket, picket,
Pickett, pricket, spigot,
stickit, thicket, ticket,
wicket, Big Thicket, big-
ticket

ickett \ik-ət\ *see* ICKET

ickety \ik-ət-ē\ rickety,
thickety, pernickety,
persnickety

ickey \ik-ē\ *see* ICKY

icki \ik-ē\ *see* ICKY

ickie \ik-ē\ *see* ICKY

icking \ik-iŋ\ ticking, wicking,
brain-picking, flat-picking,
high-sticking, nit-picking,
cotton-picking, finger-
picking—*also -ing forms of
verbs listed at* ICK

ickings \ik-ənz\ *see* ICKENS

ickish \ik-ish\ hickish, sickish,
trickish

ickit \ik-ət\ *see* ICKET

ickle \ik-əl\ brickle, chicle,
fickle, mickle, nickel, pickle,
picul, prickle, sickle, stickle,
strickle, tical, tickle, trickle,
bicycle, icicle, obstacle,
Popsicle, spectacle, tricycle,
vehicle, pumpernickel

ickler \ik-lər\ stickler, tickler,
bicycler, particular

ickly \ik-lē\ fickly, prickly,
quickly, sickly, slickly,
impoliticly

ickness \ik-nəs\ lychnis,

quickness, sickness,
slickness, thickness,
airsickness, heartsickness,
homesickness, lovesickness,
seasickness

icksy \ik-sē\ *see* IXIE

icky \ik-ē\ dickey, hickey,
icky, kicky, Mickey, picky,
quickie, rickey, sickie, sticky,
tricky, Vicki, Vickie, Vicky,
doohickey

icle \ik-əl\ *see* ICKLE

¹**icly** \ik-lē\ *see* ICKLY

²**icly** \ē-klē\ *see* EEKLY

ico \ē-kō\ *see* ICOT

icope \ik-ə-pē\ *see* ICOPY

icopy \ik-ə-pē\ wicopy,
pericope

icory \ik-rē\ *see* ICKERY

icot \ē-kō\ fico, pekoe, picot,
tricot, Tampico, Puerto Rico

ics \iks\ *see* ¹IX

¹**ict** \ikt\ picked, Pict, strict,
ticked, addict, afflict,
conflict, constrict, convict,
delict, depict, edict, evict,
inflict, lipsticked, predict,
restrict, unlicked, benedict,
Benedict, contradict, derelict,
interdict, maledict, retrodict,
eggs Benedict—*also -ed
forms of verbs listed at* ICK

²**ict** \īt\ *see* ¹ITE

ictable \it-ə-bəl\ *see* ¹ITABLE

ictal \ik-tᵊl\ fictile, rictal,
edictal

icted \ik-təd\ conflicted,
evicted, restricted—*also -ed
forms of verbs listed at* ICT

icter \ik-tər\ *see* ICTOR

ictic \ik-tik\ deictic,
panmictic, amphimictic,
apodictic

ictile \ik-tᵊl\ *see* ICTAL

ictim \ik-təm\ *see* ICTUM

iction \ik-shən\ diction,
fiction, friction, stiction,

addiction, affliction,
confliction, constriction,
conviction, depiction,
eviction, indiction,
infliction, nonfiction,
prediction, reliction,
restriction, transfixion,
benediction, contradiction,
crucifixion, dereliction,
jurisdiction, malediction,
metafiction, valediction

ictional \ik-shnəl\ fictional,
frictional, nonfictional,
jurisdictional

ictionist \ik-shnəst\ fictionist,
restrictionist

ictive \ik-tiv\ fictive,
addictive, afflictive,
conflictive, constrictive,
inflictive, restrictive,
vindictive, nonrestrictive

ictment \īt-mənt\ see
ITEMENT

ictor \ik-tər\ lictor, stricter,
victor, constrictor, depicter,
evictor, inflicter,
contradictor, vasoconstrictor

ictory \ik-tə-rē\ victory,
benedictory, contradictory,
maledictory, valedictory

ictual \it-ᵊl\ see ITTLE

ictualler \it-ᵊl-ər\ see ITALER

ictum \ik-təm\ dictum,
victim, obiter dictum

icture \ik-chər\ picture,
stricture

ictus \ik-təs\ ictus, rictus,
Benedictus

icul \ik-əl\ see ICKLE

icula \ik-yə-lə\ auricula,
Canicula

iculant \ik-yə-lənt\
gesticulant, matriculant

¹**icular** \ik-yə-lər\ spicular,
acicular, articular, auricular,
canicular, clavicular,
curricular, cuticular,

fascicular, follicular,
funicular, lenticular,
navicular, orbicular,
ossicular, particular,
radicular, reticular,
testicular, vehicular,
ventricular, vermicular,
versicular, vesicular,
appendicular, perpendicular,
extracurricular,
extravehicular, intra-
articular, supraventricular

²**icular** \ik-lər\ see ICKLER

icularly \ik-lē\ see ICKLY

iculate \ik-yə-lət\ articulate,
denticulate, geniculate,
particulate, reticulate,
straticulate, vermiculate,
inarticulate

iculous \ik-yə-ləs\
meticulous, pediculous,
ridiculous

iculum \ik-yə-ləm\
curriculum, reticulum,
diverticulum

icuous \ik-yə-wəs\
conspicuous, perspicuous,
transpicuous, inconspicuous

icy \ī-sē\ dicey, icy, pricey,
spicy

¹**id** \id\ bid, chid, Cid, did,
fid, gid, grid, hid, id, kid,
Kidd, lid, mid, quid, rid,
skid, slid, squid, SQUID,
whid, amid, backslid, bifid,
El Cid, equid, eyelid, forbid,
grandkid, Madrid, nonskid,
outdid, resid, schoolkid,
trifid, undid, katydid, ootid,
overbid, overdid, pyramid,
underbid, tertium quid,
Valladolid

²**id** \ēd\ see EED

I'd \īd\ see ¹IDE

¹**ida** \ēd-ə\ see ¹EDA

²**ida** \ī-də\ Haida, Ida, Vida

¹**idable** \īd-ə-bəl\ guidable,

decidable, dividable,
subdividable

²**idable** \id-ə-bəl\ see IDDABLE

idal \īd-ᵊl\ bridal, bridle, idle,
idol, idyll, seidel, sidle, tidal,
unbridle, Barmecidal,
fratricidal, fungicidal,
genocidal, germicidal,
herbicidal, homicidal,
intertidal, lunitidal,
matricidal, parricidal,
patricidal, septicidal,
spermicidal, suicidal, viricidal,
virucidal, bactericidal,
infanticidal, insecticidal

idance \īd-ᵊns\ guidance,
stridence, abidance,
misguidance

idas \īd-əs\ Midas, nidus

iday \īd-ē\ Friday, Heidi, tidy,
vide, alcaide, man Friday,
untidy, mala fide

idays \īd-ēz\ see ¹IDES

idd \id\ see ¹ID

iddable \id-ə-bəl\ biddable,
formidable

iddance \id-ᵊns\ riddance,
forbiddance

idden \id-ᵊn\ bidden, chiden,
hidden, midden, ridden,
stridden, swidden,
backslidden, bedridden,
bestridden, forbidden,
outbidden, unbidden,
overridden

idder \id-ər\ bidder, gridder,
kidder, siddur, skidder,
consider, forbidder,
reconsider, underbidder

iddie \id-ē\ see IDDY

iddish \id-ish\ kiddish,
Yiddish

iddity \id-ət-ē\ see IDITY

iddle \id-ᵊl\ diddle, fiddle,
griddle, middle, piddle,
riddle, twiddle, unriddle,
paradiddle, taradiddle

iddler \id-lər\ diddler, fiddler,
middler, riddler, tiddler

iddling \id-liŋ\ fiddling,
middling, piddling, riddling

iddly \id-lē\ diddly, ridley,
tiddly

iddock \id-ik\ see IDIC

iddur \id-ər\ see IDDER

iddy \id-ē\ biddy, giddy,
kiddie, middy, midi, skiddy,
widdy

¹**ide** \īd\ bide, bride, chide,
Clyde, eyed, fried, glide,
guide, hide, I'd, pied, plied,
pride, ride, side, slide, snide,
stride, thighed, tide, tried,
wide, abide, allied, applied,
aside, astride, backside,
backslide, bankside,
beachside, bedside, beside,
bestride, betide, blear-eyed,
blindside, blowdried, blue-
eyed, broadside, bromide,
bug-eyed, Burnside, clear-
eyed, cockeyed, cold-eyed,
collide, confide, courtside,
cowhide, cross-eyed,
curbside, dayside, decide,
deride, divide, dockside, doe-
eyed, downside, dry-eyed,
elide, fireside, foreside, four-
eyed, freeze-dried, glass-eyed,
graveside, green-eyed,
hagride, hawkeyed, hayride,
hillside, horsehide, inside,
ironside, joyride, kingside,
lakeside, landslide, lynx-eyed,
misguide, moon-eyed,
nearside, nightside, noontide,
offside, onside, outride,
outside, pie-eyed, poolside,
pop-eyed, preside, provide,
quayside, queenside, rawhide,
reside, ringside, riptide,
roadside, seaside, sharp-eyed,
shipside, shoreside,
Shrovetide, sloe-eyed,

snowslide, springtide, squint-eyed, stateside, statewide, storewide, Strathclyde, streamside, subside, tailside, Tayside, tongue-tied, topside, trackside, trailside, untried, upside, vat-dyed, walleyed, waveguide, wayside, wide-eyed, wild-eyed, worldwide, yuletide, alkoxide, almond-eyed, alongside, Argus-eyed, Barmecide, bleary-eyed, bona fide, chicken-fried, Christmastide, citified, citywide, classified, coincide, countrified, countryside, countrywide, cut-and-dried, cyanide, deicide, demand-side, dewy-eyed, dignified, double-wide, downslide, Eastertide, eventide, feticide, fluoride, formamide, fratricide, fungicide, genocide, germicide, gimlet-eyed, glassy-eyed, goggle-eyed, googly-eyed, harbor-side, herbicide, homicide, Humberside, humified, matricide, Merseyside, misty-eyed, miticide, monoxide, mountainside, nationwide, Naugahyde, open-eyed, override, overstride, parricide, Passiontide, patricide, pesticide, planetwide, qualified, rarefied, raticide, regicide, riverside, Riverside, set-aside, silverside, sissified, slickenside, spermicide, starry-eyed, subdivide, suicide, supply-side, trisulfide, underside, verbicide, vermicide, viricide, waterside, Whitsuntide, wintertide, acrylamide, antimonide,

borohydride, dissatisfied, formaldehyde, infanticide, insecticide, interallied, Jekyll and Hyde, preoccupied, rodenticide, self-satisfied, thalidomide, Trinitytide, tyrannicide, uxoricide, monoglyceride, overqualified, parasiticide—*also* -ed *forms of verbs listed at* ¹Y

²**Ide** \ēd\ *see* EED

idean \id-ē-ən\ *see* IDIAN

ided \īd-əd\ sided, lopsided, misguided, one-sided, slab-sided, two-sided, many-sided, sobersided—*also* -ed *forms of verbs listed at* ¹IDE

ideless \īd-ləs\ idlesse, tideless

iden \īd-ᵊn\ guidon, Haydn, widen, Poseidon

idence \īd-ᵊns\ *see* IDANCE

ideness \id-nəs\ *see* EYEDNESS

ident \īd-ᵊnt\ strident, trident

ideon \id-ē-ən\ *see* IDIAN

ideous \id-ē-əs\ *see* IDIOUS

¹**ider** \īd-ər\ bider, cider, eider, glider, guider, hider, rider, slider, spider, strider, stridor, abider, backslider, confider, decider, derider, divider, insider, joyrider, misguider, outrider, outsider, presider, provider, resider, rough rider, Top-Sider, subdivider, supply-sider, supercollider—*also* -er *forms of adjectives listed at* ¹IDE

²**ider** \id-ər\ *see* IDDER

¹**ides** \id-ēz\ Fridays, Aristides—*also* -s, -'s, *and* -s' *forms of nouns listed at* IDAY, *and* -s *forms of verbs listed there*

²ides \īdz\ ides, besides, burnsides, silversides, sobersides—*also -s, -'s, and -s' forms of nouns listed at* ¹IDE, *and -s forms of verbs listed there*

idge \ij\ bridge, fridge, fridge, midge, ridge, abridge, Blue Ridge, browridge, drawbridge, footbridge, Oxbridge, teethridge

idged \ijd\ ridged, unabridged—*also -ed forms of verbs listed at* IDGE

idgen \ij-ən\ *see* YGIAN

idget \ij-ət\ Brigitte, digit, fidget, midget, widget, double-digit

idgin \ij-ən\ *see* YGIAN

idi \id-ē\ *see* IDDY

idia \i-dē-ə\ Lydia, basidia, chlamydia, clostridia, coccidia, conidia, glochidia, nephridia, Numidia, oidia, peridia, Pisidia, presidia, pycnidia, pygidia, antheridia, enchiridia, hesperidia, miricidia, ommatidia

idian \id-ē-ən\ Gideon, Lydian, Midian, ascidian, Dravidian, euclidean, Floridian, meridian, obsidian, ophidian, quotidian, viridian, enchiridion, non-euclidean

idic \id-ik\ piddock, acidic, bromidic, Davidic, druidic, fatidic, fluidic, Hasidic, nuclidic

idical \id-i-kəl\ druidical, fatidical, juridical, veridical, pyramidical

idice \id-ə-sē\ Chalcidice, Eurydice

idiem \id-ē-əm\ idiom, iridium, presidium, rubidium, post meridiem, ante meridiem

iding \īd-iŋ\ riding, Riding, siding, tiding, abiding, confiding, East Riding, joyriding, West Riding, lawabiding, nondividing—*also -ing forms of verbs listed at* ¹IDE

idiom \id-ē-əm\ *see* IDIEM

idious \id-ē-əs\ hideous, fastidious, insidious, invidious, perfidious

idity \id-ət-ē\ quiddity, acidity, aridity, avidity, cupidity, fluidity, flaccidity, floridity, frigidity, gelidity, gravidity, hispidity, humidity, hybridity, limpidity, liquidity, lividity, lucidity, morbidity, rabidity, rapidity, rigidity, sapidity, solidity, stupidity, tepidity, timidity, torridity, turbidity, turgidity, validity, vapidity, viridity, viscidity, illiquidity, insipidity, intrepidity, invalidity

idium \id-ē-əm\ *see* IDIEM

idle \īd-ᵊl\ *see* IDAL

idlesse \id-ləs\ *see* IDELESS

idley \id-lē\ *see* IDDLY

idney \id-nē\ kidney, Sidney, Sydney

¹ido \īd-ō\ dido, Dido, fido, Hokkaido

²ido \ēd-ō\ *see* ¹EDO

idol \īd-ᵊl\ *see* IDAL

¹ids \idz\ Beskids, rapids, Grand Rapids—*also -s, -'s, and -s' forms of nouns listed at* ¹ID, *and -s forms of verbs listed there*

²ids \ēdz\ *see* EEDS

idst \idst\ didst, midst, amidst

¹idual \ij-wəl\ residual, individual

²idual \ij-əl\ *see* IGIL

idulent \ij-ə-lənt\ *see* IGILANT

idulous \ij-ə-ləs\ stridulous,
acidulous

idus \ìd-əs\ see IDAS

iduum \ij-ə-wəm\ triduum,
residuum

idy \ìd-ē\ see IDAY

idyll \ìd-ᵊl\ see IDAL

¹ie \ā\ see ¹AY

²ie \ē\ see ¹EE

³ie \ī\ see ¹Y

iece \ēs\ cease, crease,
fleece, grease, Greece,
kris, lease, Nice, niece,
peace, piece, apiece,
Bernice, Burmese, camise,
caprice, cassis, cerise,
chemise, Chinese, Clarice,
Cochise, codpiece, coulisse,
crosspiece, decease,
decrease, degrease, Denise,
Dumfries, earpiece, Elise,
eyepiece, Felice, fieldpiece,
grandniece, hairpiece,
headpiece, heelpiece,
increase, Janice, lend-lease,
Matisse, Maurice,
mouthpiece, nosepiece,
obese, one-piece, pastis,
pelisse, police, re-lease,
release, seapiece,
shankpiece, showpiece,
sidepiece, stringpiece,
sublease, surcease, tailpiece,
Therese, timepiece,
toepiece, two-piece, valise,
workpiece, afterpiece,
altarpiece, Amboinese,
Annamese, Assamese,
Balinese, Brooklynese,
Cantonese, centerpiece,
Chersonese, chimneypiece,
diocese, directrice, ex libris,
expertise, Faeroese,
frontispiece, mantelpiece,
masterpiece, Nipponese,
Pekinese, Pekingese,
Portugese, predecease,

rerelease, São Luis, Siamese,
Sinhalese, timed-release,
verdigris, archdiocese,
computerese, Dodecanese,
officialese, telegraphese,
Vietnamese, educationese

lecer \ē-sər\ see ¹EASER

¹ied \ēd\ see EED

²ied \ēt\ see ¹EAT

³ied \ìd\ see IDE

ieda \ēd-ə\ see ¹EDA

¹ief \ēf\ beef, brief, chief,
fief, grief, kef, leaf, leif,
reef, sheaf, thief, belief,
debrief, endleaf, enfeoff,
flyleaf, loose-leaf, massif,
motif, naif, O'Keefe, relief,
sharif, sherif, shinleaf, bas-
relief, cloverleaf, disbelief,
handkerchief, leatherleaf,
neckerchief, leitmotiv,
misbelief, overleaf, unbelief,
waterleaf, aperitif, Capitol
Reef, Vinson Massif, Great
Barrier Reef, Santa Cruz de
Tenerife

²ief \ēv\ see ¹EAVE

iefless \ē-fləs\ briefless,
leafless

iefly \ē-flē\ briefly, chiefly

¹ieg \ēg\ see IGUE

²ieg \ig\ see IG

¹iege \ēj\ liege, siege, besiege,
prestige

²iege \ēzh\ see ¹IGE

ieger \ē-jər\ see EDURE

iek \ēk\ see ¹EAK

¹iel \ēl\ see ²EAL

²iel \ì-əl\ see ¹IAL

iela \el-ə\ see ELLA

ield \ēld\ bield, field,
keeled, shield, weald,
wheeled, wield, yield,
afield, airfield,
backfield, brickfield,
coalfield, cornfield,
downfield, Enfield, four-

wheeled, Garfield, goldfield,
grainfield, infield, Masefield,
midfield, minefield, outfield,
playfield, Sheffield,
Smithfield, snowfield,
Springfield, subfield,
unsealed, upfield, well-
heeled, windshield, Winfield,
battlefield, broken-field,
chesterfield, Chesterfield,
color-field, Huddersfield,
track-and-field, unaneled—
also -ed *forms of verbs listed
at* ²EAL

ielder \ēl-dər\ fielder,
shielder, wielder, yielder,
infielder, outfielder

ields \ēldz\ South Shields—
also -s, -'s, *and* -s' *forms of
nouns listed at* IELD, *and* -s
forms of verbs listed there

ieler \ē-lər\ see EALER

ieless \ī-ləs\ see ILUS

¹ieling \ē-lən\ see ELIN

²ieling \ē-liŋ\ see EELING

¹iem \ē-əm\ see ¹EUM

²iem \ī-əm\ see IAM

ien \ēn\ see ³INE

ience \ī-əns\ see IANCE

iend \end\ see END

iendless \en-ləs\ see ENDLESS

iendliness \en-lē-nəs\ see
ENDLINESS

iendly \en-lē\ see ENDLY

iene \ēn\ see ³INE

¹iener \ē-nər\ see EANER

²iener \ē-nē\ see ¹INI

ienic \en-ik\ see ²ENIC

ienics \en-iks\ see ENICS

ienie \ē-nē\ see ¹INI

ienist \ē-nəst\ see ²INIST

iennes \en\ see ¹EN

ient \ī-ənt\ see IANT

ieper \ē-pər\ see EEPER

¹ier \ir\ see ²EER

²ier \ē-ər\ see ¹EER

³ier \ir\ see ¹IRE

ierate \ir-ət\ see IRIT

ierce \irs\ Bierce, birse, fierce,
pierce, Pierce, tierce,
transpierce

¹iere \er\ see ⁴ARE

²iere \ir\ see ²EER

iered \ird\ see ¹EARD

ieria \ir-ē-ə\ see ¹ERIA

ierial \ir-ē-əl\ see ERIAL

ierian \ir-ē-ən\ see ¹ERIAN

ierly \ir-lē\ see ¹EARLY

¹ierre \ir\ see ²EER

²ierre \er\ see ⁴ARE

iers \irz\ Algiers, Pamirs—
also -s, -'s, *and* -s' *forms of
nouns listed at* ²EER, *and* -s
forms of verbs listed there

iersman \irz-mən\ see
EERSMAN

iery \ī-rē\ see ¹IARY

¹ies \ēz\ see EZE

²ies \ē\ see ¹EE

³ies \ēs\ see IECE

¹iesel \ē-zəl\ see EASEL

²iesel \ē-səl\ see ¹ECIL

ieseling \ēz-liŋ\ see ESLING

iesian \ē-zhən\ see ¹ESIAN

iesis \ī-ə-səs\ see IASIS

iesling \ēz-liŋ\ see ESLING

iest \ēst\ see ¹EAST

iester \ē-stər\ see EASTER

iestley \ēst-lē\ see EASTLY

iestly \ēst-lē\ see EASTLY

iet \ī-ət\ diet, fiat, quiet, riot,
striate, Wyatt, disquiet,
unquiet

ietal \ī-ət-ᵊl\ parietal, societal,
varietal

ieter \ī-ət-ər\ dieter, quieter,
rioter, proprietor

ietor \ī-ət-ər\ see IETER

ietzsche \ē-chē\ see EACHY

iety \ī-ət-ē\ piety, anxiety,
dubiety, impiety, nimiety,
propriety, satiety, sobriety,
society, Society, variety,
contrariety, impropriety,

inebriety, insobriety,
notoriety

ieu \ü\ see ¹EW

ieur \ir\ see ²EER

iev \ef\ see ¹EF

ievable \ē-və-bəl\ see
EIVABLE

ieval \ē-vəl\ evil, shrieval,
weevil, coeval, khedival,
medieval, primeval, reprieval,
retrieval, upheaval

¹**ieve** \iv\ see ²IVE

²**ieve** \ēv\ see ¹EAVE

ieved \ēvd\ see EAVED

ievement \ēv-mənt\ see
EVEMENT

iever \ē-vər\ beaver, cleaver,
fever, griever, leaver, reaver,
reiver, weaver, achiever,
believer, conceiver, deceiver,
enfever, perceiver, receiver,
reliever, retriever, upheaver,
school-leaver, transceiver,
cantilever, disbeliever,
misbeliever, misconceiver,
unbeliever, overachiever,
underachiever

ievish \ē-vish\ see EEVISH

ievo \ē-vō\ see EVO

ievous \ē-vəs\ see EVOUS

ieze \ēz\ see EZE

¹**if** \if\ see IFF

²**if** \ēf\ see ¹IEF

¹**ife** \īf\ fife, Fife, knife, life,
rife, strife, wife, alewife,
drawknife, fishwife, flick-
knife, goodwife, half-life,
housewife, jackknife,
loosestrife, lowlife, midlife,
nightlife, oldwife, penknife,
pro-life, true-life, wakerife,
whole-life, wildlife, afterlife,
antilife, Duncan Phyfe,
nurse-midwife, pocketknife,
Yellowknife, right-to-life

²**ife** \ē-fə\ see EPHA

³**ife** \ēf\ see ¹IEF

ifeless \ī-fləs\ lifeless,
strifeless, wifeless

ifer \ī-fər\ see IPHER

iferous \if-ər-əs\ coniferous,
floriferous, lactiferous,
luciferous, pestiferous,
somniferous, splendiferous,
vociferous, carboniferous,
luminiferous, odoriferous,
salutiferous, seminiferous,
soporiferous, sudoriferous

iff \if\ biff, cliff, glyph, if, iff,
jiff, kif, miff, quiff, riff, Riff,
skiff, sniff, spiff, spliff, stiff,
syph, tiff, whiff, Er Rif,
midriff, Plovdiv, triglyph,
what-if, Wycliffe, anaglyph,
bindle stiff, hieroglyph,
hippogriff, logograph,
petroglyph

iffany \if-ə-nē\ see IPHONY

iffe \if\ see IFF

iffed \ift\ see IFT

iffen \if-ən\ see IFFIN

iffey \if-ē\ see IFFY

iffian \if-ē-ən\ Riffian,
Pecksniffian

iffin \if-ən\ griffin, griffon,
stiffen, tiffin

iffish \if-ish\ sniffish, stiffish

iffle \if-əl\ piffle, riffle,
skiffle, sniffle, whiffle,
Wiffle

iffler \if-lər\ riffler, sniffler,
whiffler

iffness \if-nəs\ stiffness,
swiftness

iffon \if-ən\ see IFFIN

iffy \if-ē\ iffy, cliffy, jiffy,
Liffey, sniffy, spiffy

ific \if-ik\ glyphic, calcific,
febrific, horrific, magnific,
pacific, Pacific, prolific,
salvific, specific, terrific,
vivific, anaglyphic, beatific,
calorific, colorific, felicific,
frigorific, hieroglyphic,

honorific, scientific,
soporific, sudorific,
tenebrific, prescientific

ifical \if-i-kəl\ magnifical,
pontifical

ificate \if-i-kət\ certificate,
pontificate

ificent \if-ə-sənt\ magnificent,
omnificent

ifle \ī-fəl\ rifle, stifle, trifle

ifling \ī-fliŋ\ rifling, stifling,
trifling

ift \ift\ drift, gift, grift, lift,
rift, shift, shrift, sift,
squiffed, swift, Swift, thrift,
adrift, airlift, blueshift,
downshift, face-lift,
festschrift, forklift,
frameshift, gearshift, Great
Rift, makeshift, redshift,
shoplift, snowdrift,
spendthrift, spindrift,
spoondrift, unshift, uplift,
upshift—*also* -ed *forms of
verbs listed at* IFF

ifter \if-tər\ drifter, snifter,
swifter, sceneshifter, shape-
shifter, shoplifter

ifth \ith\ *see* ²ITH

iftness \if-nəs\ *see* IFFNESS

ifty \if-tē\ drifty, fifty, nifty,
shifty, thrifty, wifty, fifty-
fifty, LD50

ig \ig\ big, brig, dig, fig, gig,
Grieg, grig, jig, pig, prig, rig,
sprig, swig, trig, twig, vig,
Whig, wig, zig, bagwig,
bigwig, bushpig, earwig,
hedgepig, lime-twig, renege,
shindig, unrig, caprifig, infra
dig, jury-rig, periwig,
thimblerig, whirligig,
WYSIWYG, Zagazig,
thingamajig

¹iga \ē-gə\ Riga, Vega, viga,
Antigua, omega, quadriga

²iga \ī-gə\ *see* AIGA

igamous \ig-ə-məs\ bigamous,
polygamous

igamy \ig-ə-mē\ bigamy,
digamy, polygamy

¹igan \ī-gən\ ligan, tigon

²igan \ig-ən\ *see* IGGIN

igand \ig-ənd\ brigand, ligand

igas \ī-gəs\ *see* YGOUS

igate \ig-ət\ *see* ¹IGOT

¹ige \ēzh\ siege, prestige,
noblesse oblige

²ige \ēj\ *see* ¹IEGE

igel \ij-əl\ *see* IGIL

igenous \ij-ə-nəs\ *see* IGINOUS

igeon \ij-ən\ *see* YGIAN

iger \ī-gər\ tiger,
braunschweiger

igerent \ij-rənt\ belligerent,
refrigerant, cobelligerent

iggan \ig-ən\ *see* IGGIN

iggard \ig-ərd\ niggard,
triggered—*also* -ed *forms of
verbs listed at* IGGER

igged \igd\ twigged, wigged,
bewigged, cat-rigged, square-
rigged, periwigged—*also* -ed
forms of verbs listed at IG

igger \ig-ər\ bigger, chigger,
digger, jigger, rigger,
rigor, snigger, swigger,
trigger, vigor, vigour,
ditchdigger, outrigger,
rejigger, reneger, square-
rigger, thimblerigger

iggered \ig-ərd\ *see* IGGARD

iggery \ig-ə-rē\ piggery,
priggery, Whiggery

iggle \ig-ē\ *see* IGGY

iggin \ig-ən\ biggin, piggin,
wigan, balbriggan

iggish \ig-ish\ biggish, piggish,
priggish, Whiggish

iggle \ig-əl\ giggle, higgle,
jiggle, niggle, sniggle,
squiggle, wiggle, wriggle

iggler \ig-lər\ giggler, higgler,
niggler, wiggler, wriggler

iggy \ig-ē\ biggie, piggy, twiggy

igh \ī\ see ¹Y

ighed \īd\ see ¹IDE

ighland \ī-lənd\ highland, Highland, island, Thailand, Long Island, Rhode Island, Staten Island, Prince Edward Island

ighlander \ī-lən-dər\ highlander, islander

ighlands \ī-lənz\ Highlands, Virgin Islands

ighly \ī-lē\ see YLY

ighness \ī-nəs\ see ¹INUS

ight \īt\ see ¹ITE

ightable \īt-ə-bəl\ see ¹ITABLE

ighted \īt-əd\ blighted, sighted, whited, attrited, benighted, clear-sighted, farsighted, foresighted, longsighted, nearsighted, sharp-sighted, shortsighted, skylighted, united, unrequited—*also* -ed *forms of verbs listed at* ¹ITE

ighten \īt-°n\ brighten, Brighton, chitin, chiton, frighten, heighten, lighten, tighten, titan, Titan, triton, Triton, whiten, enlighten

ightener \īt-nər\ brightener, lightener, tightener, whitener

ightening \īt-niŋ\ see IGHTNING

ighter \īt-ər\ see ¹ITER

ightful \īt-fəl\ frightful, rightful, spiteful, sprightful, delightful, despiteful, foresightful, insightful

ightie \īt-ē\ see ²ITE

ightily \īt-°l-ē\ flightily, mightily

ightiness \īt-ē-nəs\ flightiness, mightiness, almightiness

ighting \īt-iŋ\ see ITING

ightless \īt-ləs\ flightless, lightless, sightless

ightly \īt-lē\ brightly, knightly, lightly, nightly, rightly, sightly, slightly, sprightly, tightly, tritely, whitely, contritely, finitely, forthrightly, fortnightly, midnightly, outrightly, politely, unsightly, uprightly, eruditely, impolitely, reconditely

ightment \īt-mənt\ see ITEMENT

ightning \īt-niŋ\ lightning, tightening, belt-tightening—*also* -ing *forms of verbs listed at* IGHTEN

ightn't \īt-°nt\ see ITANT

ighton \īt-ən\ see IGHTEN

ights \īts\ lights, nights, tights, footlights, houselights, weeknights, Dolomites, Golan Heights—*also* -s, -'s, *and* -s' *forms of nouns listed at* ¹ITE, *and* -s *forms of verbs listed there*

ightsome \īt-səm\ lightsome, delightsome

ighty \īt-ē\ see ²ITE

igian \ij-ən\ see YGIAN

igid \ij-əd\ Brigid, frigid, rigid

igil \ij-əl\ Rigel, sigil, strigil, vigil, residual

igilant \ij-ə-lənt\ vigilant, acidulent

igine \ij-ə-nē\ polygyny, aborigine

iginous \ij-ə-nəs\ caliginous, fuliginous, indigenous, polygynous, vertiginous

igion \ij-ən\ see YGIAN

igious \ij-əs\ litigious, prestigious, prodigious, religious, irreligious

igit \ij-ət\ see IDGET

igitte \ij-ət\ see IDGET

iglet \ig-lət\ piglet, wiglet

¹igm \im\ see ¹IM

²igm \īm\ see ¹IME

igma \ig-mə\ sigma, stigma, enigma, kerygma

igment \ig-mənt\ figment, pigment

ign \īn\ see ¹INE

ignable \ī-nə-bəl\ see INABLE

ignancy \ig-nən-sē\ benignancy, malignancy

ignant \ig-nənt\ benignant, indignant, malignant

igned \īnd\ see ¹IND

igneous \ig-nē-əs\ igneous, ligneous

igner \ī-nər\ see ¹INER

igness \ig-nəs\ bigness, Cygnus

ignet \ig-nət\ see YGNET

igning \ī-niŋ\ see INING

ignity \ig-nət-ē\ dignity, indignity, malignity

ignly \īn-lē\ see ¹INELY

ignment \īn-mənt\ alignment, assignment, confinement, consignment, enshrinement, refinement, nonalignment, realignment

ignon \in-yən\ see INION

ignor \ē-nyər\ see ENIOR

¹igo \ī-gō\ Sligo, prurigo, vitiligo

²igo \ē-gō\ see EGO

igoe \ē-gō\ see EGO

igon \ī-gən\ see ¹IGAN

igor \ig-ər\ see IGGER

igorous \ig-rəs\ rigorous, vigorous

¹igot \ig-ət\ bigot, frigate, gigot, spigot

²igot \ik-ət\ see ICKET

igour \ig-ər\ see IGGER

igrapher \ig-rə-fər\ calligrapher, epigrapher, polygrapher, serigrapher

igraphist \ig-rə-fəst\ calligraphist, epigraphist, polygraphist

igraphy \ig-rə-fē\ calligraphy, epigraphy, pseudepigraphy

igua \ē-gə\ see ¹IGA

igue \ēg\ gigue, Grieg, league, blitzkrieg, colleague, fatigue, garigue, intrigue, squeteague, wampumpeag

iguer \ē-gər\ see EAGER

iguous \ig-yə-wəs\ ambiguous, contiguous, exiguous, unambiguous

igured \ig-ərd\ see IGGARD

ii \ī\ see ¹Y

iing \ē-iŋ\ see EEING

ija \ē-jə\ see EGIA

ijah \ī-jə\ Elijah, steatopygia

iji \ē-jē\ Fiji, squeegee

ijl \īl\ see ¹ILE

ijn \īn\ see ¹INE

ijssel \ī-sə\ see ISAL

¹ik \ik\ see ICK

²ik \ēk\ see ¹EAK

¹ika \ē-kə\ pika, theca, areca, eureka, Frederica, Fredericka, paprika, Costa Rica, Dominica, oiticica, Topeka, Tanganyika, bibliotheca

²ika \ī-kə\ see ¹ICA

¹ike \ī-kē\ Nike, Psyche, crikey, spiky

²ike \īk\ bike, caique, dike, dyke, fyke, haik, hike, like, mike, Mike, pike, psych, shrike, sike, spike, strike, trike, tyke, alike, belike, catlike, childlike, clocklike, dislike, fly-strike, garpike, godlike, handspike, hitchhike, homelike, Klondike, lifelike, mislike, pealike, prooflike, push-bike, rampike, restrike, scalelike, sheaflike, shunpike, suchlike, ten-strike,

turnpike, unlike, Updike,
Vandyke, warlike, wifelike,
winglike, berrylike,
businesslike, fatherlike,
ladylike, look-alike,
machinelike, marlinespike,
marlinspike, minibike,
motorbike, rubberlike,
Scafell Pike, soundalike,
thunderstrike, womanlike,
workmanlike,
unsportsmanlike

³**ike** \ik\ *see* ICK

¹**iked** \īkt\ liked, piked,
spiked, vandyked—*also* -ed
forms of verbs listed at ²IKE

²**iked** \ī-kəd\ *see* YCAD

iken \ī-kən\ *see* ¹ICHEN

iker \ī-kər\ biker, diker,
duiker, hiker, piker, spiker,
striker, disliker, hitchhiker,
shunpiker, minibiker

ikes \īks\ yikes—*also* -s, -'s,
and -s' *forms of nouns listed
at* ²IKE, *and* -s *forms of verbs
listed there*

ikey \ī-kē\ *see* ¹IKE

ikh \ēk\ *see* ¹EAK

¹**iki** \ik-ē\ *see* ICKY

²**iki** \ē-kē\ *see* EAKY

iking \ī-kiŋ\ liking, striking,
Viking, shunpiking—*also*
-ing *forms of verbs listed at*
²IKE

ikker \ik-ər\ *see* ¹ICKER

iky \ī-kē\ *see* ¹IKE

¹**il** \il\ *see* ILL

²**il** \ēl\ *see* ²EAL

¹**ila** \il-ə\ *see* ²ILLA

²**ila** \ē-lə\ *see* ¹ELA

³**ila** \ī-lə\ Lila, Delilah

ilae \ī-lē\ *see* YLY

ilage \ī-lij\ mileage, silage

ilah \ī-lə\ *see* ³ILA

ilament \il-ə-mənt\ filament,
habiliment, monofilament

ilar \ī-lər\ dialer, filar, flier,

hilar, miler, smiler, stylar,
styler, tiler, Tyler, beguiler,
bifilar, compiler, defiler,
freestyler, profiler,
rottweiler, stockpiler,
unifilar

ilary \il-ə-rē\ *see* ILLARY

ilate \ī-lət\ *see* ILOT

ilbe \il-be\ *see* ILBY

ilbert \il-bərt\ filbert, gilbert,
Gilbert

ilby \il-bē\ trilby, astilbe

¹**ilch** \ilk\ *see* ILK

²**ilch** \ilch\ filch, milch, zilch

¹**ild** \īld\ mild, piled, wild,
Wilde, brainchild, godchild,
grandchild, hog-wild, man-
child, pantiled, Rothschild,
schoolchild, self-styled,
stepchild—*also* -ed *forms of
verbs listed at* ¹ILE

²**ild** \il\ *see* ILL

³**ild** \ilt\ *see* ILT

⁴**ild** \ild\ *see* ILLED

ilda \il-də\ Hilda, tilde, Wilda

¹**ilde** \il-də\ *see* ILDA

²**ilde** \īld\ *see* ¹ILD

¹**ilder** \il-dər\ builder, gilder,
guilder, wilder, bewilder,
boatbuilder, shipbuilder,
upbuilder, bodybuilder,
jerry-builder

²**ilder** \īl-dər\ milder, wilder,
Wilder

ilding \il-diŋ\ building,
gilding, hilding, abuilding,
outbuilding, shipbuilding,
bodybuilding—*also* -ing
forms of verbs listed at ILLED

ildish \īl-dish\ childish,
wildish

ildly \īld-lē\ childly, mildly,
wildly

¹**ile** \īl\ aisle, bile, dial, faille,
file, guile, I'll, isle, Kyle,
lisle, Lyle, mile, Nile, phial,
pile, rile, roil, smile, spile,

stile, style, tile, trial, vial,
vile, viol, while, wile, abseil,
aedile, agile, anile, argyle,
Argyll, audile, awhile, axile,
beguile, Blue Nile, Carlyle,
compile, condyle, cross-file,
de Stijl, decile, defile, denial,
docile, ductile, enisle, ensile,
erewhile, erstwhile, espial,
exile, febrile, fictile, fissile,
flexile, fragile, gentile, gracile,
futile, genial, gentile, gracile,
habile, hairstyle, Kabyle,
labile, life-style, meanwhile,
mistrial, mobile, motile,
nubile, pantile, penile,
pensile, profile, puerile,
quartile, quintile, redial,
reptile, resile, retrial, revile,
sandpile, scissile, sectile,
senile, servile, sessile, stabile,
stockpile, sundial, tactile,
tensile, textile, turnstile,
typestyle, unpile, utile,
vagile, virile, woodpile,
worthwhile, afebrile,
airmobile, Anglophile,
chamomile, contractile,
crocodile, discophile,
domicile, endostyle, epistyle,
erectile, extensile,
Francophile, Gallophile,
halophile, homophile,
hypostyle, infantile, interfile,
juvenile, low-profile,
mercantile, oenophile,
otherwhile, pedophile,
percentile, peristyle,
prehensile, projectile,
protractile, pulsatile,
reconcile, refractile,
retractile, self-denial,
Slavophile, spermophile,
technopile, thermopile,
turophile, urostyle, versatile,
vibratile, xenophile,
ailurophile, amphiprostyle,

audiophile, bibliophile,
electrophile, fluviatile,
Germanophile, heterophile,
Italophile, nucleophile
²ile \il\ see ILL
³ile \ē-lē\ see EELY
⁴ile \ēl\ see ²EAL
⁵ile \il-ē\ see ¹ILLY
ilead \il-ē-əd\ see ILIAD
ileage \ī-lij\ see ILAGE
ileal \il-ē-əl\ see ¹ILIAL
ileless \īl-ləs\ guileless,
pileless, smileless
¹iler \ē-lər\ see EALER
²iler \ī-lər\ see ILAR
iles \īlz\ Giles, Miles, Niles,
Wade-Giles, British Isles,
Western Isles
ileum \il-ē-əm\ see ILIUM
iley \ī-lē\ see YLY
ilford \il-fərd\ Milford,
Wilford
¹ili \il-ē\ see ¹ILLY
²ili \ē-lē\ see EELY
¹ilia \il-ē-ə\ Celia, cilia,
Cecelia, Cecilia, Massilia,
Anglophilia, basophilia,
coprophilia, hemophilia,
juvenilia, necrophilia,
neophilia, pedophilia,
sensibilia, memorabilia
²ilia \il-yə\ Brasilia, sedilia,
bougainvillea, sensibilia,
memorabilia
³ilia \ēl-yə\ see ELIA
iliad \il-ē-əd\ Gilead, Iliad,
balm of Gilead
ilial \il-ē-əl\ filial, ileal,
familial, unfilial
¹ilian \il-ē-ən\ Gillian, Ilian,
Lillian, Basilian, reptilian,
Abbevillian, crocodilian,
preexilian, vespertilian
²ilian \il-yən\ see ILLION
ilias \il-ē-əs\ see ¹ILIOUS
iliate \il-ē-ət\ ciliate, affiliate
ilic \il-ik\ killick, acrylic,

allylic, Cyrillic, dactylic,
exilic, idyllic, sibylic,
amphiphilic, Anglophilic,
hemophilic, necrophilic,
pedophilic, postexilic,
zoophilic, bibliophilic

ilica \il-i-kə\ silica, basilica

ilican \il-i-kən\ see ILICON

ilicon \il-i-kən\ Millikan,
silicon, spillikin, basilican,
ferrosilicon

ilience \il-yəns\ see ILLIANCE

iliency \il-yən-sē\ see
ILLIANCY

ilient \il-yənt\ brilliant,
resilient

iliment \il-ə-mənt\ see
ILAMENT

¹iling \ī-liŋ\ filing, piling,
spiling, styling, tiling,
hairstyling

²iling \ē-liŋ\ see EELING

¹ilion \il-yən\ see ILLION

²ilion \il-ē-ən\ see ¹ILIAN

¹ilious \il-ē-əs\ punctilious,
supercilious, materfamilias,
paterfamilias

²ilious \il-yəs\ bilious,
atrabilious, supercilious

ilip \il-əp\ see ILLIP

ilitant \il-ə-tənt\ militant,
rehabilitant

ility \il-ət-ē\ ability, agility,
anility, civility, debility,
docility, ductility, facility,
fertility, fragility, futility,
gentility, gracility, hostility,
humility, lability, mobility,
motility, nobility, nubility,
scurrility, sectility, senility,
stability, sterility, suability,
tactility, tranquility, utility,
vagility, virility, actability,
affability, arability,
audibility, bearability,
biddability, breathability,
brushability, capability,

changeability, coilability,
contractility, countability,
credibility, crossability,
culpability, curability,
cutability, disability,
disutility, drapability,
drillability, drinkability,
durability, dyeability,
edibility, equability,
erectility, fallibility,
feasibility, fishability,
flammability, flexibility,
forgeability, formability,
frangibility, friability,
gullibility, imbecility,
immobility, inability,
incivility, indocility,
infantility, infertility,
instability, inutility,
juvenility, laudability,
leachability, legibility,
liability, likability, livability,
mailability, meltability,
miscibility, movability,
mutability, notability,
packability, placability,
plausibility, playability,
portability, possibility,
potability, pregnability,
prehensility, printability,
probability, puerility,
readability, risibility,
roadability, salability,
sensibility, sewability,
shareability, sociability,
solubility, solvability,
spreadability, squeezability,
stainability, stretchability,
tenability, testability,
traceability, treatability,
tunability, usability,
vendability, versatility,
viability, visibility, volatility,
washability, wearability,
wettability, workability,
absorbability, acceptability,
accessibility, accountability,

adaptability, adjustability,
admirability, admissibility,
adoptability, adorability,
advisability, affectability,
agreeability, alterability,
amenability, amiability,
amicability, appealability,
applicability,
approachability,
assumability, attainability,
automobility, availability,
believability, collapsibility,
combustability,
comparability, compatibility,
compensability,
compressability,
computability,
conceivability,
conductability,
confirmability,
contemptibility,
contractibility,
controllability,
convertibility, corrigibility,
corruptibility, cultivability,
damageability, decidability,
deductibility, defeasibility,
defensibility, delectability,
demonstrability, deniability,
dependability, desirability,
destructibility, detachability,
detectability, deterrability,
detonability, digestibility,
dilatability, dispensability,
disposability, dissociability,
dissolubility, distensibility,
distractibility, divisibility,
educability, electability,
eligibility, employability,
enforceability, equitability,
erasability, erodability,
exchangeability, excitability,
excludability, exhaustibility,
expansibility, expendability,
explosibility, exportability,
extensibility, extractibility,
extrudability, fashionability,

fatigability, filterability,
fissionability, formidability,
habitability, heritability,
illegibility, immiscibility,
immovability, immutability,
impalpability, impassability,
impassibility, impeccability,
implacability, implausibility,
impossibility, impregnability,
impressibility, improbability,
improvability, inaudibility,
incapability, incredibility,
indelibility, inductibility,
ineffability, infallibility,
infeasibility, inflammability,
inflexibility, infrangibility,
infusibility, insensibility,
insolubility, insurability,
intangibility, invincibility,
invisibility, irascibility,
irritability, knowledgeability,
machinability,
maintainability,
manageability, marketability,
merchantability,
measurability, modulability,
navigability, negligibility,
nonflammability,
openability, operability,
opposability, palatability,
penetrability, perceptibility,
perdurability, perfectibility,
performability, perishability,
permeability, permissibility,
pleasurability, practicability,
preferability, presentability,
preservability, preventability,
processibility,
programmability,
punishability, reasonability,
refundability, reliability,
renewability, repeatability,
reputability, resistibility,
respectability, responsibility,
retrievability, reusability,
reversability, salvageability,
separability, severability,

serviceability, suggestability,
supportability,
suppressibility, survivability,
susceptibility, sustainability,
tolerability, trafficability,
transferability,
translatability,
transmissibility,
transplantability,
transportability,
unflappability,
unthinkability,
untouchability, variability,
violability, vulnerability,
weatherability, alienability,
analyzability, assimilability,
codifiability,
commensurability,
communicability,
comprehensibility,
decomposability,
deliverability,
discriminability,
disrespectability,
distinguishability,
enumerability,
exceptionability,
hypnotizability, illimitability,
impenetrability,
imperishability,
impermeability,
impermissibility,
imponderability,
impracticability,
impressionability,
inaccessibility,
inadmissibility,
inadvisability, inalterability,
inapplicability,
incalculability,
incombustibility,
incomparability,
incompatibility,
incompressibility,
inconceivability,
incontestability,
inconvertibility,

incorrigibility,
incorruptibility,
indefeasibility,
indefensibility, indefinability,
indestructibility,
indigestibility,
indispensability,
indissolubility, indivisibility,
indomitability,
indubitability, ineducability,
ineffaceability, ineligibility,
ineluctability, inevitability,
inexhaustibility,
inexplicability,
inexpressibility,
inextricability, inheritability,
insatiability, inseparability,
insociability, insusceptibility,
intelligibility,
interchangeability,
intolerability, invariability,
invulnerability,
irreducibility,
irreformability,
irrefutability, irremovability,
irrepealability,
irreplaceability,
irrepressibility,
irreproachability,
irresistibility,
irresponsibility,
irretrievability,
irreversibility, irrevocability,
maneuverability,
manipulability, negotiability,
polarizability,
recognizability,
recoverability, rectifiability,
reprehensibility,
reproducibility,
substitutability,
unacceptability,
unaccountability,
understandability,
undesirability, verifiability,
biocompatability,
biodegradability,

differentiability,
inalienability,
incommensurability,
incommunicability,
incomprehensibility,
indefatigability,
indistinguishability,
ineradicability,
incontrovertibility,
irreconcilability,
irreproducibility,
interoperability
ilium \il-ē-əm\ cilium, ileum,
ilium, Ilium, milium,
trillium, beryllium,
penicillium
ilk \ilk\ bilk, ilk, milch, milk,
silk, buttermilk,
liebfraumilch
ilker \il-kər\ bilker, milker
ilky \il-kē\ milky, silky
ill \il\ bill, Bill, brill, chill,
dill, drill, fill, frill, gill, grill,
grille, hill, ill, Jill, kill, krill,
mil, mill, mille, Milne, nil,
nill, Phil, pill, prill, quill, rill,
shill, shrill, sild, sill, skill,
spill, squill, still, swill, thill,
thrill, til, till, trill, twill, vill,
will, Will, anthill, backfill,
bluegill, Brazil, Catskill,
Churchill, cranesbill,
crossbill, de Mille, dentil,
deskill, distill, doorsill,
downhill, duckbill, dullsville,
dunghill, fiberfill, foothill,
freewill, fulfill, goodwill,
Granville, gristmill, handbill,
hawksbill, hornbill,
Huntsville, instill, Knoxville,
lambkill, landfill, limekiln,
manille, Melville, molehill,
mudsill, Nashville, no-till,
playbill, quadrille, refill,
roadkill, sawmill, self-will,
Seville, sheathbill, shoebill,
sidehill, sigil, spadille,

spoonbill, stabile, standstill,
stockstill, storksbill, T-bill,
treadmill, unreal, until,
uphill, vaudeville, waxbill,
waybill, windchill, windmill,
Brazzaville, chlorophyll,
daffodil, deshabille, de
Toqueville, dishabille,
escadrille, espadrille,
Evansville, Francophil,
Hooverville, Jacksonville,
Libreville, Louisville,
minimill, overfill,
overkill, overspill,
razorbill, rototill, tormentil,
verticil, windowsill,
whippoorwill, winter-kill,
Yggdrasil, acidophil,
ivorybill, minoxydil,
Nizhni Togil, run-of-
the-mill
I'll \il\ see ¹ILE
¹illa \ē-yə\ barilla, cuadrilla,
banderilla, quesadilla
²illa \il-ə\ scilla, Scylla,
squilla, villa, Willa, ancilla,
Aquila, Attila, axilla,
Camilla, cedilla, chinchilla,
flotilla, gorilla, guerrilla,
manila, Manila, megillah,
papilla, perilla, Priscilla,
scintilla, vanilla, camarilla,
cascarilla, granadilla,
potentilla, sabadilla,
sapodilla, sarsaparilla
³illa \ē-ə\ see ¹IA
⁴illa \ēl-yə\ see ELIA
⁵illa \ē-lə\ see ¹ELA
illable \il-ə-bəl\ billable,
drillable, fillable, spillable,
syllable, tillable, disyllable,
refillable, trisyllable,
decasyllable, monosyllable,
octosyllable, polysyllable,
hendecasyllable
illage \il-ij\ grillage, millage,
pillage, spillage, tillage,

village, no-tillage, permillage,
Greenwich Village

illah \il-ə\ see ²ILLA

illain \il-ən\ see ILLON

illar \il-ər\ see ILLER

illary \il-ə-rē\ Hilary, Hillary,
phyllary, codicillary

illate \il-ət\ see ILLET

¹**ille** \il\ see ILL

²**ille** \ē\ see ¹EE

³**ille** \ēl\ see ²EAL

illea \il-yə\ see ²ILIA

illed \ild\ build, dilled, drilled,
gild, gilled, guild, skilled,
twilled, willed, Brynhild,
engild, gold-filled,
goodwilled, rebuild, self-
willed, spoonbilled, unbuild,
unskilled, upbuild, wergild,
jerry-build, overbuild,
semiskilled—*also* -ed *forms
of verbs listed at* ILL

illedness \il-nəs\ see ILLNESS

illein \il-ən\ see ILLON

iller \il-ər\ biller, chiller,
driller, filler, giller, griller,
hiller, killer, miller, Miller,
pillar, schiller, spiller,
swiller, thriller, tiller, triller,
axillar, distiller, fulfiller,
painkiller, pralltriller, von
Schiller, caterpillar, lady-
killer, Rototiller—*also* -er
forms of adjectives listed at
ILL

illery \il-rē\ pillory, artillery,
distillery

illes \il-ēz\ see ILLIES

illet \il-ət\ billet, fillet,
millet, rillet, skillet, willet,
distillate

illful \il-fəl\ skillful, willful,
unskillful

¹**illi** \il-ē\ see ¹ILLY

²**illi** \ē-lē\ see EELY

¹**illian** \il-ē-ən\ see ¹ILIAN

²**illian** \il-yən\ see ILLION

illiance \il-yəns\ brilliance,
resilience

illiancy \il-yən-sē\ brilliancy,
resiliency

illiant \il-yənt\ see ILIENT

illick \il-ik\ see ILIC

illie \il-ē\ see ¹ILLY

illies \il-ēz\ willies, Achilles,
Antilles, Greater Antilles,
Lesser Antilles, Netherlands
Antilles—*also* -s, -'s, *and* -s'
forms of nouns listed at ¹ILLY

illikan \il-i-kən\ see ILICON

illikin \il-i-kən\ see ILICON

¹**illin** \il-əm\ see ILLUM

²**illin** \il-ən\ see ILLON

illing \il-iŋ\ billing, drilling,
filling, killing, milling,
schilling, shilling, skilling,
twilling, willing, fulfilling,
spine-chilling,
unwilling—*also* -ing *forms of
verbs listed at* ILL

illion \il-yən\ billion, jillion,
Lillian, million, pillion,
trillion, zillion, caecilian,
Castilian, centillion, civilian,
cotillion, decillion,
modillion, nonillion,
octillion, pavilion, postilion,
quadrillion, Quintilian,
quintillion, reptilian,
septillion, sextillion,
toubillion, vaudevillian,
vermilion, crocodilian,
Maximilian, preexilian,
quindecillion, sexdecillion,
tredecillion, undecillion,
vespertilian, vigintillion,
duodecillion,
novemdecillion,
octodecillion,
septendecillion,
quattuordecillion

illip \il-əp\ fillip, Philip

illis \il-əs\ see ILLUS

illium \il-ē-əm\ see ILIUM

illness \il-nəs\ chillness, illness, shrillness, stillness

¹**illo** \il-ō\ billow, pillow, willow, Negrillo, tornillo, Amarillo, armadillo, cigarillo, coyotillo, peccadillo, tamarillo

²**illo** \ē-ō\ see ²IO

illon \il-ən\ billon, Dylan, Uilleann, villain, villein, tefillin, penicillin, amoxycillin

illory \il-rē\ see ILLERY

illous \il-əs\ see ILLUS

¹**illow** \il-ə\ see ²ILLA

²**illow** \il-ō\ see ¹ILLO

illowy \il-ə-wē\ billowy, pillowy, willowy

ills \ilz\ Black Hills, no-frills, Alban Hills—*also* -s, -'s, *and* -s' *forms of nouns listed at* ILL, *and* -s *forms of verbs listed there*

illum \il-əm\ chillum, vexillum

illus \il-əs\ Phyllis, villous, Willis, bacillus, lapillus, amaryllis, toga virilis

¹**illy** \il-ē\ Billie, billy, Chile, chili, chilly, dilly, filly, frilly, gillie, hilly, illy, Lillie, lily, Lily, Millie, really, Scilly, silly, stilly, Willie, Willy, bacilli, Caerphilly, daylily, fusilli, guidwillie, hillbilly, piccalilli, rockabilly, willy-nilly

²**illy** \il-lē\ shrilly, stilly

¹**iln** \il\ see ILL

²**iln** \iln\ kiln, Milne

¹**ilne** \iln\ see ²ILN

²**ilne** \il\ see ILL

¹**ilo** \ī-lō\ milo, Milo, phyllo, silo

²**ilo** \ē-lō\ helo, kilo, phyllo, Iloilo

ilom \ī-ləm\ see ILUM

iloquence \il-ə-kwəns\ grandiloquence, magniloquence

iloquent \il-ə-kwənt\ grandiloquent, magniloquent

iloquist \il-ə-kwəst\ soliloquist, ventriloquist

iloquy \il-ə-kwē\ soliloquy, ventriloquy

ilot \ī-lət\ eyelet, islet, Pilate, pilot, stylet, copilot, autopilot, Pontius Pilate

ils \ils\ fils, grilse, Nils

ilse \ils\ see ILS

ilt \ilt\ built, gilt, guilt, hilt, jilt, kilt, lilt, milt, quilt, silt, stilt, tilt, wilt, atilt, bloodguilt, Brunhild, homebuilt, inbuilt, rebuilt, unbuilt, uptilt, carvel-built, clinker-built, custom-built, purpose-built

ilter \il-tər\ filter, kilter, milter, philter, off-kilter

ilth \ilth\ filth, spilth, tilth

iltie \il-tē\ see ILTY

ilton \ilt-ᵊn\ Hilton, Milton, Stilton, Wilton

ilty \il-tē\ guilty, kiltie, milty, silty, bloodguilty

ilum \ī-ləm\ filum, hilum, phylum, whilom, xylem, asylum

ilus \ī-ləs\ eyeless, pilus, stylus, tieless

¹**ily** \ī-lē\ see YLY

²**ily** \il-ē\ see ¹ILLY

¹**im** \im\ bream, brim, dim, glim, grim, Grimm, gym, him, hymn, Jim, Kim, limb, limn, mim, nim, prim, rim, scrim, shim, skim, slim, swim, Tim, trim, vim, whim, bedim, dislimn, forelimb, passim, prelim, Purim, Sikkim, slim-jim, snap-brim, acronym, anonym, antonym, eponym, homonym, metonym, paradigm, paronym, pseudonym,

seraphim, synonym, tautonym, toponym, underbrim, ad interim, heteronym

²**im** \ĕm\ see ¹EAM

I'm \īm\ see ¹IME

ima \ē-mə\ see EMA

imable \ī-mə-bəl\ climable, sublimable, unclimbable

imace \im-əs\ grimace, tzimmes

image \im-ij\ image, scrimmage, self-image, afterimage

iman \ē-mən\ see ¹EMON

imate \ī-mət\ climate, primate, acclimate

¹**imb** \im\ see ¹IM

²**imb** \īm\ see ¹IME

imba \im-bə\ limba, kalimba, marimba

imbable \ī-mə-bəl\ see IMABLE

imbal \im-bəl\ see IMBLE

imbale \im-bəl\ see IMBLE

imbed \imd\ limbed, rimmed, clean-limbed—*also* -ed *forms of verbs listed at* ¹IM

¹**imber** \im-bər\ limber, timber, sawtimber, unlimber

²**imber** \ī-mər\ see ¹IMER

imble \im-bəl\ cymbal, gimbal, nimble, symbol, thimble, timbal, timbale, wimble

imbo \im-bō\ bimbo, limbo, akimbo, gumbo-limbo

imbral \am-brəl\ see AMBREL

imbre \am-bər\ see ²AMBAR

imbrel \im-brəl\ timbrel, whimbrel

imbus \im-bəs\ limbus, nimbus

¹**ime** \īm\ chime, climb, clime, crime, dime, disme,

grime, I'm, lime, mime, prime, rhyme, rime, slime, stime, thyme, time, airtime, all-time, bedtime, begrime, big time, birdlime, daytime, downtime, dreamtime, enzyme, flextime, foretime, halftime, lifetime, longtime, lunchtime, Mannheim, Maytime, mealtime, meantime, nighttime, noontime, old-time, onetime, part-time, pastime, peacetime, playtime, quicklime, ragtime, schooltime, seedtime, small-time, sometime, space-time, springtime, sublime, teatime, two-time, uptime, wartime, aftertime, Anaheim, anytime, beforetime, Christmastime, dinnertime, double-time, harvesttime, Jotunheim, lysozyme, maritime, monorhyme, overtime, pantomime, paradigm, summertime, wintertime, nickel-and-dime

²**ime** \ĕm\ see ¹EAM

imel \im-əl\ gimel, gimmal, kümmel

imeless \īm-ləs\ rhymeless, timeless

imely \īm-lē\ primely, timely, untimely

imen \ī-mən\ flyman, hymen, Hymen, limen, Lyman, Simon

imeon \im-ē-ən\ see IMIAN

imeous \ī-məs\ see IMIS

¹**imer** \ī-mər\ chimer, climber, dimer, mimer, primer, rhymer, timer, trimer, full-time, old-timer, small-timer, sublimer, two-timer, wisenheimer

²imer \im-ər\ see IMMER

imerick \im-rik\ see YMRIC

¹imes \īmz\ times, betimes, daytimes, sometimes, betweentimes, oftentimes—also -s, -'s, and -s' forms of nouns listed at ¹IME, and -s forms of verbs listed there

²imes \ēm\ see ¹EAM

imeter \im-ət-ər\ dimeter, limiter, scimitar, trimeter, altimeter, delimiter, perimeter, tachymeter

imetry \im-ə-trē\ symmetry, gravimetry, polarimetry, sypersymmetry

imian \im-ē-ən\ Simeon, simian, Endymion, prosimian

imic \im-ik\ see ²YMIC

imical \im-i-kəl\ inimical, metonymical, synonymical, toponymical

imicry \im-i-krē\ gimmickry, mimicry

imilar \im-ə-lər\ similar, dissimilar

imile \im-ə-lē\ simile, swimmily, facsimile

¹iminal \im-ən-²l\ criminal, liminal, subliminal, supraliminal

²iminal \im-nəl\ see YMNAL

iminy \im-ə-nē\ see IMONY

imis \ī-məs\ primus, thymus, timeous, imprimis, untimeous

imitable \im-ət-ə-bəl\ imitable, illimitable, inimitable

imitar \im-ət-ər\ see IMETER

imiter \im-ət-ər\ see IMETER

imits \im-its\ limits, Nimitz

imity \im-ət-ē\ dimity, proximity, sublimity, anonymity, equanimity, longanimity, magnanimity, pseudonymity, synonymity, unanimity, pusillanimity

imitz \im-its\ see IMITS

imm \im\ see ¹IM

immable \im-ə-bəl\ dimmable, swimmable

immage \im-ij\ see IMAGE

immal \im-əl\ see IMEL

imme \i-mē\ see IMMY

immed \imd\ see IMBED

immer \im-ər\ brimmer, dimmer, glimmer, krimmer, limmer, limner, primer, shimmer, simmer, skimmer, slimmer, swimmer, trimmer—also -er forms of adjectives listed at ¹IM

immes \im-əs\ see IMACE

immick \im-ik\ see ²YMIC

immickry \im-i-krē\ see IMICRY

immily \im-ə-lē\ see IMILE

immy \im-ē\ gimme, jimmy, limby, shimmy, swimmy

imn \im\ see ¹IM

imner \im-ər\ see IMMER

imo \ē-mō\ primo, sentimo

imon \i-mən\ see IMEN

imony \im-ə-nē\ simony, niminy-piminy

imothy \im-ə-thē\ timothy, Timothy, polymathy

imp \imp\ blimp, chimp, crimp, gimp, guimpe, imp, limp, pimp, primp, scrimp, shrimp, simp, skimp, wimp

impe \imp\ see IMP

imper \im-pər\ limper, shrimper, simper, whimper

imping \im-pən\ see YMPAN

impish \im-pish\ blimpish, impish

imple \im-pəl\ dimple, pimple, simple, wimple, oversimple

imply \im-plē\ dimply, limply, pimply, simply

impy \im-pē\ crimpy, gimpy,
scrimpy, shrimpy, skimpy,
wimpy
imsy \im-zē\ flimsy, slimsy,
whimsy
imulus \im-yə-ləs\ limulus,
stimulus
imus \ī-məs\ see IMIS
imy \i-mē\ grimy, limey,
limy, rimy, slimy, stymie,
thymy, old-timey
¹in \in\ been, bin, blin, chin,
din, fin, Finn, gin, grin,
Gwyn, hin, in, inn, kin, linn,
Lynn, Lynne, pin, shin,
Shin, sin, skin, spin, thin,
tin, twin, whin, win, wyn,
yin, zin, again, agin, akin,
all-in, backspin, bearskin,
begin, Benin, Berlin,
Boleyn, bowfin, break-in,
buckskin, built-in, burn-in,
calfskin, capeskin, cave-in,
chagrin, check-in,
Chongjin, close-in,
clothespin, coonskin,
Corinne, crankpin, cut-in,
deerskin, doeskin, drive-in,
drop-in, duckpin, dustbin,
fade-in, fill-in, foreskin,
goatskin, Guilin, hairpin,
Harbin,
has-been, headpin, herein,
Jilin, Kerin, kidskin,
kingpin, lambskin, lead-in,
lie-in, linchpin, live-in,
lived-in, lobe-fin, locked-in,
look-in, love-in, moleskin,
munchkin, Nankin, ninepin,
no-win, oilskin, Pekin,
phone-in, pigskin, pinyin,
plug-in, pushpin, ruin, run-
in, saimin, scarfpin,
scarfskin, sealskin, set-in,
sharkskin, sheepskin, shoo-
in, shut-in, sidespin, sit-in,
sleep-in, snakeskin, stand-in,

step-in, stickpin, swanskin,
tailspin, take-in, tap-in,
teach-in, tenpin, therein,
tholepin, threadfin, throw-
in, tie-in, tiepin, tip-in, toe-
in, trade-in, tuned-in, turn-
in, unpin, walk-in, weigh-in,
wherein, wineskin, within,
woolskin, write-in,
candlepin, catechin,
Ha-erh-pin, Ho Chi Minh,
Lohengrin, lying-in,
mandolin, maximin, Mickey
Finn, onionskin, palanquin,
Tianjin, underpin,
underspin, Vietminh, violin,
whipper-in, canthaxanthin
²in \ēn\ see ³INE
³in \an\ see ⁵AN
⁴in \aⁿ\ Chopin, doyen,
Gauguin, moulin, Petain,
Rodin, serin, coq au vin,
coup de main, fleur de coin,
Mazarin
⁵in \ən\ see ¹UN
¹ina \ī-nə\ china, China,
Dina, Dinah, Heine, Ina,
mina, mynah, Aegina,
angina, Lucina, nandina,
piscina, Regina, salina,
shechinah, vagina, Cochin
China, Carolina, Indochina,
kamaaina, Poland China,
North Carolina, South
Carolina
²ina \ē-nə\ Deena, Dena,
kina, Lena, Nina, plena,
Shina, Tina, vena, vina,
arena, Athena, cantina,
catena, Christina, coquina,
corbina, corvina, czarina,
Edwina, euglena, farina,
fontina, Georgina, hyena,
kachina, Kristina, marina,
Marina, medina, Medina,
Messina, nandina, novena,
patina, piscina, platina,

Regina, retsina, Rowena,
salina, sestina, Shechinah,
subpoena, verbena,
Agrippina, amberina,
Angelina, Argentina,
ballerina, casuarina,
Carolina, Catalina, catilena,
cavatina, Chianina,
concertina, Filipina, javelina,
Katerina, ocarina, Palestrina,
Pasadena, Saint Helena,
semolina, signorina, sonatina,
Taormina, Teresina,
Wilhelmina, Herzegovina,
Pallas Athena, Strait of
Messina

inable \ī-nə-bəl\ minable,
consignable, declinable,
definable, inclinable,
indeclinable, indefinable

inach \in-ich\ Greenwich,
spinach

¹inah \ē-nə\ see ²INA

²inah \ī-nə\ see ¹INA

¹inal \īn-ᵊl\ clinal, final,
rhinal, spinal, trinal, vinyl,
matutinal, officinal,
quarterfinal, semifinal,
serotinal

²inal \ēn-ᵊl\ see ENAL

inally \īn-ᵊl-ē\ clinally, finally,
spinally, matutinally

inary \ī-nə-rē\ binary, trinary

¹inas \ī-nəs\ see ¹INUS

²inas \ē-nəs\ see ¹ENUS

inative \in-ət-iv\ see INITIVE

inc \iŋk\ see INK

inca \iŋ-kə\ Dinka, Inca,
vinca, Mandinka

incal \iŋ-kəl\ see INKLE

incan \iŋ-kən\ Incan, Lincoln

¹ince \ins\ blintz, chintz,
mince, prince, quince, rinse,
since, wince, convince,
evince, shinsplints, Port-au-
Prince

²ince \ans\ see ³ANCE

incely \in-slē\ princely,
tinselly

incer \in-chər\ see INCHER

inch \inch\ chinch, cinch,
clinch, finch, flinch, grinch,
inch, lynch, pinch, squinch,
winch, bullfinch, goldfinch,
greenfinch, hawfinch,
unclinch

incher \in-chər\ clincher,
flincher, lyncher, pincer,
pincher, wincher,
affenpinscher, penny-
pincher, Doberman pinscher

inching \in-chiŋ\ unflinching,
penny-pinching—*also* -ing
forms of verbs listed at INCH

incible \in-sə-bəl\ principal,
principle, vincible, evincible,
invincible, inconvincible

incing \in-siŋ\ ginseng,
mincing, convincing,
unconvincing—*also* -ing
forms of verbs listed at ¹INCE

incipal \in-sə-bəl\ see INCIBLE

inciple \in-sə-bəl\ see INCIBLE

inck \iŋk\ see INK

incky \iŋ-kē\ see INKY

incoln \iŋ-kən\ see INCAN

inct \iŋt\ linked, kinked, tinct,
distinct, extinct, instinct,
precinct, succinct, unlinked,
indistinct

inction \iŋ-shən\ distinction,
extinction, contradistinction

inctive \iŋ-tiv\ distinctive,
extinctive, instinctive,
indistinctive

incture \iŋ-chər\ cincture,
tincture

¹ind \īnd\ bind, blind, find,
grind, hind, kind, mind, rind,
signed, spined, tined, wind,
wynd, affined, behind,
confined, inclined, in-kind,
night-blind, purblind,
refined, remind, rewind,

sand-blind, snow-blind,
spellbind, stone-blind,
streamlined, unbind,
unkind, unwind, color-
blind, double-blind,
gavelkind, gravel-blind,
hoodman-blind,
humankind, mastermind,
nonaligned, single-blind,
unaligned, undersigned,
well-defined, womankind—
also -ed *forms of verbs listed*
at ¹INE

²ind \ind\ finned, Ind, Sind,
skinned, wind,
buckskinned, crosswind,
downwind, exscind,
prescind, rescind, soft-
finned, thick-skinned, thin-
skinned, upwind, whirlwind,
woodwind, Amerind, spiny-
finned, tamarind—*also* -ed
forms of verbs listed at ¹IN

³ind \int\ see INT

inda \in-də\ Linda, Lucinda,
Melinda, Samarinda

indar \in-dər\ see ²INDER

¹inded \in-dəd\ minded,
rinded, broad-minded, fair-
minded, high-minded, large-
minded, like-minded, low-
minded, right-minded, small-
minded, strong-minded,
tough-minded, weak-minded,
absentminded, bloody-
minded, civic-minded, evil-
minded, feebleminded,
narrow-minded, open-
minded, simpleminded,
single-minded, social-minded,
tender-minded—*also* -ed
forms of verbs listed at ¹IND

²inded \in-dəd\ brinded,
long-winded, short-winded,
broken-winded—*also* -ed
forms of verbs listed at ²IND

¹inder \in-dər\ binder,

blinder, finder, grinder,
hinder, minder, winder,
bookbinder, faultfinder,
highbinder, netminder,
pathfinder, reminder, ring
binder, self-binder,
sidewinder, spellbinder,
stem-winder, viewfinder,
organ-grinder—*also* -er
forms of adjectives listed at
¹IND

²inder \in-dər\ cinder,
hinder, Pindar, tinder

indful \in-fəl\ mindful,
remindful, unmindful

indhi \in-dē\ see INDY

indi \in-dē\ see INDY

indic \in-dik\ Indic, syndic

indie \in-dē\ see INDY

inding \in-diŋ\ binding,
finding, winding,
bookbinding, fact-finding,
faultfinding, pathfinding,
self-winding, spellbinding,
stem-winding—*also* -ing
forms of verbs listed at ¹IND

indlass \in-ləs\ see INLESS

indle \in-d²l\ brindle,
dwindle, kindle, spindle,
swindle, enkindle

indless \in-ləs\ kindless,
mindless, spineless

¹indling \in-lən\ pindling,
kindling

²indling \ind-liŋ\ dwindling,
kindling, pindling,
spindling—*also* -ing *forms of*
verbs listed at ¹INDLE

¹indly \in-lē\ see INLY

²indly \in-lē\ see ¹INELY

indness \in-nəs\ blindness,
fineness, kindness,
purblindness, unkindness,
loving-kindness

indowed \in-dəd\ see ²INDED

indus \in-dəs\ Indus, Pindus

indy \in-dē\ Cindy, Hindi,

indie, lindy, shindy, Sindhi,
windy, Rawalpindi

'ine \in\ bine, brine, chine,
cline, dine, dyne, eyen, fine,
Jain, kine, line, Line, Main,
mine, nine, pine, Rhein,
Rhine, rind, shine, shrine,
sign, spine, spline, stein,
Stein, swine, syne, thine, tine,
trine, twine, vine, whine,
wine, A-line, affine, airline,
align, alkyne, alpine, assign,
balkline, baseline, beeline,
benign, Bernstein, bloodline,
bovine, bowline, branchline,
breadline, buntline, bustline,
byline, canine, caprine,
carbine, carmine, cervine,
clothesline, coastline,
combine, compline, condign,
confine, consign, corvine,
cutline, dateline, deadline,
decline, define, design,
divine, dragline, driveline,
earthshine, Einstein, eiswein,
enshrine, ensign, entwine,
equine, ethyne, feline, ferine,
fraulein, frontline, gantline,
grapevine, guideline, hairline,
hard-line, headline, hemline,
hipline, Holbein, Holstein,
incline, indign, in-line,
jawline, landline, lang syne,
lifeline, longline, lupine,
mainline, malign, midline,
moline, moonshine, off-line,
old-line, opine, outline,
outshine, ovine, Pauline,
Pennine, Petrine, pipeline,
piscine, plotline, pontine,
Pontine, porcine, potline,
propine, quinine, rapine,
recline, redline, refine, reline,
repine, resign, ridgeline,
roofline, Sabine, saline,
setline, shoreline, sideline,
Sixtine, skyline, soft-line,

straight-line, strandline,
streamline, strychnine,
subline, sunshine, supine,
syncline, taurine, tie-line,
time-line, topline, touchline,
towline, tramline, trapline,
trephine, trotline, truckline,
tumpline, turbine, untwine,
ursine, vespine, vulpine,
waistline, woodbine, zayin,
zebrine, aerodyne, alkaline,
androgyne, Angeline,
anodyne, anserine, anticline,
aquiline, argentine, asinine,
auld lang syne, borderline,
bottom-line, Byzantine,
calamine, calcimine,
Caroline, catarrhine,
Catiline, celandine,
centerline, cisalpine,
Cisalpine, clandestine,
colubrine, columbine,
Columbine, concubine,
Constantine, countermine,
countersign, crystalline,
cytokine, disincline,
eglantine, endocrine,
exocrine, falconine,
fescennine, Frankenstein,
gregarine, infantine,
interline, intertwine, iodine,
Johannine, leonine,
Liechtenstein, monkeyshine,
muscadine, opaline, palatine,
Palestine, passerine,
porcupine, psittacine,
realign, redefine, redesign,
riverine, Rubenstein,
saccharine, sapphirine,
saturnine, serpentine,
sibylline, sixty-nine,
subalpine, Theatine,
timberline, turnverein,
turpentine, underline,
undermine, Ursuline,
uterine, valentine, vespertine,
viperine, vulturine, waterline,

zibeline, accipitrine,
adamantine, adulterine,
alexandrine, amaranthine.
Capitoline, elephantine,
Evangeline, Frankfurt am
Main, Rembrandt van Rijn,
Schleswig-Holstein,
nonoxynol-9, Newcastle-
upon Tyne

²**ine** \ē-nä\ fine, wahine

³**ine** \ēn\ bean, clean, dean,
Dean, Deane, dene, e'en,
gene, Gene, glean, green,
Green, greene, jean, Jean,
Jeanne, keen, lean, lien,
mean, mesne, mien, peen,
preen, quean, queen, scene,
screen, seen, sheen, shin,
sin, skean, skene, spean,
spleen, teen, tween, wean,
ween, wheen, yean, Aileen,
Arlene, baleen, beguine,
Beguine, Benin, Bernstein,
between, boreen, bovine,
buckbean, caffeine,
canteen, carbine, careen,
Carlene, Cathleen,
Charlene, chlorine,
chopine, chorine, Christine,
citrine, Claudine, codeine,
colleen, Colleen, convene,
Coreen, cotquean, cuisine,
Darlene, dasheen, dauphine,
demean, demesne, dentine,
Doreen, dry-clean, dudeen,
eighteen, Eileen, Essene,
Eugene, fanzine, fascine,
fifteen, fourteen, Francine,
gamine, gangrene, glassine,
gyrene, Helene, Hellene,
Hermine, hoatzin, holstein,
Holstein, horsebean,
houseclean, hygiene, Ilene,
Irene, Jacqueline, Jeanine,
Jeannine, Jolene, Justine,
Kathleen, khamsin,
Kristine, Ladin, lateen,

latrine, Lorene, Lublin,
machine, malines, marine,
Marlene, Maureen,
Maxine, moline, moreen,
morphine, Nadine,
nankeen, naphthene,
Nicene, nineteen, nongreen,
Noreen, obscene, offscreen,
on-screen, patine, Pauline,
piscine, Pontine, poteen,
praline, preteen, pristine,
propine, protein, quinine,
Rabin, Racine, ratteen,
ravine, routine, saline,
saltine, Salween, sardine,
sateen, scalene, serene,
shagreen, Sharlene, shebeen,
siren, Sistine, sixteen,
Slovene, soybean, spalpeen,
strychnine, subteen,
sunscreen, Szczecin, takin,
taurine, terrene, terrine,
thirteen, Tolkien, tontine,
tureen, umpteen, unclean,
undine, unseen, vaccine,
vitrine, windscreen,
yestreen, Yibin, zechin,
Aberdeen, almandine,
Angeline, argentine,
Argentine, Augustine,
barkentine, bengaline,
Bernadine, bombazine,
Borodin, brigandine,
brigantine, brilliantine,
Byzantine, carotene,
carrageen, celandine,
clandestine, columbine,
Constantine, contravene,
crepe de chine, crystalline,
damascene, Dexedrine,
Dramamine, duvetyn,
eglantine, endocrine,
Eocene, epicene,
Ernestine, estaurine,
evergreen, fescennine,
figurine, Florentine,
fluorine, fukerene,

gabardine, gaberdine, gadarene, galantine, gasoline, Geraldine, Ghibelline, go-between, grenadine, Gretna Green, guillotine, Halloween, haute cuisine, Hippocrene, histamine, Holocene, Imogene, in-between, indigene, intervene, Jeraldine, Josephine, Kalinin, kerosene, langoustine, legatine, libertine, limousine, M16, magazine, mangosteen, margravine, Medellín, melamine, messaline, Methedrine, mezzanine, Miocene, mousseline, Nazarene, nectarine, nicotine, overseen, opaline, organzine, palanquin, palatine, pelerine, percaline, peregrine, philhellene, Philistine, plasticene, plasticine, Pleistocene, Pliocene, riverine, quarantine, reserpine, saccharine, Sakhalin, Saladin, San Joaquin, San Martin, sapphirine, schizophrene, serpentine, seventeen, silkaline, Stelazine, submarine, subroutine, supervene, tambourine, tangerine, Theatine, tourmaline, trampoline, transmarine, travertine, Tridentine, Vaseline, velveteen, wintergreen, wolverine, Ursuline, adamantine, alexandrine, amphetamine, aquamarine, Benedictine, bromocriptine, carbon 13, doxycycline, elephantine, Evangeline, internecine, leukotirene, methylxanthene,

mujahideen, niphedipine, nouvelle cuisine, Oligocene, Paleocene, pentamedine, tricothecene, ultramarine, antihistamine, benzoapyrene, diphenhydramine, Mary Magdalene, NC-17, polybutadiene, alpha-fetaprotein, apolipoprotein, buckminsterfullerene, General San Martin, oleomargarine

⁴ine \in-ē\ see INNY

⁵ine \ē-nē\ see ¹INI

⁶ine \ən\ see UN

inea \in-ē\ see INNY

ineal \in-ē-əl\ finial, lineal, matrilineal, patrilineal, unilineal

ined \īnd\ see ¹IND

inee \ī-nē\ see ¹INY

ineless \īn-ləs\ see INDLESS

¹inely \īn-lē\ blindly, finely, kindly, affinely, condignly, equinely, felinely, purblindly, unkindly

²inely \ēn-lē\ see ¹EANLY

inement \īn-mənt\ see IGNMENT

ineness \īn-nəs\ see INDNESS

ineous \in-ē-əs\ gramineous, sanguineous, consanguineous, ignominious

¹iner \ī-nər\ briner, diner, finer, liner, miner, minor, shiner, Shriner, signer, twiner, whiner, airliner, aligner, baseliner, byliner, combiner, confiner, cosigner, definer, designer, diviner, eyeliner, hardliner, headliner, incliner, jetliner, long-liner, moonshiner, one-liner, recliner, refiner, repiner, sideliner, soft-liner, streamliner, Asia Minor,

Canis Minor, forty-niner, party-liner, Ursa Minor, superliner

²**iner** \\-ē-nər\\ see EANER

¹**inery** \\in-rē\\ finery, pinery, vinery, winery, refinery

²**inery** \\ēn-rē\\ see EANERY

¹**ines** \\ēn\\ see ³INE

²**ines** \\ēnz\\ see EENS

³**ines** \\īnz\\ Mainz, Appenines—*also* -s, -'s, *and* -s' *forms of nouns listed at* ¹INE, *and* -s *forms of verbs listed there*

inest \\i-nəst\\ see ¹INIST

inet \\in-ət\\ see INNET

inew \\in-yü\\ see INUE

infield \\in-fēld\\ infield, Winfield

ing \\iŋ\\ bring, Ching, cling, ding, fling, king, King, ling, Ming, ping, ring, sing, sling, spring, sting, string, swing, thing, wing, wring, zing, backswing, Baoding, bedspring, Beijing, bi-swing, bitewing, bowstring, bullring, Chongqing, clearwing, downswing, drawstring, D ring, earring, first-string, forewing, G-string, greenwing, hairspring, hamstring, handspring, headspring, heartstring, Kunming, lacewing, lapwing, latchstring, mainspring, Nanjing, Nanning, O-ring, offspring, Paoting, plaything, redwing, shoestring, showring, unsling, unstring, upspring, upswing, wellspring, whitewing, windwing, wingding, Xining, à la king, anything, buck-and-wing, ding-a-ling, double-ring, everything, innerspring,

Liaoning, pigeonwing, superstring, underwing

inga \\iŋ-gə\\ anhinga, syringa

inge \\inj\\ binge, cringe, dinge, fringe, hinge, singe, springe, swinge, tinge, twinge, whinge, impinge, infringe, syringe, unhinge

inged \\iŋd\\ ringed, stringed, winged, net-winged—*also* -ed *forms of verbs listed at* ING

ingement \\inj-mənt\\ impingement, infringement

ingency \\in-jən-sē\\ stringency, astringency, contingency

ingent \\in-jənt\\ stringent, astringent, constringent, contingent, refringent

¹**inger** \\iŋ-ər\\ bringer, clinger, dinger, flinger, pinger, ringer, singer, springer, stinger, stringer, swinger, winger, wringer, zinger, folksinger, gunslinger, humdinger, left-winger, mudslinger, right-winger, mastersinger, Meistersinger, minnesinger

²**inger** \\iŋ-gər\\ finger, linger, five-finger, forefinger, malinger, ladyfinger

³**inger** \\in-jər\\ ginger, Ginger, injure, singer, swinger

ingery \\inj-rē\\ gingery, injury

inghy \\iŋ-ē\\ see ¹INGY

ingi \\iŋ-ē\\ see ¹INGY

ingian \\in-jən\\ Thuringian, Carlovingian, Carolingian, Merovingian

inging \\iŋ-iŋ\\ ringing, springing, stringing, swinging, folksinging, free-swinging, gunslinging, handwringing, mudslinging, upbringing—*also* -ing *forms of verbs listed at* ING

ingit \\iŋ-kət\\ see INKET

ingle \iŋ-gəl\ cringle, dingle, jingle, mingle, shingle, single, tingle, atingle, commingle, immingle, Kriss Kringle, surcingle, intermingle

ingler \iŋ-glər\ jingler, shingler

inglet \iŋ-lət\ kinglet, ringlet, winglet

ingletree \iŋ-gəl-trē\ singletree, swingletree

ingli \iŋ-lē\ see INGLY

inglish \iŋ-glish\ see ENGLISH

ingly \iŋ-glē\ jingly, shingly, singly, tingly, Zwingli

ingo \iŋ-gō\ bingo, dingo, jingo, lingo, pingo, flamingo, Mandingo, Santo Domingo

ings \iŋz\ Kings, springs, eyestrings, Hot Springs, Colorado Springs—*also* -s, -'s, *and* -s' *forms of nouns listed at* ING, *and* -s *forms of verbs listed there*

ingue \aŋ\ see ²ANG

inguish \iŋ-wish\ distinguish, extinguish

¹ingy \iŋ-ē\ clingy, dinghy, springy, stringy, swingy, zingy, shilingi

²ingy \in-jē\ dingy, mingy, stingy

inh \in\ see ¹IN

¹ini \ē-nē\ beanie, djinni, genie, greeny, Jeanie, Jeannie, meanie, meany, jinni, Meany, sheeny, spleeny, teeny, weanie, weeny, wienie, Alcmene, Athene, Bellini, Bernini, bikini, Bikini, Cabrini, Cellini, Eugenie, linguine, martini, Mazzini, Mbini, Mycenae, Puccini, rappini, Rossini, Selene, tahini, wahine, zucchini, fantoccini, fettucine, kundalini,

malihini, Mussolini, Mytilene, nota bene, scaloppine, spaghettini, teeny-weeny, tetrazzini, tortellini

²ini \in-ē\ see INNY

inia \in-ē-ə\ zinnia, Bithynia, Gdynia, gloxinia, Lavinia, Sardinia, Virginia, Abyssinia, West Virginia

inial \in-ē-əl\ see INEAL

¹inian \in-ē-ən\ dynein, Arminian, Darwinian, Latinian, Sardinian, Socinian, Apollinian, Argentinian, Augustinian, Carolinian

²inian \in-yən\ see INION

¹inic \ē-nik\ Enoch, nicotinic

²inic \in-ik\ clinic, cynic, Finnic, platinic, rabbinic, Jacobinic, mandarinic, misogynic, muscarinic, nicotinic, parafinic

inical \in-i-kəl\ binnacle, clinical, cynical, finical, pinnacle, dominical, Jacobinical

inican \in-i-kən\ see INIKIN

inikin \in-i-kən\ minikin, Dominican

inim \in-əm\ minim, Houyhnhnm

ining \ī-niŋ\ lining, mining, shining, declining, designing, inclining, long-lining, interlining, undesigning—*also* -ing *forms of verbs listed at* ¹INE

inion \in-yən\ minion, minyan, pinion, piñon, champignon, dominion, Justinian, opinion, Sardinian, Abyssinian

¹inis \in-əs\ finis, pinnace, Erinys

²inis \ī-nəs\ see ¹INUS

inish \in-ish\ finish, Finnish,

thinnish, diminish, refinish

¹**inist** \ī-nəst\ dynast, finest

²**inist** \ē-nəst\ hygienist, machinist, Orleanist, Byzantinist, magazinist, trampolinist

initive \in-ət-iv\ carminative, definitive, infinitive

inity \in-ət-ē\ trinity, Trinity, affinity, bovinity, concinnity, divinity, felinity, feminity, infinity, latinity, salinity, sanguinity, vicinity, virginity, alkalinity, aquitinity, clandestinity, consanguinity, crystallinity, femininity, inconcinnity, masculinity, saccharinity

inium \in-ē-əm\ delphinium, triclinium, condominium

injure \in-jər\ see ³INGER

injury \inj-rē\ see INGERY

ink \iŋk\ blink, brink, chink, clink, dink, drink, fink, gink, ink, jink, kink, link, mink, pink, plink, prink, rink, shrink, sink, skink, slink, stink, swink, sync, think, wink, zinc, bethink, chewink, cross-link, eyewink, groupthink, hoodwink, iceblink, lip-synch, misthink, outthink, preshrink, rethink, snowblink, unkink, bobolink, countersink, distelfink, doublethink, interlink, kitchen-sink, Maeterlinck, rinky-dink

inka \iŋ-kə\ see INCA

inkable \iŋ-kə-bəl\ drinkable, sinkable, thinkable, undrinkable, unsinkable, unthinkable

inkage \iŋ-kij\ linkage, shrinkage, sinkage

inke \iŋ-kē\ see INKY

inked \iŋt\ see INCT

inker \iŋ-kər\ blinker, clinker, drinker, pinker, sinker, skinker, stinker, tinker, winker, diesinker, freethinker, headshrinker

inket \iŋ-kət\ Tlingit, trinket

inkey \iŋ-kē\ see INKY

inkgo \iŋ-kō\ see INKO

inkl \iŋ-kē\ see INKY

inkle \iŋ-kē\ see INKY

inking \iŋ-kiŋ\ freethinking, unblinking, unthinking—also -ing forms of verbs listed at INK

inkle \iŋ-kəl\ crinkle, inkle, sprinkle, tinkle, twinkle, winkle, wrinkle, besprinkle, periwinkle, Rip van Winkle

inkling \iŋ-kliŋ\ inkling, sprinkling, twinkling—also -ing forms of verbs listed at INKLE

inkly \iŋ-klē\ crinkly, pinkly, tinkly, twinkly, wrinkly

inko \iŋ-kō\ ginkgo, pinko

inks \iŋs\ see INX

inky \iŋ-kē\ dinkey, dinky, inky, kinky, pinkie, pinky, slinky, stinky, zincky, Helsinki, Malinke

inland \in-lənd\ Finland, inland, Vinland

inless \in-ləs\ chinless, sinless, skinless, spinless, windlass

inley \in-lē\ see INLY

inly \in-lē\ inly, spindly, thinly, McKinley, Mount McKinley

inn \in\ see ¹IN

innace \in-əs\ see ¹INIS

innacle \in-i-kəl\ see INICAL

inned \ind\ see ²IND

inner \in-ər\ dinner, ginner, grinner, inner, pinner, sinner, skinner, spinner,

spinor, thinner, tinner,
winner, beginner,
breadwinner, prizewinner,
money-spinner
innet \in-ət\ linnet, minute,
spinet
inney \in-ē\ see INNY
inni \ē-nē\ see ¹INI
innia \in-ē-ə\ see INIA
innic \in-ik\ see ²INIC
innie \in-ē\ see INNY
inning \in-iŋ\ ginning, inning,
spinning, winning, beginning,
breadwinning, prizewinning,
underpinning—*also* -ing
forms of verbs listed at ¹IN
innish \in-ish\ see INISH
innity \in-ət-ē\ see INITY
innow \in-ō\ minnow,
winnow, topminnow
inny \in-ē\ cine, finny, ginny,
guinea, Guinea, hinny, mini,
Minnie, ninny, pinny, Pliny,
shinny, skinny, spinney,
squinny, tinny, whinny,
Winnie, ignominy,
micromini, Papua New
Guinea, Equatorial Guinea
¹ino \ī-nō\ lino, rhino, Taino,
wino, albino
²ino \ē-nō\ beano, chino, fino,
keno, leno, Pinot, vino,
Zeno, bambino, casino,
cioppino, ladino, merino,
sordino, zecchino,
andantino, Angeleno,
Bardolino, campesino,
cappuccino, concertino,
Filipino, maraschino,
palomino, Philipino, San
Marino, pecorino, sopranino,
Cape Mendocino, San
Bernardino
³ino \ē-nə\ see ²INA
iñon \in-yən\ see INION
¹inor \in-ər\ see INNER
²inor \ī-nər\ see ¹INER

inos \ī-nəs\ see INNS
inot \ē-nō\ see ²INO
inous \ī-nəs\ see ¹INUS
inscher \in-chər\ see INCHER
inse \ins\ see INCE
inselly \in-slē\ see INCELY
inseng \in-siŋ\ see INCING
insk \insk\ Minsk,
Dzerzhinsk, Semipalatinsk
insky \in-skē\ buttinsky,
kolinsky, Nijinsky,
Stravinsky
inster \in-stər\ minster,
spinster, Axminster,
Westminster, Kidderminster
int \int\ bint, Clint, dint, flint,
Flint, glint, hint, lint, mint,
print, quint, skint, splint,
sprint, squint, stint, suint,
tint, blueprint, catmint,
footprint, forint, gunflint,
handprint, hoofprint,
horsemint, imprint, in-print,
large-print, newsprint,
offprint, preprint, remint,
reprint, skinflint, spearmint,
thumbprint, voiceprint,
aquatint, calamint,
cuckoopint, fingerprint,
mezzotint, monotint,
overprint, peppermint,
photoprint, wunderkind,
Septuagint
intage \int-ij\ mintage,
vintage
intager \int-i-jər\ see
INTEGER
intain \int-ᵊn\ see INTON
¹intal \int-ᵊl\ lintel, pintle,
quintal, Septuagintal
²intal \ant-ᵊl\ see ANTLE
integer \int-i-jər\ integer,
vintager
intel \int-ᵊl\ see ¹INTAL
inter \int-ər\ hinter, linter,
minter, printer, sinter,
splinter, sprinter, squinter,

tinter, winter, imprinter, midwinter, reprinter, overwinter, teleprinter

intery \int-ə-rē\ printery, splintery

inth \inth\ plinth, synth, helminth, colocynth, labyrinth, terebinth

inthia \in-thē-ə\ Cynthia, Carinthia

inthian \in-thē-ən\ Corinthian, labyrinthian

inthine \in-thən\ hyacinthine, labyrinthine

inting \int-iŋ\ imprinting, unstinting—*also* -ing *forms of verbs listed at* INT

intle \int-ᵊl\ *see* ¹INTAL

¹into \in-tō\ pinto, Shinto, spinto

²into \in-tü\ thereinto, whereinto

inton \int-ᵊn\ Clinton, quintain, Winton, badminton

ints \ins\ *see* INCE

inty \int-ē\ flinty, linty, minty, squinty, pepperminty

intz \ins\ *see* INCE

inue \in-yü\ sinew, continue, discontinue

inuous \in-yə-wəs\ sinuous, continuous, discontinuous

¹inus \ī-nəs\ dryness, finis, highness, Minas, Minos, minus, shyness, sinus, slyness, spinous, vinous, wryness, Aquinas, Delphinus, echinus, Quirinus, Antoninus, Pontus Euxinus

²inus \ē-nəs\ *see* ¹ENUS

inute \in-ət\ *see* INNET

inx \iŋs\ jinx, links, lynx, minx, sphinx, hijinks, tiddledywinks

¹iny \ī-nē\ briny, heinie, liny, piny, shiny, spiny, tiny,

twiny, viny, whiny, winy, enshrinee, sunshiny

²iny \in-ē\ *see* INNY

inya \ē-nyə\ *see* ²ENIA

inyan \in-yən\ *see* INION

inyl \in-ᵊl\ *see* ¹INAL

inys \in-əs\ *see* ¹INIS

¹io \ī-ō\ bayou, bio, Clio, Io, Lucayo, Ohio

²io \ē-ō\ brio, Cleo, clio, guyot, Krio, Leo, Rio, trio, caudillo, con brio, Negrillo, tornillo, Trujillo, cigarillo, Hermosillo, Manzanillo, ocotillo

iocese \ī-ə-səs\ *see* IASIS

iolate \ī-ə-lət\ *see* ¹IOLET

¹iolet \ī-ə-lət\ triolet, violate, violet, Violet, inviolate, ultraviolet, near-ultraviolet

²iolet \ē-ə-lət\ *see* EOLATE

¹ion \ī-ən\ ayin, Brian, Bryan, cyan, ion, lion, Lyon, Mayan, Ryan, scion, Sion, Zion, Amphion, anion, Bisayan, Ixion, Orion, Visayan, counterion, dandelion, zwitterion

²ion \ē-ən\ *see* ¹EAN

³ion \ē-än\ *see* ²EON

ior \īr\ *see* ¹IRE

iory \ī-rē\ *see* ¹IARY

iot \ī-ət\ *see* IET

ioter \ī-ət-ər\ *see* IETER

iouan \ü-ən\ *see* UAN

ious \ī-əs\ *see* IAS

ioux \ü\ *see* ¹EW

ip \ip\ blip, chip, clip, dip, drip, flip, grip, grippe, gyp, hip, kip, lip, nip, pip, quip, rip, scrip, ship, sip, skip, slip, snip, strip, tip, trip, whip, yip, zip, airship, airstrip, atrip, bullwhip, catnip, chiefship, clerkship, courtship, cowslip, deanship, equip, fieldstrip, filmstrip,

flagship, friendship,
guildship, gunship, half-slip,
handgrip, hardship, harelip,
headship, horsewhip, inclip,
judgeship, kingship, kinship,
landslip, lightship, lordship,
nonslip, outstrip, oxlip, pip-
pip, princeship, Q-ship,
queenship, reship, round-
trip, saintship, sheep-dip,
sideslip, spaceship,
steamship, thaneship,
township, transship,
troopship, unship, unzip,
wardship, warship,
airmanship, authorship,
battleship, biochip,
brinkmanship, censorship,
chairmanship, chaplainship,
chieftainship,
churchmanship, coverslip,
dealership, draftsmanship,
ego-trip, externship,
fellowship, fingertip,
gamesmanship, Gaza Strip,
grantsmanship,
helmsmanship,
horsemanship, internship,
ladyship, leadership,
lectureship, listenership,
marksmanship, membership,
microchip, oarsmanship,
overslip, ownership,
partnership, penmanship,
pogonip, premiership,
readership, ridership,
rulership, salesmanship,
scholarship, seamanship,
showmanship, skinny-dip,
speakership, sponsorship,
sportsmanship,
statesmanship, stewardship,
studentship, swordsmanship,
trusteeship, underlip,
upmanship, viewership,
workmanship, assistantship,
attorneyship, championship,

chancellorship, citizenship,
companionship,
containership, cross-
ownership, dictatorship,
directorship, good-
fellowship, guardianship,
instructorship,
landownership, laureateship,
governorship, musicianship,
one-upmanship,
outdoorsmanship,
professorship, protectorship,
receivership, relationship,
survivorship, treasurership,
ambassadorship,
associateship, bipartisanship,
entrepreneurship,
librarianship,
nonpartisanship,
proprietorship,
secretaryship, solicitorship,
interrelationship

ipal \ē-pəl\ see EOPLE
ipari \ip-rē\ see IPPERY
ipatus \ip-ət-əs\ see IPITOUS
ipe \i-p\ Cuyp, gripe, hype,
pipe, ripe, slype, snipe, stipe,
stripe, swipe, tripe, type,
wipe, bagpipe, blowpipe,
downpipe, drainpipe,
hornpipe, hosepipe, lead-
pipe, n-type, p-type, panpipe,
pinstripe, rareripe, sideswipe,
standpipe, stovepipe, tintype,
touch-type, unripe,
windpipe, archetype,
calotype, Dutchman's-pipe,
guttersnipe, haplotype,
Linotype, liripipe, logotype,
monotype, overripe,
prototype, stenotype,
Teletype, electrotype,
stereotype, daguerreotype,
anti-idiotype
¹iped \i-ped\ biped,
parallelepiped
²iped \ipt\ stiped, striped, pin-

striped—*also* -ed *forms of verbs listed at* IPE

ipend \ī-pənd\ ripened, stipend

iper \ī-pər\ diaper, griper, hyper, piper, riper, sniper, striper, viper, wiper, bagpiper, sandpiper, candy-striper, stereotyper

iperous \ī-prəs\ see YPRESS

ipetal \ip-ət-ᵊl\ basipetal, bicipital, centripetal, occipital

ipety \ip-ət-ē\ snippety, peripety, serendipity

iph \if\ see IFF

iphany \if-ə-nē\ see IPHONY

ipher \ī-fər\ cipher, lifer, rifer, decipher, encipher, pro-lifer, right-to-lifer

iphery \if-rē\ see IFERY

iphon \ī-fən\ see YPHEN

iphony \if-ə-nē\ tiffany, Tiffany, antiphony, epiphany, polyphony

ipi \ē-pē\ see EEPY

ipid \ip-əd\ lipid, insipid

ipience \ip-ē-əns\ incipience, percipience, impercipience

ipient \ip-ē-ənt\ excipient, incipient, percipient, recipient, impercipient

iping \ī-piŋ\ piping, striping, blood-typing—*also* -ing *forms of verbs listed at* IPE

ipit \ip-ət\ see IPPET

ipital \ip-ət-əl\ see IPETAL

ipitance \ip-ət-əns\ see IPOTENCE

ipitant \ip-ət-ənt\ see IPOTENT

ipitous \ip-ət-əs\ peripatus, precipitous, serendipitous

ipity \ip-ət-ē\ see IPETY

¹**iple** \ip-əl\ see IPPLE

²**iple** \ī-pəl\ see YPAL

ipless \ip-ləs\ dripless, lipless, zipless

ipling \ip-liŋ\ Kipling, stripling—*also* -ing *forms of verbs listed at* IPPLE

ipment \ip-mənt\ shipment, equipment, transshipment

ipo \ēp-ō\ see EPOT

ipoli \ip-ə-lē\ see IPPILY

ipotence \ip-ət-əns\ omnipotence, precipitance

ipotent \ip-ət-ənt\ omnipotent, plenipotent, pluripotent, precipitant

¹**ippe** \ip\ see IP

²**ippe** \ip-ē\ see IPPY

³**ippe** \ēp\ see EEP

ipped \ipt\ see IPT

ippee \ip-ē\ see IPPY

ippen \ip-ən\ lippen, pippin

ipper \ip-ər\ chipper, clipper, dipper, dripper, flipper, gripper, hipper, kipper, nipper, ripper, shipper, sipper, skipper, slipper, snipper, stripper, tipper, tripper, whipper, zipper, blue-chipper, day-tripper, mudskipper, Yom-Kippur, double-dipper, gallinipper, lady's slipper, skinny-dipper

ippery \ip-rē\ frippery, Lipari, slippery

ippet \ip-ət\ pipit, sippet, snippet, tippet, trippet, whippet

ippety \ip-ət-ē\ see IPETY

ippi \ip-ē\ see IPPY

ipple \ip-ē\ see IPPY

ippily \ip-ə-lē\ nippily, tripoli, Tripoli, Gallipoli

ippin \ip-ən\ see IPPEN

ipping \ip-iŋ\ chipping, clipping, dripping, lipping, nipping, ripping, shipping, double-dipping, skinny-dipping—*also* -ing *forms of verbs listed at* IP

ippingly \ip-iŋ-lē\ grippingly, nippingly, trippingly

ipple \ip-əl\ cripple, nipple, ripple, stipple, tipple, triple, participle

ippur \ip-ər\ see IPPER

ippy \ip-ē\ chippy, dippy, drippy, flippy, grippy, hippie, hippy, Lippi, lippy, nippy, slippy, snippy, tippy, trippy, whippy, yippee, yippie, zippy, Xanthippe, Mississippi

ips \ips\ snips, thrips, yips, eclipse, ellipse, midships, amidships, athwartships, fish-and-chips, tidytips, apocalypse—*also* -s, -'s, *and* -s' *forms of nouns listed at* IP, *and* -s *forms of verbs listed there*

ipse \ips\ see IPS

ipso \ip-sō\ dipso, calypso, Calypso

ipster \ip-stər\ hipster, quipster, tipster

ipsy \ip-sē\ see YPSY

ipt \ipt\ crypt, hipped, lipped, ripped, script, tipped, conscript, decrypt, encrypt, harelipped, postscript, prescript, rescript, subscript, tight-lipped, transcript, typescript, eucalypt, filter-tipped, manuscript, nondescript, superscript, swivel-hipped—*also* -ed *forms of verbs listed at* IP

ipter \ip-tər\ scripter, lithotripter

iptic \ip-tik\ see YPTIC

iption \ip-shən\ ascription, conniption, conscription, decryption, description, Egyptian, encryption, inscription, prescription,

proscription, subscription, transcription, circumscription, nonprescription

iptive \ip-tiv\ ascriptive, descriptive, inscriptive, prescriptive, proscriptive

iptych \ip-tik\ see YPTIC

ipular \ip-yə-lər\ stipular, manipular

ipy \ī-pē\ stripy, typey, stenotypy, daguerrotypy, stereotypy

iquant \ē-kənt\ see ECANT

ique \ēk\ see ¹EAK

iquey \ē-kē\ see EAKY

iquish \ē-kish\ see EAKISH

iquitous \ik-wət-əs\ iniquitous, ubiquitous

iquity \ik-wət-ē\ antiquity, iniquity, obliquity, ubiquity

iquor \ik-ər\ see ¹ICKER

¹ir \ir\ see ²EER

²ir \ər\ see ¹EUR

¹ira \ir-ə\ see ²ERA

²ira \ī-rə\ see YRA

irable \ī-rə-bəl\ wirable, acquirable, desirable, respirable, undesirable

iracle \ir-i-kəl\ see ²ERICAL

irae \īr-ē\ see ¹IRY

iral \ī-rəl\ chiral, gyral, spiral, viral

irant \ī-rənt\ spirant, tyrant, aspirant, retirant

irate \ir-ət\ see IRIT

irby \ər-bē\ see ERBY

irca \ər-kə\ see ¹URKA

irce \ər-sē\ see ERCY

irch \ərch\ see URCH

¹irchen \ər-chən\ see URCHIN

²irchen \ər-kən\ see IRKIN

ircher \ər-chər\ Bircher, lurcher, nurture

irchist \ər-chəst\ Birchist, researchist

ircon \ər-kən\ see IRKIN

ircuit \ər-kət\ circuit, trifurcate, microcircuit

ircular \ər-kyə-lər\ circular, opercular, tubercular, semicircular

ird \ərd\ bird, burred, curd, furred, gird, heard, herd, nerd, spurred, surd, third, word, absurd, begird, bellbird, blackbird, bluebird, buzzword, byword, Cape Verde, catbird, catchword, cowbird, cowherd, crossword, cussword, engird, goatherd, headword, jailbird, jaybird, kingbird, loanword, lovebird, lyrebird, oilbird, password, potsherd, railbird, rainbird, redbird, reword, ricebird, seabird, Sigurd, shorebird, snakebird, snowbird, songbird, sunbird, surfbird, swearword, swineherd, textured, ungird, unheard, watchword, yardbird, afterword, bowerbird, butcher-bird, cedarbird, dollybird, hummingbird, ladybird, mockingbird, ovenbird, overheard, riflebird, tailorbird, thunderbird, undergird, wattlebird, weaverbird, whirlybird—*also* -ed *forms of verbs listed at* ¹EUR

irder \ərd-ər\ see ERDER

irdie \ərd-ē\ see URDY

irdle \ərd-ᵊl\ see URDLE

irdum \ərd-əm\ dirdum, reductio ad absurdum

¹ire \īr\ briar, brier, byre, choir, dire, drier, fire, flier, friar, fryer, gyre, hire, ire, liar, lyre, mire, prier, prior, pyre, quire, shire, sire, Speyer, spier, spire, squire, tier, tire, trier, tyer, Tyre, wire, zaire, acquire, admire, afire, Altair, aspire, attire, backfire, balefire, barbed wire, barbwire, bemire, Blantyre, blow-dryer, bonfire, brushfire, bushfire, catbrier, cease-fire, complier, conspire, defier, denier, desire, drumfire, empire, Empire, entire, esquire, expire, flytier, grandsire, greenbrier, gunfire, haywire, hellfire, highflier, hot-wire, inquire, inspire, misfire, outlier, perspire, pismire, prior, quagmire, require, respire, retire, rimfire, samphire, sapphire, satire, Shropshire, spitfire, surefire, suspire, sweetbrier, tightwire, transpire, umpire, vampire, wildfire, amplifier, Biedermeier, butterflyer, classifier, fly-by-wire, fortifier, lammergeier, magnifier, modifier, multiplier, nitrifier, nullifier, pacifier, qualifier, quantifier, rapid-fire, rectifier, retrofire, sanctifier, signifier, testifier, versifier, identifier, intensifier, Second Empire, down-to-the-wire—*also* -er *forms of adjectives listed at* ¹Y

²ire \ir\ see ²EER

³ire \ī-rē\ see ¹ARY

⁴ire \ir-ē\ see ¹RY

⁵ire \ər\ see EUR

ired \īrd\ fired, spired, tired, wired, hardwired, retired— *also* -ed *forms of verbs listed at* ¹RE

ireless \īr-ləs\ tireless, wireless

ireman \īr-mən\ fireman, wireman

irement \īr-mənt\ environment, requirement, retirement

iren \i-rən\ Byron, gyron, Myron, siren, environ, ribavirin

irge \ərj\ see URGE

irgin \ər-jən\ see URGEON

irgo \ər-gō\ see ERGO

iri \ir-ē\ see EARY

iriam \ir-ē-əm\ see ERIUM

iric \ir-ik\ see ²ERIC

irile \ir-əl\ see ¹ERAL

irin \i-rən\ see IREN

irine \ī-rən\ see IREN

iring \ir-iŋ\ firing, wiring, retiring—*also* -ing *forms of verbs listed at* ¹IRE

irious \ir-ē-əs\ see ERIOUS

iris \ī-rəs\ see IRUS

irish \īr-ish\ Irish, squirish

irit \ir-ət\ Meerut, spirit, dispirit, emirate, inspirit, vizierate

irium \ir-ē-əm\ see ERIUM

irius \ir-ē-əs\ see ERIOUS

¹irk \irk\ birk, dirk, Dirk, kirk

²irk \ərk\ see ¹ORK

irker \ər-kər\ see ¹ORKER

irkie \ər-kē\ see ERKY

irkin \ər-kən\ firkin, gherkin, jerkin, zircon, Gelsenkirchen

irky \ər-kē\ see ERKY

¹irl \ərl\ birl, burl, churl, curl, dirl, earl, Earl, Earle, furl, girl, hurl, knurl, merle, Merle, pearl, Pearl, purl, skirl, squirrel, swirl, thirl, thurl, tirl, twirl, virl, whirl, whorl, aswirl, awhirl, cowgirl, impearl, pas seul, playgirl, salesgirl, schoolgirl, showgirl, uncurl, unfurl, mother-of-pearl

²irl \irl\ dirl, skirl

irler \ər-lər\ birler, curler, pearler, twirler, whirler

irley \ər-lē\ see URLY

irlie \ər-lē\ see URLY

irling \ər-liŋ\ see URLING

irlish \ər-lish\ see URLISH

irly \ər-lē\ see URLY

irm \ərm\ see ¹ORM

irma \ər-mə\ see ERMA

irmary \ərm-rē\ spermary, infirmary

irmess \ər-məs\ see ERMIS

irmity \ər-mət-ē\ furmity, infirmity

irmy \ər-mē\ see ERMY

¹irn \irn\ firn, girn, pirn

²irn \ərn\ see URN

¹iro \ir-ō\ see ³ERO

²iro \ē-rō\ see ¹ERO

³iro \ī-rō\ see ¹YRO

¹iron \irn\ iron, andiron, environ, flatiron, gridiron

²iron \ī-rən\ see IREN

ironment \īr-mənt\ see IREMENT

irp \ərp\ see URP

irps \ərps\ stirps, turps— *also* -s, -'s, *and* -s' *forms of nouns listed at* URP, *and* -s *forms of verbs listed there*

irpy \ər-pē\ chirpy, Euterpe

irque \ərk\ see ¹ORK

¹irr \ir\ see ²EER

²irr \ər\ see ¹EUR

irra \ir-ə\ see ²ERA

irrah \ir-ə\ see ²ERA

¹irrel \ərl\ see ¹IRL

²irrel \ər-əl\ see ERRAL

irrely \ər-lē\ see URLY

irrer \ər-ər\ see ERRER

irrhous \ir-əs\ see EROUS

irrhus \ir-əs\ see EROUS

irring \ər-iŋ\ see URRING

irror \ir-ər\ see ²EARER

irrous \ir-əs\ see EROUS

irrup \ər-əp\ chirrup, stirrup, syrup

irrupy \ər-ə-pē\ chirrupy, syrupy

irrus \ir-əs\ see EROUS

irry \ər-ē\ see URRY

irs \irz\ see IERS

irsch \irsh\ see IRSH

¹irse \irs\ see IERCE

²irse \ərs\ see ERSE

irsh \irsh\ girsh, kirsch

irst \ərst\ see URST

irsty \ər-stē\ thirsty, bloodthirsty

irt \ərt\ see ¹ERT

irted \ərt-əd\ see ERTED

irter \ərt-ər\ see ERTER

irth \ərth\ berth, birth, dearth, earth, firth, girth, mirth, Perth, worth, childbirth, Fort Worth, rebirth, self-worth, stillbirth, unearth, Wordsworth, afterbirth, down-to-earth, pennyworth

irthful \ərth-fəl\ mirthful, worthful

irthless \ərth-ləs\ mirthless, worthless

irtinent \ərt-nənt\ pertinent, appurtenant, impertinent

irting \ərt-iŋ\ see ERTING

irtle \ərt-ᵊl\ see ERTILE

irtually \ərch-lē\ see URCHLY

irtue \ər-chə\ see ERCHA

irty \ərt-ē\ dirty, QWERTY, shirty, thirty

irus \ī-rəs\ Cyrus, iris, Iris, Skyros, virus, desirous, Epirus, Osiris, papyrus, lentivirus, parvovirus, rotavirus, papillomavirus

irv \ərv\ see ERVE

irving \ər-viŋ\ see ERVING

irwin \ər-wən\ see ERWIN

¹iry \īr-ē\ eyrie, friary, miry, spiry, wiry, expiry, inquiry, venire, praemunire, anno hegirae

²iry \ī-rē\ see ¹IARY

i's \īz\ see IZE

¹is \is\ see ¹ISS

²is \iz\ see ¹IZ

³is \ē\ see ¹EE

⁴is \ēs\ see IECE

⁵is \ish\ see ¹ISH

¹isa \ē-zə\ see EZA

²isa \ī-zə\ Lisa, Liza, Elisa, Eliza

isabeth \iz-ə-bəth\ see IZABETH

isable \ī-zə-bəl\ see IZABLE

¹isal \ī-səl\ Faisal, Ijssel, sisal, skysail, trysail, radisal

²isal \ī-zəl\ Geisel, incisal, reprisal, revisal, surprisal, paradisal

isan \is-ᵊn\ see ISTEN

isbane \iz-bən\ see ISBON

isbe \iz-bē\ Frisbee, Thisbe

isbee \iz-bē\ see ISBE

isbon \iz-bən\ Brisbane, Lisbon

isc \isk\ see ISK

iscable \is-kə-bəl\ confiscable, episcopal

iscan \is-kən\ see ISKIN

iscate \is-kət\ see ISKET

isce \is\ see ¹ISS

¹iscean \ī-sē-ən\ Piscean, Dionysian

²iscean \is-kē-ən\ Piscean, saurischian, ornithischian

³iscean \is-ē-ən\ see ¹YSIAN

iscence \is-ᵊns\ puissance, dehiscence, impuissance, indehiscence, reminiscence, reviviscence

iscent \is-ᵊnt\ puissant, dehiscent, impuissant, indehiscent, reminiscent, reviviscent

isces \ī-sēz\ see ICES

ische \ēsh\ see ²ICHE

ischian \is-kē-ən\ see ²ISCEAN

iscia \ish-ə\ see ITIA

iscible \is-ə-bəl\ see ISSIBLE

iscience \ish-əns\ see ICIENCE

iscient \ish-ənt\ see ICIENT

isco \is-kō\ cisco, disco, Francisco, Jalisco, Morisco, San Francisco

iscopal \is-kə-bəl\ see ISCABLE

iscous \is-kəs\ see ISCUS

iscuit \is-kət\ see ISKET

iscus \is-kəs\ discus, viscous, viscus, hibiscus, meniscus

¹ise \ēs\ see IECE

²ise \ēz\ see EZE

³ise \īs\ see ¹ICE

⁴ise \īz\ see IZE

¹ised \īst\ see ¹IST

²ised \īzd\ see IZED

isel \iz-əl\ see IZZLE

iseled \iz-əld\ see IZZLED

iseler \iz-lər\ see IZZLER

isement \īz-mənt\ advisement, chastisement, despisement, disguisement, advertisement, disfranchisement, enfranchisement, disenfranchisement

iser \ī-zər\ see IZER

ises \ī-sēz\ see ICES

¹ish \ish\ dish, fiche, fish, flysch, Nis, pish, squish, swish, whish, wish, blackfish, blowfish, bluefish, bonefish, catfish, codfish, crawfish, crayfish, dogfish, filefish, finfish, flatfish, garfish, globefish, goldfish, goosefish, Irtysh, kingfish, knish, lungfish, lumpfish, monkfish, pigfish, pipefish, ratfish, redfish, rockfish, sailfish, sawfish, shellfish, spearfish, starfish, stonefish, sunfish, swordfish, tilefish, unwish, weakfish, whitefish, angelfish, anglerfish, archerfish, butterfish, candlefish, cuttlefish, damselfish, devilfish, jellyfish, John Bullish, ladyfish, lionfish, microfiche, muttonfish, needlefish, overfish, paddlefish, ribbonfish, silverfish, surgeonfish, triggerfish

²ish \ēsh\ see ²ICHE

isha \ish-ə\ see ITIA

ishable \ish-ə-bəl\ fishable, justiciable

ished \isht\ dished, whisht—also -ed forms of verbs listed at ¹ISH

isher \ish-ər\ fisher, fissure, swisher, ill-wisher, kingfisher, well-wisher

ishery \ish-rē\ fishery, Tishri, shellfishery

ishi \ē-shē\ chichi, specie, maharishi

ishing \ish-iŋ\ bonefishing, fly-fishing, sportfishing, well-wishing—also -ing forms of verbs listed at ¹ISH

ishioner \ish-nər\ see ITIONER

ishna \ish-nə\ Krishna, Mishnah

ishnah \ish-nə\ see ISHNA

isht \isht\ see ISHED

ishu \ish-ü\ see ¹ISSUE

ishy \ish-ē\ dishy, fishy, squishy, swishy

¹isi \ē-zē\ see ¹EASY

²isi \ē-sē\ see EECY

¹isia \izh-ə\ baptisia, Dionysia, artemisia

²isia \ē-zhə\ see ²ESIA

¹isian \izh-ən\ see ISION

²isian \ē-zhən\ see ¹ESIAN

isible \iz-ə-bəl\ risible, visible, divisible, invisible, indivisible

isin \i-zən\ see ²ISON

ising \ī-ziŋ\ see IZING

ision \izh-ən\ fission, Frisian, scission, vision, abscission, collision, concision, decision, derision, division, elision, elysian, envision, excision, incision, misprision, precisian, precision, prevision, provision, recision, rescission, revision, circumcision, Dionysian, imprecision, indecision, subdivision, supervision, television

isional \izh-nəl\ visional, collisional, decisional, divisional, excisional, previsional, provisional

isis \ī-səs\ crisis, Isis, lysis, nisus, Dionysus, stare decisis

isit \iz-ət\ visit, exquisite, revisit

isite \iz-ət\ see ISIT

isitive \iz-ət-iv\ acquisitive, inquisitive

isitor \iz-ət-ər\ visitor, acquisitor, inquisitor

¹isive \ī-siv\ visive, decisive, derisive, divisive, incisive, indecisive

²isive \iz-iv\ visive, derisive, divisive

isk \isk\ bisque, brisk, disc, disk, fisc, frisk, risk, whisk, lutefisk, asterisk, basilisk, blastodisc, compact disc, laserdisc, obelisk, odalisque, tamarisk, videodisc

isker \is-kər\ brisker, frisker, risker, whisker

isket \is-kət\ biscuit, brisket, frisket

iskey \is-kē\ see ISKY

iskie \is-kē\ see ISKY

iskin \is-kən\ siskin, Franciscan

isky \is-kē\ frisky, pliskie, risky, whiskey

island \ī-lənd\ see IGHLAND

islander \ī-lən-dər\ see IGHLANDER

islands \ī-lənz\ see IGHLANDS

isle \īl\ see ¹ILE

isles \īlz\ see ILES

islet \ī-lət\ see ILOT

isling \iz-liŋ\ brisling, quisling

isly \iz-lē\ see IZZLY

ism \iz-əm\ chrism, chrisom, ism, prism, schism, abysm, autism, baalism, baptism, Birchism, bossism, Buddhism, casteism, centrism, charism, Chartism, chemism, classism, cubism, cultism, czarism, deism, dwarfism, faddism, fascism, fauvism, Gaullism, Grecism, Hobbism, holism, Jainism, Klanism, leftism, lyrism, Mahdism, Maoism, Marxism, monism, mutism, Nazism, nudism, Orphism, priggism, purism, racism, Ramism, rightism, sadism, Saivism, sapphism, Scotism, sexism, Shaktism, Shiism, Sikhism, simplism, snobbism, sophism, statism, Sufism, tachism, Tantrism, Taoism, theism, Thomism, tourism, tropism, truism, Turkism, verism, Whiggism, Yahwism, absurdism, activism, Adventism, alarmism, albinism, alpinism, altruism, amorphism, anarchism, aneurysm, anglicism, animism, aphorism, Arabism, archaism, asterism, atavism, atheism, atomism, atticism, Bahaism, barbarism, Benthamism, biblicism, blackguardism, bolshevism, boosterism, botulism, bourbonism,

Brahmanism, Briticism,
Byronism, cabalism,
Caesarism, Calvinism,
careerism, Castroism,
cataclysm, catechism,
Catharism, centralism,
chauvinism, chimerism,
classicism, colorism,
communism, concretism,
conformism, cretinism,
criticism, cronyism,
cynicism, dadaism,
dandyism, Darwinism,
defeatism, de Gaullism,
despotism, die-hardism,
dimorphism, dirigisme,
Docetism, do-goodism,
dogmatism, Donatism, Don
Juanism, druidism, dualism,
dynamism, egoism, egotism,
elitism, embolism,
endemism, erethism,
ergotism, erotism, escapism,
Essenism, etatism,
eunuchism, euphemism,
euphuism, exorcism,
expertism, extremism,
fairyism, familism, fatalism,
feminism, feudalism, fideism,
Fidelism, fogyism,
foreignism, formalism,
futurism, Galenism,
gallicism, galvanism,
gangsterism, genteelism,
Germanism, giantism,
gigantism, globalism,
gnosticism, Gongorism,
Gothicism, gourmandism,
gradualism, grangerism,
greenbackism, Hasidism,
heathenism, Hebraism,
hedonism, Hellenism,
helotism, hermetism,
hermitism, heroism,
highbrowism, Hinduism,
hipsterism, hirsutism,
hispanism, Hitlerism,

hoodlumism, hoodooism,
hucksterism, humanism,
Hussitism, hybridism,
hypnotism, Ibsenism,
idealism, imagism, Irishism,
Islamism, Jansenism,
jingoism, journalism, John
Bullism, Judaism, Junkerism,
kaiserism, Krishnaism, Ku
Kluxism, laconism, laicism,
Lamaism, Lamarckism,
landlordism, Latinism,
legalism, Leninism,
lobbyism, localism, locoism,
Lollardism, luminism,
lyricism, magnetism,
mammonism, mannerism,
Marcionism, masochism,
mechanism, melanism,
meliorism, Menshevism,
Mendelism, mentalism,
mesmerism, methodism, me-
tooism, modernism,
Mohockism, monachism,
monadism, monarchism,
mongolism, Montanism,
moralism, Mormonism,
morphinism, mullahism,
mysticism, narcissism,
nationalism, nativism,
nepotism, neutralism, new
dealism, nihilism, nomadism,
occultism, onanism,
optimism, oralism,
Orangeism, organism,
ostracism, pacifism,
paganism, Pan-Slavism,
pantheism, paroxysm,
Parsiism, passivism,
pauperism, pessimism,
phallicism, pianism, pietism,
plagiarism, Platonism,
pleinairism, Plotinism,
pluralism, pointillism,
populism, pragmatism,
presentism, privatism,
prosaism, Prussianism,

puerilism, pugilism,
Puseyism, Pyrrhonism,
Quakerism, quietism,
rabbinism, racialism,
rationalism, realism,
reformism, rheumatism,
rigorism, robotism,
Romanism, Rousseauism,
rowdyism, royalism,
satanism, savagism,
scapegoatism, schematism,
scientism, sciolism,
Scotticism, Semitism,
Shakerism, Shamanism,
Shintoism, skepticism,
socialism, solecism,
solipsism, Southernism,
specialism, speciesism,
Spartanism, Spinozism,
spiritism, spoonerism,
Stalinism, standpattism,
stoicism, syllogism,
symbolism, synchronism,
syncretism, synergism,
talmudism, tarantism,
tectonism, tenebrism,
terrorism, Teutonism,
titanism, Titoism, tokenism,
Toryism, totalism, totemism,
transvestism, traumatism,
tribalism, tritheism,
Trotskyism, ultraism,
unionism, urbanism,
utopism, Vaishnavism,
vampirism, vandalism,
vanguardism, Vedantism,
veganism, verbalism,
virilism, vitalism, vocalism,
volcanism, voodooism,
vorticism, voyeurism,
vulcanism, vulgarism,
Wahhabism, warlordism,
welfarism, Wellerism,
witticism, yahooism,
Yankeeism, Yiddishism,
Zionism, zombiism,
absenteeism, absolutism,

abstractionism, adoptionism,
adventurism, aestheticism,
Africanism, agnosticism,
alcoholism, alienism,
amateurism, amoralism,
anabaptism, anachronism,
Anglicanism, animalism,
antagonism, Arianism,
astigmatism, athleticism,
asynchronism, Atlanticism,
atonalism, Australianism,
automatism, avant-gardism,
behaviorism, Big Brotherism,
bilingualism, biologism,
bipedalism, biracialism,
Bonapartism, bureaucratism,
cannibalism, capitalism,
Cartesianism, catastrophism,
Catholicism, cavalierism,
charlatanism, clericalism,
collectivism, Colonel
Blimpism, commensalism,
commercialism,
communalism,
Confucianism, conservatism,
constructivism,
consumerism, corporatism,
creationism, credentialism,
determinism, diabolism,
didacticism, diffusionism,
dilettantism, doctrinairism,
do-nothingism, eclecticism,
ecumenism, egocentrism,
Eleatism, empiricism,
epicenism, epicurism,
epigonism, eremitism,
eroticism, erraticism,
essentialism, ethnocentrism,
eudaemonism, euhemerism,
evangelism, exceptionalism,
exclusivism, exoticism,
expansionism,
expressionism, externalism,
Fabianism, factionalism,
factualism, fanaticism,
favoritism, federalism,
Fenianism, feuilletonism,

fifth columnism,
flagellantism, Fourierism,
fraternalism, freneticism,
Freudianism, funambulism,
functionalism, gallicanism,
gutturalism, henotheism,
hermeticism, Hispanicism,
historicism, hooliganism,
Huguenotism, hypocorism,
idiotism, illiberalism,
illuminism, illusionism,
immanentism, immobilism,
impressionism, indifferentism,
Indianism, infantilism,
inflationism, initialism,
insularism, invalidism,
iotacism, irredentism,
Ishmaelitism, Italianism,
Jacobinism, Jacobitism,
jesuitism, Keynesianism,
know-nothingism, legitimism,
lesbianism, liberalism,
libertinism, literalism,
Lutheranism, Lysenkoism,
Magianism, malapropism,
mandarinism, McCarthyism,
medievalism, mercantilism,
messianism, metabolism,
metamorphism, militarism,
minimalism, misoneism,
monasticism, monetarism,
monotheism, mosaicism,
mutualism, naturalism,
Naziritism, necrophilism,
negativism, neologism, neo-
Nazism, neuroticism, nice-
nellyism, nominalism,
nonconformism, objectivism,
obscurantism, obstructionism,
officialism, opportunism,
organicism, pacificism,
Pantagruelism, parallelism,
parasitism, pastoralism,
paternalism, patriotism,
Peeping Tomism,
perfectionism, personalism,
pharisaism, physicalism,

plebeianism, poeticism,
polyglotism, polytheism,
positivism, postmodernism,
pragmaticism, primitivism,
probabilism, progressivism,
proselytism, protectionism,
Protestantism, provincialism,
pseudomorphism,
psychologism, puritanism,
radicalism, rationalism,
recidivism, reductionism,
refugeeism, regionalism,
relativism, restrictionism,
revisionism, revivalism,
ritualism, romanticism,
ruffianism, Sadduceeism,
salvationism, sansculottism,
sardonicism, scholasticism,
secessionism, sectarianism,
sectionalism, secularism,
sensualism, separatism,
serialism, Slavophilism,
solidarism, somnambulism,
sovietism, Stakhanovism,
structuralism, subjectivism,
suprematism, surrealism,
Sybaritism, sycophantism,
systematism, Tammanyism,
teetotalism, theocentrism,
triumphalism, Uncle Tomism,
vagabondism, ventriloquism,
vigilantism, voluntarism,
volunteerism, Wesleyanism,
workaholism, Zwinglianism,
abolitionism, academicism,
agrarianism, Americanism,
analphabetism,
anthropomorphism,
anthropopathism, anti-
Semitism, Arminianism,
autoerotism, barbarianism,
bibliophilism, bicameralism,
biculturalism, biloquialism,
bipartisanism, bohemianism,
colloquialism, colonialism,
conceptualism,
confessionalism,

constitutionalism,
conventionalism,
corporativism,
cosmopolitism, deviationism,
ecumenicism, emotionalism,
esotericism, Europocentrism,
evolutionism, exhibitionism,
existentialism, expatriatism,
fundamentalism,
governmentalism,
Hegelianism,
hermaphroditism,
hypercriticism, hyperrealism,
hyperurbanism, imperialism,
incendiarism,
incrementalism,
indeterminism, industrialism,
instrumentalism,
interventionism,
introspectionism,
irrationalism, isolationism,
Malthusianism,
Manichaeanism,
manorialism, materialism,
millennialism,
Monarchianism,
mongolianism,
Monophysitism,
Muhammadanism,
multilingualism,
neoclassicism,
Neoplatonism, neorealism,
Nestorianism,
Occidentalism, operationism,
orientalism, Palladianism,
parajournalism,
parochialism, particularism,
pedestrianism, Pelagianism,
Pentecostalism,
phenomenalism,
photojournalism,
pictorialism, pococurantism,
Postimpressionism,
professionalism,
pseudoclassicism,
reconstructionism,
republicanism,

Rosicrucianism,
sacerdotalism,
sacramentalism, self-
determinism,
sadomasochism,
sectarianism, sensationalism,
sentimentalism,
socinianism, spiritualism,
theatricalism, Tractarianism,
traditionalism,
transcendentalism,
transsexualism, trilateralism,
ultramontanism,
universalism, utopianism,
vernacularism,
Victorianism, vocationalism,
voluntaryism,
Albigensianism,
anticlericalism,
antiquarianism,
apocalypticism,
assimilationism,
associationism,
Augustinianism,
autoeroticism,
ceremonialism,
collaborationism,
congregationalism,
cosmopolitanism,
ecclesiasticism,
ecumenicalism,
environmentalism,
Evangelicalism,
Hamiltonianism,
homoeroticism,
epicureanism,
experimentalism,
immaterialism,
individualism,
institutionalism,
intellectualism,
internationalism,
libertarianism, middle-of-
the-roadism,
millenarianism, neo-
conservatism, neo-
impressionism,

operationalism, Pan-
Americanism, Peripateticism,
photoperiodism, Pre-
Raphaelitism,
Presbyterianism,
Pythegoreanism,
Rastafarianism,
reactionaryism,
Sabbatarianism,
supernaturalism,
Swedenborgianism,
territorialism,
Trinitarianism, unitarianism,
vegetarianism,
Zoroastrianism,
Aristotelianism,
authoritarianism,
egalitarianism,
Episcopalianism,
humanitarianism,
Machiavellianism,
neocolonialism, neo-
Expressionism,
predestinarianism,
representationalism,
utilitarianism,
establishmentarianism,
latitudinarianism

isma \iz-mə\ charisma,
melisma

ismal \iz-məl\ see YSMAL

¹isme \īm\ see ¹IME

²isme \iz²m\ see ISM

ismo \ēz-mō\ machismo,
verismo, caudillismo

iso \ē-sō\ miso, piso

isom \iz-əm\ see ISM

¹ison \īs-²n\ bison, hyson,
Meissen, streptomycin,
Aureomycin, erythromycin

²ison \iz-²n\ dizen, mizzen,
prison, risen, weasand,
wizen, arisen, imprison, Tok
Pisin, uprisen

isor \ī-zər\ see IZER

isored \ī-zərd\ guisard,
visored

isory \īz-rē\ advisory,
provisory, revisory,
supervisory

isp \isp\ crisp, lisp, LISP,
wisp, will-o-the-wisp

isper \is-pər\ crisper, lisper,
whisper

ispy \is-pē\ crispy, wispy

isque \isk\ see ISK

iss \is\ bis, bliss, cis, Chris,
cuisse, Dis, hiss, kiss, miss,
sis, Swiss, this, vis, wis,
abyss, amiss, coulisse,
dehisce, dismiss, iwis,
koumiss, remiss, submiss,
ambergris, hit-and-miss, hit-
or-miss, reminisce, verdigris

issa \is-ə\ abscissa, mantissa,
Melissa, Orissa, vibrissa

issable \is-ə-bəl\ see ISSIBLE

issal \is-əl\ see ISTLE

issance \is-²ns\ see ISCENCE

issant \is-²nt\ see ISCENT

¹isse \is\ see ISS

²isse \ēs\ see IECE

issed \ist\ see ²IST

issel \is-əl\ see ISTLE

isser \is-ər\ hisser, kisser

issible \is-ə-bəl\ kissable,
miscible, admissible,
immiscible, municipal,
omissible, permissible,
remissible, transmissible,
impermissible, inadmissible

issile \is-əl\ see ISTLE

¹ission \ish-ən\ see ITION

²ission \izh-ən\ see ISION

issionable \ish-nə-bəl\
fissionable, conditionable

issioner \ish-nər\ see ITIONER

issive \is-iv\ missive,
admissive, derisive,
dismissive, emissive,
permissive, submissive,
transmissive

issome \is-əm\ lissome,
alyssum

issor \iz-ər\ scissor, whizzer

¹issue \ish-ü\ fichu, issue, tissue, reissue, Mogadishu, overissue

²issue \ish-ə\ see ITIA

issure \ish-ər\ see ISHER

issus \is-əs\ byssus, missus, Mrs., narcissus, Narcissus

issy \is-ē\ hissy, missy, prissy, sissy

¹ist \īst\ Christ, feist, heist, hist, tryst, zeitgeist, Antichrist, black-a-vised, poltergeist—*also* -ed *forms of verbs listed at* ¹ICE

²ist \ist\ cist, cyst, fist, gist, grist, kist, list, Liszt, mist, schist, tryst, twist, whist, wist, wrist, assist, backlist, blacklist, checklist, consist, delist, desist, encyst, enlist, entwist, exist, handlist, insist, persist, playlist, protist, Rehnquist, resist, shortlist, subsist, untwist, catechist, coexist, dadaist, exorcist, intertwist, preexist, love-in-a-mist—*also* -ed *forms of verbs listed at* ISS

³ist \ēst\ see ¹EAST

¹ista \ē-stə\ turista, camorrista, Fidelista

²ista \is-tə\ crista, vista, arista, ballista, sacahuiste

istaed \is-təd\ see ISTED

istal \is-t³l\ Bristol, crystal, Crystal, distal, listel, pistil, pistol

istan \is-tən\ see ISTON

istance \is-təns\ see ISTENCE

istant \is-tənt\ see ISTENT

¹iste \is-tē\ see ²ICITY

²iste \ēst\ see ¹EAST

³iste \is-tə\ see ²ISTA

isted \is-təd\ twisted, vistaed, closefisted, enlisted, ham-fisted, hardfisted, limp-

wristed, tightfisted, two-fisted, unlisted, untwisted, white-listed, ironfisted, unassisted—*also* -ed *forms of verbs listed at* ²IST

istel \is-t³l\ see ISTAL

isten \is-³n\ christen, glisten, listen, Nisan

istenable \is-nə-bəl\ listenable, medicinable

istence \is-təns\ distance, assistance, consistence, existence, insistence, outdistance, persistence, resistance, subsistence, coexistence, inconsistence, inexistence, nonexistence, nonresistance, preexistence

istency \is-tən-sē\ consistency, insistency, persistency, inconsistency

istent \is-tənt\ distant, assistant, consistent, existent, insistent, persistent, resistant, subsistent, coexistent, equidistant, inconsistent, inexistent, nonexistent, nonpersistent, nonresistant, preexistent

ister \is-tər\ bister, blister, clyster, glister, klister, lister, Lister, mister, sister, twister, resister, resistor, solicitor, stepsister, transistor

istery \is-trē\ see ISTORY

istful \ist-fəl\ tristful, wistful

isthmus \is-məs\ see ISTMAS

isti \is-tē\ see ²ICITY

istic \is-tik\ cystic, distich, fistic, mystic, artistic, autistic, ballistic, cladistic, cubistic, eristic, fascistic, faunistic, floristic, heuristic, holistic, hubristic, juristic, linguistic, logistic, meristic, monistic, patristic, phlogistic, puristic, sadistic, simplistic, sophistic, statistic, stylistic, Taoistic, theistic, Thomistic, touristic, truistic, veristic, wholistic, Yahwistic, activistic, agonistic, alchemistic, altruistic, amoristic, anarchistic, animistic, aphoristic, archaistic, atavistic, atheistic, atomistic, belletristic, cabalistic, Calvinistic, casuistic, catechistic, Catharistic, centralistic, chauvinistic, communistic, crosslinguistic, dadaistic, dualistic, dyslogistic, egoistic, egotistic, essayistic, eucharistic, eulogistic, euphemistic, euphuistic, exorcistic, fabulistic, familistic, fatalistic, feministic, fetishistic, feudalistic, fideistic, formalistic, futuristic, gongoristic, haggadistic, Hebraistic, hedonistic, Hellenistic, humanistic, humoristic, idealistic, imagistic, inartistic, Jansenistic, jingoistic, journalistic, Judaistic, Lamaistic, legalistic, masochistic, mechanistic, melanistic, mentalistic, methodistic, modernistic, moralistic, narcissistic, nationalistic, nativistic, nepotistic, nihilistic, novelistic, onanistic, optimistic, pantheistic, pessimistic, pianistic, pietistic, plagiaristic, Platonistic, pluralistic, pointillistic, populistic, pugilistic, quietistic, realistic, Romanistic, sciolistic, shamanistic, shintoistic,

socialistic, solecistic, solipsistic, specialistic, surrealistic, syllogistic, symbolistic, synchronistic, syncretistic, synergistic, terroristic, totalistic, totemistic, ultraistic, unrealistic, urbanistic, utopistic, vandalistic, verbalistic, vitalistic, voodooistic, voyeuristic, Zionistic, absolutistic, adventuristic, anachronistic, animalistic, anomalistic, antagonistic, behavioristic, cannibalistic, capitalistic, characteristic, collectivistic, contortionistic, deterministic, evangelistic, eudaemonistic, euhemeristic, expansionistic, expressionistic, extralinguistic, functionalistic, Hinayanistic, hypocoristic, immanentistic, impressionistic, liberalistic, literalistic, Mahayanistic, melioristic, mercantilistic, militaristic, mediumistic, metalinguistic, misogynistic, monopolistic, monotheistic, naturalistic, negativistic, neologistic, opportunistic, paternalistic, physicalistic, polytheistic, probabilistic, propagandistic, psycholinguistic, rationalistic, recidivistic, reductionistic, relativistic, revivalistic, ritualistic, secularistic, sensualistic, separatistic, sociolinguistic, somnambulistic, ventriloquistic, violinistic, voluntaristic, colonialistic, commercialistic, Deuteronomistic, emotionalistic, exhibitionistic,

fundamentalistic,
existentialistic, imperialistic,
indeterministic,
introspectionistic,
irrationalistic, materialistic,
oligopolistic,
Postimpressionistic,
sadomasochistic,
sensationalistic,
sociolinguistic, spiritualistic,
traditionalistic,
individualistic

istical \is-ti-kəl\ mystical,
deistical, eristical, linguistical,
logistical, monistical,
patristical, sophistical,
statistical, theistical,
alchemistical, atheistical,
casuistical, egoistical,
egotistical, exorcistical,
pantheistical, anomalistical,
hypocoristical,
monotheistical, polytheistical

istich \is-tik\ see ISTIC

istics \is-tiks\ ballistics,
ekistics, linguistics, logistics,
patristics, statistics,
stylistics, futuristics,
criminalistics—*also* -s, -'s,
and -s' *forms of nouns listed
at* ISTIC

istle \is-tē\ see ²ICITY

istil \is-t²l\ see ISTAL

istin \is-tən\ see ISTON

istine \is-tən\ see ISTON

istle \is-əl\ bristle, fissile,
gristle, missal, missile,
scissile, thistle, whistle,
abyssal, dickcissel,
dismissal, epistle,
pennywhistle

istler \is-lər\ whistler,
Whistler, epistler

istless \ist-ləs\ listless,
resistless

istly \is-lē\ bristly, gristly,
thistly, sweet cicely

istmas \is-məs\ Christmas,
isthmus, Kiritimati

isto \is-tō\ aristo, Callisto

istol \is-t²l\ see ISTAL

iston \is-tən\ Kristin, piston,
Tristan, Philistine,
phlogiston, amethystine

istor \is-tər\ see ISTER

istory \is-trē\ blistery,
history, mystery, consistory,
prehistory

istral \is-trəl\ mistral,
sinistral

istress \is-trəs\ mistress,
headmistress, postmistress,
schoolmistress, sinistrous,
taskmistress, toastmistress

istrophe \is-trə-fē\
antistrophe, epistrophe

istrous \is-trəs\ see ISTRESS

isty \is-tē\ see ¹ICITY

isus \ī-səs\ see ISIS

iszt \ist\ see ²IST

¹It \it\ bit, bitt, brit, Brit,
chit, dit, fit, flit, frit, git,
grit, hit, it, kit, knit, lit,
mitt, nit, pit, Pitt, quit, sit,
skit, slit, snit, spit, split,
Split, sprit, teat, tit, twit,
whit, wit, writ, zit, acquit,
admit, armpit, backbit,
backfit, befit, bowsprit,
Brigitte, bushtit, cesspit,
close-knit, cockpit, commit,
culprit, demit, Dewitt,
dimwit, emit, fleapit, gaslit,
godwit, half-wit, henbit,
house-sit, legit, lit crit,
misfit, mishit, moonlit,
nitwit, obit, omit, outfit,
outwit, peewit, permit,
pinch-hit, Prakrit, pulpit,
refit, remit, sandpit,
Sanskrit, snakebit, starlit,
submit, sunlit, switch-hit,
tidbit, tight-knit, titbit,
tomtit, transmit, turnspit,

twilit, two-bit, unfit, unknit, well-knit, baby-sit, benefit, candlelit, counterfeit, hypocrite, intermit, intromit, manumit, megahit, recommit, retrofit, cost-benefit, lickety-split, overcommit, jack-in-the-pulpit

²it \ē\ see ¹EE

³it \ēt\ see ¹EAT

¹ita \īt-ə\ vita, baryta, amanita

²ita \ēt-ə\ cheetah, eta, Greta, Nita, pita, Rita, theta, vita, zeta, Akita, Anita, Bonita, bonito, casita, excreta, Granita, Juanita, Lolita, partita, Suita, amanita, arboreta, feterita, incognita, manzanita, margarita, senhorita, senorita, Bhagavad Gita

¹itable \īt-ə-bəl\ citable, writable, excitable, indictable, copyrightable, extraditable

²itable \it-ə-bəl\ see ITTABLE

itae \īt-ē\ see ²ITE

itain \it-n\ see ITTEN

¹ital \īt-ᵊl\ title, vital, detrital, entitle, nontitle, recital, requital, subtitle, disentitle, intravital, supravital

²ital \it-ᵊl\ see ITTLE

italer \īt-ᵊl-ər\ whittler, victualler, belittler, Hospitaler

italist \īt-ᵊl-əst\ titlist, vitalist, recitalist

itan \īt-ᵊn\ see IGHTEN

itant \īt-ᵊnt\ mightn't, excitant, incitant, renitent

itany \īt-ᵊn-ē\ Brittany, dittany, litany

itch \ich\ bitch, ditch, fitch, flitch, glitch, hitch, itch,

kitsch, niche, pitch, quitch, rich, snitch, stitch, such, switch, twitch, which, witch, backstitch, bewitch, cross-stitch, enrich, fast-twitch, hemstitch, lockstitch, slow-pitch, slow-twitch, topstitch, unhitch, whipstitch, czarevitch, featherstitch, microswitch

itchen \ich-ən\ kitchen, richen

itchener \ich-nər\ Kitchener, Michener

itcher \ich-ər\ hitcher, pitcher, richer, snitcher, stitcher, switcher, enricher, hemstitcher, Lubavitcher, water witcher

itchery \ich-ə-rē\ bitchery, obituary, stitchery, witchery, bewitchery

itches \ich-əz\ britches, riches, Dutchman's-breeches—*also* -s, -'s, *and* -s' *forms of nouns listed at* ITCH, *and* -s *forms of verbs listed there*

itchman \ich-mən\ pitchman, switchman

itchment \ich-mənt\ bewitchment, enrichment

itchy \ich-ē\ bitchy, itchy, kitschy, pitchy, twitchy, witchy

it'd \it-əd\ see ITTED

¹ite \īt\ bight, bite, blight, bright, byte, cite, dight, dite, Dwight, fight, flight, fright, height, hight, kite, knight, krait, kyte, light, lite, might, mite, night, plight, quite, right, rite, sight, site, sleight, slight, smite, spite, sprite, tight, trite, white, White, wight, Wight, wite, wright, Wright, write, affright, airtight, albite, alight, all right, all-night, aright, backbite, backlight, bedight, Birchite, birthright, bobwhite, bombsight, bullfight, campsite, cockfight, contrite, Cushite, daylight, deadlight, delight, despite, dogfight, downright, droplight, earthlight, excite, eyebright, eyesight, fanlight, finite, firefight, firelight, fistfight, flashlight, fleabite, floodlight, foresight, forthright, fortnight, frostbite, Gadite, gaslight, gastight, ghostwrite, graphite, gunfight, Gunite, half-light, Hamite, handwrite, headlight, highlight, hindsight, Hittite, homesite, hoplite, Hussite, ignite, illite, infight, in-flight, incite, indict, indite, insight, invite, jacklight, jadeite, lamplight, Levite, lighttight, lignite, limelight, lintwhite, lowlight, Lucite, Luddite, lyddite, Melchite, midnight, millwright, miswrite, moonlight, night-light, off-site, off-white, on-site, outright, outsight, partite, penlight, playwright, polite, prizefight, pyrite, recite, requite, respite, rushlight, safelight, searchlight, Semite, Servite, Shemite, Shiite, shipwright, sidelight, skintight, skylight, skywrite, smectite, snakebite, snow-white, spaceflight, speedlight, spotlight, starlight, sticktight, stoplight, streetlight, sunlight, Sunnite, taillight, termite, tonight, torchlight, trothplight,

twilight, twi-night, typewrite, unite, unsight, upright, uptight, wainwright, weeknight, wheelwright, acolyte, aconite, Ammonite, Amorite, amosite, anchorite, anthracite, antiwhite, apartheid, appetite, Bakelite, Benthamite, bipartite, black-and-white, blatherskite, bleacherite, chalcocite, Canaanite, Carmelite, castroite, catamite, cellulite, copyright, disinvite, disunite, dynamite, erudite, expedite, extradite, Fahrenheit, featherlight, fly-by-night, gelignite, gesundheit, gigabyte, Hashemite, Hepplewhite, Himyarite, Hitlerite, hug-me-tight, impolite, Ishmaelite, Israelite, Jacobite, Josephite, Kimberlite, laborite, Leninite, leukocyte, lily-white, localite, malachite, manganite, Marcionite, Masonite, Mennonite, Minorite, Moabite, muscovite, Nazirite, out-of-sight, overbite, overflight, overnight, oversight, overwrite, parasite, perovskite, plebiscite, proselyte, Puseyite, pyrrhotite, recondite, reunite, satellite, shergottite, socialite, sodalite, sodomite, Stagirite, stalactite, stalagmite, Sybarite, time-of-flight, transfinite, transvestite, tripartite, troglodyte, Trotskyite, ultralight, underwrite, urbanite, Wahhabite, watertight, Wycliffite, yesternight, adipocyte, anthophyllite, cosmopolite, exurbanite, gemütlichkeit, hermaphrodite, Indo-Hittite, McCarthyite, multipartite, quadripartite, suburbanite, theodolite, Areopagite, Pre-Raphaelite, Great Australian Bight

²**ite** \it-ē\ flighty, mighty, nightie, righty, whity, almighty, Almighty, Venite, Aphrodite, aqua vitae, arborvitae, lignum vitae

³**ite** \it\ see ¹IT

⁴**ite** \ēt\ see ¹EAT

ited \it-əd\ see IGHTED

iteful \it-fəl\ see IGHTFUL

itely \it-lē\ see IGHTLY

item \it-əm\ item, ad infinitum

itement \it-mənt\ alightment, excitement, incitement, indictment

iten \it-ᵊn\ see IGHTEN

itener \it-nər\ see IGHTENER

itent \it-ᵊnt\ see ITANT

iteor \ēt-ē-ər\ see ETEOR

¹**iter** \it-ər\ blighter, fighter, lighter, miter, niter, titer, writer, all-nighter, braillewriter, exciter, first-nighter, lamplighter, nail-biter, one-nighter, prizefighter, screenwriter, scriptwriter, songwriter, speechwriter, sportswriter, states righter, typewriter, copywriter, expediter, fly-by-nighter, Gastarbeiter, underwriter, teletypewriter—*also* -er *forms of adjectives listed at* ¹ITE

²**iter** \it-ər\ see ITTER

³**iter** \ēt-ər\ see ¹EATER

iteral \it-ə-rəl\ clitoral, literal, littoral, sublittoral, triliteral

iterally \it-ər-lē\ see ITTERLY

iterate \it-ə-rət\ literate, illiterate, nonliterate, postliterate, preliterate, presbyterate, subliterate, semiliterate

¹**ites** \īt-ēz\ barytes, sorites, Thersites—*also* -s, -'s, *and* -s' *forms of nouns listed at* ²ITE

²**ites** \īts\ see IGHTS

itey \it-ē\ see ²ITE

ith \ith\ fifth, frith, grith, kith, myth, pith, sith, smith, Smith, swith, with, withe, blacksmith, forthwith, goldsmith, Goldsmith, gunsmith, herewith, locksmith, songsmith, therewith, tinsmith, tunesmith, wherewith, whitesmith, wordsmith, coppersmith, eolith, Granny Smith, Hammersmith, megalith, metalsmith, microlith, monolith, neolith, silversmith, paleolith

³**ith** \ēt\ see ¹EAT

⁴**ith** \ēth\ see ¹EATH

¹**ithe** \ith\ blithe, kithe, lithe, scythe, tithe, withe, writhe

²**ithe** \ith\ see ²ITH

³**ithe** \ith\ see ¹ITH

¹**ithee** \ith-ē\ see ²ITHY

²**ithee** \ith-ē\ see ¹ITHY

ither \ith-ər\ blither, cither, dither, hither, slither, swither, thither, whither, wither, zither, come-hither, nowhither, somewhither

itherward \ith-ər-wərd\ thitherward, whitherward

ithesome \ith-səm\ blithesome, lithesome

ithia \ith-ē-ə\ see YTHIA

ithic \ith-ik\ lithic, ornithic, batholithic, Eolithic, granolithic, megalithic,

Mesolithic, monolithic, neolithic, Paleolithic

ithing \ī-<u>th</u>in\ tithing, trithing—*also* -ing *forms of verbs listed at* ¹ITHE

ithmic \i<u>th</u>-mik\ *see* YTHMIC

¹**ithy** \i<u>th</u>-ē\ prithee, withy

²**ithy** \i<u>th</u>-ē\ mythy, pithy, prithee, smithy, withy

iti \ēt-ē\ *see* EATY

¹**itia** \ish-ə\ Lycia, Mysia, wisha, Alicia, Cilicia, comitia, episcia, Galicia, indicia, Letitia, militia, Patricia, Phoenicia, Dionysia

²**itia** \ē-shə\ *see* ¹ESIA

itial \ish-əl\ *see* ICIAL

¹**itian** \ish-ən\ *see* ITION

²**itian** \ē-shən\ *see* ¹ETION

itiate \ish-ət\ initiate, novitiate, uninitiate

itic \it-ik\ clitic, critic, arthritic, bronchitic, dendritic, enclitic, granitic, graphitic, Hamitic, jaditic, mephitic, proclitic, pruritic, rachitic, Sanskritic, Semitic, Shemitic, Sinitic, anaclitic, analytic, anchoritic, catalytic, cenobitic, copralitic, crystallitic, diacritic, dialytic, dynamitic, eremitic, Himyaritic, hypercritic, jesuitic, paralytic, parasitic, sodomitic, stalactitic, stalagmitic, sybaritic, thallophytic, thrombolytic, troglodytic, cryptanalytic, electrolytic, hermaphroditic, meteoritic, Monophysitic, psychoanalytic

itical \it-i-kəl\ critical, Levitical, political, analytical, apolitical, cenobitical, diacritical, eremitical, hypercritical,

hypocritical, impolitical, Jacobitical, jesuitical, parasitical, sodomitical, supercritical, geopolitical, meteoritical, sociopolitical

itics \it-iks\ Semitics, analytics, meteoritics—*also* -s, -'s, *and* -s' *forms of nouns listed at* ITIC

itid \it-əd\ *see* ITTED

itimati \is-məs\ *see* ISTMAS

itin \it-ᵊn\ *see* IGHTEN

iting \it-in\ biting, flyting, lighting, whiting, writing, backbiting, bullfighting, cockfighting, daylighting, exciting, freewriting, frostbiting, handwriting, infighting, inviting, newswriting, prewriting, prizefighting, skywriting, songwriting, sportswriting, typewriting—*also* -ing *forms of verbs listed at* ¹ITE

ition \ish-ən\ fission, hycian, mission, titian, Titian, addition, admission, ambition, attrition, audition, beautician, clinician, cognition, coition, commission, condition, contrition, demission, dentition, dismission, Domitian, edition, emission, ethician, fruition, ignition, lenition, logician, magician, monition, mortician, munition, musician, nutrition, omission, optician, partition, patrician, perdition, permission, petition, Phoenician, physician, position, punition, remission, rendition, sedition, submission, suspicion, tactician, technician, tradition,

transition, transmission,
tuition, volition, abolition,
acquisition, admonition,
aesthetician, air-condition,
ammunition, apparition,
apposition, coalition,
competition, composition,
cosmetician, decommission,
decondition, definition,
demolition, deposition,
dietitian, Dionysian,
disposition, disquisition,
electrician, erudition,
exhibition, expedition,
exposition, extradition,
imposition, inhibition,
inquisition, intermission,
intromission, intuition,
linguistician, logistician,
malnutrition, malposition,
manumission,
mathematician, micturition,
mechanician, obstetrician, opposition,
Ordovician, parturition,
phonetician, politician,
precognition, precondition,
premonition, preposition,
prohibition, proposition,
recognition, recondition,
repetition, requisition,
rhetorician, statistician,
submunition, superstition,
supposition, transposition,
academician, arithmetician,
decomposition,
diagnostician, dialectician,
disinhibition, geometrician,
geriatrician, indisposition,
interposition, juxtaposition,
metaphysician,
onomastician, pediatrician,
presupposition, redefinition,
semiotician, theoretician,
superimposition

itionable \ish-nə-bəl\ see
ISSIONABLE

itional \ish-nəl\ additional,
attritional, cognitional,
coitional, conditional,
nutritional, positional,
traditional, transitional,
tuitional, volitional,
apparitional, appositional,
compositional, definitional,
depositional, expositional,
inquisitional, oppositional,
prepositional, propositional,
repetitional, suppositional,
transpositional,
unconditional,
juxtapositional,
presuppositional

itioner \i-shə-nər\ missioner,
commissioner, conditioner,
parishioner, partitioner,
petitioner, practitioner,
exhibitioner,
malpractitioner, nurse-
practitioner

itionist \i-shə-nəst\
nutritionist, partitionist,
abolitionist, coalitionist,
demolitionist, exhibitionist,
intuitionist, oppositionist,
prohibitionist

itious \ish-əs\ see ¹ICIOUS

itis \it-əs\ situs, Titus,
arthritis, botrytis, bronchitis,
bursitis, colitis, cystitis,
detritus, gastritis, iritis,
mastitis, nephritis, neuritis,
phlebitis, dermatitis,
enteritis, gingivitis, hepatitis,
Heracleitus, ileitis, laryngitis,
meningitis, pharyngitis,
pneumonitis, prostatitis,
retinitis, sinusitis, tonsillitis,
spondylitis, tendinitis,
urethritis, vaginitis,
appendicitis, conjunctivitis,
encephalitis, endocarditis,
endometritus, folliculitis,
Hermaphroditus, peritonitis,

analysis situs, diverticulitis, gastroenteritis, poliomyelitis

itish \it-ish\ British, skittish

itius \ish-əs\ see ICIOUS

itle \it-ᵊl\ see ¹ITAL

it'll \it-ᵊl\ see ITTLE

itment \it-mənt\ fitment, commitment, remitment, recommitment, overcommitment

itness \it-nəs\ fitness, witness, earwitness, eyewitness, unfitness

itney \it-nē\ jitney, Whitney, Mount Whitney

¹ito \ēt-ō\ keto, Leto, Quito, Tito, veto, bonito, burrito, graffito, magneto, Miskito, mosquito, Negrito, Hirohito, incognito, sanbenito

²ito \ēt-ə\ see ²ITA

¹iton \it-ᵊn\ see ITTEN

²iton \it-ᵊn\ see IGHTEN

itoral \it-ə-rəl\ see ITERAL

itra \ē-trə\ see ²ETRA

itral \ī-trəl\ mitral, nitrile

itrile \ī-trəl\ see ITRAL

it's \its\ see ITS

its \its\ blitz, ditz, Fritz, glitz, grits, it's, its, quits, spitz, Chemnitz, Saint Kitts, slivovitz—*also* -s, -'s, *and* -s' *forms of nouns listed at* ¹IT, *and* -s *forms of verbs listed there*

itsail \it-səl\ see ITZEL

itsch \ich\ see ITCH

itschy \ich-ē\ see ITCHY

itsy \it-sē\ see ITZY

itt \it\ see ¹IT

itta \it-ə\ shittah, vitta

ittable \it-ə-bəl\ committable, habitable, hospitable, remittable, transmittable, inhospitable

ittah \it-ə\ see ITTA

ittal \it-ᵊl\ see ITTLE

ittance \it-ᵊns\ pittance, quittance, acquittance, admittance, emittance, immittance, remittance, transmittance, intermittence

ittany \it-ᵊn-ē\ see ITANY

itte \it\ see ¹IT

itted \it-əd\ fitted, it'd, nitid, pitted, teated, witted, committed, dim-witted, half-witted, quick-witted, sharp-witted, slow-witted, thick-witted, unbitted, unfitted, uncommitted—*also* -ed *forms of verbs listed at* ¹IT

ittee \it-ē\ see ITTY

itten \it-ᵊn\ bitten, Britain, Briton, Britten, kitten, litten, Lytton, mitten, smitten, witting, written, backbitten, flea-bitten, Great Britain, hard-bitten, New Britain, rewritten, snakebitten, unwritten

ittence \it-ᵊns\ see ITTANCE

ittent \it-ᵊnt\ remittent, intermittent, intromittent

itter \it-ər\ bitter, chitter, critter, fitter, flitter, fritter, glitter, hitter, jitter, knitter, litter, quitter, quittor, sitter, skitter, slitter, spitter, titter, twitter, aglitter, atwitter, bed-sitter, embitter, emitter, hairsplitter, no-hitter, outfitter, rail-splitter, remitter, shipfitter, steamfitter, switch-hitter, transmitter, benefiter, counterfeiter, intromitter

itterer \it-ər-ər\ fritterer, litterer, twitterer

itterly \it-ər-lē\ bitterly, literally

ittern \it-ərn\ bittern, cittern, gittern

ittery \it-ə-rē\ glittery, jittery, littery, skittery, twittery

ittie \it-ē\ see ITTY

ittier \it-ē-ər\ grittier, prettier, Whittier, wittier

ittiness \it-ē-nəs\ grittiness, prettiness, wittiness

¹itting \it-iŋ\ fitting, sitting, splitting, witting, befitting, earsplitting, fence-sitting, formfitting, hairsplitting, hard-hitting, house-sitting, resitting, sidesplitting, unfitting, unwitting, unremitting—*also* -ing *forms of verbs listed at* ¹IT

²itting \it-ᵊn\ see ITTEN

ittish \it-ish\ see ITISH

ittle \it-ᵊl\ brittle, it'll, kittle, little, skittle, spital, spittle, tittle, victual, whittle, wittol, acquittal, belittle, committal, embrittle, hospital, lickspittle, remittal, transmittal, noncommittal, recommittal

ittler \it-ᵊl-ər\ see ITALER

ittol \it-ᵊl\ see ITTLE

ittor \it-ər\ see ITTER

ittoral \it-ə-rəl\ see ITERAL

itts \its\ see ITS

itty \it-ē\ bitty, city, ditty, gritty, kitty, Kitty, pity, pretty, tittie, witty, committee, self-pity, itty-bitty, Kansas City, megacity, nitty-gritty, Salt Lake City, subcommittee, supercity, Walter Mitty, Ho Chi Minh City

itual \ich-ə-wəl\ ritual, habitual

ituary \ich-ə-rē\ see ¹ITCHERY

itum \it-əm\ see ITEM

itus \it-əs\ see ITIS

¹ity \it-ē\ see ITTY

²ity \it-ē\ see ²ITE

itz \its\ see ITS

¹itza \ēt-sə\ pizza, czaritza, Chichén Itza, Katowice

²itza \it-sə\ czaritza, tamburitza

itzel \it-səl\ schnitzel, spritsail, Wiener schnitzel

itzi \it-sē\ see ITZY

itzy \it-sē\ bitsy, glitzy, Mitzi, ritzy, schizy

iu \ü\ see ¹EW

¹ius \ē-əs\ see ¹EUS

²ius \ī-əs\ see ¹IAS

¹iv \iv\ see ²IVE

²iv \ēf\ see ¹IEF

³iv \if\ see IFF

⁴iv \ēv\ see EAVE

¹iva \ī-və\ Saiva, gingiva, Godiva, saliva

²iva \ē-və\ diva, Eva, kiva, Shiva, siva, Siva, viva, geneva, Geneva, yeshiva

³iva \iv-ə\ Shiva, Siva

¹ivable \ī-və-bəl\ drivable, derivable, revivable, survivable

²ivable \iv-ə-bəl\ livable, forgivable

ival \ī-vəl\ rival, archival, arrival, revival, survival, adjectival, conjunctival, genitival, substantival, infinitival

ivalent \iv-ə-lənt\ ambivalent, equivalent, unambivalent

ivan \iv-ən\ see IVEN

ivance \ī-vəns\ connivance, contrivance, survivance

ivative \iv-ət-iv\ privative, derivative

¹ive \īv\ chive, dive, drive, five, gyve, hive, I've, jive, live, rive, shrive, skive, strive, thrive, wive, alive, archive, Argive, arrive, beehive, connive, contrive, deprive, derive, endive, nosedive, ogive, revive, self-drive, skin-dive, survive, test-drive, forty-five, overdrive, power-dive

²ive \iv\ give, live, sheave, shiv, sieve, spiv, forgive, misgive, outlive, relive, unlive, underactive

³ive \ēv\ see ¹EAVE

ivel \iv-əl\ civil, drivel, frivol, shrivel, snivel, swivel

iven \iv-ən\ driven, given, riven, Sivan, striven, thriven, forgiven, menu-driven

¹iver \ī-vər\ diver, driver, fiver, arriver, cabdriver, conniver, contriver, deriver, reviver, screwdriver, survivor

²iver \iv-ər\ flivver, giver, liver, quiver, river, shiver, sliver, almsgiver, aquiver, deliver, downriver, forgiver, lawgiver, quicksilver, upriver, Guadalquivir

¹ivers \ī-vərz\ divers, vivers—*also* -s, -'s, *and* -s' *forms of nouns listed at* ¹IVER

²ivers \ē-vərz\ see EAVERS

ivery \iv-rē\ livery, shivery, delivery

ives \īvz\ fives, hives, Ives—*also* -s, -'s, *and* -s' *forms of nouns listed at* ¹IVE, *and* -s *forms of verbs listed there*

ivet \iv-ət\ civet, divot, pivot, privet, rivet, swivet, trivet

¹ivi \iv-ē\ see IVVY

²ivi \ē-vē\ see EAVEY

ivia \iv-ē-ə\ Bolivia, Olivia

ivial \iv-ē-əl\ trivial, convivial, quadrivial

ivid \iv-əd\ livid, vivid

ivil \iv-əl\ see IVEL

ivilly \iv-ə-lē\ civilly, privily, uncivilly

ivily \iv-ə-lē\ see IVILLY

iving \iv-iŋ\ giving, living, almsgiving, forgiving, free-living, misgiving, thanksgiving—*also* -ing *forms of verbs listed at* ²IVE

ivion \iv-ē-ən\ Vivian, oblivion

ivious \iv-ē-əs\ lascivious, oblivious

ivir \iv-ər\ see ²IVER

ivity \iv-ət-ē\ privity, acclivity, activity, captivity, declivity, festivity, motivity, nativity, proclivity, absorptivity, adaptivity, additivity, affectivity, aggressivity, coercivity, cognitivity, collectivity, compulsivity, conductivity, connectivity, creativity, destructivity, diffusivity, directivity, effectivity, emissivity, emotivity, exclusivity, exhaustivity, expansivity, expressivity, impassivity, inactivity, infectivity, negativity, perceptivity, perfectivity, permittivity, positivity, primitivity, productivity, progressivity, reactivity, receptivity, reflexivity, relativity, resistivity, retentivity, selectivity, sensitivity, subjectivity, susceptivity, transitivity, distributivity, hyperactivity, insensitivity, overactivity, retroactivity, radioactivity, hypersensitivity

ivium \iv-ē-əm\ trivium, quadrivium

iviut \ē-vē-ət\ see EVIATE

ivo \ē-vō\ see EVO

ivocal \iv-ə-kəl\ equivocal, univocal, unequivocal

ivol \iv-əl\ see IVEL

ivor \ī-vər\ see ¹IVER

ivorous \iv-rəs\ carnivorous, granivorous, omnivorous, insectivorous

ivot \iv-ət\ see IVET

ivus \ē-vəs\ see EVOUS

ivver \iv-ər\ see ²IVER

ivvy \iv-ē\ chivy, civvy, divvy, Livy, privy, skivvy, tantivy, divi-divi

ivy \iv-ē\ see IVVY

iw \ef\ see ¹EF

iwi \ē-wē\ see EEWEE

¹ix \iks\ Brix, Dix, fix, nix, pyx, six, Styx, admix, affix, blanc fixe, commix, deep-six, immix, infix, postfix, prefix, premix, prix fixe, prolix, subfix, suffix, transfix, unfix, antefix, cicatrix, crucifix, eighty-six, intermix, politics, six-o-six, superfix, geopolitics, RU 486—*also* -s, -'s, *and* -s' *forms of nouns listed at* ICK, *and* -s *forms of verbs listed there*

²ix \ē\ see ¹EE

ixal \ik-səl\ pixel, affixal, prefixal, suffixal

¹ixe \ēks\ breeks, prix fixe, idée fixe, Macgillicuddy's Reeks—*also* -s, -'s, *and* -s' *forms of nouns listed at* ¹EAK, *and* -s *forms of verbs listed there*

²ixe \iks\ see ¹IX

³ixe \ēsh\ see ²ICHE

ixed \ikst\ fixed, mixed, twixt, betwixt, well-fixed—*also* -ed *forms of verbs listed at* ¹IX

ixel \ik-səl\ see IXAL

ixen \ik-sən\ vixen, Nixon, Mason-Dixon

ixer \ik-sər\ fixer, mixer, elixir

ixia \ik-sē-ə\ asphyxia, panmixia

ixie \ik-sē\ Dixie, nixie, Nixie, pixie, pyxie, tricksy

ixion \ik-shən\ see ICTION

ixir \ik-sər\ see IXER

ixit \ik-sət\ quixote, ipse dixit

ixon \ik-sən\ see IXEN

ixote \ik-sət\ see IXIT

ixt \ikst\ see IXED

ixture \iks-chər\ fixture, mixture, admixture, commixture, intermixture

iya \ē-ə\ see ¹IA

iyeh \ē-ə\ see ¹IA

¹iz \iz\ biz, fizz, frizz, his, is, Ms., phiz, quiz, 'tis, whiz, wiz, gee-whiz, show biz

²iz \ēz\ see EZE

¹iza \ē-zə\ see EZA

²iza \ē-thə\ see ETHA

izabeth \iz-ə-bəth\ Elisabeth, Elizabeth, Port Elizabeth

izable \ī-zə-bəl\ sizable, advisable, cognizable, devisable, excisable, amortizable, analyzable, criticizable, dramatizable, exercisable, fertilizable, hypnotizable, inadvisable, localizable, magnetizable, mechanizable, memorizable, pulverizable, recognizable, vaporizable, computerizable, generalizable, uncompromisable

izar \ī-zər\ see IZER

izard \iz-ərd\ blizzard, gizzard, izzard, lizard, vizard, wizard

ize \īz\ guise, prise, prize, rise, size, wise, abscise, advise, apprise, apprize, arise, assize, baptize, breadthwise, capsize, chastise, clockwise, cognize, comprise, crabwise, crosswise, demise, despise,

devise, disguise, disprize,
downsize, earthrise,
edgewise, emprise, endwise,
excise, fanwise, franchise,
full-size, grecize, high-rise,
incise, king-size, leastwise,
lengthwise, Levi's, life-size,
likewise, low-rise, man-size,
midsize, misprize, moonrise,
nowise, outsize, piecewise,
pint-size, premise, quantize,
remise, reprise, revise,
slantwise, streetwise, stylize,
suffice, sunrise, surmise,
surprise, twin-size, uprise,
advertise, aggrandize,
agonize, alchemize,
amortize, analyze, anglicize,
anywise, aphorize, arabize,
atomize, authorize, autolyze,
balkanize, barbarize,
bastardize, bestialize,
bolshevize, botanize,
bowdlerize, brutalize,
burglarize, canalize,
canonize, capsulize,
caramelize, carbonize,
cartelize, catalyze, catechize,
cauterize, centralize,
channelize, Christianize,
cicatrize, circumcise,
civilize, classicize, colonize,
communize, compromise,
concertize, concretize,
creolize, criticize, crystalize,
customize, demonize,
deputize, dialyze, digitize,
disfranchise, dogmatize,
dramatize, elegize,
empathize, emphasize,
energize, enfranchise,
enterprise, equalize, erotize,
eternize, etherize, eulogize,
euphemize, exercise,
exorcise, factorize, fantasize,
fascistize, feminize, fertilize,
feudalize, fictionize, finalize,

formalize, formulize,
fossilize, fragmentize,
fraternize, gallicize,
galvanize, germanize,
ghettoize, glamorize,
globalize, gormandize,
gothicize, gourmandize,
grecianize, harmonize,
heathenize, hebraize,
hellenize, hierarchize,
humanize, hybridize,
hypnotize, idolize,
immunize, improvise, ionize,
ironize, Islamize, itemize,
jeopardize, journalize,
Judaize, laicize, latinize,
legalize, lionize, liquidize,
localize, magnetize,
marbleize, martyrize,
maximize, mechanize,
melanize, melodize,
memorize, merchandise,
mesmerize, methodize,
metricize, minimize,
mobilize, modernize,
moisturize, monetize,
mongrelize, moralize,
motorize, mythicize,
narcotize, nasalize,
neutralize, normalize,
notarize, novelize, obelize,
odorize, optimize, organize,
ostracize, otherwise,
oversize, oxidize, paganize,
paradise, paralyze,
pasteurize, patronize,
pauperize, penalize,
penny-wise, pidginize,
plagiarize, plasticize,
Platonize, pluralize,
pocket-size, poetize,
polarize, polemize,
pressurize, privatize,
prussianize, publicize,
pulverize, randomize,
realize, recognize,
rhapsodize, robotize,

romanize, rubberize, sanitize, satirize, scandalize, schematize, schismatize, scrutinize, sensitize, sermonize, signalize, simonize, sinicize, slenderize, sloganize, socialize, sodomize, solarize, sonnetize, specialize, stabilize, Stalinize, standardize, sterilize, stigmatize, strategize, subsidize, summarize, supervise, syllogize, symbolize, sympathize, synchronize, syncretize, synopsize, synthesize, systemize, tantalize, televise, temporize, tenderize, terrorize, tetanize, teutonize, texturize, theorize, thermalize, totalize, tranquilize, traumatize, tyrannize, unionize, unitize, urbanize, utilize, valorize, vandalize, vaporize, verbalize, vernalize, victimize, vitalize, vocalize, vulcanize, vulgarize, weather-wise, weatherize, westernize, winterize, womanize, worldly-wise, accessorize, acclimatize, actualize, allegorize, alphabetize, analogize, anatomize, anesthetize, animalize, annualize, antagonize, anthologize, anticlockwise, apologize, apostatize, apostrophize, arabicize, aromatize, baby blue-eyes, bureaucratize, cannibalize, capitalize, categorize, catholicize, characterize, commercialize, communalize, computerize, conservatize, containerize, contrariwise, conveyorize,

cosmeticize, counterclockwise, criminalize, cryptanalize, decentralize, decolonize, de-emphasize, de-energize, dehumanize, deionize, demagnetize, demobilize, democratize, demoralize, deodorize, depersonalize, depolarize, desalinize, desensitize, destabilize, digitalize, disenfranchise, disorganize, economize, emotionalize, epitomize, epoxidize, eroticize, eternalize, euthanatize, evangelize, extemporize, externalize, familiarize, fanaticize, federalize, fictionalize, formularize, gelatinize, generalize, geologize, Hispanicize, homogenize, hospitalize, hypothesize, idealize, illegalize, immobilize, immortalize, impersonalize, Indianize, indigenize, initialize, internalize, italicize, legitimize, liberalize, literalize, lobotomize, lysogenize, macadamize, metabolize, metastasize, militarize, mineralize, monopolize, mythologize, nationalize, naturalize, parenthesize, philosophize, politicize, popularize, proselytize, regularize, reorganize, revitalize, romanticize, secularize, sexualize, sovietize, subjectivize, suburbanize, subvocalize, systematize, temporalize, theologize, traditionalize, transistorize, trivialize, ventriloquize, visualize, Americanize,

apotheosize, colonialize,
compartmentalize,
conceptualize,
contextualize, decriminalize,
demilitarize, denaturalize,
departmentalize,
depoliticize, desexualize,
Europeanize, exteriorize,
ideologize, immaterialize,
individualize, industrialize,
internationalize,
legitimatize, materialize,
miniaturize, particularize,
politicalize, psychoanalyze,
self-actualize,
sentimentalize, spiritualize,
underutilize, universalize,
constitutionalize,
dematerialize, editorialize,
intellectualize,
deinstitutionalize—*also* -s,
-'s, *and* -s' *forms of nouns
listed at* ¹Y, *and* -s *forms of
verbs listed there*
²ize \ēz\ *see* EZE
ized \īzd\ sized, advised,
outsized, ergotized, ill-
advised, pearlized,
Sanforized, unadvised,
undersized, varisized, well-
advised, elasticized,
modularized, unexercised,
immunocompromised—*also*
-ed *forms of verbs listed at*
¹IZE
¹izen \īz-ᵊn\ bison, dizen,
greisen, bedizen, horizon,
spiegeleisen
²izen \īz-ᵊn\ *see* ²ISON
izer \ī-zər\ Dreiser, geyser,
kaiser, miser, prizer, riser,
sizar, visor, wiser, adviser,

divisor, incisor, appetizer,
atomizer, energizer,
enterpriser, equalizer,
exerciser, fertilizer,
organizer, oxidizer,
stabilizer, supervisor,
synthesizer, totalizer,
tranquilizer, tyrannizer,
vaporizer, complementizer,
deodorizer
izing \ī-ziŋ\ rising, sizing,
uprising, appetizing,
enterprising, merchandising,
self-sufficing, unsurprising,
self-sacrificing,
uncompromising—*also* -ing
forms of verbs listed at ¹IZE
¹izo \ē-zō\ sleazo, chorizo,
mestizo
²izo \ē-sō\ *see* ISO
izon \īz-ᵊn\ *see* ¹IZEN
izy \it-sē\ *see* ITZY
izz \iz\ *see* ¹IZ
izza \ēt-sə\ *see* ¹ITZA
izzard \iz-ərd\ *see* IZARD
izzen \iz-ᵊn\ *see* ²ISON
izzer \iz-ər\ *see* ISSOR
izzical \iz-i-kəl\ *see* YSICAL
izzie \i-zē\ *see* IZZY
izzle \iz-əl\ chisel, drizzle,
fizzle, frizzle, grizzle,
mizzle, pizzle, sizzle, swizzle
izzled \iz-əld\ chiseled,
grizzled—*also* -ed *forms of
verbs listed at* IZZLE
izzler \iz-lər\ chiseler, sizzler,
swizzler
izzly \iz-lē\ drizzly, grisly,
grizzly, mizzly
izzy \iz-ē\ busy, dizzy, fizzy,
frizzy, tizzy, tin lizzie

O

¹o \ü\ see ¹EW

²o \ō\ see ¹OW

³o \ər\ see ¹EUR

¹oa \ō-ə\ boa, Goa, koa, moa, Noah, proa, stoa, aloha, balboa, Balboa, jerboa, Samoa, Krakatoa, Mauna Loa, Shenandoah, Sinaloa, Guanabacoa, João Pessoa

²oa \ō\ see ¹OW

oable \ü-ə-bəl\ see UABLE

oach \ōch\ broach, brooch, coach, loach, poach, roach, abroach, approach, caroche, cockroach, encroach, reproach, stagecoach

oachable \ō-chə-bəl\ coachable, approachable, inapproachable, irreproachable, unapproachable

oacher \ō-chər\ broacher, coacher, cloture, poacher, encroacher

¹oad \ōd\ see ODE

²oad \öd\ see ¹AUD

oader \ōd-ər\ see ODER

oadie \ōd-ē\ see ²ODY

oady \ōd-ē\ see ²ODY

oaf \ōf\ loaf, oaf, qoph, meatloaf, witloof, sugarloaf

oafer \ō-fər\ see OFER

oagie \ō-gē\ see OGIE

oah \ō-ə\ see ¹OA

oak \ōk\ see OKE

oaken \ō-kən\ see OKEN

oaker \ō-kər\ see OKER

oakum \ō-kəm\ see OKUM

oaky \ō-kē\ see OKY

oal \ōl\ see ¹OLE

oalie \ō-lē\ see ¹OLY

¹oam \ō-əm\ see OEM

²oam \ōm\ see ¹OME

oamer \ō-mər\ see ¹OMER

oaming \ō-miŋ\ coaming, combing, gloaming, Wyoming—*also* -ing *forms of verbs listed at* ¹OME

oamy \ō-mē\ foamy, homey, loamy, show-me, Suomi, Dahomey, Naomi, Salome

¹oan \ō-ən\ Owen, roan, rowan, Minoan, Samoan, waygoing, Eskimoan, protozoan

²oan \ōn\ see ¹ONE

oaner \ō-nər\ see ¹ONER

oaning \ō-niŋ\ see ²ONING

oap \ōp\ see OPE

oaper \ō-pər\ see OPER

oapy \ō-pē\ see OPI

oar \ȯr\ see ¹OR

oard \ȯrd\ board, bored, chord, cord, cored, floored, ford, Ford, gourd, hoard, horde, lord, Lord, oared, pored, poured, sward, sword, toward, ward, Ward, aboard, accord, afford, award, backboard, backsword, baseboard, billboard, blackboard, breadboard, broadsword, buckboard, cardboard, chalkboard, chessboard, chipboard, clapboard, clipboard, concord, corkboard, dashboard, discord, duckboard, fjord, flashboard, floorboard, footboard, freeboard, garbord, Gaylord,

greensward, hardboard,
headboard, inboard,
keyboard, kickboard,
landlord, lapboard, leeboard,
longsword, matchboard,
moldboard, onboard,
outboard, packboard,
pasteboard, patchboard,
pegboard, pressboard,
punchboard, rearward,
record, reward, sailboard,
scoreboard, seaboard,
shipboard, sideboard,
signboard, skateboard,
slumlord, smallsword,
snowboard, soundboard,
splashboard, springboard,
surfboard, switchboard,
tailboard, untoward,
wallboard, washboard, word-
hoard, warlord, whipcord,
aboveboard, bungee cord,
centerboard, checkerboard,
clavichord, disaccord,
fiberboard, fingerboard,
harpsichord, mortarbord,
motherboard, overboard,
overlord, paddleboard,
paperboard, pinafored,
plasterboard, pompadoured,
shuffleboard, smorgasbord,
storyboard, teeterboard,
tetrachord, untoward,
weatherboard, misericord,
particleboard—*also* -ed
forms of verbs listed at
¹OR
oarder \órd-ər\ see ORDER
oarding \órd-iŋ\ see ¹ORDING
oared \órd\ see OARD
oarer \ór-ər\ see ORER
oaring \ór-iŋ\ see ORING
oarious \ór-ē-əs\ see ORIOUS
oarish \ór-ish\ see ¹ORISH
oarse \órs\ see ¹ORSE
oarsen \órs-²n\ coarsen,
hoarsen, whoreson

oarsman \órz-mən\ oarsman,
outdoorsman
oart \órt\ see ¹ORT
oary \ór-ē\ see ORY
oast \ōst\ see ²OST
oastal \ōs-t²l\ see ¹OSTAL
oaster \ō-stər\ coaster, poster,
roaster, throwster, toaster,
billposter, four-poster,
roller-coaster, roller coaster
oasty \ō-stē\ see OSTY
oat \ōt\ bloat, boat, coat,
cote, dote, float, gloat, goat,
groat, haute, moat, mote,
note, oat, phot, quote, rote,
shoat, smote, stoat, throat,
tote, vote, wrote, afloat,
airboat, bareboat, bluecoat,
bumboat, capote, catboat,
compote, connote, coyote,
cutthroat, demote, denote,
devote, dovecote, eighth
note, emote, endnote,
fireboat, fistnote, flatboat,
footnote, greatcoat, gunboat,
half note, headnote, Hohhot,
houseboat, housecoat,
iceboat, keelboat, keynote,
lifeboat, longboat, one-note,
pigboat, promote, Q-boat,
quarter note, raincoat,
Rajkot, redcoat, remote,
rewrote, rowboat, sailboat,
scapegoat, sheepcote,
showboat, speedboat,
steamboat, stoneboat,
Sukkot, Sukkoth, surfboat,
tailcoat, topcoat, towboat,
tugboat, turncoat, U-boat,
unquote, wainscot,
whaleboat, whitethroat,
whole note, woodnote,
workboat, anecdote,
antidote, asymptote,
creosote, entrecote,
ferryboat, Huhehot,
motorboat, overcoat,

paddleboat, papillote,
petticoat, powerboat,
redingote, riverboat,
rubythroat, Shabuoth,
Sialkot, sugarcoat, symbiote,
table d'hôte, sixteenth note,
undercoat, yellowthroat,
thirty-second note

oate \ō-ət\ see ¹OET

oated \ōt-əd\ coated, noted,
throated, devoted, tailcoated,
petticoated—*also* -ed *forms
of verbs listed at* OAT

oaten \ōt-ⁿn\ see OTON

oater \ōt-ər\ bloater, boater,
coater, doter, floater,
gloater, motor, noter, oater,
rotor, scoter, toter, voter,
houseboater, iceboater,
keynoter, promoter,
pulmotor, sailboater, tilt-
rotor, trimotor, locomotor,
motorboater

oath \ōth\ see OWTH

oathe \ōth\ see OTHE

oathing \ō-thiŋ\ see OTHING

oating \ōt-iŋ\ boating,
coating, floating, free
floating, sailboating,
scapegoating, speedboating,
wainscoting, motorboating,
undercoating—*also* -ing
forms of verbs listed at OAT

oatswain \ōs-ⁿn\ see OSIN

oaty \ōt-ē\ see ¹OTE

oax \ōks\ coax, hoax—*also* -s,
-'s, *and* -s' *forms of nouns
listed at* OKE, *and* -s *forms of
verbs listed there*

¹ob \äb\ Ab, blob, bob, Bob,
cob, daub, fob, glob, gob,
hob, job, knob, lob, mob,
nob, Ob, rob, slob, snob,
sob, squab, stob, swab,
throb, yob, bedaub, corncob,
demob, doorknob,
heartthrob, hobnob, kabob,

macabre, nabob, nawab,
Punjab, skibob, memsahib,
shish kebab, thingamabob

²ob \ōb\ see ¹OBE

oba \ō-bə\ arroba, jojoba,
algaroba, Manitoba

obably \äb-lē\ see OBBLY

obal \ō-bəl\ see OBLE

obally \ō-bə-lē\ globally,
primum mobile

obar \ō-bər\ see OBER

obber \äb-ər\ bobber, caber,
clobber, cobber, jobber,
robber, slobber, swabber,
throbber, hobnobber,
Micawber, Skibobber,
stockjobber

obbery \äb-rē\ bobbery,
jobbery, robbery, slobbery,
snobbery, corroboree

obbes \äbz\ Hobbes—*also* -s,
-'s, *and* -s' *forms of nouns
listed at* ¹OB, *and* -s *forms of
verbs listed there*

obbet \äb-ət\ gobbet, probit

obbie \äb-ē\ see OBBY

obbin \äb-ən\ see OBIN

obbish \äb-ish\ slobbish,
snobbish

obble \äb-əl\ see ¹ABBLE

obbler \äb-lər\ cobbler,
gobbler, hobbler, nobbler,
squabbler, wobbler

obbly \äb-lē\ knobbly,
probably, wobbly, Wobbly

obby \äb-ē\ Bobbie, bobby,
Bobby, cobby, dobby,
globby, hobby, knobby,
lobby, nobby, snobby,
swabbie, Mesabi, Punjabi,
Wahhabi, Abu Dhabi,
Hammurabi

¹obe \ōb\ daube, globe, Job,
lobe, probe, robe, strobe,
bathrobe, conglobe, disrobe,
earlobe, enrobe, microbe,
wardrobe, Anglophobe,

claustrophobe,
Francophobe, homophobe,
negrophobe, xenophobe,
ailurophobe, computerphobe
²obe \ō-bē\ see OBY
obeah \ō-bē-ə\ see OBIA
obee \ō-bē\ see OBY
obelus \äb-ə-ləs\ see ABILIS
ober \ō-bər\ lobar, sober,
October
obi \ō-bē\ see OBY
obia \ō-bē-ə\ cobia, obeah,
phobia, acrophobia,
algophobia, Anglophobia,
claustrophobia,
homophobia, hydrophobia,
negrophobia, photophobia,
technophobia, xenophobia,
agoraphobia,
triskaidekaphobia
obic \ō-bik\ phobic, aerobic,
anaerobic, claustrophobic,
homophobic, hydrophobic,
photophobic, xenophobic
¹obile \ō-bə-lē\ see OBALLY
²obile \ō-bəl\ see OBLE
obin \äb-ən\ bobbin, dobbin,
graben, robin, Robin,
Robyn, round-robin
¹obit \ō-bət\ obit, Tobit, post-
obit
²obit \äb-ət\ see OBBET
oble \ō-bəl\ coble, global,
mobile, noble, airmobile,
ennoble, Grenoble, ignoble,
immobile, San Cristóbal
obo \ō-bō\ gobo, hobo, kobo,
lobo, oboe, adobo
oboe \ō-bō\ see OBO
obol \ō-bəl\ see ¹ABBLE
oboree \äb-ə-rē\ see OBBERY
obot \ō-bət\ see ¹OBIT
obra \ō-brə\ cobra, dobra
obster \äb-stər\ lobster,
mobster
obular \äb-yə-lər\ globular,
lobular

obule \äb-yül\ globule, lobule
oby \ō-bē\ Gobi, goby, Kobe,
obi, Obie, toby, Toby, adobe,
Nairobi, Okeechobee
obyn \äb-ən\ see OBIN
¹oc \ōk\ see OKE
²oc \äk\ see ¹OCK
³oc \ōk\ see ALK
oca \ō-kə\ coca, mocha, oca,
Asoka, carioca, Fukuoka,
mandioca, Shizuoka, tapioca
ocable \ō-kə-bəl\ smokable,
vocable, evocable
ocage \äk-ij\ see OCKAGE
ocal \ō-kəl\ focal, local, socle,
vocal, yokel, bifocal,
subvocal, trifocal, unvocal
ocally \ō-kə-lē\ locally,
vocally
ocative \äk-ət-iv\ locative,
vocative, evocative,
provocative
occa \äk-ə\ see ¹AKA
occer \äk-ər\ see OCKER
occie \äch-ē\ see OTCHY
occhi \ō-kē\ see ALKIE
occo \äk-ō\ socko, taco,
cheechako, guanaco,
morocco, Morocco, scirocco,
sirocco
occule \äk-yül\ floccule,
locule
occulent \äk-yə-lənt\
flocculent, inoculant
occulus \äk-yə-ləs\ flocculus,
loculus, oculus
oce \ō-chē\ see ¹OCHE
ocean \ō-shən\ see OTION
ocent \ōs-ᵊnt\ docent, nocent
ocess \äs-əs\ Knossos,
process, colossus, proboscis
¹och \ōk\ see OKE
²och \äk\ see ¹OCK
³och \òsh\ see ²ASH
⁴och \òk\ see ALK
ocha \ō-kə\ see OCA
ochal \äk-əl\ see OCKLE

ochan \ä-kən\ see ACHEN

¹oche \ō-chē\ Kochi, Sochi, penoche, sotto voce, veloce, mezza voce

²oche \ōsh\ cloche, gauche, skosh, brioche, caroche, guilloche

³oche \ō-kē\ see OKY

⁴oche \ōch\ see OACH

⁵oche \ōsh\ see ²ASH

ochee \ō-kē\ see OKY

ocher \ō-kər\ see OKER

ochi \ō-chē\ see ¹OCHE

ochle \ək-əl\ see UCKLE

ochs \äks\ see OX

ochum \ō-kəm\ see OKUM

ocia \ō-shə\ see ¹OTIA

ociable \ō-shə-bəl\ sociable, associable, dissociable, insociable, negotiable, unsociable, indissociable, renegotiable

ocial \ō-shəl\ social, asocial, dissocial, precocial, unsocial, antisocial

ocile \äs-əl\ see OSSAL

ocious \ō-shəs\ atrocious, ferocious, precocious, Theodosius

¹ock \äk\ Bach, bloc, block, bock, brock, chock, clock, cock, croc, crock, doc, dock, floc, flock, frock, hock, Jacque, Jacques, jock, knock, lakh, loch, lock, Locke, lough, Mach, moc, mock, nock, pock, roc, rock, schlock, shock, smock, sock, stock, wok, yak, yock, acock, ad hoc, aftershock, amok, Arak, backblock, Balzac, bangkok, Bangkok, baroque, Bartok, bawcock, bedrock, bemock, bibcock, bitstock, blackcock, blesbok, bloodstock, bois d'arc, Brecknock, breechblock,

burdock, buttstock, caprock, coldcock, Comstock, deadlock, debacle, defrock, dry dock, duroc, Dvořák, earlock, en bloc, epoch, fatstock, feedstock, fetlock, firelock, flintlock, forelock, foreshock, gamecock, gemsbok, gridlock, gunlock, Hancock, havelock, haycock, headlock, headstock, hemlock, Hickock, Iraq, jazz-rock, Kanak, Kazak, Kazakh, kapok, kneesock, Languedoc, livestock, lovelock, matchlock, Mohock, Nisroch, nostoc, o'clock, oarlock, padlock, peacock, penstock, petcock, pibroch, picklock, pinchcock, post doc, post hoc, rhebok, rimrock, roadblock, rootstock, Rorschach, Rostock, rowlock, shamrock, Sheetrock, sherlock, shylock, Sirach, slick rock, Slovak, springbok, steenbok, stopcock, Tarlak, tarok, ticktock, traprock, van Gogh, warlock, wedlock, woodcock, wristlock, zwieback, alpenstock, Anahuac, antiknock, antilock, Antioch, Arawak, Ayers Rock, billycock, hockablock, hammerlock, hollyhock, interlock, John Hancock, lady's-smock, laughingstock, Little Rock, manioc, mantlerock, monadnock, Offenbach, Otomac, poppycock, Ragnarok, Sarawak, shuttlecock, spatterdock, turkey-cock, weathercock, Czechoslovak, Bialystok, electroshock,

Inupiaq, Pontianak,
Vladivostok

²ock \ók\ see ALK

ockage \äk-ij\ blockage,
brockage, dockage,
lockage, socage

ocke \äk\ see ¹OCK

ocked \äkt\ blocked,
crocked, concoct, decoct,
entr'acte, half-cocked,
landlocked, periproct,
entoproct—*also* -ed *forms
of verbs listed at* ¹OCK

ocker \äk-ər\ blocker,
clocker, cocker, docker,
hocker, knocker, locker,
makar, mocker, rocker,
shocker, soccer, stocker,
footlocker, appleknocker,
beta-blocker,
knickerbocker

ockery \äk-rē\ crockery,
mockery, rockery

ocket \äk-ət\ brocket,
crocket, Crockett, docket,
locket, pocket, rocket,
socket, sprocket,
pickpocket, skyrocket,
out-of-pocket, retro-rocket

ockett \äk-ət\ see OCKET

ockey \äk-ē\ see OCKY

ockian \äk-ē-ən\
Comstockian, Slovakian,
Czechoslovakian

ockiness \äk-ē-nəs\ cockiness,
rockiness, stockiness

ocking \äk-iŋ\ flocking,
shocking, smocking,
stocking, bluestocking,
silk-stocking—*also* -ing
forms of verbs listed at ¹OCK

ockish \äk-ish\ blockish,
stockish

ockle \äk-əl\ coccal, cockle,
socle, debacle, epochal

ockney \äk-nē\ see cockney,
Procne

ocko \äk-ō\ see OCCO

ocks \äks\ see OX

ocky \äk-ē\ blocky, cocky,
hockey, jockey, pocky,
rocky, Rocky, sake,
schlocky, stocky, Yaqui,
Abnaki, Iraqi, Ontake,
peacocky, rumaki,
jabberwocky, Kawasaki,
Miyazaki, Nagasaki,
Okazaki, sukiyaki, teriyaki,
Amagasaki, enokidake

ocle \ō-kəl\ see OCAL

ocne \äk-nē\ see OCKNEY

oco \ō-kō\ coco, cocoa, loco,
poco, Bioko, iroko, rococo,
crème de cacao, Locofoco,
Orinoco, poco a poco

ocoa \ō-kō\ see OCO

ocracy \äk-rə-sē\ autocracy,
bureaucracy, democracy,
hypocrisy, mobocracy,
plutocracy, slavocracy,
technocracy, theocracy,
aristocracy, gerontocracy,
gynecocracy, meritocracy,
thalassocracy

ocre \ō-kər\ see OKER

ocrisy \äk-rə-sē\ see
OCRACY

ocsin \äk-sən\ see OXIN

oct \äkt\ see OCKED

oction \äk-shən\ concoction,
decoction

octor \äk-tər\ doctor,
proctor, concocter

oculant \äk-yə-lənt\ see
OCCULENT

ocular \äk-yə-lər\ jocular,
locular, ocular, binocular,
monocular, intraocular

ocule \äk-yül\ see OCCULE

oculus \äk-yə-ləs\ see
OCCULUS

ocum \ō-kəm\ see OKUM

ocus \ō-kəs\ crocus, focus,
hocus, locus, prefocus,

refocus, soft-focus, hocus-pocus

ocused \ō-kəst\ see OCUST

ocust \ō-kəst\ locust, unfocused

ocutor \äk-yət-ər\ prolocutor, interlocutor

¹**od** \äd\ bod, clod, cod, fade, Fahd, gaud, god, hod, mod, nod, od, odd, plod, pod, prod, quad, quod, rod, scrod, shod, sod, squad, tod, trod, wad, Akkad, amphipod, Arad, aubade, ballade, gaud, god, Beograde, bipod, Cape Cod, couvade, croustade, dry-shod, ephod, facade, fantod, glissade, hot-rod, jihad, lingcod, Nimrod, oeillade, pomade, peasecod, ramrod, Riyadh, roughshod, roulade, saccade, scalade, seedpod, slipshod, synod, tie-rod, tightwad, tomcod, torsade, tripod, accolade, arthropod, Ashkhabad, Bacolod, bigarade, carbonnade, chiffonade, defilade, demigod, enfilade, esculade, esplanade, fusillade, gallopade, gastropod, goldenrod, hexapod, lycopod, monkeypod, Novgorod, Novi Sad, octopod, promenade, pseudopod, Ahmadabad, Allahabad, cephalopod, Faisalabad, Islamabad, ornithopod, prosauropod, rodomontade, dégringolade, fanfaronade, Upanishad, Scheherazade, Nizhni Novgorod

²**od** \ō\ see ¹OW

³**od** \ōd\ see ODE

⁴**od** \ud\ see ¹OOD

⁵**od** \od\ see ¹AUD

o'd \üd\ see UDE

oda \ōd-ə\ coda, Rhoda, soda, Baroda, pagoda, sal soda

odal \ōd-²l\ Godel, modal, nodal, yodel, cathodal, intermodal

odden \äd-²n\ sodden, trodden, downtrodden, Ibadan

odder \äd-ər\ dodder, fodder, khaddar, modder, nodder, odder, plodder, prodder, solder, wadder, glissader, hot-rodder, promenader—*also* -er *forms of adjectives listed at* ¹OD

oddery \äd-rē\ see AWDRY

oddess \äd-əs\ bodice, goddess, demigoddess

oddish \äd-ish\ cloddish, kaddish

oddle \äd-²l\ coddle, model, noddle, swaddle, toddle, twaddle, waddle, remodel, mollycoddle

oddler \äd-lər\ coddler, modeler, toddler, twaddler, waddler, mollycoddler

oddly \äd-lē\ see ODLY

oddy \äd-ē\ see ¹ODY

ode \ōd\ bode, bowed, code, goad, load, lode, mode, node, ode, road, rode, Spode, strode, toad, toed, woad, wood, abode, bestrode, boatload, busload, byroad, carload, cartload, caseload, commode, corrode, crossroad, decode, displode, embowed, encode, epode, erode, explode, forebode, freeload, geode, highroad, implode, inroad, no-load, off-load, outmode, payload, planeload, postcode, railroad, rhapsode, sarod, shipload, square-toed, threnode, trainload, truckload, two-toed, unload,

upload, à la mode, antipode,
Comstock Lode,
discommode, eigenmode,
electrode, episode,
impastoed, incommode,
Kozhikode, Nesselrode,
overrode, palinode, pigeon-
toed—*also* -ed *forms of verbs
listed at* ¹OW

odeine \ōd-ē-ən\ see ODIAN

odel \ōd-ᵊl\ see ODAL

oden \ōd-ᵊn\ loden, Odin,
Woden

odeon \ōd-ē-ən\ see ODIAN

oder \ōd-ər\ coder, loader,
Oder, odor, breechloader,
decoder, freeloader,
malodor, railroader,
unloader, middle-of-the-
roader

oderate \äd-rət\ quadrate,
moderate, immoderate

odes \ōdz\ Rhodes—*also* -s,
-'s, *and* -s' *forms of nouns
listed at* ODE, *and* -s *forms
of verbs listed there*

odest \äd-əst\ Mahdist,
modest, haggadist,
immodest—*also* -est *forms
of adjectives listed at* ¹OD

odesy \äd-ə-sē\ odyssey,
geodesy, theodicy

odeum \ōd-ē-əm\ see ODIUM

odge \äj\ see ¹AGE

odger \äj-ər\ codger, dodger,
lodger, roger, Roger, Jolly
Roger, stinking roger

odgy \äj-ē\ dodgy, podgy,
stodgy, mystagogy,
pedagogy

odian \ōd-ē-ən\ Cambodian,
custodian, melodeon,
nickelodeon

odic \äd-ik\ zaddik,
cathodic, ergodic, melodic,
methodic, monodic,

prosodic, rhapsodic,
spasmodic, synodic,
threnodic, episodic,
periodic, antispasmodic,
aperiodic, upanishadic,
quasiperiodic

odical \äd-i-kəl\ methodical,
monodical, prosodical,
synodical, episodical,
immethodical, periodical

odice \äd-əs\ see ODDESS

odicy \äd-ə-sē\ see ODESY

odie \ō-dē\ see ²ODY

odin \ōd-ᵊn\ see ODEN

odious \ōd-ē-əs\ odious,
commodious, melodious,
Methodius, incommodious

odity \äd-ət-ē\ oddity,
commodity, incommodity

odium \ōd-ē-əm\ odeum,
odium, podium, rhodium,
sodium

odius \ō-dē-əs\ see ODIOUS

odless \äd-ləs\ godless,
rodless

odling \äd-liŋ\ codling,
godling—*also* -ing *forms of
verbs listed at* ODDLE

odly \äd-lē\ godly, oddly,
ungodly

odo \ōd-ō\ dodo, Komodo,
Quasimodo

odom \äd-əm\ shahdom,
Sodom

odor \ōd-ər\ see ODER

odsk \ätsk\ see ATSK

odular \äj-ə-lər\ modular,
nodular

odule \äj-ül\ module, nodule

¹ody \äd-ē\ body, cloddy,
gaudy, Mahdi, noddy,
sadhe, shoddy, toddy,
waddy, wadi, anybody,
blackbody, dogsbody,
embody, homebody,
nobody, somebody, wide-
body, antibody, busybody,

disembody, everybody,
Irrawaddy, underbody

²**ody** \ŏd-ē\ Cody, Jodie,
Jody, roadie, toady,
polypody

odyssey \äd-ə-sē\ see ODESY

odz \ŭj\ see ¹UGE

¹**oe** \ō\ see ¹OW

²**oe** \ō-ē\ see OWY

³**oe** \ē\ see ¹EE

⁴**oe** \ói\ see OY

¹**oea** \ói-ə\ see OIA

²**oea** \ē-ə\ see ¹IA

oeba \ē-bə\ see EBA

oebe \ē-bē\ see ¹EBE

oebel \ā-bəl\ see ABLE

oebus \ē-bəs\ see EBUS

oed \ōd\ see ODE

oehn \ən\ see UN

oeia \ē-ə\ see ¹IA

oeic \ē-ik\ see EIC

oek \ŭk\ see ¹OOK

oel \ō-əl\ Joel, Lowell, Noel,
bestowal, Baden-Powell,
protozoal

¹**oeless** \ō-ləs\ see OLUS

²**oeless** \ü-ləs\ see EWLESS

¹**oem** \ō-əm\ poem, proem,
jeroboam

²**oem** \ōm\ see ¹OME

³**oem** \óm\ see ¹AUM

oeman \ō-mən\ see OMAN

oena \ē-nə\ see ²INA

¹**oentgen** \en-chən\ see
ENSION

²**oentgen** \ən-chən\ see
UNCHEON

oepha \ē-fə\ see EPHA

o'er \ór\ see ¹OR

¹**oer** \ór\ see ¹OR

²**oer** \ü-ər\ see ¹EWER

³**oer** \ùr\ see ¹URE

⁴**oer** \ō-ər\ blower, knower,
lower, mower, sewer,
shower, sower, beachgoer,
churchgoer, flamethrower,
filmgoer, foregoer, forgoer,

mindblower, snowblower,
snowthrower, winegrower,
concertgoer, moviegoer,
cinemagoer, operagoer,
theatergoer, whistleblower

¹**oes** \əz\ see ¹EUSE

²**oes** \ōz\ see ²OSE

³**oes** \üz\ see ²USE

oesia \ē-shə\ see ¹ESIA

oesn't \əz-²nt\ see ASN'T

oest \ü-əst\ see OOIST

oesus \ē-səs\ see ESIS

oet \ō-ət\ poet, inchoate,
introit

²**oet** \óit\ see ¹OIT

oetess \ō-ət-əs\ coitus, poetess

oeuf \əf\ see UFF

oeur \ər\ see ¹EUR

oeuvre \ərv\ see ERVE

oey \ō-ē\ see OWY

¹**of** \äv\ see ²OLVE

²**of** \əv\ see ¹OVE

³**of** \óf\ see ²OFF

ofar \ō-fər\ see OFER

ofer \ō-fər\ chauffeur, gofer,
gopher, loafer, Ophir, shofar

¹**off** \äf\ boff, coif, doff, goif,
kaph, prof, quaff, scoff,
shroff, taw, toff, carafe,
cook-off, pilaf, Romanov

²**off** \óf\ cough, doff, off, scoff,
taw, trough, Azov, beg off,
blast-off, brush-off, cast-off,
castoff, checkoff, Chekhov,
cook-off, cutoff, die-off,
drop-off, face-off, falloff, far-
off, goof-off, hands-off, jump-
off, Khartov, kickoff, Kirov,
knockoff, Khrushchev, layoff,
leadoff, lift-off, Lvov, one-off,
Pavlov, payoff, pick-off,
pickoff, play-off, rake-off, rip-
off, roll-off, runoff, Salchow,
sawed-off, sell-off, send-off,
setoff, show-off, shutoff, spin-
off, standoff, takeoff,
Tambov, tap-off, tip-off,

trade-off, turnoff, well-off,
Wolof, write-off, Wroclaw,
better-off, cooling-off,
damping-off, Gorbachev,
Molotov, Nabokov,
philosophe, Pribilof, Rostov,
beef Stroganoff,
Rachmaninoff, Rimsky-
Korsakov

¹offal \äf-əl\ see AFEL

²offal \ȯ-fəl\ see AWFUL

offaly \ȯf-ə-lē\ see AWFULLY

offee \ȯ-fē\ coffee, toffee

¹offer \äf-ər\ coffer, gauffer,
goffer, offer, proffer,
quaffer, scoffer, troffer,
reoffer

²offer \ȯf-ər\ goffer, offer,
troffer, reoffer

offin \ȯ-fən\ coffin,
dauphin, soften, uncoffin

offit \äf-ət\ see OFIT

offle \ȯ-fəl\ see AWFUL

ofit \äf-ət\ profit, prophet,
soffit, nonprofit, not-for-
profit

ofle \ü-fəl\ see UEFUL

¹oft \ȯft\ croft, loft, oft, soft,
toft, aloft, hayloft,
undercroft——also -ed *forms
of verbs listed at* ²OFF

²oft \äft\ see ¹AFT

often \ȯ-fən\ see OFFIN

ofty \ȯf-tē\ lofty, softy,
toplofty

¹og \äg\ bog, clog, cog, flog,
fog, frog, grog, hog, jog, log,
nog, Prague, prog, quag,
shog, slog, smog, tog, agog,
backlog, bullfrog, defog,
eclogue, eggnog, footslog,
groundhog, gulag, photog,
prologue, putlog, quahog,
Rolvaag, sandhog, stalag,
warthog, analog, analogue,
antilog, apologue, catalog,
decalogue, demagogue,

dialogue, golliwog,
monologue, mummichog,
mystagogue, nouvelle vague,
pedagogue, pollywog,
semilog, sinologue,
synagogue, Taganrog,
theologue, waterlog

²og \ȯg\ bog, clog, dog, fog,
frog, hog, jog, log, smog,
backlog, bandog, befog, bird-
dog, bulldog, bullfrog,
coydog, defog, eclogue,
firedog, groundhog, hangdog,
hedgehog, hotdog, lapdog,
leapfrog, prologue, quahog,
sandhog, seadog, sheepdog,
warthog, watchdog, analog,
analogue, apologue, catalog,
decalogue, dialogue, dog-eat-
dog, duologue, epilogue,
homologue, monologue,
mummichog, overdog,
pettifog, pollywog, sinologue,
theologue, Tagalog,
travelogue, underdog,
waterlog, yellow-dog,
ideologue

³og \ōg\ see ¹OGUE

oga \ō-gə\ toga, yoga,
Conestoga

ogamous \äg-ə-məs\
endogamous, exogamous,
monogamous,
heterogamous

ogamy \äg-ə-mē\ endogamy,
exogamy, homogamy,
misogamy, monogamy

ogan \ō-gən\ brogan, Mount
Logan, shogun, slogan

ogany \äg-ə-nē\ see OGONY

ogative \äg-ət-iv\ derogative,
prerogative, interrogative

¹oge \ōj\ doge, gamboge,
horologe

²oge \ōzh\ loge, Limoges

³oge \ō-jē\ see OJI

⁴oge \üzh\ see ²UGE

ogel \ō-gəl\ see ¹OGLE

ogenous \äj-ə-nəs\
androgynous, erogenous,
homogenous, monogynous,
heterogenous

ogeny \äj-ə-nē\ progeny,
androgeny, autogeny,
homogeny, misogyny,
monogyny, ontogeny,
phylogeny, heterogeny

¹oger \äj-ər\ see ODGER

²oger \òg-ər\ see ²OGGER

oges \ōzh\ see ²OGE

¹ogey \ō-gē\ see OGIE

²ogey \ùg-ē\ see OOGIE

oggan \äg-ən\ see OGGIN

oggar \äg-ər\ see ¹OGGER

¹ogger \äg-ər\ agar, clogger,
flogger, Hoggar, jogger,
laager, lager, logger, slogger,
Ahaggar, defogger,
footslogger, agar-agar,
cataloger, pettifogger

²ogger \òg-ər\ auger, augur,
clogger, jogger, logger,
maugre, sauger, defogger,
hotdogger, cataloger,
pettifogger

¹oggery \äg-rē\ toggery,
demagoguery

²oggery \ò-gə-rē\ augury,
doggery

oggin \äg-ən\ noggin,
toboggan, Copenhagen

oggle \äg-əl\ boggle, goggle,
joggle, ogle, toggle,
boondoggle, hornswoggle,
synagogal

¹oggy \äg-ē\ boggy, foggy,
groggy, moggy, quaggy,
smoggy, soggy, yagi,
demagogy

²oggy \òg-ē\ foggy, soggy

¹ogh \ōg\ see ¹OGUE

²ogh \òk\ see OKE

³ogh \äk\ see ¹OCK

⁴ogh \ō\ see OW

ogi \ō-gē\ see OGIE

ogian \ō-jən\ see OJAN

ogic \äj-ik\ logic, choplogic,
illogic, anagogic, analogic,
biologic, chronologic,
cryptologic, cytologic,
demagogic, dendrologic,
dialogic, ecologic, ethnologic,
geologic, histologic, horologic,
hydrologic, mythologic,
neurologic, nosologic,
oncologic, pathologic,
pedagogic, pedologic,
petrologic, phonologic,
proctologic, psychologic,
serologic, technologic,
theologic, virologic, zoologic,
dermatologic, etiologic,
gerontologic, gynecologic,
hagiologic, hematologic,
ideologic, immunologic,
ophthalmologic,
ornithologic, pharmacologic,
physiologic, roentgenologic,
sociologic, teleologic,
teratologic, toxicologic,
volcanologic, bacteriologic,
endocrinologic, meteorologic,
paleontologic, parasitologic,
sedimentologic,
symptomatologic,
epidemiologic

ogical \äj-i-kəl\ logical, alogical,
illogical, anagogical,
analogical, biological,
Christological, chronological,
cosmological, cryptological,
cytological, dendrological,
ecological, enological,
ethnological, ethological,
extralogical, gemological,
geological, graphological,
histological, horological,
hydrological, limnological,
morphological, mycological,
mythological, necrological,
neurological, nomological,

oncological, pathological,
pedagogical, pedological,
penological, petrological,
philological, phonological,
phrenological, phycological,
proctological, psephological,
psychological, scatological,
seismological, serological,
sinological, tautological,
technological, theological,
topological, typological,
ufological, virological,
zoological, abiological,
anthropological,
archaeological, cardiological,
climatological,
criminological,
demonological,
dermatological,
embryological,
entomological,
eschatological, etiological,
etymological, futurological,
genealogical, gerontological,
gynecological, hagiological,
hematological,
herpetological,
ichthyological, iconological,
ideological, immunological,
Mariological, methodological,
mineralogical, musicological,
numerological,
ophthalmological,
ornithological,
pharmacological,
phraseological, physiological,
primatological,
roentgenological,
selenological, semiological,
sociological, teleological,
teratological, terminological,
thanatological, toxicological,
volcanological,
bacteriological,
characterological,
dialectological,
ecclesiological,

endocrinological,
epistemological,
geomorphological,
meteorological,
paleontological,
parasitological,
phenomenological,
sedimentological,
symptomatological,
epidemiological,
gastroenterological

ogie \ō-gē\ bogey, bogie,
dogie, fogy, hoagie, logy,
pogy, stogie, vogie, yogi,
pirogi

¹**ogle** \ō-gəl\ Gogel, ogle
²**ogle** \äg-əl\ see OGGLE
oglio \ōl-yō\ see ¹OLLO
¹**ogna** \ō-nə\ see ONA
²**ogna** \ō-nē\ see ¹ONY
³**ogna** \ōn-yə\ see ²ONIA
ogne \ōn\ see ¹ONE
ogned \ōnd\ see ¹ONED
ogo \ō-gō\ go-go, logo,
Logo, Togo, a-go-go
ogony \äg-ə-nē\ cosmogony,
mahogany, theogony
ographer \äg-rə-fər\
biographer, cartographer,
chorographer,
cryptographer,
demographer,
discographer,
ethnographer, geographer,
lithographer,
mythographer,
phonographer,
photographer,
pornographer,
stenographer, typographer,
bibliographer,
choreographer,
hagiographer, heliographer,
iconographer,
lexicographer,
oceanographer,
paleographer,

autobiographer,
biogeographer,
chromatographer,
cinematographer,
historiographer
ography \äg-rə-fē\
aerography, autography,
biography, cacography,
cartography, chorography,
chronography, cosmography,
cryptography, demography,
discography, ethnography,
filmography, geography,
holography, hydrography,
hypsography, lithography,
lymphography,
mammography,
mythography, nomography,
orthography, phonography,
photography, pictography,
planography, pornography,
reprography, sonography,
stenography, thermography,
tomography, topography,
typography, venography,
xerography, xylography,
angiography, aortography,
bibliography, cardiography,
choreography,
chromatography,
crystallography,
hagiography, heliography,
iconography, lexicography,
metallography,
oceanography, paleography,
physiography, radiography,
roentgenography,
videography,
arteriography,
autobiography,
cinematography,
encephalography,
historiography,
psychobiography,
electroencephalography
ogress \ō-grəs\ ogress,
progress

ogrom \äg-rəm\ grogram,
pogrom
¹**ogue** \ōg\ brogue, drogue,
rogue, togue, vogue, yogh,
collogue, crannog, pirogue,
prorogue, Krivoy Rog,
disembogue
²**ogue** \äg\ see ¹OG
³**ogue** \óg\ see ²OG
oguery \äg-rē\ see ¹OGGERY
oguish \ō-gish\ roguish,
voguish
ogun \ō-gən\ see OGAN
ogynous \äj-ə-nəs\ see
OGENOUS
ogyny \äj-ə-nē\ see OGENY
oh \ō\ see ¹OW
oha \ō-ə\ see ¹OA
ohl \ōl\ see ¹OLE
ohm \ōm\ see ¹OME
ohn \än\ see ¹ON
ohns \änz\ see ONZE
ohn's \ōnz\ see ONZE
ohnson \än-sən\ Johnson,
Jonson, Wisconsin
ohr \ór\ see ¹OR
¹**oi** \ä\ see ¹A
²**oi** \ói\ see OY
oia \ói-ə\ cholla, Goya, Hoya,
olla, toea, Nagoya, sequoia,
Sequoya, atemoya,
cherimoya, paranoia
oian \ói-ən\ see OYEN
oic \ō-ik\ stoic, azoic,
bistroic, echoic, heroic,
anechoic, Cenozoic,
Mesozoic, mock-heroic,
vetinoic, antiheroic,
Paleozoic
oice \óis\ choice, Joyce,
Royce, voice, devoice, Du
Bois, invoice, pro-choice,
rejoice, unvoice, sailor's-
choice
oiced \óist\ see OIST
oicer \ói-sər\ choicer, voicer,
pro-choicer, rejoicer

¹**oid** \ȯid\ Boyd, Floyd, Freud,
void, android, avoid,
chancroid, colloid, conoid,
cuboid, cycloid, deltoid,
dendroid, devoid, discoid,
factoid, fungoid, globoid,
hydroid, hypnoid, keloid,
mucoid, Negroid, ovoid,
percoid, prismoid, pygmoid,
rhizoid, rhomboid, schizoid,
scombroid, sigmoid,
spheroid, steroid, styloid,
tabloid, thalloid, thyroid,
toroid, toxoid, trochoid,
typhoid, Veddoid, viroid,
adenoid, alkaloid, amoeboid,
aneroid, anthropoid,
arachnoid, asteroid,
Australoid, carcinoid,
Caucasoid, celluloid,
crystalloid, ellipsoid,
embryoid, eunuchoid,
helicoid, hemorrhoid,
hominoid, humanoid,
hysteroid, metalloid,
Mongoloid, myeloid,
nautiloid, nucleoid, obovoid,
opioid, osteoid, overjoyed,
paranoid, philanthropoid,
planetoid, Polaroid, retinoid,
rheumatoid, solenoid,
Stalinoid, trapezoid,
unalloyed, unemployed,
cannabinoid, carotenoid,
eicosanoid, meteoroid,
tuberculoid, underemployed,
Neanderthaloid—*also* -ed
forms of verbs listed at OY

²**oid** \ä\ *see* ¹A

oidal \ȯid-³l\ chancroidal,
choroidal, colloidal,
conchoidal, cuboidal,
cycloidal, discoidal,
spheroidal, toroidal,
adenoidal, asteroidal,
ellipsoidal, emulsoidal,
hemorrhoidal, metalloidal,

planetoidal, saccharoidal,
trapezoidal, paraboloidal

older \ȯid-ər\ broider, voider,
avoider, embroider,
reembroider

oie \ä\ *see* ¹A

oif \äf\ *see* ¹OFF

oign \ȯin\ *see* ¹OIN

oil \ȯil\ boil, Boyle, broil,
coil, Doyle, foil, hoyle, moil,
loyal, noil, oil, roil, royal,
Royal, soil, spoil, toil, voile,
aboil, airfoil, assoil,
charbroil, cinquefoil,
despoil, embroil, entoil,
garboil, gargoyle, gumboil,
hard-boil, Isle Royal, langue
d'oïl, milfoil, non-oil,
parboil, recoil, subsoil,
supercoil, tinfoil, topsoil,
trefoil, turmoil, counterfoil,
disloyal, hydrofoil,
quatrefoil, rhyme royal,
surroyal, pennyroyal

oilage \ȯi-lij\ soilage, spoilage

¹**oile** \ä\ *see* ¹AL

²**oile** \ȯil\ *see* OIL

oiled \ȯild\ foiled, oiled, hard-
boiled, soft-boiled, uncoiled,
well-oiled—*also* -ed *forms of
verbs listed at* OIL

oiler \ȯi-lər\ boiler, broiler,
moiler, oiler, spoiler, toiler,
charbroiler, despoiler, Free-
Soiler, subsoiler, potboiler

oiling \ȯi-liŋ\ boiling,
moiling—*also* -ing *forms of
verbs listed at* OIL

oilless \ȯil-ləs\ soilless,
recoilless

oilsman \ȯilz-mən\ foilsman,
spoilsman

oilus \ȯi-ləs\ *see* OYLESS

oily \ȯi-lē\ doily, oily, roily

¹**oin** \ȯin\ coin, foin, groin,
groyne, join, loin, quoin,
adjoin, Burgoyne, conjoin,

Des Moines, disjoin, eloign, enjoin, essoin, purloin, recoin, rejoin, sainfoin, sirloin, subjoin, tenderloin, Assiniboin

²**oin** \aⁿ\ see ⁴IN

oine \än\ see ¹ON

oined \óind\ conjoined, uncoined—*also* -ed *forms of verbs listed at* ¹OIN

oiner \ói-nər\ coiner, joiner

oines \óin\ see ¹OIN

o-ing \ó-iŋ\ see ¹OING

¹**oing** \ó-iŋ\ bowing, going, knowing, rowing, sewing, showing, churchgoing, deep-going, foregoing, free-flowing, glassblowing, ingrowing, mind-blowing, ongoing, outgoing, seagoing, waygoing, concertgoing, easygoing, moviegoing, oceangoing, operagoing, theatergoing, thoroughgoing, whistle-blowing, to-ing and fro-ing—*also* -ing *forms of verbs listed at* ¹OW

²**oing** \ü-iŋ\ bluing, doing, Ewing, misdoing, undoing, wrongdoing, evildoing—*also* -ing *forms of verbs listed at* ¹EW

³**oing** \ó-ən\ see ¹OAN

oings \ó-iŋz\ outgoings—*also* -s, -'s, *and* -s' *forms of nouns listed at* ¹OING, *and* -s *forms of verbs listed there*

¹**oint** \óint\ joint, point, adjoint, anoint, appoint, aroint, ballpoint, bluepoint, checkpoint, conjoint, disjoint, drypoint, eyepoint, gunpoint, knifepoint, midpoint, nonpoint, outpoint, pinpoint, pourpoint, standpoint, tuck-point, viewpoint,

counterpoint, disappoint, needlepoint, petit point, silverpoint

²**oint** \ant\ see ⁵ANT

ointe \ant\ see ⁵ANT

ointed \óint-əd\ jointed, pointed, lap-jointed, loose-jointed, double-jointed, well-appointed—*also* -ed *forms of verbs listed at* ¹OINT

ointer \óint-ər\ jointer, pointer, anointer

ointing \óin-tiŋ\ finger-pointing—*also* -ing *forms of verbs listed at* ¹OINT

ointment \óint-mənt\ ointment, anointment, appointment, disappointment

¹**oir** \ir\ see ¹IRE

²**oir** \är\ see ³AR

³**oir** \óir\ see OYER

⁴**oir** \ór\ see ¹OR

¹**oire** \är\ see ³AR

²**oire** \óir\ see OYER

³**oire** \ór\ see ¹OR

¹**ois** \ä\ see ¹A

²**ois** \ói\ see OY

³**ois** \ó-əs\ Lois, Powys

⁴**ois** \óis\ see OICE

¹**oise** \äz\ poise, 'twas, vase, was, Ahwaz, bourgeoise, Lamaze, Shiraz, vichyssoise, The Afars and the Isas—*also* -s, -'s, *and* -s' *forms of nouns listed at* ¹A, *and* -s *forms of verbs listed there*

²**oise** \óiz\ hoise, noise, Noyes, poise, turquoise, counterpoise, equipoise, avoirdupois—*also* -s, -'s, *and* -s' *forms of nouns listed at* OY, *and* -s *forms of verbs listed there*

³**oise** \ói-zē\ see OISY

oison \óiz-²n\ foison, poison, empoison

oist \óist\ foist, hoist, joist, moist, voiced, unvoiced, semimoist—*also* -ed *forms of verbs listed at* OICE

oister \ói-stər\ cloister, moister, oyster, roister

oisterous \ói-strəs\ *see* OISTRESS

oistral \ói-strəl\ cloistral, coistrel

oistrel \ói-strəl\ *see* OISTRAL

oistress \ói-strəs\ cloistress, boisterous, roisterous

oisy \ói-zē\ Boise, noisy, cramoisie

¹oit \óit\ doit, droit, poet, quoit, adroit, Detroit, exploit, maladroit, Massasoit

²oit \āt\ *see* ¹ATE

³oit \ō-ət\ *see* ¹OET

⁴oit \ä\ *see* ¹A

oite \āt\ *see* ¹OT

oiter \óit-ər\ goiter, loiter, exploiter, reconnoiter

oitus \ō-ət-əs\ *see* OETESS

oivre \äv\ *see* ¹OLVE

¹oix \ä\ *see* ¹A

²oix \ói\ *see* OY

oiz \óis\ *see* ²OISE

ojan \ō-jən\ Trojan, theologian

oje \ō-jē\ *see* OJI

oji \ō-jē\ Moji, shoji, anagoge, Hachioji

¹ok \äk\ *see* ¹OCK

²ok \ək\ *see* UCK

³ok \ók\ *see* ALK

oka \ō-kə\ *see* OCA

okable \ō-kə-bəl\ *see* OCABLE

¹oke \ōk\ bloke, broke, choke, cloak, coke, Coke, croak, folk, hoke, joke, moke, oak, oke, poke, Polk, roque, smoke, soak, soke, spoke, stoke, stroke, toke, toque, woke, yogh, yoke, yolk, ad hoc, awoke,

backstroke, baroque, bespoke, breaststroke, chain-smoke, convoke, cowpoke, downstroke, evoke, heatstroke, housebroke, in-joke, invoke, keystroke, kinfolk, kinsfolk, menfolk, Nisroch, outspoke, presoak, provoke, revoke, she-oak, sidestroke, slowpoke, sunchoke, sunstroke, townsfolk, uncloak, unyoke, upstroke, workfolk, artichoke, equivoque, fisherfolk, gentlefolk, herrenvolk, masterstroke, okeydoke, Roanoke, thunderstroke, womenfolk, Mount Revelstoke

²oke \ō-kē\ *see* OKY

³oke \ō\ *see* ¹OW

⁴oke \ùk\ *see* ¹OOK

oked \ōkt\ stoked, yolked

okee \ō-kē\ *see* OKY

okel \ō-kəl\ *see* OCAL

oken \ō-kən\ broken, oaken, spoken, token, woken, awoken, bespoken, betoken, fair-spoken, foretoken, free-spoken, heartbroken, housebroken, outspoken, plainspoken, short-spoken, soft-spoken, unbroken, well-spoken, wind-broken

oker \ō-kər\ broker, choker, croaker, joker, ocher, poker, soaker, smoker, stoker, stroker, chain-smoker, invoker, pawnbroker, provoker, revoker, stockbroker, mediocre

okey \ō-kē\ *see* OKY

oki \ō-kē\ *see* OKY

oking \ō-kiŋ\ broking, choking—*also* -ing *forms of verbs listed at* ¹OKE

oko \ō-kō\ *see* OCO

okum \ō-kəm\ Bochum, hokum, locum, oakum

oky \ō-kē\ choky, croaky, folkie, hokey, Loki, pokey, poky, smoky, troche, trochee, yolky, enoki, Great Smoky, hokeypokey, karaoke, Okefenokee

¹ol \ōl\ see ¹OLE

²ol \äl\ see ¹AL

³ol \ȯl\ see ALL

ola \ō-lə\ bola, cola, Kola, Lola, tola, Zola, Angola, boffola, Canola, gondola, granola, mandola, payola, pergola, plugola, scagliola, Savonarola, viola, Viola, acerola, ayatollah, braciola, Española, gladiola, Gorgonzola, hemiola, Hispaniola, moviola, Osceola, roseola, Victrola

olable \ō-lə-bəl\ see OLLABLE

olace \äl-əs\ see OLIS

olan \ō-lən\ see OLON

oland \ō-lənd\ see OWLAND

olander \əl-ən-dər\ colander, Jullundur

¹olar \ō-lər\ see OLLER

²olar \äl-ər\ see OLLAR

olas \ō-ləs\ see OLUS

olater \äl-ət-ər\ bardolater, idolater, bibliolater, Mariolater

olatrous \äl-ə-trəs\ idolatrous, bibliolatrous, heliolatrous

olatry \äl-ə-trē\ bardolatry, idolatry, statolatry, zoolatry, bibliolatry, heliolatry, iconolatry, Mariolatry

¹old \ōld\ bold, bowled, cold, fold, gold, hold, mold, mould, old, polled, scold, sold, soled, souled, told, wold, acold, age-old, ahold, behold, billfold, blindfold, controlled,

Cotswold, cuckold, enfold, fanfold, foothold, foretold, freehold, gatefold, handhold, household, ice-cold, infold, leasehold, pinfold, potholed, roothold, scaffold, sheepfold, stone-cold, stronghold, threshold, toehold, twice-told, unfold, unmold, untold, uphold, whole-souled, withhold, centerfold, copyhold, fingerhold, manifold, manyfold, marigold, multifold, oversold, petioled, severalfold, stranglehold, throttlehold—*also* -ed *forms of verbs listed at* ¹OLE

²old \ōld\ see ALD

oldan \ōl-dən\ see OLDEN

olden \ōl-dən\ golden, holden, olden, soldan, beholden, embolden

¹older \ōl-dər\ boulder, folder, holder, molder, polder, scolder, shoulder, smolder, beholder, bondholder, cardholder, householder, jobholder, landholder, placeholder, shareholder, slaveholder, stadtholder, stakeholder, stallholder, stockholder, toolholder, officeholder, titleholder, policyholder—*also* -er *forms of adjectives listed at* ¹OLD

²older \äd-ər\ see ODDER

oldi \ōl-dē\ see ALDI

oldie \ōl-dē\ see OLDY

olding \ōl-diŋ\ folding, holding, molding, hand-holding, inholding, landholding, slaveholding—*also* -ing *forms of verbs listed at* ¹OLD

oldster \ōl-stər\ see OLSTER

oldt \ōlt\ see ¹OLT

oldy \ōl-dē\ moldy, oldie

¹ole \ōl\ bole, boll, bowl, coal, cole, Cole, dhole, dole, droll, foal, goal, hole, knoll, kohl, Kohl, mole, ole, pole, Pole, poll, prole, role, roll, scroll, Seoul, shoal, skoal, sol, sole, soul, stole, stroll, thole, tole, toll, troll, vole, whole, armhole, atoll, bankroll, beanpole, bedroll, blowhole, bolthole, borehole, bunghole, cajole, catchpole, charcoal, chuckhole, condole, console, Creole, control, creole, drumroll, enroll, ensoul, extol, eyehole, fishbowl, flagpole, foxhole, frijol, hellhole, Huichol, inscroll, insole, keyhole, kneehole, knothole, logroll, loophole, manhole, maypole, midsole, Mongol, Nicole, outsole, parole, patrol, payroll, peephole, pesthole, pinhole, pistole, pitchpole, porthole, posthole, pothole, redpoll, resole, ridgepole, Sheol, sinkhole, sotol, stokehole, tadpole, taphole, thumbhole, top-hole, touchhole, turnsole, unroll, Walpole, washbowl, wormhole, amatol, aureole, banderole, bannerol, barcarole, buttonhole, cabriole, camisole, capriole, caracole, carmagnole, casserole, croquignole, cubbyhole, decontrol, Demerol, escarole, farandole, fumarole, girandole, grand guignol, innersole, methanol, oriole, oversoul, petiole, pick-and-roll, pigeonhole, protocol, rigmarole, Seminole, cholesterol, Costa del Sol

²ole \ō-lē\ see ¹OLY

³ole \ól\ see ALL

olean \ō-lē-ən\ see ¹OLIAN

oled \ōld\ see ¹OLD

oleful \ōl-fəl\ doleful, soulful

olely \ō-lē\ see ¹OLY

¹olem \ō-ləm\ golem, solum

²olem \ā-ləm\ see ALAAM

olemn \äl-əm\ see OLUMN

¹oleon \ō-lē-ən\ see ¹OLIAN

²oleon \ōl-yən\ see ²OLIAN

¹oler \ō-lər\ see OLLER

²oler \äl-ər\ see OLLAR

olery \ōl-rē\ see OLLERY

olesome \ōl-səm\ dolesome, Folsom, wholesome

oless \ō-ləs\ see OLUS

oleum \ō-lē-əm\ see OLIUM

oleus \ō-lē-əs\ coleus, soleus

oley \ō-lē\ see ¹OLY

¹olf \álf\ golf, Rolf, Adolph, Randolph, Rudolph, Lake Rudolf

²olf \ólf\ see ULF

olfing \óf-iŋ\ see OFFING

olga \äl-gə\ Olga, Volga

oli \ō-lē\ see ¹OLY

olia \ō-lē-ə\ Mongolia, pignolia, Anatolia, melancholia, Inner Mongolia, Outer Mongolia

olian \ō-lē-ən\ aeolian, Aeolian, eolian, Mongolian, napoleon, Napoleon, simoleon, Tyrolean, Anatolian

¹olic \äl-ik\ colic, frolic, Gaelic, rollick, Aeolic, bucolic, carbolic, embolic, Mongolic, symbolic, systolic, alcoholic, anabolic, apostolic, catabolic, diabolic, hyperbolic, melancholic, metabolic, parabolic, vitriolic, workaholic

²olic \ō-lik\ colic, fumarolic, bibliopolic

olicking \ä-lik-iŋ\ frolicking, rollicking

olicy \äl-ə-sē\ policy, Wallasey

olid \äl-əd\ solid, squalid, stolid

¹olin \äl-ən\ see ⁵OLLEN

²olin \ō-lən\ see OLON

olis \äl-əs\ braless, Hollis, polis, solace, tallith, Wallace, Wallis, Cornwallis, Manizales, torticollis

olish \äl-ish\ polish, abolish, demolish, apple-polish

olitan \äl-ət-ʰn\ cosmopolitan, megapolitan, metropolitan, Neapolitan, megalopolitan

olity \äl-ət-ē\ see ¹ALITY

olium \ō-lē-əm\ scholium, linoleum, petroleum, trifolium

olivar \äl-ə-vər\ see OLIVER

¹olk \elk\ see ¹ELK

²olk \ōk\ see OKE

³olk \əlk\ see ULK

⁴olk \ȯk\ see ALK

olked \ōkt\ see OKED

olkie \ō-kē\ see OKY

olky \ō-kē\ see OKY

¹oll \ōl\ see ¹OLE

²oll \äl\ see ¹AL

³oll \ȯl\ see ALL

¹olla \äl-ə\ see ²ALA

²olla \ȯi-ə\ see OIA

ollable \ō-lə-bəl\ controllable, inconsolable, uncontrollable

ollack \äl-ək\ see OLOCH

¹ollah \ō-lə\ see OLA

²ollah \äl-ə\ see ²ALA

³ollah \əl-ə\ see ¹ULLAH

ollands \äl-ənz\ see OLLINS

ollar \äl-ər\ choler, collar, dollar, dolor, haler, holler, loller, Mahler, scholar, squalor, taler, thaler, blue-collar, brass-collar, half-

dollar, white-collar, Emmentaler, Eurodollar, petrodollar

ollard \äl-ərd\ bollard, collard, collered, hollered, Lollard, pollard

olled \ōld\ see ¹OLD

ollee \ō-lē\ see ¹OLY

ollege \äl-ij\ see OWLEDGE

¹ollen \ō-lən\ see OLON

²ollen \əl-ə\ see ¹ULLAH

³ollen \äl-ən\ see ULLEN

⁴ollen \ȯ-lən\ see ALLEN

⁵ollen \äl-ən\ Colin, pollen, Rollin, Nordrhein-Westfalen

oller \ō-lər\ bowler, choler, dolor, droller, molar, polar, poler, poller, roller, solar, stroller, troller, bankroller, cajoler, comptroller, controller, extoller, patroller, premolar, steamroller, antisolar, buttonholer, logroller, Maryknoller, pigeonholer

ollery \ōl-rē\ drollery, cajolery

ollet \äl-ət\ collet, Smollett, tallith, wallet, whatchamacallit

ollett \äl-ət\ see OLLET

olley \äl-ē\ see ¹OLLY

ollick \äl-ik\ see ¹OLIC

ollicking \ä-lik-iŋ\ see OLICKING

ollie \äl-ē\ see ¹OLLY

ollin \äl-ən\ see ⁵OLLEN

olling \ō-liŋ\ bowling, logrolling—also -ing *forms of verbs listed at* ¹OLE

ollins \äl-ənz\ collins, Hollands, Tom Collins

ollis \äl-əs\ see OLIS

ollity \äl-ət-ē\ see ¹ALITY

¹ollo \ōl-yō\ imbroglio, arroz con pollo

²ollo \ō-yō\ yo-yo, criollo

³ollo \äl-ō\ see ¹OLLOW

ollop \äl-əp\ collop, dollop, lollop, polyp, scallop, scollop, trollop, wallop, codswallop, escallop

¹ollow \äl-ō\ follow, hollo, hollow, swallow, wallow, Apollo, robalo, Leoncavallo

²ollow \äl-ə\ see ²ALA

ollower \äl-ə-wər\ follower, swallower, wallower

ollster \ōl-stər\ see OLSTER

¹olly \äl-ē\ Bali, Cali, brolly, collie, colly, dolly, folly, golly, Halle, holly, Holly, jolly, Lally, lolly, Mali, Mollie, molly, Molly, Ollie, Pali, poly, Polly, quale, Raleigh, trolley, volley, Denali, finale, Kigali, loblolly, Nepali, petrale, Somali, Svengali, tamale, melancholy, pastorale, teocalli

²olly \ò-lē\ see AWLY

olm \ōm\ see ¹OME

olman \ōl-mən\ dolman, dolmen, patrolman

olmen \ōl-mən\ see OLMAN

olmes \ōmz\ Holmes—*also* -s, -'s, *and* -s' *forms of nouns listed at* ¹OME, *and* -s *forms of verbs listed there*

olo \ō-lō\ bolo, kolo, nolo, polo, solo, Barolo, Marco Polo

oloch \äl-ək\ Moloch, pollack, rowlock

ologer \äl-ə-jər\ astrologer, chronologer, horologer, mythologer

ologist \äl-ə-jəst\ anthologist, biologist, cetologist, conchologist, cosmologist, cryptologist, cytologist, dendrologist, ecologist, enologist, ethnologist,

ethologist, fetologist, gemologist, geologist, graphologist, histologist, horologist, hydrologist, Indologist, limnologist, mixologist, morphologist, mycologist, mythologist, necrologist, nephrologist, neurologist, oncologist, ontologist, oologist, pathologist, pedologist, penologist, petrologist, philologist, phonologist, phrenologist, phycologist, psychologist, seismologist, serologist, sexologist, sinologist, technologist, topologist, typologist, ufologist, virologist, zoologist, anthropologist, archaeologist, climatologist, cosmetologist, criminologist, dermatologist, Egyptologist, embryologist, entomologist, enzymologist, escapologist, etymologist, futurologist, genealogist, gerontologist, gynecologist, hematologist, herpetologist, ichthyologist, ideologist, immunologist, kremlinologist, lexicologist, martyrologist, methodologist, mineralogist, musicologist, nematalogist, numerologist, oceanologist, ophthalmologist, ornithologist, osteologist, papyrologist, pharmacologist, phraseologist, physiologist, planetologist, primatologist, rheumatologist, roentgenologist, semiologist, sociologist, speleologist, teleologist, teratologist, thanatologist, toxicologist,

urbanologist, volcanologist,
bacteriologist, diabetologist,
dialectologist,
endocrinologist,
epistemologist, liturgiologist,
meteorologist, neonatologist,
paleontologist, parasitologist,
phenomenologist,
sedimentologist,
anesthesiologist,
epidemiologist,
gastroenterologist,
otolaryngologist

ologous \äl-ə-gəs\
heterologous, homologous,
tautologous

ology \äl-ə-jē\ anthology,
apology, astrology, biology,
bryology, cetology,
Christology, chronology,
conchology, cosmology,
cryptology, cytology,
dendrology, doxology,
ecology, enology, ethnology,
ethology, fetology, gemology,
geology, graphology,
haplology, histology,
homology, horology,
hydrology, hymnology,
Indology, limnology,
lithology, mixology,
morphology, mycology,
myology, mythology,
necrology, nephrology,
neurology, nosology,
oncology, ontology, oology,
pathology, pedology,
penology, petrology,
philology, phlebology,
phonology, phrenology,
phycology, proctology,
psychology, scatology,
seismology, serology,
sexology, sinology,
symbology, tautology,
technology, tetralogy,
theology, topology,

trichology, typology, ufology,
urology, virology, zoology,
angelology, anthropology,
archaeology, audiology,
axiology, cardiology,
climatology, codicology,
cohomology, cosmetology,
craniology, criminology,
dactylology, demonology,
deontology, dermatology,
Egyptology, embryology,
entomology, enzymology,
escapology, eschatology,
etiology, etymology,
futurology, genealogy,
gerontology, gynecology,
hematology, herpetology,
ichthyology, iconology,
ideology, immunology,
kremlinology, laryngology,
lexicology, lichenology,
Mariology, martyrology,
methodology, mineralogy,
museology, musicology,
narratology, nematology,
numerology, oceanology,
opthalmology, ornithology,
osteology, pharmacology,
phraseology, physiology,
planetology, primatology,
radiology, reflexology,
rheumatology,
roentgenology, semiology,
sociology, speleology,
sumerology, teleology,
teratology, terminology,
thanatology, toxicology,
urbanology, volcanology,
vulcanology, bacteriology,
chronobiology,
cryptozoology, dialectology,
ecclesiology, endocrinology,
epistemology, liturgiology,
metapsychology,
meteorology, microbiology,
micromorphology,
neonatology, onomatology,

paleontology,
parapsychology,
parasitology,
phenomenology,
sedimentology,
symptomatology,
anesthesiology,
epidemiology,
ethnomusicology,
gastroenterology,
otolaryngology,
paleobiology,
paleopathology,
periodontology,
otorhinolaryngology

olon \ō-lən\ bowline, Colin,
colon, Nolan, solon, stoien,
stollen, stolon, swollen,
eidolon, semicolon

olonel \ərn-ᵊl\ see ERNAL

olonist \äl-ə-nəst\ colonist,
Stalinist

¹olor \əl-ər\ color, cruller,
culler, muller, sculler,
bicolor, discolor, off-color,
three-color, tricolor,
Technicolor, watercolor

²olor \ō-lər\ see OLLER

³olor \äl-ər\ see OLLAR

olored \əl-ərd\ colored,
dullard, bicolored, rose-
colored, varicolored

olp \ōp\ see OPE

olpen \ō-pən\ see OPEN

olph \älf\ see OLF

ols \älz\ hols, Casals

olsom \ōl-səm\ see OLESOME

olster \ōl-stər\ bolster, holster,
oldster, pollster, upholster

¹olt \ōlt\ bolt, colt, dolt, holt,
jolt, molt, poult, smolt, volt,
eyebolt, Humboldt, kingbolt,
revolt, ringbolt, unbolt,
thunderbolt

²olt \ōlt\ see ALT

olta \äl-tə\ see ALTA

olter \ōl-tər\ bolter, coulter

oltish \ōl-tish\ coltish, doltish

oluble \äl-yə-bəl\ soluble,
voluble, dissoluble,
insoluble, irresoluble,
resoluble, indissoluble

olum \ō-ləm\ see OLEM

olumn \äl-əm\ column,
slalom, solemn, Malayalam

olus \ō-ləs\ bolas, bolus,
solus, snowless, toeless,
Coriolis, electroless,
gladiolus, holus-bolus

olvable \äl-və-bəl\ solvable,
dissolvable, evolvable,
insolvable, resolvable,
revolvable, irresolvable

¹olve \älv\ salve, solve,
absolve, au poivre,
convolve, devolve, dissolve,
evolve, involve, resolve,
revolve, coevolve

²olve \äv\ grave, of, salve,
Slav, suave, taw, waw,
moshav, thereof, whereof,
Zouave, Tishah-b'Ab,
unheard-of, well-thought-of

olvement \älv-mənt\
evolvement, involvement,
noninvolvement

olvent \äl-vənt\ solvent,
dissolvent

olver \äl-vər\ solver,
absolver, dissolver, involver,
revolver

¹oly \ō-lē\ goalie, holey, holy,
lowly, mole, moly, pollee,
slowly, solely, aioli, amole,
anole, cannoli, frijole,
pinole, unholy, guacamole,
ravioli, roly-poly

²oly \äl-ē\ see ¹OLLY

olyp \äl-əp\ see OLLOP

¹om \äm\ balm, bomb,
bombe, calm, from, gaum,
Guam, glom, malm, mom,
palm, Pom, pram, prom,
psalm, qualm, rhomb, ROM,

tom, A-bomb, aplomb, ashram, becalm, Ceram, cheongsam, coulomb, Coulomb, dive-bomb, embalm, EPROM, firebomb, grande dame, H-bomb, imam, Islam, Long Tom, napalm, nizam, noncom, phenom, pogrom, pom-pom, reclame, rhabdom, salaam, seram, sitcom, Songnam, tam-tam, therefrom, tom-tom, wherefrom, wigwam, cardamom, diatom, intercom, Peeping Tom, Uncle Tom, Vietnam, Dar es Salaam, Omar Khayyám

²**om** \ōm\ see ¹OME

³**om** \üm\ see ¹OOM

⁴**om** \əm\ see ¹UM

⁵**om** \üm\ see ²UM

⁶**om** \ȯm\ see ¹AUM

oma \ō-mə\ chroma, coma, Roma, soma, aroma, diploma, glaucoma, sarcoma, Tacoma, carcinoma, granuloma, melanoma, Oklahoma, glioblastoma, neurofibroma

omac \ō-mik\ see ²OMIC

¹**omace** \äm-əs\ see OMISE

²**omace** \əm-əs\ see UMMOUS

omach \əm-ək\ see UMMOCK

omache \äm-ə-kē\ see OMACHY

omachy \äm-ə-kē\ Andromache, logomachy

omal \ō-məl\ domal, stomal, prodromal, chromosomal

omaly \äm-ə-lē\ balmily, homily, anomaly

oman \ō-mən\ bowman, foeman, gnomon, nomen, omen, Roman, showman, snowman, yeoman, agnomen, cognomen, crossbowman, longbowman, praenomen,

Sertoman

omany \äm-ə-nē\ see OMINY

omas \äm-əs\ see OMISE

omathy \äm-ə-thē\ chrestomathy, stichomythy

¹**omb** \ōm\ see ¹OME

²**omb** \üm\ see ¹OOM

³**omb** \äm\ see ¹OM

⁴**omb** \əm\ see ¹UM

omba \äm-bə\ see AMBA

¹**ombe** \ōm\ see ¹OME

²**ombe** \üm\ see ¹OOM

³**ombe** \äm\ see ¹OM

ombed \ümd\ see OOMED

¹**omber** \äm-ər\ bomber, calmer, palmar, palmer, Palmer, dive-bomber, embalmer, fighter-bomber

²**omber** \äm-bər\ ombre, sambar, somber

³**omber** \ō-mər\ see ¹OMER

ombic \ō-mik\ see ²OMIC

ombical \ō-mi-kəl\ see ²OMICAL

ombie \äm-bē\ zombie, Abercrombie

ombing \ō-miŋ\ see OAMING

¹**ombo** \äm-bō\ combo, mambo, sambo

²**ombo** \əm-bō\ see UMBO

¹**ombre** \äm-brē\ hombre, ombre

²**ombre** \äm-bər\ see ²OMBER

³**ombre** \əm-brē\ see UMBERY

ombus \äm-bəs\ rhombus, thrombus

¹**ome** \ōm\ brougham, chrome, comb, combe, dome, foam, gloam, gnome, holm, home, loam, mome, nome, ohm, om, poem, pome, roam, Rom, Rome, tome, airdrome, at-home, bichrome, cockscomb, coulomb, coxcomb, defoam, down-home, Jerome, Nichrome, ogham, seadrome, shalom, sholom, Stockholm,

syndrome, aerodrome, astrodome, catacomb, chromosome, currycomb, double-dome, gastronome, halidrome, hecatomb, hippodrome, honeycomb, metronome, monochrome, motordrome, palindrome, ribosome, stay-at-home, Styrofoam

²**ome** \ō-mē\ see OAMY

³**ome** \əm\ see ¹UM

omedy \äm-əd-ē\ comedy, psalmody, tragicomedy

omely \əm-lē\ see ²UMBLY

omen \ō-mən\ see OMAN

omenal \äm-ən-ᵊl\ see OMINAL

omene \äm-ə-nē\ see OMINY

¹**omer** \ō-mər\ comber, foamer, homer, Homer, omer, roamer, vomer, beachcomber, Reaumur, Lag b'Omer, misnomer

²**omer** \əm-ər\ see UMMER

omery \əm-ə-rē\ see UMMERY

omet \äm-ət\ comet, grommet, vomit

ometer \äm-ət-ər\ barometer, chronometer, cyclometer, drunkometer, ergometer, gasometer, geometer, hydrometer, hygrometer, kilometer, manometer, micrometer, odometer, pedometer, photometer, pulsometer, pyrometer, rheometer, seismometer, spectrometer, speedometer, tachometer, thermometer, anemometer, audiometer, diffractometer, electrometer, magnetometer, alcoholometer

ometry \äm-ə-trē\

astrometry, barometry, chronometry, cytometry, geometry, isometry, micrometry, optometry, photometry, psychometry, seismometry, thermometry, craniometry, sociometry, trigonometry

omey \ō-mē\ see OAMY

omi \ō-mē\ see OAMY

omia \ō-mē-ə\ peperomia, Utsunomia

¹**omic** \äm-ik\ comic, anomic, atomic, coelomic, Islamic, tsunamic, agronomic, anatomic, antinomic, autonomic, economic, ergonomic, gastronomic, metronomic, subatomic, taxonomic, tragicomic, Deuteronomic, heroicomic, physiognomic, polyatomic, seriocomic, macroeconomic, microeconomic, socioeconomic

²**omic** \ō-mik\ gnomic, oghamic, Potomac, rhizomic, catacombic, monochromic, palindromic

¹**omical** \äm-i-kəl\ comical, domical, agronomical, anatomical, astronomical, economical, gastronomical, metronomical, tragicomical, heroicomical, physiognomical

²**omical** \ō-mi-kəl\ domical, coxcombical

omics \äm-iks\ atomics, Islamics, tectonics, bionomics, economics, ergonomics, macroeconomics, microeconomics—also -s, -'s, and -s forms of nouns listed at ¹OMIC

omily \äm-ə-lē\ see OMALY

ominal \äm-ən-ᵊl\ nominal,

abdominal, cognominal,
phenomenal, epiphenomenal

ominance \äm-nəns\
dominance, prominence,
predominance

ominant \äm-nənt\ dominant,
prominent, predominant,
semidominant, subdominant,
superdominant

ominate \äm-ə-nət\
innominate, prenominate

omine \äm-ə-nē\ see OMINY

ominence \äm-nəns\ see
OMINANCE

ominent \äm-nənt\ see
OMINANT

¹oming \əm-iŋ\ coming,
plumbing, becoming,
forthcoming, homecoming,
incoming, oncoming,
shortcoming, upcoming,
unbecoming, up-and-
coming—*also* -ing *forms of
verbs listed at* ¹UM

²oming \ō-miŋ\ see OAMING

omini \äm-ə-nē\ see OMINY

ominous \äm-ə-nəs\ ominous,
prolegomenous

ominy \äm-ə-nē\ hominy,
Romany, Melpomene, anno
Domini, eo nomine

omise \äm-əs\ pomace,
promise, shammes, shamus,
Thomas, Saint Thomas,
doubting Thomas

omit \äm-ət\ see OMET

omium \ō-mē-əm\ chromium,
holmium, encomium,
prostomium

¹omma \äm-ə\ see ²AMA

²omma \əm-ə\ see UMMA

¹ommel \äm-əl\ pommel,
Jamil, Rommel, trommel

²ommel \əm-əl\ pommel,
pummel, Beau Brummell

ommet \äm-ət\ see OMET

ommie \äm-ē\ see ¹AMI

ommon \äm-ən\ Amon,
Brahman, common, shaman,
yamen, Roscommon,
Tutankhamen

ommoner \äm-ə-nər\ almoner,
commoner, gewürztraminer

¹ommy \äm-ē\ see ¹AMI

²ommy \əm-ē\ see UMMY

omo \ō-mō\ bromo, Como,
homo, Pomo, promo, Oromo,
majordomo

omon \ō-mən\ see OMAN

¹omp \ämp\ champ, chomp,
clomp, comp, pomp, romp,
stamp, stomp, swamp, tramp,
tromp, whomp

²omp \əmp\ see UMP

ompany \əmp-nē\ company,
accompany, intracompany

ompass \əm-pəs\ compass,
rumpus, encompass,
gyrocompass

omper \äm-pər\ romper,
stamper, stomper, swamper,
wafflestomper

ompers \äm-pərz\ Gompers—
also -s, -'s, *and* -s' *forms of
nouns listed at* OMPER

ompey \äm-pē\ see OMPY

omplement \äm-plə-mənt\
complement, compliment

ompliment \äm-plə-mənt\ see
OMPLEMENT

ompo \äm-pō\ campo, compo

ompous \äm-pəs\ see ¹OMPASS

ompson \äm-sən\ see AMSUN

ompt \aúnt\ see ²OUNT

ompy \äm-pē\ Pompey,
swampy

omythy \äm-ə-thē\ see
OMATHY

¹on \än\ ban, Bonn, chon,
con, conn, dawn, don, Don,
Donn, drawn, Fan, faun,
fawn, gone, guan, Han, John,
Jon, khan, maun, mon, on,
pan, pawn, phon, prawn,

Ron, Shan, spawn, swan,
Vaughn, wan, yawn, yon,
yuan, aeon, add-on, agon,
agone, Akan, alençon,
Amman, ancon, anon,
Anshan, Anton, archon,
argon, Argonne, Aswan,
atman, Avon, axon,
barchan, baton, blouson,
bon ton, bonbon, boron,
boson, bouillon, Brython,
bygone, caisson, Calgon,
canton, capon, Ceylon,
chaconne, chiffon, chignon,
Chiron, chiton, chrismon,
cistron, clip-on, codon,
come-on, cordon, coupon,
crampon, crayon, crepon,
cretonne, crouton, Dacron,
dead-on, Dear John, dewan,
doggone, doggoned, Dogon,
Don Juan, eon, exon, far-
gone, flacon, foregone,
Freon, fronton, Fujian,
Garonne, Gibran, gluon,
gnomon, Golan, Gosplan,
guidon, hadron, Hainan,
hazan, Henan, hogan,
Huainan, Hunan, icon,
Inchon, intron, Ivan, Jinan,
Kanban, kaon, Kashan,
Kazan, Kerman, Khoisan,
Kirman, koan, krypton,
kurgan, Kurgan, lauan,
Leon, lepton, liman, log on,
Luzon, macron, Massan,
Medan, Memnon, meson,
micron, Milan, mod con,
moron, mouton, Multan,
muon, natron, neon,
nephron, neuron, neutron,
ninon, nylon, odds-on,
Oman, Oran, Orlon,
outgone, pacon, parton,
Pathan, pavane, pecan,
peon, Phaethon, photon,
phyton, pion, pinon, piton,

plankton, pluton, pompon,
prion, proton, Pusan, put-
on, pylon, python, Qur'an,
radon, rayon, recon, rhyton,
run-on, Saint John, Saipan,
salon, San Juan, Schumann,
Shaban, shaman, shaitan,
Shingon, Simplon, Sjoelland,
slip-on, snap-on, solon,
soupçon, soutane, Stefan,
stolon, Suwon, Szechuan,
Szechwan, Tainan, Taiwan,
taipan, tampon, taxon,
Teflon, teston, Tétouan,
Tetuán, thereon, tisane,
torchon, toucan, toyon,
trigon, Tristan, triton,
trogon, Tucson, Typhon,
tzigane, uhlan, Ulsan, upon,
walk-on, witan, whereon,
Wonsan, wonton, Wuhan,
xenon, Xi'an, yaupon,
Yukon, Yunnan, Yvonne,
zircon, Abadan, Abijan,
Acheron, Ahriman, aileron,
amazon, Amazon, amnion,
Aragon, autobahn,
Avalon, Babylon,
Bakhtaran, Balaton,
balmacaan, Bantustan,
Barbizon, baryon, Basilan,
betatron, biathlon, abochon,
calutron, carillon, carryon,
celadon, chorion, colophon,
Culiacán, cyclotron,
decagon, decathlon,
demijohn, deuteron,
dipteron, echelon, electron,
elevon, epsilon, etymon,
fermion, follow-on, Fujisan,
Genghis Khan, goings-on,
gonfalon, Grand Teton,
graviton, harijan, helicon,
heptagon, hexagon,
hopping John,
Huascarán, Ilion, Irian,
Isfahan, Kazakhstan, Kublai

Khan, Kyrgyzstan, Lake
Huron, Lebanon, leprechaun,
lexicon, liaison, Lipizzan,
logion, macédoine, marathon,
Marathon, marzipan,
mastodon, Mazatlán,
Mbabane, Mellotron,
Miquelon, morion,
myrmidon, negatron,
nonagon, noumenon,
nucleon, Oberon, octagon,
omicron, Oregon, organon,
ostracon, Pakistan, Palawan,
pantheon, paragon,
Parmesan, parmigiana,
Parthenon, pentagon,
Percheron, Phaethon,
Phlegethon, polygon,
positron, Procyon, put-upon,
Rajasthan, Ramadan,
Rubicon, silicon, Suleiman,
tachyon, Taiyuan, talkathon,
Teheran, telamon, telethon,
thereupon, Tian Shan,
Tucumán, undergone,
upsilon, virion, walkathon,
whereupon, woebegone,
Yerevan, Zahedan, abutilon,
Agamemnon, archenteron,
arrière-ban, asyndeton,
automaton, Azerbaijan,
Bellerophon, bildungsroman,
carrying-on, Diazenon,
dimetrodon, dodecagon,
encephalon, ephemeron,
himation, interferon,
kakiemon, Laocoön,
mesenteron, Michoacán,
millimicron, oxymoron,
phenomenon, protozoon,
Saskatchewan, septentrion,
sine qua non, t'ai chi ch'uan,
Taklimakan, Vientiane, West
Irian, Xiangtan, anacoluthon,
diencephalon, ferrosilicon,
mesencephalon,
metencephalon,

prolegomenon, prothalamion,
prosencephalon, pteranodon,
spermatozoon, telencephalon,
ultramarathon,
epiphenomenon,
myelencephalon, kyrie
eleison, San Miguel de
Tucumán

²**on** \ōⁿ\ fond, ton, ballon,
baton, bouillon, Dijon,
flacon, fourgon, frisson,
Gabon, garçon, lorgnon,
Lyons, maçon, marron,
Marron, mouflon, soupçon,
Toulon, Villon, Aubusson,
bourguignon, feuilleton,
Ganelon, gueridon, limaçon,
papillon, filet mignon, Saint
Emilion

³**on** \on\ awn, Bonn, bonne,
brawn, dawn, Dawn, drawn,
faun, fawn, gone, lawn, maun,
on, pawn, prawn, Sean, spawn,
Vaughn, won, yawn, add-on,
agon, agone, begone, bygone,
chaconne, clip-on, come-on,
dead-on, doggone, far-gone,
foregone, hands-on, hard-on,
head-on, hereon, impawn,
indrawn, Kherson, odds-on,
outgone, Puchon, put-on,
Quezon, run-on, slip-on, snap-
on, Taejon, thereon, turned-
on, upon, walk-on, whereon,
wiredrawn, withdrawn,
bourguignonne, carryon,
follow-on, goings-on, hanger-
on, hereupon, looker-on, put-
upon, thereupon, undergone,
whereupon, woebegone,
carrying-on

⁴**on** \ōn\ see ¹ONE

⁵**on** \ən\ see UN

¹**ona** \ō-nə\ dona, Dona,
Jonah, krone, Mona, Nona,
Rhona, Rona, Shona, trona,
Ancona, Bellona, bologna,

Bologna, cinchona, corona, kimono, Leona, madrona, Pamplona, persona, Ramona, Verona, Arizona, Barcelona, Desdemona, in propria persona

²ona \än-ə\ see ¹ANA

oña \ōn-yə\ see ³ONIA

onachal \än-i-kəl\ see ONICAL

onae \ō-nē\ see ¹ONY

onah \ō-nə\ see ONA

¹onal \ōn-ᵊl\ clonal, tonal, zonal, atonal, coronal, hormonal, baritonal, microtonal, polyclonal, polytonal, semitonal

²onal \än-ᵊl\ Donal, Ronal

onald \än-ᵊld\ Donald, Ronald, MacDonald

onant \ō-nənt\ see ONENT

onas \ō-nəs\ see ²ONUS

onative \ō-nət-iv\ conative, donative

onc \äŋk\ see ¹ONK

¹once \äns\ see ²ANCE

²once \əns\ see UNCE

¹onch \äŋk\ see ¹ONK

²onch \änch\ see ¹AUNCH

oncha \äŋ-kə\ see ANKA

oncho \än-chō\ honcho, poncho, rancho

onchus \äŋ-kəs\ bronchus, rhonchus

onco \äŋ-kō\ bronco, Franco

¹ond \änd\ blond, bond, fond, frond, Gond, pond, rand, sonde, wand, yond, abscond, Armand, beau monde, beyond, despond, fishpond, Gironde, gourmand, haut monde, millpond, neoned, pairbond, respond, allemande, towmond, correspond, demimonde, Eurobond, Trebizond, Trobriand,

vagabond, radiosonde, slough of despond—*also* -ed *forms of verbs listed at* ¹ON

²ond \ō̃\ see ²ON

³ond \ónt\ see ¹AUNT

onda \än-də\ Lahnda, Rhonda, Rhondda, Ronda, Wanda, Golconda, Luganda, Ruanda, Rwanda, Uganda, anaconda, Campo Grande

ondam \än-dəm\ see ¹ONDOM

ondant \än-dənt\ see ONDENT

onday \ən-dē\ see UNDI

ondays \ən-dēz\ see UNDAYS

ondda \än-də\ see ONDA

onde \änd\ see ¹OND

ondeau \än-dō\ see ONDO

ondel \än-dᵊl\ condyle, fondle, rondel

ondence \än-dəns\ correspondence, despondence

ondency \än-dən-sē\ despondency, correspondency

ondent \än-dənt\ fondant, despondent, respondent, corespondent, correspondent

¹onder \än-dər\ bonder, condor, maunder, ponder, squander, wander, yonder, zander, absconder, responder, transponder—*also* -er *forms of adjectives listed at* ¹OND

²onder \ən-dər\ see UNDER

ondly \än-lē\ see ¹ANLY

ondness \än-nəs\ see ANNESS

ondo \än-dō\ condo, Hondo, rondeau, rondo, secondo, tondo, forzando, glissando, lentando, parlando, scherzando, sforzando, allargando, rallentando, ritardando, accelerando

¹ondom \än-dəm\ condom, quondam

²ondom \ən-dəm\ see UNDUM

ondor \än-dər\ see ¹ONDER

ondrous \ən-drəs\ see UNDEROUS

ondyle \än-dᵊl\ see ONDEL

¹one \ōn\ blown, bone, clone, cone, crone, drone, flown, groan, grown, hone, Joan, known, loan, lone, moan, Mon, mown, none, own, phone, pone, prone, Rhône, roan, Saône, scone, sewn, shone, shoon, shown, sone, sown, stone, throne, thrown, tone, trone, won, zone, agon, aitchbone, alone, atone, backbone, bemoan, birthstone, Blackstone, breastbone, brimstone, brownstone, capstone, cheekbone, chinbone, cogon, cologne, Cologne, colon, Colón, condone, curbstone, cyclone, daimon, debone, depone, dethrone, disown, drystone, earphone, enthrone, fieldstone, flagstone, flyblown, freestone, full-blown, gallstone, gemstone, Gijón, Gladstone, gravestone, grindstone, hailstone, halftone, handblown, headphone, headstone, high-flown, hipbone, homegrown, hormone, impone, ingrown, inkstone, intone, jawbone, keystone, León, leone, limestone, lodestone, Mount Mayon, milestone, millstone, misknown, moonstone, oilstone, outgrown, outshown, ozone, peon, pinbone, pinecone, pinon, pinyon, postpone, propone,

Ramon, rezone, rhinestone, sandstone, shade-grown, shinbone, Shoshone, soapstone, T-bone, tailbone, thighbone, tombstone, touchstone, Touch-Tone, tritone, trombone, turnstone, twelve-tone, two-tone, Tyrone, unknown, unthrone, well-known, whalebone, wheel-thrown, whetstone, windblown, wishbone, Yangon, allophone, anglophone, anklebone, barbitone, Barbizon, barytone, Bayamon, bombardon, Canal Zone, chaperon, cherrystone, cobblestone, collarbone, cornerstone, cortisone, cuttlebone, diaphone, Dictaphone, epigone, francophone, free-fire zone, Gaborone, gramophone, herringbone, homophone, ironstone, knucklebone, marrowbone, megaphone, mellophone, methadone, microphone, microtone, minestrone, monotone, overblown, overflown, overgrown, overthrown, overtone, Picturephone, polyphone, rottenstone, sacaton, saxophone, semitone, shacklebone, silicone, sousaphone, speakerphone, stepping-stone, telephone, Toreón, undertone, vibraphone, xylophone, Yellowstone, anticyclone, Asunción, bred-in-the-bone, Concepción, eau de cologne, mesocyclone, norethindrone, Nuevo León, radiophone, sine qua non, testosterone, videophone,

Darby and Joan, Ponce de
León, Sierra Leone,
radiotelephone

²one \ō-nē\ see ¹ONY

³one \än\ see ¹ON

⁴one \ən\ see UN

⁵one \ŏn\ see ³ON

onean \ō-nē-ən\ see ¹ONIAN

¹oned \ōnd\ boned, stoned,
toned, cologned, high-toned,
pre-owned, rawboned,
rhinestoned, two-toned,
cobblestoned—also -ed
forms of verbs listed at ¹ONE

²oned \än\ see ¹ON

oneless \ŏn-ləs\ boneless,
toneless

onely \ōn-lē\ lonely, only,
pronely

onement \ŏn-mənt\
atonement, cantonment,
dethronement, disownment,
enthronement

oneness \ən-nəs\ dunness,
doneness, oneness,
rotundness

onent \ō-nənt\ sonant,
component, deponent,
exponent, opponent,
proponent, bicomponent

oneous \ō-nē-əs\ see
ONIOUS

¹oner \ō-nər\ boner, donor,
droner, groaner, honer,
loaner, loner, moaner,
stoner, toner, zoner,
condoner, dethroner,
intoner, landowner,
shipowner, telephoner

²oner \ŏn-ər\ see ¹AWNER

onerous \än-ə-rəs\ onerous,
sonorous

ones \ōnz\ Jones, nones,
sawbones, Davy Jones,
lazybones, skull and
crossbones—also -s, -'s, and
-s' forms of nouns listed at

¹ONE, and -s forms of verbs
listed there

onest \än-əst\ honest,
dishonest, Hinayanist,
Mahayanist

¹oney \ō-nē\ see ¹ONY

²oney \ən-ē\ see UNNY

³oney \ü-nē\ see OONY

¹ong \äŋ\ Chang, Fang, gong,
hong, Huang, prong, Shang,
Tang, tong, yang, Anyang,
barong, biltong, Da Nang,
dugong, Guiyang, Hanyang,
Heng-yang, Hong Kong,
kiang, liang, Mah-Jongg,
Malang, Padang, satang,
Wuchang, Zhejiang,
Zhenjiang, billabong,
Chittagong, Liaoyang,
Pyong-yang, Semarang,
scuppernong, Shenyang,
Sturm und Drang, Vietcong,
Shijiazhuang, Ujung
Pandang, Wollongong,
ylang-ylang, Heilongjiang

²ong \ŏŋ\ bong, dong, gong,
long, prong, song, strong,
thong, throng, tong, wrong,
agelong, along, Armstrong,
barong, belong, biltong,
birdsong, chaise longue,
daylong, dingdong,
diphthong, dugong, endlong,
erelong, furlong, Geelong,
Haiphong, headlong,
headstrong, Kaesong,
kampong, lifelong, livelong,
Mekong, monthlong,
Nanchang, nightlong,
oblong, oolong, part-song,
ping-pong, Ping-Pong,
plainsong, prolong, sarong,
Shandong, sidelong,
singsong, so long, souchong,
weeklong, yard-long,
yearlong, billabong,
Chittagong, cradlesong,

evensong, Palembang,
scuppernong, sing-along,
summerlong, tagalong,
Vietcong

³**ong** \əŋ\ see ¹UNG

⁴**ong** \ùng\ see ²UNG

onga \äŋ-gə\ conga, panga,
tonga, Tonga, Kananga,
mridanga, Alba Longa,
Zamboanga, Bucaramanga

onge \ənj\ see UNGE

onged \ónd\ pronged,
thonged, multipronged—*also*
-ed *forms of verbs listed at*
²ONG

¹**onger** \əŋ-gər\ hunger,
monger, younger,
fellmonger, fishmonger,
ironmonger, newsmonger,
phrasemonger, scaremonger,
warmonger, whoremonger,
wordmonger, costermonger,
fashionmonger,
gossipmonger,
rumormonger,
scandalmonger

²**onger** \ən-jər\ see ¹UNGER

ongery \əŋ-grē\ hungry,
fellmongery, ironmongery

ongful \óŋ-fəl\ wrongful,
songful

ongin \ən-jən\ see UNGEON

ongish \óŋ-ish\ longish,
strongish

ongo \äŋ-gō\ bongo, Congo,
congou, Kongo, mongo,
Niger-Congo, Pago Pago

ongous \əŋ-gəs\ see UNGOUS

¹**ongue** \əŋ\ see ¹UNG

²**ongue** \óŋ\ see ²ONG

ongued \əŋd\ lunged, tongued

ongy \ən-jē\ see UNGY

onhomous \än-ə-məs\ see
ONYMOUS

oni \ō-nē\ see ¹ONY

¹**onia** \ō-nē-ə\ bignonia,
clintonia, Estonia, Laconia,

Livonia, mahonia,
paulownia, Polonia,
Slavonia, Snowdonia,
tithonia, valonia, zirconia,
Amazonia, Caledonia,
Catalonia, Macedonia

²**onia** \ō-nyə\ Konya, Sonia,
Sonja, Sonya, ammonia,
Bologna, pneumonia,
Polonia, tithonia, valonia,
anhedonia, Caledonia,
Macedonia, New Caledonia,
Patagonia

³**onia** \ōn-yə\ doña, begonia

onial \ō-nē-əl\ baronial,
colonial, ceremonial,
matrimonial, testimonial

¹**onian** \ō-nē-ən\ chthonian,
aeonian, Antonian,
Baconian, Clactonian,
demonian, Devonian,
draconian, Estonian,
Etonian, favonian,
gorgonian, Ionian,
Jacksonian, Oxonian,
plutonian, Samsonian,
Shoshonean, Slavonian,
Amazonian, Apollonian,
Arizonian, Babylonian,
calypsonian, Chalcedonian,
Hamiltonian, parkinsonian

²**onian** \ō-nyən\ Zonian,
Amazonian, Babylonian,
Estonian, Macedonian

onic \än-ik\ chronic,
chthonic, conic, dornick,
phonic, sonic, tonic,
Aaronic, agonic, atonic,
benthonic, bionic, Brittonic,
Brythonic, bubonic, Byronic,
canonic, carbonic, cryonic,
cyclonic, daimonic, demonic,
draconic, euphonic,
gnomonic, harmonic,
hedonic, iconic, Ionic, ironic,
laconic, Masonic, mnemonic,
planktonic, platonic,

plutonic, pneumonic,
Puranic, Pythonic, sardonic,
Saronic, sermonic, Slavonic,
symphonic, synchronic,
tectonic, Teutonic,
ultrasonic, zirconic,
catatonic, diachronic,
diatonic, disharmonic,
electronic, embryonic,
hegemonic, histrionic,
homophonic, hydroponic,
inharmonic, isotonic,
macaronic, megaphonic,
microphonic, monophonic,
monotonic, nonionic,
pharaonic, Philharmonic,
polyphonic, quadraphonic,
semitonic, Solomonic,
supersonic, supertonic,
telephonic, thermionic,
architectonic, chameleonic,
cardiotonic, electrotonic,
geotectonic, Neoplatonic,
stereophonic,
extraembryonic

onica \än-i-kə\ Monica,
harmonica, japonica,
Salonika, veronica, Veronica,
Thessalonica

onical \än-i-kəl\ chronicle,
conical, monachal, monocle,
canonical, demonical,
ironical, deuterocanonical

onicals \än-i-kəlz\ Chronicles,
canonicals

onicker \ä-ni-kər\ see
ONNICKER

onicle \än-i-kəl\ see ONICAL

onicles \än-i-kəlz\ see
ONICALS

onics \än-iks\ onyx, phonics,
bionics, cryonics,
mnemonics, Ovonics,
photonics, sardonyx,
tectonics, avionics,
electronics, histrionics,
hydroponics, microphonics,

nucleonics, quadriphonics,
radionics, supersonics,
thermionics,
architectonics—*also* -s, -'s,
and -s' *forms of nouns listed
at* ONIC

onika \än-i-kə\ see ONICA

oniker \ä-ni-kər\ see
ONNICKER

¹**oning** \än-iŋ\ awning,
couponing—*also* -ing *forms
of verbs listed at* ¹on

²**oning** \ō-niŋ\ loaning,
jawboning,
landowning—*also* -ing *forms
of verbs listed at* ¹one

onion \ən-yən\ see UNION

onious \ō-nē-əs\ erroneous,
euphonious, felonious,
harmonious, Polonius,
Suetonius, symphonious,
acrimonious, ceremonious,
disharmonious,
inharmonious, parsimonious,
sanctimonious, Marcus
Antonius, unceremonious

¹**onis** \ō-nəs\ see ²ONUS

²**onis** \än-əs\ see ¹ONUS

onish \än-ish\ donnish,
monish, admonish, astonish,
premonish, leprechaunish

onishment \än-ish-mənt\
admonishment, astonishment

onium \ō-nē-əm\ euphonium,
harmonium, plutonium,
pandemonium,
Pandemonium

onius \ō-nē-əs\ see ONIOUS

onja \ō-nyə\ see ²ONIA

onjon \ən-jən\ see UNGEON

onjure \än-jər\ conjure,
rondure

¹**onk** \äŋk\ ankh, bronc,
clonk, conch, conk, Franck,
honk, Planck, plonk, zonk,
honkytonk

²**onk** \əŋk\ see UNK

onker \äŋ-kər\ conker, conquer, honker

¹onkey \äŋ-kē\ see ONKY

²onkey \əŋ-kē\ see UNKY

onkian \äŋ-kē-ən\ conquian, Algonkian

onky \äŋ-kē\ conkey, donkey, wonky, yanqui

onless \ən-ləs\ see UNLESS

only \ōn-lē\ see ONELY

onment \ōn-mənt\ see ONEMENT

¹onn \än\ see ¹ON

²onn \ȯn\ see ³ON

¹onna \ȯn-ə\ donna, Donna, fauna, prima donna, megafauna

²onna \än-ə\ see ¹ANA

onnage \ən-ij\ see UNNAGE

¹onne \än\ see ¹ON

²onne \ən\ see UN

³onne \ȯn\ see ³ON

onner \än-ər\ see ¹ONOR

onnet \än-ət\ bonnet, sonnet, bluebonnet, sunbonnet, warbonnet

onnicker \ä-ni-kər\ donnicker, doniker, monicker, moniker

onnie \än-ē\ see ¹ANI

onnish \än-ish\ see ONISH

onnor \än-ər\ see ¹ONOR

¹onny \än-ē\ see ¹ANI

²onny \ən-ē\ see UNNY

¹ono \ō-nō\ phono, cui bono, kimono, pro bono, kakemono, makimono

²ono \ō-nə\ see ONA

³ono \än-ō\ see ¹ANO

onocle \än-i-kəl\ see ONICAL

onomer \än-ə-mər\ monomer, astronomer, comonomer

onomist \än-ə-məst\ agronomist, autonomist, economist, ergonomist, gastronomist, synonymist, taxonomist, Deuteronomist

onomous \än-ə-məs\ see ONYMOUS

onomy \än-ə-mē\ agronomy, antonymy, astronomy, autonomy, economy, eponymy, gastronomy, homonomy, metonymy, synonymy, taphonomy, taxonomy, toponymy, Deuteronomy, diseconomy, heteronomy, teleonomy

¹onor \än-ər\ Bonner, fawner, goner, honor, pawner, pawnor, spawner, wanner, yawner, dishonor, O'Connor, Lipizzaner, marathoner, Afrikaner, weimaraner

²onor \ō-nər\ see ¹ONER

onorous \än-ə-rəs\ see ONEROUS

onquer \äŋ-kər\ see ONKER

onquian \äŋ-kē-ən\ see ONKIAN

¹ons \änz\ see ONZE

²ons \ōⁿ\ see ²ON

onsil \än-səl\ see ONSUL

onsin \än-sən\ see OHNSON

onson \än-sən\ see OHNSON

onsor \än-sər\ panzer, sponsor

onsul \än-səl\ consul, tonsil

on't \ōnt\ don't, won't

¹ont \ənt\ blunt, brunt, bunt, front, grunt, hunt, lunt, punt, runt, shunt, strunt, stunt, want, wont, affront, beachfront, bowfront, breakfront, confront, forefront, housefront, lakefront, manhunt, outfront, seafront, shirtfront, shorefront, storefront, swellfront, up-front, witch-hunt, battlefront, oceanfront, riverfront, waterfront

²ont \änt\ see ²ANT

³ont \ȯnt\ see ¹AUNT

¹ontal \änt-ᵊl\ pontil, fontal, quantal, horizontal, periodontal

²ontal \ᵊnt-ᵊl\ see UNTLE

ontan \änt-ⁿ\ see ONTON

ontas \änt-əs\ see ONTUS

¹onte \änt-ē\ see ANTI

²onte \än-tā\ see ¹ANTE

onted \ónt-əd\ vaunted, wonted, undaunted—*also* -ed *forms of verbs listed at* ¹AUNT

onter \ənt-ər\ see UNTER

onth \ᵊnth\ month, billionth, millionth, trillionth, twelvemonth

ontian \änt-ē-ən\ Zontian, post-Kantian

ontic \änt-ik\ ontic, deontic, Vedantic, orthodontic, anacreontic

ontil \änt-ᵊl\ see ¹ONTAL

ontinent \änt-ᵊn-ənt\ continent, incontinent, subcontinent, supercontinent

ontis \än-təs\ see ²ANTOS

ontist \änt-əst\ Vedantist, orthodontist, prosthodontist

onto \än-tō\ see ¹ANTO

onton \änt-ᵊn\ ponton, wanton, Lahontan

ontra \än-trə\ contra, mantra, tantra, per contra

ontre \änt-ər\ see ¹AUNTER

ontus \änt-əs\ Pontus, Pocahontas

onty \änt-ē\ see ANTI

¹onus \än-əs\ Cronus, Faunus, Adonis

²onus \ō-nəs\ bonus, Cronus, Jonas, onus, slowness, Adonis, colonus

¹ony \ō-nē\ bony, coney, crony, phony, pony, stony, Toni, tony, Tony, yoni, baloney, Benoni, bologna, canzone, Marconi, Moroni, Oenone, padrone, spumoni, tortoni, abalone, acrimony, agrimony, alimony, antimony, cannelloni, ceremony, chalcedony, colophony, macaroni, mascarpone, matrimony, minestrone, palimony, parsimony, patrimony, pepperoni, provolone, rigatoni, sanctimony, telephony, testimony, zabaglione, con espressione, conversazione, dramatis personae

²ony \än-ē\ see ¹ANI

onya \ō-nyə\ see ²ONIA

onymist \än-ə-məst\ see ONOMIST

onymous \än-ə-məs\ bonhomous, anonymous, antonymous, autonomous, eponymous, homonymous, pseudonymous, synonymous, heteronomous

onymy \än-ə-mē\ see ONOMY

¹onyon \än-yən\ ronyon, wanion

²onyon \ən-yən\ see UNION

onyx \än-iks\ see ONICS

onze \änz\ bonze, bronze, pons, long johns, Saint John's, Afrikaans, solitons, islet of Langerhans—*also* -s, -'s, *and* -s *forms of nouns listed at* ¹ON, *and* -s *forms of verbs listed there*

onzi \än-zē\ see ONZY

onzy \än-zē\ bronzy, Ponzi

¹oo \ü\ see ¹EW

²oo \ō\ see ¹OW

oob \üb\ see UBE

oober \ü-bər\ see UBER

ooby \ü-bē\ booby, looby, ruby, Ruby

¹ooch \üch\ brooch, hooch,

mooch, pooch, smooch, capuche, scaramouch

²**ooch** \ōch\ see OACH

oocher \ü-chər\ see UTURE

oochy \ü-chē\ smoochy, Baluchi, penuche, Vespucci, Kawaguchi

¹**ood** \ud\ good, hood, pud, rudd, should, stood, wood, would, yod, basswood, bentwood, blackwood, boxwood, brushwood, childhood, cordwood, deadwood, do-good, dogwood, driftwood, Ellwood, Elwood, falsehood, fatwood, feel-good, firewood, fruitwood, girlhood, godhood, greasewood, greenwood, groundwood, gumwood, hardwood, ironwood, kingwood, knighthood, maidhood, manhood, monkhood, monkshood, Mount Hood, no-good, pinewood, plywood, priesthood, pulpwood, redwood, rosewood, sainthood, selfhood, Sherwood, softwood, sonhood, statehood, stinkwood, Talmud, teakwood, unhood, Wedgwood, wifehood, withstood, wormwood, arrowwood, bachelorhood, brotherhood, buttonwood, candlewood, cedarwood, cottonwood, fatherhood, hardihood, Hollywood, likelihood, livelihood, maidenhood, motherhood, nationhood, neighborhood, parenthood, personhood, Robin Hood, sandalwood, scattergood, servanthood, sisterhood, spinsterhood,

toddlerhood, tulipwood, understood, widowhood, womanhood, misunderstood, unlikelihood, widowerhood

²**ood** \ōd\ see ODE

³**ood** \ud\ see UDE

⁴**ood** \ud\ see ¹UD

¹**ooded** \əd-əd\ blooded, cold-blooded, full-blooded, half-blooded, hot-blooded, pure-blooded, red-blooded, star-studded, warm-blooded—*also* -ed *forms of verbs listed at* ¹UD

²**ooded** \ud-əd\ hooded, wooded, hard-wooded, soft-wooded

¹**ooder** \ud-ər\ see UDER

²**ooder** \əd-ər\ see UDDER

ooding \ud-iŋ\ pudding, do-gooding, unhooding

oodle \ud-ᵊl\ boodle, doodle, feudal, noodle, poodle, strudel, caboodle, flapdoodle, paludal, Yankee-Doodle

oodman \ud-mən\ goodman, woodman

oodoo \ud-ü\ doo-doo, hoodoo, kudu, voodoo

oods \udz\ backwoods, dry goods, piney woods—*also* -s, -'s, *and* -s' *forms of nouns listed at* ¹OOD, *and* -s *forms of verbs listed there*

oodsman \udz-mən\ woodsman, backwoodsman, ombudsman

¹**oody** \ud-ē\ broody, Judi, Judie, Judy, moody, Rudy, Trudy

²**oody** \ud-ē\ cuddy, goody, hoody, woody, goody-goody

³**oody** \əd-ē\ see ¹UDDY

ooer \ü-ər\ see ¹EWER

ooey \ü-ē\ see EWY

¹**oof** \üf\ goof, kloof, poof, pouf, proof, roof, spoof,

woof, aloof, behoof, disproof, fireproof, foolproof, forehoof, rustproof, shadoof, soundproof, sunroof, Tartuffe, unroof, bulletproof, opera bouffe, shatterproof, waterproof, weatherproof

²**oof** \úf\ hoof, poof, roof, woof, forehoof, Tartuffe

³**oof** \ôf\ see OAF

⁴**oof** \üv\ see ³OVE

oofah \ü-fə\ see UFA

¹**oofer** \ü-fər\ proofer, roofer, twofer, waterproofer

²**oofer** \úf-ər\ hoofer, woofer

oofy \ü-fē\ goofy, spoofy, Sufi

ooga \ü-gə\ see UGA

ooge \üj\ see ¹UGE

ooger \úg-ər\ see UGUR

oogie \úg-ē\ bogey, boogie, boogie-woogie

oo-goo \ü-gü\ see UGU

ooh \ü\ see ¹EW

ooh-pooh \ü-pü\ hoopoe, pooh-pooh

ooi \ü-ē\ see EWY

ooist \ü-əst\ doest, tattooist, voodooist—*also -est forms of adjectives listed at* ¹EW

¹**ook** \úk\ book, brook, Brooke, chook, cook, Cook, crook, gook, hook, look, nook, rook, schnook, shook, snook, stook, took, bankbook, betook, billhook, caoutchouc, chapbook, checkbook, Chinook, cookbook, forsook, fishhook, guidebook, handbook, hornbook, hymnbook, Innsbruck, Kobuk, logbook, matchbook, mistook, Mount Cook, notebook, outlook,

partook, passbook, Pembroke, playbook, pothook, promptbook, psalmbook, retook, schoolbook, scrapbook, sketchbook, skyhook, songbook, studbook, textbook, unhook, Windhoek, workbook, yearbook, buttonhook, copybook, donnybrook, gerenuk, inglenook, Leeuwenhoek, overbook, overlook, overtook, pocketbook, storybook, tenterhook, undertook, Volapuk, gobbledygook

²**ook** \ük\ see UKE

ooka \ü-kə\ yuca, bazooka, felucca, palooka, Toluca, verruca, Juan de Fuca

ookah \úk-ə\ hookah, sukkah

ooke \úk\ see ¹OOK

ooker \úk-ər\ booker, cooker, hooker, Hooker, looker, snooker, good-looker, onlooker

ookery \úk-ə-rē\ crookery, rookery

ookie \úk-ē\ bookie, brookie, cookie, cooky, hooky, rookie, rooky, Takatsuki, walkie-lookie

ooking \úk-iŋ\ booking, cooking, good-looking, onlooking—*also -ing forms of verbs listed at* ¹OOK

ooklet \úk-lət\ booklet, brooklet, hooklet

¹**ooks** \úks\ deluxe, gadzooks—*also -s, -'s, and - s' forms of nouns listed at* UKE, *and -s forms of verbs listed there*

²**ooks** \úks\ Brooks, crux, luxe, zooks, deluxe,

gadzooks—*also* -s, -'s, *and*
-s' *forms of nouns listed at*
¹OOK, *and* -s *forms of verbs
listed there*

¹**ooky** \ü-kē\ kooky, spooky,
bouzouki, Kabuki, saluki,
tanuki

²**ooky** \ùk-ē\ see OOKIE

¹**ool** \ül\ boule, boulle, buhl,
cool, drool, fool, fuel, ghoul,
gul, joule, mewl, mule, pool,
Poole, pul, pule, rule, school,
spool, stool, tool, tulle,
you'll, yule, air-cool,
ampoule, babul, Banjul,
befool, Blackpool, carpool,
cesspool, curule, Elul,
faldstool, footstool, hangul,
Kabul, Kurnool, misrule,
Mosul, preschool, retool,
self-rule, synfuel, toadstool,
tomfool, uncool, vanpool,
whirlpool, Barnaul,
fascicule, gallinule,
graticule, groupuscule,
Hartlepool, Istanbul,
lenticule, Liverpool,
majuscule, minuscule,
molecule, monticule,
overrule, reticule, ridicule,
vestibule, water-cool,
biomolecule

²**ool** \ùl\ see ¹UL

oola \ü-lə\ see ULA

oole \ül\ see ¹OOL

oolean \ü-lē-ən\ see ULEAN

ooled \üld\ bejeweled,
unschooled, vestibuled—*also*
-ed *forms of verbs listed at*
¹OOL

ooler \ü-lər\ cooler, gular,
puler, ruler, carpooler,
grade-schooler, high
schooler, preschooler,
ridiculer, watercooler

oolie \ü-lē\ see ULY

oolish \ü-lish\ coolish,

foolish, ghoulish, mulish,
pound-foolish

¹**oolly** \ü-lē\ see ULY

²**oolly** \ùl-ē\ see ²ULLY

¹**oom** \üm\ bloom, boom,
broom, brougham, brume,
combe, cwm, doom, flume,
fume, gloom, glume, groom,
Hume, khoum, loom,
neume, plume, rheum, room,
spume, tomb, toom, vroom,
whom, womb, zoom,
abloom, assume, backroom,
ballroom, barroom,
bathroom, bedroom,
boardroom, bridegroom,
broadloom, checkroom,
classroom, cloakroom,
coatroom, consume,
costume, courtroom,
darkroom, dayroom,
entomb, enwomb, exhume,
foredoom, greenroom,
guardroom, headroom,
heirloom, homeroom,
houseroom, illume, inhume,
jibboom, Khartoum,
legroom, legume,
lunchroom, mudroom,
mushroom, newsroom,
perfume, playroom,
poolroom, pressroom,
presume, proofroom,
relume, resume, salesroom,
schoolroom, showroom,
sickroom, simoom,
stateroom, stockroom,
storeroom, subsume,
taproom, Targum, tearoom,
toolroom, wardroom,
washroom, workroom,
anteroom, checkerbloom,
dyer's broom, elbowroom,
impostume, locker-room,
miniboom, nom de plume,
smoke-filled room, witches'-
broom

²**oom** \ùm\ see ²UM

oomed \ümd\ groomed, plumed, wombed, well-groomed—*also* -ed *forms of verbs listed at* ¹OOM

oomer \ü-mər\ see UMER

oomily \ü-mə-lē\ gloomily, contumely

¹**ooming** \ü-mən\ see UMAN

²**ooming** \ü-miŋ\ see UMING

oomlet \üm-lət\ boomlet, plumelet

oomy \ü-mē\ bloomy, boomy, doomy, fumy, gloomy, plumy, rheumy, roomy, spumy, costumey

¹**oon** \ün\ boon, Boone, coon, croon, dune, goon, hewn, June, loon, lune, moon, noon, prune, rune, shoon, soon, spoon, swoon, strewn, toon, tune, aswoon, attune, baboon, balloon, bassoon, buffoon, Calhoun, cardoon, cartoon, cocoon, commune, doubloon, dragoon, festoon, fine-tune, forenoon, gaboon, gadroon, galloon, Gudrun, half-moon, harpoon, immune, impugn, jargoon, jejune, Kowloon, Kunlun, lagoon, lampoon, lardoon, maroon, monsoon, Neptune, oppugn, Pashtun, patroon, platoon, poltroon, pontoon, premune, puccoon, quadroon, raccoon, ratoon, repugn, rockoon, rough-hewn, saloon, shalloon, soupspoon, spittoon, spontoon, teaspoon, Torun, tribune, triune, tuchun, tycoon, typhoon, untune, Walloon, afternoon, barracoon, Brigadoon, Cameroon, demilune, dessertspoon, honeymoon, importune, macaroon, octoroon, opportune, pantaloon, picaroon, picayune, rigadoon, saskatoon, Saskatoon, tablespoon, contrabassoon, inopportune

²**oon** \ōn\ see ¹ONE

oona \ü-nə\ see UNA

oonal \ü-nᵊl\ see UNAL

oone \ün\ see ¹OON

ooner \ü-nər\ crooner, crowner, lunar, pruner, schooner, sooner, swooner, tuner, harpooner, lacunar, lampooner, oppugner, honeymooner, importuner, semilunar

¹**oonery** \ün-rē\ buffoonery, lampoonery, poltroonery

²**oonery** \ü-nə-rē\ see UNARY

ooney \ü-nē\ see OONY

oonie \ü-nē\ see OONY

ooning \ü-niŋ\ nooning, ballooning, cartooning, gadrooning—*also* -ing *forms of verbs listed at* ¹OON

oonish \ü-nish\ moonish, buffoonish, cartoonish, picayunish

oonless \ün-ləs\ moonless, tuneless, woundless

oons \ünz\ lunes, zounds, eftsoons, afternoons—*also* -s, -'s, *and* -s' *forms of nouns listed at* ¹OON, *and* -s *forms of verbs listed there*

oony \ü-nē\ gooney, loony, luny, Moonie, moony, muni, puisne, puny, spoony, Zuni, Mulroney

o-op \üp\ see ¹OOP

oop \üp\ bloop, coop, croup, droop, drupe, dupe, goop, group, hoop, loop, loupe, poop, roup, scoop, sloop, snoop, soup, stoop, stoup,

stupe, swoop, troop, troupe,
whoop, age-group, in-group,
out-group, recoup, regroup,
subgroup, T-group, alley-
oop, cock-a-hoop,
Guadalupe, Guadeloupe,
nincompoop, paratroop,
supergroup

ooped \üpd\ looped—*also -ed
forms of verbs listed at* OOP

oopee \ü-pē\ see OOPY

ooper \ü-pər\ blooper,
cooper, Cooper, Cowper,
duper, grouper, looper,
scooper, snooper, stupor,
swooper, super, trooper,
trouper, party pooper,
paratrooper, pooper-scooper,
super-duper

ooping \ü-piŋ\ grouping,
trooping, trouping—*also -ing
forms of verbs listed at* OOP

oopoe \ü-pü\ see OOH-POOH

oops \ùps\ hoops, oops,
whoops, woops

oopy \ü-pē\ croupy, droopy,
groupie, Kewpie, loopy,
snoopy, soupy, Tupi,
whoopee

¹oor \ör\ see ¹OR

²oor \ùr\ see ¹URE

¹oorage \ùr-ij\ moorage,
sewerage

²oorage \ör-ij\ see ²ORAGE

¹oore \ör\ see ¹OR

²oore \ùr\ see ¹URE

oored \örd\ see OARD

oorer \ör-ər\ see ORER

oori \ùr-ē\ see ¹URY

¹ooring \ör-iŋ\ see ORING

²ooring \ùr-iŋ\ see URING

¹oorish \ùr-ish\ boorish,
Moorish, poorish

²oorish \ör-ish\ see ¹ORISH

oorly \ùr-lē\ see URELY

oorman \ör-mən\ see ORMAN

oors \örz\ Bors, drawers,

yours, Azores, indoors,
outdoors, underdrawers,
withindoors, withoutdoors,
Louis Quatorze—*also -s, -'s,
and -s' forms of nouns listed
at* ¹OR, *and -s forms of verbs
listed there*

oorsman \örz-mən\ see
OARSMAN

oort \órt\ see ¹ORT

oosa \ü-sə\ see ¹USA

¹oose \üs\ see ¹USE

²oose \üz\ see ²USE

¹ooser \ü-sər\ see UCER

²ooser \ü-zər\ see USER

oosey \ü-sē\ see UICY

¹oosh \üsh\ see OUCHE

²oosh \ùsh\ see ²USH

oost \üst\ boost, juiced,
Proust, roost, langouste,
produced, self-induced,
Zlatoust—*also -ed forms of
verbs listed at* ¹USE

oosy \ü-zē\ see OOZY

¹oot \üt\ foot, put, root, Root,
soot, afoot, barefoot,
bigfoot, bird's-foot,
Blackfoot, clubfoot, crow's-
foot, enroot, flatfoot,
forefoot, hotfoot, input,
kaput, outfoot, output,
Rajput, shot put, snakeroot,
splayfoot, taproot,
throughput, uproot, acre-
foot, arrowroot, bitterroot,
cajeput, candle-foot,
gingerroot, orrisroot,
pussyfoot, tenderfoot,
underfoot

²oot \üt\ see UTE

³oot \ət\ see ¹UT

¹ootage \üt-ij\ fruitage,
rootage, scutage

²ootage \ùt-ij\ footage,
rootage

¹ooted \üt-əd\ booted, fruited,
muted, suited, abluted, deep-

rooted, jackbooted, pantsuited, voluted—*also* -ed *forms of verbs listed at* UTE

²**ooted** \üt-əd\ footed, barefooted, clubfooted, deep-rooted, duckfooted, fleet-footed, four-footed, light-footed, slow-footed, splayfooted, surefooted, web-footed, wing-footed, cloven-footed—*also* -ed *forms of verbs listed at* ¹OOT

¹**ooter** \üt-ər\ footer, putter, shot-putter, pussyfooter

²**ooter** \üt-ər\ *see* UTER

¹**ooth** \üth\ smooth, soothe, tooth

²**ooth** \üth\ booth, Booth, couth, crwth, routh, ruth, Ruth, scouth, sleuth, sooth, tooth, truth, Truth, youth, bucktooth, Duluth, eyetooth, forsooth, half-truth, sawtooth, selcouth, tollbooth, uncouth, untruth, vermouth, snaggletooth

oothe \üth\ *see* ¹OOTH

oothed \ütht\ toothed, gap-toothed, snaggletoothed

oothless \üth-ləs\ *see* UTHLESS

oothly \üth-lē\ soothly, uncouthly

oothy \ü-thē\ couthie, toothy

ootie \üt-ē\ *see* ¹OOTY

¹**ooting** \üt-iŋ\ footing, off-putting—*also* -ing *forms of verbs listed at* ¹OOT

²**ooting** \üt-iŋ\ *see* UTING

ootle \üt-ᵊl\ *see* UTILE

ootless \üt-ləs\ bootless, fruitless

ootlet \üt-lət\ fruitlet, rootlet

oots \üts\ boots, firstfruits, grassroots, slyboots, Vaduz, shoot-the-chutes—*also* -s, -'s, *and* -s' *forms of nouns listed*

at UTE, *and* -s *forms of verbs listed there*

ootsie \üt-sē\ footsie, tootsie

¹**ooty** \üt-ē\ beauty, booty, Clootie, cootie, cutie, duty, footy, fluty, fruity, hooty, rooty, snooty, sooty, tutti, zooty, agouti, Djibouti, Funafuti, heavy-duty, persecutee, tutti-frutti

²**ooty** \üt-ē\ rooty, sooty, tutti

³**ooty** \ət-ē\ *see* UTTY

oove \üv\ *see* ³OVE

oover \ü-vər\ *see* ³OVER

oovy \ü-vē\ groovy, movie

ooze \üz\ *see* ²USE

oozer \ü-zər\ *see* USER

oozle \ü-zəl\ *see* ²USAL

oozy \ü-zē\ bluesy, boozy, choosy, floozy, newsy, oozy, Susie, woozy, Jacuzzi

¹**op** \äp\ bop, chap, chop, clop, cop, crop, drop, flop, fop, glop, hop, knop, lop, mop, op, plop, pop, prop, scop, shop, slop, sop, stop, strop, swap, top, whop, Aesop, airdrop, atop, backdrop, backstop, bakeshop, barhop, bebop, bellhop, blacktop, bookshop, carhop, cartop, chop-chop, clip-clop, clop-clop, coin-op, cooktop, co-op, desktop, dewdrop, doorstop, dramshop, Dunlop, eardrop, eavesdrop, ESOP, estop, f-stop, fire-stop, flattop, flip-flop, foretop, grogshop, gumdrop, hardtop, hedgehop, high-top, hilltop, hip-hop, hockshop, housetop, joypop, maintop, milksop, nonstop, one-stop, outcrop, pawnshop, pop-top, ragtop, raindrop, redtop, ripstop, rooftop, sharecrop,

shortstop, skin-pop, slipslop,
snowdrop, soursop,
stonecrop, sweatshop,
sweetshop, teardrop, tip-top,
treetop, unstop, workshop,
agitprop, barbershop,
carrottop, countertop,
double-crop, double-stop,
Ethiop, island-hop, lollipop,
malaprop, mom-and-pop,
mountaintop, overtop, table-
hop, tabletop, techno-pop,
teenybop, turboprop,
whistle-stop, window-shop,
Babelthuap

²**op** \ō\ see ¹OW

opa \ō-pə\ opa, opah, Europa

opah \ō-pə\ see OPA

opal \ō-pəl\ copal, nopal,
opal, Opal, Simferopol,
Constantinople

ope \ōp\ cope, coup, dope,
grope, holp, hope, Hope,
lope, mope, nope, ope, pope,
Pope, rope, scop, scope,
slope, soap, stope, taupe,
tope, trope, aslope,
borescope, downslope, elope,
gantlope, gantelope, Good
Hope, myope, nightscope,
pyrope, sandsoap, soft-soap,
tightrope, towrope, antelope,
antipope, calliope,
cantaloupe, chronoscope,
envelope, epitope, Ethiope,
gyroscope, horoscope,
interlope, isotope, kinescope,
microscope, misanthrope,
periscope, phalarope,
radarscope, sniperscope,
snooperscope, stethoscope,
telescope, heliotrope,
kaleidoscope, stereoscope

opean \ō-pē-ən\ see OPIAN

opee \ō-pē\ see OPI

open \ō-pən\ holpen, open,
reopen, wide-open

opence \əp-əns\ see UPPANCE

openny \əp-nē\ threepenny,
twopenny

oper \ō-pər\ coper, doper,
groper, loper, moper, roper,
soaper, toper, eloper,
no-hoper, soft-soaper,
interloper

opera \äp-rə\ see OPRA

opey \ō-pē\ see OPI

oph \ōf\ see OAF

ophagous \äf-ə-gəs\
coprophagous, esophagus,
necrophagous, sarcophagus,
zoophagous,
anthropophagous

ophagy \äf-ə-jē\ geophagy,
coprophagy, anthropophagy

¹**ophe** \ō-fē\ see OPHY

²**ophe** \ōf\ see ²OFF

opher \ō-fər\ see OFER

ophet \äf-ət\ see OFIT

¹**ophic** \äf-ik\ strophic,
antistrophic, apostrophic,
catastrophic

²**ophic** \ō-fik\ strophic,
trophic, atrophic

ophical \äf-i-kəl\
philosophical, theosophical

ophie \ō-fē\ see OPHY

ophir \ō-fər\ see OFER

ophonous \äf-ə-nəs\
cacophonous, homophonous

ophony \äf-ə-nē\ cacophony,
colophony, homophony,
monophony, theophany,
heterophony, stereophony

ophy \ō-fē\ Sophie, sophy,
strophe, trophy

opi \ō-pē\ dopey, Hopi,
mopey, ropy, soapy, topee,
topi

opia \ō-pē-ə\ dystopia,
myopia, sinopia, utopia,
cornucopia, Ethiopia

opian \ō-pē-ən\ Aesopian,
cyclopean, dystopian,

utopian, Ethiopian, cornucopian

¹opic \äp-ik\ topic, tropic, Aesopic, anthropic, ectopic, Ethiopic, subtropic, gyroscopic, hygroscopic, macroscopic, microscopic, misanthropic, periscopic, philanthropic, semitropic, stethoscopic, telescopic, kaleidoscopic, stereoscopic

²opic \ō-pik\ tropic, myopic, Ethiopic, psychotropic

opical \äp-i-kəl\ topical, tropical, anthropical, subtropical, microscopical, philanthropical, semitropical, Neotropical

oplar \äp-lər\ see OPPLER

ople \ō-pəl\ see OPAL

opol \ō-pəl\ see OPAL

¹opolis \äp-ə-ləs\ propolis, acropolis, cosmopolis, necropolis, Heliopolis, megalopolis, metropolis, Florianopolis

²opolis \äp-ləs\ see OPLESS

opolist \äp-ə-ləst\ monopolist, bibliopolist

opoly \äp-ə-lē\ choppily, floppily, sloppily, duopoly, monopoly, vox populi, oligopoly, Tiruchirappalli

oppa \äp-ə\ see ¹APA

opped \äpt\ see OPT

oppel \äp-əl\ see OPPLE

opper \äp-ər\ bopper, chopper, copper, cropper, dropper, flopper, hopper, lopper, mopper, popper, proper, shopper, stopper, swapper, topper, whopper, yapper, clodhopper, eavesdropper, eyedropper, eyepopper, grasshopper, hedgehopper, improper, job-hopper, joypopper,

leafhopper, namedropper, rockhopper, sharecropper, showstopper, skin-popper, table-hopper, teenybopper, treehopper, woodchopper, window-shopper

oppery \äp-rē\ coppery, foppery

oppet \äp-ət\ moppet, poppet

oppily \äp-ə-lē\ see OPOLY

oppiness \äp-ē-nəs\ choppiness, floppiness, sloppiness

opping \äp-iŋ\ hopping, sopping, topping, whopping, clodhopping, eye-popping, job-hopping, name-dropping, outcropping—*also* -ing *forms of verbs listed at* ¹OP

opple \äp-əl\ popple, stopple, topple, estoppel

oppler \äp-lər\ Doppler, poplar

oppy \äp-ē\ choppy, copy, crappie, floppy, gloppy, hoppy, kopje, poppy, sloppy, soppy, stroppy, jalopy, okapi, serape, microcopy, Nahuel Huapi, photocopy

opra \äp-rə\ copra, opera

ops \äps\ chops, copse, Ops, tops, beechdrops, cyclops, eyedrops, Pelops, pinedrops, sundrops, muttonchops, triceratops—*also* -s' *forms of nouns listed at* ¹OP, *and* -s *forms of verbs listed there*

opse \äps\ see OPS

opsy \äp-sē\ dropsy, autopsy, biopsy, necropsy

opt \äpt\ Copt, knopped, opt, topped, adopt, close-cropped, co-opt, end-stopped—*also* -ed *forms of verbs listed at* ¹OP

opter \äp-tər\ copter, adopter,
helicopter, ornithopter

optic \äp-tik\ Coptic, optic,
panoptic, synoptic, electro-
optic

optimist \äp-tə-məst\
optimist, Optimist,
Soroptimist

option \äp-shən\ option,
adoption, co-option

optric \äp-trik\ catoptric,
dioptric

opula \äp-yə-lə\ copula,
scopula

opulace \äp-yə-ləs\ populace,
populous

opulate \äp-yə-lāt\ copulate,
populate, over-populate

opuli \äp-ə-lē\ see OPOLY

opulous \äp-yə-ləs\ see
OPULACE

opus \ō-pəs\ opus, Canopus,
magnum opus,
pithecanthropus

¹opy \ō-pē\ see OPI

²opy \äp-ē\ see OPPY

¹oque \ōk\ see OKE

²oque \äk\ see ¹OCK

³oque \ók\ see ALK

oquial \ō-kwē-əl\ colloquial,
ventriloquial

¹or \ór\ boar, Boer, Bohr,
bore, chore, core, corps,
crore, door, drawer, floor,
for, fore, four, frore, gore,
Gore, hoar, hoer, kor, lore,
Moore, mor, more, More,
nor, o'er, oar, or, ore, poor,
pore, pour, roar, score,
shore, snore, soar, sore,
splore, spoor, spore, store,
swore, Thor, tor, tore, torr,
war, whore, wore, yore,
your, you're, abhor, actor,
adore, afore, and/or, ashore,
backdoor, bailor, bandore,
Beardmore, bedsore, before,

bezoar, bookstore, candor,
captor, centaur, claymore,
closed-door, condor, decor,
deplore, dime-store, donor,
downpour, drugstore,
encore, ephor, explore,
Exmoor, eyesore, feoffor,
fetor, Fillmore, folklore,
footsore, forebore, forswore,
forscore, galore, hardcore,
ichor, ignore, implore,
Indore, indoor, inpour,
inshore, Lahore, lakeshore,
Lenore, lessor, memoir,
mentor, Mysore, nearshore,
Nestor, offshore, onshore,
outdoor, outpour, outsoar,
outwore, pastor, psywar,
rancor, rapport, raptor,
Realtor, restore, rhetor,
savior, seafloor, seashore,
sector, seignior, senhor,
señor, sensor, settlor,
Seymour, signor,
smoothbore, sophomore,
stentor, stertor, stressor,
stridor, subfloor, temblor,
tensor, therefor, therefore,
threescore, Timor, trapdoor,
turgor, uproar, vendor,
wherefore, woodlore,
albacore, alongshore,
anaphor, anymore,
archosaur, Baltimore,
Bangalore, Barrymore,
brontosaur, carnivore, CD4,
Coimbatore, commodore,
comprador, confessor,
consignor, corridor,
cuspidor, devisor, dinosaur,
door-to-door, Ecuador,
either-or, Eleanor, Eleanore,
elector, Elinor, en rapport,
evermore, franchisor,
furthermore, guarantor,
Gwalior, hackamore,
hadrosaur, hellebore,

herbivore, heretofore, humidor, Labrador, louis d'or, man-of-war, manticore, matador, metaphor, meteor, millepore, Minotaur, mirador, Mount Rushmore, nevermore, omnivore, out-of-door, petit four, picador, pinafore, pompadour, predator, promisor, pterosaur, reservoir, sagamore, Salvador, Salvatore, semaphore, Singapore, stegosaur, stevedore, superstore, sycamore, Theodore, theretofore, troubador, tug-of-war, two-by-four, uncalled-for, underscore, vavasor, warrantor, alienor, ambassador, ankylosaur, conquistador, conservator, Corregidor, de Pompadour, El Salvador, esprit de corps, forevermore, hereinbefore, ichthyosaur, insectivore, legislator, plesiosaur, San Salvadore, toreador, tyrannosaur, Ulan Bator, administrator, lobster thermidor, Talleyrand-Perigord

²or \ór\ see ¹EUR

ora \ór-ə\ aura, bora, Cora, Dora, flora, Flora, hora, Laura, Lora, mora, Nora, sora, Torah, Andorra, angora, aurora, Aurora, begorra, camorra, fedora, gemara, Gomorrah, Lenora, Masora, menorah, pandora, Pandora, remora, senhora, señora, signora, Sonora, grandiflora, Juiz de Fora, Leonora, Simchas Torah, Tuscarora, Lomas de Zamora

orable \ór-ə-bəl\ horrible, pourable, storable, adorable, deplorable, restorable

orace \ór-əs\ see AURUS

oracle \ór-ə-kəl\ coracle, oracle

¹orage \är-ij\ barrage, borage, forage, porridge

²orage \ór-ij\ borage, floorage, forage, porridge, storage

orah \ór-ə\ see ORA

¹oral \ór-əl\ aural, choral, coral, Coral, floral, laurel, Laurel, moral, oral, quarrel, sorrel, aboral, amoral, auroral, balmoral, binaural, immoral, monaural, peroral, restoral, sororal

²oral \órl\ see ²ORL

oram \ór-əm\ see ORUM

orate \ór-ət\ see ORET

orative \ór-ət-iv\ explorative, pejorative, restorative

oray \ə-rē\ see URRY

orb \órb\ forb, orb, sorb, Sorb, absorb, adsorb, desorb, resorb

orbate \ór-bət\ see ORBIT

orbeil \ór-bəl\ see ORBEL

orbel \ór-bəl\ corbeil, corbel, warble

orbent \ór-bənt\ absorbent, immunosorbent

orbet \ór-bət\ see ORBIT

orbit \ór-bət\ orbit, sorbet, adsorbate

orc \órk\ see ²ORK

orca \ór-kə\ orca, Majorca, Minorca, Palma de Mallorca

orcas \ór-kəs\ Dorcas, orchis

orce \órs\ see ¹ORSE

orced \órst\ see ¹ORST

orceful \órs-fəl\ see ORSEFUL

orcement \ór-smənt\ see ORSEMENT

orcer \ór-sər\ courser, forcer,

discourser, enforcer, reinforcer—*also -er forms of adjectives listed at* ¹ORSE

orch \órch\ porch, scorch, torch, blowtorch, sunporch

orcher \ór-chər\ scorcher, torture

orchid \ór-kəd\ forked, orchid, cryptorchid, monorchid

orchis \ór-kəs\ see ORCAS

¹ord \órd\ see OARD

²ord \ərd\ see IRD

³ord \ór\ see ¹OR

ordan \órd-ᵊn\ see ²ARDEN

ordancy \órd-ᵊn-sē\ mordancy, discordancy

ordant \órd-ᵊnt\ mordant, mordent, accordant, concordant, discordant

orde \órd\ see OARD

orded \órd-əd\ see ²ARDED

ordent \órd-ᵊnt\ see ORDANT

order \órd-ər\ boarder, border, corder, hoarder, order, warder, awarder, disorder, keyboarder, recorder, reorder, rewarder, skateboarder, surfboarder, made-to-order

ordered \órd-ərd\ bordered, ordered—*also -ed forms of verbs listed at* ORDER

orders \órd-ərz\ Borders—*also -s, -'s, and -s' forms of nouns listed at* ORDER, *and -s forms of verbs listed there*

ordial \órd-ē-əl\ exordial, primordial

ordid \órd-əd\ see ²ARDED

¹ording \órd-iŋ\ boarding, hoarding, lording, recording, rewarding, skateboarding, weatherboarding—*also -ing forms of verbs listed at* OARD

²ording \ərd-iŋ\ see ERDING

ordingly \órd-iŋ-lē\ accordingly, rewardingly

ordion \órd-ē-ən\ accordion, Edwardian

ordist \órd-əst\ recordist, clavichordist, harpsichordist

ordon \órd-ᵊn\ see ²ARDEN

ordure \órd-jər\ see ORGER

¹ordy \órd-ē\ Geordie, Lordy, awardee

²ordy \ərd-ē\ see URDY

ore \ór-ē\ see ORY

²ore \ùr\ see ¹URE

³ore \ər-ə\ see ¹OROUGH

⁴ore \ór\ see ¹OR

oreal \ór-ē-əl\ see ORIAL

orean \ór-ē-ən\ see ORIAN

oreas \ór-ē-əs\ see ORIOUS

ored \órd\ see OARD

oredom \órd-əm\ boredom, whoredom

orehead \ór-əd\ see ORRID

¹oreign \är-ən\ see ARIN

²oreign \ór-ən\ see ¹ORIN

oreigner \ór-ə-nər\ see ORONER

orem \ór-əm\ see ORUM

oreman \ór-mən\ see ORMAN

orence \ór-ən(t)s\ see AWRENCE

oreous \ór-ē-əs\ see ORIOUS

orer \ór-ər\ borer, corer, floorer, horror, pourer, roarer, scorer, schnorrer, snorer, soarer, sorer, abhorer, adorer, deplorer, explorer—*also -er forms of adjectives listed at* ¹OR

¹ores \ór-əs\ see AURUS

²ores \órz\ see OORS

oreson \órs-ᵊn\ see OARSEN

orest \ór-əst\ see ORIST

orester \ór-ə-stər\ see ORISTER

oret \ór-ət\ floret, sororate

oreum \ór-ē-əm\ see ORIUM

oreward \ȯr-wərd\ see ORWARD

oreword \ȯr-wərd\ see ORWARD

orey \ȯr-ē\ see ORY

orf \ȯrf\ see ORPH

¹org \ȯrg\ morgue, cyborg

²org \ȯr-ē\ see ORY

organ \ȯr-gən\ gorgon, morgan, Morgan, organ, Glamorgan, Demogorgon, Mid Glamorgan, South Glamorgan, West Glamorgan

orge \ȯrj\ forge, George, gorge, scourge, disgorge, drop-forge, engorge, Lloyd George, reforge, Olduvai Gorge

orger \ȯr-jər\ bordure, forger, gorger, ordure

orgi \ȯr-gē\ see ORGY

orgia \ȯr-jə\ Borgia, Georgia, Strait of Georgia

orgian \ȯr-jən\ Georgian, Swedenborgian

orgon \ȯr-gən\ see ORGAN

orgue \ȯrg\ see ORG

orgy \ȯr-gē\ corgi, porgy

ori \ȯr-ē\ see ORY

oria \ȯr-ē-ə\ gloria, Gloria, noria, scoria, centaurea, euphoria, Peoria, Pretoria, victoria, Victoria, Vitoria, phantasmagoria

orial \ȯr-ē-əl\ boreal, oriel, oriole, arboreal, armorial, auctorial, authorial, cantorial, censorial, corporeal, cursorial, factorial, fossorial, manorial, marmoreal, memorial, pictorial, praetorial, proctorial, raptorial, rectorial, sartorial, seignorial, sensorial, sponsorial, tonsorial, tutorial, uxorial, vectorial,

conductorial, consistorial, curatorial, dictatorial, directorial, editorial, equatorial, immemorial, incorporeal, janitorial, monitorial, monsignorial, natatorial, piscatorial, preceptorial, professorial, purgatorial, reportorial, senatorial, territorial, ambassadorial, conservatorial, combinatorial, conspiratorial, extracorporeal, gladiatorial, gubernatorial, imperatorial, inquisitorial, legislatorial, procuratorial, propriatorial, prosecutorial, extraterritorial, improvisatorial

oriam \ȯr-ē-əm\ see ORIUM

orian \ȯr-ē-ən\ Dorian, saurian, Taurean, aurorean, Gregorian, historian, Nestorian, praetorian, stentorian, victorian, dinosaurian, hyperborean, Oratorian, prehistorian, senatorian, terpsichorean, salutatorian, valedictorian

oriant \ȯr-ē-ənt\ see ORIENT

oriat \ȯr-ē-ət\ see ²AUREATE

oric \ȯr-ik\ auric, choric, Doric, toric, Armoric, caloric, clitoric, dysphoric, euphoric, folkloric, historic, phosphoric, plethoric, pyloric, anaphoric, cataphoric, metaphoric, meteoric, paregoric, prehistoric, sophomoric, aleatoric, phantasmagoric

orical \ȯr-i-kəl\ auricle, historical, rhetorical, ahistorical, allegorical, categorical, metaphorical,

oratorical, transhistorical,
sociohistorical

orics \ór-iks\ see ORYX

orid \ór-əd\ see ORRID

oriel \ór-ē-əl\ see ORIAL

orient \ór-ē-ənt\ orient,
Orient, euphoriant

¹orin \ór-ən\ chlorine, florin,
foreign, Lauren, Orrin,
sporran, warren, Warren,
cyclosporine, cephalosporin

²orin \är-ən\ see ARIN

orine \ór-ən\ see ¹ORIN

oring \ór-iŋ\ boring, flooring,
roaring, shoring, inpouring,
longshoring, outpouring, rip-
roaring—*also* -ing *forms of
verbs listed at* ¹OR

öring \ər-iŋ\ see URRING

oriole \ór-ē-əl\ see ORIAL

orious \ór-ē-əs\ aureus,
Boreas, glorious, arboreous,
censorious, inglorious,
laborious, notorious,
sartorius, uproarious,
uxorious, vainglorious,
victorious, meritorious

oris \ór-əs\ see AURUS

¹orish \ór-ish\ boarish,
poorish, whorish, folklorish

²orish \ùr-ish\ see ¹OORISH

orist \ór-əst\ florist, forest,
Forrest, sorest, afforest,
Black Forest, deforest,
folklorist, reforest, allegorist,
Petrified Forest—*also* -est
forms of adjectives listed at
¹OR

orister \ór-ə-stər\ chorister,
forester

ority \ór-ət-ē\ authority,
majority, minority, priority,
seniority, sonority, apriority,
exteriority, inferiority,
interiority, posteriority,
superiority

orium \ór-ē-əm\ castoreum,

ciborium, emporium,
pastorium, scriptorium,
sensorium, auditorium,
crematorium, in memoriam,
moratorium, natatorium,
sanitorium, sudatorium

¹ork \árk\ burke, Burke,
chirk, cirque, clerk, dirk,
Dirk, irk, jerk, kirk, Kirk,
lurk, murk, perk, quirk,
shirk, smirk, stirk, Turk,
work, yerk, zerk, artwork,
berserk, breastwork,
brickwork, bridgework,
brightwork, brushwork,
capework, casework,
clockwork, coachwork, de
Klerk, ductwork, Dunkirk,
earthwork, falsework,
fieldwork, firework,
flatwork, footwork,
formwork, framework,
goldwork, groundwork,
guesswork, hackwork,
handwork, headwork,
homework, housework,
ironwork, knee-jerk,
legwork, lifework, make-
work, meshwork, millwork,
network, outwork,
paintwork, patchwork,
piecework, presswork,
quillwork, rework,
roadwork, salesclerk,
schoolwork, Selkirk,
Southwark, spadework,
steelwork, stickwork,
stonework, teamwork,
timework, topwork,
waxwork, webwork,
woodwork, basketwork,
busywork, crewelwork,
donkeywork, fancywork,
handiwork, journeywork,
laquerwork, masterwork,
needlework, openwork,
overwork, paperwork,

plasterwork, soda jerk,
wonderwork, cabinetwork

²**ork** \ȯrk\ cork, Cork, dork,
fork, pork, quark, stork,
torque, York, bulwark, Cape
York, futhorc, hayfork, New
York, North York,
pitchfork, uncork

¹**orked** \ȯrkt\ corked, forked,
uncorked

²**orked** \ȯr-kəd\ see ORCHID

¹**orker** \ər-kər\ jerker, lurker,
shirker, worker, berserker,
caseworker, dockworker,
fieldworker, handworker,
ironworker, outworker,
pieceworker, steelworker,
tearjerker, wageworker,
woodworker, autoworker,
metalworker, needleworker,
wonderworker

²**orker** \ȯr-kər\ corker,
forker, porker, torquer

orkie \ȯr-kē\ see ORKY

orking \ər-kiŋ\ hardworking,
tear-jerking, woodworking,
wonder-working—*also* -ing
forms of verbs listed at ¹ORK

orky \ȯr-kē\ corky, dorky,
forky, Gorky, porky, Yorkie

¹**orl** \ərl\ see ¹IRL

²**orl** \ȯrl\ schorl, whorl, ceorl

orld \ərld\ burled, knurled,
whorled, world, dreamworld,
New World, old-world,
demiworld, microworld,
netherworld, otherworld,
underworld—*also* -ed *forms
of verbs listed at* ¹IRL

orled \ərld\ see ORLD

¹**orm** \ərm\ berm, firm, germ,
herm, perm, Perm, sperm,
squirm, term, therm, worm,
affirm, bookworm,
budworm, confirm,
cutworm, deperm, deworm,
earthworm, flatworm,

glowworm, heartworm,
hookworm, hornworm,
inchworm, infirm, long-term,
lugworm, lungworm,
midterm, pinworm,
ringworm, roundworm,
sandworm, screwworm,
short-term, silkworm,
tapeworm, woodworm,
angleworm, armyworm,
caddis worm, disaffirm,
disconfirm, gymnosperm,
pachyderm, reconfirm,
angiosperm, echinoderm

²**orm** \ȯrm\ corm, dorm,
form, norm, storm, swarm,
warm, aswarm, barnstorm,
brainstorm, conform,
deform, Delorme, firestorm,
free-form, hailstorm, inform,
L-form, landform, life-form,
lukewarm, perform,
planform, platform,
postform, preform,
rainstorm, re-form,
reform, sandstorm,
snowstorm, transform,
triform, windstorm,
chloroform, cruciform,
dendriform, dentiform,
disciform, fungiform,
funnelform, fusiform,
letterform, microform,
multiform, nonconform,
thunderstorm, uniform,
vermiform

ormable \ȯr-mə-bəl\
formable, conformable,
performable, transformable

ormal \ȯr-məl\ formal,
normal, abnormal,
conformal, informal,
subnormal, paranormal,
semiformal, supernormal

ormally \ȯr-mə-lē\ formally,
formerly, normally, stormily,
abnormally, informally,

subnormally, paranormally, supernormally

orman \ór-mən\ corpsman, doorman, foreman, Mormon, Norman, longshoreman, Anglo-Norman

ormance \ór-məns\ conformance, performance, nonconformance

ormant \ór-mənt\ dormant, formant, informant

ormative \ór-mət-iv\ formative, normative, informative, performative, reformative, transformative

orme \órm\ see ²ORM

ormed \órmd\ formed, normed, informed, malformed, unformed—*also* -ed *forms of verbs listed at* ²ORM

¹ormer \ór-mər\ dormer, former, swarmer, warmer, barnstormer, benchwarmer, brainstormer, conformer, heart-warmer, informer, performer, reformer, transformer

²ormer \ər-mər\ see URMUR

ormerly \ór-mə-lē\ see ORMALLY

ormie \ór-mē\ see ¹ORMY

ormily \ór-mə-lē\ see ORMALLY

orming \ór-miŋ\ brainstorming, heartwarming, housewarming, habit-forming, nonperforming—*also* -ing *forms of verbs listed at* ²ORM

ormist \ór-məst\ warmest, conformist, reformist, nonconformist

ormity \ór-mət-ē\ conformity, deformity, enormity, nonconformity, uniformity

ormless \órm-ləs\ formless, gormless

ormon \ór-mən\ see ORMAN

¹ormy \ór-mē\ stormy, dormie

²ormy \ər-mē\ see ERMY

¹orn \órn\ born, borne, bourn, corn, horn, lorn, morn, mourn, Norn, porn, scorn, shorn, sworn, thorn, torn, warn, worn, acorn, adorn, airborne, alphorn, althorn, baseborn, bicorne, bighorn, blackthorn, boxthorn, broomcorn, buckthorn, bullhorn, Cape Horn, careworn, Christ's-thorn, Dearborn, dehorn, earthborn, einkorn, firethorn, firstborn, foghorn, foreborn, foresworn, forewarn, forlorn, forworn, freeborn, greenhorn, hartshorn, hawthorn, Hawthorne, highborn, inborn, inkhorn, krummhorn, leghorn, longhorn, lovelorn, lowborn, newborn, outworn, popcorn, pronghorn, reborn, seaborne, shipborne, shoehorn, shopworn, shorthorn, skyborne, soilborne, staghorn, stillborn, stinkhorn, suborn, timeworn, tinhorn, tricorne, trueborn, twice-born, unborn, unworn, wayworn, wellborn, well-worn, windborne, alpenhorn, barleycorn, Capricorn, flügelhorn, foreign-born, Golden Horn, Matterhorn, peppercorn, unicorn, waterborne, waterworn, weatherworn, winterbourne

²orn \ȯrn\ see URN

ornament \ȯr-nə-mənt\ ornament, tournament

orne \ȯrn\ see ¹ORN

orned \ȯrnd\ horned, thorned, unadorned—*also* -ed *forms of verbs listed at* ¹ORN

orner \ȯr-nər\ warner, Warner, Cape Horner, dehorner, suborner

ornery \än-rē\ see ¹ANNERY

orney \ər-nē\ see ¹OURNEY

ornful \ȯrn-fəl\ mournful, scornful

ornice \ȯr-nəs\ cornice, ornice, notornis

orning \ȯr-niŋ\ morning, mourning, warning, aborning

ornis \ȯr-nəs\ see ORNICE

ornment \ərn-mənt\ see ERNMENT

orny \ȯr-nē\ corny, horny, porny, thorny, tourney

¹**oro** \ər-ə\ see ¹OROUGH

²**oro** \ȯ-rō\ Chamorro, Mindoro, Rio de Oro

oroner \ȯr-ə-nər\ coroner, foreigner, warrener

¹**orough** \ər-ə\ borough, burgh, burro, burrow, curragh, furrow, ore, thorough, Gainsborough, Greensboro, Roxborough, Scarborough, Yarborough, Edinburgh, kookaburra, Peterborough, Soke of Peterborough, Huntingdon and Peterborough

²**orough** \ər-ō\ see ¹URROW

orous \ȯr-əs\ see AURUS

orp \ȯrp\ dorp, gorp, thorp, warp, Australorp,

Krugersdorp, octothorp, Oglethorpe

orpe \ȯrp\ see ORP

orper \ȯr-pər\ dorper, torpor

orph \ȯrf\ corf, dwarf, morph, Düsseldorf, anthropomorph

orphan \ȯr-fən\ orphan, endorphin, beta-endorphin

orpheus \ȯr-fē-əs\ Morpheus, Orpheus

orphic \ȯr-fik\ orphic, ectomorphic, endomorphic, mesomorphic, pseudomorphic, metamorphic, anthropomorphic

orphin \ȯr-fən\ see ORPHAN

orphous \ȯr-fəs\ amorphous, isomorphous

orphrey \ȯr-frē\ orphrey, porphyry

orphyrin \ȯr-fə-rən\ see ARFARIN

orphyry \ȯr-frē\ see ORPHREY

orpoise \ȯr-pəs\ see ORPUS

orpor \ȯr-pər\ see ORPER

orps \ȯr\ see ¹OR

orpsman \ȯr-mən\ see ORMAN

orpus \ȯr-pəs\ corpus, porpoise, habeas corpus

orque \ȯrk\ see ²ORK

orquer \ȯr-kər\ see ²ORKER

orr \ȯr\ see ¹OR

¹**orra** \är-ə\ see ¹ARA

²**orra** \ȯr-ə\ see ORA

orrader \är-əd-ər\ see ORRIDOR

¹**orrah** \ȯr-ə\ see ORA

²**orrah** \är-ə\ see ¹ARA

¹**orran** \är-ən\ see ARIN

²**orran** \ȯr-ən\ see ¹ORIN

orrence \ȯr-əns\ see AWRENCE

orrel \ȯr-əl\ see ¹ORAL

orrent \ȯr-ənt\ horrent, torrent, warrant, abhorrent

orrer \ór-ər\ see ORER

orres \ór-əs\ see AURUS

orrest \ór-əst\ see ORIST

orrible \ór-ə-bəl\ see ORABLE

orrid \ór-əd\ florid, horrid, torrid

¹orridge \är-ij\ see ¹ORAGE

²orridge \ór-ij\ see ²ORAGE

orridor \är-əd-ər\ corridor, forrader

¹orrie \är-ē\ see ¹ARI

²orrie \ór-ē\ see ORY

orrier \ór-ē-ər\ see ARRIOR

¹orrin \är-en\ see ARIN

²orrin \ór-ən\ see ¹ORIN

¹orris \är-əs\ charas, Juárez, Maurice, morris, Morris, Norris, orris, Banaras, Benares, Polaris, Ciudad Juárez

²orris \ór-əs\ see AURUS

orro \ó-rō\ see ²ORO

orror \ór-ər\ see ORER

¹orrow \är-ō\ borrow, claro, morrow, sorrow, taro, Pizarro, saguaro, tomorrow, Catanzaro, Kilimanjaro, Mohenjo-Daro

²orrow \ór-ə\ see ¹ARA

¹orry \är-ē\ see ¹ARI

²orry \ər-ē\ see URRY

ors \órz\ see OORS

orsal \ór-səl\ see ORSEL

¹orse \órs\ coarse, corse, course, force, gorse, hoarse, horse, Morse, Norse, source, clotheshorse, concourse, deforce, discourse, divorce, endorse, enforce, extrorse, introrse, midcourse, packhorse, perforce, post-horse, racecourse, racehorse, recourse, remorse, resource, retrorse, sawhorse, stringcourse, unhorse, war-horse, Whitehorse, workhorse, charley horse,

Crazy Horse, hobbyhorse, intercourse, nonrecourse, reinforce, stalking-horse, telecourse, tour de force, watercourse

²orse \órs\ see ERSE

orseful \órs-fəl\ forceful, remorseful, resourceful

orsel \ór-səl\ dorsal, morsel

orseman \ór-smən\ horseman, Norseman

orsement \ór-smənt\ deforcement, divorcement, endorsement, enforcement, reinforcement

orsen \órs-²n\ see ERSON

orser \ər-sər\ see URSOR

orset \ór-sət\ corset, Dorset

orsey \ór-sē\ see ORSY

orsion \ór-shən\ see ORTION

¹orst \órst\ forced, horst—also -ed forms of verbs listed at ¹ORSE

²orst \ərst\ see URST

orsted \ər-stəd\ see ERSTED

orsum \ór-səm\ dorsum, foursome

orsy \ór-sē\ gorsy, horsey

¹ort \órt\ boart, bort, court, fort, forte, mort, Oort, ort, port, Porte, quart, short, snort, sort, sport, swart, thwart, tort, torte, wart, wort, abort, airport, amort, aport, assort, athwart, backcourt, bellwort, birthwort, bistort, Bridgeport, cavort, cohort, colewort, comport, consort, contort, crosscourt, deport, disport, distort, downcourt, effort, escort, exhort, export, extort, forecourt, frontcourt, glasswort, gosport, half-court, homeport, milkwort, Newport, outport, passport, presort, purport, ragwort,

report, re-sort, resort, retort,
seaport, Shreveport,
spaceport, spoilsport,
Stockport, support,
transport, bladderwort,
davenport, life-support,
nonsupport, pennywort,
Saint-John's wort, teleport,
ultrashort, worrywart,
pianoforte, underreport

²ort \òr\ see ¹OR

³ort \ärt\ see ¹ERT

ortable \òrt-ə-bəl\ portable,
deportable, exportable,
importable, reportable,
supportable, transportable,
insupportable

ortage \òrt-ij\ portage,
shortage, colportage

ortal \òrt-ᵊl\ chortle, mortal,
portal, quartile, immortal

ortar \òrt-ər\ see ORTER

ortative \òrt-ət-iv\ hortative,
portative, assortative,
exhortative

¹orte \òrt\ see ¹ORT

²orte \òrt-ē\ see ORTY

orted \òrt-əd\ warted,
assorted, ill-sorted—also -ed
forms of verbs listed at ¹ORT

ortedly \òrt-əd-lē\
purportedly, reportedly

orten \òrt-ᵊn\ quartan,
shorten, foreshorten

orter \òrt-ər\ mortar, porter,
Porter, quarter, snorter,
sorter, thwarter, aborter,
colporteur, distorter,
exhorter, exporter, extorter,
headquarter, importer,
lambs-quarter, reporter,
resorter, ripsnorter,
transporter—also -er forms
of adjectives listed at
¹ORT

orteur \òrt-ər\ see ORTER

¹orth \òrth\ forth, Forth,

fourth, north, North,
thenceforth, Firth of Forth

²orth \ärth\ see IRTH

orthful \ärth-fəl\ see IRTHFUL

orthless \ärth-ləs\ see
IRTHLESS

orthy \ər-thē\ earthy, worthy,
airworthy, blameworthy,
Galsworthy, newsworthy,
noteworthy, praiseworthy,
seaworthy, trustworthy,
creditworthy

ortic \òrt-ik\ see ²ARTIC

ortical \òrt-i-kəl\ cortical,
vortical

ortie \òrt-ē\ see ORTY

orting \òrt-iŋ\ sporting, self-
supporting

ortion \òr-shən\ portion,
torsion, abortion, apportion,
contortion, distortion,
extorsion, extortion,
proportion, retortion,
disproportion, proabortion,
reapportion, antiabortion

ortionate \òr-shnət\
extortionate, proportionate,
disproportionate

ortionist \òr-shnəst\
abortionist, contortionist,
extortionist

ortis \òrt-əs\ fortis, mortise,
tortoise, aquafortis, rigor
mortis

ortise \òrt-əs\ see ORTIS

ortive \òrt-iv\ sportive,
abortive, contortive,
extortive

ortle \òrt-ᵊl\ see ORTAL

ortly \òrt-lē\ courtly, portly,
shortly, thwartly

ortment \òrt-mənt\
assortment, comportment,
deportment, disportment

ortoise \òrt-əs\ see ORTIS

orton \òrt-ᵊn\ Morton,
Norton, Wharton

orts \òrts\ quartz, shorts, sports, undershorts—*also* -s, -'s, *and* -s' *forms of nouns listed at* ¹ORT, *and* -s *forms of verbs listed there*

ortunate \órch-nət\ fortunate, importunate, unfortunate

orture \òr-chər\ see ORCHER

orty \òrt-ē\ forty, shorty, sortie, sporty, warty, mezzo forte, pianoforte

orum \ór-əm\ foram, forum, jorum, quorum, decorum, Mizoram, ad valorem, cockalorum, indecorum, Karakoram, variorum, pons asinorum, sanctum sanctorum, schola cantorum

orus \òr-əs\ see AURUS

orward \òr-wərd\ forward, foreward, shoreward, henceforward, carryforward

ory \òr-ē\ Corey, corrie, dory, glory, gory, hoary, Laurie, Lori, lorry, lory, nori, quarry, saury, sorry, story, Tory, zori, centaury, clerestory, John Dory, outlawry, satori, vainglory, a priori, allegory, amatory, auditory, cacciatore, castratory, category, con amore, crematory, damnatory, decretory, desultory, dilatory, dormitory, expletory, feudatory, fumitory, Goteborg, gustatory, gyratory, hortatory, hunky-dory, inventory, laudatory, lavatory, mandatory, migratory, minatory, monitory, Montessori, nugatory, offertory, oratory, overstory, predatory, prefatory, probatory, promissory, promontory,

purgatory, repertory, Ruwenzori, signatory, statutory, sudatory, territory, transitory, understory, vibratory, vomitory, yakitori, accusatory, admonitory, adulatory, a fortiori, aleatory, ambulatory, amendatory, applicatory, approbatory, celebratory, circulatory, combinatory, commendatory, compensatory, condemnatory, confirmatory, confiscatory, conservatory, consolatory, contributory, copulatory, cosignatory, declamatory, declaratory, dedicatory, defamatory, denigratory, depilatory, depository, derogatory, designatory, dispensatory, divinatory, escalatory, excitatory, exclamatory, exculpatory, excusatory, exhibitory, exhortatory, expiatory, expiratory, explanatory, explicatory, exploratory, expository, expurgatory, incantatory, incubatory, indicatory, inflammatory, informatory, innovatory, inspiratory, inundatory, invitatory, judicatory, laboratory, Lake Maggiore, masticatory, masturbatory, memento mori, millefiori, modulatory, obfuscatory, obligatory, observatory, performatory, persecutory, predicatory, premonitory, preparatory, prohibitory, reformatory, regulatory, repository, retributory, revelatory, respiratory,

salutatory, stipulatory,
supplicatory, transmigratory,
undulatory, adjudicatory, a
posteriori, annihilatory,
annunciatory, anticipatory,
appreciatory, assimilatory,
circumlocutory,
classificatory, concilliatory,
confabulatory,
congratulatory, de-
escalatory, denunciatory,
depreciatory, discriminatory,
ejaculatory, hallucinatory,
improvisatore,
improvisatory, interrogatory,
intimidatory, investigatory,
participatory, propitiatory,
recommendatory,
recriminatory, renunciatory,
reverberatory, viola d'amore,
amelioratory,
overcompensatory,
reconciliatory,
supererogatory,
immunoregulatory

oryx \ór-iks\ oryx, Armorics,
combinatorics

orze \órz\ see OORS

¹os \äs\ boss, doss, dross,
floss, fosse, gloss, joss, Maas,
os, pross, stoss, toss, Argos,
bathos, benthos, bugloss,
chaos, Chios, cosmos, Delos,
demos, Ellás, emboss, Eos,
epos, Eros, ethos, Hyksos,
kaross, kudos, kvass, Lagos,
Laplace, Lemnos, Lesbos,
Logos, Madras, Melos,
mythos, nol-pros, nonpros,
Paros, pathos, peplos,
pharos, ringtoss, Samos,
telos, topos, tripos, coup de
grace, demitasse, extrados,
gravitas, intrados, isogloss,
omphalos, reredos,
semigloss, Thanatos,
underboss, volte-face

²os \ō\ see ¹OW

³os \ós\ see ¹OSE

⁴os \ós\ see ¹OSS

¹osa \ō-sə\ Xhosa, Formosa,
mimosa, Reynosa, curiosa,
virtuosa, anorexia nervosa

²osa \ō-zə\ mimosa, mucosa,
serosa, Spinoza, sub rosa,
curiosa, virtuosa, Zaragoza

¹osable \ō-zə-bəl\ closable,
disposable, erosible,
explosible, opposable,
reclosable, supposable,
decomposable, superposable,
indecomposable,
superimposable

²osable \ü-zə-bəl\ see USABLE

osal \ō-zəl\ hosel, losel,
deposal, disposal, proposal,
reposal, supposal

osan \ōs-ⁿn\ see OSIN

osch \äsh\ see ²ASH

¹oschen \ō-shən\ see OTION

²oschen \ó-shən\ see AUTION

oscible \äs-ə-bəl\ see OSSIBLE

osco \äs-kō\ see OSCOE

oscoe \äs-kō\ Bosco, roscoe,
Roscoe, fiasco

oscopy \äs-kə-pē\
arthroscopy, microscopy,
spectroscopy, sigmoidoscopy

¹ose \ōs\ close, dose, gross, os,
arkose, Carlos, cosmos,
crustose, cymose, dextrose,
engross, erose, fructose,
globose, glucose, jocose,
lactose, maltose, mannose,
megadose, morose, mythos,
nodose, pappose, pathos,
pentose, pilose, plumose,
ramose, rhamnose, ribose,
rugose, scapose, schistose,
setose, spinose, strigose,
sucrose, Sukkoth, triose,
vadose, ventricose, verbose,
viscose, adios, adipose,
bellicose, calvados, cellulose,

comatose, diagnose,
grandiose, granulose, Helios,
lachrymose, otiose, overdose,
racemose, Shabuoth,
tuberose, varicose, inter
alios, inter vivos,
metamorphose, religiose

²ose \ōz\ brose, Broz, chose,
close, clothes, cloze, doze,
froze, gloze, hose, nose,
pose, prose, rose, Rose,
Ambrose, appose, aros,
bedclothes, bluenose,
brownnose, bulldoze,
Burroughs, compose, depose,
dextrose, disclose, dispose,
enclose, expose, foreclose,
fructose, glucose, hardnose,
impose, nightclothes,
oppose, plainclothes,
primrose, propose,
quickfroze, repose, rockrose,
suppose, transpose, tuberose,
unclose, uprose, viscose,
wind rose, Berlioz,
counterpose, decompose,
diagnose, discompose,
indispose, interpose,
juxtapose, letters close,
pettitoes, predispose,
presuppose, pussytoes,
recompose, shovelnose,
superpose, underclothes,
anastomose, metamorphose,
overexpose, superimpose,
underexpose—*also* -s, -'s,
and -s' *forms of nouns listed
at* ¹OW, *and* -s *forms of verbs
listed there*

³ose \üz\ see ²USE

osed \ōzd\ closed, nosed,
composed, exposed, hard-
nosed, opposed, pug-nosed,
snub-nosed, stenosed,
supposed, unclosed,
indisposed, shovel-nosed,
toffee-nosed, well-

disposed—*also* -ed *forms of
verbs listed at* ²OSE

osee \ō-zē\ see OSY

osel \ō-zəl\ see OSAL

osen \ōz-ⁿn\ chosen, frozen,
quickfrozen, lederhosen

¹oser \ō-zər\ closer, dozer,
poser, proser, brownnoser,
bulldozer, composer,
discloser, disposer, exposer,
imposer, opposer, proposer,
decomposer, interposer,
photocomposer

²oser \ü-zər\ see USER

¹oset \ō-zət\ see ²OSIT

²oset \äz-ət\ see ¹OSIT

³oset \äs-ət\ see OSSET

osey \ō-zē\ see OSY

¹osh \ȯsh\ see ²ASH

²osh \ōsh\ see ¹OCHE

¹oshed \ȧsht\ sloshed,
galoshed—*also* -ed *forms of
verbs listed at* ¹ASH

²oshed \ȯsht\ see ¹ASHED

oshen \ō-shən\ see OTION

osher \ȧsh-ər\ see ¹ASHER

osia \ō-shə\ see ¹OTIA

osible \ō-zə-bəl\ see ¹OSABLE

osier \ō-zhər\ see OSURE

osily \ō-zə-lē\ cozily, nosily,
rosily

osin \ōs-ⁿn\ boatswain,
Mosan, pocosin

osing \ō-ziŋ\ closing, nosing,
disclosing, imposing,
supposing—*also* -ing *forms of
verbs listed at* ²OSE

osion \ō-zhən\ plosion,
corrosion, displosion,
erosion, explosion, implosion

osis \ō-səs\ gnosis, hypnosis,
narcosis, necrosis, neurosis,
orthosis, osmosis, prognosis,
psychosis, sclerosis,
thrombosis, brucellosis,
cyanosis, dermatosis,
diagnosis, halitosis, heterosis,

psittacosis, scoliosis, silicosis, symbiosis, anaplasmosis, autohypnosis, coccidiosis, hyperhidrosis, pediculosis, psychoneurosis, tuberculosis, mononucleosis, immunodiagnosis, neurofibromatosis

¹osit \äz-ət\ closet, posit, composite, deposit, exposit

²osit \ō-zət\ prosit, roset

osite \äz-ət\ see ¹OSIT

ositive \äz-ət-iv\ positive, appositive, seropositive

ositor \äz-ət-ər\ compositor, depositor, expositor

osius \ō-shəs\ see OCIOUS

osive \ō-siv\ plosive, corrosive, erosive, explosive, implosive, purposive

osk \äsk\ mosque, kiosk, abelmosk

¹oso \ō-sō\ proso, maestoso, rebozo, arioso, furioso, gracioso, grandioso, mafioso, Mato Grosso, oloroso, spiritoso, vigoroso, virtuoso, concerto grosso

²oso \ō-zō\ bozo, rebozo, furioso, gracioso, grandioso, spiritoso, vigoroso

³oso \ü-sō\ see USOE

osophy \äs-ə-fē\ philosophy, theosophy, anthroposophy

osque \äsk\ see OSK

¹oss \ös\ boss, cross, crosse, floss, gloss, loss, moss, Ross, sauce, toss, across, bugloss, crisscross, emboss, Kinross, kouros, lacrosse, outcross, pathos, ringtoss, topcross, uncross, albatross, applesauce, autocross, double-cross, intercross, motocross, semigloss

²oss \ōs\ see ¹OSE

³oss \äs\ see ¹OS

ossa \äs-ə\ see ¹ASA

ossable \äs-ə-bəl\ see OSSIBLE

ossal \äs-əl\ docile, dossal, fossil, glossal, jostle, tassel, throstle, warsle, wassail, apostle, colossal, indocile, isoglossal

¹osse \äs\ see ¹OS

²osse \äs-ē\ see ¹OSSY

³osse \ös\ see ¹OSS

ossed \öst\ see ³OST

osser \ö-sər\ Chaucer, crosser, saucer, double-crosser

osset \äs-ət\ cosset, faucet, Osset, posset, Samoset

ossible \äs-ə-bəl\ possible, cognoscible, embossable, impossible

ossic \äs-ik\ see OSSICK

ossick \äs-ik\ fossick, isoglossic

ossil \äs-əl\ see OSSAL

ossity \äs-ət-ē\ adiposity, atrocity, callosity, ferocity, gibbosity, monstrosity, pomposity, porosity, precocity, velocity, viscosity, zygosity, animosity, bellicosity, curiosity, generosity, grandiosity, hideosity, luminosity, nebulosity, preciosity, reciprocity, scrupulosity, sensuosity, sinuosity, strenuosity, tortuosity, tuberosity, varicosity, virtuosity, impetuosity, religiosity, voluminosity, impecuniosity

ossly \ös-lē\ costly, crossly

osso \ō-sō\ see ¹OSO

ossos \äs-əs\ see OCESS

ossular \äs-ə-lər\ grossular, wassailer

ossum \äs-əm\ blossom, passim, possum, opossum

ossus \äs-əs\ see OCESS

¹ossy \äs-ē\ Aussie, bossy, dassie, drossy, flossy, glossy, posse, quasi, dalasi, Kumasi, Likasi, sannyasi

²ossy \ȯ-sē\ Aussie, bossy, lossy, mossy

¹ost \äst\ sol-faist, Pentecost, teleost—also -ed forms of verbs listed at ¹OS

²ost \ōst\ boast, coast, ghost, host, most, oast, post, roast, toast, almost, bedpost, compost, doorpost, endmost, foremost, gatepost, goalpost, Gold Coast, guidepost, headmost, hindmost, impost, inmost, midmost, milepost, Milquetoast, outmost, outpost, provost, rearmost, riposte, seacoast, signpost, sternmost, sternpost, topmost, upcoast, upmost, utmost, aftermost, ante-post, bottommost, coast-to-coast, easternmost, farthermost, fingerpost, furthermost, headforemost, hithermost, innermost, Ivory Coast, lowermost, nethermost, northernmost, outermost, rudderpost, southernmost, sternforemost, undermost, uppermost, uttermost, westernmost

³ost \ȯst\ cost, frost, lost, accost, defrost, exhaust, hoarfrost, star-crossed, holocaust, Pentecost, permafrost—also -ed forms of verbs listed at ¹OSS

⁴ost \əst\ see ¹UST

osta \äs-tə\ costa, pasta

¹ostal \äs-t²l\ coastal, postal, bicoastal, intercostal

²ostal \äs-t²l\ see OSTEL

ostasy \äs-tə-sē\ apostasy, isostasy

oste \ōst\ see ²OST

ostel \äs-t²l\ hostel, hostile, Pentecostal

¹oster \äs-tər\ coster, foster, Foster, roster, impostor, piaster, Double Gloucester, paternoster, snollygoster

²oster \ȯs-tər\ foster, Foster, roster, Double Gloucester

³oster \ō-stər\ see OASTER

ostic \äs-tik\ Gnostic, acrostic, agnostic, prognostic, diagnostic

ostile \äs-t²l\ see OSTEL

ostle \äs-əl\ see OSSAL

¹ostly \ōst-lē\ ghostly, hostly, mostly

²ostly \ȯs-lē\ see OSSLY

ostomy \äs-tə-mē\ ostomy, colostomy, enterostomy

oston \ȯs-tən\ Austin, Boston, Godwin Austen

ostor \äs-tər\ see ¹OSTER

¹ostral \ȯs-trəl\ austral, rostral

²ostral \äs-trəl\ see OSTREL

ostrel \äs-trəl\ austral, costrel, nostril, rostral, wastrel, colostral

ostril \äs-trəl\ see OSTREL

ostrum \äs-trəm\ nostrum, rostrum, colostrum

osty \ō-stē\ ghosty, toasty

osure \ō-zhər\ closure, crosier, osier, composure, disclosure, disposure, enclosure, exclosure, exposure, foreclosure, discomposure, overexposure, underexposure

osy \ō-zē\ cozy, dozy, mosey, nosy, Osee, posy, prosy, rosy, ring-around-a-rosy

osyne \äs-²n-ē\ Euphrosyne, Mnemosyne

osz \òsh\ see ²ASH

oszcz \òsh\ see ²ASH

¹ot \ät\ aught, baht, blot, boite, bot, chott, clot, cot, dot, ghat, got, grot, hot, jat, jot, khat, knot, kyat, lot, Lot, lotte, motte, naught, not, plot, pot, rot, scot, Scot, Scott, shot, skat, slot, snot, sot, spot, squat, swat, swot, tot, trot, watt, Watt, what, wot, yacht, allot, ascot, begot, besot, big shot, bloodshot, bowknot, boycott, buckshot, bullshot, cachepot, calotte, cannot, Connacht, crackpot, Crockpot, culotte, dashpot, despot, dreadnought, earshot, ergot, escot, eyeshot, eyespot, feedlot, fiat, firepot, fleshpot, forgot, fox-trot, fusspot, fylfot, garrote, gavotte, grapeshot, gunshot, half-knot, have-not, highspot, hotchpot, hotshot, ikat, jackpot, Korat, kumquat, long shot, loquat, marplot, mascot, motmot, nightspot, one-shot, Pequot, potshot, Rabat, red-hot, robot, Sadat, sandlot, sexpot, Shabbat, shallot, Shebat, sheepcote, slingshot, slipknot, slungshot, snapshot, somewhat, stinkpot, stockpot, subplot, sunspot, teapot, tin-pot, topknot, tosspot, try-pot, upshot, wainscot, whatnot, white-hot, woodlot, aeronaut, aliquot, apparat, apricot, aquanaut, argonaut, astronaut, bergamot, cachalot, Camelot, caveat, carry-cot, coffeepot, cosmonaut, counterplot, diddley-squat, doodley-squat, flowerpot, gallipot, guillemot, Gujarat, Hottentot, Huguenot, kilowatt, Lancelot, megawatt, microdot, Nouakchott, ocelot, overshot, paraquat, patriot, Penobscot, peridot, polka dot, polyglot, samizdat, sansculotte, scattershot, terawatt, tommyrot, touch-me-not, underplot, undershot, Willemstadt, Wyandot, wyandotte, compatriot, forget-me-not, immunoblot, Inupiat, requiescat, Johnny-on-the-spot

²ot \ō\ see ¹OW

³ot \òt\ see OAT

⁴ot \òt\ see ¹OUGHT

ôt \ō\ see ¹OW

ota \ōt-ə\ bota, flota, lota, quota, rota, biota, Dakota, iota, Lakota, pelota, Toyota, Minnesota, North Dakota, South Dakota

otable \ōt-ə-bəl\ notable, potable, quotable

otage \ōt-ij\ dotage, flotage, anecdotage

otal \ōt-ºl\ dotal, motile, scrotal, total, immotile, subtotal, teetotal, anecdotal, antidotal, sacerdotal

otalist \ōt-ºl-əst\ teetotalist, anecdotalist, sacerdotalist

otamus \ät-ə-məs\ see OTOMOUS

otany \ät-ºn-ē\ botany, cottony, monotony

otarist \ōt-ə-rəst\ motorist, votarist

otary \ōt-ə-rē\ coterie, rotary, votary, locomotory, prothonotary

otas \ō-təs\ see OTUS

otch \äch\ blotch, botch, crotch, hotch, notch, scotch, Scotch, splotch, swatch, watch, bird-watch, deathwatch, debauch, dogwatch, hopscotch, hotchpotch, Sasquatch, stopwatch, top-notch, wristwatch, butterscotch

otchet \äch-ət\ crotchet, rochet

otchman \äch-mən\ Scotchman, watchman

otchy \äch-ē\ blotchy, boccie, botchy, splotchy, hibachi, huarache, huisache, Karachi, vivace, mariachi

¹ote \ōt-ē\ dhoti, floaty, loti, roti, throaty, cenote, coyote, chayote, peyote, quixote

²ote \ōt\ see OAT

³ote \ät\ see ¹OT

otea \ōt-ē-ə\ protea, scotia

oted \ōt-əd\ see OATED

otem \ōt-əm\ see OTUM

oten \ōt-ⁿn\ see OTON

oter \ōt-ər\ see OATER

oterie \ōt-ə-rē\ see OTARY

¹oth \äth\ broth, cloth, froth, Goth, moth, sloth, swath, troth, wroth, betroth, breechcloth, broadcloth, cheesecloth, dishcloth, facecloth, floorcloth, loincloth, Naboth, oilcloth, sackcloth, sailcloth, washcloth, Alioth, behemoth, Ostrogoth, tablecloth, Visigoth

²oth \ōs\ see ¹OSE

³oth \ōt\ see OAT

⁴oth \ōth\ see OWTH

othal \ōth-əl\ see OTHEL

othe \ōth\ clothe, loathe,

betroth, unclothe

othel \ōth-əl\ brothel, betrothal

¹other \əth-ər\ brother, mother, nother, other, rather, smother, tother, another, foremother, godmother, grandmother, housemother, stepbrother, stepmother

²other \äth-ər\ see ¹ATHER

otherly \əth-ər-lē\ brotherly, motherly, southerly, grandmotherly

othes \ōz\ see ²OSE

othesis \äth-ə-səs\ prothesis, hypothesis

othic \äth-ik\ gothic, neo-Gothic, Ostrogothic, Visigothic

othing \ō-thiŋ\ clothing, loathing, underclothing—*also* -ing *forms of verbs listed at* OTHE

otho \ō-thō\ see ¹OTO

¹oti \ōt-ē\ see ¹OTE

²oti \ôt-ē\ see AUGHTY

¹otia \ō-shə\ scotia, Scotia, agnosia, dystocia, Cappadocia, Nova Scotia

²otia \ōt-ē-ə\ see OTEA

otiable \ō-shə-bəl\ see OCIABLE

otiant \ō-shənt\ see OTIENT

¹otic \ät-ik\ Scotic, aquatic, biotic, chaotic, demotic, despotic, erotic, exotic, hypnotic, narcotic, necrotic, neurotic, Nilotic, osmotic, psychotic, quixotic, robotic, sclerotic, semiotic, abiotic, anecdotic, asymptotic, bibliotic, embryotic, epiglottic, homeotic, Huguenotic, idiotic, macrobiotic, melanotic, patriotic, posthypnotic, sanculottic, symbiotic, antibiotic, autoerotic, compatriotic, homoerotic

²otic \ŏt-ik\ lotic, photic, aphotic, aprotic, dichotic, robotic

³otic \ŏt-ik\ see AUTIC

otica \ät-i-kə\ erotica, exotica

otice \ŏt-əs\ see OTUS

otics \ät-iks\ robotics, astronautics, bibliotics—*also* -s, -'s, *and* -s' *forms of nouns listed at* ¹OTIC

otid \ät-əd\ see OTTED

otient \ō-shənt\ quotient, negotiant

otile \ŏt-ᵊl\ see OTAL

¹oting \ŏt-iŋ\ see OATING

²oting \ät-iŋ\ see OTTING

¹otinous \ät-nəs\ see OTNESS

²otinous \ät-ᵊn-əs\ see ¹OTONOUS

otion \ō-shən\ Goshen, groschen, lotion, motion, notion, ocean, potion, commotion, demotion, devotion, emotion, Laotian, promotion, slow-motion, locomotion

otional \ō-shnəl\ motional, notional, devotional, emotional, promotional, unemotional

otis \ŏt-əs\ see OTUS

otist \ŏt-əst\ protist, Scotist, anecdotist

otive \ŏt-iv\ motive, votive, emotive, promotive, automotive, locomotive

otl \ät-ᵊl\ see OTTLE

otle \ät-ᵊl\ see OTTLE

otley \ät-lē\ see OTLY

otly \ät-lē\ Atli, hotly, motley

otment \ät-mənt\ allotment, ballottement

otness \ät-nəs\ hotness, squatness

oto \ō-tō\ koto, photo, roto,

Sotho, Basotho. con moto, de Soto, ex-voto, in toto, Kyoto, Lesotho, Mosotho, Sesotho, Kumamoto, telephoto

otomous \ät-ə-məs\ dichotomous, hippopotamus

otomy \ät-ə-mē\ dichotomy, lobotomy, tracheotomy, episiotomy

oton \ŏt-ᵊn\ croton, Jotun, oaten, Lofoten, verboten

¹otonous \ät-ᵊn-əs\ rottenness, monotonous, serotinous

²otonous \ät-nəs\ see OTNESS

otor \ŏt-ər\ see OATER

otorist \ŏt-ə-rəst\ see OTARIST

otory \ŏt-ə-rē\ see OTARY

ots \äts\ Graz, hots, lots, Scots, Spaatz, swats, ersatz, Galati—*also* -s, -'s, *and* -s' *forms of nouns listed at* ¹OT, *and* -s *forms of verbs listed there*

otsk \ätsk\ see ATSK

otsman \ät-smən\ Scotsman, yachtsman

ott \ät\ see ¹OT

otta \ät-ə\ see ¹ATA

ottage \ät-ij\ cottage, plottage, pottage, wattage

ottal \ät-ᵊl\ see OTTLE

¹otte \ät\ see ¹OT

²otte \ŏt\ see ¹OUGHT

otted \ät-əd\ knotted, potted, spotted, carotid, proglottid, polka-dotted—*also* -ed *forms of verbs listed at* ¹OT

ottement \ät-mənt\ see OTMENT

otten \ät-ᵊn\ cotton, gotten, gratin, ratton, rotten, shotten, au gratin, begotten, forgotten, guncotton, ill-gotten, misbegotten, sauerbraten

ottenness \ät-ᵊn-əs\ see ¹OTONOUS

otter \ät-ər\ blotter, cotter, daughter, dotter, knotter, otter, plotter, potter, Potter, Qatar, rotter, spotter, squatter, swatter, Tatar, totter, trotter, water, alotter, backwater, bathwater, blackwater, boycotter, breakwater, cutwater, dewater, deepwater, dishwater, firewater, floodwater, flyswatter, freshwater, garroter, globe-trotter, goddaughter, groundwater, headwater, jerkwater, limewater, meltwater, pinspotter, rainwater, rosewater, saltwater, sandlotter, sea otter, seawater, shearwater, springwater, tailwater, tidewater, wastewater, alma mater, imperator, milk-and-water, polywater, teeter-totter, underwater—*also -er forms of adjectives listed at* ¹OT

ottery \ät-ə-rē\ lottery, pottery, Tatary, tottery, watery

ottic \ät-ik\ see ¹OTIC

ottid \ät-əd\ see OTTED

ottie \ät-ē\ see ATI

otting \ät-iŋ\ jotting, wainscoting—*also -ing forms of verbs listed at* ¹ot

ottis \ät-əs\ glottis, clematis, epiglottis, literatus

ottische \ät-ish\ see OTTISH

ottish \ät-ish\ hottish, schottische, Scottish, sottish, sanculottish

ottle \ät-ᵊl\ bottle, dottle, glottal, mottle, pottle, ratel, rotl, throttle, wattle, atlatl, bluebottle, Aristotle, monocotyl, Nahuatl, epiglottal, Quetzalcoatl

¹**otto** \ät-ō\ see ¹ATO

²**otto** \ot-ō\ see ¹AUTO

ottom \ät-əm\ see ¹ATUM

otty \ät-ē\ see ATI

otum \ōt-əm\ notum, scrotum, totem, factotum, teetotum

otun \ōt-ᵊn\ see OTON

oture \ō-chər\ see OACHER

otus \ōt-əs\ lotus, notice, Otis, denotice, Pelotas

oty \ot-ē\ see ¹AUGHTY

otyl \ät-ᵊl\ see OTTLE

¹**ou** \ō\ see ¹OW

²**ou** \ü\ see ¹EW

³**ou** \au̇\ see ²OW

oubled \ə-bəld\ see UBBLED

ouble \əb-əl\ see UBBLE

oubler \əb-lər\ doubler, bubbler, troubler

oubly \əb-lē\ see UBBLY

oubt \au̇t\ see ³OUT

oubted \au̇t-əd\ see OUTED

oubter \au̇t-ər\ see ²OUTER

¹**ouc** \ü\ see ¹EW

²**ouc** \ük\ see UKE

³**ouc** \u̇k\ see ¹OOK

ouce \üs\ see ¹USE

¹**oucester** \äs-tər\ see ¹OSTER

²**oucester** \os-tər\ see ²OSTER

¹**ouch** \üch\ see ¹OOCH

²**ouch** \üsh\ see OUCHE

³**ouch** \əch\ see ¹UTCH

⁴**ouch** \au̇ch\ couch, crouch, grouch, ouch, pouch, slouch, vouch, avouch, debouch, scaramouch, retort pouch

ouche \üsh\ douche, louche, ruche, squoosh, swoosh, whoosh, barouche, capuche, cartouche, debouch, farouche, kurus, tarboosh, scaramouch

¹**ouchy** \ch-ē\ see UCHY

²**ouchy** \au̇-chē\ grouchy, pouchy, slouchy

ou'd \üd\ see UDE

¹**oud** \üd\ see UDE

²**oud** \au̇d\ boughed, bowed, cloud, crowd, loud, proud, shroud, stroud, aloud, becloud, enshroud, highbrowed, house-proud, purse-proud, Red Cloud, unbowed, overcrowd, thundercloud—*also* -ed *forms of verbs listed at* ²OW

ouda \üd-ə\ see UDA

oudy \au̇d-ē\ see OWDY

oue \ü\ see ¹EW

ouf \üf\ see ¹OOF

ouffe \üf\ see ¹OOF

oug \əg\ see UG

¹**ouge** \üj\ see ¹UGE

²**ouge** \üzh\ see ²UGE

³**ouge** \au̇j\ gouge, scrouge

¹**ough** \ō\ see ¹OW

²**ough** \ü\ see ¹EW

³**ough** \au̇\ see ²OW

⁴**ough** \äk\ see ¹OCK

⁵**ough** \əf\ see UFF

⁶**ough** \óf\ see ²OFF

¹**ougham** \ōm\ see ¹OME

²**ougham** \üm\ see ¹OOM

oughed \au̇d\ see ²OUD

oughen \əf-ən\ see UFFIN

ougher \əf-ər\ see UFFER

oughie \əf-ē\ see UFFY

oughish \əf-ish\ see UFFISH

oughly \əf-lē\ see UFFLY

oughs \ōz\ see ²OSE

¹**ought** \ót\ aught, bought, brought, caught, dot, fought, fraught, ghat, lotte, naught, nought, ought, sought, taught, taut, thought, wrought, besought, distraught, dreadnought, forethought, handwrought, high-wrought, onslaught,

self-taught, store-bought, unthought, aeronaut, aforethought, afterthought, aquanaut, argonaut, astronaut, cosmonaut, juggernaut, overbought, overwrought

²**ought** \au̇t\ see ³OUT

oughten \ót-ᵊn\ see AUTEN

oughty \au̇t-ē\ doughty, droughty, gouty, pouty, snouty, trouty

¹**oughy** \ō-ē\ see OWY

²**oughy** \ü-ē\ see EWY

ouie \ü-ē\ see EWY

ouille \ü-ē\ see EWY

¹**ouis** \ü-ē\ see EWY

²**ouis** \ü-əs\ lewis, Lewis, Louis, Luis, Port Louis, Saint Louis

ouk \ük\ see UKE

ouki \ü-kē\ see ¹OOKY

¹**oul** \ōl\ see ¹OLE

²**oul** \ül\ see ¹OOL

³**oul** \au̇l\ see ²OWL

¹**ould** \ōld\ see ¹OLD

²**ould** \ud\ see ¹OOD

oulder \ōl-dər\ see ¹OLDER

ouldered \ōl-dərd\ bouldered, shouldered, round-shouldered, square-shouldered—*also* -ed *forms of verbs listed at* ¹OLDER

ouldest \ud-əst\ couldest, shouldest, wouldest, Talmudist

ouldn't \ud-ᵊnt\ shouldn't, wouldn't

¹**oule** \ü-lē\ see ULY

²**oule** \ül\ see ¹OOL

ouled \ōld\ see ¹OLD

oulee \ü-lē\ see ULY

¹**ouleh** \ü-lə\ see ULA

²**ouleh** \ü-lē\ see ULY

ouli \ü-lē\ see ULY

oulie \ü-lē\ see ULY

ouling \au̇-liŋ\ see ²OWLING

oulish \ü-lish\ see OOLISH

¹ou'll \ül\ see ¹OOL

²ou'll \úl\ see ¹UL

oulle \ül\ see ¹OOL

oulli \ü-lē\ see ULY

oully \aú-lē\ see ²OWLY

oult \ōlt\ see ¹OLT

oulter \ōl-tər\ see OLTER

oum \üm\ see ¹OOM

oumenal \ü-mən-ᵊl\ see UMINAL

¹oun \aún\ see ²OWN

²oun \ün\ see ¹OON

ounce \aúns\ bounce, flounce, jounce, ounce, pounce, trounce, announce, denounce, enounce, pronounce, renounce, mispronounce

ouncement \aún-smənt\ announcement, denouncement, pronouncement

ouncer \aún-sər\ bouncer, announcer

ouncil \aún-səl\ see OUNSEL

ouncy \aún-sē\ bouncy, flouncy, jouncy, viscountcy

¹ound \ünd\ stound, swound, wound—also -ed forms of verbs listed at ¹OON

²ound \aúnd\ bound, crowned, found, ground, hound, mound, pound, Pound, round, sound, stound, swound, wound, abound, aground, all-round, around, astound, background, black-crowned, bloodhound, campground, chowhound, compound, confound, coonhound, dachshund, deerhound, deskbound, earthbound, eastbound, elkhound, expound, fairground, fogbound, foot-pound,

foreground, foxhound, go-round, greyhound, hardbound, hellhound, hidebound, homebound, horehound, housebound, icebound, impound, inbound, newfound, northbound, outbound, playground, pot-bound, profound, propound, rebound, redound, resound, rockbound, snowbound, softbound, southbound, spellbound, stone-ground, stormbound, strikebound, surround, unbound, well-found, westbound, white-crowned, wolfhound, year-round, aboveground, all-around, belowground, battleground, decompound, go-around, muscle-bound, outward-bound, paperbound, Puget Sound, runaround, turnaround, ultrasound, underground, weather-bound, wraparound, merry-go-round, superabound—also -ed forms of verbs listed at ²OWN

oundal \aún-dᵊl\ poundal, roundel

oundary \aún-drē\ see OUNDRY

ounded \aún-dəd\ drownded, rounded, confounded, unbounded, unfounded, well-founded, well-grounded

oundel \aún-dᵊl\ see OUNDAL

ounder \aún-dər\ bounder, flounder, founder, grounder, hounder, pounder, rounder, sounder, all-rounder, backgrounder, compounder, confounder, dumbfounder, tenpounder

ounding \aún-diŋ\ drownding,

grounding, sounding, astounding, high-sounding, rockhounding—*also* -ing *forms of verbs listed at* ²OUND

¹**oundless** \ün-ləs\ *see* OONLESS

²**oundless** \aùn-ləs\ groundless, soundless

oundlet \aùn-lət\ *see* OWNLET

oundling \aùn-liŋ\ foundling, groundling

oundly \aùnd-lē\ roundly, soundly

oundness \aùn-nəs\ roundness, unsoundness

oundry \aùn-drē\ boundary, foundry

¹**ounds** \ünz\ *see* OONS

²**ounds** \aùnz\ hounds, zounds, inbounds, Barren Grounds, out-of-bounds— *also* -s, -'s, *and* -s' *forms of nouns listed at* ²OUND, *and* -s *forms of verbs listed there*

oundsel \aùn-səl\ *see* OUNSEL

oundsman \aùnz-mən\ *see* OWNSMAN

ounge \aùnj\ lounge, scrounge, chaise lounge

¹**ounger** \aùn-jər\ lounger, scrounger

²**ounger** \əŋ-gər\ *see* ¹ONGER

ounker \əŋ-kər\ *see* UNKER

ounsel \aùn-səl\ council, counsel, groundsel

¹**ount** \änt\ *see* ²ANT

²**ount** \aùnt\ count, fount, mount, account, amount, demount, discount, dismount, high-count, miscount, recount, remount, seamount, surmount, viscount, catamount, paramount, rediscount, tantamount, undercount

ountable \aùnt-ə-bəl\ countable, accountable,

demountable, discountable, surmountable, insurmountable, unaccountable

ountain \aùnt-³n\ fountain, mountain, transmountain, cat-a-mountain, Riding Mountain

ountcy \aùnt-sē\ *see* OUNCY

ounter \aùnt-ər\ counter, mounter, discounter, encounter, recounter, rencounter

ountess \aùnt-əs\ countess, viscountess

ountie \aùnt-ē\ *see* OUNTY

ounting \aùnt-iŋ\ mounting, accounting—*also* -ing *forms of verbs listed at* ²OUNT

ounty \aùnt-ē\ bounty, county, Mountie, viscounty

¹**oup** \ōp\ *see* OPE

²**oup** \ü\ *see* ¹EW

³**oup** \üp\ *see* OOP

¹**oupe** \ōp\ *see* OPE

²**oupe** \üp\ *see* OOP

ouper \ü-pər\ *see* OOPER

oupie \ü-pē\ *see* OOPY

ouping \ü-piŋ\ *see* OOPING

ouple \əp-əl\ *see* ¹UPLE

ouplet \əp-lət\ *see* ¹UPLET

oupous \ü-pəs\ *see* UPUS

oupy \ü-pē\ *see* OOPY

¹**our** \ór\ *see* ¹OR

²**our** \ùr\ *see* ¹URE

³**our** \aùr\ *see* ²OWER

⁴**our** \är\ *see* ³AR

⁵**our** \ər\ *see* ¹EUR

oura \ùr-ə\ *see* URA

ourable \ór-ə-bəl\ *see* ORABLE

ourage \ər-ij\ courage, demurrage, discourage, encourage

¹**ourbon** \ər-bən\ *see* ¹URBAN

ourbon \ùr-bən\ *see* ²URBAN

ource \órs\ *see* ¹ORSE

ourceful \órs-fəl\ see
ORSEFUL

ourcing \ór-siŋ\
outsourcing—*also* -ing
forms of verbs listed at
¹ORSE

ourd \órd\ see OARD

ourde \ùrd\ see ¹URED

¹**ou're** \ór\ see ¹OR

²**ou're** \ü-ər\ see ¹EWER

³**ou're** \ùr\ see ¹URE

⁴**ou're** \ər\ see ¹EUR

oured \órd\ see OARD

¹**ourer** \ór-ər\ see ORER

²**ourer** \ùr-ər\ see ¹URER

³**ourer** \aùr-ər\ flowerer,
scourer, showerer,
deflowerer, devourer—*also*
-er *forms of adjectives listed
at* ²OWER

¹**ourg** \ùr\ see ¹URE

²**ourg** \ərg\ see ERG

¹**ourge** \ərj\ see URGE

²**ourge** \órj\ see ORGE

ourger \ər-jər\ see ERGER

ouri \ùr-ē\ see ¹URY

¹**ourier** \ùr-ē-ər\ courier,
couturier, couturiere, vaunt-
courier

²**ourier** \ər-ē-ər\ see URRIER

¹**ouring** \ór-iŋ\ see ORING

²**ouring** \ùr-iŋ\ see URING

ourish \ər-ish\ currish,
flourish, nourish, amateurish

ourist \ùr-əst\ see URIST

ourly \aùr-lē\ dourly, hourly,
sourly

¹**ourn** \órn\ see ¹ORN

²**ourn** \ərn\ see URN

ournal \ərn-ᵊl\ see ERNAL

ournament \ór-nə-mənt\ see
ORNAMENT

ourne \órn\ see ¹ORN

¹**ourney** \ər-nē\ Bernie, Ernie,
ferny, gurney, journey,
tourney, attorney

²**ourney** \ór-nē\ see ORNY

ourneyer \ər-nē-ər\
journeyer, vernier

ournful \órn-fəl\ see ORNFUL

ourning \ór-niŋ\ see ORNING

ournment \ərn-mənt\ see
ERNMENT

¹**ours** \órz\ see OORS

²**ours** \ärz\ see ARS

³**ours** \aùrz\ ours, after-
hours—*also* -s, -'s, *and* -s'
forms of nouns listed at
²OWER, *and* -s *forms of verbs
listed there*

⁴**ours** \ùr\ see ¹URE

ourse \órs\ see ¹ORSE

oursome \ór-səm\ see ORSUM

¹**ourt** \órt\ see ¹ORT

²**ourt** \ùrt\ see ¹URT

ourtesy \ərt-ə-sē\ courtesy,
curtesy, discourtesy

ourth \órth\ see ¹ORTH

ourtier \ór-chər\ see ORCHER

ourtly \órt-lē\ see ORTLY

oury \aùr-ē\ see OWERY

¹**ous** \ü\ see ¹EW

²**ous** \üs\ see ¹USE

¹**ousa** \ü-sə\ see ¹USA

²**ousa** \ü-zə\ see ²USA

ousal \aù-zəl\ housel, spousal,
tousle, arousal, carousal

ousand \aùz-ᵊn\ see OWSON

¹**ouse** \üs\ see ¹USE

²**ouse** \aùs\ blouse, chiaus,
chouse, douse, Gauss,
grouse, house, Klaus, Laos,
louse, mouse, scouse, souse,
spouse, Strauss, baghouse,
bathhouse, Bauhaus,
birdhouse, blockhouse,
bughouse, bunkhouse,
cathouse, chophouse,
clubhouse, cookhouse,
courthouse, deckhouse,
degauss, delouse, doghouse,
dollhouse, dormouse,
espouse, farmhouse,
firehouse, flophouse,

gashouse, gatehouse, glasshouse, greenhouse, guardhouse, henhouse, hothouse, icehouse, in-house, jailhouse, lighthouse, lobscouse, longhouse, madhouse, Manaus, nuthouse, outhouse, penthouse, playhouse, poorhouse, roadhouse, roughhouse, roundhouse, schoolhouse, smokehouse, springhouse, statehouse, storehouse, teahouse, titmouse, tollhouse, warehouse, washhouse, wheelhouse, White House, whorehouse, workhouse, boardinghouse, clearinghouse, coffeehouse, countinghouse, customhouse, house-to-house, meetinghouse, Mickey Mouse, overblouse, pilothouse, porterhouse, powerhouse, slaughterhouse, sugarhouse, summerhouse, treasure-house, Westinghouse

³ouse \aúz\ blouse, bouse, bowse, browse, douse, dowse, drowse, house, mouse, rouse, spouse, touse, arouse, carouse, delouse, doss-house, espouse, rehouse, roughhouse, warehouse—*also* -s, -'s, *and* -s' *forms of nouns listed at* **²OW,** *and* -s *forms of verbs listed there*

⁴ouse \üz\ see **²USE**

ousel \aú-zəl\ see **OUSAL**

ouser \aú-zər\ dowser, houser, mouser, schnauzer, trouser, wowser, carouser, espouser, warehouser, rabble-rouser

ousin \əz-ᵊn\ see **¹OZEN**

ousinage \əz-ᵊn-ij\ cousinage, cozenage

ousing \aú-ziŋ\ housing, rousing, rabble-rousing—*also* -ing *forms of verbs listed at* **³OUSE**

¹ousle \ü-zəl\ see **²USAL**

²ousle \aú-zəl\ see **OUSAL**

ousse \üs\ see **¹USE**

ousseau \ü-sō\ see **USOE**

¹oust \aúst\ Faust, joust, oust, roust—*also* -ed *forms of verbs listed at* **²OUSE**

²oust \üst\ see **OOST**

ouste \üst\ see **OOST**

¹ousy \aú-zē\ see **OWSY**

²ousy \aú-sē\ mousy, Firdawsi

¹out \ü\ see **¹EW**

²out \üt\ see **UTE**

³out \aút\ bout, clout, doubt, drought, flout, glout, gout, grout, knout, kraut, lout, out, pout, rout, route, scout, shout, snout, spout, sprout, stout, tout, trout, ablaut, about, all-out, bailout, blackout, blissed-out, blowout, breakout, breechclout, brownout, burned-out, burnout, checkout, clapped-out, closeout, cookout, cop-out, cutout, devout, dishclout, downspout, dropout, dugout, eelpout, fade-out, fallout, far-out, flameout, flat-out, foldout, force-out, freak-out, freeze out, full-out, gross-out, groundout, handout, hangout, hideout, holdout, ice-out, knockout, layout, lights-out, lockout, lookout, misdoubt, payout, phaseout, pitchout, printout, psych-out, pullout, punch-out, putout, rainspout, readout,

redoubt, rollout, sellout,
setout, shakeout, shoot-out,
shutout, sick-out, sold-out,
spaced-out, speak-out,
spinout, stakeout, standout,
straight-out, stressed-out,
stretch-out, strikeout,
takeout, thought-out,
throughout, throw out, time-
out, tryout, turnout, umlaut,
veg out, walkout, washed-
out, washout, way-out,
whacked-out, whiteout,
wigged-out, wipeout, without,
workout, worn-out, zonked-
out, all get-out, carryout,
diner-out, down-and-out,
falling-out, gadabout,
hereabout, knockabout,
layabout, out-and-out,
roundabout, rouseabout,
roustabout, runabout,
sauerkraut, stirabout,
thereabout, turnabout,
walkabout, waterspout

¹oute \üt\ see UTE

²oute \aút\ see ³OUT

outed \aút-əd\ snouted,
spouted, undoubted—*also*
-ed *forms of verbs listed at*
³OUT

¹outer \üt-ər\ see UTER

²outer \aút-ər\ doubter,
flouter, grouter, outer,
pouter, router, scouter,
shouter, spouter, touter,
come-outer, down-and-outer,
out-and-outer—*also -er forms
of adjectives listed at* ³OUT

¹outh \üth\ see ²OOTH

²outh \aúth\ mouth, routh,
scouth, south, bad-mouth,
goalmouth, loudmouth, poor-
mouth, blabbermouth,
cottonmouth, hand-to-
mouth, motormouth, word-
of-mouth

outherly \əth-ər-lē\ see
OTHERLY

outhey \aú-thē\ see OUTHY

outhful \üth-fəl\ see UTHFUL

outhie \ü-thē\ see OOTHY

outhly \üth-lē\ see OOTHLY

outhy \aú-thē\ mouthy,
Southey

outi \üt-ē\ see ¹OOTY

outing \aút-iŋ\ outing,
scouting—*also -ing forms of
verbs listed at* ³OUT

outish \aút-ish\ loutish,
snoutish

outre \üt-ər\ see UTER

outrement \ü-trə-mənt\ see
UTRIMENT

outs \aúts\ hereabouts, ins
and outs, thereabouts,
whereabouts

outy \aút-ē\ see OUGHTY

ou've \üv\ see ³OVE

ouver \ü-vər\ see ³OVER

oux \ü\ see ¹EW

ouy \ē\ see ¹EE

ouyhnhnm \in-əm\ see INIM

ouzel \ü-zəl\ see ²USAL

¹ov \äf\ see ¹OFF

²ov \óf\ see ²OFF

ova \ō-və\ nova, Cralova,
Jehovah, Moldova, bossa
nova, Casanova,
Czestochowa, Kemerovo,
supernova

ovable \ü-və-bəl\ movable,
provable, approvable,
disprovable, immovable,
improvable, removable,
irremovable

ovah \ō-və\ see OVA

oval \ü-vəl\ approval,
removal, disapproval

ovat \ō-ət\ see OVET

¹ove \əv\ dove, glove, love, of,
shove, above, foxglove,
hereof, kid-glove, ringdove,
thereof, truelove, whereof,

ladylove, light-o'-love,
roman-fleuve, turtledove,
unheard of, well-thought-of,
hereinabove

²ove \ōv\ clove, cove, dove,
drove, fauve, grove, hove,
Jove, mauve, rove, stove,
strove, throve, trove, wove,
alcove, behove, cookstove,
mangrove, woodstove,
Garden Grove, interwove,
treasure trove

³ove \üv\ groove, move, poof,
prove, you've, approve,
behoove, commove,
disprove, improve, remove,
reprove, disapprove

¹ovel \äv-əl\ grovel, novel,
antinovel, Yaroslavl

²ovel \əv-əl\ grovel, hovel,
shovel

ovement \üv-mənt\
movement, improvement

¹oven \əv-ən\ coven, oven,
sloven

²oven \ō-vən\ cloven, coven,
woven, Beethoven,
handwoven, interwoven

¹over \əv-ər\ cover, glover,
hover, lover, plover,
bedcover, discover,
dustcover, hardcover, re-
cover, recover, slipcover,
softcover, uncover,
windhover, undercover

²over \ō-vər\ clover, Dover,
drover, Grover, over, plover,
rover, stover, trover, allover,
changeover, crossover,
cutover, flashover, flopover,
flyover, hangover,
Hannover, Hanover,
holdover, layover, leftover,
makeover, moreover, once-
over, Passover, popover,
pullover, pushover, rollover,
runover, slipover, spillover,

stopover, strikeover,
takeover, turnover, voice-
over, walkover, warmed-
over, carryover, crossing-
over, going-over, Strait of
Dover

³over \ü-vər\ groover,
Hoover, louver, mover,
prover, earthmover,
improver, maneuver,
remover, reprover,
Vancouver, disapprover

⁴over \äv-ər\ see ¹AVER

overable \əv-rə-bəl\
discoverable, recoverable,
irrecoverable

overly \əv-ər-lē\ loverly, Sir
Roger de Coverley

overt \ō-vərt\ covert, overt

overy \əv-rē\ discovery,
recovery

ovet \əv-ət\ covet, lovat

ovey \ə-vē\ covey, lovey-
dovey

ovian \ō-vē-ən\ Jovian,
Markovian, Pavlovian,
Varsovian

ovie \ü-vē\ see OOVY

ovo \ō-vō\ Provo, ab ovo, de
novo, Porto Novo

ovost \äv-əst\ see AVIST

ovsk \ófsk\ Dnepropetrovsk,
Petropavlovsk

¹ow \ō\ beau, blow, bow,
bro, Chou, crow, do, doe,
dough, ewe, floe, flow, foe,
fro, froe, frow, glow, go,
grow, ho, hoe, jo, Jo, joe,
Joe, know, lo, low, mho,
mot, mow, no, No, O, oh,
owe, Po, Poe, pow, pro,
rho, roe, row, schmo, sew,
shew, show, sloe, slow,
snow, so, sow, stow, Stowe,
strow, though, throe,
throw, toe, tow, trow,
whoa, woe, yo, aglow, ago,

airflow, airglow, alow,
although, backflow,
backhoe, bandeau, Baotou,
barlow, bateau, below,
bestow, bon mot, Bordeaux,
bravo, by-blow, cachepot,
caló, Carlow, chapeau,
chateau, Chi-Rho, cockcrow,
cornrow, crossbow, Day-Glo,
dayglow, Defoe, de trop,
deathblow, deco, down-bow,
elbow, escrow, fencerow,
flambeau, flyblow, fogbow,
forego, foreknow, forgo,
Fuzhou, galop, Gateau,
genro, gigot, go-slow,
Gounod, Guangzhou, gung
ho, hallo, Hangzhou,
Hankow, heave-ho,
hedgerow, heigh-ho, hello,
hollo, hullo, inflow, jabot,
Jane Doe, jim crow, Jinzhou,
John Doe, Hounslow, kayo,
KO, Kwangchow, Lanzhou,
longbow, low-low, macho,
mahoe, maillot, manteau,
Marlowe, matelot, merlot,
Meursault, Miró, misknow,
Moho, mojo, Monroe,
morceau, Moscow, mucro,
mudflow, nightglow, no-no,
no-show, nouveau, outflow,
outgo, outgrow, oxbow,
Paot'ou, Pernod, picot,
Pinot, plateau, pronto,
Quanzhou, rainbow, reflow,
regrow, repo, reseau,
rondeau, rondo, Roseau,
rouleau, Rousseau, sabot,
salchow, scarecrow, self-sow,
serow, shadblow, Shantou,
sideshow, skid row, Soho, so-
so, sourdough, sunbow,
Suzhou, tableau, Taizhou,
tiptoe, Thoreau, tonneau,
trousseau, Trudeau, uh-oh,
unsew, up-bow, upthrow,

van Gogh, Watteau,
windrow, windthrow,
Xuzhou, Zhangzhou,
Zhengzhou, Zhuzhon, Zibo,
afterglow, aikido, alpenglow,
Angelo, apropos, art deco,
art nouveau, audio, Baguio,
Bamako, barrio, Bergamo,
bibelot, Bilbao, bordereau,
Borneo, buffalo, Buffalo,
bungalow, Bushido, buteo,
calico, cameo, cachalot,
cembalo, centimo, CEO,
chassepot, cheerio, Cicero,
Clemenceau, cogito,
comedo, comme il faut,
Comoro, counterflow,
curaçao, Curaçao, curassow,
curio, daimyo, danio,
dataflow, Delano, Diderot,
do-si-do, domino, dynamo,
embryo, entrepôt, Erato,
escargot, Eskimo, extrados,
fabliau, folio, fricandeau,
furbelow, gigolo, go-no-go,
guacharo, hammertoe,
haricot, heel-and-toe, hetero,
HMO, Holy Joe, Idaho,
indigo, Jericho, kakapo,
Kosciuszko, latigo, long-ago,
Maceió, Manchukuo, Mario,
massicot, medico, Mexico,
mistletoe, modulo, Monaco,
Navaho, Navajo, NCO,
nuncio, oleo, olio, overflow,
overgrow, overthrow, ovolo,
Pamlico, Papago, patio,
peridot, picaro, piccolo,
Pierrot, polio, pomelo,
pompano, portico, PPO,
Prospero, proximo, quid pro
quo, radio, raree-show, ratio,
Richard Roe, Rochambeau,
rococo, rodeo, Romeo,
saddlebow, Sapporo,
sapsago, Scorpio, semipro,
sloppy joe, so-and-so, SRO,

standing O, status quo, stereo, stop-and-go, studio, subito, tallyho, tangelo, Taranto, ticktacktoe, tic-tac-toe, tit-tat-toe, TKO, to-and-fro, Tokyo, tombolo, touch-and-go, touraco, tournedos, tremolo, tuckahoe, tupelo, UFO, ultimo, undergo, undertow, Veneto, vertigo, vibrio, virago, vireo, zydeco, Antonio, Arapaho, centesimo, con spirito, continuo, DMSO, Etobicoke, ex nihilo, fantastico, fellatio, Fernando Póo, fortissimo, Geronimo, get-up-and-go, Guantanamo, hereinbelow, in utero, in vacuo, La Rochefoucauld, lentissimo, lothario, magnifico, malapropos, milesimo, New Mexico, oregano, politico, portfolio, presidio, prestissimo, punctilio, Querétaro, Quintana Roo, Rosario, quo warranto, Sarajevo, scenario, simpatico, Zhangjiakou, ab initio, archipelago, braggadocio, duodecimo, ex officio, generalissimo, impresario, internuncio, oratorio, Paramaribo, pianissimo, rose of Jericho

²ow \aú\ bough, bow, brow, chiao, chow, ciao, cow, dhow, Dou, dow, Dow, Frau, hao, how, howe, Howe, jow, Lao, mow, now, ow, plow, pow, prau, prow, row, scow, slough, sough, sow, Tao, tau, thou, vow, wow, Yao, allow, avow, Belau, Bissau, bowwow, cacao, cahow, Callao, Davao, chowchow, chow chow, Cracow, Donau,

endow, enow, erenow, eyebrow, gangplow, Haikou, Hankow, hausfrau, haymow, highbrow, hoosegow, Jungfrau, know-how, kowtow, Krakow, landau, lowbrow, luau, Lucknow, Macao, meow, miaow, Moscow, Niihau, nohow, Pelau, powwow, Qing-dao, snowplow, somehow, Zwickau, anyhow, curaçao, Curaçao, disallow, disavow, disendow, middlebrow, Guinea-Bissau, Marianao, Mindanao, holier-than-thou

³ow \óv\ see ²OFF

owa \ō-və\ see OVA

¹owable \ō-ə-bəl\ knowable, sewable, unknowable

²owable \aú-ə-bəl\ plowable, allowable, disavowable

owage \ō-ij\ flowage, stowage, towage

¹owal \ō-əl\ see OEL

²owal \aúl\ see ²OWL

¹owan \ō-ən\ see ¹OAN

²owan \aú-ən\ Gawain, gowan, rowan, rowen, Bandar Seri Begawan

¹oward \órd\ see OARD

²oward \aúrd\ see OWERED

¹owd \üd\ see UDE

²owd \aúd\ see ²OUD

owdah \aúd-ə\ see ³AUDE

owder \aúd-ər\ chowder, powder, gunpowder, five-spice powder—*also* -er *forms of adjectives listed at* ²OUD

owdown \ō-daún\ blowdown, lowdown, showdown, slowdown

owdy \aúd-ē\ cloudy, dowdy, howdy, rowdy, cum laude, pandowdy, magna cum laude, summa cum laude

owe \ō\ see ¹OW

¹**owed** \ōd\ see ODE

²**owed** \aud\ see ²OUD

owedly \au̇-əd-lē\ allowedly, avowedly

owel \au̇l\ see ²OWL

oweling \au̇-liŋ\ see ²OWLING

¹**owell** \au̇l\ see ²OWL

²**owell** \ō-əl\ see OEL

¹**owen** \au̇-ən\ see ²OWAN

²**owen** \ō-ən\ see ¹OAN

¹**ower** \o̊r\ see ¹OR

²**ower** \au̇r\ bower, cower, dour, dower, flour, flower, gaur, giaour, glower, hour, lower, our, plower, power, scour, shower, sour, tour, tower, vower, avower, cornflower, deflower, devour, embower, empower, firepower, high-power, man-hour, mayflower, moonflower, off-hour, pasqueflower, Peshawar, repower, safflower, sunflower, wallflower, watchtower, wildflower, willpower, candlepower, cauliflower, disendower, Eisenhower, overpower, passionflower, person-hour, Schopenhauer, superpower, sweet-and-sour, thundershower, waterpower, womanpower

³**ower** \ō-ər\ see ⁴OER

owered \au̇rd\ coward, flowered, powered, towered, high-powered, ivory-towered, superpowered, underpowered—*also* -ed *forms of verbs listed at* ²OWER

owerer \au̇r-ər\ see ³OURER

owerful \au̇r-fəl\ flowerful, powerful

owering \au̇-riŋ\ lowering, nonflowering—*also* -ing *forms of verbs listed at* ²OWER

owery \au̇r-ē\ bowery, cauri, dowry, floury, flowery, kauri, Maori, showery

owff \au̇f\ howff, langlauf

owhee \ō-ē\ see OWY

owie \au̇-ē\ Maui, zowie

owing \ō-iŋ\ see ¹OING

¹**owl** \ōl\ see ¹OLE

²**owl** \au̇l\ bowel, cowl, dowel, foul, fowl, growl, Howell, howl, jowl, owl, prowl, rowel, scowl, towel, trowel, vowel, yowl, avowal, batfowl, befoul, embowel, peafowl, seafowl, wildfowl, disavowal, disembowel, waterfowl

owland \ō-lənd\ lowland, Poland, Roland

owledge \äl-ij\ college, knowledge, acknowledge, foreknowledge

¹**owler** \ō-lər\ see OLLER

²**owler** \au̇-lər\ growler, howler, prowler, scowler, waterfowler

owless \ō-ləs\ see OLUS

owline \ō-lən\ see OLON

¹**owling** \ō-liŋ\ see OLLING

²**owling** \au̇-liŋ\ cowling, growling, howling, toweling, antifouling, biofouling, waterfowling—*also* -ing *forms of verbs listed at* ²OWL

owlock \äl-ək\ see OLOCH

¹**owly** \ō-lē\ see ¹OLY

²**owly** \au̇-lē\ foully, growly, jowly

¹**owman** \ō-mən\ see OMAN

²**owman** \au̇-mən\ bowman, cowman, plowman

ow-me \ō-mē\ see OAMY

¹**own** \ōn\ see ¹ONE

²**own** \au̇n\ brown, Brown, clown, crown, down, Down, drown, frown, gown, lown, noun, town, blowdown,

boomtown, breakdown,
Bridgetown, bringdown,
Capetown, clampdown,
closedown, comedown,
cooldown, countdown,
crackdown, crosstown,
downtown, drawdown,
embrown, facedown,
Freetown, Georgetown,
George Town, godown,
hoedown, hometown,
Jamestown, knockdown,
letdown, lockdown,
lookdown, lowdown,
markdown, meltdown,
nightgown, pastedown,
phasedown, pronoun,
pushdown, put-down,
renown, rubdown, rundown,
scale-down, shakedown,
showdown, shutdown, sit-
down, slowdown,
Southdown, splashdown,
stand-down, step-down,
stripped-down, sundown,
thumbs-down, tie-down, top-
down, touchdown,
turndown, uncrown,
uptown, Von Braun, write-
down, Youngstown,
Allentown, broken-down,
buttondown, Charlottetown,
Chinatown, dressing-down,
eiderdown, Germantown,
hand-me-down, reach-me-
down, shantytown,
tumbledown, upside down,
watered-down, man-about-
town

ownded \aún-dəd\ see
    OUNDED
ownding \aún-diŋ\ see
    OUNDING
¹**owned** \ōnd\ see ¹ONED
²**owned** \aúnd\ see ²OUND
¹**owner** \ō-nər\ see ¹ONER
²**owner** \ü-nər\ see OONER

³**owner** \aú-nər\ browner,
    crowner, downer, frowner,
    sundowner
owness \ō-nəs\ see ²ONUS
ownia \ō-nē-ə\ see ¹ONIA
ownie \aú-nē\ see OWNY
¹**owning** \ō-niŋ\ see ²ONING
²**owning** \aú-niŋ\
    Browning—also -ing forms of
    verbs listed at ²OWN
ownish \aú-nish\ brownish,
    clownish
ownlet \aún-lət\ roundlet,
    townlet
ownsman \aúnz-mən\
    gownsman, groundsman,
    roundsman, townsman
owny \aú-nē\ brownie,
    browny, downy, townie
owper \ü-pər\ see OOPER
owry \aúr-ē\ see OWERY
owse \aúz\ see ²OUSE
owser \aú-zər\ see OUSER
owson \aúz-ᵊn\ thousand,
    advowson
owster \ō-stər\ see OASTER
owsy \aú-zē\ blousy, blowsy,
    drowsy, lousy
owth \ōth\ both, growth,
    loath, loth, oath, quoth,
    sloth, troth, wroth, betroth,
    outgrowth, upgrowth,
    Alioth, intergrowth,
    overgrowth, undergrowth
owy \ō-ē\ blowy, Chloe,
    doughy, joey, Joey, showy,
    snowy, towhee, echoey,
    kalanchoe
owys \ō-əs\ see ²OIS
ox \äks\ box, cox, fox, Fox,
    gox, Knox, lox, ox, pax,
    phlox, pox, aurochs,
    bandbox, boondocks,
    cowpox, detox, dreadlocks,
    firebox, Fort Knox, gearbox,
    gravlax, hatbox, hotbox,
    icebox, jukebox, lockbox,

mailbox, matchbox, musk-ox, outfox, pillbox, postbox, redox, saltbox, sandbox, skybox, smallpox, snuffbox, soapbox, strongbox, sweatbox, toolbox, unbox, volvox, witness-box, workbox, Xerox, chatterbox, equinox, orthodox, Orthodox, paradox, pillarbox, shadowbox, Skinner box, tinderbox, econobox, Greek Orthodox, heterodox, homeobox, jack-in-the-box, unorthodox, neoorthodox, dementia praecox—*also* -s, -'s, *and* -s' *forms of nouns listed at* ¹OCK, *and* -s *forms of verbs listed there*

oxen \äk-sən\ oxen, Niedersachsen

oxer \äk-sər\ boxer, Boxer, bobby-soxer

oxie \äk-sē\ *see* OXY

oxin \äk-sən\ coxswain, tocsin, toxin, dioxin, aflatoxin, mycotoxin

oxswain \äk-sən\ *see* OXIN

oxy \äk-sē\ boxy, doxy, foxy, moxie, oxy, proxy, epoxy, orthodoxy, Orthodoxy, heterodoxy, neoorthodoxy

oy \öi\ boy, buoy, cloy, coy, foy, goy, hoy, joy, Joy, koi, ploy, poi, Roy, soy, strawy, toy, troy, Troy, ahoy, alloy, Amoy, annoy, batboy, bellboy, bok choy, borzoi, busboy, callboy, carboy, charpoy, choirboy, convoy, cowboy, decoy, deploy, destroy, doughboy, employ, enjoy, envoy, fly-boy, footboy, Hanoi, hautbois, highboy, houseboy, killjoy, Khoikhoi, Leroy, linkboy, lowboy, McCoy, newsboy,

pak choi, playboy, plowboy, po'boy, postboy, potboy, Quemoy, Rob Roy, Saint Croix, Savoy, schoolboy, sepoy, tallboy, teapoy, Tolstoy, tomboy, travois, viceroy, Adonai, attaboy, bullyboy, copyboy, corduroy, hoi polloi, Illinois, Iroquois, Kawagoe, maccaboy, Niterói, overjoy, paperboy, redeploy, reemploy, Tinkertoy, Helen of Troy

oya \öi-ə\ *see* OIA

oyable \öi-ə-bəl\ deployable, employable

¹oyal \īl\ *see* ¹ILE

²oyal \öil\ *see* OIL

oyalist \öi-ə-ləst\ loyalist, royalist

oyalty \öil-tē\ loyalty, royalty, disloyalty, viceroyalty

oyance \öi-əns\ buoyance, joyance, annoyance, chatoyance, clairvoyance, flamboyance

oyancy \öi-ən-sē\ buoyancy, chatoyancy, flamboyancy

oyant \öi-ənt\ buoyant, chatoyant, clairvoyant, flamboyant

oyce \ois\ *see* OICE

oyd \öid\ *see* ¹OID

oyden \öi-dᵊn\ Croydon, hoyden

oydon \öi-dᵊn\ *see* OYDEN

oyed \öid\ *see* ¹OID

oyen \öi-ən\ doyen, Goyen, Iroquoian

oyer \öir\ coir, foyer, moire, caloyer, destroyer

oyes \oiz\ *see* ²OISE

oying \öiŋ\ *see* AWING

oyle \öil\ *see* OIL

oyless \öi-ləs\ joyless, Troilus

oyment \öi-mənt\

deployment, employment,
enjoyment, unemployment
oyne \óin\ see ¹OIN
¹oyo \ói-ō\ boyo, arroyo
²oyo \ói-ə\ see OIA
o-yo \ō-yō\ see ²OLLO
oyster \ói-stər\ see OISTER
¹oz \əz\ see ¹EUSE
²oz \óz\ see ¹AUSE
³oz \ōz\ see ²OSE
oza \ō-zə\ see ²OSA
oze \ōz\ see ²OSE
¹ozen \əz-³n\ cousin, cozen,
dozen, cater-cousin

²ozen \ōz-³n\ see OSEN
ozenage \əz-³n-ij\ see
  OUSINAGE
ozer \ō-zər\ see ¹OSER
ozily \ō-zə-lē\ see OSILY
¹ozo \ō-sō\ see ¹OSO
²ozo \ō-zō\ see ²OSO
ozy \ō-zē\ see OSY
ozzer \äz-ər\ rozzer, alcazar
ozzle \äz-əl\ Basel, Basil,
  nozzle, schnozzle

U

¹u \ü\ see ¹EW

²u \ə\ Chang-de, Lao-tzu

¹ua \ü-ə\ skua, Karlsruhe, lehua, Quechua, Timucua

²ua \ä\ see ¹A

uable \ü-ə-bəl\ chewable, doable, suable, viewable, accruable, construable, renewable

ual \ü-əl\ see ¹UEL

uan \ü-ən\ bruin, ruin, Siouan, yuan

uancy \ü-ən-sē\ see UENCY

uant \ü-ənt\ see UENT

uart \ürt\ see ¹URT

ub \əb\ blub, chub, club, cub, drub, dub, flub, grub, hub, nub, pub, rub, scrub, shrub, slub, snub, stub, sub, tub, bathtub, flubdub, hubbub, nightclub, washtub, overdub, Beelzebub

uba \ü-bə\ Cuba, juba, scuba, tuba, Aruba, Santiago de Cuba

ubal \ü-bəl\ Jubal, nubile, ruble, tubal

uban \ü-bən\ see EUBEN

ubbard \əb-ərd\ cupboard, Mother Hubbard

ubber \əb-ər\ blubber, clubber, drubber, dubber, grubber, lubber, rubber, scrubber, slubber, snubber, tubber, landlubber, nightclubber, money-grubber

ubbery \əb-rē\ blubbery, rubbery, shrubbery

ubbily \əb-ə-lē\ bubbly, chubbily, grubbily

ubbin \əb-ən\ dubbin, nubbin

ubbing \əb-iŋ\ drubbing, rubbing, slubbing, landlubbing—*also* -ing *forms of verbs listed at* UB

ubble \əb-əl\ bubble, double, nubble, rubble, stubble, trouble, abubble, redouble, undouble, hubble-bubble

ubbled \ə-bəld\ bubbled, doubled, troubled, redoubled

ubbler \əb-lər\ see OUBLER

¹ubbly \əb-lē\ bubbly, doubly, nubbly, stubbly

²ubbly \əb-ə-lē\ see UBBILY

ubby \əb-ē\ chubby, clubby, cubby, grubby, hubby, nubby, Rabi, scrubby, shrubby, snubby, stubby, tubby

ube \üb\ boob, cube, lube, rube, tube, blowtube, Danube, flashcube, haboob, jujube, hypercube

uben \ü-bən\ see EUBEN

ubens \ü-bənz\ Rubens—*also* -s, -'s, *and* -s' *forms of nouns listed at* EUBEN

uber \ü-bər\ Buber, cuber, goober, tuber

uberance \ü-brəns\ exuberance, protuberance

uberant \ü-brənt\ exuberant, protuberant

uberous \ü-brəs\ see UBRIS

ubic \ü-bik\ cubic, pubic, cherubic

ubile \ü-bəl\ see UBAL

ubious \ü-bē-əs\ dubious, rubious

ubis \ü-bəs\ pubis, rubus, Anubis

uble \ü-bəl\ see UBAL

ublic \əb-lik\ public, republic

ublican \əb-li-kən\ publican, republican

ubman \əb-mən\ clubman, Tubman

ubric \ü-brik\ lubric, rubric

ubrious \ü-brē-əs\ lugubrious, salubrious, insalubrious

ubris \ü-brəs\ hubris, tuberous

ubtile \ət-ᵊl\ see UTTLE

ubus \ü-bəs\ see UBIS

uby \ü-bē\ see OOBY

uca \ü-kə\ see OOKA

ucal \ü-kəl\ ducal, nuchal, archducal

ucan \ü-kən\ glucan, kuchen, Lucan, interleukin

ucat \ək-ət\ see UCKET

¹**ucca** \ü-kə\ see OOKA

²**ucca** \ək-ə\ see UKKA

uccal \ək-əl\ see UCKLE

ucci \ü-chē\ see OOCHY

ucco \ək-ō\ see UCKO

uccor \ək-ər\ see UCKER

uccory \ək-rē\ see UCKERY

ucculence \ək-yə-ləns\ see UCULENCE

uce \üs\ see ¹USE

uced \üst\ see OOST

ucement \ü-smənt\ inducement, seducement

ucence \üs-ᵊns\ nuisance, translucence

ucer \ü-sər\ juicer, looser, adducer, Bull Mooser, inducer, lime-juicer, producer, transducer, introducer, reproducer

¹**uch** \ich\ see ITCH

²**uch** \ük\ see UKE

³**uch** \əch\ see ¹UTCH

uchal \ü-kəl\ see UCAL

¹**uche** \ü-chē\ see OOCHY

²**uche** \ich\ see ¹OOCH

³**uche** \üsh\ see OUCHE

uchen \ü-kən\ see UCAN

ucher \ü-chər\ see UTURE

uchin \ü-shən\ see UTION

uchsia \ü-shə\ see UTIA

uchy \əch-ē\ duchy, smutchy, touchy, archduchy

ucia \ü-shə\ see UTIA

ucial \ü-shəl\ crucial, fiducial

ucian \ü-shən\ see UTION

ucible \ü-sə-bəl\ crucible, deducible, educible, inducible, producible, protrusible, irreducible, reproducible, irreproducible

ucid \ü-səd\ deuced, lucid, pellucid, Seleucid

ucifer \ü-sə-fər\ crucifer, Lucifer

ucity \ü-sət-ē\ abstrusity, caducity

ucive \ü-siv\ see USIVE

¹**uck** \ək\ buck, Buck, chuck, cluck, cruck, duck, guck, huck, luck, muck, pluck, puck, Puck, ruck, schmuck, shuck, snuck, struck, stuck, suck, truck, Truk, tuck, yech, yuck, amok, awestruck, bushbuck, Canuck, dumbstruck, Kalmuck, lame-duck, light-struck, moonstruck, mukluk, muktuk, potluck, reedbuck, roebuck, sawbuck, shelduck, stagestruck, starstruck, sunstruck, unstuck, upchuck, woodchuck, geoduck, Keokuk, Habakkuk, megabuck, muckamuck, nip and tuck, high-muck-a-muck

²**uck** \ük\ see ¹OOK

ukar \ək-ər\ see UCKER

ucker \ək-ər\ bucker, chukar,

chukker, ducker, mucker, plucker, pucker, shucker, succor, sucker, trucker, tucker, bloodsucker, sapsucker, seersucker

uckery \ək-rē\ puckery, succory

ucket \ək-ət\ bucket, ducat, tucket, gutbucket, Nantucket

uckle \ək-əl\ buccal, buckle, chuckle, knuckle, suckle, truckle, Arbuckle, bare-knuckle, parbuckle, pinochle, swashbuckle, turnbuckle, unbuckle, honeysuckle

uckled \ək-əld\ cuckold, knuckled, bare-knuckled—also -ed forms of verbs listed at UCKLE

uckler \ək-lər\ buckler, knuckler, swashbuckler

uckling \ək-lin\ duckling, suckling, swashbuckling—also -ing forms of verbs listed at UCKLE

ucko \ək-ō\ bucko, stucco

uckold \ək-əld\ see UCKLED

uckoo \ü-kü\ cuckoo, Maluku

ucks \əks\ see ¹UX

uckus \úk-əs\ ruckus, Sukkoth

ucky \ək-ē\ ducky, lucky, mucky, plucky, yucky, Kentucky, unlucky, happy-go-lucky

uco \ü-kō\ pachuco, osso buco

ucre \ü-kər\ euchre, lucre

uct \ əkt\ duct, abduct, adduct, conduct, construct, deduct, destruct, eruct, induct, instruct, obstruct, aqueduct, deconstruct, reconstruct, usufruct,

viaduct—also -ed forms of verbs listed at ¹UCK

uctable \ək-tə-bəl\ see UCTIBLE

uctal \ək-t²l\ ductal, ductile

uctance \ək-təns\ conductance, inductance, reluctance

uctible \ək-tə-bəl\ conductible, constructible, deductible, destructible, indestructible, ineluctable, reconstructible

uctile \ək-t²l\ see UCTAL

ucting \ək-tin\ ducting, semiconducting—also -ing forms of verbs listed at UCT

uction \ək-shən\ fluxion, ruction, suction, abduction, adduction, conduction, construction, deduction, destruction, eduction, effluxion, induction, instruction, obstruction, production, reduction, seduction, deconstruction, introduction, reconstruction, reproduction, photoreproduction

uctive \ək-tiv\ adductive, conductive, constructive, deductive, destructive, inductive, instructive, productive, reductive, seductive, reconstructive, reproductive, self-destructive, counterproductive

uctor \ək-tər\ abductor, adductor, conductor, constructor, destructor, eductor, inductor, instructor, obstructor, deconstructor, reconstructor, semiconductor, superconductor

uctress \ək-trəs\ conductress, instructress, seductress

uculence \ək-yə-ləns\ succulence, truculence

ucy \ü-sē\ see UICY

¹ud \əd\ blood, bud, crud, cud, dud, flood, fud, Judd, mud, rudd, scud, spud, stud, sudd, thud, coldblood, disbud, full-blood, half-blood, hotblood, lifeblood, oxblood, redbud, rosebud, warmblood, stick-in-the-mud

²ud \üd\ see UDE

³ud \ud\ see ¹OOD

uda \üd-ə\ Buddha, Gouda, Judah, Barbuda, Bermuda, remuda, barracuda, Buxtehude, Gautama Buddha

udable \üd-ə-bəl\ excludable, extrudable, includable, ineludible

udah \üd-ə\ see UDA

udal \üd-ᵊl\ see OODLE

udas \üd-əs\ Judas, Santa Gertrudis

¹udd \ud\ see ¹OOD

²udd \əd\ see ¹UD

udded \əd-əd\ see ¹OODED

udder \əd-ər\ budder, flooder, judder, rudder, shudder, udder

uddha \üd-ə\ see UDA

uddhist \üd-əst\ see ¹UDIST

uddie \əd-ē\ see ¹UDDY

¹udding \əd-iŋ\ budding, studding—*also* -ing *forms of verbs listed at* ¹UD

²udding \ud-iŋ\ see OODING

uddle \əd-ᵊl\ buddle, cuddle, fuddle, huddle, muddle, puddle, ruddle, befuddle

uddly \əd-lē\ cuddly, Dudley, muddly, studly

¹uddy \əd-ē\ bloody, buddy, Buddy, cruddy, cuddy,

duddie, muddy, ruddy, study, fuddy-duddy, understudy

²uddy \ud-ē\ see ²OODY

¹ude \üd\ brood, crowd, crude, dude, feud, food, hued, Jude, lewd, mood, nude, oud, pood, prude, pseud, rood, rude, shrewd, snood, stewed, who'd, wood, wud, you'd, allude, collude, conclude, delude, denude, elude, etude, exclude, extrude, exude, fast-food, Gertrude, include, intrude, obtrude, occlude, postlude, preclude, prelude, protrude, quaalude, Quaalude, seafood, seclude, subdued, transude, unglued, altitude, amplitude, aptitude, attitude, certitude, consuetude, crassitude, desuetude, finitude, fortitude, gratitude, habitude, hebetude, interlude, lassitude, latitude, longitude, magnitude, mansuetude, multitude, negritude, platitude, plenitude, plentitude, promptitude, pulchritude, quietude, rectitude, seminude, servitude, solitude, turpitude, vastitude, beatitude, correctitude, decrepitude, exactitude, inaptitude, incertitude, ineptitude, infinitude, ingratitude, inquietude, similitude, solicitude, vicissitude, dissimilitude, inexactitude, verisimilitude

²ude \üd-ə\ see UDA

udel \üd-ᵊl\ see OODLE

udence \ü-dᵊn(t)s\ Prudence,

students, imprudence, jurisprudence

udeness \üd-nəs\ see UDINOUS

udent \üd-ᵊnt\ prudent, imprudent, student, jurisprudent

udents \ü-dᵊn(t)s\ see UDENCE

uder \üd-ər\ brooder, Tudor, concluder, deluder, excluder, extruder, intruder, obtruder, preluder—*also* -er *forms of adjectives listed at* ¹UDE

¹**udge** \əj\ budge, drudge, fudge, grudge, judge, nudge, sludge, smudge, trudge, adjudge, begrudge, forejudge, misjudge, prejudge

²**udge** \üj\ see ¹UGE

udgeon \əj-ən\ bludgeon, dudgeon, gudgeon, curmudgeon

udget \əj-ət\ budget, fussbudget

udgie \əj-ē\ see UDGY

udging \əj-iŋ\ drudging, grudging—*also* -ing *forms of verbs listed at* ¹UDGE

udgy \əj-ē\ budgie, pudgy, sludgy, smudgy

udible \üd-ə-bəl\ see UDABLE

udi \ü-dē\ see ¹OODY

udie \ü-dē\ see ¹OODY

udinal \üd-nəl\ altitudinal, aptitudinal, attitudinal, latitudinal, longitudinal, platitudinal

udinous \üd-nəs\ crudeness, lewdness, rudeness, shrewdness, altitudinous, multitudinous, platitudinous, plenitudinous, pulchritudinous

udis \üd-əs\ see UDAS

udish \üd-ish\ dudish, prudish

¹**udist** \üd-əst\ Buddhist, feudist, nudist—*also* -est *forms of adjectives listed at* ¹UDE

²**udist** \üd-əst\ see OULDEST

udity \üd-ət-ē\ crudity, nudity

udley \əd-lē\ see UDDLY

udly \əd-lē\ see UDDLY

udo \üd-ō\ judo, kudo, pseudo, scudo, escudo, Matsudo, testudo

udor \üd-ər\ see UDER

udsman \üdz-mən\ see OODSMAN

udson \əd-sən\ Hudson, Judson

udu \üd-ü\ see OODOO

¹**udy** \ü-dē\ see ¹OODY

²**udy** \əd-ē\ see ¹UDDY

¹**ue** \ü\ see ¹EW

²**ue** \ā\ see ¹AY

ued \üd\ see UDE

ueful \ü-fəl\ rueful, pantofle

ueghel \ü-gəl\ see UGAL

ueil \əi\ Arauil, Argentueil

¹**uel** \ü-əl\ crewel, cruel, dual, duel, gruel, jewel, Jewel, Jewell, newel, Newell, accrual, eschewal, refuel, renewal, Pantagruel

²**uel** \ül\ see ¹OOL

uely \ü-lē\ see ULY

uement \ü-mənt\ see EWMENT

uence \ü-əns\ affluence, confluence, congruence, effluence, influence, pursuance, refluence, incongruence

uency \ü-ən-sē\ fluency, truancy, affluency, congruency, nonfluency

ueness \ü-nəs\ see EWNESS

uenster \ən-stər\ see UNSTER

uent \ü-ənt\ fluent, suint, truant, affluent, confluent, congruent, effluent, influent, incongruent

uer \ü-ər\ see ¹EWER

uerdon \ərd-ᵊn\ see URDEN

uerile \ür-əl\ see URAL

ues \üz\ see ²USE

uesman \üz-mən\ see EWSMAN

uesome \ü-səm\ gruesome, twosome

uesy \ü-zē\ see OOZY

uet \ü-ət\ bluet, cruet, peewit, suet, conduit, intuit

uette \et\ see ¹ET

uey \ü-ē\ see EWY

ufa \ü-fə\ loofah, tufa, opera buffa

uff \əf\ bluff, buff, chough, chuff, cuff, duff, fluff, gruff, guff, huff, luff, muff, puff, rough, ruff, scruff, scuff, slough, snuff, sough, stuff, tough, tuff, dyestuff, earmuff, enough, foodstuff, handcuff, rebuff, oeil-de-boeuf, overstuff

uffa \ü-fə\ see UFA

¹**uffe** \üf\ see ¹OOF

²**uffe** \üf\ see ²OOF

uffed \əft\ chuffed, ruffed, tuft, candytuft—*also -ed forms of verbs listed at* UFF

uffel \əf-əl\ see ¹UFFLE

uffer \əf-ər\ bluffer, buffer, duffer, puffer, rougher, snuffer, stuffer, suffer, candlesnuffer—*also -er forms of adjectives listed at* UFF

uffet \əf-ət\ buffet, tuffet

uffin \əf-ən\ muffin, puffin, roughen, toughen, ragamuffin

uffish \əf-ish\ huffish, roughish

¹**uffle** \əf-əl\ duffel, muffle, ruffle, scuffle, shuffle, snuffle, truffle, kerfuffle, reshuffle, unmuffle

²**uffle** \ü-fəl\ see UEFUL

uffled \əf-əld\ truffled, unruffled—*also -ed forms of verbs listed at* ¹UFFLE

uffler \əf-lər\ muffler, shuffler, snuffler

uffly \əf-lē\ bluffly, gruffly, roughly, ruffly

uffy \əf-ē\ chuffy, fluffy, huffy, puffy, scruffy, snuffy, stuffy, toughie

ufi \ü-fē\ see OOFY

ufous \ü-fəs\ rufous, Rufus

uft \əft\ see UFFED

ufti \əf-tē\ mufti, tufty

ufty \əf-tē\ see UFTI

ufus \ü-fəs\ see UFOUS

ug \əg\ bug, chug, Doug, drug, dug, fug, hug, jug, lug, mug, plug, pug, rug, shrug, slug, smug, snug, thug, trug, tug, ugh, vug, bedbug, billbug, debug, earplug, firebug, fireplug, goldbug, humbug, lovebug, stinkbug, unplug, antidrug, chugalug, doodlebug, jitterbug, ladybug, litterbug, mealybug, shutterbug

uga \ü-gə\ beluga, Cayuga, Kaluga, Sevruga, Tortuga, Chattanooga

ugal \ü-gəl\ Brueghel, bugle, frugal, fugal, fugle, kugel, conjugal

ugar \ùg-ər\ see UGUR

¹**uge** \üj\ huge, kludge, Lodz, scrooge, scrouge, stooge, deluge, centrifuge, subterfuge

²**uge** \üzh\ Bruges, luge, rouge, deluge, gamboge, refuge, Baton Rouge

ugel \ü-gəl\ see UGAL

uges \üzh\ see ²UGE

uggaree \əg-rē\ see ¹UGGERY

¹**ugger** \əg-ər\ bugger,

chugger, lugger, mugger, plugger, rugger, slugger, Bavagar, Jamnagar, Srinagar, hugger-mugger, Navanagar

²**ugger** \ùg-ər\ see UGUR

¹**uggery** \əg-rē\ buggery, puggaree, snuggery, thuggery, skulduggery

²**uggery** \ùg-rē\ see UGARY

ugget \əg-ət\ drugget, nugget

uggie \əg-ē\ see UGGY

uggish \əg-ish\ sluggish, thuggish

uggle \əg-əl\ guggle, juggle, smuggle, snuggle, struggle

uggler \əg-lər\ juggler, smuggler, struggler

uggy \əg-ē\ buggy, druggie, druggy, fuggy, luggie, muggy

¹**ugh** \əg\ see UG

²**ugh** \ü\ see ¹EW

ughes \üz\ see ²USE

ugle \ü-gəl\ see UGAL

ugli \ə-glē\ see UGLY

uglia \ùl-yə\ see ULIA

ugly \əg-lē\ smugly, Ugli, ugly, plug-ugly

ugn \ün\ see ¹OON

ugner \ü-nər\ see OONER

ugric \ü-grik\ tugrik, Ugric, Finno-Ugric

ugrik \ü-grik\ see UGRIC

ugu \ü-gü\ fugu, goo-goo

ugur \ùg-ər\ booger, bugger, sugar

uhe \ü-ə\ see UA

uhl \ül\ see ¹OOL

¹**uhr** \ər\ see ¹EUR

²**uhr** \ùr\ see ¹URE

ührer \ùr-ər\ see ¹URER

¹**ui** \ā\ see ¹AY

²**ui** \ē\ see ¹EE

uice \üs\ see ¹USE

uiced \üst\ see OOST

uiceless \ü-sləs\ see USELESS

uicer \ü-sər\ see UCER

uicy \ü-sē\ goosey, juicy,

Lucy, sluicy, sprucy, Brancusi, Watusi, acey-deucey, Arginusae, loosey-goosey

uid \ü-id\ Clwyd, druid, fluid

uidable \īd-ə-bəl\ see ¹IDABLE

uidance \īd-ᵊns\ see IDANCE

uide \īd\ see ¹IDE

uided \īd-əd\ see IDED

uider \īd-ər\ see ¹IDER

uidon \īd-ᵊn\ see IDEN

uiker \ī-kər\ see IKER

uild \ild\ see ILLED

uilder \il-dər\ see ILDER

uilding \il-diŋ\ see ILDING

uile \īl\ see ¹ILE

uileless \īl-ləs\ see ILELESS

uiler \ī-lər\ see ILAR

uilleann \i-lən\ see ILLON

uilt \ilt\ see ILT

uimpe \amp\ see ³AMP

¹**uin** \ü-ən\ see UAN

²**uin** \ən\ see UN

³**uin** \aᵊn\ see ⁴IN

uing \ü-iŋ\ see ²OING

uint \ü-ənt\ see UENT

uir \ùr\ see ¹URE

uirdly \ùr-lē\ see URELY

uis \ü-əs\ see ²OUIS

uisance \üs-ᵊns\ see UCENCE

uisard \ī-zərd\ see ISORED

¹**uise** \üz\ see ²USE

²**uise** \īz\ see IZE

uiser \ü-zər\ see USER

uish \ü-ish\ see EWISH

uisne \ü-nē\ see OONY

uiste \is-tē\ see ²ICITY

¹**uit** \ü-ət\ see UET

²**uit** \üt\ see UTE

uitable \üt-ə-bəl\ see UTABLE

uitage \üt-ij\ see ¹OOTAGE

uite \üt\ see UTE

uited \üt-əd\ see ¹OOTED

uiter \üt-ər\ see UTER

uiterer \üt-ər-ər\ fruiterer, pewterer

uiting \üt-iŋ\ see UTING
uitless \üt-ləs\ see OOTLESS
uitlet \üt-lət\ see OOTLET
uitor \üt-ər\ see UTER
uitous \ü-ət-əs\ circuitous, fortuitous, gratuitous
uits \üts\ see OOTS
¹**uittle** \üt-ᵊl\ see UTILE
²**uittle** \ət-ᵊl\ see UTTLE
¹**uity** \ü-ət-ē\ acuity, annuity, circuity, congruity, fatuity, fortuity, gratuity, vacuity, ambiguity, assiduity, conspicuity, contiguity, continuity, incongruity, ingenuity, perpetuity, promiscuity, superfluity, discontinuity
²**uity** \üt-ē\ see ¹OOTY
¹**uk** \ük\ see UKE
²**uk** \ùk\ see ¹OOK
³**uk** \ək\ see UCK
ukar \ə-kər\ see UCKER
uke \ük\ cuke, duke, fluke, gook, juke, kook, Luke, nuke, puke, snook, souk, spook, suq, tuque, uke, yeuk, archduke, Baruch, caoutchouc, Chinook, Kirkuk, Mamluk, rebuke, Heptateuch, Hexateuch, Pentateuch
uki ¹ \ü-kē\ see ¹OOKY
²**uki** \ù-kē\ see OOKIE
ukka \ək-ə\ chukka, pukka, yucca, felucca
ukkah \úk-ə\ see OOKAH
ukker \ək-ər\ see UCKER
ukkoth \úk-əs\ see UCKUS
uku \ü-kü\ see UCKOO
¹**ul** \úl\ bull, Bull, full, pull, shul, wool, you'll, armful, bagful, bellpull, brimful, bulbul, canful, capful, carful, cheekful, chestful, chock-full, cupful, drawerful, earful, eyeful,

fistful, forkful, glassful, handful, houseful, jarful, John Bull, jugful, leg-pull, mouthful, outpull, pailful, panful, pipeful, plateful, potful, push-pull, rackful, roomful, sackful, scoopful, shelfful, skinful, spoonful, stickful, tankful, tinful, topful, trainful, trayful, trunkful, tubful, barrelful, basketful, bellyful, teaspoonful, dyed-in-the-wool, tablespoonful
²**ul** \ül\ see ¹OOL
³**ul** \əl\ see ¹ULL
ula \ü-lə\ Beulah, Fula, hula, moola, pula, Tula, ampulla, tabbouleh, Ashtabula, San Pedro Sula
ular \ü-lər\ see OOLER
ulcent \əl-sənt\ see ULSANT
ulcer \əl-sər\ see ULSER
ulch \əlch\ cultch, gulch, mulch
¹**ule** \ü-lē\ see ULY
²**ule** \ül\ see ¹OOL
ulean \ü-lē-ən\ Boolean, Acheulean, cerulean
uled \üld\ see OOLED
ulep \ü-ləp\ see ULIP
uler \ü-lər\ see OOLER
ules \ülz\ Jules—also -s, -'s, and -s' forms of nouns listed at ¹OOL, and -s forms of verbs listed there
ulet \əl-ət\ see ¹ULLET
¹**uley** \ü-lē\ see ULY
²**uley** \úl-ē\ see ²ULLY
ulf \əlf\ golf, gulf, Gulf, engulf, Beowulf, Saronic Gulf
ulgar \əl-gər\ see ULGUR
ulge \əlj\ bulge, divulge, indulge, overindulge
¹**ulgence** \əl-jəns\ divulgence, indulgence, refulgence

²**ulgence** \úl-jəns\ effulgence, refulgence

ulgent \əl-jənt\ fulgent, indulgent

ulgur \əl-gər\ bulgur, vulgar

ulhas \əl-əs\ see ULLUS

uli \úl-ē\ see ²ULLY

ulia \ül-yə\ Julia, Puglia, Apulia, Friuli-Venezia Guilia

ulie \ü-lē\ see ULY

ulip \ü-ləp\ julep, tulip

ulish \ü-lish\ see OOLISH

ulity \ü-lət-ē\ credulity, garrulity, sedulity, incredulity

ulk \əlk\ bulk, hulk, skulk, sulk, yolk

ulky \əl-kē\ bulky, sulky

¹**ull** \əl\ cull, dull, gull, hull, Hull, lull, mull, null, scull, skull, stull, trull, annul, Choiseul, mogul, numskull, pas seul, monohull, multihull, Sitting Bull, Solihull, Kingston upon Hull

²**ull** \úl\ see ¹UL

ulla \úl-ə\ bulla, mullah, Sulla, ampulla

²**ulla** \ü-lə\ see ULA

³**ulla** \əl-ə\ see ¹ULLAH

ullage \əl-ij\ sullage, ullage

¹**ullah** \əl-ə\ Gullah, mullah, nullah, stollen, medulla, ayatollah

²**ullah** \úl-ə\ see ¹ULLA

ullan \əl-ən\ see ULLEN

ullard \əl-ərd\ see OLORED

ullate \əl-ət\ see ¹ULLET

ulle \ül\ see ¹OOL

ullein \əl-ən\ see ULLEN

ullen \əl-ən\ mullein, stollen, sullen, Lucullan

¹**uller** \úl-ər\ fuller, puller

²**uller** \əl-ər\ see ¹OLOR

ulles \əl-əs\ see ULLUS

¹**ullet** \əl-ət\ culet, cullet, gullet, mullet, cucullate

²**ullet** \úl-ət\ bullet, Bullitt, pullet

ulley \úl-ē\ see ²ULLY

ullion \əl-yən\ cullion, mullion, scullion, slumgullion

ullis \əl-əs\ see ULLUS

ullitt \úl-ət\ see ²ULLET

ullman \úl-mən\ fulmine, Pullman

ullus \əl-əs\ Dulles, Agulhas, Catullus, portcullis, Cape Agulhas

¹**ully** \əl-ē\ cully, dully, gully, sully

²**ully** \úl-ē\ bully, fully, gully, muley, puli, pulley, woolly

ulmine \úl-mən\ see ULLMAN

ulp \əlp\ gulp, pulp, insculp

ulsant \əl-sənt\ pulsant, convulsant, demulcent

ulse \əls\ dulse, pulse, avulse, convulse, expulse, impulse, repulse

ulser \əl-sər\ pulser, ulcer

ulsion \əl-shən\ pulsion, avulsion, compulsion, convulsion, emulsion, evulsion, expulsion, impulsion, propulsion, repulsion, revulsion

ulsive \əl-siv\ compulsive, convulsive, emulsive, expulsive, impulsive, propulsive, repulsive

ult \əlt\ cult, adult, consult, exult, incult, indult, insult, occult, penult, result, tumult, catapult, antepenult

ultancy \əlt-ⁿn-sē\ consultancy, exultancy

ultant \əlt-ⁿnt\ consultant, exultant, resultant

ultch \əlch\ see ULCH

ulter \əl-tər\ consultor, insulter, occulter

ultery \əl-trē\ see ULTRY

ultor \əl-tər\ see ULTER

ultry \əl-trē\ sultry, adultery

ulture \əl-chər\ culture,
multure, vulture, subculture,
agriculture, apiculture,
aquaculture, aviculture,
counterculture, floriculture,
horticulture, mariculture,
monoculture, silviculture,
viniculture, arboriculture

ulty \əl-tē\ see ¹ALTI

ulu \ü-lü\ lulu, Sulu, Zulu,
Bangweulu, Honolulu

ulunder \əl-ən-dər\ see
OLANDER

ulva \əl-və\ ulva, vulva

ulvar \əl-vər\ see ULVER

ulver \əl-vər\ culver, vulvar

uly \ü-lē\ bluely, boule,
coolie, coolly, coulee, duly,
ghoulie, Julie, muley, newly,
puli, ruly, stoolie, Thule,
truly, tule, Bernoulli,
guayule, patchouli,
tabbouleh, unduly, unruly,
ultima Thule

¹um \əm\ bum, chum, come,
crumb, cum, drum, dumb,
from, glum, gum, hum, lum,
mum, numb, plum, plumb,
rhumb, rum, scrum, scum,
slum, some, strum, sum,
swum, them, thrum, thumb,
alum, aplomb, become,
benumb, degum, dim sum,
dumdum, eardrum, ho-hum,
humdrum, income, outcome,
subgum, succumb,
therefrom, Tom Thumb,
tom-tom, wherefrom, yum-
yum, bubblegum,
kettledrum, overcome,
sugarplum, hop-o'my-thumb

²um \u̇m\ cum, groom, Qom,
Targum, mare librum

³um \u̇m\ see ¹OOM

uma \ü-mə\ duma, pneuma,

puma, satsuma, Ancohuma,
Montezuma

umable \ü-mə-bəl\ assumable,
consumable, presumable,
subsumable, inconsumable

umage \əm-ij\ see UMMAGE

uman \ü-mən\ blooming,
crewman, human, lumen,
Newman, numen, Truman,
Yuman, acumen, albumen,
albumin, bitumen,
ichneumon, illumine,
inhuman, panhuman,
subhuman, antihuman,
catechumen, protohuman,
superhuman

umanist \ü-mə-nəst\ see
UMENIST

umanous \ü-mə-nəs\ see
UMINOUS

umb \əm\ see ¹UM

umbar \əm-bər\ see ¹UMBER

umbed \əmd\ green-thumbed,
unplumbed

umbel \əm-bəl\ see UMBLE

umbency \əm-bən-sē\
incumbency, recumbency

umbent \əm-bənt\
decumbent, incumbent,
procumbent, recumbent,
superincumbent

¹umber \əm-bər\ cumber,
Humber, lumbar, lumber,
number, slumber, umber,
cucumber, encumber,
outnumber, renumber,
disencumber, Reynolds
number, Avogadro's number

²umber \əm-ər\ see UMMER

umbered \əm-bərd\
unnumbered,
unencumbered—also -ed
forms of verbs listed at
¹UMBER

umberland \əm-bər-lənd\
Cumberland,
Northumberland

umberous \əm-brəs\ see
UMBROUS

umbery \əm-brē\ ombre,
slumbery

umbing \əm-iŋ\ see OMING

umble \əm-bəl\ bumble,
crumble, fumble, grumble,
humble, jumble, mumble,
rumble, scumble, stumble,
tumble, umbel, rough-and-
tumble

umbler \əm-blər\ bumbler,
fumbler, grumbler, humbler,
mumbler, rumbler, stumbler,
tumbler

umbling \əm-bliŋ\ rumbling,
tumbling—*also* -ing *forms of
verbs listed at* UMBLE

¹**umbly** \əm-blē\ crumbly,
grumbly, humbly, mumbly,
rumbly

²**umbly** \əm-lē\ comely,
dumbly, dumly, numbly

umbness \əm-nəs\ dumbness,
glumness, numbness,
alumnus

umbo \əm-bō\ gumbo, jumbo,
umbo, Colombo, mumbo
jumbo

umbra \əm-brə\ umbra,
penumbra

umbral \əm-brəl\ see UMBRIL

umbria \əm-brē-ə\ Cumbria,
Umbria, Northumbria

umbril \əm-brəl\ tumbril,
umbral, penumbral

umbrous \əm-brəs\
cumbrous, slumberous

ume \üm\ see ¹OOM

umed \ümd\ see OOMED

umedly \ü-məd-lē\
consumedly, presumedly

umelet \üm-lət\ see OOMLET

umely \ü-mə-lē\ see OOMILY

umen \ü-mən\ see UMAN

umenist \ü-mə-nəst\
humanist, luminist,

ecumenist, illuminist,
phillumenist

umer \ü-mər\ bloomer,
Bloomer, groomer, humor,
roomer, rumor, Sumer,
tumor, consumer, costumer,
exhumer, perfumer,
presumer, schussboomer

umeral \üm-rəl\ humeral,
humoral, numeral

umerous \üm-rəs\ see
UMOROUS

umerus \üm-rəs\ see
UMOROUS

umey \ü-mē\ see OOMY

umf \əmf\ see UMPH

umi \ü-mē\ see OOMY

umice \əm-əs\ see UMMOUS

umid \ü-məd\ humid, tumid

¹**umin** \əm-ən\ cumin,
summon

²**umin** \ü-mən\ see UMAN

uminal \ü-mən-ᵊl\ luminal,
noumenal

uminate \ü-mə-nət\
acuminate, illuminate

umine \ü-mən\ see UMAN

uming \ü-miŋ\ blooming,
consuming, everblooming,
time-consuming,
unassuming—*also* -ing *forms
of verbs listed at* ¹OOM

uminist \ü-mə-nəst\ see
UMENIST

uminous \ü-mə-nəs\
luminous, numinous,
albuminous, aluminous,
bituminous, leguminous,
quadrumanous, voluminous

umma \əm-ə\ gumma,
momma, summa

ummage \əm-ij\ rummage,
West Brumage

¹**ummary** \əm-rē\ see
²UMMERY

²**ummary** \əm-ə-rē\ see
¹UMMERY

ummate \əm-ət\ see UMMET
ummel \əm-əl\ see ²OMMEL
ummell \əm-əl\ see ²OMMEL
ummer \əm-ər\ bummer, comer, drummer, gummer, hummer, mummer, plumber, rummer, slummer, strummer, summer, latecomer, midsummer, newcomer, overcomer, up-and-comer—*also* -er *forms of adjectives listed at* ¹UM
ummery \əm-ə-rē\ flummery, mummery, summary, summery, Montgomery
ummet \əm-ət\ grummet, plummet, summit, consummate
ummie \əm-ē\ see UMMY
ummit \əm-ət\ see UMMET
ummock \əm-ək\ hummock, stomach
ummon \əm-ən\ see ¹UMIN
ummoner \əm-nər\ see UMNAR
ummous \əm-əs\ gummous, hummus, pomace, pumice
ummox \əm-əks\ flummox, hummocks, lummox, stomachs
ummus \əm-əs\ see UMMOUS
ummy \əm-ē\ chummy, crummie, crummy, dummy, gummy, mommy, mummy, plummy, rummy, scummy, slummy, tummy, yummy
umnar \əm-nər\ summoner, Sumner, columnar
umner \əm-nər\ see UMNAR
umness \əm-nəs\ see UMBNESS
umnus \əm-nəs\ see UMBNESS
umor \ü-mər\ see UMER
umoral \üm-rəl\ see UMERAL
umorous \üm-rəs\ humerus, humorous, numerous, tumorous, innumerous

umous \ü-məs\ brumous, humus, spumous, posthumous
ump \əmp\ bump, chump, clomp, clump, comp, crump, dump, flump, frump, grump, hump, jump, lump, mump, plump, pump, rump, slump, stump, sump, thump, trump, tump, ump, whump, mugwump, no-trump, tub-thump, callithump, overtrump
umper \əm-pər\ bumper, dumper, jumper, lumper, plumper, pumper, stumper, thumper, tub-thumper, Bible-thumper
umph \əmf\ bumf, humph, galumph, harrumph
umpish \əm-pish\ dumpish, frumpish, lumpish, plumpish
umpkin \əŋ-kən\ see UNKEN
umple \əm-pəl\ crumple, rumple
umply \əm-plē\ crumply, plumply, rumply
umps \əms\ dumps, mumps—*also* -s, -'s, *and* -s' *forms of nouns listed at* UMP, *and* -s *forms of verbs listed* there
umption \əm-shən\ gumption, assumption, consumption, presumption, resumption, subsumption
umptious \əm-shəs\ bumptious, scrumptious, presumptuous
umptive \əm-tiv\ assumptive, consumptive, presumptive
¹**umptuous** \əm-chəs\ sumptuous, presumptuous
²**umptuous** \əm-shəs\ see UMPTIOUS
umpus \əm-pəs\ see ²OMPASS
umpy \əm-pē\ bumpy,

clumpy, dumpy, frumpy,
grumpy, humpy, jumpy,
lumpy, stumpy

umulous \ü-myə-ləs\ see
UMULUS

umulus \ü-myə-ləs\
cumulous, cumulus, tumulus

umus \ü-məs\ see UMOUS

umy \ü-mē\ see OOMY

¹un \ən\ bun, done, Donne,
dun, fen, foehn, fun, gun,
hon, Hun, jun, maun, none,
nun, one, pun, run, shun,
son, spun, stun, sun, sunn,
ton, tonne, tun, won, A-1,
begun, blowgun, chaconne,
Chang-chun, Chaplin,
finespun, first-run, flashgun,
forerun, godson, grandson,
handgun, hard-won,
homespun, long run,
outdone, outgun, outrun,
popgun, pressrun, rerun, sea-
run, shotgun, six-gun,
stepson, undone, V-1, well-
done, Acheron, Algonquin,
allemande, all-or-none,
Balzacian, hit-and-run,
kiloton, machine-gun,
megaton, one-on-one,
one-to-one, overdone,
overrun, PL/1, Sally Lunn,
scattergun, tommy gun,
twenty-one, underdone,
underrun, Xiamen,
alexandrine

²un \ün\ see ¹OON

³un \ùn\ Fushun, Lushun,
tabun

una \ü-nə\ Buna, Cunha,
Luna, Poona, puna, tuna,
Altoona, kahuna, lacuna,
laguna, vicuña, Tristan da
Cunha

¹uña \ü-nə\ see UNA

²uña \ün-yə\ see UNIA

unal \ün-ᵊl\ communal,

jejunal, lagoonal, monsoonal,
tribunal

unar \ü-nər\ see OONER

unary \ü-nə-rē\ unary,
festoonery, sublunary,
superlunary

unate \ü-nət\ unit, lacunate,
tribunate

unc \ənk\ see UNK

uncan \əŋ-kən\ see UNKEN

unce \əns\ dunce, once—*also
-s, -'s, and -s' forms of nouns
listed at ¹ONT, and -s forms of
verbs listed there*

unch \ənch\ brunch, bunch,
Bunche, crunch, hunch,
lunch, munch, punch,
scrunch, keypunch,
ploughman's lunch

unche \ənch\ see UNCH

uncheon \ən-chən\ luncheon,
puncheon, truncheon

uncher \ən-chər\ cruncher,
luncher, muncher,
cowpuncher, keypuncher,
counterpuncher

unchy \ən-chē\ bunchy,
crunchy, punchy

uncial \ən-sē-əl\ uncial,
internuncial

uncle \əŋ-kəl\ nuncle, uncle,
carbuncle, caruncle,
furuncle, granduncle,
peduncle

¹unco \əŋ-kō\ bunco, junco,
unco

²unco \əŋ-kə\ see UNKAH

unct \əŋt\ trunked, adjunct,
conjunct, defunct,
disjunct—*also -ed forms of
verbs listed at UNK*

unction \əŋ-shən\ function,
junction, unction,
compunction, conjunction,
disjunction, dysfunction,
injunction, malfunction,
extreme unction

unctional \əŋ-shnəl\
functional, junctional,
dysfunctional

unctious \əŋ-shəs\
compunctious, rambunctious

unctory \əŋ-trē\ emunctory,
perfunctory

uncture \əŋ-chər\ juncture,
puncture, acupuncture,
conjuncture, disjuncture

uncular \əŋ-kyə-lər\
avuncular, carbuncular,
peduncular

unculus \əŋ-kyə-ləs\
homunculus, ranunculus

¹und \ənd\ bund, fund,
gunned, defund, obtund,
refund, rotund, secund,
cummerbund, orotund,
pudibund, rubicund,
underfund—*also* -ed *forms of
verbs listed at* ¹UN

²und \und\ bund, dachshund

³und \unt\ see ¹UNT

⁴und \aund\ see ²OUND

unda \ən-də\ Munda, Sunda,
osmunda, rotunda,
barramunda, floribunda

undae \ən-dē\ see ¹UNDI

undant \ən-dənt\ abundant,
redundant, superabundant

unday \ən-dē\ see ¹UNDI

undays \ən-dēz\ Mondays,
Sundays, undies—*also* -s, -'s,
and -s' *forms of nouns listed
at* ¹UNDI

undem \ən-dəm\ see UNDUM

under \ən-dər\ Bandar,
blunder, plunder, sunder,
thunder, under, wonder,
asunder, hereunder,
thereunder

underous \ən-drəs\
plunderous, wondrous,
thunderous

¹undi \ən-dē\ Monday,
sundae, Sunday,

Whitmonday, Whitsunday,
barramundi, Bay of Fundy,
jaguarundi, Mrs. Grundy,
salmagundi, coatimundi

²undi \un-dē\ Burundi,
Ruanda-Urundi

undies \ən-dēz\ see UNDAYS

undity \ən-dət-ē\ fecundity,
profundity, rotundity,
moribundity, orotundity,
rubicundity

undle \ən-dᵊl\ bundle, rundle,
trundle, unbundle

undness \ən-nəs\ see
ONENESS

undum \ən-dəm\ corundum,
ad eundem, Carborundum

undy \ən-dē\ see ¹UNDI

une \ün\ see ¹OON

uneau \ü-nō\ see UNO

uneless \ün-ləs\ see OONLESS

uner \ü-nər\ see OONER

unes \ünz\ see OONS

¹ung \əŋ\ bung, clung, dung,
flung, hung, lung, pung,
rung, slung, sprung, strung,
stung, sung, swung, tongue,
tung, wrung, young, Young,
among, bee-stung, far-flung,
high-strung, Kaifeng, low-
slung, unstrung, unsung,
well-hung, adder's-tongue,
double-hung, double-tongue,
triple-tongue, overhung,
overstrung, underslung

²ung \ùŋ\ Jung, Kung, Sung,
Antung, Bandung, Dandong,
Dadong, Hamhung, Tatung,
Kaohsiung, Zigong,
Nibelung, geländesprung,
Götterdämmerung

ungal \ən-gəl\ see UNGLE

unge \ənj\ lunge, plunge,
sponge, expunge

unged \əŋd\ see ONGUED

ungeon \ən-jən\ donjon,
dungeon, spongin

¹unger \ən-jər\ lunger, plunger, sponger, expunger

²unger \əŋ-gər\ see ¹ONGER

ungible \ən-jə-bəl\ fungible, inexpungible

ungle \əŋ-gəl\ bungle, fungal, jungle, pungle

ungo \əŋ-gō\ fungo, mungo

ungous \əŋ-gəs\ fungous, fungus, humongous

ungry \ən-grē\ see ONGERY

ungus \əŋ-gəs\ see UNGOUS

ungy \ən-jē\ grungy, spongy

unha \ü-nə\ see UNA

uni \ü-nē\ see OONY

unia \ün-yə\ petunia, vicuña

unic \ü-nik\ eunuch, Munich, Punic, runic, tunic

unicate \ü-ni-kət\ tunicate, excommunicate

unich \ü-nik\ see UNIC

union \ən-yən\ bunion, grunion, onion, ronyon, trunnion, Paul Bunyan

unis \ü-nəs\ see EWNESS

¹unish \ən-ish\ Hunnish, punish

²unish \ü-nish\ see OONISH

unit \ü-nət\ see UNATE

unitive \ü-nət-iv\ punitive, unitive

unity \ü-nət-ē\ unity, community, disunity, immunity, impunity, importunity, opportunity, European Community

unk \əŋk\ bunk, chunk, clunk, drunk, dunk, flunk, funk, gunk, hunk, junk, monk, plunk, punk, shrunk, skunk, slunk, spunk, stunk, sunk, thunk, trunk, bohunk, chipmunk, debunk, Podunk, punch-drunk, quidnunc

unkah \əŋ-kə\ punkah, unco

unkard \əŋ-kərd\ bunkered,

drunkard, Dunkard, hunkered

unked \əŋt\ see UNCT

unken \əŋ-kən\ Duncan, drunken, pumpkin, shrunken, sunken

unker \əŋ-kər\ bunker, Bunker, clunker, Dunker, flunker, hunker, junker, lunker, plunker, punker, younker, debunker, spelunker

unkie \əŋ-kē\ see UNKY

unkin \əŋ-kən\ see UNCAN

unks \əŋs\ hunks, quincunx—also -s, -'s, and -s' forms of nouns listed at UNK, and -s forms of verbs listed there

unky \əŋ-kē\ chunky, clunky, donkey, flunky, funky, gunky, hunky, Hunky, junkie, junky, monkey, punkie, punky, spunkie, spunky

unless \ən-ləs\ runless, sonless, sunless

unn \ən\ see UN

unnage \ən-ij\ dunnage, tonnage, megatonnage

unned \ənd\ see UND

unnel \ən-ᵊl\ funnel, gunnel, gunwale, runnel, trunnel, tunnel

unner \ən-ər\ cunner, gunner, runner, scunner, shunner, stunner, tonner, forerunner, front-runner, gunrunner, roadrunner, rumrunner

unnery \ən-rē\ gunnery, nunnery

unness \ən-nəs\ see ONENESS

unning \ən-iŋ\ cunning, running, stunning—also -ing forms of verbs listed at ¹UN

unnion \ən-yən\ see UNION

unnish \ən-ish\ see ¹UNISH

unny \ən-ē\ bunny, funny, gunny, honey, money, runny,

sonny, sunny, tunny,
Ballymoney

uno \ü-nō\ Bruno, Juneau,
Juno, numero uno

unster \ən-stər\ Muenster,
punster

¹unt \ünt\ dachshund,
Dortmund, exeunt

²unt \ənt\ see ¹ONT

untal \ənt-ᵊl\ see UNTLE

unter \ənt-ər\ blunter,
bunter, chunter, grunter,
hunter, punter, shunter,
confronter, foxhunter,
headhunter, pothunter,
witch-hunter

unting \ənt-iŋ\ bunting,
foxhunting, head-hunting,
witch-hunting—*also* -ing
forms of verbs listed at ¹ONT

untle \ənt-ᵊl\ frontal, gruntle,
confrontal, disgruntle,
contrapuntal

unty \ənt-ē\ punty, runty

unwale \ən-ᵊl\ see UNNEL

unx \əŋs\ see UNKS

uny \ü-nē\ see OONY

unyan \ən-yən\ see UNION

uoth \ü-əs\ see EWESS

¹uoy \ü-ē\ see EWY

²uoy \ȯi\ see OY

uoyance \ü-əns\ see OYANCE

uoyancy \ȯi-ən-sē\ see
OYANCY

uoyant \ȯi-ənt\ see OYANT

up \əp\ cup, dup, hup, pup,
scup, sup, tup, up, yup,
backup, balls-up, bang-up,
beat-up, blowup, breakup,
brush up, buildup, built-up,
call-up, catch-up, change-
up, checkup, chin-up,
cleanup, close-up, cock-up,
crack-up, cutup, dried-up,
dustup, eggcup, eyecup,
faceup, fill-up, flare-up,
foul-up, frame-up, fry-up,

getup, giddap, grown-up,
hang-up, heads-up, hepped
up, het up, holdup, hookup,
hopped-up, jack-up, jam-up,
kickup, kingcup, lash-up,
lay-up, lead-up, letup, line
up, linkup, lockup, lookup,
louse up, made-up, makeup,
markup, matchup, mix-up,
mixed-up, mock-up, mop-
up, mug up, nip-up, one-up,
pasteup, pickup, pileup,
pinup, pop-up, pull-up,
punch-up, push-up, put-up,
re-up, roundup, run-up,
scaleup, screwup, send-up,
setup, shack up, shake-up,
shape-up, shook-up, shoot
up, sign up, sit-up, slap-up,
slipup, smashup, speedup,
stand-up, start-up, step up,
stepped-up, stickup, stuck-
up, sum-up, sunup, take-up,
teacup, thumbs-up, tie-up,
toss-up, touch-up, trumped-
up, tune-up, turnup, walk-
up, warm-up, washed-up,
washup, windup, wised-up,
workup, wrap-up, write-up,
belly up, buttercup, button-
up, cover-up, dial-up,
follow-up, higher-up, hurry-
up, pick-me-up, pony up,
runner-up, seven-up, shoot-
em-up, summing-up, up-
and-up, wickiup, winding-
up, Johnny-jump-up, sunny-
side up

upa \ü-pə\ pupa, stupa

upas \ü-pəs\ see UPUS

upboard \əb-ərd\ see
UBBARD

upe \üp\ see ¹OOP

upel \ü-pəl\ see ²UPLE

upelet \ü-plət\ see ²UPLET

uper \ü-pər\ see OOPER

upi \ü-pē\ see OOPY

upid \ü-pəd\ Cupid, stupid

upil \ü-pəl\ see ²UPLE

¹**uple** \əp-əl\ couple, supple, decouple

²**uple** \ü-pəl\ cupel, duple, pupil, scruple, quadruple, quintuple, sextuple

³**uple** \üp-ºl\ supple, quadruple, quintuple, sextuple

¹**uplet** \əp-lət\ couplet, gradruplet, quintuplet, sextuplet

²**uplet** \ü-plət\ drupelet, quadruplet

uplicate \ü-pli-kət\ duplicate, quadruplicate, quintuplicate, sextuplicate

upor \ü-pər\ see OOPER

uppance \əp-əns\ threepence, twopence, comeuppance

upper \əp-ər\ crupper, scupper, supper, upper, stand-upper

uppie \əp-ē\ see UPPY

¹**upple** \üp-əl\ see ³UPLE

²**upple** \əp-əl\ see ¹UPLE

uppy \əp-ē\ cuppy, guppy, puppy, yuppie

upt \əpt\ abrupt, corrupt, disrupt, erupt, irrupt, developed, incorrupt, interrupt—*also* -ed *forms of verbs listed at* UP

upter \əp-tər\ corrupter, disrupter, interrupter

uptible \əp-tə-bəl\ corruptible, eruptible, irruptible, incorruptible, interruptible

uption \əp-shən\ abruption, corruption, disruption, eruption, irruption, interruption

uptive \əp-tiv\ corruptive, disruptive, eruptive, irruptive, interruptive

upus \ü-pəs\ croupous, lupus, upas

uq \ük\ see UKE

uque \ük\ see UKE

¹**ur** \ȯr\ see ¹OR

²**ur** \ úr\ see ¹URE

³**ur** \ər\ see ¹EUR

ura \úr-ə\ dura, durra, Jura, sura, surah, Agoura, bravura, caesura, datura, Madura, tamboura, tempura, aqua pura, Arafura, Bujumbura, appoggiatura, Bonaventura, coloratura, Telanaipura, Anuradhapura, camera obscura

urable \úr-ə-bəl\ curable, durable, thurible, endurable, incurable, insurable, perdurable

uracy \úr-ə-sē\ curacy, obduracy

urae \úr-ē\ see ¹URY

urah \úr-ə\ see URA

ural \úr-əl\ crural, jural, mural, neural, plural, puerile, rural, Ural, caesural, commissural, extramural, intramural

uralist \úr-ə-ləst\ muralist, pluralist, ruralist

uran \ü-rən\ see ²URIN

urance \úr-əns\ durance, assurance, endurance, insurance, coinsurance, reassurance, reinsurance

urate \úr-ət\ curate, turret, obdurate, barbiturate

urative \úr-ə-tiv\ curative, durative

urb \ərb\ see ERB

¹**urban** \ər-bən\ bourbon, Durban, rurban, turban, turbine, urban, Urban, exurban, suburban, interurban

²**urban** \úr-bən\ bourbon, Bourbon, rurban

urber \ər-bər\ Berber, Ferber, Thurber, disturber

urbia \ər-bē-ə\ Serbia, exurbia, suburbia

urbid \ər-bəd\ turbid, verbid

urbine \ər-bən\ see ¹URBAN

urbit \ər-bət\ burbot, sherbet, turbit, turbot

urble \ər-bəl\ see ERBAL

urbot \ər-bət\ see URBIT

urcate \ər-kət\ see IRCUIT

urch \ərch\ birch, church, Church, curch, lurch, perch, search, smirch, besmirch, Christchurch, research, unchurch

urchin \ər-chən\ birchen, urchin

urchly \ərch-lē\ churchly, virtually

urcia \ər-shə\ see ERTIA

¹**urd** \ùrd\ see ¹URED

²**urd** \ərd\ see IRD

urdane \ərd-ᵊn\ see URDEN

urden \ərd-ᵊn\ burden, guerdon, lurdane, verdin, disburden, unburden, overburden

urder \ərd-ər\ see ERDER

urderer \ərd-ər-ər\ murderer, verderer

urdle \ərd-ᵊl\ curdle, girdle, hurdle, engirdle

urdu \ər-dü\ see ERDU

urdum \ərd-əm\ see IRDUM

urdy \ərd-ē\ birdie, sturdy, wordy, hurdy-gurdy, Mesa Verde, Monteverdi

¹**ure** \ùr\ Boer, boor, bourg, cure, dour, ewer, fewer, lure, moor, Moor, Moore, Muir, poor, pure, Ruhr, sewer, skewer, spoor, stour, sure, tour, Tours, your, you're, abjure, adjure, Adour, allure, amour, Ashur, assure, brochure, ceinture, cocksure, coiffure, conjure, contour, couture, demure, detour, dirt-poor, endure, ensure, Exmoor, faubourg, Fraktur, grandeur, gravure, guipure, hachure, immure, impure, insure, inure, kultur, land-poor, langur, ligure, manure, mature, mohur, obscure, parure, perdure, procure, secure, siddur, tambour, tandoor, tenure, Uighur, unmoor, velour, velure, amateur, aperture, armature, blackamoor, carrefour, carte du jour, coinsure, commissure, confiture, connoisseur, coverture, cubature, curvature, cynosure, debouchure, embouchure, epicure, filature, forfeiture, garniture, geniture, green-manure, haute couture, immature, insecure, ligature, manicure, overture, paramour, pedicure, plat du jour, portraiture, prelature, premature, quadrature, reassure, Reaumur, reinsure, saboteur, sepulture, sequitur, signature, simon-pure, sinecure, soup du jour, tablature, temperature, troubadour, white amur, vavasour, Yom Kippur, candidature, caricature, discomfiture, distemperature, divestiture, entablature, entrepreneur, expenditure, imprimatur, investiture, literature, miniature, musculature, nomenclature, nonsequitur,

primogeniture,
ultraminiature

²**ure** \ùr-ē\ see ¹URY

urean \ùr-ē-ən\ see URIAN

ureau \ùr-ō\ see URO

¹**ured** \ùrd\ gourde, Kurd,
urd, assured, steward,
underinsured—*also* -ed
forms of verbs listed at ¹URE

²**ured** \ərd\ see IRD

urely \ùr-lē\ buirdly, poorly,
purely, surely, cocksurely,
demurely, impurely,
maturely, obscurely,
immaturely, insecurely,
prematurely

urement \ùr-mənt\
allurement, immurement,
inurement, procurement,
securement

uren \ùr-ən\ see ²URIN

ureous \ùr-ē-əs\ see URIOUS

¹**urer** \ùr-ər\ curer, führer,
furor, furore, juror, lurer,
tourer, abjurer, assurer,
insurer, manurer, procurer,
tambourer, coinsurer,
reinsurer—*also* -er *forms of
adjectives listed at* ¹URE

²**urer** \ər-ər\ see ERRER

¹**urety** \ùr-ət-ē\ see URITY

²**urety** \ùrt-ē\ see URTI

urey \ùr-ē\ see ¹URY

urf \ərf\ kerf, scurf, serf,
surf, turf, enserf, bodysurf

urfy \ər-fē\ Murphy, scurfy,
turfy

urg \ərg\ see ERG

urgative \ər-gə-tiv\ see
URGATIVE

urge \ərj\ dirge, merge, purge,
scourge, serge, splurge,
spurge, surge, urge, verge,
converge, deterge, diverge,
emerge, immerge, resurge,
submerge, upsurge,
dramaturge

urgence \ər-jəns\ see
ERGENCE

urgency \ər-jən-sē\ see
ERGENCY

urgent \ər-jənt\ urgent,
assurgent, convergent,
detergent, divergent,
emergent, insurgent,
resurgent, preemergent

urgeon \ər-jən\ burgeon,
sturgeon, surgeon, virgin

¹**urger** \ər-gər\ burgher,
turgor, cheeseburger,
hamburger, Limburger

²**urger** \ər-jər\ see ERGER

urgery \ərj-rē\ see ERJURY

¹**urgh** \ər-ə\ see ¹OROUGH

²**urgh** \ər-ō\ see ¹URROW

³**urgh** \ərg\ see ERG

urgher \ər-gər\ see ¹URGER

urgic \ər-jik\ see ERGIC

urgical \ər-ji-kəl\ surgical,
liturgical, theurgical,
dramaturgical

urgid \ər-jəd\ turgid, synergid

urgle \ər-gəl\ burgle, gurgle

urgor \ər-gər\ see ¹URGER

urgy \ər-jē\ clergy,
dramaturgy, metallurgy

uri \ùr-ē\ see ¹URY

¹**urial** \ùr-ē-əl\ curial, urial,
Uriel, mercurial, seigneurial,
tenurial, entrepreneurial

²**urial** \er-ē-əl\ see ARIAL

urian \ùr-ē-ən\ durian,
Hurrian, Arthurian,
centurion, epicurean

uriance \ùr-ē-əns\ see
URIENCE

uriant \ùr-ē-ənt\ see URIENT

¹**urible** \ùr-ə-bəl\ see URABLE

²**urible** \ər-ə-bəl\ see ERABLE

uric \ùr-ik\ uric, mercuric,
sulfuric

urid \ùr-əd\ lurid, murid

urie \ùr-ē\ see ¹URY

uriel \ùr-ē-əl\ see ¹URIAL

urience \ùr-ē-əns\ prurience, luxuriance

urient \ùr-ē-ont\ esurient, luxuriant, parturient

¹**urier** \er-ē-ər\ see ERRIER

²**urier** \ùr-ē-ər\ see ¹OURIER

uriere \ùr-ē-ər\ see ¹OURIER

¹**urin** \ər-ən\ burin, murrain

²**urin** \ùr-ən\ burin, Huron, urine, Belgian Tervuren

urine \ùr-ən\ see ²URIN

uring \ùr-iŋ\ during, mooring, touring—*also* -ing *forms of verbs listed at* ¹URE

urion \ùr-ē-ən\ see URIAN

urious \ùr-ē-əs\ curious, furious, spurious, incurious, injurious, luxurious, penurious, perjurious, sulfureous, usurious

uris \ùr-əs\ see URUS

urist \ùr-əst\ purist, tourist, manicurist, pedicurist, caricaturist, chiaroscurist, miniaturist—*also* -est *forms of adjectives listed at* ¹URE

urity \ùr-ət-ē\ purity, surety, futurity, impurity, maturity, obscurity, security, immaturity, insecurity, prematurity

urk \ərk\ see ¹ORK

¹**urka** \ər-kə\ charka, circa, Gurkha, mazurka

²**urka** \ùr-kə\ Gurkha, mazurka

urke \ərk\ see ¹ORK

urker \ər-kər\ see ¹ORKER

urkey \ər-kē\ see ERKY

¹**urkha** \ùr-kə\ see ²URKA

²**urkha** \ər-kə\ see ¹URKA

urki \ər-kē\ see ERKY

urky \ər-kē\ see ERKY

url \ərl\ see ¹IRL

urled \ərld\ see ORLD

urlew \ərl-ü\ curlew, purlieu

urlieu \ərl-ü\ see URLEW

urlin \ər-lən\ see ERLIN

urling \ər-liŋ\ curling, hurling, sterling—*also* -ing *forms of verbs listed at* ¹IRL

urlish \ər-lish\ churlish, girlish

urly \ər-lē\ burley, burly, curly, early, girlie, hurly, knurly, pearly, squirrely, surly, swirly, twirly, whirly, hurly-burly

urman \ər-mən\ see ERMAN

urmity \ər-mət-ē\ see IRMITY

urmur \ər-mər\ firmer, infirmer, murmur, termer, wormer

urn \ərn\ burn, churn, curn, earn, erne, fern, kern, learn, pirn, quern, spurn, stern, tern, terne, turn, urn, yearn, adjourn, astern, attorn, casern, concern, discern, downturn, epergne, eterne, extern, heartburn, intern, lucerne, nocturn, nocturne, outturn, return, sauternes, secern, sojourn, sunburn, unlearn, upturn, U-turn, windburn, Comintern, overturn, taciturn, unconcern

urnable \ər-nə-bəl\ burnable, discernible, returnable, indiscernible

urnal \ərn-ᵊl\ see ERNAL

urne \ərn\ see URN

urned \ərnd\ burned, durned, concerned, unearned, unlearned, well-turned, windburned—*also* -ed *forms of verbs listed at* URN

urner \ər-nər\ burner, earner, turner, discerner, returner, afterburner

urnery \ər-nə-rē\ see ERNARY

urney \ər-nē\ see ¹OURNEY

urnian \ər-nē-ən\ see ERNIAN

urnish \ər-nish\ burnish, furnish

urnt \ərnt\ see EARNT

urnum \ər-nəm\ sternum, alburnum, laburnum, viburnum

uro \u̇r-ō\ bureau, duro, euro, enduro, maduro, politburo, chiaroscuro

uron \u̇r-ən\ see ²URIN

uror \u̇r-ər\ see ¹URER

urore \u̇r-ər\ see ¹URER

urous \u̇r-əs\ see URUS

urp \ərp\ burp, chirp, slurp, stirp, twerp, usurp

urphy \ər-fē\ see URFY

urple \ər-pəl\ purple, empurple

urplice \ər-pləs\ see URPLUS

urplus \ər-pləs\ surplice, surplus

urps \ərps\ see IRPS

urr \ər\ see ¹EUR

¹urra \u̇r-ə\ see URA

²urra \ər-ə\ see ¹OROUGH

urrage \ər-ij\ see OURAGE

urragh \ər-ə\ see ¹OROUGH

urrain \ər-ən\ see ¹URIN

urral \ər-əl\ see ERRAL

urrant \ər-ənt\ see URRENT

urray \ər-ē\ see URRY

urre \ər\ see ¹EUR

urred \ərd\ see IRD

urrence \ər-əns\ concurrence, conference, deterrence, incurrence, occurrence, transference, countertransference

urrent \ər-ənt\ currant, current, weren't, concurrent, crosscurrent, decurrent, deterrent, occurrent, recurrent, susurrant, countercurrent, undercurrent, supercurrent

urrer \ər-ər\ see ERRER

urret \u̇r-ət\ see URATE

urrey \ər-ē\ see URRY

urrian \u̇r-ē-ən\ see URIAN

urrie \ər-ē\ see URRY

urrier \ər-ē-ər\ courier, currier, furrier, hurrier, worrier—*also* -er *forms of adjectives listed at* URRY

urring \ər-iŋ\ furring, shirring, stirring, skiöring—*also* -ing *forms of verbs listed at* ¹EUR

urrish \ər-ish\ see OURISH

¹urro \ər-ə\ see ¹OROUGH

²urro \ər-ō\ see ¹URROW

¹urrow \ər-ō\ borough, burgh, burro, burrow, furrow, thorough

²urrow \ər-ə\ see ¹OROUGH

urry \ər-ē\ blurry, burry, curry, flurry, furry, dhurrie, gurry, hurry, Moray, Murray, murrey, scurry, slurry, spurrey, surrey, Surrey, whirry, worry, hurry-scurry

ursa \ər-sə\ see ERSA

ursal \ər-səl\ see ¹ERSAL

ursar \ər-sər\ see URSOR

ursary \ərs-rē\ bursary, cursory, mercery, nursery, anniversary

urse \ərs\ see ERSE

ursed \ərst\ see URST

ursement \ər-smənt\ see ERCEMENT

urser \ər-sər\ see URSOR

ursery \ərs-rē\ see URSARY

ursion \ər-zhən\ see ¹ERSION

ursionist \ərzh-nəst\ see ERSIONIST

ursive \ər-siv\ see ERSIVE

ursor \ər-sər\ bursar, cursor, mercer, nurser, purser, worser, disburser, disperser, precursor, rehearser, reverser, traverser

ursory \ərs-rē\ see URSARY

urst \ərst\ burst, cursed, durst, erst, first, Hearst, thirst, verst, worst, wurst, accursed, airburst, Amherst, athirst, cloudburst, downburst, emersed, feetfirst, groundburst, headfirst, outburst, sunburst, liverwurst, microburst—*also* -ed *forms of verbs listed at* ERSE

ursus \ər-səs\ *see* ERSUS

¹ursy \ər-sē\ *see* ERCY

²ursy \əs-ē\ *see* USSY

¹urt \ùrt\ yurt, Erfurt, Frankfurt, Betancourt

²urt \ərt\ *see* ¹ERT

urtain \ərt-ᵊn\ *see* ERTAIN

urtal \ərt-ᵊl\ *see* ERTILE

urtenance \ərt-ᵊn-əns\ *see* ERTINENCE

urtenant \ərt-nənt\ *see* IRTINENT

urter \ərt-ər\ *see* ERTER

urtesy \ərt-ə-sē\ *see* OURTESY

urthen \ər-thən\ burthen, earthen

urther \ər-thər\ further, murther

urti \ùrt-ē\ pretty, surety, Trimurti

urtium \ər-shəm\ nasturtium, sestertium

urtive \ərt-iv\ *see* ERTIVE

urtle \ərt-ᵊl\ *see* ERTILE

urton \ərt-ᵊn\ *see* ERTAIN

urture \ər-chər\ *see* IRCHER

uru \ùr-ü\ guru, kuru, Nauru

urus \ùr-əs\ urus, Arcturus, mercurous, sulfurous, Epicurus, sui juris, tinea cruris

urve \ərv\ *see* ERVE

urved \ərvd\ *see* ERVED

urviness \ər-vē-nəs\ *see* ERVINESS

urvy \ər-vē\ curvy, nervy, scurvy, topsy-turvy

¹ury \ùr-ē\ curie, Curie, fleury, fury, houri, Jewry, jury, Kure, Urey, Bhojpuri, de jure, Missouri, tandoori, lusus naturae

²ury \er-ē\ *see* ¹ARY

urze \ərz\ *see* ERS

urzy \ər-zē\ *see* ERSEY

¹us \əs\ bus, buss, crus, cuss, fuss, Gus, Huss, muss, plus, pus, Russ, suss, thus, truss, us, airbus, concuss, cost-plus, discuss, nonplus, percuss, railbus, untruss, autobus, blunderbuss, microbus, minibus

²us \ü\ *see* ¹EW

³us \üs\ *see* ¹USE

⁴us \ùsh\ *see* OUCHE

⁵us \üz\ *see* ²USE

¹usa \ü-sə\ Sousa, Azusa, Medusa, Appaloosa, Gebel Musa, Jebel Musa

²usa \ü-zə\ Sousa, Susa, Medusa, Arethusa

usable \ü-zə-bəl\ fusible, losable, usable, abusable, diffusible, excusable, infusible, reusable, transfusible, inexcusable, irrecusable

usae \ü-sē\ *see* UICY

¹usal \ü-səl\ streusel, occlusal

²usal \ü-zəl\ foozle, fusil, ouzel, snoozle, streusel, accusal, bamboozle, occlusal, perusal, refusal

usc \əsk\ *see* USK

uscan \əs-kən\ buskin, Ruskin, Tuscan, Etruscan, molluscan

uscat \əs-kət\ *see* USKET

uscle \əs-əl\ *see* USTLE

uscular \əs-kyə-lər\ muscular,

corpuscular, crepuscular,
majuscular

uscule \əs-kyül\ crepuscule,
opuscule

¹**use** \üs\ Bruce, crouse, crus,
cruse, deuce, douce, goose,
juice, loose, moose, mousse,
noose, nous, puce, rhus,
ruse, Russ, schuss, sluice,
spruce, truce, use, Zeus,
Aarhus, abstruse, abuse,
adduce, Arhus, Atreus,
burnoose, caboose, Cayuse,
Cepheus, ceruse, conduce,
couscous, deduce, diffuse,
disuse, educe, effuse, excuse,
footloose, induce, Lanús,
misuse, mongoose,
Morpheus, negus, obtuse,
Orpheus, papoose, Peleus,
Perseus, prepuce, produce,
profuse, Proteus, Purus,
recluse, reduce, refuse,
retuse, reuse, Sanctus,
seduce, Tereus, Theseus,
traduce, transduce, unloose,
vamoose, Belarus,
Betelgeuse, calaboose,
charlotte russe, introduce,
mass-produce, Odysseus,
Prometheus, reproduce, self-
abuse, Syracuse, Typhoeus,
hypotenuse, Sancti Spiritus

²**use** \üz\ blues, booze, bruise,
choose, cruise, cruse, Druze,
flews, fuse, Hughes, lose,
Meuse, muse, news, ooze,
roose, ruse, schmooze,
snooze, trews, use, whose,
abuse, accuse, amuse,
Andrews, bemuse, berceuse,
chanteuse, chartreuse,
coiffeuse, confuse, contuse,
danseuse, defuse, diffuse,
diseuse, disuse, effuse,
Elbrus, enthuse, excuse, ill-
use, infuse, masseuse,

misuse, perfuse, peruse,
recluse, recuse, refuse, reuse,
suffuse, Toulouse, transfuse,
vendeuse, Betelgeuse,
disabuse, interfuse,
mitrailleuse, Newport News,
p's and q's, Santa Cruz, Vera
Cruz, Goody Two-shoes

used \üzd\ used, confused,
underused—*also -ed forms of
verbs listed at* ²USE

useless \ü-sləs\ juiceless,
useless

user \ü-zər\ boozer, bruiser,
chooser, cruiser, doozer,
loser, snoozer, user, abuser,
accuser, amuser, diffuser,
excuser, infuser, peruser,
multiuser

¹**ush** \əsh\ blush, brush,
crush, flush, gush, hush,
Cush, lush, mush, plush,
rush, shush, slush, squush,
thrush, tush, airbrush,
bulrush, bum's rush,
hairbrush, hush-hush,
inrush, nailbrush, onrush,
paintbrush, sagebrush,
toothbrush, uprush,
bottlebrush, Hindu Kush,
underbrush

²**ush** \ush\ bush, Bush, mush,
push, shush, squoosh,
swoosh, tush, whoosh,
ambush, Hindu Kush,
rosebush, thornbush

ushabel \ə-shə-bəl\ crushable,
flushable

¹**usher** \əsh-ər\ blusher,
brusher, crusher, gusher,
musher, rusher, usher, four-
flusher, goldrusher—*also -er
forms of adjectives listed at*
¹USH

²**usher** \ush-ər\ pusher,
ambusher

ushi \ush-ē\ see ²USHY

ushing \əsh-iŋ\ onrushing, toothbrushing, unblushing—*also* -*ing forms of verbs listed at* ¹USH

ushu \ü-shü\ Kyushu, Kitakyushu

¹ushy \əsh-ē\ brushy, gushy, mushy, plushy, rushy, slushy

²ushy \ùsh-ē\ bushy, cushy, mushy, pushy, sushi

usi \ü-sē\ see UICY

usian \ü-zhən\ see USION

¹usible \ü-sə-bəl\ see UCIBLE

²usible \ü-zə-bəl\ see USABLE

usic \ü-zik\ music, Tungusic

usie \ü-zē\ see OOZY

usil \ü-zəl\ see ²USAL

using \əs-iŋ\ busing, trussing, antibusing—*also* -*ing forms of verbs listed at* ¹US

usion \ü-zhən\ fusion, affusion, allusion, Carthusian, collusion, conclusion, confusion, contusion, delusion, diffusion, effusion, elusion, exclusion, extrusion, illusion, inclusion, infusion, intrusion, Malthusian, obtrusion, occlusion, perfusion, prelusion, profusion, prolusion, protrusion, reclusion, seclusion, transfusion, Venusian, Andalusian, disillusion, malocclusion, autotransfusion

usionist \üzh-nəst\ fusionist, diffusionist, exclusionist, illusionist, perfusionist

usity \ü-sət-ē\ see UCITY

usive \ü-siv\ abusive, allusive, amusive, collusive, conclusive, conducive, delusive, diffusive, effusive, elusive, exclusive, extrusive, illusive, inclusive, intrusive,

obtrusive, occlusive, prelusive, protrusive, reclusive, inconclusive

usk \əsk\ brusque, cusk, dusk, husk, musk, rusk, tusk, subfusc

usker \əs-kər\ busker, husker, tusker

usket \əs-kət\ muscat, musket

uskie \əs-kē\ see USKY

uskin \əs-kən\ see USCAN

usky \əs-kē\ dusky, husky, muskie, musky

usly \əs-lē\ pussley, thusly

uso \ü-sō\ see USOE

usoe \ü-sō\ trousseau, whoso, Caruso, Robinson Crusoe

usory \üs-ə-rē\ delusory, prolusory, illusory

usque \əsk\ see USK

¹uss \ùs\ puss, Russ, schuss, chartreuse, sea puss, sourpuss, glamour-puss, octopus, platypus

²uss \üs\ see ¹USE

³uss \əs\ see ¹US

ussant \əs-²nt\ mustn't, discussant

ussate \əs-ət\ see USSET

usse \üs\ see ¹USE

ussel \əs-əl\ see USTLE

ussell \əs-əl\ see USTLE

usset \əs-ət\ gusset, russet, decussate

ussia \əsh-ə\ Prussia, Russia, Belorussia

ussian \əsh-ən\ see USSION

ussing \əs-iŋ\ see USING

ussion \əsh-ən\ Prussian, Russian, concussion, discussion, percussion, Belorussian, repercussion

ussive \əs-iv\ jussive, tussive, concussive, percussive, repercussive

ussle \əs-əl\ see USTLE

ussley \əs-lē\ see USLY

ussy \əs-ē\ fussy, hussy, mussy, pursy, pussy

¹ust \əst\ bust, crust, dost, dust, gust, just, lust, must, musth, rust, thrust, trust, wast, adjust, adust, august, combust, degust, disgust, distrust, encrust, entrust, mistrust, moondust, piecrust, robust, stardust, upthrust, antitrust, dryasdust, unitrust, wanderlust—*also* -ed *forms of verbs listed at* ¹US

²ust \əs\ *see* ¹US

³ust \üst\ *see* OOST

ustable \əs-tə-bəl\ *see* USTIBLE

ustard \əs-tərd\ bustard, custard, mustard—*also* -ed *forms of verbs listed at* USTER

usted \əs-təd\ busted, disgusted, maladjusted, well-adjusted—*also* -ed *forms of verbs listed at* ¹UST

uster \əs-tər\ bluster, buster, cluster, Custer, duster, fluster, luster, muster, thruster, adjuster, blockbuster, combustor, deluster, gangbuster, lackluster, sodbuster, trustbuster, antitruster, filibuster

ustful \əst-fəl\ lustful, thrustful, trustful, distrustful

usth \əst\ *see* ¹UST

ustian \əs-chən\ *see* USTION

ustible \əs-tə-bəl\ adjustable, combustible, incombustible

ustin \əs-tən\ Justin, Augustine

ustine \əs-tən\ *see* USTIN

ustic \əs-tik\ fustic, rustic

ustion \əs-chən\ fustian, combustion

ustious \əs-chəs\ robustious, rumbustious

ustive \əs-tiv\ adjustive, combustive, maladjustive

ustle \əs-əl\ bustle, hustle, muscle, mussel, Russell, rustle, trestle, tussle, corpuscle, crepuscle, Jack Russell

ustn't \əs-ᵊnt\ *see* USSANT

ustom \əs-təm\ custom, frustum, accustom, disaccustom

ustor \əs-tər\ *see* USTER

ustrious \əs-trē-əs\ illustrious, industrious

ustrous \əs-trəs\ blustrous, lustrous

ustule \əs-chül\ frustule, pustule

ustum \əs-təm\ *see* USTOM

ustus \əs-təs\ Justus, Augustus

usty \əs-tē\ busty, crusty, dusty, fusty, gusty, lusty, musty, rusty, trusty

usy \iz-ē\ *see* IZZY

¹ut \ət\ but, butt, cut, glut, gut, hut, jut, mutt, nut, putt, rut, scut, shut, slut, smut, soot, strut, tut, ut, what, abut, beechnut, catgut, chestnut, clean-cut, clear-cut, cobnut, cockshut, crosscut, groundnut, haircut, locknut, offcut, peanut, pignut, rebut, recut, rotgut, shortcut, somewhat, tut-tut, uncut, walnut, woodcut, butternut, congregate, hazelnut, overcut, scuttlebutt, undercut, uppercut, open-and-shut

²ut \ü\ *see* ¹EW

³ut \üt\ *see* UTE

⁴ut \ut\ *see* ¹OOT

uta \üt-ə\ Baruta, likuta, valuta

utable \üt-ə-bəl\ mutable,

scrutable, suitable,
commutable, computable,
disputable, immutable,
inscrutable, permutable,
statutable, executable,
incommutable, indisputable,
incomputable, indisputable,
irrefutable, prosecutable,
substitutable

utage \üt-ij\ see ¹OOTAGE

utal \üt-ᵊl\ see UTILE

utan \üt-ᵊn\ cutin, gluten,
Luton, mutine, Newton,
Teuton, Laputan, rambutan,
Rasputin, highfalutin

utant \üt-ᵊnt\ mutant,
disputant, pollutant

utative \üt-ət-iv\ putative,
commutative, imputative

¹**utch** \əch\ clutch, crutch,
cutch, dutch, Dutch, grutch,
hutch, much, scutch,
smutch, such, touch,
nonesuch, retouch, double-
clutch, overmuch

²**utch** \úch\ butch, putsch

utcher \əch-ər\ scutcher,
retoucher

utchy \əch-ē\ see UCHY

ute \üt\ boot, bruit, brut,
brute, bute, Bute, butte,
chute, cloot, coot, cute,
flute, fruit, glout, hoot, jute,
Jute, loot, lute, moot, mute,
newt, pood, root, Root, rout,
route, scoot, scute, shoot,
snoot, soot, suit, suite, toot,.
tout, ut, Ute, acute, astute,
Asyût, beetroot, Beirut,
birthroot, bloodroot,
breadfruit, butut, cahoot,
Canute, cheroot, clubroot,
commute, compute, confute,
crapshoot, deaf-mute,
depute, dilute, dispute, elute,
en route, enroot, folkmoot,
freeboot, galoot, grapefruit,

hardboot, hirsute, imbrute,
impute, jackboot, jackfruit,
jumpsuit, kashruth, lawsuit,
minute, nonsuit, offshoot,
outshoot, Paiute, pantsuit,
permute, playsuit, pollute,
pursuit, recruit, refute,
repute, salute, seaboot,
snowsuit, solute, sunsuit,
swimsuit, taproot, tracksuit,
transmute, uproot, volute,
absolute, Aleut, arrowroot,
Asyût, attribute, autoroute,
bandicoot, bitterroot,
bodysuit, boilersuit,
bumbershoot, constitute,
convolute, Denver boot,
destitute, disrepute,
dissolute, evolute, execute,
gingerroot, institute,
involute, kiwifruit,
malamute, overshoot,
parachute, persecute,
prosecute, prostitute, qiviut,
resolute, restitute, revolute,
subacute, substitute,
troubleshoot, undershoot,
electrocute, Hardecanute,
Inuktitut, irresolute,
reconstitute

uted \üt-əd\ see ¹OOTED

utee \üt-ē\ see ¹OOTY

utely \üt-lē\ cutely, mutely,
accutely, astutely, minutely,
absolutely, dissolutely,
irresolutely

uten \üt-ᵊn\ see UTAN

uteness \üt-nəs\ cuteness,
glutenous, glutinous,
muteness, mutinous,
acuteness, diluteness,
hirsuteness, absoluteness,
destituteness, dissoluteness,
irresoluteness

utenist \üt-ᵊn-əst\ lutenist,
Teutonist

utenous \üt-nəs\ see UTENESS

uteous \üt-ē-əs\ beauteous, duteous, gluteous, luteous

uter \üt-ər\ cooter, neuter, fluter, hooter, looter, pewter, rooter, router, scooter, shooter, souter, suiter, suitor, tooter, tutor, accoutre, commuter, computer, confuter, crapshooter, diluter, disputer, freebooter, peashooter, recruiter, saluter, sharpshooter, six-shooter, trapshooter, two-suiter, zoot-suiter, coadjutor, executor, instituter, persecutor, prosecutor, prostitutor, troubleshooter, microcomputer, minicomputer, superminicomputer—*also* -er *forms of adjectives listed at* UTE

utes \üts\ see OOTS

uteus \üt-ē-əs\ see UTEOUS

¹**uth** \üt\ see UTE

²**uth** \üth\ see ²OOTH

¹**uther** \ü-thər\ Luther, Uther

²**uther** \ə-<u>th</u>er\ see ¹OTHER

uthful \üth-fəl\ ruthful, truthful, youthful, untruthful

uthless \üth-ləs\ ruthless, toothless

uti \üt-ē\ see ¹OOTY

utia \ü-shə\ fuchsia, minutia, Saint Lucia

utian \ü-shən\ see UTION

utic \üt-ik\ maieutic, scorbutic, toreutic, hermeneutic, parachutic, propaedeutic, therapeutic

utical \üt-i-kəl\ cuticle, hermeneutical, pharmaceutical

uticle \üt-i-kəl\ see UTICAL

utie \üt-ē\ see ¹OOTY

utiful \üt-i-fəl\ beautiful, dutiful

utile \üt-ᵊl\ brutal, cuittle, footle, futile, tootle, utile, inutile, Kwakiutl

utin \üt-ᵊn\ see UTAN

utine \üt-ᵊn\ see UTAN

uting \üt-iŋ\ fluting, luting, suiting, hip-shooting, sharpshooting, trapshooting—*also* -ing *forms of verbs listed at* UTE

¹**utinous** \üt-ᵊn-əs\ glutinous, mutinous

²**utinous** \üt-nəs\ see UTENESS

utiny \üt-ᵊn-ē\ mutiny, scrutiny

ution \ü-shən\ Lucian, ablution, Aleutian, capuchin, Confucian, dilution, elution, locution, pollution, solution, absolution, allocution, attribution, comminution, consecution, constitution, contribution, convolution, destitution, devolution, diminution, dissolution, distribution, elocution, evolution, execution, exsolution, institution, involution, lilliputian, persecution, prosecution, prostitution, resolution, restitution, retribution, revolution, Rosicrucian, substitution, antipollution, circumlocution, electrocution, irresolution, maldistribution, reconstitution, redistribution

utionary \ü-shə-ner-ē\ illocutionary, revolutionary

utionist \ü-shnəst\ devolutionist, elocutionist, evolutionist, revolutionist, redistributionist

utish \üt-ish\ brutish, Vutish

utist \üt-əst\ chutist, flutist, absolutist, parachutist—*also* -est *forms of adjectives listed at* UTE

utive \üt-iv\ dilutive, constitutive, persecutive, substitutive

utl \ü-t°l\ see UTILE

utland \ət-lənd\ Jutland, Rutland

utlass \ət-ləs\ cutlass, gutless

utler \ət-lər\ butler, Butler, cutler, sutler

utless \ət-ləs\ see UTLASS

utlet \ət-lət\ cutlet, nutlet

utment \ət-mənt\ hutment, abutment

utney \ət-nē\ chutney, gluttony, Ascutney

uto \üt-ō\ Bhutto, Pluto, putto, Basuto, cornuto, Maputo, tenuto, sostenuto

uton \üt-ⁿ\ see UTAN

utor \üt-ər\ see UTER

utriment \ü-trə-mənt\ nutriment, accoutrement

uts \əts\ see UTZ

utsch \üch\ see ²UTCH

utsi \üt-sē\ see ²UZZI

utsk \ütsk\ Irkutsk, Yakutsk

utsy \ət-sē\ gutsy, klutzy

utt \ət\ see ¹UT

uttack \ət-ək\ see UTTOCK

uttal \ət-°l\ see UTTLE

utte \üt\ see UTE

uttee \ət-ē\ see UTTY

¹utter \ət-ər\ butter, clutter, cutter, flutter, gutter, mutter, nutter, putter, scutter, shutter, splutter, sputter, strutter, stutter, utter, abutter, aflutter, haircutter, price-cutter, rebutter, stonecutter, unclutter, woodcutter

²utter \üt-ər\ see ¹OOTER

uttery \ət-ə-rē\ buttery, fluttery, spluttery

¹utti \üt-ē\ see ¹OOTY

²utti \üt-ē\ see ²OOTY

utting \üt-iŋ\ see ¹OOTING

uttish \ət-ish\ ruttish, sluttish

uttle \ət-°l\ cuittle, scuttle, shuttle, subtile, subtle, rebuttal

utto \üt-ō\ see UTO

uttock \ət-ək\ buttock, Cuttack, futtock

utton \ət-ⁿn\ button, glutton, mutton, Sutton, keybutton, unbutton, leg-of-mutton

uttony \ət-nē\ see UTNEY

utty \ət-ē\ butty, gutty, jutty, nutty, puttee, putty, rutty, smutty

utum \üt-əm\ scutum, sputum

uture \ü-chər\ blucher, future, moocher, suture

uty \üt-ē\ see ¹OOTY

utz \əts\ futz, klutz, lutz, nuts, blood-and-guts—*also* -s, -'s, *and* -s' *forms of nouns listed at* ¹UT, *and* -s *forms of verbs listed there*

utzy \ət-sē\ see UTSY

uu \ü\ see ¹EW

uvial \ü-vē-əl\ fluvial, pluvial, alluvial, colluvial, diluvial, eluvial

uvian \ü-vē-ən\ alluvion, diluvian, Peruvian, vesuvian, Vesuvian, postdiluvian, antediluvian

uvion \ü-vē-ən\ see UVIAN

uvium \ü-vē-əm\ alluvium, colluvium, effluvium, eluvium

¹ux \əks\ crux, flux, lux, tux, afflux, aw-shucks, conflux, deluxe, efflux, influx, redux, reflux, Benelux—*also* -s, -'s, *and* -s' *forms of nouns listed* at ¹UCK, *and* -s *forms of verbs listed there*

²ux \ùks\ see ²OOKS

¹uxe \ùks\ see ¹OOKS

²uxe \ùks\ see ²OOKS

³uxe \əks\ see ¹UX

uxion \ək-shən\ see UCTION

uy \ī\ see ¹Y

uygur \ē-gər\ see EAGER

uyot \ē-ō\ see ²IO

uyp \īp\ see IPE

¹uz \üts\ see OOTS

²uz \úz\ see ²USE

uze \üz\ see ²USE

uzz \əz\ see ¹BUSE

¹uzzi \ü-zē\ see OOZY

²uzzi \üt-sē\ Tutsi, Abruzzi

uzzle \əz-əl\ guzzle, muzzle, nuzzle, puzzle

uzzler \əz-lər\ guzzler, puzzler, gas-guzzler

uzzy \əz-ē\ fuzzy, muzzy, scuzzy

Y

¹y \ī\ ai, ay, aye, bi, buy, by, bye, chi, cry, die, dry, dye, eye, fie, fly, fry, guy, Guy, hi, hie, high, i, I, lie, lye, my, nigh, phi, pi, pie, ply, pry, psi, rye, scythe, sei, shy, sigh, sky, sly, spry, spy, sty, Tai, Thai, thigh, thy, tie, try, vie, why, wry, wye, xi, Y, aby, agley, air-dry, ally, Altai, anti, apply, assai, awry, aye-aye, Bacchae, Baha'i, banzai, barfly, Belgae, belie, bigeye, birds-eye, blackfly, blow-dry, blowby, blowfly, blue-sky, Bottai, bone-dry, bonsai, botfly, Brunei, buckeye, bugeye, bulls-eye, bye-bye, canaille, catchfly, cat's-eye, cockeye, cockshy, comply, cross-eye, deadeye, decry, deep-fry, deep-sky, deerfly, defy, Delphi, deny, descry, drip-dry, Dubai, elhi, Eli, espy, firefly, fish-eye, flyby, forby, freeze-dry, frogeye, gadfly, gallfly, GI, good-bye, greenfly, grisaille, gun-shy, Haggai, Hawkeye, hereby, hi-fi, hog-tie, horsefly, housefly, imply, jai alai, July, Katmai, Kauri, Kenai, knee-high, lanai, Lanai, lay-by, Levi, magpie, mao-tai, Masai, medfly, Moirai, mooneye, nearby, necktie, nisi, outbye, outcry, oxeye, Panay, panfry, Parcae, piece-dye, pigsty, pinkeye, Po Hai, pop eye, potpie, Qinghai, quasi, rabbi, re-try, red-eye,

rely, reply, rocaille, rough-dry, Sakai, sci-fi, semi, Sendai, serai, shanghai, Shanghai, shoofly, shut-eye, Sinai, sky-high, small-fry, sockeye, stand by, standby, stir-fry, supply, swing-by, terai, test-fly, thereby, tie-dye, titi, tongue-tie, two-ply, untie, Versailles, walleye, watcheye, well-nigh, whereby, whitefly, wise guy, worms-eye, Adonai, alibi, alkali, amplify, apple-pie, argufy, basify, beautify, butterfly, by-and-by, calcify, certify, Chou En-lai, citify, clarify, classify, cockneyfy, codify, crucify, cut-and-dry, DIY, damnify, damselfly, dandify, deify, densify, dignify, dobsonfly, do-or-die, dragonfly, edify, falsify, fancify, fortify, frenchify, fructify, gasify, Gemini, gentrify, glorify, goggle-eye, goldeneye, gratify, Haggai, hexerei, horrify, Iceni, justify, lignify, liquefy, lithify, Lorelei, lullaby, Madurai, magnify, Malachi, Maracay, modify, mollify, Molokai, Mordecai, mortify, multi-ply, multiply, mummify, mystify, nazify, nitrify, notify, nullify, occupy, Olduvai, ossify, overbuy, overfly, overlie, pacify, Paraguay, passerby, peccavi, petrify, PPI, preachify, prettify, prophesy,

purify, putrefy, qualify,
quantify, ramify, rarefy,
ratify, RBI, rectify, reify, res
gestae, resupply, Russify,
samurai, sanctify, satisfy,
scarify, semidry, signify,
simplify, sine die, specify,
speechify, stratify, stultify,
stupefy, Tenebrae, terrify,
testify, tigereye, typify,
uglify, ultrahigh, underlie,
unify, Uruguay, Veneti,
verify, versify, vilify, vinify,
vitrify, vivify, zombify,
acetify, acidify, a priori,
beatify, decertify, declassify,
demystify, denazify,
detoxify, Dioscuri,
disqualify, dissatisfy,
diversify, electrify,
exemplify, facetiae, Helvetii,
humidify, identify,
indemnify, intensify,
objectify, personify,
preoccupy, reliquiae,
reunify, revivify, rigidify,
saponify, solemnify,
solidify, syllabify,
transmogrify, undersupply,
vox populi, a fortiori,
caravanserai, corpus
delicti, deacidify,
dehumidify, ex hypothesi,
modus vivendi, nolle
prosequi, oversimplify,
amicus curiae, curriculum
vitae, modus operandi

²y \ē\ see ¹EE
ya \ē-ə\ see ¹IA
yable \ī-ə-bəl\ see ¹IABLE
yad \ī-əd\ dryad, dyad, naiad,
  sayyid, triad, hamadryad,
  jeremiad
yan \ī-ən\ see ¹ION
yant \ī-ənt\ see IANT
yatt \ī-ət\ see IET
ybe \īb\ see ¹IBE

ybele \ib-ə-lē\ Cybele,
  ambiboly
yber \ī-bər\ see IBER
ybia \ī-bē-ə\ see IBIA
ybris \ī-brəs\ see IBROUS
ycad \ī-kəd\ cycad, spiked
ycan \ī-kən\ see ¹ICHEN
yce \īs\ see ¹ICE
¹ych \ik\ see ICK
²ych \īk\ see ²IKE
yche \ī-kē\ see ¹IKE
ychnis \ik-nəs\ see ICKNESS
ycia \ish-ə\ see ¹ITIA
ycian \ish-ən\ see ITION
ycin \īs-ⁿn\ see ¹ISON
¹ycle \ī-kəl\ cycle, Michael,
  recycle, Calvin cycle,
  epicycle, Exercycle,
  hemicycle, kilocycle,
  motorcycle, unicycle,
  Wanne-Eickel
²ycle \ik-əl\ see ICKLE
ycler \ik-lər\ see ICKLER
yd \ü-id\ see UID
yde \īd\ see ¹IDE
ydia \i-dē-ə\ see IDIA
ydian \id-ē-ən\ see IDIAN
ydice \id-ə-sē\ see IDICE
ydney \id-nē\ see IDNEY
ye \ī\ see ¹Y
yeable \ī-ə-bəl\ see ¹IABLE
yed \īd\ see ¹IDE
yer \īr\ see ¹IRE
yeth \ī-əth\ see ¹IATH
yfe \īf\ see ¹IFE
yfed \ər-əd\ see OVED
yg \ig\ see IG
ygamous \ig-ə-məs\ see
  IGAMOUS
ygamy \ig-ə-mē\ see IGAMY
ygia \ī-jə\ see IJAH
ygian \ij-ən\ Phrygian, pidgin,
  pigeon, smidgen, stygian,
  wigeon, religion,
  Cantabrigian, irreligion,
  callipygian
ygiene \ī-jēn\ see AIJIN

ygma \ig-mə\ see IGMA

ygnet \ig-nət\ cygnet, signet

ygnus \ig-nəs\ see IGNESS

ygos \ī-gəs\ see YGOUS

ygous \ī-gəs\ gigas, azygos,
callipygous, hemizygous,
homozygous, steatopygous

ygrapher \ig-rə-fər\ see
IGRAPHER

ygraphist \ig-rə-fəst\ see
IGRAPHIST

ygyny \ij-ə-nē\ see IGINE

ying \ī-iŋ\ crying, flying,
lying, trying, high-flying,
low-lying, outlying, undying,
nitrifying, terrifying,
underlying

yke \īk\ see ²IKE

yked \īkt\ see ¹IKED

yl \ēl\ see ²EAL

ylan \il-ən\ see ILLON

ylar \ī-lər\ see ILAR

yle \īl\ see ¹ILE

ylem \ī-ləm\ see ILUM

yler \ī-lər\ see ILAR

ylet \ī-lət\ see ILOT

yley \ī-lē\ see YLY

yli \ē-lē\ see EELY

ylic \il-ik\ see ILIC

ylie \ī-lē\ see YLY

yling \ī-liŋ\ see ¹ILING

yll \īl\ see ¹ILE

ylla \il-ə\ see ²ILLA

yllable \il-ə-bəl\ see ILLABLE

yllary \il-ə-rē\ see ILLARY

yllic \il-ik\ see ILIC

yllis \il-əs\ see ILLUS

yllium \il-ē-əm\ see ILIUM

¹yllo \ē-lō\ see ²ILO

²yllo \ī-lō\ see ¹ILO

ylum \ī-ləm\ see ILUM

ylus \ī-ləs\ see ILUS

yly \ī-lē\ dryly, highly, maile,
Philae, riley, shyly, slyly,
smiley, Wiley, wily, Wyley,
wryly, life of Riley

ym \im\ see ¹IM

yma \ī-mə\ Chaima, cyma

yman \ī-mən\ see IMEN

ymathy \im-ə-thē\ see
IMOTHY

ymbal \im-bəl\ see IMBLE

ymbalist \im-bə-ləst\
cymbalist, symbolist

ymbol \im-bəl\ see IMBLE

ymbolist \im-bə-ləst\ see
YMBALIST

yme \īm\ see ¹IME

ymeless \īm-ləs\ see IMELESS

ymen \ī-mən\ see IMEN

ymer \ī-mər\ see ¹IMER

¹ymic \ī-mik\ thymic,
enzymic

²ymic \im-ik\ gimmick,
mimic, bulimic, acronymic,
antonymic, eponymic,
homonymic, matronymic,
metonymic, patronymic,
synonymic, toponymic

ymical \im-i-kəl\ see IMICAL

ymie \ī-mē\ see IMY

ymion \im-ē-ən\ see IMIAN

ymity \im-ət-ē\ see IMITY

ymmetry \im-ə-trē\ see
IMETRY

ymn \im\ see ¹IM

ymp \imp\ see IMP

ymph \imf\ lymph, nymph

ymric \im-rik\ Cymric,
limerick

ymus \ī-məs\ see IMIS

ymy \ī-mē\ see IMY

yn \in\ see ¹IN

ynah \ī-nə\ see ¹INA

ynast \ī-nəst\ see ¹INIST

¹ynch \inch\ see INCH

²ynch \iŋk\ see INK

yncher \in-chər\ see INCHER

ynd \īnd\ see ¹IND

yndic \in-dik\ see INDIC

yne \īn\ see ¹INE

ynein \in-ē-ən\ see ¹INIAN

yness \ī-nəs\ see ¹INUS

ynia \in-ē-ə\ see INIA

ynic \in-ik\ see ²INIC
ynical \in-i-kəl\ see INICAL
ynn \in\ see ¹IN
ynne \in\ see ¹IN
ynth \inth\ see INTH
ynthia \in-thē-ə\ see INTHIA
ynx \iŋs\ see INX
yon \ī-ən\ see ¹ION
yone \i-ə-nē\ see YONY
yony \i-ə-nē\ bryony, Alcyone
yp \ip\ see IP
ypal \ī-pəl\ typal, disciple, archetypal, prototypal
ype \īp\ see IPE
yper \ī-pər\ see IPER
ypey \i-pē\ see IPY
yph \if\ see IFF
yphen \ī-fən\ hyphen, siphon
yphic \if-ik\ see IFIC
yphony \if-ə-nē\ see IPHONY
ypic \ip-ik\ typic, philippic, genotypic, holotypic, stereotypic
yping \ī-piŋ\ see IPING
ypo \ī-pō\ hypo, typo
ypress \ī-prəs\ cypress, Cyprus, viperous
yprus \ī-prəs\ see YPRESS
ypse \ips\ see IPS
ypso \ip-sō\ see IPSO
ypsy \ip-sē\ gypsy, Gypsy, tipsy
ypt \ipt\ see IPT
yptian \ip-shən\ see IPTION
yptic \ip-tik\ cryptic, diptych, styptic, triptych, ecliptic, elliptic, apocalyptic
ypy \ī-pē\ see IPY
yr \ir\ see ²EER
yra \ī-rə\ Ira, Lyra, Myra, naira, bell-lyra, hegira, hetaira, palmyra, spirogyra
yral \ī-rəl\ see IRAL
yrant \ī-rənt\ see IRANT
yre \īr\ see ¹IRE
yreal \ir-ē-əl\ see ERIAL
yria \ir-ē-ə\ see ¹ERIA

yriad \ir-ē-əd\ see ERIOD
yrian \ir-ē-ən\ see ¹ERIAN
yric \ī-rik\ pyric, oneiric, panegyric, see ²ERIC
yrical \ir-i-kəl\ see ²ERICAL
¹yrie \ir-ē\ see EARY
²yrie \ī-rē\ see ¹IARY
yril \ir-əl\ see ¹ERAL
yrist \ir-əst\ see ¹ERIST
yrium \ir-ē-əm\ see ERIUM
yrna \ər-nə\ see ERNA
¹yro \ī-rō\ biro, Cairo, gyro, Gyro, tyro
²yro \ir-ō\ see ³ERO
yron \ir-ən\ see IREN
yros \ī-rəs\ see IRUS
yrrh \ər\ see ¹EUR
yrrha \ir-ə\ see ²ERA
yrrhic \ir-ik\ see ²ERIC
yrrhus \ir-əs\ see EROUS
yrse \ərs\ see ERSE
yrsus \ər-səs\ see ERSUS
yrtle \ərt-ᵊl\ see ERTILE
yrup \ər-əp\ see IRRUP
yrupy \ər-ə-pē\ see IRRUPY
yrus \ī-rəs\ see IRUS
ysail \ī-səl\ see ¹ISAL
ysch \ish\ see ¹ISH
yse \īs\ see ¹ICE
ysh \ish\ see ¹ISH
¹ysia \ish-ə\ see ITIA
²ysia \izh-ə\ see ISIA
¹ysian \is-ē-ən\ Piscean, Odyssean, Dionysian
²ysian \ish-ən\ see ITION
³ysian \izh-ən\ see ISION
⁴ysian \ī-sē-ən\ see ¹ISCEAN
ysical \iz-i-kəl\ physical, quizzical, metaphysical
ysis \ī-səs\ see ISIS
ysm \iz-əm\ see ISM
ysmal \iz-məl\ dismal, abysmal, baptismal, cataclysmal, catechismal
yson \īs-ᵊn\ see ¹ISON
yss \is\ see ¹ISS
yssal \is-əl\ see ISTLE

yssean \is-ē-ən\ see ¹YSIAN
ysseus \ish-əs\ see ¹ICIOUS
yssum \is-əm\ see ISSOME
yssus \is-əs\ see ISSUS
yst \ist\ see ²IST
ystal \is-t°l\ see ISTAL
¹yster \is-tər\ see ISTER
²yster \ī-stər\ see ¹EISTER
ystery \is-trē\ see ISTORY
ystic \is-tik\ see ISTIC
ystical \is-ti-kəl\ see ISTICAL
ystine \is-tən\ see ISTON
¹ysus \ē-səs\ see ESIS
²ysus \ī-səs\ see ISIS
yta \īt-ə\ see ¹ITA
yte \īt\ see ¹ITE
yterate \it-ə-rət\ see ITERATE
ytes \īt-ēz\ see ITES
¹ythe \ī\ see ¹Y
²ythe \ith\ see ¹ITHE

ythia \ith-ē-ə\ lithia, Scythia,
  forsythia, stichomythia
ythian \ith-ē-ən\ Pythian,
  Scythian
ythmic \ith-mik\ rhythmic,
  arrhythmic, eurythmic,
  logarithmic
ythy \i-thē\ see ITHY
ytic \it-ik\ see ITIC
ytical \it-i-kəl\ see ITICAL
ytics \it-iks\ see ITICS
yting \īt-iŋ\ see ITING
ytis \ī-təs\ see ITIS
ytton \it-°n\ see ITTEN
yve \īv\ see ¹IVE
yx \iks\ see ¹IX
yxia \ik-sē-ə\ see IXIA
yxie \ik-sē\ see IXIE
yze \īz\ see IZE